LITERACY INSTRUCTION FOR ADOLESCENTS

D1568277

Literacy Instruction for Adolescents

Research-Based Practice

EDITED BY
Karen D. Wood
William E. Blanton

THE GUILFORD PRESS
New York   London

© 2009 The Guilford Press
A Division of Guilford Publications, Inc.
72 Spring Street, New York, NY 10012
www.guilford.com

Printed in the United States of America

This book is printed on acid-free paper.

Last digit is print number: 9   8   7   6   5   4   3   2   1

Library of Congress Cataloging-in-Publication Data

Literacy instruction for adolescents: research-based practice / edited by Karen D.
Wood and William E. Blanton.
     p. cm.
  Includes bibliographical references and index.
  ISBN 978-1-60623-123-4 (hardcover: alk. paper) — ISBN 978-1-60623-118-0
(pbk.: alk. paper)
  1. Reading (Secondary)   2. Reading (Secondary)—Research.   I. Wood, Karen D.
II.   Blanton, William E.
  LB1632.L55 2009
  428.4—dc22

                                                                2008054618

To Eric, Ryan, Lauren, and Kevin
—K.D.W.

To Ellie and Bill
—W.E.B.

About the Editors

Karen D. Wood, PhD, is Professor in the Department of Reading and Elementary Education at the University of North Carolina at Charlotte. A former middle school reading teacher and K–12 literacy specialist in the public schools, she is the author of over 200 articles, chapters, and books focusing on various topics, including integrating literacy across the curriculum, meeting the needs of diverse learners, vocabulary and comprehension development, and translating research and theory into classroom practice. These articles have appeared in journals such as *The Reading Teacher, Journal of Reading, Reading and Writing Quarterly, Reading Psychology, Language Arts*, and the *Middle School Journal*. Dr. Wood began writing the "Research into Practice" column for the *Middle School Journal* in 1986 and continues as its author today. She was a member of the authorship team of the McGraw-Hill Basal Reading Series from 1989 to 2004 and was the former coeditor, along with William E. Blanton, of the journal *Reading Research and Instruction*. Her recent books include *Guiding Readers through Text: Strategy Guides in New Times, Strategies for Integrating Reading and Writing in Middle and High School Classrooms, Teaching Literacy in Sixth Grade, Literacy Strategies across the Subject Areas* (2nd edition), and *Instructional Strategies for Teaching Content Vocabulary: Grades 4–12*.

William E. Blanton, EdD, is Professor in the Language and Literacy Learning in Multilingual Settings Program at the University of Miami in Coral Gables, Florida. A 1970 graduate of the Reading Education Program of the University of Georgia, he has held faculty appointments at Indiana University and Appalachian State University. Formerly he was associated with the Education Resources Information Center (ERIC) Clearinghouse on Reading Education at Indiana University, and he was a cofounder of the Laboratory of Technology and Learning at Appalachian State University. Dr. Blanton has coauthored reading instruction programs; edited journals in reading education; served on editorial boards of major journals; written extensively for journals such as *The Elementary School Journal, Reading Research Quarterly, Reading Psychology, Journal of Adolescent and Adult Literacy*, and *The Reading Teacher*; and contributed chapters to many books. His current research studies the role of culture in development, with a dual focus on characterizing children's development and the development of the social institutions in which this process occurs.

Contributors

Richard L. Allington, PhD, College of Education, University of Tennessee, Knoxville, Tennessee

Donna E. Alvermann, PhD, Department of Language and Literacy Education, University of Georgia, Athens, Georgia

Patricia L. Anders, PhD, College of Education, University of Arizona, Tucson, Arizona

Mary A. Avalos, PhD, School of Education, University of Miami, Coral Gables, Florida

Rita M. Bean, PhD, Department of Instruction and Learning, University of Pittsburgh, Pittsburgh, Pennsylvania

Thomas W. Bean, PhD, Curriculum and Instruction Department, University of Nevada, Las Vegas, Nevada

William E. Blanton, EdD, School of Education, University of Miami, Coral Gables, Florida

William G. Brozo, PhD, Graduate School of Education, George Mason University, Fairfax, Virginia

Julie Coiro, PhD, School of Education, University of Rhode Island, Kingston, Rhode Island

Patricia M. Cunningham, PhD, Department of Education, Wake Forest University, Winston-Salem, North Carolina

Danielle V. Dennis, PhD, Department of Childhood Education and Literacy Studies, University of South Florida, Tampa, Florida

Brock Dubbels, PhD, The Center for Cognitive Sciences, University of Minnesota, Minneapolis, Minnesota

Pamela J. Dunston, PhD, Department of Reading Education, Clemson University, Clemson, South Carolina

Ellen Eisenberg, MEd, The Pennsylvania High School Coaching Initiative, The Annenberg Foundation, Radnor, Pennsylvania

Douglas Fisher, PhD, School of Teacher Education, San Diego State University, San Diego, California

Nancy Frey, PhD, School of Teacher Education, San Diego State University, San Diego, California

Linda B. Gambrell, PhD, Department of Reading Education, Clemson University, Clemson, South Carolina

Courtney Gaskins, MEd, Youth for Tomorrow, Bristow, Virginia

Jane Hansen, PhD, Curry School of Education, University of Virginia, Charlottesville, Virginia

Janis M. Harmon, PhD, Department of Interdisciplinary Learning and Teaching, University of Texas at San Antonio, San Antonio, Texas

Helen Harper, PhD, Curriculum and Instruction Department, University of Nevada, Las Vegas, Nevada

Alison Heron-Hruby, PhD, College of Education and Human Development, George Mason University, Fairfax, Virginia

Kara K. Keeling, PhD, Department of English, Christopher Newport University, Newport News, Virginia

Brian Kissel, PhD, Department of Reading and Elementary Education, University of North Carolina at Charlotte, Charlotte, North Carolina

Diane Lapp, EdD, College of Education, San Diego State University, San Diego, California

Evan Lefsky, PhD, literacy consultant, Crawfordville, Florida

Miriam Martinez, PhD, Department of Interdisciplinary Learning and Teaching, University of Texas at San Antonio, San Antonio, Texas

Patrick McCabe, PhD, PhD Program in Literacy, St. John's University, Queens, New York

Rachel L. McCormack, EdD, School of Education, Roger Williams University, Bristol, Rhode Island

Beverly K. McIntyre, MS, College of Education, University of North Carolina at Charlotte, Charlotte, North Carolina

Adriana L. Medina, PhD, Department of Reading and Elementary Education, University of North Carolina at Charlotte, Charlotte, North Carolina

David W. Moore, PhD, College of Teacher Education and Leadership, Arizona State University, Phoenix, Arizona

Maryann Mraz, PhD, College of Education, University of North Carolina at Charlotte, Charlotte, North Carolina

William Dee Nichols, PhD, College of Education and Allied Professions, Western Carolina University, Cullowhee, North Carolina

David G. O'Brien, PhD, Department of Curriculum and Instruction, University of Minnesota, Minneapolis, Minnesota

Nancy D. Padak, PhD, Department of Education, Kent State University, Kent, Ohio

Jeanne R. Paratore, EdD, School of Education, Boston University, Boston, Massachusetts

Paola Pilonieta, PhD, Department of Reading and Elementary Education, University of North Carolina at Charlotte, Charlotte, North Carolina

Kristy Pytash, MA, Teaching, Leadership, and Curriculum Studies Department, Kent State University, Kent, Ohio

Timothy Rasinski, PhD, Reading and Writing Center, Kent State University, Kent, Ohio

Robert J. Rickelman, PhD, College of Education, University of North Carolina at Charlotte, Charlotte, North Carolina

Nancy Roser, PhD, College of Education, University of Texas at Austin, Austin, Texas

Donna Ross, PhD, School of Teacher Education, San Diego State University, San Diego, California

Jeanne Shay Schumm, PhD, School of Education, University of Miami, Coral Gables, Florida

Marsha M. Sprague, EdD, Department of English, Christopher Newport University, Newport News, Virginia

Richard T. Vacca, PhD, Emeritus, Department of Teaching Leadership and Curriculum Studies, Kent State University, Kent, Ohio

Barbara J. Walker, PhD, College of Education, Oklahoma State University, Tulsa, Oklahoma

Thomas DeVere Wolsey, EdD, Richard W. Riley College of Education and Leadership, Walden University, Minneapolis, Minnesota

Karen D. Wood, PhD, College of Education, University of North Carolina at Charlotte, Charlotte, North Carolina

Preface

This text is about research-based methods for promoting the literacy of adolescent learners in all content fields. Its major purpose is to engage the reader in reading, thinking, and engaging in conversation about issues that affect the acquisition and improvement of adolescent literacy. To that end, we asked the experts, the researchers whose names are most associated with all dimensions of adolescent literacy, to contribute their best and latest work. The outcome is this volume, a synthesis of the current research and its application to adolescent learners' acquisition of literacy and to teachers' instruction of subject matter.

Adolescent Literacy Instruction: A Brief History

The field of content-area literacy, although not a fledgling area of inquiry, is receiving new and abundant attention in the professional literature (see Chapter 1 by David W. Moore on advocating literacy and Chapter 4 by Maryann Mraz, Robert J. Rickelman, and Richard T. Vacca, which chronicles the past, present, and future of content-area literacy). Prior to 1970, content-area reading instruction focused on providing students with assistance in reading and locating, comprehending, summarizing, and remembering information obtained by reading subject-matter textbooks and other materials (Herber, 1970; Moore, Readence, & Rickelman, 1983; Moorman & Blanton, 1990; Wood & Muth, 1991). In the mid-1970s, researchers pointed out that the textual organization of subject matter such as literature, physical science, biology, mathematics, chemistry, social studies, health, music appreciation, and art appreciation, varies from one subject area to another. Studies of successful and unsuccessful readers yielded evidence that more successful readers utilized metacognitive strategies, such as accessing and activating prior knowledge relevant to material to be read, developing a purpose for reading, monitoring progress toward attaining purpose, recruiting fix-up strategies to overcome disruptions and breakdowns during reading, and actively updating their prior knowledge.

The fields of cultural psychology, anthropology, sociology, technology, and the learning sciences influenced a transformation from the idea of literacy as simply the ability to read and write to the idea of *multiple literacies* that comprise a mosaic of cultural activities, including speaking, listening, viewing, reading, and writing. Fundamentally, literacies are intentional acts that involve skill in coordinating the interrelationship among thinking, language, speaking, listening, writing, reading, subject-matter, and instrumental and conceptual tools to accomplish intellectual and everyday tasks. Scientists, historians, geographers, mathematicians, physicians, musicians, teachers, artists, legislators, dairy workers, and others enact literacies differently—in current parlance, literacies express different ways of thinking, knowing, and doing.

About This Book

In this volume, we present multiple ways to improve literacy—from devising ways to use picture books with older readers to integrating writing instruction in the content areas, to grouping students to promote discussion and interaction. The book opens with a comprehensive look at adolescent literacy instruction today by David W. Moore and then is divided into two parts. Part I, "Literacy and the Adolescent Learner," comprises 10 chapters, opening with a chapter by Thomas W. Bean and Helen Harper on the adolescent learner in today's society. Part II, "Teaching the Adolescent Learner: Research-Based Instructional Practices," contains 13 chapters, opening with a chapter by Patricia L. Anders on the challenges and opportunities of research-based instruction. Each chapter begins with a set of questions that develop a purpose for reading the chapter and ends with a set of questions for discussion, along with further readings and World Wide Web resources for accessing further information on the chapter content. Within these chapters, you will find the most current thinking in the field of adolescent literacy from the leaders themselves. We envision this book as a resource for graduate students, teachers in the field, and undergraduate students just entering the teaching profession. The book includes topics that, according to our experiences, are the top concerns of our nation's middle- and secondary-level teachers. To this end, we proudly present *Literacy Instruction for Adolescents: Research-Based Practice*.

Acknowledgments

We would like to thank Lynne Newton and Kendall Kiser, University of North Carolina at Charlotte doctoral students, for their helpful comments on various aspects of this book. We value the opinions and editorial suggestions of these practicing teachers and future scholars.

KAREN D. WOOD
WILLIAM E. BLANTON

References

Herber, H. L. (1970). *Teaching reading in the content areas.* Englewood Cliffs, NJ: Prentice Hall.

Moore, D., Readence, J., & Rickelman, R. (1983). An historical exploration of content area reading instruction. *Reading Research Quarterly, 18*(4), 419–438.

Moorman, G. B., & Blanton, W. E. (1990). The information text reading activity (ITRA): Engaging students in meaningful learning. *Journal of Reading, 34*(3), 174–183.

Wood, K. D., & Muth, D. (1991). The case for improved instruction in the middle grades. *Journal of Reading, 35*(2), 84–90.

Contents

PART II. Teaching the Adolescent Learner: Research-Based Instructional Practices

Contents xvii

The Case for Improving Adolescent Literacy Instruction

William E. Blanton
Karen D. Wood

The publication of this book occurs at one of the most challenging times for middle and high school students and teachers. On the one hand, the academic performance of students is described as being on the cusp of average to mediocre performance. The future our nation's adolescents confront is one of a world that opens with the touch of a keyboard or eludes them as a result of insufficient levels of literacies. Their ability to enact literacies will have a profound effect on their level of participation in social and political activities, personal relationships, success in chosen vocations, health and well-being, and their understanding of themselves in relation to an expanding and complex world. On the other hand, we as educators have assumed the enormous task of arranging for students to acquire literacies and subject-matter knowledge. In undertaking this task, we must continually seek out better ways to solve the literacy and subject-matter instructional problems presented by students who express themselves through their cultural, linguistic, ethnic, and educational diversity.

The purpose of our introduction is to provide a context for reading and discussing the chapters presented in this text. To that end, we begin with a discussion of the state of adolescent literacy and subject-matter achievement. Then, we present three varied aspects of literacy that illustrate the importance of providing adolescents with research-based instruction in content-area classrooms. While our book contains more illustrations of literacy, we include these three dimensions to provide additional emphasis. The first dimension focuses on the crucial issue of health literacy, the need to promote literacy instruction to influence students' development of personal health and well-being, a by-product of proficient literacy that is often unmentioned in the field of content-area reading. The second dimension is the need to promote proficiency through multiliteracy experiences and, in this context, we describe a scenario of a student who is engaged in learning activity through the activation, coordination, and utilization of multimodel processes to participate in a lesson. The final dimension focuses on what we have chosen to call "commercial literacy," when the improvement of literacy is pursued almost exclusively through commercially prepared and published programs. Here, we describe how schools attempt to solve the problems of struggling adolescents by using commercial programs and the cognitive energy a teacher must marshal in order to shape these programs to meet the instructional needs of these students.

Accountability and the Acquisition of Literacies

The nation's schools are held accountable for providing instruction that enables students to access and to apply literacies. The National Assessment of Educational Progress (NAEP) monitors the extent to which American students are acquiring literacies. State agencies monitor student achievement by administering statewide achievement tests. Other agencies monitor and report on dropout rates and the number of students entering and completing postsecondary education, and compare the achievement of American students with that of students of other countries.

The NAEP reports student performance for 4th, 8th, and 12th grades according to three levels of achievement. Students who perform at the Basic level have *partially* mastered the prerequisite knowledge and skills fundamental to proficient academic performance on grade level tasks. Students who reach the Proficient level demonstrate *strong* performance on challenging tasks, including reading, interpreting, critically analyzing, and writing about subject matter and its application to challenging academic activities, work activities, and everyday activities. Attaining the Advanced level represents *superior* performance. We should expect middle and high school students to perform at the Proficient level or higher.

The results reported by NAEP are disturbing. The latest assessment of reading revealed that 31% of 8th graders and 35% of 12th graders scored at the Proficient level (Grigg, Donahue, & Dion, 2007). Thirty-one percent of 8th graders and 35% of 12th graders achieved the Proficient level in writing (Salahu-Din, Persky, & Miller, 2008). On subject matter assessments, 32% of 8th graders and 23% of 12th graders reached the Proficiency level in mathematics (Grigg et al., 2007). In science, 29% of 8th graders and 18% of 12th graders reached the Proficiency level (Grigg, Lauko, & Brockway, 2006). The percentage of 8th graders and 12th graders attaining the Proficient level in history were 17% and 13%, respectively (Lee & Weiss, 2007), whereas 22%

of 8th graders and 27% of 12th graders reached the Proficient level in civics (Lutkus & Weiss, 2007). The first assessment of economics was limited to the 12th grade, in which 42% of students scored at the Proficient level (Mead & Sandene, 2007). In short, the preponderance of middle and high school students have a history of performing poorly on tasks requiring the comprehension, interpretation, critical analysis, and application of information obtained by reading subject matter texts (Campbell, Hombo, & Mazzeo, 2000; Donahue, Daane, & Jin, 2005; Donahue, Voelkl, Campbell, & Mazzeo, 1999; Lutkus, Rampey, & Donahue, 2005).

Most adolescents continue to need some kind of instructional support as they progress through middle and high school, and enter postsecondary education. Struggling students who do not reach the Proficient level have not mastered core reading knowledge (e.g., phonemic awareness, decoding, phonics, and word meaning), and have not developed skill in coordinating that knowledge to acquire subject matter knowledge and present a constellation of deficiencies (Buly & Valencia, 2002). Struggling students require intense remedial instruction. When available, remedial instruction is usually provided through pullout programs, intensive reading classrooms, and computerized instruction. Students who have reached the Proficient level of literacy often struggle with comprehending, interpreting, critically analyzing, and understanding information presented in different textual genres, and formulating and communicating their results to others in writing (Biancarosa & Snow, 2003). These students need to participate in instruction that promotes the acquisition of a metalanguage for understanding *how* reading and writing, and their complementary tools, work and for what purposes in academic and work tasks and everyday activities.

Adolescents who pass statewide literacy tests and enter postsecondary education often struggle (American Diploma Project, 2004) and require support in developing reading and study skills as they encounter heavy reading assignment of conceptually dense subject matter texts. Over one-third of America's university and college students are enrolled in remedial courses that provide them with assistance with reading, writing, speaking, and study skills (Strong American Schools, 2009). The cost of this remediation is approximately $2.5 billion per year. In addition, many students who need remedial help often reduce their academic workload and extend the time it takes to complete their programs of study. When they do so, many colleges and universities increase their tuition.

A number of concerns dominate discussions of the status of American adolescents' attainment of literacies. First, school dropout rates now approach 1.1 million per year in the nation's largest cities (Swanson, 2008). Students who struggle to acquire literacies are likely to drop out of school (Joftus & Maddox-Dolan, 2003; Carnevale, 2001; Kamil, 2003; Snow & Biancarosa, 2003) and not take advantage of postsecondary education, have limited choices for employment, have lower incomes over their lifespan, and do not accumulate sufficient resources for retirement in comparison to their more successful peers who acquire proficiency in literacies. Second, insufficient reading and writing ability puts students at risk for failure in acquiring subject matter knowledge (Biancarosa & Snow, 2003). Finally, compared to adolescents in the worlds' most industrialized nations, American adolescents consistently score below average on measures of reading, mathematics, and science literacies (Baldi, Jin, Skemar, Greden, & Herget, 2007; Lemke et al., 2001). Low levels of literacies jeopardize America's ability to compete in the global economy.

Health Literacy

Health literacy is crucial to understanding, navigating, and negotiating America's complex health care system (American Medical Association, 1999; Selden, Zorn, Ratzan, & Parker, 2000). What is often referred to as the *American lifestyle* has gradually become a problem that threatens the future of many Americans, regardless of their cultural background, ethnicity, language, age, or gender. Approximately 75 million adults, adolescents, and children carry a diagnosis of type I or type II diabetes. At present, one child in three will eventually become diabetic (Ogden, Flegal, Carroll, & Johnson, 2002). As children and adolescents who carry this diagnosis progress through school and enter adulthood, they generally find themselves left to self-manage their disease, a task requiring proficiency in applying multiliteracies. They must monitor and interpret blood glucose levels; calculate insulin dosage on a sliding scale; adhere to diet plans that are coordinated with glucose level, insulin dosage, and carbohydrate intake; comprehend and interpret prescription labels, appointment slips, and nutrition labels; manage multiple medications; be astutely aware of problems of poor sensation and circulation caused by polyneuropathy; visit multiple health care providers; and maintain a regimen of physical exercise (Rothman et al., 2004a; Schillinger et al., 2002). Their level of multiliteracy proficiency affects the extent to which they can successfully manage their disease (Rothman et al., 2004b; Rothman, Housam, Weiss, & Davis, 2006).

As can be seen in the previous scenario, proficient health literacy is the outcome of the interplay among thinking, speaking, listening, viewing, writing, and reading, and their complementary tools, and knowledge of subject matter, such as health, biology, and mathematics. The critical period for the acquisition of health literacy is during adolescence, when health and biology subject matter are acquired, metacognition develops, and health and well-being behaviors are in their formative stages. It is virtually impossible for a person who has not acquired proficiency in coordinating and applying multiple literacies to be agentive, and to act with knowledge and understanding of information, institutional structures, social networks, and other resources necessary for making crucial everyday decisions.

Multiliteracies

Literacies are multimodal processes that include the reading and writing and thinking that utilizes print-based and electronic texts, and visual, spatial, gestural, and aural representations. *Multimodality* is about making meaning with diverse communicative modes, such as language, images, music, sound, texture, and gesture, and how they may differ and be combined. Teachers do not engage students in learning subject matter with a single tool and a single modality. It is crucial that students participate in multimodal activities that utilize multiple sources of subject matter (see Chapter 22 by Julie Coiro, and Chapter 23 by David G. O'Brien and Brock Dubbels, this volume, for more information on promoting technological literacy) to negotiate successfully the tasks presented by a world that is becoming increasingly reliant on multiple sources of information (New London Group, 2000; O'Brien & Bauer, 2005).

As we learned by observing Eduardo, a student in a mathematics class on quadratics, student learning is inextricably interwoven among learning activity, texts, concepts, representations (e.g., diagrams, tables, and tools), gestures, and social interactions. Three weeks before this particular observation, we observed Eduardo's class as his teacher was finishing a gallery walk to overview a transition from the previous content that students had been studying to a new unit on quadratics. Eduardo's teacher used the gallery walk to assess students' prior knowledge and skills necessary for the unit on quadratics; to determine gaps in their knowledge that might interfere with learning content; to introduce them to the central concepts of the unit, kinds of learning assignments, and tools they would be using; and to stress the importance of writing notes, redescribing their learning, and reflecting on the meaning of what they were learning to gauge their personal understandings of the material they would use to learn about quadratics.

As our observation began, Eduardo was listening to his teacher's lecture and demonstration on solving quadratic equations, along with analyzing the diagrams, equations, and solutions written on the chalkboard and presented on a screen connected to the teacher's laptop computer. Eduardo listened and attended to his classmates' questions, the teacher's responses and follow-up questions, and the comments offered by his classmates, then turned back to his own thoughts. Now and then, he looked back to his textbook and read, then closed his eyes for a few moments. We inferred that he was generating links between his prior knowledge and the content of the lesson. At one point, Eduardo whispered to himself, and then to his neighbor, as he followed the teacher's explanation and step-by-step procedures to solve an equation on the chalkboard. All of a sudden he picked up his calculator, computed a solution before the teacher finished, and showed it to his neighbor. Intermittently, he made entries in his notebook or in the margins of his textbook, using his own shorthand to scribble down meanings that only he would be able to interpret. Eduardo and his classmates jokingly called these interactions VMJ, "virtual multitasking jive." The ability to coordinate these interactions enabled students to assign importance and meaning to particular instructional events, images, statements, and gestures.

Eduardo relied on his recall of the meanings of technical vocabulary, concepts, and procedures presented in previous lessons; information he had read and noted in his textbook; and conversations he had had with his peers. He was constantly predicting, anticipating, integrating, translating, comparing, synthesizing, and coordinating information presented in sentences, phrases, lists, question–answer interactions, written texts, diagrams, and the lecture and procedures demonstrated by the teacher, as well as thinking with the special language of mathematics. Eduardo's notes represented his interpretations and syntheses of teacher and student comments during the lesson and his redescriptions of learning activity—all written in his unique shorthand.

As the class was closing, the teacher passed out a sign-up sheet for students to indicate their choice from a set of optional assignments that they would complete in small groups and present to the class. Among the selections were developing a digital story on the history of quadratic equations; visiting Internet sites to learn about everyday uses of quadratic equations; and creating a poster on real problems located beyond the walls of school and how they could be solved with quadratics.

Students who struggle with the acquisition of literacies are often limited to singular experiences to construct meaning and understanding of subject matter. Subject matter instruction that supports multimodal activity is more powerful, interesting, engaging, and motivating, particularly when students like Eduardo are encouraged to redescribe and reflect on their learning activity. The understanding of subject matter is enhanced through conversations about meanings of technical vocabulary, symbols, graphs, text structure, and other tools that specialized disciplines use.

The scenarios presented earlier are representative of the issues with which schools and subject matter teachers deal every day. Many students *do* enter subject matter classrooms as struggling readers and present complex instructional problems for teachers to solve. Nonetheless, we are responsible for *arranging* effective subject matter instruction for students of all ability levels. Arranging appropriate instruction is facilitated when we take advantage of what we have learned through decades of reading research on the most effective research-based ways of teaching adolescent learners. The dissemination of research-based instruction is our main purpose for compiling the chapters for this book.

Commercial Literacy

We have chosen to call this dimension of literacy *commercial literacy,* in which improvement of reading achievement is pursued through commercial, published programs. Surprisingly, there are very few effective, commercial reading programs for adolescents who struggle with the acquisition of literacy. The programs that are available lack research supporting their effectiveness. Slavin et al. (2008) applied rigorous criteria to select 33 reading programs to include in a best-evidence evaluation and synthesis study of reading programs designed for adolescents. Based on their analysis, none of the programs demonstrated strong evidence of effectiveness; four demonstrated moderate evidence of effectiveness; and six demonstrated limited evidence of effectiveness. Most of the programs demonstrating the best evidence of effectiveness promoted social interactions, cooperative learning, and improvement in classroom instruction.

Our experience with READ 180, a computer-based commercial reading program, is representative of the unanticipated outcomes obtained when reading programs that lack strong evidence of their effectiveness are adopted by school systems. Many schools systems have turned to intensive reading classrooms and computerized reading instruction as the intervention of choice to improve the reading ability of struggling readers, even though evidence of their effectiveness is not available. READ 180 is one of the more popular programs being used. The program is currently used by over 5,000 elementary, middle, and high schools throughout the United States (Campbell, 2006).

Briefly, READ 180 provides students with instruction on phonemic awareness, phonics, fluency, vocabulary, spelling, writing, and comprehension. Test scores obtained by the Scholastic Reading Inventory are used to place students in the program and to match students with leveled texts for independent reading. Students participate in a set of instructional rotations, including computerized instruction, modeled/independent reading with audiobooks and paperbacks, and teacher-directed guided reading with the whole class and small groups. At the computer, students engage with CDs that present prior knowledge relevant to practice texts they will read. Students move through a set of learning zones to meet their individual needs. The Word Zone provides instruction on basic decoding skills and structural analysis. The Spelling Zone provides instruction on the acquisition and transfer of spelling patterns and sounds, and the Success Zone assesses comprehension, word recognition, and fluency skills. There is also a 10-minute, whole-class wrap-up at the end of the 90-minute instructional framework.

We had an opportunity to work with a teacher responsible for providing reading instruction to struggling middle school students in an intensive reading classroom. Students who were not making adequate yearly progress in reading were selected for the classroom. The backbone of instruction was READ 180. Prior to the beginning of school, the teacher attended a set of READ 180 workshops provided by Scholastic and the school system. The teacher was required to implement READ 180 as outlined by Scholastic, along with two requirements imposed by the school system. First, the teacher was required to conduct teacher-directed guided reading instruction every day in a literature text adopted for the grade level of the students. As we learned, the level of difficulty of the text was 2 years or more beyond the instructional and independent reading levels of students. Second, the teacher was required to follow scripted lessons for guided reading, written by a committee of teachers during the summer.

Our first visit with the teacher was a month after the beginning of school. At that time, the teacher had seriously considered resigning at the end of the semester. As the teacher described it, "This situation is nothing like my image of meeting the needs of students who are on their last reading legs!" Our observations revealed that the scripted guided reading instruction and the adopted grade-level text were the causes of a serious problem. The students were experiencing great difficulty in reading material that was beyond their instructional reading and independent reading levels and in participating in discussions of the material. For example, the scripted lessons directed the teacher to engage students in discussion of reading selections by asking them a list of randomly selected literal questions and a few inferential questions, inviting students to respond, asking other students to comment, then moving on to the next question.

In a meeting with the teacher and principal we suggested that the requirements for guided reading instruction imposed by the school system be waived. We explained why students needed to read and discuss material with a level of difficulty as close as possible to their instructional and independent reading levels; why a reading discussion had to have a predictable structure to promote cognitive clarity for students and to coordinate the interactions among struggling readers who need to learn how to attend to instructional events and the language used by the teacher and other students, and how to use strategies used by accomplished readers to read and comprehend text. Otherwise, it was doubtful that students would improve their reading ability. The principal agreed to contact the central office and was surprised to receive a waiver during the telephone call. Apparently, this was not the first call about reading-intensive classrooms; although, it was the first to request a change in the rules and procedures governing instruction.

To meet each student's needs, the teacher and media specialist managed to put together three sets of reading material written 1, 2, and 3 years below students' instructional and independent reading levels. Three guided reading groups were organized. The new routine for conducting discussion focused on the teacher developing his own discussion questions; on asking text-based questions first, followed by inferential questions; and ending with author's craft questions. A few weeks later, the teacher reported that students seemed to have increased their level of attention and participation in guided reading.

At the teacher's beckoning, we returned at the end of the semester. According to the teacher, guided reading was going fairly well; however, some of the better students were not making much progress in comprehension, although they could decode the text presented by the computer program and the leveled text used for independent reading. As the teacher explained it, "They could decode the words, but the words had little or no meaning."

The teacher was also concerned that the students' interest in reading had not improved. With the teacher, we agreed that the problem might be solved by providing students with an opportunity to read age-appropriate material on their independent reading level. Fortunately, the media specialist had just received classroom libraries of information text written at the midrange of the students' instructional and independent reading levels from Newbridge Educational Publishing (*www.newbridgeonline.com*).

With our help, the teacher reorganized the guided reading groups into a set of Core Reading Circles that focused on engaging students in reading and discussion about *how* reading works. The groups were coordinated with Reading Role cards that provided tasks for students to accomplish as they read. For example, the task of the *Code Breaker* was to list the words that were hard to say; the *Meaning Maker* noted words that did not make sense; the *Main Idea Maker* was responsible for figuring out the main idea of the text; the *Text User* figured out what kind of text was being read; the *Purpose Pusher* was responsible for deciding why the author wrote the text; the *Pedantic Prober* was responsible for asking questions about what others were thinking and feeling as they read; the *Timekeeper* kept track of time; a *Bookish Bookworm* selected group members to share what they thought were the most interesting parts of the text; the *Word Rapper* made a chart of interesting words in the text, and the *Techno Technician* started, rewound, and later played back a tape of the discussion. Before reading a selection, the students and the teacher discussed why people might read the text and how. Then the group members reviewed their tasks and read the text. After the reading, the teacher facilitated a discussion that focused on the tasks, how they were accomplished, and how to do better next time. In a few weeks, the teacher reported that the students had learned the new routine easily and were eager to finish their work at the computer to get to the guided reading. Most of all, they were excited about what they were going to read during their Core Reading Circles.

The scenario above provides a number of cautions. First, let the preemptor be aware! Publishers often claim that research evidence demonstrates the effectiveness of their programs. We are led to think that publication of such claims on their homepages means that the claims are based on scientific research. The place to verify claims of program effectiveness is in the published literature. It is extremely important for school systems to be informed of the extent to which the instructional programs they adopt are evidenced-based. For example, a federally funded, large-scale, randomized, experimental-control group study was conducted on the most popular computerized reading programs, including READ 180 (Dynarski et al., 2007). The central findings reported to Congress by the researchers for every program investigated were that (1) reading test scores were not significantly higher in classrooms that used the selected computerized reading programs compared to scores of classrooms that received regular reading instruction, and (2) reading test scores were correlated with local classroom conditions.

Second, classroom contexts are extremely diverse. We should expect that a program with strong evidence of its effectiveness will probably need to be adjusted to meet the needs of struggling students. When students are struggling to make satisfactory progress in attaining proficient literacies, their struggle cannot be overcome by simply unpacking commercial programs and exposing students to them. Last, and most important, we are obligated to remediate (rearrange) instruction—not to *remediate* students by plugging them into isolated, computerized instruction and scripted lessons arranged by arbitrary rules and procedures. Remediation is fashioned by teachers who modify the elements of instruction, such as rules and procedures for engaging students; change the social organization of instruction; select materials that are appropriate for reading levels and interests of students; modify inappropriate materials; and create learning activities that promote the acquisition of literacies.

References

American Diploma Project. (2004). *Ready or not: Creating a high school diploma that counts.* Washington, DC: Achieve.

American Medical Association. (1999). Health literacy: Report of the Council on Scientific Affairs. *Journal of the American Medical Association, 281*(6), 552–557.

Baldi, S., Jin, Y., Skemer, M., Green, P. J., & Herget, D. (2007). *Highlights from PISA 2006: Performance of U.S. 15-year-old students in science and mathematics literacy in an international context* (NCES 2008-016). Washington, DC: National Center for Education Statistics, Institute of Education Sciences, U.S. Department of Education. Available online at *nces.ed.gov/pubs2008/2008016.pdf.*

Biancarosa, G., & Snow, C. E. (2003). *A vision for action and research in middle and high school literacy.* New York: Carnegie Foundation. Available online at *www.all4ed. org/files/archive/publications/readingnext/readingnext.pdf.*

Buly, M. R., & Valencia, S. W. (2002). Below the bar: Profiles of students who fail state reading assessments. *Educational Evaluation and Policy Analysis, 24*(3), 219–239. Available online at *epa.sagepub./com/cgi/reprint/24/3/219.*

Campbell, J. R., Hombo, C. M., & Mazzeo, M. (2000, August). *NAEP 1999 Trends in academic progress: Three decades of student performance.* Washington, DC. Available online at *nces.ed.gov/naep/pdf/main1999/200049pdf.*

Campbell, Y. C. (2006). *Effects of an integrated learning system on the reading achievement of middle school students.* Unpublished doctoral dissertation, University of Miami, Miami, FL.

Carnevale, A. P. (2001). *Help wanted . . . college required* [Leadership 2000 Series]. Princeton, NJ: Educational Testing Service.

Donahue, P. L., Daane, M. C., & Jin, Y. (2005). *The nation's report card: Reading 2003* (NCES 2005-453). Washington, DC: U.S. Department of Education, Institute of Education Sciences, National Center for Education Statistics, U.S. Government Printing Office. Available online at *nces.ed.gov/nation/reportcard/pdf/ main2003/2005453.pdf.*

Donahue, P. L., Voekl, K. C., Campbell, J. R., & Mazzeo, J. (1999). *NAEP 1998 Read-*

ing Report Card for the nation and the states. Washington, DC: U.S. Department of Education, Office of Educational Research & Improvement. Available online at *nces.ed.gov/nationsreportcard/pubs/main1998/1999500.shtml.*

Dynarski, M., Agodini, R., Heaviside, S., Novak, T., Carey, N., & Campuzano, L. (2007). *Effectiveness of reading and mathematics software products: Findings from the first student cohort.* Washington, DC: U.S. Department of Education, Institute of Education Sciences. Available online at *ies.ed.gov/ncee/pdf/20074005.pdf.*

Grigg, W., Donahue, P., & Dion, G. (2007). *The nation's report card: 12th-grade reading and mathematics 2005.* Washington, DC: U.S. Department of Education, National Center for Education Statistics, U.S. Government Printing Office.

Grigg, W. S., Lauko, M. A., & Brockway, D. M. (2006). *The nation's report card: Science 2005.* Washington, DC: National Center for Education Statistics.

Joftus, S., & Maddox-Dolan, B. (2003, April). *Left out and left behind: NCLB and the American high school.* Washington, DC: Alliance for Excellent Education.

Kamil, M. L. (2003). *Adolescents and literacy: Reading for the 21st century.* New York: Alliance for Excellent Education.

Lee, J., & Weiss, A. (2007). *The nation's report card: U.S. history 2006* (NCES 2007-474). Washington, DC: U.S. Department of Education, National Center for Education Statistics, U.S. Government Printing Office.

Lemke, M., Calsyn, C., Lippman, L., Jocelyn, L., Kastberg, D., Liu, Y., et al. (2001). *Outcomes of learning: Results from the 2000 Program for International Student Assessment of 15-year-olds in reading, mathematics, and science literacy.* Washington, DC: U.S. Department of Education. Available online at *nces.ed.gov/pubs2002/2002115.pdf.*

Lutkus, A. D., Rampey, B. D., & Donahue, D. (2005). *The nation's report card: Trial urban district assessment reading 2005* (NCES 2006-455). Washington, DC: U.S. Department of Education, National Center for Education Statistics, U.S. Government Printing Office. Available online at *nces.ed.gov/nationsreportcard/pdf/dst2007/2008455.pdf.*

Lutkus, A. D., & Weiss, A. (2007). *The nation's report card: Civics 2006* (NCES 2007-476). Washington, DC: U.S. Department of Education, National Center for Education Statistics, U.S. Government Printing Office. Available online at *eric.ed.gov/EricDocs/data/ericdocs2sql/content_storage-01/0000019b/80/29/es/da.pdf.*

Mead, N., & Sandene, B. (2007). *The nation's report card: Economics 2006* (NCES 2007-475). Washington, DC: National Center for Education Statistics, Institute of Education Sciences, U.S. Department of Education. Available online at *nces.ed.gov/nationsreport/pdf/main2006/2007475.pdf.*

New London Group. (2000). A pedagogy of multiliteracies: Designing social futures. In B. Cope & M. Kalantzis (Eds.), *Multiliteracies: Literacy learning and the design of social futures* (pp. 9–38). New York: Routledge.

O'Brien, D. G., & Bauer, E. (2005). New literacies and the institution of old learning. *Reading Research Quarterly, 40,* 120–131.

Ogden C. L., Flegal, K. M., Carroll, M. D., & Johnson, C. L. (2002). Prevalence and trends in overweight among US children and adolescents, 1999–2000. *Journal of the American Medical Association, 288*(14), 1728–1732.

Rothman, R. L., DeWalt, A., Malone, R., Bryant, B., Shintani, A., Crigler, B., et al. (2004a). Influence of patient literacy on the effectiveness of a primary care–based diabetes disease management program. *Journal of the American Medical Association, 292,* 1711–1716.

Rothman, R. L., Housam, R., Weiss, H., & Davis, D. (2006). Patient understanding of food labels: The role of literacy and numeracy. *American Journal of Preventive Medicine, 1*(5), 391–398.

Rothman, R. L., Malone, R., Bryant, B., Horlen, C., Dewalt, D., & Pignone, M. (2004b). The relationship between literacy and glycemic control in a diabetes disease management program. *Diabetes Education, 30,* 263–273.

Salahu-Din, D., Persky, H., & Miller, J. (2008). *The writing report card: Writing 2007.* Washington, DC: National Center for Education Statistics. Available online at *nces.ed.gov/nationsreportcard/pdf/main2007/2008468.pdf.*

Schillinger, D., Grumbach, K., Piette, J., Wang, F., Osmond, D., Daher, C., et al. (2002). Association of health literacy with diabetes outcomes. *Journal of the American Medical Association, 288,* 475–482.

Selden, C. R., Zorn, M., Ratzan, S. C., & Parker, R. M. (2000). *Current bibliographies in medicine 2000-1: Health literacy.* Bethesda, MD: U.S. Department of Health and Human Resources. Available online at *www.nlm.nih.gov/archive//20061214/pubs/cbm/hliteracy.html.*

Slavin, R. E., Cheung, A., Grovv, C., & Lake, C. (2008). Effective reading programs for middle and high schools: A best-evidenced synthesis. *Reading Research Quarterly, 45*(3), 290–313.

Snow, C. E., & Biancarosa, G. (2003). *Adolescent literacy and the achievement gap: What do we know and where do we go from here?* New York: Carnegie Corporation.

Strong American Schools. (2008). *Diploma to nowhere.* Washington, DC: Author. Available online at *www.edin08.com/uploadedfiles/issues/issues_pages/diplomatonowhere.pdf.*

Swanson, C. B. (2008) .*Cities in crisis: A special analytic report on high school graduation.* Bethesda, MD: Editorial Projects Research Center.

Chapter 1

Advocating Reading Instruction in Middle and High School Classrooms

David W. Moore

Although reading educators have researched and advocated secondary school reading instruction since the early 1900s (Moore, Readence, & Rickelman, 1983; Singer, 1983), the current attention to it is extraordinary. Nearly half of the states in the United States now require high school students to pass reading exams to receive diplomas (Callahan, 2007), and the federal No Child Left Behind Act requires schools to generate nearly universal reading proficiency or to replace their governance (U.S. Department of Education, n.d., a). Expectations for all secondary school youth to read well have never been so urgent.

Between 1999 and 2007, national governmental agencies, educational associations, and advocacy groups published an unprecedented number of major documents on literacy instruction in secondary school classrooms (see Figure 1.1). These documents review the knowledge base on improving literacy instruction in middle and high school classrooms, and recommend ways to implement needed reforms. Additionally, several national groups recently have sponsored websites that spotlight literacy in middle and high school classrooms (see Figure 1.2). Most of these sites focus on classroom instruction, although a few address school policies.

The Advancing Literacy grant-making initiative that the Carnegie Corporation of New York (n.d.) began in 2003 is a noteworthy example of this recent advocacy of secondary school literacy instruction. The *Reading Next* report (Biancarosa & Snow, 2004), which today's policymakers, practitioners, publishers, and researchers cite frequently, is one especially visible outcome of this initiative.

Alvermann, D. E. (2001). *Effective literacy instruction for adolescents.* Executive summary and paper commissioned by the National Reading Conference. Chicago, IL: National Reading Conference. Available at *www.nrconline.org.*

Biancarosa, F., & Snow, C. E. (2004). *Reading next: A vision for action and research in middle and high school literacy—a report to Carnegie Corporation of New York.* Washington, DC: Alliance for Excellent Education. Available at *www.all4ed.org/ adolescent_literacy/index.html.*

Kamil, M. (2003). *Adolescents and literacy: Reading for the 21st century.* Washington, DC: Alliance for Excellent Education. Available at *www.all4ed.org/adolescent_ literacy/index.html.*

Moore, D. W., Bean, T. W., Birdyshaw, D., & Rycik, J. A., for the Commission on Adolescent Literacy of the International Reading Association. (1999). *Adolescent literacy: A position statement.* Newark, DE: International Reading Association. Available at *www.reading.org/resources/issues/positions_adolescent.html.*

National Association of Secondary School Principals. (2005). *Creating a culture of literacy.* Reston, VA: Author. Available at *www.principals.org/s_nassp/sec. asp?cid=62&did=62.*

National Council of Teachers of English. (2006). *NCTE principles of adolescent literacy reform: A policy research brief.* Urbana, IL: Author. Available at *www.ncte.org/ edpolicy/literacy.*

National Governor's Association Center for Best Practices. (2005). *Reading to achieve: A governor's guide to adolescent literacy.* Washington, DC: Author. Available at *www.nga.org.*

Phelps, S. (2005). *Ten years of research on adolescent literacy, 1994–2004: A review.* Naperville, IL: Learning Point Associates. Available at *www.learningpt.org/pdfs/ literacy/tenyears.pdf.*

Short, D. J., & Fitzsimmons, S. (2007). *Double the work: Challenges and solutions to acquiring language and academic literacy for adolescent English language learners—a report to Carnegie Corporation of New York.* Washington, DC: Alliance for Excellent Education. Available at *www.all4ed.org/adolescent_literacy/index.html.*

Torgesen, J. K., Houston, D. D., Rissman, L. M., Decker, S. M., Roberts, G., Vaughn, S., et al. (2007). *Academic literacy instruction for adolescents: A guidance document from the Center on Instruction.* Portsmouth, NH: RMC Research Corporation, Center on Instruction. Available at *www.centeroninstruction.org.*

FIGURE 1.1. Sponsored reports on adolescent literacy.

In 2003, U.S. Senator Patty Murray (D-WA) first introduced the PASS Act (Pathways for All Students to Succeed), a $1 billion plan for U.S. secondary schools to hire at least one literacy coach for every 20 teachers (PASS Act, n.d.). In 2007, the U.S. Department of Education (n.d., b) appropriated $31,870,000 for its Striving Readers program. The goals of this federal program are to improve struggling middle and high school students' reading skills and to build a research base around instruction that improves those skills. Finally, in 2007, a collection of prominent educational leaders who follow literacy trends identified adolescent literacy as the reading and writing movement currently receiving the most attention (Cassidy & Cassidy, 2008).

AdLit.org

www.adlit.org

"A national multimedia project offering information and resources to the parents and educators of struggling adolescent readers and writers."

Adolescent Literacy

www.literacy.uconn.edu/adolit.htm

Contains links to "policy statements and effective practices, articles about adolescent literacy instruction, instructional resources, [and] booklists for adolescents."

Alliance for Excellent Education

www.all4ed.org

"Founded in 2001, the Alliance focuses on America's six million most at-risk secondary school students—those in the lowest achievement quartile—who are most likely to leave school without a diploma or to graduate unprepared for a productive future."

Carnegie Corporation's Advancing Literacy Initiative

www.carnegie.org/literacy/initiative.html

Advancing Literacy "was created in 2003, after an extensive review that included consultations with the nation's leading practitioners and researchers. . . . Carnegie Corporation's response . . . was to create the Advancing Literacy subprogram and charge it with the daunting task of advancing literacy by affecting policy, practice and research."

International Reading Association: Focus on Adolescent Literacy

www.reading.org/resources/issues/focus_adolescent.html

"Offers resources for those who work with adolescent learners—whether they struggle with reading or are achieving at grade level."

Learning Point Associates

www.learningpt.org/literacy/adolescent

"Help[s] practitioners, administrators, policymakers, and other stakeholders gather and apply knowledge of necessary elements of curriculum and instruction for adolescents with the goal of helping all students achieve success."

Literacy Matters

www.literacy matters.org

Works to "improve the literacy development of middle grades and secondary school students, especially those students who are struggling to succeed. The content within this web site focuses on what matters most in adolescent literacy development."

National Council of Teachers of English: Adolescent Literacy Teaching Resource Collection

www.ncte.org/collections/adolescentliteracy

Offers professional development, publications, and programs on helping teachers recognize and value the "multiple literacy resources students bring to the acquisition of school literacy."

FIGURE 1.2. Online resources for improving adolescent literacy.

This chapter surveys reasons for the current widespread advocacy of secondary school literacy instruction. Understanding this support can provide perspective on the reforms being recommended and inform instructional decision making. This chapter's first section connects influential recommendations for comprehensive secondary school reforms with literacy reforms. The second section presents assessments of adolescents' reading achievement that reformers frequently invoke. The third section surveys adolescents' uses of reading inside and outside secondary schools that contribute to calls for change. The final section reflects on the current advocacy of secondary school reading instruction.

Comprehensive Secondary School Reforms

> Every year our country loses thousands of young people—
> students who leave school without graduating or without
> the skills and knowledge to succeed in life. . . . Our
> schools, particularly our high schools, must prepare
> students for the demands of college, work, and citizenship.
> —BILL AND MELINDA GATES FOUNDATION (n. d., p. 2)

Bill Gates, the billionaire founder of Microsoft Corporation, currently is considered one of the most influential leaders of U.S. education policy (Swanson & Barlage, 2006). The Bill and Melinda Gates Foundation's rhetoric about the need to improve U.S. secondary schools, exemplified in the proclamation just presented, extends untold documents epitomized by landmarks such as *A Nation at Risk* (National Commission on Excellence in Education, 1983), *Turning Points* (Carnegie Council on Adolescent Development, 1989), and *Breaking Ranks* (National Association of Secondary School Principals, 1996). Educators and educational policymakers have for decades been rethinking and restructuring secondary schools largely in the name of national competitiveness and social justice.

National Competitiveness

> The Bill and Melinda Gates Foundation's Education Division
> is investing heavily in reforms to equip all U.S. youth with
> advanced knowledge and skills. These reforms are based on a
> revised set of the three R's: rigor, relationships, and relevance.
> —BILL AND MELINDA GATES FOUNDATION (n. d.)

Rigorous course work is exacting. Schools that advocate rigor align their academics with high standards, eliminate curricular tracking, and maintain course work requirements for graduation that involve complex thinking and challenging levels of literacy. Teachers and students are accountable for success.

Schools that advocate relationships promote personal affiliations that center about academic success. To personalize educational settings, they create small schools of 300–500 students, perhaps within larger structures, and usually keep class sizes fewer than 25. They emphasize a culture of caring, endorsing respectful interactions and civil discourse inside and outside classrooms. They involve students in school organizations and committees. Teachers display professional responsibility for their students' learning.

Relevance is stressed, so that youth see the value of formal education. These schools focus on clear, measurable goals, such as increasing literacy performance. Business and community groups partner with the schools, offering programs such as internships and service learning opportunities. Students have access to rich learning materials, including contemporary print and information–communication technology.

Social Justice

Notable comprehensive school reforms that accentuate social justice go beyond the Bill and Melinda Gates Foundation's three R's (see, e.g., Campaign for High School Equity, n.d.; Friedlander & Darling-Hammond, 2007). These school improvement efforts work to provide youth of color and poverty the educational opportunities they frequently lack. Emphasis is on securing experienced, certified personnel to teach within their college major or minor, then supporting these teachers with effective professional development.

Another emphasis is learning English. Newcomer centers are provided, so that recent adolescent immigrants can acquire the basic U.S. customs and language needed to participate in school. Teachers bridge students' languages spoken at home with the academic languages of the school disciplines. When necessary, translation services are provided.

Targeted interventions also are offered. Common interventions include extended class periods and school days, afterschool and summer programs, and bridges between the lower and upper grades. Special classes in academic literacy typify many of these interventions. In-class supports, such as heterogeneous grouping, multilevel reading materials, and scaffolded instruction in the literacy of the disciplines, are provided.

Commentary

The sense of urgency underlying these comprehensive secondary school reforms in general and adolescent literacy instruction in particular comes from many factors. Massive changes in the workplace, resulting from technological innovations, globalization, and emerging economies, are raising expectations of the schools (Barton, 2006; Stein, 2000). Students now require updated approaches and new sets of skills to be competitive. Demographic shifts in the United States, resulting from new patterns of immigration and birth rates, are obliging schools to change (Kirsch, Braun, Yamamoto, & Sum, 2007). Educators, more than in the recent past, are now realizing the need to accommodate students from different backgrounds.

Finally, high school graduation rates are driving many reforms. Although about 70% of youth currently are receiving diplomas in 4 years, only about 50% of African American and Hispanic youth do so (Editorial Projects in Education, 2007). Youth who abandon high school these days diminish their futures, and educators realize that limited reading proficiencies contribute to dropping out (Legters, McPartland, & Balfanz, 2004).

In conclusion, most comprehensive secondary school reforms embrace literacy instruction. Past advocates, who asserted that students deserve advanced literacy instruction whenever they encounter advanced literacy challenges (Bond & Bond, 1941; Graham, 1981; Whipple, 1925), now are being supported forcefully by the advocates represented here. Whether focusing on national competitiveness in the global economy, social justice in the nation, or personal fulfillment by individuals, reformers share a widespread belief that U.S. youth ought to receive ongoing reading and writing instruction (Heller & Greenleaf, 2007; Jacobs, 2008). Large-scale assessments of literacy achievement provide grounds for many of these assertions.

Reading Achievement

America's adolescents face a literacy crisis.
—ALLIANCE FOR EXCELLENT EDUCATION
(2006, p. 1)

As this quote exemplifies, reading and writing achievement of U.S. youth often is considered disastrous. This section surveys international, national, and state reading assessments that shed light on this claim.

International

A trustworthy international comparison of reading achievement of U.S. youth comes from the Programme for International Student Assessment (PISA; Topping, 2006). Other notable comparisons are on hand, but they include only fourth-grade students (Progress in International Reading Literacy Study [PIRLS]) or focus just on mathematics and science (Trends in International Mathematics and Science Study [TIMSS]) (cf. TIMSS & PIRLS International Study Center website: *timss.bc.edu*).

The PISA, administered by the Organisation for Economic Co-operation and Development (OECD), a voluntary intergovernmental organization of 30 industrialized nations, is a standardized assessment that compares the academic performance of 15-year-old students across countries. It typically is administered to 4,500–10,000 youth in each country. The first PISA assessment occurred in 2000, and the second in 2003. The third assessment was in 2006, but the reading scores for U.S. youth were invalidated because their test booklets contained a major formatting error.

PISA assesses what it calls *reading literacy*, that is, "understanding, using, and reflecting on written texts, in order to achieve one's goals, to develop one's knowledge and potential, and to participate in society" (Organisation for Economic Co-operation and Development, n.d., p. 108). The PISA test makers added *literacy* to *reading* to connote application, the idea that the test goes beyond mastery of school curricula to knowledge and skills needed in adulthood.

In brief, U.S. youth on average scored about the same as youth from most other industrialized countries (Lemke & Gonzales, 2006). In 2000, the U.S. average score of 504 did not differ measurably from 19 other countries' scores (Lemke & Gonzales, 2006). Youth from 3 countries—Finland, Canada, and New Zealand—measurably outperformed U.S. youth, whereas U.S. youth measurably outperformed youth from 7 countries—Greece, Portugal, Luxembourg, Mexico, Russian Federation, Latvia, and Brazil. The U.S. scores did not change significantly from 2000 to 2003, and the U.S. average scores roughly equaled the OECD averages in both PISA administrations (Lemke et al., 2004).

Characterizations of this PISA performance by U.S. youth vary considerably. One group states, "In virtually every international assessment of academic performance, the United States' performance varies from mediocre to poor . . . particularly for secondary school students" (Alliance for Excellent Education, 2007, p. 1). However, another asserts, "U.S. students perform relatively well in reading literacy compared with their international peers" (Kober, 2006, p. 26). Expectations seem to be the factor that determines the acceptability of national reading performance of U.S. youth relative to youth in other nations.

A noteworthy PISA finding that goes beyond average performance involves the way U.S. test scores vary according to students' socioeconomic status (SES). The proportion of U.S. youth with low SES and correspondingly low test scores is greater than the proportion in every industrialized country but one (Lemke et al., 2005). This means that the United States is among the least effective industrialized countries in ameliorating the results of low social and economic status on academic performance.

National

The National Assessment of Educational Progress (NAEP) is a highly visible measure of adolescents' literacy achievement at the national level. Youth readiness for college is another well-known indicator of national reading achievement.

National Assessment of Educational Progress

The NAEP (n.d.), which calls itself the "nation's report card", serves as the only nationally representative and continuing assessment of students' academic performance. NAEP periodically assesses 4th-, 8th-, and 12th-grade students in all U.S. states. Educators consider it the information source that currently influences educational policy the most (Swanson & Barlage, 2006).

Following general guidelines from the U.S. Congress, NAEP has assessed the reading achievement of U.S. youth since 1969. The National Center for Education Statistics (NCES), which is part of the U.S. Department of Education, is responsible for this test. The Educational Testing Service, which also administers assessments such as the Scholastic Aptitude Test (SAT) for college entrance and Advanced Placement tests for college course credit, has been contracted to develop and administer the NAEP since 1983 (Yeager, 2007).

NAEP comprises two series of tests: a main test that addresses 11 subjects, and a long-term trend test that includes only reading and math. NAEP changes the contents of its main series about once a decade to correspond to educational movements, but it has kept the contents of its long-term trend series nearly the same. The most trustworthy comparison of reading achievement of U.S. youth across time comes from NAEP's long-term series, which reports scores from 1971 to 2004.

OVERALL SCORES

Eighth-grade students' reading achievement scores barely rose during the past 30-year period, whereas 12th-grade students' scores remained virtually unchanged (National Center for Education Statistics, n.d., a). As shown in Table 1.1, eighth-grade students' 1971 Reading Scale score was 255, and their 2004 Reading Scale score was 259. This 4-point difference is statistically significant, although its practical significance is questionable. Twelfth-grade students' 1971 Reading Scale score was 285. Their scores rose slightly during the early 1990s, and their 2004 Reading Scale score returned to its original point of 285.

DEMOGRAPHIC GROUPS' SCORES

Along with comparing average reading scores, NAEP has documented reading scores broken down according to demographic groups. Table 1.2 displays the differences that persisted between Black and White students' reading achievement scores from 1971 to 2004, with White students consistently out-

TABLE 1.1. NAEP Reading Scale Scores

Year	8th-grade students	12th-grade students
1971	255	285
2004	259	285

**TABLE 1.2. NAEP Reading Scale Score
Differences between Black and White Students**

Year	13-year-old students	17-year-old students
1971	39	53
2004	22	29

performing Black students. The difference decreased measurably over the years, although it remains substantial.

Table 1.3 shows the differences that persisted between Hispanic and White students' reading achievement scores at nearly the same time. Although the amount of difference did not change measurably across time for 13-year-olds, it decreased appreciably for 17-year-olds. Nevertheless, the gap between Hispanic and White students' reading scores remains substantial.

English language learners (ELLs), a group with myriad ethnicities, comprise a rapidly growing population whose literacy achievement is dramatically lower than others (Batalova, Fix, & Murray, 2007; Short & Fitzsimmons, 2007). The reading score differences between eighth-grade ELL and non-ELL students exceeded the differences among all other comparison groups, including students with and without disabilities (Perie, Grigg, & Donahue, 2005).

Finally, NAEP displays reading achievement gaps by gender. As Table 1.4 reveals, reading achievement of females consistently has been higher than that of males from 1971 to 2004.

College Readiness

College faculty tend to claim that new students generally are not ready for a college education (American College Testing [ACT], 2006; Intersegmental Committee for the Academic Senates, 2002). Evidence to support the faculty members' claims comes from several sources. A measure derived from high school graduation rates, academic course work, and reading tests indicate that only 34% of high school students were ready for college in 2002 (Greene & Winters, 2005). This measure also demonstrated gaps among demographic groups, with 40% of White students, 23% of African American students, and 20% of Hispanic students with diplomas and ready for college in 2002.

**TABLE 1.3. NAEP Reading Scale Score
Differences between Hispanic and White Students**

Year	13-year-old students	17-year-old students
1975	30	41
2004	24	29

**TABLE 1.4. NAEP Reading Scale Score
Differences between Female and Male Students**

Year	13-year-old students	17-year-old students
1971	11	12
2004	10	14

Several indicators go straight to reading performance. The College Readiness Benchmark for Reading, derived from high school students' performance on the ACT college entrance test, indicated that half of 2004–2005 students were ready for college reading requirements (ACT, 2006). A large number of faculty members designate students' lack of analytical reading skills as a contributor to their learning difficulties (Intersegmental Committee for the Academic Senates, 2002). And large numbers of college students enroll in remedial reading course work (Alliance for Excellent Education, 2007b).

A particularly relevant finding that points directly to secondary school reading instruction is that high school students tend to lose reading momentum. High school students tend to be on track for college-level reading more in 8th- and 10th grade than when they reach 12th grade and graduate (ACT, 2006).

State

State tests, which commonly involve 10th-grade students (Callahan, 2007), provide mixed information about adolescents' reading achievement. A perplexing feature is that state reading tests tend to be more difficult to pass in upper grades than in earlier grades (Cronin, Dahlin, Adkins, & Kingsbury, 2007). Taking into account obvious increases in complexity across grade-level reading materials, more students in the upper grades than students in the lower grades are at risk of failing to reach proficiency. This greater risk seems due to different cut scores for proficiency. In nearly half the states, students in the upper grades need to score nearly 10 percentile points higher than students in the lower grades to be considered proficient.

Year-to-year trends in adolescents' reading achievement based on state tests need to be interpreted with caution. According to one analysis, since 2002, the youth in seven states showed moderate-to-large reading test score gains (Center on Education Policy, 2007). However, such year-to-year growth needs to be scrutinized because states frequently move to new measurement scales or amend the scores that readers need in order to be considered proficient (Cronin et al., 2007). Changes in state testing programs may explain gains in state reading test scores.

State-to-state comparisons of reading test scores also need to be interpreted with caution (McCombs, Kirby, Barney, Darilek, & Magee, 2004;

Cronin et al., 2007; National Center for Education Statistics, 2007). As Table 1.5 illustrates, the percentage of South Carolina and Wyoming eighth-grade students demonstrating proficiency on their state assessments in 2004 is about the same as those demonstrating proficiency on NAEP (Moore, Moore, Cunningham, & Cunningham, 2006). However, markedly different percentages of North Carolina and Texas eighth graders demonstrated proficiency on the two assessments. Far more students performed well on the North Carolina and Texas state tests than on NAEP. Such differences confirm inconsistencies among state tests, with some expecting readers to perform at higher levels than others.

Commentary

The claims of a literacy crisis can be mediated in light of the literacy achievement measures just presented. International testing programs such as PISA reveal similarities and differences among reading test scores, but they do not reveal economic productivity. In 2007-2008 the U.S. ranked first among all nations in global competitiveness, sustained economic productivity, and prosperity (World Economic Forum, n.d.). Perhaps the U.S. scores are satisfactory, indicating an appropriate balance of test-taking abilities along with habits of the mind and spirit like initiative, independence, and inquiry. Reading scores do not necessarily indicate national wealth or quality of life.

The NAEP long-term trend in reading achievement of U.S. youth has been virtually stationary. This trend can be viewed positively on the one hand, with the realization that U.S. demographics have shifted toward a greater representation of traditionally underserved students. On the other hand, it can be viewed negatively given the ever-increasing economic, work force, and social demands.

U.S. adolescents' reading achievement gaps among racial, ethnic, and language lines, such as the ones just presented through international and national comparisons, have led to much legitimate unrest (Snow & Biancarosa, 2003). Many of the school reforms described in this chapter's earlier section focus directly on resisting the effects of poverty and racism that underlie disparities in academic performance. Yet efforts are needed to move beyond only the redesign of schools' instructional offerings (Berliner, 2006). Youth

TABLE 1.5. Percentage of Eighth-Grade Students Scoring at Proficient Level in Reading

State	State assessment	NAEP
South Carolina	21%	24%
Wyoming	39%	34%
North Carolina	86–88%	29%
Texas	86–88%	26%

can be expected to benefit from afterschool and summer programs that support academics, as well as cultural, athletic, and organizational experiences. Addressing disparities in teaching and learning conditions would seem to go far in addressing disparities in academics.

Reading Use

> There is a general decline in reading
> among teenage and adult Americans.
> —NATIONAL ENDOWMENT
> FOR THE ARTS (2007, p. 3)

Along with pointing to social, economic, and educational concerns and consulting measures of reading achievement, secondary school literacy advocates often support their activism by considering adolescents' existing uses of print. This section surveys youth reading inside and outside school.

Reading in School

Because reading is a valuable path to subject matter knowledge, most reports of in-school reading appraise the reading that youth do to learn assigned subject matter. In general, U.S. high school youth report that they read and study very little for their classes. One survey of 81,499 adolescents, in 110 schools within 26 states, reports that in a typical 7-day week, 55% of the youth say they read/study 0 to 1 hour for class (Yazzie-Mintz, 2007); 35% say they read/study 2–5 hours.

Youth seem to be reading a slight bit more for their schoolwork and homework than in the past (National Center for Education Statistics, n.d., b). As shown in Table 1.6, 13-year-old students reported reading more pages per day for school in 2004 than did 13-year-olds in 1984. Measurably fewer students read 5 or fewer pages per day, and measurably more students read more than 20 pages per day.

During this same 1984–2004 time period, however, 17-year-olds reported no appreciable differences in the number of pages they read daily for school and homework. Table 1.7 shows that 21% of these students in 2004 reported reading 5 or fewer pages each day, whereas 23% reported reading more than 20 pages daily. These figures do not differ appreciably from this age group's reported reading in 1984.

Although many secondary school classrooms have been shown to engage students in rich literacy experiences and to develop advanced reading proficiencies (Applebee, Langer, Nystrand, & Gamoran, 2003; Langer, 2002), many practices associated with limited reading growth persist (Alvermann & Moore, 1991; Sosniak & Perlman, 1990; Wade & Moje, 2000). Many teachers focus on students' acquisition of factual textbook information presented in brief portions, with few expectations for noting relationships among the

**TABLE 1.6. Number of Pages Read per Day
for School and Homework: 13-Year-Old Students**

Year	5 or fewer pages	More than 20 pages
1984	27%	11%
2004	21%	21%

ideas or organization of the texts. Students often use print in extremely short bursts, less than 1 minute at a time, to support their acquisition of directly specified ideas and information. Responses often are stated according to the precise language of the textbook. Struggling high school readers who remain in such courses with limited literacy experiences rarely improve their reading performance (Cappella & Weinstein, 2001).

If a state's high-stakes literacy testing accentuates single, simple responses, then schools serving traditionally low-performing populations are at risk of decreasing emphases on reading for sophisticated understandings (Au, 2007; Zabala & Minnici, 2007). These schools often limit the richness of the materials for students to read and the responses for students to produce. They limit their curricula to preparing students only for what they will encounter on the tests. Indeed, instituting rich literacy experiences across the curriculum, with subject matter teachers featuring the disciplinary literacies of their academic specializations, continues to be an ongoing issue in many schools (Bacevich & Salinger, 2006; Sunderman, Amoa, & Meyers, 2001).

Finally, focused reading instruction in secondary school tends to occur in regular English/language arts classes, where the reading materials mostly comprise prose fiction, humanities, and social science texts (ACT, 2007; Barry, 1997). Practically no natural science, mathematics, or functional everyday texts are used.

Another setting for focused reading instruction in secondary schools is supplemental classes devoted to ELLs, special needs students, or struggling readers (ACT, 2007; Barry, 1997). Boosting struggling readers' competencies in these classes continues to be challenging, especially at the high school level. Highly rated interventions have been shown to accelerate struggling ninth-grade readers' performance only about 25% over regular instruction, helping move students' average reading performance from the 16th to just the 25th percentile (Kemple et al., 2008).

**TABLE 1.7. Number of Pages Read per Day
for School and Homework: 17-Year-Old Students**

Year	5 or fewer pages	More than 20 pages
1984	21%	21%
2004	21%	23%

Reading Outside School

Today's youth live in a world saturated with print and nonprint media. Their access to ideas, to information, and to one another outside of school is unprecedented. Youth literacies in these outside-of-school settings range between those involving only print and those involving digital communications.

Print Literacies

Examinations of print usage outside of school typically focus on what adolescents read voluntarily, what they choose to read on their own rather than school requirements. Supporters of avid voluntary reading call attention to its link with intellectual proficiencies, as well as its recreational and aesthetic experiences (Cunningham & Stanovich, 1998; Krashen, 2004).

High school youth report that the amount of reading/studying they do for themselves outside of school parallels the reading they do inside school (Yazzie-Mintz, 2007). In a typical 7-day week, 56% report voluntarily reading 0 to 1 hour for themselves; 30% report reading 2–5 hours for themselves in a typical week.

The numbers of U.S. youth who report not reading voluntarily seems to be growing slightly (National Endowment for the Arts, 2007). Between 1984 and 2004, the percentage of 13-year-olds who reported reading nothing for pleasure grew from 8% to 13%; the percentage of 17-year-olds who reported reading nothing for pleasure grew from 9% to 19%. Between 1992 and 2002, the percentage of youth ages 18–24 who reported not reading any books for pleasure grew from 41% to 49%.

Voluntary reading diminishes as young Americans age (McKenna, Kear, & Ellsworth, 1995; National Endowment for the Arts, 2007). About one out of every two 9-year-olds reports reading for fun almost daily, whereas only about one out of every five 17-year-olds reports doing this.

Digital Literacies

Literacy tools of the 21st century, such as video screens, websites, and text messaging are joining the literacy tools of previous centuries, such as paper, books, and pencils (New London Group, 1996). The reading and writing of today's youth outside of school are moving to different, nonlinear forms as they engage in social networking sites (e.g., Facebook and MySpace), video sharing sites (e.g., YouTube), virtual worlds (e.g., Second Life), and personal interest websites about celebrities, current events, music, and so on. Their blogging, chatting, and video-gaming involve new ways of reading and writing. As information–communication technologies increase, youth are going beyond the traditional role of media consumers to new roles as media producers and distributors (Jacobs, 2006).

U.S. youth report using online communications more than ever (Lenhart, Madden, Macgill, & Smith, 2007). About 93% use the Internet, and this use centers more and more on social networking sites and blogging. Some 55% of teens have posted their profiles on a social networking site, and at least 70% of this group have read and responded to others' blogs.

Digital literacies are prime candidates for transforming schools into institutions attuned to the sensibilities of current youth and the demands of the new world economy (Knobel & Lankshear, 2007; O'Brien & Bauer, 2005). The new information–communication technologies might provide breakthroughs in helping students in general, and exceptional students in particular, access what they need to learn well. A huge majority of members of the U.S. public believe that schools need to prepare students differently than they did 20 years ago, with new attention to computer and technology skills, critical thinking and problem solving, and teamwork and collaboration (Partnership for 21st Century Skills, 2007).

Students and teachers will need help along the digital highway. Students' abilities to navigate, evaluate, and make sense of the wealth of information available through digital technology frequently are imperfect (Katz, 2005). Digital illiteracy can exist. Teachers require support incorporating information–communication technology into their classroom norms and academic expectations (Cuban, 2001; McGrail, 2006). New conceptions of literacy entail new conceptions of literacy instruction.

Commentary

As with the claim of a crisis in reading achievement, claims of a decline in reading use can be mediated. This section consistently shows that U.S. adolescents read rather moderate amounts of print now and in the past, inside and outside school. It shows that print is losing traction in the lives of many youth as they develop capacities and interests in other areas. Rather than blaming youth or schools, an ecological view focuses on the overall situation, examining its conditions and circumstances (Franzak, 2006; Moore, 1996). Youth probably would read more if their environment supported reading more.

The prevalence of digital literacies indicates that youth are thriving in this new environment. Rather than privileging print, schools might do well to endorse multiple literacies—the reading and writing done in many situations with many tools. Characterizing individuals as illiterate (can't read) or aliterate (won't read) often overstates their condition and misses their capacity. Youth seem to enjoy and to control print well in situations that speak to them.

Conclusion

The case for middle- and high-school reading instruction presented here avoids the rhetoric of crisis, as well as complacence. It might seem to accentuate the negative, but this is the catch-22 of literacy instruction (Myers, 1984).

Educational needs change along with national needs; schools regularly are expected to meet new standards. Resting on past accomplishments in reading instruction is not an option; we always need to do better.

The meaning of reading changes across time (Leu, 2006; Resnick & Resnick, 1977). Long ago, accurate oral recitations of print or verbatim recall of ideas might have counted as proficient reading, but times have changed. Youth now are expected to discern authors' intentions and to synthesize ideas across texts, to name a few advanced competencies.

Helping all youth achieve advanced levels of reading requires new ways of thinking, because it never before has been done (Bracey, 2004; Kantor & Lowe, 2004). The United States never had a golden age, in which all youth from all walks of life read at the levels expected today. High achievers certainly graduated in the past, but many youth remained at limited levels. Students from poor families, students with restricted English, and students with special learning needs had especially limited expectations and opportunities.

Attention to high levels of reading for all youth currently is at unprecedented levels. Educators now have the opportunity—and the challenge—to ensure that this attention serves youth well.

References

Alliance for Excellent Education. (2006, June). *Why the crisis in adolescent literacy demands a national response: Policy brief.* Washington, DC: Author. Retrieved December 6, 2007, from *www.all4ed.org/publication_material/fact_sheets/crisis_adlit.*

Alliance for Excellent Education. (2007a, September). *International comparisons of academic achievement: Fact sheet.* Washington, DC: Author. Retrieved December 6, 2007, from *www.all4ed.org/intl_comp.*

Alliance for Excellent Education. (2007b, September). *High school teaching for the twenty-first century: Preparing students for college: Issue brief.* Washington, DC: Author. Retrieved November 15, 2007, from *www.all4ed.org/publication_material/issue_policy_briefs.*

Alvermann, D. E., & Moore, D. W. (1991). Secondary school reading. In R. Barr, M. Kamil, P. Mosenthal, & P. D. Pearson (Eds.), *Handbook of reading research* (Vol. 2, pp. 951–983). New York: Longman.

American College Testing (ACT). (2006). *Reading between the lines: What the ACT reveals about college readiness in reading.* Iowa City, IA: Author. Retrieved September 8, 2006, from *www.act.org/path/policy/reports/reading.html.*

American College Testing (ACT). (2007). *ACT National Curriculum Survey, 2005–2006.* Iowa City, IA: Author. Retrieved December 8, 2007, from *www.act.org/research/policymakers/reports/curriculum.html.*

Applebee, A. N., Langer, J. L., Nystrand, M., & Gamoran, A. (2003). Discussion-based approaches to developing understanding: Classroom instruction and student performance in middle and high school English. *American Educational Research Journal, 40,* 685–730.

Au, W. (2007). High-stakes testing and curricular control: A qualitative metasynthesis. *Educational Researcher, 36,* 258–267.

Bacevich, A., & Salinger, T. (2006). *Lessons and recommendations from the Alabama Reading Initiative: Sustaining focus on secondary reading.* Washington, DC: American Institutes for Research. Retrieved September 21, 2006, from *www.air.org.*

Barry, A. (1997). High school reading programs revisited. *Journal of Adolescent & Adult Literacy, 40,* 525–531.

Barton, P. E. (2006). *What jobs require: Literacy, education, and training, 1940–2006.* Princeton, NJ: Educational Testing Service. Retrieved September 15, 2006, from *www.ets.org/research/pic.*

Batalova, J., Fix, M., & Murray, J. (2007). *Measures of change: The demography and literacy of adolescent English language learners—a report to Carnegie Corporation of New York.* Washington, DC: Migration Policy Institute. Retrieved March 15, 2008, from *www.migrationpolicy.org/pubs/measures_of_change.pdf.*

Berliner, D. (2006). *Our impoverished view of educational reform.* Tempe, AZ: Education Policy Studies Laboratory. Retrieved October 26, 2007, from *epsl.asu.edu/epru/documents/epsl-0508-116-epru.pdf.*

Biancarosa, F., & Snow, C. E. (2004). *Reading next: A vision for action and research in middle and high school literacy—a report to Carnegie Corporation of New York.* Washington, DC: Alliance for Excellent Education. Retrieved October 26, 2006, from *www.all4ed.org/adolescent_literacy/index.html.*

Bill and Melinda Gates Foundation. (n.d.). *High schools for the new millennium.* Seattle, WA: Author. Retrieved January 18, 2008, from *www.gatesfoundation.org/unitedstates/education/transforminghighschools/default.htm.*

Bond, G. L., & Bond, E. (1941). *Developmental reading in high school.* New York: Macmillan.

Bracey, G. (2004). *Setting the record straight* (2nd ed.). Portsmouth, NH: Heinemann.

Callahan, J. (2007). High school assessments 2006–07. *Diplomas count: Ready for what?* Retrieved June 12, 2007, from *www.edweek.org/ew/articles/2007/06/07/40policy3.h26.html.*

Campaign for High School Equity. (n.d.). *A plan for success: Communities of color define policy priorities for high school reform.* Washington, DC: Author. Retrieved January 18, 2008, from *www.highschoolequity.org/home.*

Cappella, E., & Weinstein, R. S. (2001). Turning around reading achievement: Predictors of high school students' academic resilience. *Journal of Educational Psychology, 93,* 758–771.

Carnegie Corporation of New York. (n.d.). *Advancing Literacy.* New York: Author. Retrieved June 28, 2007, from *www.carnegie.org/literacy/index.html.*

Carnegie Council on Adolescent Development. (1989). *Turning points: Preparing American youth for the 21st century.* Washington, DC: Author.

Cassidy, J., & Cassidy, D. (2008, February/March). What's hot for 2008. *Reading Today, 25*(4), 1, 10, 11. Retrieved February 5, 2008, from *www.reading.org/publications/reading_today/samples/rty-0802-hotlist.html.*

Center on Education Policy. (2007, June). *Answering the questions that matter most: Has student achievement increased since No Child Left Behind?* Retrieved June 28, 2007, from *www.cep-dc.org.*

Cronin, J., Dahlin, M., Adkins, D., & Kingsbury, G. G. (2007). *The proficiency illusion.* Washington, DC: Thomas B. Fordham Institute. Retrieved January 13, 2008, from *www.edexcellence.net/institute/publication/publication.cfm?id=376.*

Cuban, L. (2001). *Oversold and underused: Computers in the classroom.* Cambridge, MA: Harvard University Press.

Cunningham, A. E., & Stanovich, K. E. (1998). What reading does to the mind. *American Educator, 22*(1), 8–15.

Editorial Projects in Education. (2007, June). *Diplomas count 2007: Ready for what? Education Week* [Special issue]. Retrieved June 12, 2007, from *www.edweek.org/ew/articles/2007/06/12/40gradprofiles.h26.html?print=1.*

Franzak, J. K. (2006). Zoom: A review of the literature on marginalized adolescent readers, literacy theory, and policy implications. *Review of Educational Research, 76,* 209–248.

Friedlander, D., & Darling-Hammond, L. (2007). *High schools for equity: Policy supports for student learning in communities of color.* Stanford, CA: School Redesign Network. Retrieved January 19, 2008, from *www.srnleads.org.*

Graham, P. (1981). Literacy: A goal for secondary schools. *Daedalus, 110*(3), 119–134.

Greene, J., & Winters, M. (2006). *Public high school graduation and college-readiness rates: 1991–2002.* New York: Manhattan Institute for Policy Research. Retrieved January 13, 2008, from *www.manhattan-institute.org/html/ewp_08.htm.*

Heller, R., & Greenleaf, C. L. (2007). *Literacy instruction in the content areas: Getting to the core of high school improvement.* Washington, DC: Alliance for Excellent Instruction. Retrieved January 15, 2008, from *www.all4ed.org/publication_material/reports.*

Intersegmental Committee for the Academic Senates. (2002). *Academic literacy: A statement of the competencies expected of students entering California's public colleges and universities.* Sacramento, CA: Author. Retrieved January 23, 2007, from *www.academicsenate.cc.ca.us/icas.html.*

Jacobs, G. (2006). Fast times and digital literacy: Participation roles and portfolio construction with instant messaging. *Journal of Literacy Research, 38,* 171–196.

Jacobs, V. (2008). Adolescent literacy: Putting the crisis in context. *Harvard Educational Review, 78,* 7–39.

Kantor, H., & Lowe, R. (2004). Reflections on history and quality education. *Educational Researcher, 33*(5), 6–10.

Katz, I. R. (2005). *Beyond technical competence: Literacy in information and communication technology.* Princeton, NJ: Educational Testing Service. Retrieved January 24, 2008, from *www.ets.org.*

Kemple, J., Corrin, W., Nelson, E., Salinger, T., Herrmann, S., & Drummond, K. (2008). *The Enhanced Reading Opportunities Study: Early impact and implementation findings* (NCEE 2008-4015). Washington, DC: National Center for Education Evaluation and Regional Assistance, Institute of Education Sciences, U.S. Department of Education. Retrieved February 17, 2008, from *ies.ed.gov/ncee/pubs/20084015.asp.*

Kirsch, I., Braun, H., Yamamoto, K., & Sum, A. (2007). *America's perfect storm: Three forces changing our nation's future.* Princeton, NJ: Educational Testing Service. Retrieved February 10, 2007, from *www.ets.org/research/pic.*

Knobel, M., & Lankshear, C. (2007). *A new literacies sampler.* New York: Peter Lang.

Kober, N. (2006). *A public education primer: Basic (and sometimes surprising) facts about the U.S. education system.* Washington, DC: Center on Education Policy. Retrieved December 6, 2007, from *www.cep-dc.org.*

Krashen, S. (2004). *The power of reading* (2nd ed.). Englewood, CO: Libraries Unlimited.

Langer, J. A. (2002). *Effective literacy instruction: Building successful reading and writing programs.* Urbana, IL: National Council of Teachers of English.

Legters, N. E., McPartland, J. M., & Balfanz, R. (2004). Scaling up talent development high schools: Lessons learned from comprehensive high school reform. In T. K. Glennan, Jr., S. J. Bodily, J. R. Galegher, & K. A. Kerr (Eds.), *Expanding the reach of education reforms: Perspectives from leaders in the scale-up of educational interventions* (pp. 379–432). Santa Monica, CA: RAND Corporation. Retrieved January 13, 2008, from *www.rand.org/pubs/monographs/MG248.*

Lemke, M., & Gonzales, P. (2006). *U.S. student and adult performance on international assessments of educational achievement: Findings from the Condition of Education 2006* (NCES 2006-073). Washington, DC: U.S. Department of Education, National Center for Education Statistics. Retrieved January 16, 2007, from *nces.ed.gov/pubsearch/pubsinfo.asp?pubid=2006073.*

Lemke, M., Sen, A., Johnston, J., Pahlke, E., Williams, T., Kastberg, D., et al. (2005). *Characteristics of U.S. 15-year-old low achievers in an international context: Findings from PISA 2000* [U.S. Department of Education Sciences]. Washington, DC: National Center for Education Statistics. Retrieved January 25, 2008, from *nces. ed.gov/pubsearch/pubsinfo.asp?pubid=2006010.*

Lemke, M., Sen, A., Pahlke, E., Partelow, L., Miller, D., Williams, T., et al. (2004). *International outcomes of learning in mathematics literacy and problem solving: PISA 2003 results from the U.S. perspective* [U.S. Department of Education Sciences]. Washington, DC: National Center for Education Statistics. Retrieved January 25, 2008, from *nces.ed.gov/pubsearch/pubsinfo.asp?pubid=2005003.*

Lenhart, A., Madden, M., Macgill, A. R., & Smith, A. (2007). *Teens and social media.* Washington, DC: Pew Internet and American Life Project. Retrieved January 16, 2008, from *www.pewinternet.org/ppf/r/230/report_display.asp.*

Leu, D. J. (2006). New literacies, reading research, and the challenges of change: A deictic perspective. In J. V. Hoffman, D. L. Schallert, C. M. Fairbanks, J. Worthy, & B. Maloch (Eds.), *55th yearbook of the National Reading Conference* (pp. 1–20). Oak Creek, WI: National Reading Conference.

McCombs, J. S., Kirby, S. N., Barney, H., Darilek, H., & Magee, S. J. (2004). *Achieving state and national literacy goals: A long uphill road* [A report to Carnegie Corporation of New York]. Santa Monica, CA: RAND Corporation. Retrieved December 18, 2004, from *www.rand.org/publications/tr/tr180.*

McGrail, E. (2006). "It's a double-edged sword, this technology business": Secondary English teachers' perspectives on a schoolwide laptop technology initiative. *Teachers College Record, 108,* 1055–1079.

McKenna, M. C., Kear, D. J., & Ellsworth, R. A. (1995). Children's attitudes toward reading: A national survey. *Reading Research Quarterly, 30,* 934–956.

Moore, D. W. (1996). Contexts for literacies in secondary schools. In K. Hinchman, D. J. Leu, & C. K. Kinzer (Eds.), *Literacies for the 21st century: Research and practice: 45th yearbook of the National Reading Conference* (pp. 15–46). Chicago: National Reading Conference.

Moore, D. W., Moore, S. A., Cunningham, P. M., & Cunningham, J. W. (2006). *Developing readers and writers in the content areas: K–12* (5th ed.). Boston: Allyn & Bacon.

Moore, D. W., Readence, J. E., & Rickelman, R. (1983). An historical exploration of content area reading instruction. *Reading Research Quarterly, 18,* 419–438.

Myers, M. (1984). Shifting standards of literacy—the teacher's Catch 22. *English Journal, 73*(4), 26–32.

National Assessment of Educational Progress. (n.d.). *Reading.* Retrieved October 7, 2006, from *nces.ed.gov/nationsreportcard/reading.*

National Association of Secondary School Principals. (1996). *Breaking ranks: Changing an American institution.* Reston, VA: Author.

National Center for Education Statistics. (2007). *Mapping 2005 state proficiency standards onto the NAEP scales.* Retrieved March 15, 2008, from *nces.ed.gov/nationsreportcard/pubs/studies/2007482.asp.*

National Center for Education Statistics. (n.d., a). *National trends in reading by average scale scores.* Retrieved September 19, 2007, from *nces.ed.gov/nationsreportcard/ltt/results2004/nat-reading-scalescore.asp.*

National Center for Education Statistics. (n.d., b). *Trends in pages read per day for school and for homework.* Retrieved September 19,2007, from *nces.ed.gov/nationsreportcard/ltt/results2004/exp-reading-percentage.asp.*

National Commission on Excellence in Education. (1983). *A nation at risk: The imperative for educational reform.* Retrieved January 13, 2008, from *www.ed.gov/pubs/natatrisk/index.html.*

National Endowment for the Arts. (2007). *To read or not to read: A question of national consequence.* Washington, DC: Author. Retrieved January 17, 2008, from *www.arts. gov/pub/publit.php.*

New London Group. (1996). A pedagogy of multiliteracies: Designing social futures. *Harvard Educational Review, 66*(1), 60–92.

O'Brien, D., & Bauer, E. B. (2005). New literacies and the institution of old learning. *Reading Research Quarterly, 40,* 120–131.

Organisation for Economic Co-operation and Development. (n.d.). *The PISA 2003 assessment framework—mathematics, reading, science and problem solving knowledge and skills.* Retrieved January 25, 2008, from *www.pisa.oecd.org.*

Partnership for 21st Century Skills. (2007). *Beyond the 3 Rs: Voter attitudes toward 21st century skills.* Tucson, AZ: Author. Retrieved February 12, 2008, from *www.21stcenturyskills.org.*

PASS Act—Pathways for All Students to Succeed. (n.d.). Retrieved June 2, 2007, from *murray.senate.gov/pass.*

Perie, M., Grigg, W., & Donahue, P. (2005). *The nation's report card: Reading 2005* (NCES 2006–451; U.S. Department of Education, National Center for Education Statistics). Washington, DC: U.S. Government Printing Office. Retrieved January 16, 2007, from *nces.ed.gov/pubsearch/pubsinfo.asp?pubid=2006451.*

Resnick, D. P., & Resnick, L. B. (1977). The nature of literacy: An historical exploration. *Harvard Educational Review, 47,* 370–385.

Short, D. J., & Fitzsimmons, S. (2007). *Double the work: Challenges and solutions to acquiring language and academic literacy for adolescent English language learners—a report to Carnegie Corporation of New York.* Washington, DC: Alliance for Excellent Education. Retrieved November 25, 2006, from *www.all4ed.org/adolescent_literacy/index. html.*

Singer, H. (1983). A century of landmarks in reading and learning from text at the high school level: Research, theories, and instructional strategies. *Journal of Reading, 26,* 332–342.

Snow, C. E., & Biancarosa, G. (2003). *Adolescent literacy and the achievement gap: What do we know and where do we go from here?* New York: Carnegie Corporation of New York. Retrieved November 25, 2006, from *www.carnegie.org/literacy/pdf/alff1.pdf.*

Sosniak, L. A., & Perlman, C. L. (1990). Secondary education by the book. *Journal of Curriculum Studies, 22,* 427–442.

Stein, S. (2000). *Equipped for the future: What adults need to know and be able to do in the*

21st century. Washington, DC: National Institute for Literacy. Retrieved March 8, 2006, from *www.nifl.gov*.

Sunderman, G. L., Amoa, M., & Meyers, T. (2001). California's reading initiative: Constraints on implementation in the middle and high schools. *Educational Policy, 15*, 674–698.

Swanson, C. B., & Barlage, J. (2006). *Influence: A study of the factors shaping educational policy*. Bethesda, MD: Editorial Projects in Education Research Center. Retrieved September 26, 2007, from *www.edweek.org/rc/articles/2006/12/13/influentials. html*.

Topping, K. (2006). PISA/PIRLS data on reading achievement: Transfer into international policy and practice. *Reading Teacher, 59*, 289–290.

U.S. Department of Education. (n.d., a). *Public law print of PL 107-110, the No Child Left Behind Act of 2001*. Retrieved May 14, 2006, from *www.ed.gov/policy/elsec/leg/ esea02/index.html*.

U.S. Department of Education. (n.d., b). *Striving Readers*. Retrieved May 14, 2006, from *www.ed.gov/programs/strivingreaders/index.html*.

Wade, S., & Moje, E. B. (2000). The role of text in classroom learning. In M. J. Kamil, P. B. Mosenthal, P. D. Pearson, & R. Barr (Eds.), *Handbook of reading research* (Vol. 3, pp. 609–627). Mahwah, NJ: Erlbaum.

Whipple, G. M. (1925). *Report of the National Committee on Reading: 24th yearbook of the National Society for the Study of Education* (Pt. 1). Bloomington, IL: Public School Publishing Company.

World Economic Forum. (n.d.). *The global competitiveness report, 2007–2008*. Retrieved February 12, 2008, from *www.gcr.weforum.org*.

Yazzie-Mintz, E. (2007). *Voices of students on engagement: A report on the 2006 High School Survey of Student Engagement*. Center for Evaluation and Education Policy, Indiana University School of Education. Retrieved November 24, 2007, from *ceep. indiana.edu/hsse*.

Yeager, M. (2007). *Understanding NAEP: Inside the nation's education report card*. Washington, DC: Education Sector. Retrieved February 3, 2008, from *www.educationsector.org*.

Zabala, D., & Minnici, A. (2007). *It's different now: How exit exams are affecting teaching and learning in Jackson and Austin*. Washington, DC: Center on Education Policy. Retrieved September 21, 2007, from *www.cep-dc.org*.

Part I

LITERACY AND
THE ADOLESCENT LEARNER

Chapter 2

The "Adolescent" in Adolescent Literacy
A Preliminary Review

Thomas W. Bean
Helen Harper

GUIDING QUESTIONS

---

1. What has the field of adolescent literacy revealed about adolescents and their current literacy practices?
2. How has the field itself constructed adolescents and their literacy?
3. What does this mean for future research in adolescent literacy?

Students stream into class, oozing an array of emotions ranging from wild enthusiasm to absolute indifference. It is Thursday afternoon, which means it is Ms. Campinello's senior English Literature class. Four new students have recently transferred into Ms. Campinello's class. Rafael, one of these newly transferred students, enters the classroom. He has his black hood pulled up against the winter cold. His iPod earbuds are in and he's listening to an old Bob Marley reggae tune. His touch screen cell phone is on, and he's watching a rough clip of a YouTube video he and other class members are creating to promote recycling and the banning of plastic bags at his school. Alongside Rafael is Tiffany, swinging a large, Hello Kitty bag, which, among an incredibly large assortment of other items, carries her favorite novel (she will carefully tuck it inside the class-assigned text, *The Merchant of Venice*, and read surreptitiously during class, then text her friends about later). Damian, who trips in behind her, has already read *The Merchant of Venice* in its entirety and loved it. He has set as a secret project to read as many Shakespearean plays as possible this semester. Anna, who struggles to understand English, despite many years in an English language learner (ELL) class, slinks in behind them, hoping to escape the teacher's attention and hide her failure yet again to complete the class reading assignment. She pauses to write her boyfriend's name, along with a heart, on the inside cover of her English/ Polish dictionary. She smiles. The heart and name will help distract her from whatever impossible task she'll be asked to do in this class.

Ms. Campinello picks up her own well-marked copy of *The Merchant of Venice* and looks out at the class. This is a large class and, as usual, there are not enough desks, not enough books, not enough help, and not enough time. Moreover, she feels a huge gap between her students and herself. They are worlds apart from each other. She knows so little about them and their lives. Ms. Campinello sighs; she needs to time think about and get to know these students of hers, collectively and individually. But for now, with the sound of the buzzer, she begins the lesson.

The Adolescent and Society

It may seem that Ms. Campinello does not know her students. Certainly she feels this. And in truth she has not had much interaction with them, or at least not as much as she would like, but Ms. Campinello is in many respects already very familiar with "adolescents" and perhaps even with their "adolescent literacies." For following the teacher and the students into the classroom are both individual histories of how the "adolescent" life has been lived out, and the broader social history of how "adolescence" has been named, characterized, and categorized in our society. To some degree the teacher and her students already know each other, or more accurately, know *of* each other through these histories.

Individual and social histories are not unrelated. How society names, organizes, and structures adolescence affects how individuals may live out their lives as a teenagers at any given moment. It is society, or more precisely, the state that determines when an adolescent can get a drivers license, quit school, enter the labor market, or be married. Such government policies and common social practices name and separate the adolescent from the adult and the child. These policies and practices, and notions about the adolescent that underwrite them, help at least to some degree to standardize or normalize adolescent life in and out of school. Those adolescents whose lives do not conform to policies or practices and the assumptions that support them must negotiate the problem of being defined as deviant, odd, or strangely exceptional. And they must cope with myriad programmatic remedies concocted by adults to cure them of such labels.

Ms. Campinello wants to know her students to better educate them, and she already knows something about adolescents from her own history, from her previous students, and from what she knows about the social history and organization of adolescents. All of this equips her with what might be deemed "commonsense" or common knowledge about adolescents. Of course, as a high school teacher, she is also educated in the practices, policies, and organization of schooling in America and its history that determine how adolescents are named and understood. Her classroom, the school building itself, and indeed all classrooms and school buildings, with their structure, location, texts, equipment, and artifacts, embody to various degrees what is and what has been thought about the education of high school students. Curricula, class schedules, extracurricular events, and administrative structure all indicate something about how adolescent learners and their education are understood. Both Ms. Campinello and her students enter into a site that is imbued with a history that precedes them, and that organizes and influences their interactions, learning, and teaching experiences.

As is evident in the opening vignette, Ms. Campinello is not just any high school teacher; she is an English teacher. Indeed, she is a literacy specialist working on an advanced degree in adolescent literacy. As will be shown, the field of adolescent literacy itself offers "readings" or particular understandings of adolescence and adolescent literacy practices that also help to construct and organize Ms. Campinello's knowledge of her students and of the kind of literacy education she can and will provide them. Knowing how *adolescence* is defined in society, in school, and in the field of adolescent literacy may be a first step toward the possibility of truly knowing and providing for the students that Ms. Campinello and all of us meet in our literacy classrooms.

In this chapter we focus on how adolescence is configured in the field of adolescent literacy. The three guiding questions at the beginning of the chapter organize our thinking. We begin by briefly situating these questions in the context of the larger milieu of contemporary America that informs the ways that adolescence has been defined and understood, that is, produced in our classrooms, our schools, and our field.

Defining Adolescence

The vignette that opens this chapter offers a quick sketch of adolescent life, adolescent literacies, and literacies of the adolescents' teacher. It is a representation, perhaps familiar, but not a particularly comprehensive one. However, as described in the work of Nancy Lesko (2001), more all-encompassing constructions of adolescence that are apparent in both popular and academic discourses are indeed quite powerful, serving to name and organized adolescence systematically in many fields of endeavor, including the law, government, psychology, medicine, and education. Lesko defines these constructions as (1) biological or developmental and (2) sociohistorical. According to Lesko, of the two, the view of adolescent life as a biological or development stage of life is the most dominant. From this perspective, adolescence is viewed as a natural biological phenomenon, universal and predictable in its characteristics and onset, and all aspects of adolescent life, including the cognitive, social, and psychological aspects, are affected by it. Because adolescence is not a static state but one that changes over time as the individual matures, teachers working within this perspective focus on teens' developmental achievements, including emotional stability, self-control, rationality, and conformity to adult norms and standards, all of which are seen as sequential and cumulative.

Myriad assumptions arise from this view; for example, that adolescents "come of age"; that adolescents are controlled by raging hormones; that they are peer-oriented, and best understood and represented by age (Lesko, 2001, p. 2). In general, this perspective suggests that teenagers, in comparison with adults, are "unfinished products" whose age-related biological and developmental condition requires particular care and protection to ensure their optimal development.

The sociohistoric view posits adolescence as an invention of the 20th century, more specifically, not as a product of biology, but of cultural, economic, and educational circumstances. From this perspective, adolescence in North America and Europe is said to have begun in the late 1800s, when child labor laws, industrialization, and union organization limited employment, in particular, the apprenticeships that youth traditionally entered after some modicum of public schooling. Extending compulsory education proved to be one means of dealing with the threat of idle, unemployed youth. Because of their economic dependence, all adolescents were defined through their collective lives as high school students, and they became the "teenagers" of the 20th and now 21st century. Economic, institutional, and social changes allowed for the development of teen-based popular culture that in turn created a generation of youth quite different from those in previous generations.

Because of its emphasis on context, this perspective acknowledges differences rather than universalities among youth. Gender, race, ethnicity, and social class, for example, are seen as dramatically affecting the nature and experience of adolescent life. Moreover, it is possible that some individuals, particularly youth living in places with different economic, social, and cultural practices, might never experience an "adolescence" at all.

These two perspectives have informed, or at least have provided a backdrop, and it stands to reason that adolescence is understood and explained in schools, in the field of adolescent literacy, to which we now turn.

The Field of Adolescent Literacy

Adolescent literacy as a field was developed and formalized in large measure through the efforts of the International Reading Association (IRA) and its creation of the Commission on Adolescent Literacy in the mid-1990s (Richardson, 2008). Although interest in the reading skills of teenagers goes back to the early 20th century, and research in the content-area literacy of adolescents back to the 1970s, these areas of research and scholarship by the 1990s were largely subsumed by the category of *adolescent literacy* (Vacca, 1998). In an effort to address growing interest in the adolescent learner, the Commission on Adolescent Literacy created a position paper to drive curriculum policy and funding decisions (Moore, Bean, Birdyshaw, & Rycik, 1999). Now, 10 years later, the field of adolescent literacy is on a firmer footing, and in part because of the history of the field it encompasses, multiple views of adolescence, some of which hint at a biological or developmental framing; others, the majority of views, seem to suggest a sociohistorical understanding of both adolescence and adolescent literacy. In general, our preliminary review of the documents and major texts indicates that amid lingering unanswered questions and assumptions about what comprises adolescence, the field is certainly challenging simplistic and universal views, while offering its own particular and bounded reading of teens' lives and their literacies. We all need to be aware of these readings, if we ever hope to know or at least acknowledge the complexity and diversity of the adolescents we teach.

Views of Adolescence and Adolescent Literacy Practices

We examined in this preliminary review the following texts, policies, and position statements:

1. Edited texts, including the first and second editions of *Reconceptualizing the Literacies in Adolescents' Lives* (Alvermann, Hinchman, Moore, Phelps, & Waff, 1998, 2006); *Literacy for the New Millennium: Volume 3. Adolescent Literacy* (Guzzetti, 2007); *Adolescent Literacy Research and Practice* (Jetton & Dole, 2004); and *Adolescent Literacy Instruction: Policies and Promising Practices* (Lewis & Moorman, 2007).

2. Journals and journal articles including an examination of the publishing history and content of the *Journal of Adolescent & Adult Literacy* and selected articles and editorials appearing in general literacy journals, such as *Reading Research Quarterly*, and *English Journal*.

3. Policy documents and position papers, including *Adolescent Literacy: A Position Statement for the Commission on Adolescent Literacy of the International Reading Association* (Moore et al., 1999); a related Carnegie Corporation case study report and book, *Principled Practices for Adolescent Literacy: A Framework for Instruction and Policy* (Sturtevant et al., 2006); two Carnegie-funded reports, *Reading Next* (Biancarosa & Snow, 2006) and *Writing Next* (Graham & Perin, 2007); and the annual report in the IRA's publication *Reading Today* on "What's Hot for 2008" (Cassidy & Cassidy, 2008), as well as a related 10-year analysis of this column, published in the *Journal of Adolescent and Adult Literacy* (Cassidy, Garrett, & Barrera, 2006).

Each of these policy and position papers charts the growing interest in adolescent literacy, often attributed to the extension of the No Child Left Behind legislation to include adolescent learners and related federal funding for striving reader grants (Cassidy et al., 2006). Based on our reading and interpretive analysis of these and other documents characterizing adolescent learners, we examine four major ways in which adolescence has been configured in the field.

Adolescence as a Grade- or Age-Level Designation

The growing body of work aimed at understanding adolescent literacy practices reveals a rich and complex terrain, but one in which, with rare exception,[1] adolescence is not directly theorized. Instead, adolescence is taken as a given, named, if defined at all, by grade- or age-level designation. This is particularly true in state and federal policy documents, and in position papers by various interest groups. The National Institute of Child Health and Human Development (NICHD), for example, in its literacy initiatives, defines *adolescents* as middle and high school students. This would seem practical, indeed commonsensical, but as Terry Salinger (2007) points out, middle school entry can occur at fifth grade or later. The IRA position statement on adolescent literacy also uses a grade-level designation, defining *adolescents* as "the more than 20,000,000 students currently enrolled in U.S. middle and high schools" (Moore et al., 1999, p. 3). The *Journal of Adolescent & Adult Literacy*, which we edit, has a history of using the designation "age 12 and up" for adolescents. We suspect that this designation has been used to differentiate the journal from *The Reading Teacher*, which focuses on elementary school reading.

The age- or grade-level designation of the adolescent may be in response to government initiatives that have focused exclusively on ensuring that all students can read by grade 3. The use of grade 3 as an endpoint designation is critical. In 1999, Carol Santa, then President of the IRA, stated, "In the United States, most Title 1 budgets are allocated for early intervention—little is left over for the struggling adolescent reader. Even if all children do learn to read by Grade 3, the literacy needs of the adolescent reader are far different from those of primary-grade children" (Moore et al., 1999, p. 1). Santa's statements create a distinct separation of primary grade students from adolescent students of middle and high school, even if basic literacy is attained. This common position is evident in the field. However, it has been challenged by some, including Patricia Alexander (2005/2006) whose work draws on developmental psychology but nonetheless suggests that literacy "evolves and matures over time in ways not governed by grade-level designations" (cited in Salinger, 2007, p. 7). Alexander is troubled by simplistic notions of ado-

---

[1]Although not specific to and about the field of adolescent literacy, the most explicit theorizing about adolescence we reviewed was apparent in *Re/Constructing "the Adolescent": Sign, Symbol, and Body* (Vadeboncoeur & Stevens, 2005).

lescents and their literacies as fixed by age or grade-level. Other ways that adolescents and their literacies have been defined in the field speak more to literacy needs and practices, irrespective of, or at least with less emphasis on, specific age or grade levels, or the developmental or biological assumptions that underlie these designations.

Adolescence Defined by Literacy Needs

Another way that adolescents are defined in the field is through their literacy needs, which are positioned as separate and distinct from the literacy needs of others. Thus, adolescence is understood as a time when one's literacy needs shift, so that appropriate and particular forms of instruction are required.

Evident in the literature are two major literacy needs of adolescents: (1) teens need more advanced literacy instruction for the increasingly complex materials they face in their classes, and (2) many teens need basic literacy instruction. In the first case, many in the field would agree that literacy is a continuum, and that learning to read and write is just the beginning, or it occurs near the beginning, of an individual's literacy education, certainly not the end. The IRA adolescent literacy position statement reads: "Reading success in the early grades certainly pays off later, but early achievement is not the end of the story. . . . There are developmental stages—reading and [early literacy accomplishments] are only the first steps of growth into full literacy" (cited by Salinger, 2007, p. 3).

Although a developmental or biological perspective is suggested in these statements, in much of what we read, the need for further literacy education, or "full literacy," is not brought about by an individual's cognitive or psychological development per se, but by the academic literacy demands placed on individuals in secondary classrooms (Bean, Readence, & Baldwin, 2008). Context, then, rather than one's internal psychology or biology (i.e., age) is the key factor in understanding the literacy of adolescents. Thus, *adolescence* is not defined in terms of age or grade, but in terms of literacy needs that expand due to the demands of schooling and the individual's expanding interests and abilities. These reading skills include comprehending multiple-content texts laden with technical vocabulary and sometimes arcane text structures. Each content area (e.g., biology, mathematics, history, and English) has its own idiosyncratic ways of conveying information and concepts, of naming evidence, and of assessing validity and quality. Coupled with the vast array of content material on the Internet, often organized according to a particular Web authors' logic, a huge array of information in various forms and of varying quality and credibility confronts contemporary students (McNabb, 2006). Moreover the ideological and political context and foundation of informational and narrative material also require consideration. For many, this suggests a need for critical reading and critical literacy practices, in addition to more standard content-area reading support (Morrell, 2008; King, Hart, & Kozdras, 2007; Stevens & Bean, 2007).

As outlined, many perceived adolescent reading needs are described as being distinct from those of primary school children, shifting from a learning-to-read to a reading-to-learn stance, and a potentially more sophisticated set of skills, knowledge, and attitudes. However, another way in which adolescent needs have been defined in the field is in relation to deficiencies in basic literacy; to adolescents as illiterates or aliterates, or, more euphemistically, as struggling or striving readers. These adolescents are deemed to need specialized or at least appropriate teaching instruction and literacy materials to improve and encourage reading. This a major area of concern and, indeed, much of the attention toward adolescents and adolescent literacy is centered on the needs of *struggling readers,* often defined as those students performing below grade-level expectations (Biancarosa & Snow, 2006; Jetton & Dole, 2004).

If discussed at all, the ultimate origins of low achievement are not usually attributed to biological conditions. Rather, low achievement is attributed to socioeonomic, cultural, and institutional or pedagogical factors. Whatever the cause, the category of struggling or striving readers is often undifferentiated in policy, with little attention to adolescents as individuals with radically different histories and unique social contexts, with strengths as well as deficiencies. Williams Dee Nichols (2007) notes that "classifying struggling readers as illiterate often overgeneralizes their true reading identity and does not completely acknowledge their literacy capacities" (p. 7). Supportive instructional efforts that recognize local funds of knowledge on which adolescents may draw in their out-of-school lives (writing hip-hop songs, poetry, music, etc.), taps into this resource as a way to engage struggling readers in bridging to content-area material, sometimes through a critique of how diverse cultures are erroneously portrayed in the media (Morrell, 2008).

Whatever their circumstances and strengths, the number of students performing below grade level is a critical factor in the field for teachers, researchers, and policymakers. Various policy documents that now drive funding for adolescent struggling readers sound a note of alarm. The economic well-being of the nation, as well as the individual, is at risk. Widely quoted national reports, including *Reading Next* (Biancarosa & Snow, 2006) and *Writing Next* (Graham & Perin, 2007), suggest a crisis in need of immediate research-based solutions. Recognizing the absence of a fully developed research base in adolescent literacy, the *Reading Next* report uses the best current scientifically based quantitative studies to craft a call to action. Pointing to a lack of reading skills as one of the most commonly cited reasons for adolescents' departure from high school, the authors have developed a reasonably sound series of cognitive instructional recommendations.

Similarly, *Writing Next* (Graham & Perin, 2007) paints a grim picture of adolescent learners, with fully 70% described as low-achieving writers who compare poorly to their international peers. Citing research syntheses in much the same fashion as its sister report *Reading Next,* this report points to specific writing strategies (e.g., summarization instruction) that are supported in the research and offer, again, a solid cognitive solution to the perceived problem of a growing population of struggling adolescent writers. In essence, if we can boost adolescents' reading and writing skills, using what we know about strategies that work (e.g., graphic organizers), then the crisis may be solved.

This deficit view of adolescent struggling readers has received considerable attention in the literature, with a number of critiques aimed at deconstructing and countering an exclusively cognitivist view of instruction for adolescent learners. For example, Hall (2006) explored how middle-grade struggling readers coped with metacognitive comprehension and study strategies that their well-meaning social studies, mathematics, and science teachers offered to help them with text reading. These students were well aware of how they were being positioned as struggling readers, and the comprehension strategies simply elevated their visibility as deficient in reading. As an alternative coping strategy that preserved their identity with their peers as "good" students, they chose to listen carefully to text discussions and to use alternative routes to obtain meaning from texts. Rather than adopt a learned helplessness view of adolescent struggling readers, Hall recommended that educators move beyond an obsession with effective methodology and strategies. Rather, teachers should carefully consider students' social and cultural worlds better to fashion whole-school interventions that are useful to all students and unlikely to marginalize struggling readers (Fisher & Ivey, 2006).

With the cautionary statement that adolescent struggling readers are more complex than recent national reports reveal, these prominent reports and their instructional recommendations are not without considerable merit. Indeed, they offer very well grounded research syntheses, pulling together a wide array of instructional studies supporting strategy instruction. However, with respect to struggling adolescent readers, they do represent a particular stance that needs to be tempered with a broader, sociocultural critique. Are adolescents in crisis as learners? The answer may be more complex than those typically offered in policy documents, in grant calls for proposals to benefit "striving readers," and in common wisdom and conversation. For example, Franzak (2006) argues that a deficit medical model that disenfranchises and marginalizes struggling readers persists in policy documents. But many adolescents are well aware of their struggling reader status and take active measures to protect their social identities as learners.

A curriculum that acknowledges and enhances students' feelings of competence and control across reading ability levels is preferable to isolated metacognitive strategy instruction. For example, Franzak (2006) recommends multimedia material as a powerful and engaging vehicle for adolescent readers. Books based on video games such as Halo, as well as popular movies, are natural bridges to contemporary students' interest in visual media. In addition, well-designed sustained silent reading (SSR) programs with self-selected reading materials and contemporary young-adult literature hold promise within a whole-school literacy program for all students (Bean et al., 2008; Fisher & Ivey, 2006). In a carefully crafted study of a high school intervention program in which 35% of the students were reading one or more grade levels below grade placement, Fisher and Ivey found that four key elements supported measurable increases in students' achievement and motivation to read. A combination of SSR, using young adult novels in conjunction with content-area learning, offering alternative texts to struggling readers and advanced readers in content classrooms, and buddy reading to elementary school students produced positive results. The point is that simply adopting well-researched cognitive strategy instruction is not enough. Intervention efforts, such as that described by Fisher and Ivey, as well as other notable efforts (e.g., Brozo & Hargis, 2003), hold promise because they adopt a whole-school stance that neither names nor marginalizes struggling readers, nor does it place places high-performing students in an elevated status.

Defining *adolescence* as a time of changing literacy needs that are not being addressed or fully addressed by the educational community has been a key way that the field has named its mission. Certainly, this definition has served to galvanize recent research and government initiatives. Although important, these initiatives and the interventions that result need to be tempered by the complexity of literacy learners, who cannot simply be defined by their "neediness," which then directs our adult "generosity" and "responsibility." The field of adolescent literacy, as represented in the policy documents, texts, and articles we examined, uses and at times complicates the definition of *adolescence* in relation to literacy "needs." In part, this has been done through recognition of literacy strengths, as previously discussed. Receiving perhaps the most attention recently has been adolescents' new literacies practices (i.e., their use of communication technologies). These new practices are viewed not only as strengths but also as unique gifts, if you will, that define a generation. We turn now to this particular construction of adolescence.

Adolescents Defined by Their New and Multiple Literacy Practices: The Millennials

In addition to defining *adolescents* in relation to their literacy needs, another area dominating the field concerns the new literacies of adolescents. The term *new literacies* refers to the practices, skills, and knowledge involved with new and emerging information and communication technologies (ICTs). Here, *adolescence* is defined by one's comfort and expertise with various forms of new and emerging computer-mediated technologies. More specifically, to be an *adolescent* is equated with being a "native" user rather than adult "immigrant" user of technology (Moorman & Horton, 2007). As producers of texts in an Internet-based world, it is argued, today's adolescents read and write more than did previous generations, but the nature of this social interaction is dramatically different for millennials than for previous generations. *Millennials* are defined chronologically and with reference to the evolution of personal computers. Students born between 1982 and 2002 comprise a generation that has never known a world without computers, cell phones, and other forms of ICTs (Moorman & Horton, 2007). This is a generation that is accustomed to writing their views on Weblogs (blogs), text messaging friends, and playing complex, multiplayer video games spanning global boundaries. Each of these distinctly new literacy practices combines elements of older, print-based forms with newer, visual media dimensions in which design and composition are important. Indeed, ethnographic studies and thoughtful analyses of adolescents' literacy practices show that teens occupy a world in which ever-changing text forms coexist with older, print-bound forms of text (Alvermann & Eakle, 2007; Moorman & Horton, 2007; Moje & Hinchman, 2004). However, it has been argued that these out-of-school literacy competencies are not always acknowledged or capitalized upon in the classroom (Moore & Cunningham, 2006; O'Brien, 2006; Smith & Wilhelm, 2002, 2006).

David G. O'Brien has argued that struggling readers often are misperceived based on narrow views of literacy competency that fail to recognize a host of new literacy practices these readers may well engage in outside of school. These practices include creating multimedia music productions in Apple's GarageBand, podcasts for YouTube, and iMovie productions, all of which demand a high tolerance for ambiguity and an aesthetic sensibility for design. Thus, providing opportunities for struggling readers to display competencies in new literacies may be a more powerful way to bridge within-school and out-of-school contexts. For example, engaging in digital media literacy critiques aimed at viewing and evaluating productions (e.g., podcasts and YouTube clips) places struggling readers in a role quite different from that of learned helplessness.

According to this view, today's teachers are seen as needy. They require both the knowledge and the environment (i.e., a technologically rich classroom) that can capitalize on millennial adolescents' so-called "natural affinity" for and competence with new literacies. They also need an open attitude toward change. The attitude is crucial because of the claim that a growing array of multimedia tools are altering the print-based landscape and changing the nature of what it means to be literate, despite the intensification of high-stakes and standardized testing in traditional print literacy (Bean & Wimmer, 2007; Lewis, Leander, & Wang, 2007; Luke & Elkins, 1998).

This construction of adolescence often celebrates not only those whose practices include them in this category but also the new technologies themselves. Although a critical perspective is evident in the field (see, e.g., Wilder & Dressman, 2006), it has been easier to offer more exuberant portrayals of teens and their new literacies that universalize adolescents as the amazing "native" users of technology. Undoubtedly, this exuberance is a response to the ongoing, relentless reinscription of traditional literacies in classrooms despite changing times and changing literacy patterns in these "new times." However, the concern is whether this rendering of adolescence is indeed an accurate portrayal of all youth, locally or globally, and whether the comfort and expertise suggested by the term *native-user* best describes all those who chronologically fit the designation of millennial.

Adolescence as a Diverse and Dynamic Population of Literacy Learners

This final construction of adolescence that is evident in the field names and highlights social difference rather than universality across the population defined conventionally as *adolescents*. Much of this largely ethnographic research examines how gender, race, ethnicity, social class, sexuality, home language, citizenship, and so on, are organized by and organize school and home literacy practices (e.g., Blair, 2007; Lytle, 2006; Smith & Wilhelm, 2002, 2004; Blackburn, 2002, 2003; Gunderson, 2000; Moje, 2006; Finders, 1997). Drawing strongly on a sociocultural perspective, this research presents a much more complex picture of the lives and literacies of any group of adolescents.

The intense study of individual and group cases emphasizes difference to the extent that even categories of race and ethnicity cannot be assumed to be definitive: Moje (2006) comments that "individual difference is a complex intersection of all of those qualities of difference, so that a third-generation Latina living in Detroit may be more like an African American girl living in Detroit than she is like a Latino living in New Mexico" (p. 123). To extend Moje's comment further, it is possible to consider that, in terms of literacy practices, a third-generation Latina might at times be more like working-class boys in her class or, in some aspects, more like her Latino parents.

Ethnographic work complicates any particular notion of what might constitute *adolescence*. Certainly, it makes any generalization about youth difficult. Also undercutting the category is the idea of identity, which, under the guise of postmodern thought, speaks to a more multiple and fluid sense of self. This self is constructed not by personality, but discursively, that is, through the use of linguistic and material resources that organize and reorganize social scripts, or what James Gee (2000, 2006) calls *identity kits*. These resources also include the discourses on adolescence found in popular culture (Hagood, 2007; Moje & van Helden, 2004). Most important, in much of what we reviewed, literacy practices were deeply implicated in the formation of self. Many of the chapters in Alvermann et al. (2006) demonstrate the ways that identities are formulated with and against literacy texts and literacy practices available in and out of schools (see chapters in Alvermann et al. by Neilsen, Marsh, and Stolle; O'Brien; Moje & Dillion; and Moore). Identity within this perspective is not fixed, stable, or unified for anyone, particularly when new literacy practices emerge.

The emphasis on differences among teens, and the fluid and multiple identity formations–reformations of individual teens (and all of us) threatens to undo entirely the category of adolescence or, at the very least, to complicate any generalization that can be made. This suggests care in forming any absolutes that seem to construct the category of *adolescence.*

Tentative Conclusions and Future Research on Adolescence and Adolescent Literacy

This is a preliminary review, and certainly for future reference, we would like to extend and intensify our reading and analysis of the various texts that make up the field. In particular, we would like to look at more international texts and contexts in relation to adolescent literacy, because much of what we have reviewed is American. Because this is a preliminary review, our observations and conclusions are tentative. Nonetheless, we believe that the four patterns we found are worthy of thought and further inquiry.

What seems apparent is that the various ways in which adolescence and adolescent literacy together are configured in the field create a complex and multifaceted picture of adolescent life and literacy. It seems to us that the four constructions of adolescence act as foils for each other, each naming and limiting the next. We see good reason to remember each of these constructions individually and collectively as the field continues to develop. For example, we suggest that taking a strictly cognitive stance toward understanding struggling or, indeed, any readers and their needs may be seriously limited when the various understandings of *adolescence* are considered.

We want to issue a call for more theorizing about adolescence and adolescent literacy practices in complex and instructionally useful ways. In this effort, we are adding to Donna Alvermann's initial challenge in 1998 to "question simplistic notions of adolescence and literacy" (cited in Phelps, 2006, p. 3), and to those researchers who have already begun to answer her challenge. What we highlight is the importance of critical self-reflection about the field, from the field, and remaining vigilant to the possibility of universalizing adolescence in a fashion that creates new boundaries that may limit our thinking and our actions, even as we enthusiastically create and embrace new research on adolescents and their literacies.

In relation to the opening vignette with Ms. Campinello and her class, including Rafael, Tiffany, Damian, and Anna, the explicit theorizing about adolescence, and the exposure and critique of the various ways that adolescents and their literacies are defined, may help both teacher and students to know, understand, and define each other with, against, and, most importantly, beyond not only the frames provided to them but also to all of us within and outside the field of adolescent literacy. We consider this to be freedom.

QUESTIONS FOR DISCUSSION

1. How do we hold on to the complexity and individuality of adolescents and their literacies in our teaching and research?

2. When and how does the category of adolescents divide, collide, and meld with the categories of children and adults? When should this occur?

3. Most important, what is the work of these categories (socially, psychologically, pedagogically, institutionally), and whose interest do they service?

Resources

Further Reading

Alvermann, D. E., Hinchman, K. A., Moore, D. W., Phelps, S. F., & Waff, D. R. (Eds.). (2006). *Reconceptualizing the literacies in adolescents' lives* (2nd ed.). Mahwah, NJ: Erlbaum.

Biancarosa, C., & Snow, C. E. (2006). *Reading next: A vision for action and research in middle and high school literacy: A report to the Carnegie Corporation of New York* (2nd ed.). Washington, DC: Alliance for Excellent Education. Available at *www.all4ed. org/publications/readingnext/readingnext.pdf.*

Cassidy, J., Garrett, D., & Barrera, E. S. (2006). What's hot in adolescent literacy 1997–2006. *Journal of Adolescent and Adult Literacy, 50*(1), 30–36.

Graham, S., & Perin, D. (2007). *Writing next: Effective strategies to improve writing of adolescents in middle and high schools: A report to the Carnegie Corporation of New York.* Washington, DC: Alliance for Excellent Education. Available at *www.all4ed.org/ publications/writingnext/writingnext.pdf.*

Guzzetti, B. J. (Ed.). (2007). *Literacy for the new millennium: Vol. 3. Adolescent literacy.* Westport, CT: Praeger.

Jetton, T. L., & Dole, J. A. (Eds.). (2004). *Adolescent literacy research and practice.* New York: Guilford Press.

Lesko, N. (2001). *Act your age!: A cultural construction of adolescence.* New York: Routledge.

Lewis, J., & Moorman, G. (Eds.). (2007). *Adolescent literacy instruction: Policies and promising practices.* Newark, DE: International Reading Association.

Moore, D. W., Bean, T. W., Birdyshaw, D., & Rycik, J. A. (1999). *Adolescent literacy: A position statement for the Commission on Adolescent Literacy of the International Reading Association.* Newark, DE: International Reading Association.

Sturtevant, E. G., Boyd, F. B., Brozo, W. G., Hinchman, K. A., Moore, D. W., & Alvermann, D. E. (Eds.). (2006). *Principled practices for adolescent literacy: A framework for instruction and policy.* Mahwah, NJ: Erlbaum.

Vadeboncoeur, J. A., & Stevens, L. (2005). *Re/constructing "the adolescent": Sign, symbol, and body.* New York: Peter Lang.

Website

www.reading.org—the website of the International Reading Association. It contains information on the *Journal of Adolescent & Adult Literacy* and other publications of the International Reading Association.

References

Alexander, P. A. (2005/2006). The path to competence: A lifespan developmental perspective on reading. *Journal of Literacy Research, 37*(4), 413–436.

Alvermann, D. E., & Eakle, J. A. (2007). Challenging literacy theories and practices from the outside. In J. Lewis & G. Moorman (Eds.), *Adolescent literacy instruction: Policies and promising practices* (pp. 64–81). Newark, DE: International Reading Association.

Alvermann, D. E., Hinchman, K., Moore, D. W., Phelps, S. W., & Waff, D. (Eds.). (1998). *Reconceptualizing the literacies in adolescents' lives.* Mahwah, NJ: Erlbaum.

Alvermann, D. E., Hinchman, K. A., Moore, D. W., Phelps, S. F., & Waff, D. R. (Eds.). (2006). *Reconceptualizing the literacies in adolescents' lives* (2nd ed.). Mahwah, NJ: Erlbaum.

Bean, T. W., Readence, J. E., & Baldwin, R. S. (2008). *Content area literacy: An integrated approach* (9th ed.). Dubuque, IA: Kendall/Hunt.

Bean, T. W., & Wimmer, J. (2007). Resources for adolescent literacy. In B. J. Guzzetti (Ed.), *Literacy for the new millennium: Vol. 3. Adolescent literacy* (pp. 265–278). Westport, CT: Praeger.

Biancarosa, C., & Snow, C. E. (2006). *Reading next: A vision for action and research in middle and high school literacy: A report to Carnegie Corporation of New York* (2nd ed.). Washington, DC: Alliance for Excellent Education. Retrieved January 8, 2007 from, *www.all4ed.org/publications/readingnext/readingnext.pdf.*

Blackburn, M. (2002). Disrupting the (hetero)normative: Exploring literacy performances and identity work with queer youth. *Journal of Adolescent & Adult Literacy, 46,* 312–324.

Blackburn, M. (2003). Exploring literacy performances and power dynamics at The Loft: Queer youth reading the word and the world. *Research in the Teaching of English, 37,* 467–490.

Blair, H. (2007). I used to treat all the boys and the girls the same: Gender and literacy. In B. Guzzetti (Ed.), *Literacy for the new millennium: Vol. 3: Adolescent literacy* (pp. 189–206). Westport, CT: Praeger.

Brozo, W. G., & Hargis, C. H. (2003). Taking seriously the idea of reform: One high school's efforts to make reading more responsive to all students. *Journal of Adolescent & Adult Literacy, 47,* 14–23.

Cassidy, J., & Cassidy, D. (2008). What's hot for 2008. *Reading Today, 25*(4), 1, 10.

Cassidy, J., Garrett, D., & Barrera, E. S. (2006). What's hot in adolescent literacy 1997–2006. *Journal of Adolescent & Adult Literacy, 50*(1), 30–36.

Finders, M. (1997). *Just girls: Hidden literacies and life in junior high.* New York: Teachers College Press.

Fisher, D., & Ivey, G. (2006). Evaluating the interventions for struggling adolescent readers. *Journal of Adolescent & Adult Literacy, 50*(3), 180–189.

Franzak, J. K. (2006). Zoom: A review of the literature on marginalized adolescent readers, literacy theory, and policy implications. *Review of Educational Research, 76,* 209–248.

Gee, J. P. (2000). Teenagers in new times: A new literacy study perspective. *Journal of Adolescent & Adult Literacy, 43,* 412–420.

Gee, J. P. (2006). Self-fashioning and shape-shifting: Language, identity, and social class. In D. E. Alvermann, K. A. Hinchman, D. W. Moore, S. F. Phelps, & D. R.

Waff (Eds.), *Reconceptualizing the literacies in adolescents' lives* (2nd ed., pp. 165–185), Mahwah, NJ: Erlbaum.

Graham, S., & Perin, D. (2007). *Writing next: Effective strategies to improve writing of adolescents in middle and high schools: A report to Carnegie Corporation of New York.* Washington, DC: Alliance for Excellent Education. Retrieved February 12, 2007, from *www.all4ed.org/publications/writingnext/writingnext.pdf.*

Gunderson, L. (2000). Voices of the teenage diasporas. *Journal of Adolescent & Adult Literacies, 43,* 692–706.

Guzzetti, B. J. (Ed.). (2007). *Literacy for the new millennium: Vol. 3: Adolescent literacy.* Westport, CT: Praeger.

Hagood, M. (2007). Linking popular culture to literacy learning and teaching in the twenty-first century. In B. Guzzetti (Ed.), *Literacy for the new millennium: Vol. 3. Adolescent literacy* (pp. 223–238). Westport, CT: Praeger.

Hall, L. A. (2006). Anything but lazy: New understandings about struggling readers, teaching, and text. *Reading Research Quarterly, 41*(4), 424–426.

Jetton, T. L., & Dole, J. A. (2004). Introduction. In T. L. Jetton & J. A. Dole (Eds.), *Adolescent literacy research and practice* (pp. 1–11). New York: Guilford Press.

King, J., Hart, S., & Kozdras, D. (2008). Critical literacy and adolescents. In B. Guzzetti (Ed.) *Literacy for the new millennium: Vol. 3. Adolescent literacy* (pp. 173–188). Westport, CT: Praeger.

Lesko, N. (2001). *Act our age!: A cultural construction of adolescence.* New York: Routledge.

Lewis, C., Leander, K., & Wang, X. (2007). Digital literacies. In B. Guzzetti (Ed.), *Literacy for the new millennium: Vol. 3. Adolescent literacy* (pp. 207–222). Westport, CT: Praeger.

Lewis, J., & Moorman, G. (2007). *Adolescent literacy instruction: Policies and promising practices.* Newark, DE: International Reading Association.

Luke, A., & Elkins, J. (1998). Reinventing literacy in "new times." *Journal of Adolescent & Adult Literacy, 42,* 4–7.

Lytle, S. (2006). The literacies of teaching urban adolescents in these times. In D. E. Alvermann, K. A. Hinchman, D. W. Moore, S. F. Phelps, & D. R. Waff (Eds.), *Reconceptualizing the literacies in adolescents' lives* (2nd ed., pp. 257–278). Mahwah, NJ: Erlbaum

McNabb, M. (2006). *Literacy learning in networked classrooms: Using the Internet with middle-level students.* Newark, DE: International Reading Association.

Moje, E. B. (2006). A scholar's response to Principle 7: Adolescents need opportunities to connect reading with their life and their learning inside and outside of school. In E. G. Sturtevant, F. B. Boyd, W. G. Brozo, K. A. Hinchman, D. W. Moore, & D. E. Alvermann (Eds.), *Principled practices for adolescent literacy: A framework for instruction and policy* (pp. 110–124). Mahwah, NJ: Erlbaum.

Moje, E. B., & Hinchman, K. (2004). Culturally responsive practices for youth literacy learning. In T. L. Jetton, & J. A. Dole (Eds.), *Adolescent literacy research and practices* (pp. 321–350). New York: Guilford Press.

Moje, E. B., & van Helden, C. (2004). Doing popular culture: Troubling discourses about youth. In J. Vadeboncoeur & L. Stevens (Eds.), *Re/constructing "the Adolescent": Sign, symbol, and body* (pp. 211–248). New York: Peter Lang.

Moore, D. W., Bean, T. W., Birdyshaw, D., & Rycik, J. A. (1999). *Adolescent literacy: A position statement for the Commission on Adolescent Literacy of the International Reading Association.* Newark, DE: International Reading Association.

Moore, D. W., & Cunningham, J. W. (2006). Adolescent agency and literacy. In

D. E. Alvermann, K. A. Hinchman, D. W. Moore, S. F. Phelps, & D. R. Waff (Eds.),*Reconceptualizing the literacies in adolescents' lives* (2nd ed., pp. 129–146). Mahwah, NJ: Erlbaum.

Moorman, G., & Horton, J. (2007). Millenials and how to teach them. In J. Lewis & G. Moorman (Eds.), *Adolescent literacy instruction: Policies and promising practices* (pp. 263–285). Newark, DE: International Reading Association.

Morrell, E. (2008). *Critical literacy and urban youth: Pedagogies of access, dissent, and liberation.* New York: Routledge.

Nichols, W. D. (2007). Introduction to the adolescent reader [Special issue]. *Reading Psychology, 28*(1), 5–10.

O'Brien, D. (2006). "Struggling" adolescents engagement in multimediating: Countering the institutional construction of incompetence. In D. E. Alvermann, K. A. Hinchman, D. W. Moore, S. F. Phelps, & D. R. Waff (Eds.), *Reconceptualizing the literacies in adolescents' lives* (2nd ed., pp. 29–46). Mahwah, NJ: Erlbaum.

Phelps, S. F. (2006). Introduction to Part I: Situating adolescents' literacies. In D. E. Alvermann, K. A. Hinchman, D. W. Moore, S. F. Phelps, & D. R. Waff (Eds.), *Reconceptualizing the literacies in adolescents' lives* (2nd ed., pp. 3–4). Mahwah, NJ: Erlbaum.

Richardson, J. S. (2008). Content area reading: A 50-year history. In M. J. Fresh (Ed.), *An essential history of current reading practices* (pp. 120–143). Newark, DE: International Reading Association.

Salinger, T. (2007). Setting the agenda for adolescent literacy. In J. Lewis & G. Moorman (Eds.), *Adolescent literacy instruction: Policies and promising practices* (pp. 3–19). Newark, DE: International Reading Association.

Smith, M. W., & Wilhelm, J. D. (2002). *"Reading don't fix no Chevys": Literacy in the lives of young men.* Portsmouth, NH: Heinemann.

Smith, M. W., & Wilhelm, J. D. (2004). "I just like being good at it": The importance of competence in the literate lives of young men. *Journal of Adolescent & Adult Literacy, 47,* 454–461.

Smith, M. W., & Wilhelm, J. D. (2006). *Going with the flow: How to engage boys (and girls) in their literacy learning.* Portsmouth, NH: Heinemann.

Sturtevant, E. G., Boyd, F. B., Brozo, W. G., Hinchman, K. A., Moore, D. W., & Alvermann, D. E. (2006). *Principled practices for adolescent literacy: A framework for instruction and policy.* Mahwah, NJ: Erlbaum.

Vacca, R. T. (1998). Let's not marginalize adolescent literacy. *Journal of Adolescent & Adult Literacy, 41,* 604–609.

Vadeboncoeur, J. A., & Stevens, L. (2005). *Re/constructing "the adolescent": Sign, symbol, and body.* New York: Peter Lang.

Wilder, P., & Dressman, M. (2006). New literacies, enduring challenges?: The influence of capital on adolescent readers' Internet practices. In D. E. Alvermann, K. A. Hinchman, D. W. Moore, S. F. Phelps, & D. R. Waff (Eds.), *Reconceptualizing the literacies in adolescents' lives* (2nd ed., pp. 29–46). Mahwah, NJ: Erlbaum.

Chapter 3

Enhancing Adolescent Self-Efficacy for Literacy

Patrick McCabe

GUIDING QUESTIONS

1. What is self-efficacy?
2. How does self-efficacy develop?
3. How does self-efficacy affect motivation?
4. What is the relationship between years in school and self-efficacy?
5. How can middle and high-school students' low self-efficacy for literacy be increased?

In 1982, Irene Athey decried the lack of proportional interest in motivation and in other affective factors compared to cognitive factors that influence learning to read, but countless research articles on motivation and literacy have appeared since that time. This volume is a testament to that gradual but seismic change in focus. Supporting this comprehensive and important collection is a research-based understanding of motivation as it relates to the learning and psychological characteristics of adolescence.

In the following pages, I explain how the theory of motivation articulated by Albert Bandura (1986, 1995) can help middle and high school teachers engage reluctant students in literacy tasks. *Self-efficacy*, the personal belief in one's ability to be successful on a prospective task, is a critical aspect of motivation in this theory. Although a number of individual or combined factors (i.e., interest, compliance, social acceptance, and competition) may influence an adolescent's decision to become involved in an activity, consistent research evidence (Bandura, 1986, 1997; Pintrich & Schunk, 2002; Schunk & Zimmerman, 2007; Zimmerman,1995) confirms that self-efficacy plays a particularly catalytic, significant, and influential role in initiating and sustaining engagement in an activity.

Waning Motivation

Many adolescents become engaged in literacy tasks in school without hesitation; however, others rarely become involved. Educational researchers and organizations (Ivey & Broaddus, 2001; National Endowment for the Arts, 2007; Nelson & DeBacker, 2008; Schunk & Meece, 2006; Unrau & Schlackman, 2006) have documented a decline in academic motivation and achievement for literacy during adolescence that becomes especially evident during the year of transition from elementary to junior high or middle school (Snow, Porche, Tabors, & Harris, 2007). Adolescents' low motivation for academic tasks has long-term, significant, and pernicious results: poor grades; frustration with academics; hopelessness; pessimism; and, all too often, the decision to drop out of school.

Fortunately, a growing body of research (Baker & Wigfield, 1999; Brophy, 2004; Dweck, 2006; Henk & Melnick, 1995; Hughes-Hassell & Rodge, 2007; Ivey & Broaddus, 2001; Morgan & Fuchs, 2007; Pintrich & Schunk, 2002; Pitcher et al., 2007; Schunk & Zimmerman, 2007; Unrau & Schlackman, 2006; Watkins & Coffey, 2004) on motivation provides a framework for understanding and addressing this important but historically overlooked aspect of instruction. Researchers in education and psychology have presented numerous models of motivation based on slightly different frameworks. Important in one model (expectancy–value) is the value and expectation of results; in another (attribution), it is human to be curious about the nature of events and objects in the environment; in a third (social-cognitive), the interaction among personal, social, and environmental factors explains motivation (for an excellent summary of these positions, see Pintrich & Schunk, 2002).

This chapter and Chapter 14 by Pamela J. Dunston and Linda B. Gambrell (this volume) describe the complex nature of motivation and suggest ways for teachers to align and to anchor literacy instruction to reflect current research. I focus on the social-cognitive theory of Albert Bandura (1986, 1995) because of its wealth of research evidence and its practical application for teaching and learning.

A Perspective on Motivation

As teachers, we usually judge student motivation by degree of observable action in relation to a task. Two useful definitions of motivation include this behavioral, observable aspect. One is "the initiation, direction, intensity, persistence, and quality of behavior, especially goal-directed behavior" (Brophy, 2004, p. 3); the other is "the process whereby goal-directed behavior is instigated and sustained" (Pintrich & Schunk, 2002, p. 5). As the research has revealed, motivation is a complex psychological construct influenced by environmental and conscious or subconscious personal factors, acting individually or in combination. These factors include challenge, competition, compliance, curiosity, grades, importance, interest, recognition by others, self-efficacy, social reasons, and work avoidance (Baker & Wigfield, 1999; Watkins & Coffey, 2004). For example, a student with a compelling interest in hammerhead sharks may start to read about sharks, although he or she anticipates that the written material will be difficult. A compliant student may become involved in an activity when told to do so, and a competitive student may be motivated to do better than his or her peers. Extrinsic rewards, such as a pizza, a ticket to a sporting event, or a CD with the student's favorite music, can also influence motivation, because they have personal value and importance. As a final example, many students are motivated to do homework to avoid a poor grade.

Observable behavior alone, however, obscures the complex, multidimensional nature of motivation and prevents us from recognizing and, therefore, addressing reasons for low student motivation. If you understand why a student is not motivated to read, you can plan a course of action to resolve this problem with confidence; if you lack an understanding, you will probably be unable to address the problem with confidence in the outcome.

Based on both social factors and individuals' cognitive processes, Bandura's (1986, 1997) theory has particular relevance to teaching and learning. *Social* refers to the classroom environment: student–student interaction; the teacher's personality, feedback and management systems; feedback from others; and physical features of the room that facilitate or inhibit learning. *Cognitive* refers to not only a student's personal learning strategies and thoughts but also his or her beliefs about personal intelligence and level of confidence for academic tasks, personal goals, and values. A third dimension of this theory, *personal behavior,* results from the interaction of the social and cognitive dimensions. Personal behavior can range from full engagement and persistence in an activity (i.e., high motivation) to moderate or no engagement (i.e., low or no motivation, respectively).

A critical component of motivation in Bandura's framework is *self-efficacy,* a "belief in one's capabilities to organize and execute the courses of action required to produce given attainments" (1997, p. 3). Self-efficacy is the degree to which an individual perceives him- or herself to be capable of successfully completing a specific and prospective task. The value of high self-efficacy in relation to both motivation and achievement cannot be underestimated. Research evidence demonstrates that when task ability is about the same, individuals with higher self-efficacy do better than do those with lower self-efficacy (Bandura, 1995; Pintrich & Schunk, 2002; Zimmerman, 1995). An even more interesting finding is that, for the same task, individuals with less ability, although not drastically so, and high self-efficacy do better than those with more ability but lower self-efficacy (Pintrich & Schunk, 2002).

Self-efficacy beliefs result from prior experiences, vary in strength, are task specific, and exert strong influence on the decision to become involved in prospective tasks. Positive prior experiences in and out of school related to literacy activities likely result in high self-efficacy for literacy; a history of negative experiences results in low self-efficacy.

Next, I briefly explain how self-efficacy develops. According to Bandura (1986, 1997), we collect information about personal ability from four sources and use this information to make a self-efficacy judgment. These sources or modalities are enactive mastery, verbal persuasion, vicarious experiences, and personal physiological–affective reaction. *Enactive mastery* is the recognition that one has successfully completed a task. If you experience success in a task, you have obvious, irrefutable, and thoroughly convincing evidence of your ability. According to Bandura (1997), "Enactive mastery experiences are the most influential source of efficacy information because they provide the most authentic evidence of whether one can muster whatever it takes to succeed" (p. 80). Therefore, I devote a considerable portion of this chapter to principles that ensure enactive mastery for literacy tasks with adolescent students.

A second source of self-efficacy is vicariousness. *Vicarious* means "experienced or realized through imaginative or sympathetic participation in the experience of another" (*Merriam-Webster's Collegiate Dictionary*, 11th edition). Bandura refers to the individual performing the task as the model, and to the person watching as the observer. Vicariousness is facilitated to the degree that the model resembles or can relate to the observer in some significant way. A struggling reader, for example, is more likely to see him- or herself accomplishing the same task as a peer who looks, dresses, and speaks like him- or herself than one who lacks these characteristics.

A third source of self-efficacy is *verbal persuasion*. Although not as powerful as enactive mastery, verbal persuasion can also influence how one feels about his or her competence, especially when a credible persuader attributes success on the task to the listener's personal effort. When a respected other person (e.g., teacher, friend, family member) who possesses a skill tells a listener that he or she can also acquire that skill, the listener is likely to internalize that belief. Although there are exceptions, persuading someone that he or she can acquire a skill is not likely to be successful unless the speaker possesses the skill.

The final source of self-efficacy information is through *physiological* or *affective feedback*. Increased heartbeat or excessive fidgeting is a physiological, autonomous response that might be related to a past, current, or impending event. When interpreted positively (e.g., "My rapid heartbeat is a signal I am `psyched' to be the batter" or "My fidgeting tells me I am ready for the soccer game"), the individual is likely to have high self-efficacy for that activity or skill. When interpreted negatively (i.e., "My rapid heartbeat tells me I am not relaxed enough to be the batter" or "My fidgeting tells me I am too stressed to play soccer"), the individual is likely to develop low self-efficacy for the activity or skill. Examples of affective reactions include relief, joy, and pride, if one is successful on a task, or tension, disappointment, and embarrassment, if he or she is not successful.

Finally, it is not merely the recognition of information from any of these sources that results in a self-efficacy judgment; it is how the information is processed, interpreted, or evaluated. "A host of factors, including personal, social, situational, and temporal circumstances under which events occur, affect how personal experiences are cognitively appraised" (Bandura, 1986, p. 401). When developing a self-efficacy judgment, an individual consciously or subconsciously weighs the information from these four sources and decides which source(s) have the most value. Unfortunately, this cognitive process may be faulty for many reasons because people, especially adolescents who have struggled in school and have learned to protect their egos in learning situations that they perceive as threatening, ignore or discard important information that might be interpreted positively.

There is a marked difference between the thoughts and behaviors of students with high self-efficacy and of those with low self-efficacy. Personal qualities associated with high self-efficacy are persistence, optimism in relation to successful task completion, willingness to try alternative strategies, and explaining success or failure as related to strategy use rather than to innate intelligence. These qualities sustain motivation. Personal qualities associated with low self-efficacy are lack of persistence, pessimism in relation to successful task completion, inability or lack of desire to try alternative strategies when encountering difficulty, and explaining success or failure as related to innate, immutable low intelligence rather than to strategy use. Individuals with low self-efficacy are not likely to involve themselves or to persist with literacy tasks, especially when they encounter difficulty.

As students mature physically, psychologically, and socially, and move from elementary to middle and high school, they become more reflective and judgmental about their ability to learn (Bruning, Schraw, Norby, & Ronning, 2004). After years in the academic setting, adolescents gather evidence about their ability from report card grades; teacher, peer, and parental feedback; and personal reactions in relation to school tasks. An adolescent's opinion about personal ability to learn becomes stronger and may even approach intransigence. This uncompromising self-belief, based on years of evidence, benefits those who do well but is damaging to those who struggle with literacy and other tasks. For adolescents with a long school history of frustration, failure, and poor performance, conclusions about personal ability to read are likely to be negative, detrimental, corrosive, and self-destructive.

In the remainder of this chapter, I provide suggestions for enhancing the self-efficacy of adolescents based on the sources of self-efficacy.

Enactive Mastery

There are, of course, scores of books and thousands of journal articles on ways to increase mastery in literacy. In addition, the International Reading Association (IRA; *www.reading.org*) is an invaluable source for those interested in all aspects of literacy development. The following five principles, however, can frame instruction and enhance the likelihood of students' experiencing enactive mastery with reading tasks.

Influence Students' First Glance at Text

At times, people make "snap" decisions, without deliberating or considering all the relevant variables, and adolescent students are certainly no exception to this truism. A term from the field of visualization studies, *preattentive processing*, loosely defined, refers to visual features that we instantly notice, before we consciously focus attention on what is important to us. More technically, *preattentive processing* refers to visual recognition tasks performed in less than 200 milliseconds (Healey, Booth, & Enns, 1996). There is evidence that results of preattentive processing affect individuals not only consciously but also subconsciously and autonomically, with especially deleterious results for individuals with high anxiety (Najström & Jansson, 2006). Researchers found that the higher a person's anxiety, the more likely he or she perceived real or imagined threat in rapid exposure to a stimulus.

This line of research has particular relevance and promise for understanding the development of self-efficacy for literacy, especially for students who have struggled with reading and writing in the past and are anxious about literacy tasks in the immediate and distant future. Although not technically considered preattentive, a student glancing at textual material may also detect salient visual information and use it to make a self-efficacy judgment. I have seen and heard many adolescent and young adult students react instantly to the appearance of a book, especially one with expository or informational content area text. Some were overjoyed and automatically exclaimed, "Yes!" or "Cool!" and looked forward to reading; others, however, reacted with dread and expressed negative sentiments such as "Ugh!" or "Oh no!" and never became involved in reading. At the college bookstore of the university where I teach, I recently observed a first-year student looking at the books for his course. Upon opening one, he immediately exclaimed to his friend, "This is whack! I'll never get through this. Look at this `stuff'!" I do not know whether this student struggled with literacy tasks in high school, but I do know that he made a self-efficacy judgment that contributed to and reinforced a weak self-belief about learning. Unless he subsequently became convinced that he did have the ability to do well with that material, this student created, albeit perhaps temporarily, an unnecessary obstacle to his learning. Additionally, some colleagues and I (McCabe, Kraemer, Miller, Parmar, & Ruscica, 2006) found that initial judgment of text difficulty based on visual features had an influential effect on subsequent comprehension.

A student who struggles with reading, and who perceives textual material as difficult or intimidating, will likely not choose to read that material. Therefore, it is your job to reduce the chances of a student perceiving a textbook or other written material negatively. One way to do this is to conduct a considerateness analysis of the reading material you are about to assign. *Considerateness* in this context refers to the degree of user-friendliness of a textbook. Individually or in combination some text features that students immediately notice, and that influence perception of user-friendliness, are font size and type; amount of white space; presence or absence of headings; quantity and quality of drawings, political cartoons, and photographs; color usage; and presence or absence of summaries and questions before or after sections or chapters. Sentence length and word length are additional elements (and can be quantified with a readability technique), but a judgment based on these elements requires perusal of the material. Many researchers have related degree of text considerateness to comprehension (Armbruster; 1984; Crismore, 1983; Kantor, Anderson, & Armbruster, 1983; Langer, 1983; McCabe, 1993; McKenna & Robinson, 2005; Singer, 1986).

If a text analysis reveals the absence of considerateness or that the nature of these or other text features will likely influence students' perception of user-friendliness negatively, involve your students in prereading activities before they view the text. For example, give students a one- or two-level outline if there are no headings, have them view PowerPoint slides or transparency projections of charts and graphs if these data are too complex in the book, and assign fewer pages or less text to read if the font is too small. Admittedly, some of the features I have mentioned are difficult, if not impossible, to alter easily in a hard copy format. However, if you prepare your students in advance by addressing possible pitfalls, you decrease their chances of developing a negative self-efficacy judgment based on a glance at reading material. With electronic text that can be edited, teachers have the option of easily changing these features to make the material appear more user-friendly.

Bridge the Gap Created by Challenging Material

Although there are exceptions, students are not likely to experience mastery with material that is significantly above their reading ability level or conceptually too difficult. Obviously, if you suspect that a student will be unable to comprehend prospective material, avoid giving it to him or her. However, because your school may lack multilevel material, you need to provide instruction to help the student comprehend text written above his or her ability level. Below is a short list of five instructional strategies to accommodate difficult text to student ability levels. The references at the end of this chapter provide more detail and additional strategies.

Create Written and Oral Summaries of the Material

E-mail a written summary or use an MP-3 media player to allow a student to hear an oral summary before reading the material. This private, individual communication also reduces the chances of students' public embarrassment and humiliation due to difficulty with the material.

Create Marginalia

Marginalia refers to notes in text margins that highlight or explain illustrations, captions, headings, titles, and other graphic aids. To direct students' attention to this important information, create marginal notes on photocopies of pages, display a page with marginalia using an overhead projector, or scan a page with marginalia into a PowerPoint slide show.

Create Concept Maps

Use text structure diagrams to show relationships between ideas. Illustrations of cause–effect, enumeration, sequence, and other cognitive processes represented in text, for example, are especially helpful to struggling learners as they anticipate structure and understand written material (Sinatra, 2000).

Use Reading Guides

Providing written questions and statements prior to reading to focus the reader's thoughts while reading can improve comprehension. Reading guides that encourage the reader to anticipate, to react during reading, and to reflect on what is read result in more engaged readers who comprehend at enhanced levels (McKenna & Robinson, 2005).

Use the ReQuest Procedure

Introduced in 1969 by Anthony Manzo, the reciprocal questioning (ReQuest) procedure has withstood the test of time. When student and teacher (or another student) question each other as they read, student comprehension improves. This procedure is particularly appropriate for adolescent learners when creating questions, because they provide input and are able to control, to some degree, the learning situation.

Avoid Overusing Independent-Level Material

Traditionally defined, *independent-level material* is material in which a student understands 90% or more, and in which he or she can decode 98% of the words (Leslie & Caldwell, 2001). However, a more practical, flexible, and less formal definition is "the level at which the student can effortlessly handle material without teacher guidance" (McCormick, 2003, p. 90). You might intuitively feel that using independent-level material would best ensure mastery and enhance self-efficacy. However, especially with middle and junior high school students, who are becoming more reflective of their capability as learners and more sensitive to peer judgment, when instructional material is perceived as too easy and offers minimal challenge, mastery has little value and self-efficacy can be weakened as a result (Bandura, 1986). A constant, predictable diet of easy reading material suggests to the student that the teacher has low expectations and standards for him or her, reinforces a personal conclusion of low ability, and results in low self-efficacy, especially when the student recognizes that his or her peers receive more challenging material. "To succeed at an easy task is redundant with what one already knows, whereas mastery of a difficult [or moderately challenging] task conveys new efficacy information for raising one's efficacy appraisal" (Bandura, 1986, p. 402).

Provide Short-Term Goals

When a student achieves a number of goals in a relatively short period, he or she has consistent evidence of personal ability to succeed and the expectation of success (i.e., high self-efficacy) is likely to be strengthened. Therefore, for students who struggle, it is better to establish short- rather than long-term goals, because feedback on progress is frequent, immediate, and reinforcing. If a goal for your seventh graders is to know regional topography of the United States, and your social studies book has a long chapter on this topic, divide the assignment into smaller, more digestible sections. Students who have high self-efficacy and are motivated to read will persist throughout the entire chapter and complete a follow-up assignment to compare the regions. However, when you assign that same lengthy chapter to students with low self-efficacy for reading, they are likely to be hesitant and not complete the assignment. For these students, set intermediate, shorter-term goals that require less reading. In the examples that follow, the first four are shorter-term, intermediate goals; the last is the longer-term, more distant goal.

1. You will know the landform of the northeastern United States.
2. You will know the landform of the northwestern United States.
3. You will know the landform of the southeastern United States.
4. You will know the landform of the southwestern United States.
5. You will be able to compare the landforms of the regions of the United States.

Both students and teachers can set goals. When students establish or contribute to the establishment of goals, they commit to attaining goals to a greater degree than if the goals are set for them (Pintrich & Schunk, 2002). A sequence of learning contracts that lead to independent goal setting is an effective way to engage junior high and middle school students in learning and increase their possibility of experiencing success (Greenwood, 2003; McCabe & Greenwood, 2005).

Provide Appropriate, Easily Accessible In-Class Support

Provide help efficiently and as unobtrusively as possible to optimize students' chances for mastery and to enable them to attribute success to their own effort. As Bandura (1986) wrote, "Successes achieved with external aid carry less efficacy value because they are likely to be credited to external factors rather than to personal capabilities" (p. 402). This is especially true for adolescents surrounded in class by judgmental peers, who listen, overhear, and watch, then readily gossip. Admittedly, it is not easy to achieve the right balance of duration and intensity of assistance; unfortunately, no existing research has a calculus for this. A further complication is that a student's reaction to the amount of time the teacher helps him or her may be situational. The following five instructional principles help students attribute personal success to their own effort, thus enhancing self-efficacy.

Avoid Too Many Examples

An adolescent who asks for help, then perceives the number of examples the teacher provides as too many, or the explanation as too long, may interpret this as evidence of personal inability to learn easily and, consequently, develop low self-efficacy for the task. Unfortunately, because of the idiosyncratic nature of the interaction of teacher and student, I cannot give you an optimum number of examples for all students; however, asking a student whether he or she would like an additional example is one way to avoid the detrimental effects of overexplaining. An additional complication for you is that some adolescents may not admit that they need additional examples or explanation. If you suspect this is the case, it is better to return to such students as quickly as possible than to "overstay" your welcome at that time.

Circulate Regularly and Widely

Chances of stigmatizing a student as one who has trouble mastering a task increase when you communicate with that student only when helping him or her. One way to avoid this perception is to circulate frequently throughout the room, stopping to visit all students, regardless of ability level, on a regular basis. By visiting high achievers who are doing well as frequently as you visit low achievers, you minimize the chances of being perceived as a helper for a helpless student. Similarly, when you visit struggling students at times other than when they need assistance, you again avoid the automatic perception of providing help and the subsequent interpretation of your presence as evidence of student inability to learn. This reduces the likelihood that students will develop low self-efficacy, therefore increasing their chances of both experiencing mastery and attributing it to personal effort.

Use Skilled Questioning

It is not always helpful to answer a student's question automatically and immediately, although this may at times be necessary, expedient, and appropriate, especially in a large-group setting. Asking a sequence of questions that elicit answers increases students' chances of becoming independent learners who are self-efficacious. If a student expresses a lack of understanding about what he or she is reading, respond with questions similar to the following: "Can you tell me more to let me know what you do not understand?"; "Can you guess what you think it might be about?"; or "How does this differ from what we have read before?" These are examples of possible questions; others that require student self-reflection and clarification are equally acceptable.

Provide Frequent Feedback

Frequent feedback that is focused on effort and is formative helps students to recognize mastery and contributes to positive self-efficacy (Brophy, 2004; Dweck, 2006; Margolis & McCabe, 2006; Pintrich & Schunk, 2002). It is important not to overdo this, however, by complimenting students on relatively insignificant achievements in an effort to build their self-efficacy. For example, for most adolescents, praise for locating a page quickly, an elementary skill, is likely to be counterproductive feedback, and the adolescent student may even perceive it as insulting. In addition, feedback should focus on the skill mastered, so the student knows with certainty what is noteworthy. Focused feedback should also reflect achievement due to personal effort rather than to intelligence. When students are praised for effort and not intelligence, they persist and are more confident in their ability to succeed (Dweck, 2006). It is better to say, "You got that correct because you continued to use the self-questioning technique" than "You got that correct because you are smart." Finally, feedback that is formative is more effective than feedback that is summative. *Formative* refers to progress in comparison to previous efforts; *summative* refers to absolute achievement, without comparison to previous effort.

Provide Easy Access

If possible, arrange classroom seating so that you can visit students and they can visit each other with relative ease. When not optimally arranged for easy passage, furniture can become an obstacle, preventing you from responding quickly and efficiently. Additionally, arrange for easy access to materials. Unnecessary time spent searching for material reduces immediacy of feedback, allows time for student loss of focus, and jeopardizes the timely opportunity for mastery.

Vicarious Experience

According to *Merriam-Webster's Collegiate Dictionary* (11th edition), *vicarious* means "experienced or realized through imaginative or sympathetic participation in the experience of another." Under the right circumstances, individuals can use information derived from a vicarious experience to make a personal self-efficacy judgment. The positive effect upon self-efficacy of watching another person perform a task depends on the degree to which the observer perceives similarity. "Similarity to a model is one factor that increases the personal relevance of modeled performance information for the observers' perceptions of their own efficacy" (Bandura, 1986, p. 403). This similarity is critical for adolescent self-efficacy development, especially for struggling readers. Personal similarity, however, needs further elaboration, because it is a characteristic critical to vicariousness, especially for adolescents.

Teachers and peers can enable the vicarious experiences of an observer through both mastery and coping models. A mastery model demonstrates immediate success; a coping model demonstrates eventual success after using alternative strategies when not immediately successful. Some examples of coping strategies for comprehension are rereading, reading at a slower pace, or looking at illustrations.

Unlike dancing, swimming, or kicking a soccer ball, reading is usually a private, somewhat opaque activity, during which a reader uses thought processes and strategies as well as personal information to understand text. Therefore, to model reading strategies involves thinking aloud while reading. Pintrich and Schunk (2002) refer to this as *cognitive modeling*.

Two adjectives can guide you when using peer models with adolescents: sensitive and subtle. *Sensitive* refers to criteria used to match the model with the observer. When selecting a peer model, be sensitive to personal characteristics, such as age, culture, gender, race, economic level, in-school and out-of-school group membership, and even dress style. These factors, individually or in combination, can have a strong influence on perception of similarity; therefore, they affect personal vicariousness, especially with adolescents. In addition, carefully consider relative skills levels. There is little or minimal effect on development of an observer's self-efficacy when he or she recognizes a model's skills levels to be significantly superior. The perceived significant difference in skills levels prevents perception of similarity and inhibits vicariousness.

Subtle refers to that which is not obvious. An obvious or direct modeling situation is one in which one person explicitly demonstrates for another how he or she does something, often using attentional phrases, such as "Watch me as I . . . , " "Pay attention as I . . ., " or "Notice as I . . . " (McCabe, 2006). As a middle or high school teacher in a large-group situation, avoid making peer modeling obvious and public. One way to make modeling subtle is to seat the observer (the student who lacks the skill) near the model (the student who possesses the skill) to increase the likelihood of informal observation and communication. Another way to provide subtle modeling is to have two or three students work cooperatively on a project, with one or two indirectly modeling a task as the student with low self-efficacy observes. Also, rotate seating in your class on a predictable and regular basis, so that seating a student who has a skill next to one who lacks the skill does not appear prearranged.

Physiological–Affective State

People can interpret physiological and affective reactions to prospective situations negatively or positively (Bandura, 1986).

"In the social cognitive view, knowledge concerning bodily states is acquired, in large part, through social labeling processes" (Bandura, 1986, p. 407). *Labeling* is commenting on the observable behavior resulting from physiological response (i.e., facial expression, fidgeting, or clinching one's fist and saying, "Yes"). The label ascribed to the observable behavior, together with its cause, become connected information that affects self-efficacy. Individuals learn to interpret personal and private physiological responses from parents, other caretakers, siblings, peers, and even people in electronic media, such as television. "By conjuring up aversive thoughts about their ineptitude and stress reactions, people can rouse themselves to elevated levels of distress that produce the very dysfunction they fear" (Bandura, 1997, p. 107); however, success is likely to lower levels of anxiety and increase self-efficacy for that or a similar task in the future. "Students who notice they are reacting in less-agitated fashion to tasks feel more efficacious about learning" (Pintrich & Schunk, 2002, p. 172). Research has also revealed that when in a positive mood, people feel more self-efficacious and are likely to attempt more challenging tasks compared to when they are in a negative mood (Bandura, 1986; Pintrich & Schunk, 2002; Thelwell, Lane, & Weston, 2007).

In addition, people who anticipate using a recently learned skill often subconsciously recall their mood as they learned that skill (Bower, 1981, 1994). In turn, this recall may subsequently influence predicted level of performance. A student who felt a great deal of anxiety learning a task may use that level of anxiety to predict struggle and lack of success on the same or a similar task, and develop a negative self-efficacy belief. A student who enjoyed learning a task, however, is likely to recall a feeling of joy accompanied by success, and develop a positive self-efficacy belief for the same or a similar task in the future.

Affect encompasses both mood and emotion. *Moods* are "low intensity, diffuse, and enduring affective states that have no salient antecedent cause and little cognitive content. . . . Emotions are more short lived, intense phenomena that usually have a salient cause, and the person is usually aware of this cause of the emotion" (Pintrich & Schunk, 2002, p. 278). These researchers listed positive and negative emotions that can occur before, during, and after involvement in a task. Positive emotional responses before the task include hope and anticipated joy; negative ones include anxiety, hopelessness, and resignation/despair. Enjoyment, a positive response, or boredom, a negative response, can be experienced during a task. Relief, outcome-related joy, and pride are likely to be experienced after success on a task; sadness, disappointment, shame, self-anger, and guilt may be emotional responses to lack of success. Positive emotions strengthen self-efficacy; negative ones weaken it.

Those in the health professions use the term *white coat syndrome* to refer to significant increase in blood pressure when in a doctor's office or hospital, or even in the presence of a medical worker in a white coat usually worn by doctors. In this situation, interpretation of environmental cues precipitate the physiological reaction. Some students may experience a similar phenomenon as they react to the many environmental variables in the school building or classroom, especially if those variables conjure images of past struggle and failure with literacy tasks. Factors that may contribute to the academic equivalent of white coat syndrome are perception of the teacher, the teacher's management or instructional style, the student's peers, and the physical arrangement of the room, including seating assignment.

Learners' perceptions of personal characteristics of the teacher also play a significant role in their motivation. Students are more likely to be motivated to learn when they perceive the teacher to be caring, pleasant, positive, encouraging, and understanding. "You—your own personality and everyday behavior in [and out of] the classroom—can become your most powerful motivational tool" (Brophy, 2004, p. 28); I added the bracketed words to remind you that the manner in which you behave and interact in the school hallway, lunchroom, and out-of-class conversations with students and others is additional information that students use to judge your personal characteristics. For example, as a result of an informal conversation with you at a place other than the school building, a student may decide that you are an understanding and caring individual. As noted earlier, because of student social relationships in the junior high and middle school classroom, out-of-school conversations with teachers away from peers may have greater impact than those within the academic setting, surrounded by peers.

Cues from the teacher and the environment are information that students can use to develop a self-efficacy judgment. I discuss both below.

Cues from the Teacher

Excellent teachers possess and consistently demonstrate personal and professional qualities and characteristics that contribute positively to student achievement and mood. However, cultural, ethnic, or idiosyncratic family factors can affect the quality of the teacher–student interaction. For example, both teachers and students who are unaware of the mores of groups other than their own may misunderstand a facial expression, body language, or mode of communication.

The following suggestions maximize the possibility of positive, productive student mood, and minimize negative and nonproductive mood.

Incorporate Humor

Judicious use of humor lessens stress (Pollak & Freda, 1997) and can contribute to positive mood and enhance learning. "In education, humor appears to be a viable way to enhance student learning and to advance the student's knowledge base" (Dziegielewski, Jacinto, Laudadio, & Legg-Rodriguez, 2003, p. 74). Appropriate jokes and spontaneous responses to classroom events can create a relaxed ambience and mood. Benign and positive humor that does not target others has a positive relationship to cheerfulness and high self-esteem, and a negative relationship to depression and anxiety. (The caution is that some adolescents direct insulting and injurious humor at others' physical characteristics, family members, or social position. Text messaging of negative humor—as well as cyberbullying—has become particularly troublesome recently.)

Use Appropriate and Reassuring Facial Gestures

Facial gestures communicate a variety of emotions and, although affected by culture or developmental history, have a significant effect on the observer (Hansen & Ranald, 1988; Ohman, 2002). Abused children's reactions to facial expressions differ from those of nonabused children (Elfenbein, 2006; Elfenbein, Beaupre, & Levesque, 2007; Elfenbein, Mandal, Ambady, Harizuka, & Kumar, 2004). A frown may provide a cue that something is wrong; a wide-eyed look conveys surprise; and a smile, happiness or pleasure. This may vary according to observer background. Therefore, make a conscious effort to project genuine, positive, pleasant, and reassuring facial gestures that contribute to a positive student mood and, consequently, increase the possibility of positive self-efficacy. One way to do this is to smile frequently, as appropriate. Smiles should also be credible and not gratuitous. If you do not smile easily, you may appear to be serious, distant, and unapproachable, even though this is not true.

Listen Empathetically

Individuals like to know they have "gotten through" to the listener. One way to provide evidence of empathic listening is by repeating to the student what he or she has just said, although in different words. For example, "What I just heard you say was that you get nervous before tests and that affects your score. Is that correct?" is evidence that you have listened carefully to what the student has said. Rather than immediately trying to resolve or "fix" the problem, you demonstrate that you are paying attention.

Attend to Your Voice

There is evidence that listeners can detect affective and emotional state from speakers' speech rhythm and intonation (Bostanov & Kotchoubey, 2004; Nwe, Foo, & Da Silva, 2003), although this may also be affected by cultural factors (Graham, Hamblin, & Feldstein, 2001). Therefore, monitor your prosody to avoid sounding anxious, rushed, disappointed, angry, or exasperated. Adolescent learners, struggling with academic tasks, may incorrectly interpret a sigh or a higher-than-usual pitch to your voice as evidence of your exasperation at their inability to learn.

Use Names

Using the student's name when communicating with him or her is important to establish rapport, focus attention, and demonstrate respect. Some of the following suggestions are more practical than others in helping you remember the names of the many students you have on a daily basis. One is to have students wear or place name tags on their desks; another is to put the seating arrangement in your Blackberry device, creating a class map that you can access quickly; still another is to encourage your students to use each other's names in class. Also, when outside the school setting, visualize your seating arrangements and rehearse each student's name.

Cues from the Environment

Physical environment affects learning. According to Mastropieri and Scruggs (2000, p. 280), "The overall orientation of the classroom environment is also an important condition for enhancing motivation and affect." While it is clearly impossible to control for all environmental events outside and within the room, the following suggestions may help.

Manage Class Routines Well

Most students learn best with consistent, predictable, and fair class routines; capricious reactions to student behavior and inconsistent routines inhibit learning, raise student anxiety, and create a negative mood (Brophy, 2004). Lesson design and implementation can also affect student mood. When learning tasks are at an inappropriate level, lack value, and require unavailable supplies, student anxiety is likely to increase.

Maintain a Professional Environment

Rooms with broken desks, windows, and shades; peeling and chipped wall and ceiling paint; and inadequate lighting signal a neglected, unimportant, and even aversive environment. That feeling may in turn contribute to student anxiety, especially for those who learn best in highly structured and predictable surroundings. Many school buildings in this country are architecturally very pleasing, well lit, and well maintained. Unfortunately, however, too many other schools, especially in some urban areas, have suffered recent cuts in federal and state finding. Although some of this is beyond your control, be pleasantly persistent in following up with your supervisor to create a professional ambience in your room.

Establish a Pleasant Atmosphere

Establish a learning community in which you expect students to treat each other with respect and dignity. The best way to maximize chances of creating such an environment is to model such behavior yourself. When you say "Good morning," "Please," and "Thank-you" to your students, they begin to use these terms more frequently. For many reasons, too many adolescents have grown up in environments in which regular interpersonal communication with an adult may have been limited to hearing commands (i.e., "Give me that pencil!") directed toward them rather than more gentle interrogatives (i.e., "Can you give me that pencil?"). Signs posted around your room that remind students to use courtesy when speaking to each other reinforce this idea.

Advertise Literacy with Attractive, Relevant, Contemporary Artifacts

Display posters of celebrities and recognizable others reading; examples of out-of-school literacies, such as text messaging, blogging, and webpages; and lists of books popular with adolescents (for suggestions, see the IRA's Young Adults' Choices Booklists at *www.reading.org/resources/tools/choices_young_adults. html*). When asked about their reading habits, many adolescents think solely of in-school reading and ignore what they read out of school (Hughes-Hassell & Rodge, 2007; Moje, 2006; Pitcher et al., 2007). By incorporating images or artifacts representing out-of-school literacies into the classroom environment, you expand the perception of literate behavior and provide access to the learning community for those students hooked on electronic media.

Advertise Happiness

Critical placement in your room of photographs, paintings, and posters of people smiling is likely to result in positive feelings for many students. To make it easier for students to relate to such images, include items that reflect the ethnic composition of your classes. Although you should include images of all ethnicities, it is essential that students see happy people who resemble themselves to enhance the value of advertising happiness. Involve your students in the selection process and allow them to bring in personal family pictures, if they so desire.

Verbal Persuasion

Teachers can enhance motivation by helping students "set goals for their literacy and content learning and then guide them to focus on their progress toward attaining these goals" (National Institute for Literacy, 2007, p. 36). Both oral and written (electronic or handwritten) feedback can make students aware of their progress and influence self-efficacy judgments. "People who are persuaded verbally that they possess the capabilities to master given tasks are likely to mobilize greater sustained effort than if they harbor self-doubts and dwell on personal deficiencies when difficulties arise" (Bandura, 1986, p. 399); however, many factors can affect the value of such comments.

"The impact of persuasory opinions on self-efficacy is apt to be only as strong as the recipient's confidence in the person who issues them" (Bandura, 1986, p. 406). Comments designed to raise self-efficacy must be convincing. Effective comments must come from a credible source, be evidence-based, and attribute success to the effort of the learner. Also, immediate feedback after success is more effective than delayed feedback, because it is temporally associated with the success and focuses a student's attention, with minimal chance of misunderstanding. Delayed feedback increases the possibility of a student not recognizing or forgetting personal success.

For middle and high school students, however, who are replacing or augmenting their network of previous and comparatively limited social relationships in the elementary school with a larger, more complex, less familiar, and possibly intimidating social structure, public oral feedback may have disadvantages that far outweigh advantages. One major disadvantage of oral feedback for adolescent students is possible embarrassment caused by teachers' public praise in front of peers. Although it perhaps lacks the advantage of immediacy, consider communicating through handwritten or electronic messages that are private and personal.

The goal of verbal persuasion as it relates to self-efficacy is to convince a student to attribute success to his or her effort (Pintrich & Schunk, 2002). Attributing success to ease of task, luck, or even to innate intelligence may not enhance self-efficacy, because these elements are outside the individual's power to change. However, attributing success to quantity and quality of effort results in enhanced self-efficacy, because personal effort is within the individual's control. Students praised for effort, rather than intelligence, persevere to a greater degree when faced with challenge (Dweck, 2006). "Research indicates that some students struggle unnecessarily because they incorrectly attribute failure to [innate] ability rather than to lack of effort or undirected effort" (Bruning et al., 2004, p. 125). Students with low self-efficacy tend to attribute their success to luck or happenstance; those with high self-efficacy tend to attribute it to personal effort (Bruning et al., 2004; Mueller & Dweck, 1998; Pintrich & Schunk, 2002).

Interestingly, praising excessive effort can have deleterious effects on self-efficacy development. Do not say, for example, "The reason you were successful was because you worked so hard to understand what the author said." Such comments imply that the student has to expend a lot of energy to accomplish something, and that learning is not easy. Coupled with successful enactive mastery experiences, verbal persuasion that focuses on attribution retraining can bolster feelings of self-efficacy.

Below are examples of phrases, consistent with the sources of self-efficacy information described by Bandura (1986), to convince students of their ability to learn (McCabe, 2006). (The key word in the previous sentence is *convince*, because these words and phrases direct students to recognize evidence of their accomplishment.) The *italicized* words and phrases direct students' attention to the source of self-efficacy information. The nonitalicized words and phrases refer to the skill learned (using Greek roots to determine word meaning, in my example). The same skill is used in each example to enable you to focus more easily on the source of self-efficacy addressed.

Emphasize Enactive Mastery

- "*You were able to* figure out the meaning of words by looking at the Greek root."
- "*What you just said indicates that you know how to* figure out the meaning of words by looking at the Greek root."
- "*You have the idea of looking* at Greek roots to figure out the meaning of words."
- "*Now you have the knack of looking* at Greek roots to figure out the meaning of words."
- "*You have the skill of looking* at Greek roots to figure out the meaning of words."

Experience Vicariousness

- "*Watch me (Henrietta; a peer model) as I (she)* look(s) at the Greek roots."
- "*Did you see the way I (Henrietta)* located the Greek root to figure out what that word means?"
- "*Notice how I (Henrietta)* looked for Greek roots."
- "*Listen as I (Henrietta)* look for Greek roots."

Use Verbal Persuasion

- "*Because you* watched me, you were able to find the Greek roots."
- "*As a result of studying* the Greek roots, you were able to figure out the meaning of that word."
- "*You did not give up and that is why* you were able to figure out what the word means."
- "*The way you studied helped you* remember the Greek roots."

Notice Physiological–Affective State

- *"You must feel great* because you figured out the meaning of the word by locating the Greek root."

- *"Do you realize that you smiled to yourself* when you figured out the meaning of that word?"

- *"How did you feel* when you figured out the meaning of that word by using the Greek root?"

- *"You must feel proud of yourself* because you figured out the meaning of that word by using the Greek root."

QUESTIONS FOR DISCUSSION

You should now answer the questions at the beginning of this chapter, as well as the ones that follow. Based on what you have learned in this chapter:

1. Can you identify some students who have low self-efficacy for literacy tasks?
2. How will you ensure enactive mastery for students with low self-efficacy?
3. How will you change what you say to students?
4. Can you identify students who would be good peer models?
5. How could you communicate some of these ideas about self-efficacy to parents?
6. How could you communicate some of these ideas about self-efficacy to school administrators?
7. Did you ever experience low self-efficacy? What did you do if given a task for which you had low self-efficacy?
8. Did you ever experience high self-efficacy? How did you feel when anticipating that task?
9. Has your self-efficacy for any task changed?
10. Has there been anyone in your life who helped you to enhance your self-efficacy? If so, how did that person accomplish this?

Resources

www.positivepractices.com/efficacy/selfefficacy.html
www.des.emory.edu/mfp/self-efficacy.html
thrivingitsallgood.blogspot.com/2007/05/wonderful-self-efficacy-website.html
www.positivepractices.com/efficacy/selfefficacy.html
psychology.about.com/od/theoriesofpersonality/a/self_efficacy.htm
userpage.fu-berlin.de/~health/selfscal.htm
projects.coe.uga.edu/epltt/index.php?title=motivation
www.about-personal-growth.com/self-efficacy.html

References

Armbruster, B. B. (1984). The problem of inconsiderate text. In G. Duffy, L. Roehler, & J. Mason (Eds.), *Comprehension instruction: Perspectives and suggestions* (pp. 202–217). White Plains, NY: Longman.

Athey, I. J. (1982). Reading: The affective domain reconceptualized. In B. A. Hutson (Ed.), *Advances in reading/language research* (Vol. 1, pp. 203–217). Greenwich, CT: JAL Press.

Baker, L., & Wigfield, A. (1999). Dimension of children's motivation for reading and their relations to reading activity and reading achievement. *Reading Research Quarterly, 34,* 452–477.

Bandura, A. (1986). *Social foundations of thought and action.* Englewood Cliffs, NJ: Prentice-Hall.

Bandura, A. (1995). Exercise of personal and collective efficacy in changing societies. In *Self-efficacy in changing societies* (pp. 1–46). New York: Cambridge University Press.

Bandura, A. (1997). *Self-efficacy: The exercise of control.* New York: Longman

Bostonav, V., & Kotchoubey, B. (2004). Recognition of affective prosody: Continuous wavelet measures of event-related brain potentials to emotional exclamations. *Psychophysiology, 41*(2), 259–268.

Bower, G. H. (1981). Mood and memory. *American Psychologist, 36,* 129–148.

Bower, G. H. (1994). Some relations between emotions and memory. In P. Elman & R. J. Davidson (Eds.), *The nature of emotions: Fundamental questions* (pp. 303–305). New York: Oxford University Press.

Brophy, J. (2004). *Motivating students to learn* (2nd ed.). Mahwah, NJ: Erlbaum.

Bruning, R. H., Schraw, G. J., Norby, M. M., & Ronning, R. R. (2004). *Cognitive psychology and instruction* (4th ed.). Upper Saddle River, NJ: Pearson.

Crismore, A. (1983). *The rhetoric of social studies textbooks* (Research/Technical Report No. 143). Urbana–Champaign: University of Illinois. (ERIC Document Reproduction Service No. ED 239-226)

Dweck, C. (2006). *Mindset: The new psychology of success.* New York: Random House.

Dziegielewski, S. F., Jacinto, G. A., Laudadio, A., & Legg-Rodriguez, L. (2003). Humor: An essential communication tool in therapy. *International Journal of Mental Health, 32,* 74–90.

Elfenbein, H. A. (2006). Learning in emotion judgments: Training and the cross-cultural understanding of facial expressions. *Journal of Nonverbal Behavior, 30*(1), 21–36.

Elfenbein, H. A., Beaupre, M., & Levesque, M. (2007). Toward a dialect theory: Cultural differences ion the expression and recognition of posed facial expressions. *Emotion, 7*(1), 21–36.

Elfenbein, H. A., Mandal, M. K., Ambady, N., Harizuka, S., & Kumar, S. (2004). Hemifacial difference in the in-group advantage in emotion recognition. *Cognition and Emotion, 18*(5), 613–629.

Graham, C. R., Hamblin, A. W., & Feldstein, S. (2001). Recognition of emotion in English voices by speakers of Japanese, English, and Spanish. *International Review of Applied Linguistics in Language Teaching, 39*(1), 19–37.

Greenwood, S. (2003). *On equal terms: How to make the most of learning contracts in grades 4–9.* Portsmouth, NH: Heinemann.

Hansen, C., & Ranald, D. (1988). Finding a face in the crowd: An anger superiority effect. *Journal of Personality and Social Psychology, 54*(6), 917–924.

Healey, C. G., Booth, K. S., & Enns, J. T. (1996). High-speed visual estimation using preattentive processing. *ACM TOCHI, 3*(2), 107–135. Retrieved January 2, 2008, from *www.csc.ncsu.edu/faculty/healey/download/tochi.96.pdf.*

Henk, W. A., & Melnick, S. A. (1995). The reader self-perception scale. *Reading Teacher, 48*, 470–482.

Hughes-Hassell, S., & Rodge, P. (2007). The leisure reading habits of urban adolescents. *Journal of Adolescent & Adult Literacy, 51*(1), 22–32.

Ivey, G., & Broaddus, K. (2001). "Just plain reading": A survey of what makes students want to read in middle school classrooms. *Reading Research Quarterly, 36*(4), 350–377.

Kantor, R., Anderson, T., & Armbruster, B. (1983). How inconsiderate are children's textbooks? *Journal of Curriculum Studies, 15*, 61–72.

Langer, J. (1983). Inconsiderate text. In H. Singer & T. Bean (Eds.), *Proceedings of the Lake Arrowhead Conference on Learning from Text: Selection of friendly text* (pp. 143–149). Riverside: University of California, Riverside, Learning from Text Project.

Leslie, L., & Caldwell, J. (2001). *Qualitative Reading Inventory-3.* New York: Longman.

Manzo, A. V. (1969). The ReQuest procedure. *Journal of Reading, 13*, 123–126.

Margolis, H., & McCabe, P. (2006). Improving self-efficacy and motivation: What to do, what to say! *Intervention in School and Clinic, 41*(4), 218–227.

Mastropieri, M. A., & Scruggs, T. E. (2000). *The inclusive classroom: Strategies for effective instruction.* Columbus, OH: Prentice-Hall/Merrill.

McCabe, P. (1993). Considerateness of fifth-grade social studies texts. *Theory and Research in Social Education, 21*(2), 128–142.

McCabe, P. (2006). Convincing students they can learn to read: Crafting self-efficacy prompts. *The Clearing House, 79*(6), 252–257.

McCabe, P., & Greenwood, S. (2005). Using the learning contract to enhance students' self-efficacy for reading and writing in the middle school. *Middle School Journal, 36*(4), 13–19.

McCabe, P., Kraemer, L., Miller, P., Parmar, R., & Ruscica, M. (2006). The effect of text format upon underachieving first year college students' self-efficacy for reading and subsequent reading comprehension. *Journal of College Reading and Learning, 37*(1), 19–42.

McCormick, S. M. (2003). *Instructing students who have literacy problems* (4th ed.). Columbus, OH: Prentice-Hall/Merrill.

McKenna, M. C., & Robinson, R. D. (2005). *Teaching through text: Reading and writing in the content areas* (4th ed.). Boston: Allyn & Bacon.

Merriam-Webster's Collegiate Dictionary (11th ed.). Springfield, MA: Author.

Moje, E. (2006). To be part of the story: The literacy practices of gangsta adolescents. *Teachers College Record, 102*(3), 651–690.

Morgan, P. L., & Fuchs, D. (2007). Is there a bidirectional relationship between children's reading skills and reading motivation? *Exceptional Children, 73*(2), 165–183.

Mueller, C. M., & Dweck, C. S. (1998). Intelligence praise can undermine motivation and performance. *Journal of Personality and Social Psychology, 75*, 33–52.

Najström, M., & Jansson, B. (2006). Unconscious responses to threatening pictures:

Interactive effect of trait anxiety and social desirability on skin conductance responses. *Cognitive Behaviour Therapy, 35,* 11–18.

National Endowment for the Arts. (2007). *To read or not to read: A question of national consequence* (Research Report No. 47). Washington, DC: U.S. Government Printing Office.

National Institute for Literacy. (2007). *What content area teachers should know about adolescent literacy.* Washington, DC: U.S. Government Printing Office.

Nelson, R. M., & DeBacker, T. K. (2008). Achievement motivation in adolescents: The role of peer climate and best friends. *Journal of Experimental Education, 76*(2), 170–189.

Nwe, T. L., Foo, S. W., & Da Silva, L. C. (2003). Speech emotion recognition using hidden Markov models. *Speech Communication, 41*(4), 603–623.

Ohman, A. (2002). Automaticity and the amygdala: Nonconscious responses to emotional faces. *Current Directions in Psychological Science, 11*(2), 62–67.

Pintrich, P. R., & Schunk, D. H. (2002). *Motivation in education: Theory, research, and applications* (2nd ed.). Columbus, OH: Prentice-Hall/Merrill.

Pitcher, S. M., Albright, L. K., DeLaney, C. J., Walker, N. T., Seunarinesingh, K., Mogge, S., et al. (2007). Assessing adolescents' motivation to read. *Journal of Adolescent & Adult Literacy, 50,* 978–996.

Pollack, J. P., & Freda, P. D. (1997). Humor, learning, and socialization in the middle level classrooms. *Clearing House, 70*(4), 176–179.

Schunk, D. L., & Meece, J. L. (2006). Self-efficacy development in adolescence. In F. Parajes & T. Urdan (Eds.), *Self-efficacy beliefs of adolescents* (pp. 71–96). Greenwich, CT: Information Age.

Schunk, D. L., & Zimmerman, B. (2007). Influencing children's self-efficacy and self-regulation of reading and writing through modeling. *Reading & Writing Quarterly, 23*(1), 7–25.

Sinatra, R. C. (2000). Teaching learners to think, read, and write more effectively in content subjects. *Clearing House, 73,* 266–273.

Singer, H. (1986). Friendly texts: Description and criteria. In E. K. Dishner, T. W. Bean, J. E. Readance, & D. W. Moore (Eds.), *Reading in the content areas: Improving classroom instruction* (2nd ed., pp. 112–118). Dubuque, IA: Kendall Hunt.

Snow, C. E., Porche, M. V., Tabors, P. O., & Harris, S. R. (2007). *Is literacy enough?: Pathways to academic success for adolescents.* Baltimore: Brookes.

Thelwell, R. C., Lane, A. M., & Weston, N. J. (2007). Mood states, self-set goals, self-efficacy, and performance in academic examinations. *Personality and Individual Differences, 42*(3), 573–583.

Unrau, N., & Schlackman, J. (2006). Motivation and its relationship with reading achievement in an urban middle school. *Journal of Educational Research, 100*(2), 81–101.

Watkins, M. W., & Coffey, D. Y. (2004). Reading motivation: Multidimensional and

Zimmerman, B. J. (1995). Self-efficacy and educational development. In A. Bandura (Ed.), *Self-efficacy in changing societies* (pp. 202–232). New York: Cambridge University Press.

Chapter 4

Content-Area Reading

Past, Present, and Future

Maryann Mraz
Robert J. Rickelman
Richard T. Vacca

GUIDING QUESTIONS

---

1. How has the field of content-area reading evolved over time?
2. How has research informed content-area reading?
3. What elements impact content-area reading today?

Many people are familiar with the aphorism, "Every teacher a teacher of reading." The statement over time, has come to mean that teaching reading skills goes beyond teaching children to read, which most people associate with instruction that takes place in kindergarten through second or third grade. During this "learning to read" time, students learn isolated skills through direct instruction and practice them in reading materials that may or may not have links to the content they typically study in other subjects. Once students have learned the basic skills sets necessary to become proficient readers, the expectation is that, especially once students enter the middle grades, teachers will not directly teach reading skills in isolation, because the assumption is that students have already learned how to read. Although this assumption can certainly be debated, it is safe to say that middle and secondary schoolteachers see themselves more as teachers of content than as teachers of reading. During this period, from the late intermediate grades on, "reading to learn" is assumed, implying that reading skills must continue to grow beyond the

77

basics as students read to help understand content subject material. Reading at this stage becomes a vehicle to learn subject-area material rather than an end in itself. This "reading to learn" phase is linked closely to content-area reading, because the focus is on the content.

Some people attribute the statement that all teachers are responsible for teaching reading to the 1970s, when content reading regained the focus of much interest, with the publication of *Teaching Reading in the Content Areas,* by Harold Herber (1970). During this time, mandatory content reading classes for preservice teachers, especially those at the junior high and high school levels, became a common prerequisite to becoming licensed. Many states even today require a content reading course for potential teachers as a licensure requirement. But the roots of content reading actually can be traced back much further.

The Early Roots of Content Reading

Nila Banton Smith (1934/1965) wrote a comprehensive and thorough history of reading instruction in the United States, but much of her discussion of content reading focused on how basal readers included "integrated" reading that used content subject material. She did discuss secondary reading in some detail, but more from the aspect of work related to remedial reading in high schools and colleges. Moore, Readence, and Rickelman (1983) provided a focused exploration of the roots of content reading, which began in the late 19th century. Before that time, successful reading was linked for the most part to rote memorization. The focus of reading was almost exclusively on the oral elements—how well students used pronunciation, voice inflection, and gesture as they recited famous speeches or poetry they had memorized. It was assumed that if students could correctly and convincingly demonstrate oral mastery of a text, then they could be assumed to be proficient readers. Some today might find it surprising that reading comprehension at that time was not a focus for reading instruction. It would have been unusual if a teacher in the second half of the 19th century had asked students who finished an oral recitation what they thought the orator meant by his or her words, or to elaborate on thoughts presented in the oration, as teachers today might do.

However, as early as 1894, some scholars began to point out that there is more to reading than orally reproducing a text. Colonel Francis Parker discussed the active role of reading in understanding, going beyond oral elements to critical thought. He wrote that "the mental results of written or printed words upon the mind are predetermined by the mind itself" (1894, as cited in Moore et al., 1983, p. 422). In other words, what the reader brings to the text in terms of background knowledge should influence the meaning of words on a page. In the early 1900s, Huey (1908/1968) published his seminal work *The Psychology and Pedagogy of Reading.* He wrote that "reading should not be an 'exercise,' done as a formal process or end in itself. Rather, it should be meaningful, with intrinsic interest and value" (as cited in Richardson, 2008). In fact, he dedicated a chapter in his book to reading for meaning.

Thorndike's work (1917) on the roots of content reading was also seminal. He argued that rather than re-creating meanings through oral recitation, reading is a much more complex process, "involving a weighing of each of many elements in a sentence, their organization in the proper relations one to another, the selection of certain of their connotations and the rejections of others, and the cooperation of many forces to determine final response" (p. 323). He concluded:

> It appears likely that exercises in silent reading to find the answer to given questions, or to give a summary of the matter read, or to list the questions which it answers, should in large measure replace oral reading. The vice of the poor reader is to say the words to himself without actively making judgments concerning what they reveal. Reading aloud or listening to one reading aloud may leave this vice unaltered or even encouraged. Perhaps it is in their outside reading of stories and in their study of geography, history, and the like, that many school children really learn to read. (p. 332)

So, by the mid-1920s, there were distinct lines drawn between the demands of oral and silent reading, and the different purposes good readers would have for each, with different expected outcomes as well.

Researchers in the 1920s and 1930s studied the unique needs of subject-area learners, and made many recommendations for how best to meet the needs of older readers. Some (e.g., Gray, 1919) thought that generic reading skills should be taught in schools, and that students would then be able to transfer these skills to specific subject areas. Others (Yoakam, 1928) recommended that these skills be taught during subject-area instruction, because some subjects make different demands on reading than do others.

In the interim period, between recognizing that reading ability went far beyond the oral aspects and mandating courses for those seeking teaching licenses in middle and secondary school education, many changes helped to shape the field of content reading into what it is today (Moore et al., 1983). Researchers studied the differences between silent and oral reading (Mead, 1917). In 1925, William S. Gray conducted one of the first studies related to what we now consider content reading (Vacca, 2002). He studied 250 teachers of grades 4–6 to analyze the types of reading that took place during subject-area instruction. Gray also chaired the National Committee on Reading, which produced the *Yearbook for the 24th National Society for the Study of Education* (Whipple, 1925). This yearbook emphasized reading across the content fields. Beginning in 1935, Gray published annual summaries of reading research in the *Elementary School Journal* that eventually were continued by others in the *Reading Research Quarterly*. In these earlier, annual summaries, Gray recognized the unique demands placed on readers relative to different subject-area material by reporting content reading research findings as distinct from other reading focal areas. Smith (1934/1965) reported on Gray's strong interest in research related to content reading in the early 1940s, with 19 studies reported in 1940–1941 and 18 more during the following year. In subsequent years, through 1950, there were six to eight studies.

William McCallister (1936), who worked with Gray at the University of Chicago, published what is believed to be the first book to report on the differentiated reading needs across different content areas, with specific chapters devoted to different subject areas. McCallister also published some influential articles that recognized the differences across subject areas. He wrote that

> Guidance in reading should be recognized as a function of every instructor. It is generally assumed that an instructor is responsible for directing the study activities necessary to the successful pursuance of the course which he is teaching. When reading difficulties arise in the study of a subject, it is not unreasonable to expect an instructor to accept the responsibility for aiding pupils to overcome these difficulties. Such guidance is an essential phase of the instructional procedure in any course. (1930a, pp. 200–201)

He further concluded in a related study that "each content course provides the opportunity for developing new reading habits and skills. Because of the varied character of the instructional materials assigned in different courses and the varied techniques of teaching employed, pupils encounter numerous types of reading activities" (1930b, p. 284). In a later study, he outlined specific and unique skills required in different subject areas (1932), and stated that "facility in performing the reading activities required in the study of a subject, such as history, arithmetic, or science, does not necessarily result from the training usually provided in reading classes" (p. 115). He concluded that if content teachers fail to address these unique needs in their subject areas, then "pupils may be seriously handicapped by ineffective reading practices" (p. 115).

Another major influence in content reading from this period was the publication of Bond and Bond's book (1941) titled *Developmental Reading in High School*. Moore et al. (1983) reported that this text was "instrumental in establishing professional awareness of the need to provide reading instruction in high schools and to integrate it with subject matter instruction" (p. 434). The book outlined a "total reading program" by discussing the roles that school administrators, supervisors, and teachers each should play in planning and implementing high school reading instruction.

As Richardson (2008) pointed out, there was a shift away from interest in content reading between 1950 and 1970, when Herber's book was published. During this time, Rudolf Flesch (1955) proposed that the reason Johnny could not read was because phonics was not being taught in a systematic and direct way. Rather, students were being taught to read using the "look-and-say" method, which relied on using the pictures and context to identify the whole word, to the exclusion of phonics instruction. Flesch's work, even today, has a major impact on the field of reading instruction, and on content reading as a result. In the 1960s, because of some of the criticisms aimed at schools, achievement testing became popular (Richardson, 2008). Test scores were aggregated and compared across schools, school districts, states, and even different countries. When math and science test scores in the United States were reported as being lower than those in the Soviet Union, a huge influx of money was pumped into U.S. schools, especially in these areas, to ensure that we could remain competitive with other countries.

The Rebirth of Content Reading: 1970 to the Mid-1980s

Harold Herber was influential in the reemergence of interest in content reading, beginning in the 1970s. As we mentioned earlier, the publication of his book *Teaching Reading in the Content Areas* (1970) began lines of research and practice that continue to this day. According to Vacca (2002), Herber's book suggested that the "learning to read" phase is critical in allowing readers to understand subject-area materials, but good readers must adapt these skills to the unique challenges brought forth by content reading materials. Herber, who was Director of the Reading Research Center at Syracuse University, teamed up with faculty colleagues and doctoral students to issue Research in Reading in the Content Area reports, published through the Syracuse University Reading and Language Arts Center. From these research reports evolved a focus on learning from texts through the use of teaching and learning strategies, and many of Herber's doctoral students completed their dissertations by studying different strategies and how they were used by students in different content classes. For instance, Barron (1972) studied the use of graphic organizers, Shablak (1972) studied the use of anticipation guides, and Vacca (1973) studied the effects of different reading guides on text structure.

The works of Herber and his former students and associates, related to the use of reading strategies across content subjects, differed from the thinking of others during that period. Books by Robinson (1975) and Burmeister (1974) included specific chapters on teaching reading within different subjects—in math, science, social studies, the languages arts, and the fine arts, for example. But for the most part, the division of books into specific subjects ended around 1980. Rather, books like that by Readence, Bean, and Baldwin (1981) discussed theories of reading and learning in general, moved on to selection of appropriate textbooks based on readers' needs in a content classroom, then on to strategies for teaching vocabulary, comprehension, and study skills. These books had a strong focus on teaching and learning specific reading strategies, similar to that of Herber. In fact, Tierney, Readence, and Dishner (1985) organized a book around content reading strategies, to be used by teachers as a resource rather than for instruction.

The importance of using strategies to help students read and understand content-area texts was summarized by Moore and Readence (1983). They explain that a crucial issue in content-area reading instruction is instructing students so that they understand how to study and learn from their texts. They discussed four possible ways to teach both reading skills and content:

1. *Presenting isolated skills.* Skills and strategies are taught independently of content, with the hope that the skills will transfer over when needed.

2. *Aiming at content.* Focus is on the content rather than on reading skills, with the hope that, through experience, students figure out the necessary skills to learn the content.

3. *Guiding toward content.* Teachers first give students specific goals for reading, then teach the specific skills necessary for learning these goals.

4. *Presenting content and skills concurrently.* Students are taught learning strategies along with content material, with the goal of learning how to learn from their texts independently.

Moore and Readence suggested that, depending on the learning goals, the unique needs of the students, and the context for learning, each of these ways might have merit, although the fourth way seemed to make the most intuitive sense.

The Mid-1980s to the Present

Strategic Learning across the Content Areas

In traditional classrooms, especially those in which teachers did not have content reading background, assign-and-tell routines were the hallmark of content-area reading instruction: Teachers assigned a book chapter or text section to be read independently by students as homework. Often the reading included a list of literal questions to which the students were expected to respond, usually in writing. Then, in subsequent classroom lessons, teachers told the students about the material they had presumably read and asked basic questions to which the teachers already knew the answer (Vacca & Vacca, 2008). This "guess what's in my head" game required students to be little more than passive participants in the learning process. The critical analysis involved in constructing meaning and making connections remained largely within the domain of the teachers, not the students. In fact, the use of assign-and-tell routines was found to escalate as students moved from primary grades to middle and secondary grades, where teachers were found to talk three times as much as students during class interactions (Goodlad, 1984). In many classrooms today, this method is still carried on by teachers who see themselves as "deliverers of content" (Readence et al., 1981).

Strategic learning practices across the content areas sought to move beyond traditional assign-and-tell instruction by engaging students in organizing ideas, critically analyzing material, and integrating content-area concepts into broader social contexts (Vacca & Vacca, 2008). Strategy instruction provided students with the tools to better understand and synthesize content-area material (Herber & Herber, 1993). Numerous strategies were developed for content-area reading instruction. Examples included Raphael's (1986) question–answer relationship, which helped students to comprehend text by considering where answers to questions might be found. Think-alouds (Davey, 1983) showed how readers could clarify meaning by verbalizing their thoughts and questions about a text as they read. Reciprocal teaching (Brown & Palinscar, 1984) emphasized how to use the four key comprehension strategies of generating questions, summarizing, predicting, and clarifying to understand complex concepts.

More than simple classroom activities, strategy instruction was intended to teach students how to approach content-area learning in a deliberate and critical manner (Afflerbach & VanSledright, 2001). Explicit strategy instruction included the following steps:

- Assessing what students already knew how to do.
- Making students aware of strategies that could assist them in understanding content-area texts.
- Explaining the procedures for implementing a particular strategy.
- Modeling and demonstrating a strategy's use.
- Guiding students in using the strategy with a text selection or concept.
- Providing opportunities for students to apply the strategy on their own.

The emphasis on implementing strategies specifically designed for use in the content areas continued throughout the 1990s. Richardson (2008) detailed several scholarly works of this era that enhanced the understanding of strategy use in content-area reading: Bulgren and Scanlon (1997/1998) explored instructional routines. Hynd (1999) addressed the importance of teaching students to approach content-area texts from a critical stance. Alvermann, O'Brien, and Dillon (1990) studied teachers' questioning techniques and suggested types of questions that were more useful than others in providing information about students' understanding of the material. Schumm and Mangrum (1991) examined strategies for learning content-area vocabulary.

Teachers using explicit strategy instruction sought to teach students not only what strategies to use but also why certain strategies are useful in certain contexts and how these strategies may be applied to content-area reading.

Consistent with this focus on strategic teaching and learning, content-area teachers were encouraged to use an instructional framework that engaged students in applying strategies before, during, and after (BDA) reading, in a framework referred to as the BDA model. This model highlights the importance of using strategies throughout a reading lesson to engage students in active and purposeful meaning making. A complete BDA lesson does not need to take place during a single class period, nor do all the components of a BDA lesson need to receive equal emphasis during every lesson. Nevertheless, the use of strategies at different points in a lesson allows both teachers and students to monitor consistently the comprehension of text.

Prior Knowledge and Reading Engagement

Also in the 1990s, with the resurgence of constructivism, greater emphasis was placed on the social nature of learning, and on the influence of students' background knowledge in their understanding of text (McArthur, Spencer, Penland, & Anders, 2008). Constructivism espouses a student-centered approach to learning and highlights the importance of relating new concepts to one's own experiences and prior knowledge (Richardson, 2008). Schema theory helps explain how readers use their prior knowledge to organize information and to integrate new information into their existing knowledge framework. In content-area classrooms, the cognitive processes involved in understanding new concepts requires readers to evaluate and to integrate new information they encounter in texts. Students' schemas, as well as their purposes for reading, were increasingly recognized as important factors in text comprehension (Bruner, 1990).

Typically, adolescent readers are familiar with the reading process. They are capable of establishing a purpose for reading and of recalling experiences and prior knowledge related to the reading. In the application of strategies that support students in making connections between their experiences and prior knowledge, and the new material, it was increasingly recognized that content-area teachers could support student learning across subject areas.

In addition to expanding students' conceptual knowledge of content-area subjects and their use of strategies to understand new concepts, the importance of content-area learning in students' engagement in reading and their motivation to read was widely recognized (Guthrie & Wigfield, 2000). Knickerbocker and Rycik (2002) found that students' motivation for reading and learning increased when they perceived the text to be relevant to their own lives. Believing themselves to be capable of responding effectively to a text also increased students' motivation for reading.

In traditional middle and secondary school classrooms, a limited emphasis was placed on students' personal responses to reading. During this time period, however, researchers suggested that encouraging self-expression could provide students with important opportunities to construct meaning and to make personal connections across subjects (Oldfather & Dahl, 1994).

Throughout this era, emphasis was placed on instructional strategies that provided students with substantive opportunities to connect with texts.

Looking Forward

New Literacies

For many years, the term *content-area reading* described reading and learning that occurred across the subject areas, mainly in the reading of traditional print textbooks. In recent years, as the concept of content-area reading has broadened to include students' ability to use reading, writing, listening, and viewing to understand material across the curriculum, the term *content-area literacy* is now more commonly used to describe this wider range of skills (Vacca & Vacca, 2008). Content area literacy encompasses students' abilities to apply strategies for learning subject-area content and to interpret, evaluate, and communicate information (Conley, 2008).

Part of this shift in the concept of content-area reading/content-area literacy may be attributed to the rise of the new literacies that developed as a result of rapid technological advances, and the subsequent impact of those advances on teaching and learning. Traditional literacy skills in content-area classrooms focus primarily on improving students' comprehension of printed materials—in particular, textbooks. However, in the 21st century, the nature of what it means to be *literate* has changed (Leu, 2008). The term *literacy* now is expanded beyond the reading and writing of printed text to include a broad range of information and communication technologies (ICTs), such as the Internet, blogs, podcasts, and text messages (Leu, Kinzer, Coiro, & Cammack, 2004; Miners & Pascopella, 2007).

New literacies require that students develop the skills and knowledge they need to navigate complex networked environments (Kist, 2005; Leu, 2000). Content-area reading is no longer regarded by most experts as a matter of reading information from a single textbook. Instead, students must seek, evaluate, and comprehend information from a variety of print and technology sources. They are called upon to apply critical literacy skills to evaluate, process, and communicate information in print, oral, and digital forms (Anstey & Bull, 2006; Brown & Lockyer, 2006). Students' flexibility to respond to technological changes is necessary for not only understanding content-area material in school but also developing the skills needed to become productive and responsive participants in work force environments that require the application of increasingly sophisticated technology to gather and manipulate information in a variety of different formats, both analog and digital (Leu et al., 2004).

Although research suggests that there is some overlap in the literacy skills needed for print-based and technology-based reading comprehension, the latter appears to require more complex literacy skills (Chandler-Olcott, & Mahar, 2003; Coiro, 2003). Leu (2008) underscored the following skills as necessary for effective comprehension of both print- and technology-based materials:

- Identifying important questions.
- Locating information.
- Critically thinking and evaluating information.
- Synthesizing.
- Communicating.

These skills, sometimes referred to as the *new basics* (Kalantzis, Cope, & Harvey, 2003, p. 16), are now considered the building blocks of new literacies.

Implementing ICTs in content-area classrooms presents a challenge to many teachers. Often, teachers are unsure of the purpose for using ICTs:

Should they be used to enhance print-based literacy?

To support standardized testing?

To develop new literacy skills? (Labbo, 2006)

Lack of funding to support new technologies is a challenge in many school districts. Because new literacies are not included in mandated high-stakes assessments, they are not seen as a priority in some schools (Miners & Pascopella, 2007). Access to new technology further complicates its implementation across subject areas. Students from lower socioeconomic status (SES) districts are less likely, for example, to have access to ICTs both inside and outside of school. There is growing concern among researchers that the achievement gap, which currently exists across SES lines, will widen if a technology gap is allowed to persist (Coiro & Dobbler, 2007; Leu et al., 2007). New literacies will continuously change as new technologies evolve. The challenge for teachers across the content areas will be to adapt their instructional practices to respond effectively to these changes.

Multiple Literacies to Meet Diverse Learner Needs

Learning to read in the primary grades has long received the attention of researchers and policymakers. Although the importance of early reading development is not disputed, some have called for additional attention, commitment, and resources to be directed toward adolescent literacy (Kamil, 2003; Vacca & Alvermann, 1998). In recent years, positive initiatives have focused on the literacy needs of adolescent learners. For example, the International Reading Association (IRA) Commission on Adolescent Literacy developed a position statement addressing key principles that are essential to the literacy development of adolescents (Moore, Bean, Birdyshaw, & Rycik, 1999). Those principles included the need for access to the wide variety of reading materials that adolescents can and want to read, and ongoing literacy instruction that builds both the skills and the desire to read complex materials. Although some content-area teachers continue to rely on a single textbook for core instruction, many are moving beyond the single-text approach, toward the use of multiple sources that include both print- and technology-based materials (Behrman, 2003). In a report to the Carnegie Corporation, Biancarosa and Snow (2004) detailed 15 research-based elements for improving adolescent literacy programs and, in turn, adolescent literacy achievement. Those elements included motivation and self-directed learning, diverse texts, effective instructional principles embedded in content, and a strong technology component. Fisher and Ivey (2006) outlined research-based principles for evaluating critical interventions for struggling adolescent readers and found that teacher-directed practices, rather than methods and materials, made a difference, but the challenge is in building literacy expertise for secondary teachers.

Content-area literacy is increasingly informed by research that examines not only in-school literacy learning but also adolescents' use of literacy skills beyond the classroom. Students' use of out-of-school literacies suggests that their literacy lives are more complex than may be apparent from the school setting alone (Bean & Harper, 2004; Flores-Gonzalez, 2002). To understand these complexities fully and use this information to enhance literacy learning, Moje (2002) suggests that teachers learn as much as possible about adolescents' identities and their literacy use beyond the classroom. Many teachers have begun this process. In doing so, the focus of content-area reading is shifting from the text to the adolescent reader (Bean & Harper, 2008).

This shift is particularly important as the needs of adolescent learners in American schools becomes increasing diverse. It is estimated, for example, that by the year 2020, one student in four will be Hispanic (Readence, Bean, & Baldwin, 2004). These students bring an array of both English language learning needs and enriching cultural experiences to their classrooms. Content-area reading teachers will continue to be called upon to respond to a diverse range of student backgrounds and learning needs. Innovative content-area instruction, characterized by student-centered inquiry that engages adolescents in interdisciplinary learning and problem solving (Sturtevant & Linek, 2003), will be needed to respond to the evolving dynamics and technological innovations inherent in adolescent literacy learning.

QUESTIONS FOR DISCUSSION

1. In your work with other content-area teachers, describe the instructional strategies you use to help students understand subject-area material.

2. What aspects of content-area reading are challenging for your students? How have you responded to them? Discuss with colleagues other strategies you might use to address these challenges.

3. Explain the perception and use of new literacies in your school. Discuss ways in which you might revise your instructional practices to effectively integrate new literacies with traditional content-area reading.

Resources

Further Reading

Leu, D. J., Zawailinski, L., Castek, J., Banerjee, M., Housand, B. C., Liu, Y., et al. (2007). What is new about the new literacies on online reading comprehension? In L. S. Rush, A. J. Eakle, & A. Berger (Eds.), *Secondary school literacy: What research reveals for classroom practice* (pp. 37–68). Urbana, IL: National Council of Teachers of English.

Moore, D. W., Bean, T. W., Birdyshaw, D., & Rycik, J. A. (1999). *Adolescent literacy: A position statement for the Commission on Adolescent Literacy of the International Reading Association*. Newark, DE: International Reading Association.

Moore, D. W., & Readence, J. E. (1983). Approaches to content-area reading instruction. *Journal of Reading, 26,* 391–403.

Vacca, R. T., & Alvermann, D. E. (1998). The crisis in adolescent literacy: Is it real or imagined? *NASSP Bulletin, 82,* 4–9.

Websites

www.sedl.org/pubs/reading16/12.html—Contains information for addressing the needs of struggling readers across content areas.

www.literacy.matter.org/lessons/contentoverview.htm—Suggests sample lessons to be used in a variety of content areas.

www.readingrockets.org—Offers research and ideas related to engaging students in reading.

References

Afflerbach, P., & VanSledright, B. (2001). Hath! Doth! What? Middle graders reading innovative history text. *Journal of Adolescent & Adult Literacy, 44,* 696–707.

Alvermann, D. E., O'Brien, D. G., & Dillon, D. R. (1990). What teachers do when they say they're having discussions of content-area reading assignments: A qualitative analysis. *Reading Research Quarterly, 25,* 296–321.

Anstey, M., & Bull, G. (2006). *Teaching and learning multiliteracies.* Newark, DE: International Reading Association.

Barron, R. F. (1972). *An iterative–ecological investigation of vocabulary development in tenth grade biology.* Unpublished doctoral dissertation, Syracuse University, Syracuse, NY.

Bean. T. W., & Harper, H. J. (2004). Teacher education and adolescent literacy. In T. L. Jetton & J. A. Dole (Eds.), *Adolescent literacy research and practice* (pp. 392–411). New York: Guilford Press.

Bean, T. W., & Harper, H. J. (2008). Content area reading: Current state of the art. In D. Lapp, J. Flood, & N. Farnan (Eds.), *Content area reading and learning: Instructional strategies.* New York: Erlbaum.

Behrman, E. H. (2003). Reconciling content literacy with adolescent literacy: Expanding literacy opportunities in a community-focused biology class. *Reading Research and Instruction, 43,* 1–30.

Biancarosa, G., & Snow, C. (2004). *Reading next: A vision for action and research in middle and high school literacy: A report to Carnegie Corporation of New York.* Washington, DC: Alliance for Excellent Education.

Bond, G. L., & Bond, E. (1941). *Developmental reading in high school.* New York: Macmillan.

Brown, A. L., & Palinscar, A. S. (1984). Reciprocal teaching of comprehension-fostering and comprehension-monitoring activities. *Cognition and Instruction, 1,* 117–175.

Brown, I., & Lockyer, L. (2006). Exploring a learning design to operationalize new pedagogical frameworks using multi-literacies. *International Journal of Learning, 12*(10), 175–178.

Bruner, J. (1990). *Acts of meaning.* Cambridge, MA: Harvard University Press.

Bulgren, J., & Scanlon, D. (1997/1998). Instructional routines and learning strategies that promote understanding of content-area concepts. *Journal of Adolescent & Adult Literacy, 41,* 292–302.

Burmeister, L. E. (1974). *Reading strategies for secondary school teachers.* Reading, MA: Addison-Wesley.

Chandler-Olcott, K., & Mahar, D. (2003). "Tech savviness" meets multiliteracies: Exploring adolescent girls' technology-mediated literacy practices. *Reading Research Quarterly, 38,* 356–385.

Coiro, J. L. (2003). Reading comprehension on the Internet: Expanding our understanding of reading comprehension to encompass new literacies. *Reading Teacher, 56,* 458–464.

Coiro, J. L., & Dobler, E. (2007). Exploring the online reading comprehension strategies used by sixth-grade skilled readers to search for and locate information on the Internet. *Reading Research Quarterly, 42,* 214–257.

Conley, M. W. (2008). *Content area literacy: Learners in context.* Boston: Allyn & Bacon.

Davey, B. (1983). Think aloud: Modeling the cognitive processes of reading comprehension. *Journal of Reading, 27,* 44–47.

Fisher, D., & Ivey, G. (2006). Evaluating the interventions for struggling adolescent readers. *Journal of Adolescent & Adult Literacy, 50,* 180–189.

Flesch, R. (1955). *Why Johnny can't read.* New York: Harper.

Flores-Gonzalez, N. (2002). *School kids/street kids: Identity development in Latino students.* New York: Teachers College Press.

Goodlad, J. (1984). *A place called school.* New York: McGraw-Hill.

Gray, W. S. (1919). *The relation between study and reading: Proceedings of the Annual Meeting of the National Education Association.* Washington, DC: National Education Association.

Guthrie, J. T., & Wigfield, A. (2000). Engagement and motivation in reading. In M. Kamil, P. Mosenthal, P. D. Pearson, & R. Barr (Eds.), *Handbook of reading research* (Vol. III, pp. 403–424). Mahwah, NJ: Erlbaum.

Herber, H. L. (1970). *Teaching reading in the content areas.* Englewood Cliffs, NJ: Prentice-Hall.

Herber, H. L., & Herber, J. N. (1993). *Teaching in content areas with reading, writing, and reasoning.* Boston: Allyn & Bacon.

Huey, E. B. (1968). *The psychology and pedagogy of reading.* Cambridge, MA: MIT Press. (Original work published 1908)

Hynd, C. (1999). Teaching students to think critically using multiple texts in history. *Journal of Adolescent and Adult Literacy, 42,* 428–436.

Kalantzis, M., Cope, B., & Harvey, A. (2003). Assessing multiliteracies and the new basics. *Assessment in Education, 10*(3), 15–26.

Kamil, M. (2003). *Adolescents and literacy: Reading for the 21st century.* Washington, DC: Alliance for Excellent Education.

Kist, W. (2005). *New literacies in action: Teaching and learning in multiple media.* New York: Teachers College Press.

Knickerbocker, J. L., & Rycik, J. (2002). Growing into literature: Adolescents' literacy interpretation and appreciation. *Journal of Adolescent & Adult Literacy, 46,* 196–208.

Labbo, L. D. (2006). Living in the promised land . . . or can old and new literacies live happily ever after in the classroom? *College Reading Association Yearbook, 28,* 20–30.

Leu, D. J. (2000). Literacy and technology: Deictic consequences for literacy education in an information age. In M. L. Kamil, P. M. Mosenthal, P. D. Pearson, & R. Barr (Eds.), *Handbook of reading research* (Vol. III, pp. 743–770). Mahwah, NJ: Erlbaum.

Leu, D. J. (2008, April). *How reading comprehension has changed while we weren't looking.* Paper presented at the Voices of Innovation Speaker Series, William & Ida Friday Institute for Educational Innovation, Raleigh, North Carolina State University.

Leu, D. J., Kinzer, C. K., Coiro, J. L., & Cammack, D. W. (2004). Toward a theory of new literacies emerging from the Internet and other information and communication technologies. In R. B. Ruddell & N. J. Unrau (Eds.), *Theoretical models and processes of reading* (pp. 1570–1613). Newark, DE: International Reading Association.

Leu, D. J., Zawailinski, L., Castek, J., Banerjee, M., Housand, B. C., Liu, Y., et al. (2007). What is new about the new literacies on online reading comprehension? In L. S. Rush, A. J. Eakle, & A. Berger (Eds.), *Secondary school literacy: What research reveals for classroom practice* (pp. 37–68). Urbana, IL: National Council of Teachers of English.

McArthur, K. Spencer, F., Penland, T., & Anders, P. (2008). Why content-area literacy?: Focus on students. In D. Lapp, J. Flood, & N. Farnan (Eds.), *Content area reading and learning* (pp. 55–89). New York: Erlbaum.

McCallister, J. M. (1930a). Reading difficulties in studying content subjects. *Elementary School Journal, 31,* 191–201.

McCallister, J. M. (1930b). Guiding pupils' reading activities in the study of content subjects. *Elementary School Journal, 31,* 271–284.

McCallister, J. M. (1932). Determining the types of reading in studying content subjects. *School Review, 40,* 115–123.

McCallister, J. M. (1936). *Remedial and corrective instruction in reading: A program for the upper grades and high school.* New York: Appleton–Century.

Mead, C. D. (1917). Results in silent versus oral reading. *Journal of Educational Psychology, 8,* 367–368.

Miners, Z., & Pascopella, A. (2007). The new literacies. *District Administration, 43*(10), 26–34.

Moje, E. (2002). Re-framing adolescent literacy research for new times: Studying youth as a resource. *Reading Research and Instruction, 41,* 211–228.

Moore, D. W., Bean, T. W., Birdyshaw, D., & Rycik, J. A. (1999). *Adolescent literacy: A position statement for the Commission on Adolescent Literacy of the International Reading Association.* Newark, DE: International Reading Association.

Moore, D. W., & Readence, J. E. (1983). Approaches to content-area reading instruction. *Journal of Reading, 26,* 391–403.

Moore, D. W., Readence, J. E., & Rickelman, R. J. (1983). An historical exploration of content-area reading instruction. *Reading Research Quarterly, 18,* 419–438.

Oldfather, P., & Dahl, K. (1994). Toward a social constructivist reconceptualization of intrinsic motivation for literacy learning. *Journal of Reading Behavior, 26*, 139–158.

Parker, F. W. (1894). *Talks on pedagogics: An outline of the theory of concentration.* New York: E. L. Kellogg.

Raphael, T. E. (1986). Teaching question–answer relationships. *Reading Teacher, 39*, 516–520.

Readence, J. E., Bean, T. W., & Baldwin, R. S. (1981). *Content area reading: An integrated approach.* Dubuque, IA: Kendall/Hunt.

Readence, J. E., Bean, T. W., & Baldwin, R. S. (2004). *Content area literacy: An integrated approach* (8th ed.). Dubuque, IA: Kendall/Hunt.

Richardson, J. S. (2008). Content area reading: A 50-year history. In M. J. Fresch (Ed.), *An essential history of current reading practices* (pp. 120–143). Newark, DE: International Reading Association.

Robinson, H. A. (1975). *Teaching reading and study strategies: The content areas.* Boston: Allyn & Bacon.

Schumm, J. S., & Mangrum, C. (1991). FLIP: A framework for content-area reading. *Journal of Reading, 35*, 120–124.

Shablak, S. L. (1972). *The effects of different types of guide materials and manner of presentation on ninth graders' curiosity toward and response to selected short stories.* Unpublished doctoral dissertation, Syracuse University, Syracuse, NY.

Smith, N. B. (1965). American reading instruction. Newark, DE: International Reading Association. (Original work published 1934)

Sturtevant, E. G., & Linek, W. M. (2003). The instructional beliefs and decisions of middle and secondary teachers who successfully blend literacy and content. *Reading Research and Instruction, 43*, 74–90.

Thorndike, E. L. (1917). Reading as reasoning: A study of mistakes in paragraph reading. *Journal of Educational Psychology, 8*, 323–332.

Tierney, R. J., Readence, J. E., & Dishner, E. K. (1985). *Reading strategies and practices: A compendium.* Needham Heights, MA: Allyn & Bacon.

Vacca, R. T. (1973). *An investigation of a functional reading strategy in seventh grade social studies.* Unpublished doctoral dissertation, Syracuse University, Syracuse, NY.

Vacca, R. T. (2002). Making a difference in adolescents' school lives: Visible and invisible aspects of content-area reading. In A. E. Farstrup & S. J. Samuels (Eds.), *What research has to say about reading instruction* (3rd ed., pp. 184–204). Newark, DE: International Reading Association.

Vacca, R. T., & Alvermann, D. E. (1998, October). The crisis in adolescent literacy: Is it real or imagined? *NASSP Bulletin, 82*, 4–9.

Vacca, R. T., & Vacca, J. L. (2008). *Content area reading: Literacy and learning across the curriculum* (9th ed.). Boston: Allyn & Bacon.

Whipple, G. M. (Ed.). (1925). *Report of the National Committee on Reading: Twenty-fourth yearbook of the National Society for the Study of Education, Part I.* Bloomington, IL: Public School Publishing.

Yoakam, G. A. (1928). *Reading and study: More effective study through better reading habits.* New York: Macmillan.

Chapter 5

Promoting Adolescent Literacy through Parental Involvement

Making It Happen

Timothy Rasinski
Nancy D. Padak
Kristy Pytash

GUIDING QUESTIONS

1. How can teachers collaborate with parents to create a rich literacy environment at school and at home?

2. Although young adults are gaining independence and autonomy, it is important for teachers and parents to continue to be important influences during the years of adolescence. How can parents maintain strong relationships with their young adult through literacy activities?

3. Where can teachers and parents find high-quality, yet popular and interesting, reading materials for young adults?

4. Teachers and parents should have collaborative relationships; is it possible for teachers to organize their classroom instruction based on their knowledge of students' home situations? Why is it important for parents to be recognized as partners and valuable resources?

Mrs. Smith was perplexed. She was committed to involving her middle school students' parents in classroom activities, but she was feeling discouraged. Mrs. Smith had read the professional literature explaining the importance of parental involvement in effective literacy programs and wanted to create meaningful literacy experiences for her students and their families. She had told her students to invite their parents in for literature circle discussions. Only a handful of parents arrived, and although they brought the book assigned and participated in discussion, there still seemed to be a lack of interaction. Mrs. Smith realized she needed to rethink her ideas about parent involvement, and provide a variety of activities to foster and strengthen the home–school relationship.

Although fictional, this vignette illustrates many middle and high school teachers' experiences when they attempt to involve parents in their adolescents' educational experiences. Like the parents who arrived for Mrs. Smith's Reading Day, many parents are willing to be involved in their adolescents' educational experiences; however, as adolescents are gaining greater autonomy, parents might be unsure about the extent to which they should be involved. Schools and teachers can work to build and strengthen the relationships between parents and adolescents, and in the process support adolescents' literacy learning and school achievement.

Adolescence, the developmental period between ages 12 and 18, is a time of increasing awareness of the personal self in relation to others due to cognitive growth and social–emotional maturity. For many young adults, adolescence is the time when questions concerning personal identity and normative values arise. Young adults are involved in extensive social networks as they shift peer groups and experience greater levels of autonomy from parents and other family members. Although often disputed by teenagers, their gains in being able to function independently require continued parental guidance and support. In fact, because adolescents are experiencing physical, cognitive, and social–emotional changes, adult relationships are vital to their wellbeing.

Parents often recognize the importance of playing an active role in their child's early years of schooling but fail to appreciate fully the need for positive involvement in supporting educational growth in the middle and high school years. Teachers and schools can help here. Successful parent involvement can enhance adolescents' academic success, and build and strengthen relationships among parents, adolescents, and schools. Moreover, engaging adolescents and parents in literacy activities can help to foster discussions about school, peer groups, interests, and other topics of importance to teenagers and their families.

In this chapter, we provide suggestions for how educators can collaborate with parents to create effective school and home literacy practices that engage adolescents and promote literacy growth.

Parental Involvement: A View from Researchers

Researchers have found that parent involvement affects student achievement not only during elementary school years but also through the middle and high school years. In an international study, for example Postlethwaite and Ross (1992) found that parental involvement in all its various forms, when initiated by schools and teachers, was the single best predictor of student achievement in reading for grades 2 and 8.

Researchers who have delineated the effective forms of parental involvement have used various conceptualizations of involvement. Studies have defined *parental involvement* as parental aspirations for their children, parental participation in school-based activities, home involvement in students' education, and communication with students about school (Singh et al., 1995). Analyses of types of parental involvement have looked at factors that include parents' educational background, socioeconomic status (SES), ethnicity, and race. Thus, the research base offers a comprehensive view of *parent involvement* in terms of both family characteristics and types of involvement.

Communication and discussions among parents, teachers, and students have continually been found to raise student achievement. Singh et al. (1995) found that parental aspirations for their children had the strongest positive effect in terms of types of parental involvement. Parental aspirations are important because they lead to conversations about school. Studies have also revealed that in middle and high school students, communication among adolescents, teachers, parents, and administrators concerning education and future educational plans has a positive relationship with academic outcomes (Hill et al., 2004; Sui-Chu & Willms, 1996). Establishing effective communication between parents and adolescents has been associated with positive academic achievement, and talking about adolescents' school and personal lives can motivate parents to take an active role in their children's lives. Falbo, Lein, and Amador (2001) found that adolescents who successfully transition from middle school to high school had parents who monitored their teens, evaluated potential problem areas, and intervened to help their teens make decisions. Parents who helped their teens socially and participated in school activities were more apt to help their teens transition successfully to high school. Parental involvement in adolescents' lives is critical, because school achievement, particularly adolescents' literacy practices and abilities, have been found to be important in violence and risk prevention (Vanderstaay, 2006). Also important for violence and risk prevention are the attachments and bonds with adults in adolescents' lives (Vanderstaay, 2006).

Discussions between parents and adolescents about educational achievements, struggles, activities, and aspirations can be further developed with help from teachers and administrators. Research surrounding parents' educational backgrounds, ethnicity, and SES indicates that these variables affect parent involvement; however, Epstein and Dauber (1991) contend that more important than parent variables are the practices and attitudes of teachers and schools. In other words, we have an important role in helping parents become knowledgeable partners in their children's education. Parental interaction with children's education at home increases when teachers make parental involvement a component of their teaching practice, regardless of the child's age or grade level (Epstein & Dauber, 1991). Epstein and Dauber also insist that schools can help parents learn to be involved in a productive manner. Eccles and Harold (1993), whose research supports this notion, found that the school programs and teacher practices encouraging parents were the strongest predictors of parent involvement. They provide six teacher and school characteristics thought to be predictors of parent involvement:

> (a) beliefs about the appropriate amount and type of parent involvement, (b) beliefs about influences on parents' levels of participation, particularly beliefs as to why parents are not more involved, (c) sense of efficacy about their ability to affect the parents' level of participation, (d) knowledge of specific strategies for getting parents more involved, (e) plans for implementing these strategies, and (f) support for implementing specific plans. (p. 577)

As teachers, then, we should keep parents informed, but do so beyond open houses and parent–teacher conferences and try to develop more personal relationships with parents (Eccles & Harold, 1993). Brough and Irvin (2001) argue that parents must be "apprised of concrete ways and parental roles that foster student academic improvement" (p. 58). Thus, we want to approach parental involvement in a systematic, rather than haphazard, manner. To do so, the following design characteristics may prove useful (Padak & Rasinski, 2006):

1. *Identify key goals and use proven and effective strategies.* Teachers should work to help students and parents recognize the value of reading strategies that have been researched and proven effective for support and instruction.

2. *Provide ongoing training, communication, and support.* The authors challenge teachers to "find meaningful ways for all families to be involved in home reading activities" (p. 292). Many parents need teachers' guidance and support to help engage their children in literacy activities.

3. *Provide authentic reading texts.* The authors stress the importance of using authentic genres, such as newspaper and magazine articles, editorials, poems, folktales, family histories, and song lyrics. Offer materials that are engaging for both parents and their children, and guidance on how to select appropriate reading materials. Explaining to parents the various book awards for young adults, such as The American Library Association's Best Books for Young Adults Award and Outstanding Books for the College Bound, helps parents learn about literature written specifically for their adolescents. (See *www.ala.org/ala/yalsa/booklistsawards/booklistsbook.com* for more information.) It is important to remind parents that the goal is to engage their adolescent in reading; therefore, allowing adolescents to choose topics and genres they find interesting may be more important than forcing adolescents to read great literary works, which they may not find interesting. Many times, adolescents do not have a choice in the reading they do for school; therefore, it is important for adolescents to have ownership over the text they read at home.

4. *Make activities easy, enjoyable, and consistent.* The authors found that parents are more willing to complete home reading activities if "they are not too complex, take inordinate amounts of time, or change often" (p. 293). Creating routines helps students and parents consistently participate in reading activities, but make sure variation exists to subdue boredom.

5. *Provide ways to document home activities.* Simple reading logs help teachers, parents, and adolescents track their reading work. A reading log may serve as a helpful reminder for parents and teenagers to integrate reading within the home environment.

Below we offer examples of how to put these design principles to work to promote adolescents' literacy growth. But first, a note about word choice: Our use of the term *literacy* includes the reading and writing of text, whereas our discussion of literacy practices includes many ways of reading and writing, such as drama, art, dance, and speech (Moje, 2000). Moreover, we understand that many adolescents do not live with parents, but with other family members or guardians. Our use of the word *parents* refers to any person or persons who have legal guardianship or assume the role of "parent" to the adolescent. We also encourage teachers not to limit involvement to parental participation only. Extended family members can be a valuable resource, especially in families with a single parent or in which both parents work. Grandparents, aunts, uncles, and other important adults in adolescents' lives should be seen as valuable resources. During their study with male teenage readers and their parents, Love and Hamston (2004) found the boys included their extended family members, such as grandparents, aunts, and uncles, as active members in encouraging reading.

At Home

We want parents to view themselves as active participants in their adolescents' education, to support their adolescents' efforts to become better readers and writers. The first step in this process may well be to help parents see that creating a literate home environment is essential for fostering and continuing an interest in literacy. An important component of a supportive home environment is the availability of books, magazines, poetry, dramas, newspapers, comics, graphic novels, texts from the Internet, and so forth, for the entire family to browse and to read. Observing the reading preferences of their teenager is key to parents' provision of enticing literacy materials.

Educators can help parents realize that reading is not a skill taught only in elementary school; such a narrow view of literacy excludes many of the literacy practices in which adolescents engage. Many adolescents may not be reading print-based materials at home, but they are engaged and comfortable reading non-print-based materials, at times described as *out-of-school* or *new literacies.* Kist (2000) describes a *new literacies* classroom as one in which "there would be ongoing, continuous usage or multiple forms of representation" (p. 712); therefore, these literacy practices are not limited to print-based forms, but include video, audio, and graphic forms. This notion of the new literacies classroom can be extended to the literacy practices of adolescents at home. These out-of-school literacies may be very important to adolescents but are not always validated by schools or adults. Many times, graphic novels, videos, and weblogs are what adolescents read on a daily basis. It is important to encourage adolescents to read, whether reading novel or an article posted on a favorite website. Teachers might suggest that parents create their own family websites on which family members can post pictures of family trips or activities, schedules, and/or photo albums.

Adolescents must have a choice and preference of reading material to maintain their interests. Teenagers may prefer reading short, informational text, as is found on a cereal box; how-to information found in cookbooks; word games, such as crossword puzzles; in addition to the traditional literacy activities, such as reading a newspaper, a fashion magazine, a novel, or a sports magazine. It is important for parents and teachers to recognize the importance of choice and self-selection, especially while encouraging the practice of reading. Ivey and Broaddus (2001), who studied the reading interests of over 1,700 sixth graders, found that choice in selection of reading materials was strongly aligned to positive reading experiences. They also found that students' reasons for reading were personal and purposeful.

Teachers can suggest that parents buy reading material for their adolescents. Chandler (1999) found that, many times, parents supplied various genres of writing to their adolescents, and that occasionally students received books as presents from their parents and/or family members. Parents can signal the importance of books and reading in and out of school by the purchase of reading materials for holidays and celebratory events (Chandler, 1999). The focus should remain on the interests of the adolescents, and parents need to be encouraged to refrain from selecting only reading materials that deliver a moral message.

Using the American Library Association's Book Award website, teachers can create lists for parents of popular young adult literature. Teachers can also distribute copies of the *Journal of Adolescent and Adult Literacy*'s Young Adults' Choices, published each November (see also *www.reading.org/resources/tools/choices_young_adults.html* for a complete list of all Young Adults' Choices by year), or *The Reading Teacher*'s Children's Choices published in October (see also *www.reading.org/resources/tools/choices_childrens.html* for a complete list of all Children's Choices by year). Informing parents about *Booklist*, and *Horn Book Magazine,* journals with recommendations for young adult literature, can assist parents in selecting appropriate texts that appeal to their adolescent reader. A helpful aspect of a book list is making reference to book awards and journals that include book reviews for young adults. Parents also need to know where to find young adult literature. Supplying parents with websites and journals containing book awards also encourages them to notice specific sites devoted to young adult literature. Parents and teens can work together to create a home library in which each family member contributes and suggests reading recommendations for other members of the family.

Encouraging parents to take their adolescents to the library or to bookstores is crucial, especially for parents of students who might not have access to books at home. A trip to the community library or a local bookstore allows parents and adolescents to browse reading sections, to look through book selections together, and to compare reading interests. This shared experience builds a common interest in reading between the parent and the young adult. It may also extend to involvement in book clubs and other group activities for parents and their young adults at the library. These activities form partnerships in which each member plays an equal role, allowing both parents and adolescents to voice their thoughts and opinions. An informed discussion centered on what has been read is beneficial to academic achievement. Chandler (1999) found that effective home discussions are similar to school discussions, and include consideration of elements of style and talk about story predictions.

Reading with young children before bedtime is a tradition in some homes; however, few parents realize the benefits of reading with their adolescent, even for just 5–10 minutes a day. Many schools provide newspapers for classrooms; students can select or be assigned an appealing article to take home and read with their parents. Adolescents can read the article aloud to their parents and explain why they selected it. Reading the article aloud affords the adolescent additional practice in gaining reading fluency. Monitoring the child's reading expands parents' knowledge of the interests and opinions of their adolescent. This discussion format can result in critical analysis of text. Parents may not fully realize that this brief, 10-minute reading and subsequent discussion is an excellent way to support higher-order thinking. (See Appendix 5.1 for questions that prompt discussion.)

Parents can help their adolescent not only read for comprehension, but read to critique and analyze written work. This will provide parents the opportunity to move beyond just monitoring their adolescent's work; instead parents can be active participants in a discussion about a literary work.

Approaches for English Language Learner Students and Families

English language learners (ELLs) require practice reading and writing in various settings, including schools and homes. As educators, we realize that ELLs require multiple opportunities to talk, listen, read, and write. Class discussion provides effective, necessary social interaction to build skills in listening and talking. Outside the classroom or school environment, family partnerships can support students' reading and writing fluency.

Family members who are also learning English can use books on tape, recordings of speeches, and music to hear and to practice language. Allowing students to listen to language acknowledges that literacy practices include not only reading and writing but also listening and speaking. Listening to language that is read aloud provides ELL students (and their parents) a model for language structure. To read and to discuss a book on tape with an adult provides adolescents the opportunity to talk about literacy, and their struggles and accomplishments.

Because parents are children's first teachers, our sole focus should not be on what parents should be doing to engage their adolescents in reading, but on what they are doing already to influence their children's reading experience. The International Reading Association (IRA) views parent–teacher relationships as collaborative endeavors and stresses that teachers think critically about how they can organize classroom instruction based on their knowledge of students' home situations. To build on ELL students' and their families' strengths requires teachers to recognize and value the skills, life lessons, and knowledge that students bring to the classroom. In addition, recognizing parents as important partners in building language and literacy skills is crucial. This extends to recognizing the value of the literacy practices that adolescents may live out at home with their families. Cline and Necochea (2003) discuss their family backgrounds as lacking a strong print background but having "a rich tradition of oral storytelling" (p. 123). The authors relate their own experiences of how oral storytelling, music, and dancing promoted and led to a love of reading and writing. Although both authors admit that their upbringing did not consist of a "traditional print rich pathway to literacy" (p. 124), they did come from very literate homes, infused with genres such as folktales, fables, legends, family histories, music, and family and cultural traditions.

A family–school partnership is strengthened by the positive acknowledgment of family contributions to students' literacy practices. Parents' contributions when acknowledged, become available as a resource for teachers. Finding out more about children from their parents can help teachers to personalize instruction (Chandler, 1999). By relying on parents as partners and valuable resources, teachers include parents in their adolescents' education. At the Diagnostic Reading Clinic at Kent State University, for example, parents are seen as a critical source of information about their children who struggle in reading. Before clinicians at the clinic even meet a child, they talk with the parents—over the phone and in person—to gain information and insight into what may cause the child's difficulties in reading and to determine ways to overcome those difficulties. Parents are more likely to become involved in their children's reading education if we professionals view them as significant partners in the teaching and learning process. In Appendix 5.2

we provide a list of possible questions that teachers may ask parents to learn more about their students and to empower parents.

Involving Parents in School

Class newsletters are a useful and effective way to communicate with parents. The teacher may want to provide synopses of any upcoming units of study. Teachers can include calendars, test days, and due dates, as well as specific writing assignments or other types of projects students will be completing. Students can contribute as writers, editors, or featured artists. Students can write reviews on the literature they have read in class, creative short stories, or poetry. Teachers and students might want to work together to create a recommended booklist. Newsletters provide parents specific information about students' learning; they can also serve to strengthen connections between home and school.

A class website may also be used as a form of parent, teacher, and student communication. Similar to a class newsletter, a website can post a class calendar, class readings, and information about upcoming assignments. A website can also feature WebQuests for students and parents to work on together, or ways for parents and students to extend or enrich the learning that takes place at school. Creating a class website also may encourage participation from students who are not as interested in print-based reading. Adolescents are exposed to a vast quantity of information (e.g., television, advertisements, video, and the Internet); creating a classroom website may help to introduce critical literacy issues to adolescents and parents. Teachers can discuss how information is presented in these forms, and help adolescents and their parents become aware of the following critical reading issues applied to cyber-information:

- Reputability of the author/sponsoring organization.
- Purpose of the information.
- Sources to double-check accuracy of information.

An effective partnership means that parents are invited members in the classroom. Parents who attend student performances can inspire students to participate in poetry readings, readers' theatre, or debates. Repeated readings, such as rehearsing scripts, has been found to develop fluency (Rasinski, 2006), the ability to read not only "with accuracy and rate but also with good and meaningful phrasing and expression" (Rasinski et al., 2005, p. 27). Students can write and perform reader's theater scripts, poetry, and other types of performance texts. Parents can not only be a supportive audience for student performances, but they can also be encouraged to participate in the readings. Parents and adolescents can practice the performance texts at home together.

Activities for Students Who Struggle

Many adolescents who struggle with reading lack strategic reading abilities. Teachers in all content areas need to recognize the importance of teaching students how to read within the disciplines. Teachers can help parents talk about explicit reading strategies on which adults may rely. Literacy activities can be designed for parents and students to practice at home. Instructional activities help foster discussions about school and home literacy. This also helps parents assess areas in which their adolescent might excel or struggle. These activities do not always need to focus on classroom instruction; rather, they can be engaging for both parents and adolescents. Creating literacy activities can foster discussions about school-related activities and literacy.

For example, reading fluency has been identified as a significant factor in reading success, even among adolescents (National Reading Panel, 2000; Rasinski & Padak, 2005; Rasinski et al., 2005). Parents can contribute to fluency development simply by listening to their children read, commenting on their ability to read with appropriate and meaningful expression, and encouraging them to practice a given text to achieve fluency in their reading. Teachers can contribute to this home fluency scenario by assigning reading material, such as scripts, poetry, speeches, interviews, dialogues, and monologues, that students will eventually perform in class.

Many adolescents who struggle with reading may eventually become what Bintz (1993) terms *resistant readers*. Alvermann (2001) argues that schools might be creating struggling readers out of adolescents who have become reluctant readers of in-school literacy materials. Even though adolescence is a period in which young adults are gaining autonomy and independence, many times, adolescents in school do not have a choice over what material they read or the pace of their reading. Encouraging resistant adolescent readers to read at home requires that teachers and parents realize students must have a choice in reading materials. Parents need encouragement to help students find engaging reading material that aligns with their interests.

Reluctant or resistant readers need to have meaningful and purposeful reading opportunities. It is important for young adults to see teachers and parents reading for a variety of purposes. Teachers and parents should recognize the value of discussing with adolescents the reading they must do for work or to acquire new skills, for example, home manuals or a new recipe. Teachers, parents, and adolescents can compare and explore the types of reading they do for pleasure, for information, and for pragmatic purposes. Parents might be encouraged to engage adolescents in more pragmatic or purposeful reading endeavors. For example, families that are planning trips can include their adolescents in the planning. Adolescents can read guide books or Internet reviews of hotels, restaurants, and places to visit. The mundane but highly motivating reading activities of adolescents, such as reviewing driver education materials, should not be overlooked.

Adolescents who are interested in current events and politics may enjoy reading editorials or commentaries from newspapers or magazines. The family bulletin board is often the refrigerator door, and on this public posting the article or commentary is visible to all family members. Allowing all family members to read the same article can create discussions revolving around topics of interests to teenagers and their family. Adolescents and parents can also highlight or mark interesting words or phrases. The public posting of articles and commentary can go beyond politics and current events to include sports articles, fashion reviews, or the cartoon of the week.

Remember Writing

Writing is an integral literacy component. Teachers can encourage parents to share the variety of types and purposes of their writing with their children. Academic writing, such as critical analyses or research papers, is not the only type of writing that should be stressed. Grocery lists, phone messages, e-mails, blogs, thank-you notes, dairies, reminders, and letters are also items that parents and adolescents write often. It is important for adolescents not only to write but also to notice the types of writing they do in their lives for school, for pragmatic reasons, or for pleasure. Just as they discuss reading, parents and adolescents can discuss the types of writing they do on a daily basis.

Many people use journals and diaries for self-reflection. Writing allows adolescents the opportunity to reflect on their achievements and frustrations, and to think critically about their decisions. Journals may be considered personal space, but they can also be used to facilitate conversation. Dialogue journals are often used in schools to facilitate talk between students and teachers. These types of journals tend to focus on school-related readings or classroom activities. The notion of written conversations can be expanded to include parents and adolescents. Parents and adolescents can use dialogue journals to record and respond to their thoughts, feelings, and ideas. Dialogue journals may not only revolve around matters of school but also may focus on shared or individual reading experiences. Parents and adolescents can write about characters, events, places, or interesting facts from their reading. Dialogue journals allow parents and adolescent to see each other's thinking processes, and they provide a space for thoughtful written discussions. This not only provides meaningful opportunities for communication with parents but also allows students to improve their writing skills.

School, Home, and Community Connections

Adolescents are involved and spend their time in community-sponsored activities, such as church, volunteer projects, service groups, and community organizations. One way teachers can involve adolescents' parents in the school is to understand and connect the literacy practices of the community to the school. To engage adolescents, their parents, and other community members in education, teachers must recognize and use adolescents' lived experiences to help them to understand and negotiate new learning experiences. Although literacy practices occur in specific contexts, such as the school, the home, and the community, these practices are often intertwined. Kelly (2001) studied the literacy practices in a public middle school and the practices of church-based activities, including an African drumming group, an African dance troupe, and a Saturday school. She found that most of the information presented at the church was through speech, such as sermons. She then focused on one young adolescent male involved in both the Saturday school and the middle school. A persuasive writing assignment given at school allowed the adolescent the opportunity to connect his school and church literacy practices. Kelly found that the community's uses of oral language "encourage flexibility and a creativity to help them [adolescents] move between community and school-based literacies" (p. 257). Helping adolescents and parents to make connections among home, community, and school literacy practices requires that teachers know the communities in which their students live and learn. Teachers can become familiar with students' communities by attending students' sporting events, community-based activities, and local plays, and by simply talking to students.

Conclusion

Parent involvement is not just an elementary school level concern. Parents need to be involved in adolescents' education in a manner that moves past monitoring, critiquing, and ensuring that adolescents are doing the required school work. Literacy practices can increase students' academic performances, but literacy practices can also be designed to help foster and strengthen relationships. Mrs. Smith, whose story we told at the beginning of this chapter, took a positive first step by inviting parents into the classroom to share their reading experiences; however, the demands of family life, work, and other circumstances may affect parents' ability to come to their adolescents' school during the day. Mrs. Smith could have encouraged parents to send their thoughts or comments on the book to class with the students, to post them on the class website, or to e-mail them to the teacher or to their child. The parents' comments would still have been shared with the class, despite their inability to be present.

It is important to provide both parents and adolescents a choice in selecting at-home reading experiences. Activities that take place at home, during a family trip, or even while driving in the car allow for optimal participation. Mrs. Smith could also have invited other family members, such as grandparents, aunts, and uncles. Teachers need to design effective means of communication for adolescents, parents, and the school. In Mrs. Smith's case, having her students invite their parents may have not been as effective as personally contacting the parents herself. Designing a newsletter or webpage with classroom information might welcome parents into the classroom or at least informs them of classroom activities.

Teachers and parents need to be committed partners in supporting adolescents' reading and academic growth. Learning to read also takes place beyond the elementary school years and outside the school. When teachers and schools work to get parents involved in their children's reading lives, great things are bound to happen.

QUESTIONS FOR DISCUSSION

1. How can teachers learn more about the literacy traditions practiced by students and their families?
2. How can parents and teachers work together to provide young adults a choice with regard to reading materials and activities?
3. Young adults are involved in various forms of literacy, such as nonprint reading and writing. How can teachers encourage parents to accept and to make these forms of literacy accessible?

Resources

literacy.kent.edu/oasis/famlitnotebook—The Family Literacy Resource Notebook, published by the Ohio Literacy Resource Center, includes chapters about program design, developing collaborative partnerships, and obtaining funding.

literacy.kent.edu/oasis/pubs/whobenefits2003.pdf—"Family Literacy: Who Benefits" is a research review that summarizes documented effects of parental involvement in terms of children, parents, and family.

References

Alvermann, D. (2001). Reading adolescents' reading identities: Looking back to see ahead. *Journal of Adolescent & Adult Literacy, 44*, 676–690.

Bintz, W. P. (1993). Resistant readers in secondary education: Some insights and implications. *Journal of Reading, 36*(8), 604–615.

Brough, J., & Irvin, J. (2001). Parental involvement supports academic improvement among middle schoolers. *Middle School Journal, 32*(5), 56–61.

Chandler, K. (1999). Reading relationships: Parents, adolescents, and popular fiction by Stephen King. *Journal of Adolescent & Adult Literacy, 43*(3), 228–239.

Cline, Z., & Necochea, J. (2003). My mother never read to me. *Journal of Adolescent & Adult Literacy, 47*(2), 122–126.

Eccles, J., & Harold, R. (1993). Parent–school involvement during the early adolescent years. *Teachers College Record, 94*(3), 568–587.

Epstein, J., & Dauber, S. (1991). School programs and teacher practices of parent involvement in inner-city elementary and middle schools. *Elementary School Journal, 91*(3), 289–305.

Falbo, T., Lein, L., & Amador, N. (2001). Parental involvement during the transition to high school. *Journal of Adolescent Research, 16*(5), 511–529.

Hill, N., Castellino, D., Lansford, J., Nowlin, P., Dodge, K., Bates, J., et al. (2004). Parent academic involvement as related to school behavior, achievement, and aspirations: Demographic variations across adolescence. *Child Development, 75*(5), 1491–1509.

Ivey, G., & Broaddus, K. (2001). "Just plain reading": A survey of what makes students want to read in middle school classrooms. *Reading Research Quarterly, 36*(4), 350–377.

Kelly, M. (2001). The education of African American youth: Literacy practices and identity representation in church and school. In E. Moje & D. O'Brien (Eds.), *Constructions of literacy: Studies of teaching and learning in and out of secondary schools* (pp. 239–259). Mahwah, NJ: Erlbaum.

Kist, W. (2000). Beginning to create the new literacy classroom: What does the new literacy look like? *Journal of Adolescent & Adult Literacy, 43*(8), 710–718.

Love, K., & Hamston, J. (2004). Committed and reluctant male teenage readers: Beyond bedtime stories. *Journal of Literacy Research, 36*(3), 335–400.

Moje, E. (2000). To be part of the story: The literacy practices of gangsta adolescents. *Teachers College Record, 102*(3), 651–690.

National Reading Panel. (2000). *Report of the National Reading Panel: Teaching children to read: Report of the subgroups.* Washington, DC: U.S. Department of Health and Human Services, National Institutes of Health.

Padak, N., & Rasinski, T. (2006). Home–school partnerships in literacy education: From rhetoric to reality. *Reading Teacher, 60*(3), 292–296.

Postlethwaite, T. N., & Ross, K. N. (1992). *Effective schools in reading: Implications for policy planners.* The Hague: International Association for the Evaluation of Educational Achievement.

Rasinski, T. (2006). Reading fluency instruction: Moving beyond accuracy, automaticity, and prosody. *Reading Teacher, 59*(7), 704–706.

Rasinski, T., Padak, N., McKeon, C., Wilfong, L., Friedaver, J., & Heim, P. (2005). Is reading fluency a key for successful high school reading? *Journal of Adolescent & Adult Literacy, 49*(1), 22–27.

Rasinski, T. V., & Padak, N. D. (2005). Fluency beyond the primary grades: Helping adolescent readers. *Voices from the Middle, 13,* 34–41.

Singh, K., Bickley, P., Trivette, P., Keith, T., Keith, P., & Anderson, E. (1995). The effects of four components of parental involvement on eighth-grade student achievement: Structural analysis of NELS-88 data. *School Psychology Review, 24*(2), 299–317.

Sui-Chu, E., & Willms, J. (1996). Effects of parental involvement on eighth-grade achievement. *Sociology of Education, 69,* 126–141.

Vanderstaay, S. (2006). Learning from longitudinal research in criminology and the health sciences. *Reading Research Quarterly, 41*(3), 328–350.

APPENDIX 5.1. Article Discussion Prompts and Question

1. Did you learn anything new from the article?
2. What was the most interesting or surprising part of the article?
3. Did the article discuss any people who might remind you of people from your life?
4. Have you ever experienced anything similar to what you read?
5. Were any parts of the article confusing?
6. What section of the article stood out to you while you were reading?
7. Why do you think the author wrote this article and the newspaper published it?
8. What did you like or dislike about the article?
9. Look back at the first sentence of the article. Why do you think the author started with that particular sentence?
10. What do you think is the most important part of the article?

APPENDIX 5.2. Possible Questions That Teachers Might Ask of Parents of Adolescent Students

1. How does your child feel about assigned reading from school?
2. How does your child feel about reading at home for pleasure?
3. Is there a time or place at home that your child prefers for reading? Please describe.
4. Are there particular kinds of materials that your child prefers for reading? Please describe.
5. Does you child have a regular time and place for doing his or her homework? Please describe.
6. How does your child feel about assigned writing from school?
7. How does your child feel about writing at home for his own purposes?
8. What kinds of writing does your child do at home (keep a personal journal, write on the computer, write letters and notes to others, etc.)?
9. What can I do as a teacher to help your child in reading and writing?
10. What can the school do to help your child become a better reader and writer?

Chapter 6

Literacy Coaching in Middle and High Schools

Rita M. Bean
Ellen Eisenberg

GUIDING QUESTIONS

1. What is literacy coaching, and what is the rationale for literacy coaching in middle and high schools?
2. What evidence supports the presence of literacy coaching at those levels?
3. What would one expect to see in a large-scale coaching initiative?
4. What recommendations can help those interested in implementing literacy coaching at middle and high school levels to do so effectively?

Why Literacy Coaching?

We begin with this question and the usual accompanying query—"Does it work?"—because these are the questions most frequently asked by administrators, school board members, teachers, and even coaches themselves. These are legitimate questions given the meteoric increase in the numbers of literacy coaches in schools today, especially in middle and high schools. In 2003, the Alliance for Excellent Education estimated that as many as 10,000 literacy coaches would be needed to "meet the needs of the fourth through twelfth graders who read below basic levels on the National Assessment of Education Progress" (Sturtevant, 2003, p. 17).

Cassidy and Cassidy (2008), in their ongoing study of what's hot in education, identified literacy coaching as an "extremely hot" topic. Specifically, nationally known educators, with a finger on the pulse of what is occurring in education, identified coaching as one of the "hot" topics being implemented in schools across the United States in grades, K–12. At the same time, sources of information about the effects of literacy coaching are few, especially about coaching at the adolescent level. Often, educators want to know whether coaching increases student learning, or, as those concerned about accountability would ask, "Is student performance improving?" Other educators are interested in whether there are changes in classroom practices. This is particularly important in thinking about middle and high schools, where one of the primary foci of coaches is academic or disciplinary literacy, that is, supporting content-area teachers' efforts to teach science, social studies, English, math, and so forth.

Frankly, this emphasis on coaching began without much direct evidence about its success as a means of changing teacher practices and improving student learning. As indicated by Snow, Ippolito, and Schwartz (2006, p. 36), "Literacy coaching is being widely implemented based on its convergence with theory and the wisdom of practitioners, before rigorous evaluations have been carried out." At the same time, evidence from closely related studies support the presence of literacy coaching in schools. For example, studies about teachers' learning through professional development and reform efforts in schools provide us with information that highlights the need for ongoing support to help teachers address curricular, instructional, and management issues. Moreover, given the wide interest in literacy coaching, more studies are now being conducted that provide the field with evidence, about not only the effects of literacy coaching but also how it should function, if it is to be successful, and what skills and capabilities literacy coaches need to work effectively in schools.

In the next section, we discuss the available research evidence about literacy coaching. We place our emphasis on work done at middle or high school levels, although at times we include relevant studies conducted at elementary school levels.

The Evidence Base for Literacy Coaching

In this section, we first summarize research evidence on professional development and teacher learning that support literacy coaching; second, we provide information that helps to define coaching at the middle and secondary school levels; third, we summarize studies that address outcomes of coaching. Finally, we describe specific coaching initiatives at the middle or secondary school levels.

Professional Development and Teacher Learning

Because the goals of coaching are to improve classroom practices and ultimately, student learning, research about professional development is especially important. In 1993, Little called professional development the "wasteland of education," lamenting the fragmented, often sporadic attempts to provide ongoing learning for teachers in the schools. Since that time, however, there have been efforts to improve professional development in schools. The consensus seems to be that characteristics of effective professional development include (1) long-term or sustained endeavors; (2) content that is closely related to the classroom work of the teachers (i.e., job-embedded); and (3) opportunities for sustainability that include support and feedback to teachers. Standards developed by the National Staff Development Council (2001) call for attention to content, context, and process variables. In other words, those involved in professional development need to identify the content teachers need to know and the instructional approaches that enable them to teach that content to students. They also need to take into consideration the context in which such professional development is to be offered; that is, the characteristics of the school, the students, and the teachers in that environment. Finally, the processes need to reflect what is known about adult learning if they are to be effective. The adult learner brings experiences, prior knowledge, and attitudes about learning to the professional development table, and these factors need to be taken into consideration when planning such opportunities.

What is consistent about the characteristics of effective professional development (National Staff Development Council, 2001; American Educational Research Association, 2005) is the recognition that support and feedback are important elements in designing professional development; hence, the focus on coaching. Successful school literacy programs (Slavin, Madden, Doland, & Wasik, 1996; Taylor, Pressley, & Pearson, 2002) have often used coaching as an aspect of implementation although key personnel have not always been called coaches; often the term *facilitator* has been used. Moreover, facilitators have been both internal to the school (i.e., members of the school faculty) or external (i.e., employed by the initiative to visit the school on a regular, sustained basis).

Probably the most cited studies that provide support for coaching have come from the work of Joyce and Showers (1980, 2002). The model of peer coaching that evolved from their original work proposes four components: presentation of theory, modeling or demonstration, practice (often in small groups or with peers), and peer coaching. Their many investigations of various training initiatives indicated that addition of the coaching component significantly affected transfer of training, namely, that teachers used what they learned appropriately and were able to integrate their new skills into current repertoires (2002). Moreover, they found that such coaching contributed to collegiality and positive professional relationships in schools.

However, the peer coaching model differs somewhat from current models of coaching. First, in the field today, literacy coaches are generally seen as individuals who bring specific expertise to the position; that is, the literacy coach is seen as a more knowledgeable other. Second, in some models, there is more focus on "critical" feedback, not necessarily emphasized in the peer coaching model as defined by Joyce and Showers.

Secondary Literacy Coaching: What Is It?

Information provided in the position statement, *The Role and Qualifications of the Reading Coach in the United States* (International Reading Association [IRA], 2004), in *Standards for Middle and High School Literacy Coaches* (IRA, 2006), and in the brief written by Frost and Bean (2006), describing the "gold standard" for coaching, addresses issues related to both coaching qualifications and responsibilities. It is clear that coaches are expected to have a strong literacy background, excellent leadership skills, and an understanding of assessment and how to work with other adults. There is support for coaches having classroom experience, especially at the levels at which they will be coaching. Although there is still a need for more empirical evidence about the specific value of each of these qualifications, results from the Alabama Reading Initiative at the secondary school level (Bacevich & Salinger, 2006) indicated that reading coaches were more successful if they had an understanding of secondary education and adolescent literacy. The issue about qualifications is key for those involved in selecting literacy coaches for their schools. The strongest coaches are most likely those who have in-depth content knowledge in a discipline *and* an understanding of literacy instruction and assessment.

The *Standards for Middle and High School Literacy Coaches*, developed by the IRA (2006) in collaboration with the National Council of Teachers of English, the National Council of Teachers of Mathematics, the National Science Teachers Association, and the National Council for Social Studies, was a noteworthy effort to provide clarification about the role of coaches in the secondary schools and the challenges to such coaching, and to summarize what was known about coaching from a research perspective. What is most useful is its description of both leadership standards and specific content-area literacy standards for English/language arts, mathematics, science, and social studies.

Yet it would be fiscally difficult for a school to support a coach for each of the disciplines; therefore, in terms of role responsibilities, coaches at the secondary school level are generally expected to work with teachers across the various disciplines (English, math, science, social studies, etc.) to improve instruction. They are also responsible for serving as literacy leaders, promoting school change. The work with classroom teachers can occur in various ways, from work with individual teachers, which includes planning lessons, modeling various instructional strategies, and observing and providing feedback, to providing resources. At the same time, coaches can work with both small and large groups of teachers (e.g., conducting professional development workshops, leading study groups, and working with teachers in content-area team meetings).

The broader role of serving as a literacy leader involves working with the administrator to review and interpret assessment data, and to make decisions about how to improve the school as a whole, and communicating with parents, community agencies, and so forth. Coaches often have other roles and responsibilities that require them to write various school improvement plans or to collect and analyze achievement data.

The key role of the coach, however, is that of providing support to teachers that enables them to develop and implement effective instruction for students in their classrooms. Toll, in her book *The Literacy Coach's Desk Reference* (2006), explains that coaching may be brought into schools to achieve several purposes: remediation or "fixing the teacher," program implementation, or teacher growth. As Toll indicates, these purposes are not entirely compatible; she states, "I choose to emphasize teacher growth as the purpose of literacy coaching because it seems both professionally and morally sound" (p. 13). According to Toll, such a focus requires that teachers be involved in reflection and decision making, and in working toward their own goals. In our view, it is this notion of teacher growth that makes the most sense for literacy coaches working at the middle and secondary school levels. Both the teacher and the coach bring knowledge and expertise to the coaching experience; together, they must make decisions about what is needed to improve instruction for specific students in a specific context. At the same time, we recognize that coaches and teachers need to know what the goals and objectives are relative to literacy instruction in the schools; this requires that members of the school community share a vision or goal about literacy; that is, the school must have a literacy framework that undergirds the work of the coach. See Figure 6.1 for a summary of what coaching is and what it is not.

Coaching IS:	Coaching IS NOT:
• Job-embedded professional development that is ongoing and sustained.	• Evaluative in nature; that is, coaches are not there to "judge" teachers' performance.
• Support for teachers (both individual and groups).	• Administrative, with a major role of handling paperwork and budgets, and ordering and organizing materials.
• Based on teacher and student needs as identified by multiple sources.	• Serving as a teacher's aide.
• A form of inquiry and reflection.	• Assessing students only.
• Cooperative and collaborative.	• Data entry only.
• Building school capacity.	• An instructional role (e.g., teaching students with problems).
• A means of improving school achievement.	

FIGURE 6.1. Defining coaching: What it is and is not.

Sturtevant et al. (2006) state it well:

> Our review of the school change record shows that admonitions such as "every teacher should be a teacher of reading" will not lead to curricular changes in science, math, and history unless teachers (a) are adequately prepared in content-area literacy strategies, (b) can directly observe the benefits of such strategies, (c) can support one another in their attempts to implement new literacy strategies, and (d) are able to reflect on and refine strategy instruction over time. Coaches lead teaching staff through these actions. (p. 144)

We refer readers to other chapters in this book for specific information about literacy strategies to improve the teaching of content-area subjects and to develop an overall literacy framework for the school. Later in the chapter, we discuss various coaching initiatives and the literacy frameworks that guide the work of coaches in those initiatives. However, our major emphasis in this chapter is the process of coaching.

What Can Be Learned about Coaching from Research

In this section, we discuss the results of studies on instructional coaching. Most are associated with large-scale efforts to reform or to change schools, ones in which the focus is whole-school reform, that is, coaching as a mechanism for systems change. The goal of such coaching initiatives is to "build capacity within the system leading to a new professional environment in which the leadership causes change, including instructional improvement" (Brown, Stroh, Fouts, & Baker, 2005, p. 10). Coaches work with teachers to improve classroom instruction, but their work is only a component of larger systems change.

We begin, however, by describing the results of a recent, small-scale study by Smith (2007), who sought to answer the following questions: What roles do middle school coaches assume in different school settings? In what ways do contextual factors, and the coaches themselves, affect what they do? In this multiple-case study, Smith examined the work of three coaches in two school districts, all working in middle schools. Smith observed the coaches over a 5-month period, observing each for three 1-week periods. He also interviewed the coaches, teachers, and principals, and collected written reflections of the coaches. Smith categorized the roles of these coaches as *classroom instructional tasks* and *school-related tasks*. The classroom instructional roles included tasks such as planning with teacher, coteaching, or observing. School-related tasks included roles such as professional developer, principal assistant, tour guide, lunchtime librarian, or office worker. Smith indicated that, overall, the coaches spent approximately "30% of their time on peripheral tasks that seemed disconnected from either mentoring or literacy program advocacy" (p. 59). Smith indicated that because the coaches assumed many responsibilities, the coaching process became fragmented. He considered the school context to be a major influence in this fragmentation. He also highlighted his concerns that the coaching process only partially aligned with teachers' professional knowledge landscapes. For example, when coaches observed teachers but did not have the time to meet and discuss the observation, such behavior had little influence on teacher knowledge. Smith stressed the importance of recognizing that the process of influencing teacher change is potentially long and requires the support of both coaches and teachers. Smith raised concerns about coaching's potential, because it is complex and highly affected by school context, including relationships with the principal, organizational factors, school and classroom climate. Smith raised some legitimate cautions about the complexity of initiating a coaching initiative in a school—cautions that are similar to findings of larger-scale studies.

For example, as part of its grades K–12 Alabama Reading Initiative (ARI), the state of Alabama included as one of its key elements the appointment of full-time reading coaches to work with both teachers and struggling readers. A qualitative study of this initiative at the secondary school level was conducted by the American Institutes for Research (Bacevich & Salinger, 2006). Data were collected from interviews with teachers, administrators, and others to investigate the implementation and effects of this initiative. Bacevich and Salinger indicated four important lessons to be learned. First, key differences in needs of the elementary and secondary schools required the State to recognize that a one-size-fits-all approach to reading reform was not effective. Interestingly, one of the concerns was that few individuals had experience with or understood issues associated with secondary-level reading. For example, the literacy coach might have been an elementary school teacher, with little understanding of the materials and strategies that were effective for secondary-level instruction. In the report, Bacevich and Salinger quoted a high school principal: "This has been a real weak link.... The school reading coaches will tell the secondary principals, 'I don't know about secondary'" (p. 23). Second, Bacevich and Salinger called for partnerships among teachers, administrators, and schools that would enable them to create a coherent and well-defined continuum of reading instruction (K–12). Third, data indicated a need for ongoing and consistent support (human resources), if the reading initiative was to be effective. When coaches were overextended and responsible for several schools, or had other major responsibilities (teaching in addition to coaching), there was less chance of success. Finally, there must be continuing support at all levels—local, state, and national—if the emphasis on improving literacy achievement of middle and secondary school students is to continue. Bacevich and Salinger indicated positive outcomes of the ARI at secondary school levels. First, teachers seemed to have a deeper awareness of the importance of reading in their specific content areas and were also more aware of various instructional practices that could help students achieve academically. They were also collaborating more than they did before the implementation of ARI. Student outcomes were not determined by examining test scores or other quantitative indicators; however, interviews of teachers, principals, and the students themselves indicated that students were more engaged with reading and had more confidence in themselves as readers; they were able to use the various reading strategies independently. Moreover, students in the ARI schools tended to do better on standardized tests, although not all ARI schools had consistent increases in test scores. Nevertheless, the writers of the report indicated that implementation of this initiative has resulted in positive directions for secondary schools.

Another well-known coaching program is the Collaborative Coaching and Learning (CCL) initiative in the Boston public schools (Neufeld & Roper, 2003). This K–12 initiative has evolved over time. Currently, coaches work with a cohort of teachers (e.g., social studies teachers at the middle school), who meet for about 2 hours weekly for 9 weeks. This team sets goals, reads various materials, constructs model lessons, and demonstrates these lessons in a lab classroom. Often the coach models first, then teachers may volunteer to demonstrate lessons, which are observed by cohort members. The coach may also meet individually with teachers. In other words, the focus in this initiative is on the collaborative work of teachers and coach. The CCL is highly influenced by the work of Lucy Calkins: The Readers' and Writers' Workshop serves as the literacy framework for this initiative. Evidence gathered over time indicates that teachers saw coaching as a valuable model of professional development, and there has been an increase in the establishment of a collaborative culture in the schools (Neufeld, 2006).

In 2005, Kentucky passed legislation that required the development of a program to prepare literacy coaches to assist teachers, grades 4–12 (Kannapel, 2007). The program is developed and managed by the Collaborative Center for Literacy Development (CCLD) at the University of Kentucky. Although the project was designed to prepare approximately 160 coaches per year for 4 years, participation was much lower, with 22 coaches participating in 2006–2007. One of the barriers to participation was funding, because schools were required to fund the literacy coach position with the grant paying for all staff development and materials. Several universities were involved in preparing coaches and providing follow-up support. The foci in the institutes were strategic planning, effective reading/literacy instruction, strategies, coaching, and mentoring. Data from the evaluation study indicated that the most common activities reported by coaches included sharing strategies with teachers, modeling, assisting in selecting materials, providing professional development, analyzing assessment data, and linking teachers with research. Fewer coaches observed or coordinated schoolwide literacy events. Principals and teachers tended to be positive about coaching, with teachers indicating that they appreciated the sharing of strategies through demonstration lessons. There was some indication that coaching did help to improve scores on school-based assessment and also to increase student enthusiasm for reading, although Kannapel acknowledged the limitations of this aspect of the evaluation. Coaches identified factors that hindered their work, including being assigned to more than one school, lack of time to serve all teachers, lack of understanding of the coach's role, and lack of funding.

There are other large-scale coaching initiatives across this country, many of which focus on middle and secondary schools. In Figure 6.2, we list some of these initiatives, a short description, and a link to additional information.

We find from the available research that first, teachers as a whole tend to appreciate and value instructional coaching as a means of staff development, although some are resistant to such endeavors. Second, developers of coaching initiatives speak to the need for well-prepared coaches. However, because some schools have difficulty locating these qualified individuals, coaches may come to the position with credentials that are less than what might be called the "gold standard" (Frost & Bean, 2006). Third, many challenges must be addressed by those who design coaching initiatives. One of the challenges is to teach coaches to learn how to renegotiate their relationships with teachers. Coaches who have suddenly become senior among their peers must now engage in difficult conversations to guide teachers through the practice of reflective learning. Another challenge is the context; certain enabling conditions must be present if coaching is to be successful, including: well-prepared, qualified coaches with sufficient time to work with teachers; a solid instructional framework that provides practice tools for teachers and coaches; and administrators who "are on the same page as their coaches" (Knight, 2006, p. 38). Fourth, the major emphases of the research and evaluation have been on coach activities (what coaches do), on reactions and responses of various constituents to coaching, or on isolated changes in teacher practices (e.g., asking higher level questions) (Bean et al., 2008). Most often, these studies have been conducted at the elementary school level. There has been less study of the effect of coaching on student achievement, most likely because this is such a complex topic to tackle given the many other variables that influence student achievement in schools, including context of the school and its readiness for coaching, implementation of other initiatives designed for school improvement, additional time given to literacy instruction, change in materials, change in student demographics, and so forth. Finally, there is still a great deal we do not know about coaching, how it might be implemented and for whom, and its effects on teacher practices and student learning. Current studies tend to be local or state evaluation studies that provide much useful information but not the rigorous systematic data that yield more definitive information about coaching. At the same time, conclusions indicate that coaching is an initiative that has potential; it is complex and requires a long-term commitment to its implementation, and it requires support at all levels of the system. As stated by Snow et al. in the *Standards for Middle and High School Literacy Coaches*, "Waiting for that body of research to be produced before committing to coaching is neither feasible nor wise" (2006, p. 45). They argue that schools must "start with the practice as it exists.... attending to possibilities for accumulating findings across sites" (p. 46).

Coaching initiative	Summary and source
Alabama Reading Initiative (ARI), K–12	Schools must agree to join (85% commitment). The role of the coach is to help teachers learn new strategies (lead study groups, model, etc.). Evaluation indicates that secondary schools have different needs; teachers are positive; students tend to be more engaged in reading; achievement results vary. *www.air.org/publications/documents/ari%20popular%20report_final.pdf*
America's Choice (developed by National Center on Education and the Economy)	The study focused on the role of coaches and their work to help teachers implement both reading and writing workshops, not on whether students' achievement scores improved. From readingthis report, one learns more about designing coaching programs, coaches' qualifications, coaches' actual roles, and both the successes and pitfalls that coaches, principals, and school districts leaders might anticipate. *www.cpre.org/images/stories/cpre_pdfs/ac-06.pdf* Poglinco et al. (2003)
Boston Collaborative Coaching Learning (CCL) initiative, K–12	Began in 1996; evolved into a cohort model, a team of teachers meets weekly for 9 weeks, 2 hours each week. The cohort group, with a coach, develops a course of study, setting goals; discusses readings, models and demonstrates lessons. Influenced by Calkins's Readers' and Writers' Workshop. *eric.ed.gov/ericwebportal/recorddetail?accno=ed480874* Neufeld and Roper (2003)
Kansas Coaching Project	Instructional coaches are onsite professional developers who teach educators how to use proven instructional methods and adhere to three core principles: choice, dialogue, and knowledge in action. They work with teachers to promote two-way conversations that lead to partnership. Coaches are not content experts but professional developers. *www.instructionalcoach.org/theory.html*
Adolescent Literacy Coaching Project (ALP)	State initiative involving a small number of coaches in grades 4–12. Literacy coach positions were not funded by the state but by districts; the state funded the professional development for coaches. *www.kentuckyliteracy.org/alcp/research.html*
Pennsylvania High School Coaching Initiative (PAHSCI)	Statewide instructional coaching initiative funded by the Annenberg Foundation in 24 high schools across Pennsylvania. Participating districts hire their own full-time instructional coaches, one math and one literacy coach for every 600 students. Instructional coaches and school/district administrators are supported by mentors 4 days per month. Instructional coaches implement a "before, during, and after" consultation model. *www.pachoaching.org*

FIGURE 6.2. Overview of various secondary coaching initiatives.

In the following section, we describe a large-scale coaching initiative directed by Ellen Eisenberg, second author of this chapter.

The Pennsylvania High School Coaching Initiative

The Pennsylvania High School Coaching Initiative (PAHSCI) is a 3-year, $31 million high school reform model funded by the Annenberg Foundation and implemented in partnership with the Pennsylvania Department of Education. PAHSCI is a distinctive high school reform design focused on one-on-one instructional coaching, mentoring, and professional development, with the goals of improving student achievement and building teacher capacity in schools through collaborative whole-school reform practices. In addition to a thorough description of the initiative, we provide evaluators' evidence of the program's effectiveness. The initiative places one literacy and one math coach for every 600 students in 24 high-need high schools in 15 school districts across Pennsylvania, with a total enrollment of over 32,000 students.

PAHSCI helps to change the culture of schools and promote a collaborative, collegial, collective problem-solving environment that is conducive to improved teaching and learning. With five key partners—Pennsylvania Department of Education; Foundations Inc.; Penn Literacy Network; Philadelphia Foundation, and Research for Action—PAHSCI helps to improve teaching and learning in urban and rural school districts. Additional research support is provided by MPR Associates, Inc., the Academy for Educational Development (AED), National Institute for Work and Learning (NIWL), and the Success for All Foundation. This design draws on the expertise of the groups to model professional, collaborative learning communities strengthened with teams of school-based coaches; to support district administrators and coaches through onsite mentors; to focus on improving classroom instruction through content-based professional development; to study and develop the model through a cycle of documentation; to assess and evaluate the model for continuous improvement; and to allocate the fiduciary responsibility to a fiscal agent for consistent financial reporting. Teachers, coaches, and administrators attend credit-bearing centralized and regional courses, and learn about a specific literacy framework developed by the Penn Literacy Network (www.gse.upenn.edu/pln), the art and science of instructional coaching, and how to design effective, differentiated professional development.

In PAHSCI schools, instructional coaches follow a before, during, and after (BDA) consultation process. A coach meets one-on-one with a teacher prior to a classroom visitation. They plan lessons, discuss the goals of each lesson, and share resources. In the classroom, the coach focuses on the mutually agreed-upon goals and may model segments of the lesson. After the classroom visit, the coach and teacher meet for a feedback session, perhaps the most important segment of the process, reviewing how the goals were met and reflecting on the strengths and limitations of the particular lesson. These feedback sessions are confidential, involving only the teacher and coach. Coaches also work with administrators as part of the leadership team to develop strategies for schoolwide improvement. They lead professional development sessions for teams of teachers and meet with groups of teachers to discuss results and how the data can be useful in informing instructional decisions. In addition to facilitating professional learning at the school or district sites, coaches also attend professional learning sessions facilitated by their coaching colleagues and by the mentors in both statewide and regional networking events. These networking sessions enable coaches to nourish their own professional growth by collaborating and sharing their new learning with their colleagues from across the state. These sessions offer coaches an opportunity to discuss successes, challenges, and more effective ways to accomplish the goals of instructional coaching.

Mentors also play a critical role in supporting coaches and administrators in their schools. A team of three mentors—one literacy, one math, and one leadership mentor—visits each district 4 days per month, modeling the kinds of support that coaches provide for teachers. Content mentors meet with coaches to coplan, to visit classes, to observe coaches practicing their craft with teachers, and to debrief and to model the feedback loop for continuous improvement. Simultaneously, the leadership mentors meet with the leadership teams of the school and the district to discuss sustained professional development that is tied to standards, teacher practices, research, and student outcomes. Leadership mentors are advocates for one-on-one instructional coaching, mentoring, and professional development to school boards, community and business leaders, and the broader legislative community.

There is an understanding in PAHSCI that coaches are nonevaluative, and all participants—administrators, coaches, and teachers—must support this belief. What happens between teacher and coach stays between them. Coaches are there to encourage teacher collaboration; to promote the notion that everyone is a leader and a learner; to problem-solve collectively; to help teachers and administrators become reflective practitioners; and to reinforce how teaching, learning, and classroom practices can change to improve student outcomes. The key elements of PAHSCI are summarized in Figure 6.3.

Several sources of evidence support PAHSCI's effectiveness as a school improvement initiative (Brown et al., 2007). Fifteen of 21 schools with data for 2004 and 2007 exceeded the state change in the percentage of students reaching advanced or proficient levels in reading. Eighteen of 21 PAHSCI schools with data from the same time period exceeded the state change in the percentage of students reaching advanced or proficient levels in math (2007 Pennsylvania System of School Assessment [PSSA] data). Given that these instructional coaches worked with not only literacy but also math structured around a literacy framework, we believe that PAHSCI's efficacy as a one-on-

- Onsite, one-on-one, job-embedded professional development for teachers and administrators.
- Specially trained instructional coaches are teachers from participating schools.
- Improved classroom instruction through onsite, content-based professional development and facilitated, credit-bearing courses designed around research-based literacy strategies.
- Over-the-shoulder classroom support for teachers, including help in identifying academic needs to students, determining which evidence-based practices will bridge learning gaps, and planning for and debriefing on specific lessons.
- Sustainability through creation of professional, collaborative learning communities created within schools and districts.
- Support for district administrators and coaches through onsite mentors.
- Research and development of the model through ongoing documentation, assessment, and reflection for continuous improvement.

FIGURE 6.3. Key elements of PAHSCI.

one instructional coaching, mentoring, and professional development model supports teachers across content areas.

In spring 2007, 64% of queried PAHSCI teachers responded to a survey designed and administered by Research for Action. The data were analyzed and summarized by MPR Associates, Inc. and AED IWL (Medrich & Charner, 2007). Teachers reported that one-on-one (intensive) instructional coaching made a difference in classroom instruction, student engagement, and student learning. Teachers with extensive one-on-one coaching (at least once or twice a month) indicated that they understood research-based literacy strategies better, were more likely to integrate these strategies in their classrooms, and were more likely to participate in school-based professional development activities. As the surveys indicated, students of these teachers who received one-on-one coaching were more engaged and enthusiastic about learning, were able to think critically, and were better able to communicate content knowledge.

Working one-on-one (intensively) with an instructional coach positively affected teachers. Ninety-one percent of these intensively coached teachers, compared with 28% of those not intensively coached but participating in professional development activities led by a coach, reported that their instructional coach addressed their needs as teachers. Eighty-six percent of these intensively coached teachers, compared with 31% of those not intensively coached, reported that their coaches effectively communicated research-based literacy strategies to them, and 83% of these teachers, compared with 42% of those without one-on-one coaching, reported that the instructional coaches were a catalyst for learning among staff members at their school.

According to teachers' self-reports, instructional coaching changed the way they taught. Eighty-one percent of intensively coached teachers, compared with 60% of those not coached intensively, reported that their knowledge of research-based literacy strategies increased and deepened as result of working with their instructional coaches. Seventy-seven percent of intensively coached teachers, compared with 38% of those not intensively coached, reported that the quality of their instruction improved because they attended research-based professional literacy development activities. Sixty-eight percent of one-on-one coached teachers, compared with 29% of those without one-on-one coaching, reported that PAHSCI and the coaches promoted more discussion of student work among teachers.

Seventy-nine percent of intensively coached teachers reported that their coach played a significant role in improving classroom instruction and practice. Seventy-two percent of these same teachers said that their coaches played a significant role in improving student achievement. Michael Reed, Principal of SciTech High School in the Harrisburg School District, reported that the coaching in his school has lead to more collegial relationships, better instruction, and a significant increase in student performance.

The teacher surveys suggest that the more students are engaged in rigorous work and relevant learning, the more likely their performance improves. This does not happen without the effective delivery of instruction. Not surprisingly, our teacher surveys also indicated that students of intensively coached teachers are more engaged and enthusiastic than students of teachers not involved in one-on-one coaching. For example, 60% of intensively coached teachers, compared with 39% of teachers who were not intensively coached, reported that their students were engaged in reflective writing practices. Seventy-seven percent of intensively coached teachers reported that their students were able to think critically, as reflected in top students' reading, writing, and communication skills. At Bellwood-Antis High School, Principal Diane Williams declared that the frequency of writing in all content areas improved the quality of student performance: 97.2% of students in Bellwood-Antis scored proficient and above in the PSSA Writing Assessment Test for 2007—evidence that in Bellwood-Antis engaging more students in writing had a positive impact on student achievement. In fact, nine PAHSCI schools exceeded the 87.9% state average of students scoring as proficient or better in writing on the 2007 PSSA Writing Assessment Test.

Sustained one-on-one instructional coaching is expected to yield appreciable change in classroom instruction, teaching practices, and student outcomes. Although other types of interactions (small-group, whole-faculty professional development, and other activities led by coaches) yield positive results for students, it appears that the more a teacher engages with an instructional coach, the more meaningful the personal contact, and the more positive the learning environment for both teachers and students. In other words, in this initiative, there appears to be evidence that the one-on-one coaching helped teachers make remarkable changes in how they taught and improved results.

Guidelines for Literacy Coaching in Middle and Secondary Schools

As a result of our investigation of the research and literature about literacy coaching in middle and secondary schools, we conclude with guidelines that we believe are important for educators interested in developing, implementing, and evaluating coaching initiatives in their schools.

- Choose carefully. There is strong support for selecting coaches who know and understand literacy, but who, at the same time, have both a strong understanding of content in one of the disciplines and the interpersonal, communication, and leadership skills that enable them to work effectively with their colleagues. Coaching success begins with selecting a qualified coach.
- Coaching is a process—not an event. It takes time for coaches to generate support and credibility; schools have not typically functioned as places that encourage collaborative teaching and openness of teaching practices. We refer readers to the brief *Do's and Don'ts for Literacy Coaches: Advice from the Field* (Bean & DeFord, 2007), in which practicing coaches provide ideas for their coaching colleagues.
- Differentiate among coaching approaches. Just as students require differentiated instruction to meet their needs, teachers, too, have different interests, experiences, and needs. They bring the "ghosts of their past" in terms of attitude toward professional development and learning to the experience. Coaches may coplan only with some teachers; with others, they may model, and with still others they may coplan, model, observe, and provide feedback. Some teachers may be more willing to work as members of the subject or grade-level team, at least in the beginning.
- Support—and understanding—of the administrators are critical. Only if the administration supports and understands coaching will it have a good chance of success. When principals do not support the initiative, there is much less buy in from teachers, and coaches find it difficult to do their work.
- Evaluate the coaching initiative. Any school involved in a coaching initiative should include a process for obtaining feedback about its success from coaches, administrators, teachers, and students as an integral part of the initiative. In addition, coaches can self-evaluate their efforts. In May 2007, the IRA, with support from the Carnegie Corporation, released a self-assessment tool for middle and high school literacy coaches (*www.literacycoachingonline. org*). This inventory may be used by coaches to think about what they do, and how well they do it.
- Establish a means of networking, so that coaches within a district or across districts can get together to share ideas and discuss challenges and suc-

cesses. In any coaching initiative with which we have been involved, coaches speak to the importance of this sort of professional development.

• Spread the word. The value and merit of instructional coaching must be communicated to key decision makers in the school and legislative communities. Success stories, relevant data, and voices from the field can illustrate the impact of instructional coaching on teachers, classroom instruction, and student learning.

Literacy coaching has much to offer students, teachers, and schools. It has the potential to change the way that middle and high schools function, with more focus on the importance of elements of literacy—reading, writing, speaking, and listening—as key tools for all teachers at those levels.

QUESTIONS FOR DISCUSSION

1. If you were responsible for developing a literacy coaching initiative, what key points do you think would be critical to ensure such an initiative's potential for success?

2. Think about a school with which you are familiar. What are the barriers and challenges that you would face in implementing a coaching initiative in that school? What would be the reaction of the teachers in that school to this initiative? The administrators?

3. What evidence described in the chapter is most compelling to you in terms of the potential of literacy coaching? Think about ways that you might design an evaluation program for a literacy coaching initiative.

Resources

Further Reading

Duncan, M. (2006). *Literacy coaching: Developing effective teachers through instructional dialogue.* Katonah, NY: Owen.

Killion, J., & Harrison, C. (2006) *Taking the lead: New roles for teachers and school-based coaches.* Oxford, OH: National Staff Development Council.

Puig, E. A., & Froelich, K. S. (2007). *The literacy coach: Guiding in the right direction.* Boston: Pearson Education.

Rodgers, A., & Rodgers, E. M. (2007). *The effective literacy coach: Using inquiry to support teaching and learning.* New York: Teachers College Press.

Toll, C. A. (2007). Lenses on literacy coaching: Conceptualizations, functions, and outcomes. Norwood, MA: Christopher-Gordon.

Websites

www.literacycoachingonline.org
www.pa.coaching.org

References

American Educational Research Association. (2005). *Research points: Teaching teachers: Professional development to improve students achievement* (Vol. 3, Issue 1) [Brochure]. Washington, DC: Author.
Bacevich, A., & Salinger, T. (2006). *Lessons and recommendations from the Alabama Reading Initiative: Sustaining focus on secondary reading.* Washington, DC: American Institutes for Research. Retrieved May 16, 2008, from *www.air.org/publications/documents/ari%20popular%20report_final.pdf.*
Bean, R. M. (2007, Fall). The promise and potential of literacy coaching. *PASHCI Portfolio Report,* pp. 2–3.
Bean, R. M., Belcastro, B., Hathaway, J., Risko, V., Rosemary, C., & Roskos, K. (2008, March). *A review of the research on instructional coaching.* Paper presented at the American Educational Research Association Conference, New York, NY.
Bean, R. M., & DeFord, D. (2007). *Do's and don'ts for literacy coaches: Advice from the field.* Retrieved May 16, 2008, from *www.literacycoachingonline.org.*
Brown, C. J., Stroh, H. R., Fouts, J. T., & Baker, D. B. (2005, February). *Learning to change: School coaching for systemic reform.* Millcreek, WA: Fouts & Associates. Retrieved May 16, 2008, from *www.gatesfoundation.org/unitedstates/education/researchandevaluation/research/hsimprovement.htm.*
Brown, D., Reumann-Moore, R., Hugh, R., Christman, J. B., Riffer, M., duPlessis, P., et al. (2007). *Making a difference: Year two report of the Pennsylvania High School Coaching Initiative.* Philadelphia: Research for Action.
Cassidy, J., & Cassidy, D. (2008, February/March). What's hot for 2008? *Reading Today, 25*(4), 1, 10–11.
Frost, S., & Bean, R. M. (2006). *Qualifications for literacy coaches: Achieving the gold standard.* Retrieved May 16, 2008, from *www.literacycoachingonline.org/briefs/literacy-coaching.pdf.*
International Reading Association. (2004). *The role and qualifications of the reading coach in the United States: A position statement of the International Reading Association* [Brochure]. Newark, DE: Author.
International Reading Association. (2006). *Standards for middle and high school literacy coaches.* Newark, DE: Author.
International Reading Association. (2007, May). *Self-assessment for middle and high school literacy coaches.* Developed by the IRA with funding provided by the Carnegie Foundation. Retrieved May 16, 2008, from *www.literacycoachingonline.org.*
Joyce, B., & Showers, B. (1980). Improving in-service training: The messages of research. *Educational Leadership, 37*(5), 379–385.
Joyce, B., & Showers, B. (2002). *Student achievement through staff development.* Alexandria, VA: Association for Supervision and Curriculum Development.
Kannapel, P. (2007). *The Adolescent Literacy Coaching Project (ALCP): Year 1 evaluation report.* Lexington, KY: Collaborative Center for Literacy Development. Retrieved May 16, 2008, from *www.kentuckyliteracy.org/alcp/research.html.*
Knight, J. (2006). Instructional coaching: Eight factors for realizing better classroom teaching through support, feedback and intensive, individualized professional learning. *School Administrator, 63*(4), 36–40.
Little, J. (1993). Teachers' professional development in a climate of education reform. *American Education Research Association, 15*(2), 129–151.
Medrich, E,, & Charner, I. (2007). *Summary of selected results from the PAHSCI Teacher*

Survey. Berkeley, CA: MPR Associates, & Washington, DC: AED National Institute for Work and Learning.

National Staff Development Council (2001). *Standards for staff development.* Oxford, OH: Author. Retrieved October 20, 2009, from *www.nsdc.org/standards/index. cfm.*

Neufeld, B. (2006). *Summary of the report: Instructional improvement in the Boston public schools: 1996–2006.* Retrieved May 16, 2008, from *www.renniecenter.org/research_ docs/summary-instruction.pdf.*

Neufeld, B., & Roper, D. (2003). *Expanding the work: Year II of collaborative coaching and learning in the effective practice schools* (Report No. TM035-259). Cambridge, MA: Education Matters. (ERIC Document reproduction Service ED480874)

Poglinco, S., Bach, A., Hovde, K., Rosenblum, S., Saunders, M., & Supevitz, J. (2003, May). *The heart of the matter: The coaching model in America's choice schools.* Philadelphia: Consortium for Policy Research in Education.

Slavin, R. E., Madden, N. A., Dolan, L. J., & Wasik, B. A. (1996). *Every child, every school: Success for all.* Thousand Oaks, CA: Corwin Press.

Smith, A. T. (2007). The middle school literacy coach: Considering roles in context. In D. W. Rowe, R. T. Jimenez, D. L. Compton, D. K. Dickinson, Y. Kim, K. M. Leander, et al. (Eds.), *56th yearbook of the National Reading Conference* (pp. 53–67). Oak Creek, WI: National Reading Conference.

Snow, C., Ippolito, J., & Schwartz, R. (2006). What we know and what we need to know about literacy coaches in middle and high schools: A research synthesis and proposed research agenda. In International Reading Association, *Standards for middle and high school literacy coaches* (pp. 35–49). Newark, DE: Author.

Sturtevant, E. G. (2003). *The literacy coach: A key to improving teaching and learning in secondary schools.* Washington, DC: Alliance for Excellent Education. Retrieved May 16, 2008, from *www.all4ed.org/publications/literacycoach/pdf.*

Sturtevant, E. G., Boyd, F. B., Brozo, W. G., Hinchman, K. A., Moore, D. W., & Alvermann, D. E. (2006). *Principled practices for adolescent literacy: A framework for instruction and policy.* Mahwah, NJ: Erlbaum.

Taylor, B. M., Pressley, M., & Pearson, P. D. (2002). Research-supported characteristics of teachers and schools that promote reading achievement. In B. M. Taylor & P. D. Pearson (Eds.), *Teaching reading: Effective schools, accomplished teachers* (pp. 361–374). Mahwah, NJ: Erlbaum.

Toll, C. (2006). *The literacy coach's desk reference: Processes and perspectives for effective coaching.* Urbana, IL: National Council of Teachers of English.

Chapter 7

Meeting the Needs
of English Language Learners
in the Middle and Secondary Classroom

Paola Pilonieta
Adriana L. Medina

GUIDING QUESTIONS

1. What factors should teachers consider when working with English language learners (ELLs)?
2. What is the role of a student's first language in acquiring his or her second language?
3. What are some instructional principles for ELLs?
4. What strategies can teachers use with ELLs?

Consider the following statistics:

- In 2005, Hispanics, African Americans, Asian/Pacific Islanders, and Native American/Alaska Natives made up 33% of the U.S. population. Hispanics were the largest minority group, representing 14% of the population (National Center for Educational Statistics, 2007).

- By 2020, minority groups are predicted to represent 39% of the total U.S. population: Hispanics will be the largest group (National Center for Educational Statistics, 2007).

- As expected, five states (California, Texas, New York, Florida, and Illinois) accounted for 60% of all ELL students in grades 6–12 in 2000; however, these are not the states with the fastest growing ELL populations. These states are North Carolina (500% growth between 1993 and 2003), Colorado, Nevada, Nebraska, Oregon, Georgia, and Indiana (each with a more than 200% increase between 1993 and 2003; Batalova, Fix, & Murray, 2005).

- Among adolescent ELLs, 70% speak Spanish as their first language (Alliance for Excellent Education, 2007).

- Eighty-nine percent of Hispanics in middle and high school read below grade level (Perie, Grigg, & Donahue, 2005).

- Only 4% of eighth-grade ELLs and 20% of students labeled as "former ELLs" scored at the proficient or advanced levels on the reading portion of the 2005 National Assessment of Educational Progress (Perie et al., 2005).

- Among 16- to 24-year-old Hispanics, the percentage of high school dropouts among those born outside of the United States (38%) was more than twice that of their native counterparts (13%; National Center for Educational Statistics, 2007).

These statistics illustrate the changing face of our country's school-age population. These changes are not limited to certain geographic areas. States that traditionally have not been associated with ELLs are experiencing the fastest growing ELL populations. Even more alarming is the fact that most Hispanic adolescents are not reading at grade level. Therefore, it is not surprising that the high school dropout rate among Hispanics is more than double that of White adolescents. The underachievement of ELLs will have widespread economic and political ramifications unless educators take up the challenge to meet the needs of this growing school population (August & Shanahan, 2006). Unfortunately, most secondary school teachers have had little professional development in second-language literacy (Fitzgerald, 1995; Klingner & Vaughn, 2004; Short & Fitzsimmons, 2007).

Our goal in this chapter is to provide an introduction to adolescent ELLs, to inform teachers about language-minority students, and to present instructional practices that improve the academic literacy experiences of ELLs. This chapter lists factors that affect adolescent ELLs' learning, addresses second-language literacy and the role the first language plays in students' success, outlines basic instructional principles, and offers instructional strategies for adolescent ELLs.

Factors Affecting Adolescent ELLs' Learning

For purposes of clarity, a student is considered an ELL if his or her first language is not English whether or not he or she is receiving special instructional services at school. It should be noted that although we use the term ELL here, other terms are also often used to describe this population of students, for example, learners of ESL (English as a second language); second-language, or L2 learners, LEP (limited-English-proficient) learners, bilingual learners, language-minority students, and non-native speakers of English.

Many factors, such as cognitive ability, motivation, and parent–teacher expectations affect student achievement in general. However, factors such as previous education, socioeconomic status (SES), legal immigration status, and school labels play a unique role in the academic achievement of adolescent ELLs.

Education

The educational backgrounds of ELL students vary considerably. Some students may have attended elementary school in the United States but have not received enough instruction to navigate the English language with ease. Others may be recent immigrants to the United States and have a history of schooling in their home countries, resulting in a strong academic foundation in their native or first language (L1; García & Godina, 2004). Due to economic hardship or political instability, some students may have had little, if any, schooling background, or may have experienced gaps in their education (Rubinstein-Ávila, 2004). These students may lack basic literacy and content knowledge in their L1.

Socioeconomic Status

Many adolescent ELLs are of low SES (García & Godina, 2004; Rubinstein-Ávila, 2004). Therefore, it is not uncommon for ELLs to have to work after school or on the weekends to help support their families. This additional responsibility can negatively impact their academic progress (Hadaway & Mundy, 1999). Even while in the United States, families of ELLs may need to move frequently to find work, resulting in an intermittent and inconsistent educational experience for the student. Because of their work schedules, parents of ELLs may have little time to spend in their children's schools, thereby creating the erroneous impression that they lack interest in their children's education (García & Godina, 2004). In fact, August and Shanahan (2006) conclude that schools tend to underestimate and underutilize parent's interests and potential contributions.

Legal Immigration Status

Immigration status can have a negative effect on adolescent students' motivation. Only 8.9% of immigrants who arrived between 1990 and 1999 have obtained legal citizenship (National Institute for Literacy, 2007). Without citizenship or permanent residence, adolescent students may experience difficulty being admitted to colleges, may be ineligible for financial aid, and may find it nearly impossible to secure professional employment. These hardships can have a detrimental effect on academic perseverance and motivation (Rubinstein-Ávila, 2004).

The Term Struggling Reader

ELLs are overrepresented among struggling readers (August & Hakuta, 1997). Rubinstein-Ávila (2004) states that, historically, many struggling readers are from underrepresented minority groups. However, the term *struggling reader* may be misleading, because "ELLs may be quite successful at tackling the literacy demands with which they are faced outside of school walls; thus, the label *struggling reader* is intricately tied to the context of school literacy" (Rubinstein-Ávila, 2004, p. 291). In school, adolescent ELLs may be labeled as *struggling*, but their skill with the English language is considered a resource at home, because these students serve as language brokers who translate for their families (Jimenez, 2001). Additionally, it is important to remember that ELLs face high academic and cognitive demands: They are learning English and content, and simultaneously trying to meet the same academic benchmarks as their monolingual counterparts (García & Godina, 2006).

Summary

A multitude of factors affect academic achievement for all students. ELLs, particularly adolescents, face a group of unique challenges. Although a classroom teacher cannot change a student's past or erase the consequences of these factors, it is important to be aware that these factors exist. In this manner, teachers can create accepting classroom communities and better meet their students' needs.

Second-Language Literacy

There are four acknowledged stages of language development: (1) preproduction in which students listen and watch; (2) early production, in which students may understand and speak some English but are still assimilating language and vocabulary; (3) speech emergence, in which students begin communicating with some fluency; and (4) intermediate fluency, in which students function well in English (Ernst-Slavit, Moore, & Maloney, 2002). It is important to remember that some students in the preproduction stage might experience a "silent period," in which they do not communicate and may appear to be unmotivated or unengaged, but are actually absorbing and learning language (Samway & McKeon, 1999). The silent period can last from a few days to a year or more. Although four stages are listed, as with any native language speaker, language development is a continuous, life-long learning process.

Acquiring an L2 is a complex developmental process that takes several years. Adolescents who are learning another language face many challenges; however, they also have many strengths that assist them with this endeavor.

Students' First Language

Cummins (2003) asserts that children need to learn the reading and writing process only once. Regardless of the differences between the L1 and the L2, the concept of reading and writing is virtually the same. What students *do* need to learn is the vocabulary and the structure of the L2.

The interdependence hypothesis (Cummins, 1981) describes the relationship between the L1 and the L2. High levels of proficiency in the L1 assist students with L2 acquisition. In essence, the reading skills and strategies used in the L1 transfer to L2 reading. Much research has been done to substantiate the interdependence hypothesis (Avalos, 2003; Lesaux & Geva, 2006; Rubinstein-Ávila, 2004; Temple, Ogle, Crawford, & Freppon, 2005). Bernhardt's (2005) compensatory model of L2 reading posits that L1 literacy accounts for 20% of the variance in L2 performance, knowledge of the L2 (grammar, vocabulary) accounts for 30% of the variance, and the unexplained portion of the variance may be accounted for by the student's knowledge of comprehension strategies, motivation, content knowledge, and interest. Thus, a student with a strong L1 foundation, who is knowledgeable in comprehension strategies and content, and is motivated and interested, will acquire an L2 more easily than a student who does not share these characteristics.

Students who have strong literacy skills in their L1 take less time to acquire comparable literacy skills in their L2 (Bigelow & Tarone, 2004). Thomas and Collier (1996) found that ELLs proficient in their L1 benefit from instruction that focuses on higher order thinking skills and inquiry-based learning, and that respects students' native language and culture. In contrast, ELLs who were not proficient in their L1 took 7–10 years to learn L2 literacy skills in which cognitively demanding academic language was prevalent and the context was limited (Bigelow & Tarone, 2004). Some of these ELLs never seemed to catch up to their monolingual counterparts (Bigelow & Tarone, 2004). In Rubinstein-Ávila's (2004) case study of Miguel, she explains how Miguel did not know that his knowledge of reading in Spanish could help him with reading in English. Miguel said, "There's nothing to do; it's so different, 'cause like Spanish goes with Spanish and English goes with English. What I needed was English, so how Spanish was gonna help?" (Rubinstein-Ávila, 2004, p. 294). As Miguel's example demonstrates, many of these ELLs need specific and explicit instruction in applying their L1 literacy skills to their L2 (Harper & de Jong, 2004).

L1 and L2 Match

Although L1 skills and strategies can transfer to the L2, it is important to be aware how similarities and differences in the structure of the L1 and the L2 may affect this relationship. Whereas Spanish-speaking students' knowledge of the alphabet will transfer to English (however, they may need some instruction on the English phonemes), a Chinese-speaking student will need instruction on the alphabet, because Chinese is a nonalphabetic language. Hinkel (2006) writes, "Readers whose L1 orthographies (e.g., Chinese, Japanese, Hebrew) are markedly distinct from the L2 orthography may be slowed down in their reading progress by the need to attain fluent L2 word recognition before they can acquire text-processing skills" (p. 120). Other factors to consider include: how syntax (word order) in L1 and L2 compare, the directionality of print, the relationship between graphemes and phonemes (whether is it more consistent, as in Spanish or French, or whether multiple graphemes make the same phonemes, as in English), and discourse styles (Avalos, 2006). Avalos notes that understanding the students' L1 may help to explain the reason behind some L2 errors, may guide instructional objectives for the teacher, and may validate the students' language.

Oral Proficiency and Literacy

Research indicates a positive relationship between oral proficiency and reading in the L2 (August & Shanahan, 2006; Fitzgerald, 1995; Klingner & Vaughn, 2004). This is especially true for secondary school students. Klingner and Vaughn note that the best predictor of English reading for students in grades 6–8 is oral English language proficiency. It is unknown exactly how much proficiency in oral language is needed to experience success in L2 reading. This in no way suggests that instruction in reading the L2 should be postponed until oral proficiency in the L2 is reached. Avalos (2006) explains that there is a reciprocal relationship between L2 oral language proficiency and literacy: Oral language proficiency helps and improves literacy; improved literacy assists and develops oral language proficiency. August and Shanahan (2006) add that the most successful literacy programs are those that provide ELL students with instructional support for oral language development, while providing high-quality literacy instruction.

Levels of Language Proficiency

Cummins (2003) describes three levels of language proficiency. These levels are not discrete entities that develop independently; instead, they develop concurrently. The first level is basic interpersonal conversation skills (BICS), or conversational fluency. BICS is typically acquired within 1–2 years of exposure to the L2. In BICS, students use high-frequency words and simple syntax. Their communication is supported by the use of facial expressions and gestures.

The next level is discrete language skills, which comprises the specific literacy, phonological, and grammatical knowledge that students acquire through exposure to formal and informal instruction. Discrete language skills can be learned simultaneously with BICS. These skills include spelling, punctuation, and capitalization conventions, as well as grammatical rules.

The third level, cognitive academic language proficiency (CALP), comprises knowledge of less frequent vocabulary words, and the ability to produce and understand complex written and oral material. This is the abstract and complex language that is seen in content areas. Teachers are often puzzled when students who appear orally proficient in English continue to perform poorly in class. This is because they are missing CALP. Students may be orally proficient (have BICS) but still need support when it comes to academic tasks. Only when students have CALP is their academic achievement comparable to that of their monolingual counterparts.

Use of the Native Language

Use of the native language during the school day for instruction is a controversial topic. Although it may seem counterintuitive, use of the L1 can play a beneficial role in an ELL's education. Storch and Wigglesworth (2003) view L1 functioning as a psychological tool, whose use "may provide learners with additional cognitive support that allows them to analyze language and work at a higher level than would be possible were they restricted to sole use of their L2" (p. 760). Strategic use of the L1, rather than constant translation, can help students continue to develop higher order thinking skills and content knowledge as they acquire the L2 (García & Godina, 2004; Gersten & Baker, 2000). Using the L1 can be an additional strategy to assist students in acquiring English or, in the case of bilingual education, it can be a goal in and of itself.

Summary

Reading in an L2 is influenced by many factors, including students' proficiency with their L1, the relationship between the L1 and L2, and oral proficiency in the L2. Though a controversial topic, use of the L1 can benefit students' academic success. Finally, it is important to be aware of the three levels of language proficiency. Only when ELL students have CALP do they experience the same academic success as their monolingual counterparts.

Instructional Principles and Strategies

As Lesaux and Geva (2006) have noted, the reading development of adolescent ELLs has received scant research attention. The National Literacy Panel on Language-Minority Children and Youth (August & Shanahan, 2006) found that many research studies have findings consistent with those for native English speakers. This might suggest that reading instruction for ELLs and native English speakers can follow the same basic sequence, with ELLs only having to learn the differences in language, structure, and prior cultural knowledge. Much is still unknown about the process that students undergo when learning an L2, particularly when their native language is different than the L2, or when the native cultural view of literacy differs significantly from assumptions about the L2. However, we do know that effective instructional programs for ELLs value students' culture and language, and look at students' assets, not their deficits. Efforts need to be made to connect what students already know, their "funds of knowledge" (Moll & Greenberg, 1990), and what is being offered to them academically.

As previously stated, many factors influence the academic literacy development of ELLs. Although educators may not have much control over many of these factors, they do have the power to control a key factor—instruction. Although research in the area of effective instructional practices that contribute to literacy success for ELL students is limited, some evidence supports the importance of the following instructional components: vocabulary instruction, cooperative learning groups and peer-tutoring strategies, activating background knowledge, and culturally responsive instruction.

Vocabulary

According to the National Reading Panel (National Institute of Child Health and Human Development, 2000), vocabulary is a strong predictor of reading proficiency. A limited vocabulary leads to limited comprehension. This is particularly true for ELLs (Fitzgerald, 1995; Klingner & Vaughn, 2004). According to August, Carlo, Dressler, and Snow (2005), "ELLs who experience slow vocabulary development are less able to comprehend text at grade level than their English only peers and may be at risk of being diagnosed as learning disabled, when in fact their limitation is due to limited English vocabulary and poor comprehension that results in part from this limitation" (p. 50).

In addition to limited English vocabulary, ELLs are also deficient in depth of word knowledge (Verhallen & Schoonen, 1993). Ways of knowing a word in depth include knowing its denotation, connotation, etymology, morphology, and associated words (e.g., synonyms and antonyms). Therefore, depth of word knowledge is also important to reading proficiency.

A common approach to teaching vocabulary is the total physical response (TPR) method developed by James J. Asher. TPR requires students to physically do something as a response to demonstrate understanding of the language. In the classroom, this often takes the form of pantomime.

In general, plenty of research supports teaching vocabulary to improve reading comprehension (Nagy, 1988), even though there is debate over methods of instruction and how students acquire vocabulary. One method for targeted vocabulary instruction is Beck, McKeown, and Kucan's (2002) three-tiered model for selecting vocabulary for instruction. In this model, Tier 1 words are basic and require no instruction; Tier 2 words are targeted for instruction, because they add depth to a student's existing vocabulary; and Tier 3 words are ones that students are unlikely to know, and that because they are not found frequently across different subject areas, they are not targeted for instruction. Calderón et al. (2005) developed four criteria for word selection for ELLs that can be integrated into this model: the nature of the word, its cognate status, its depth of meaning, and its utility (p. 123).

Although the Beck et al. (2002) model assumes that students know Tier 1 basic words, the same cannot be assumed for ELLs. It cannot be taken for granted that ELLs know the English label for basic words, such as *desk, confused,* or *leg.* Because ELLs have not captured English oral language in the same manner as native English speakers have, basic words require direct instruction for ELLs. In many cases, these Tier 1 words are words that ELLs know in their L1, but for which they have not been explicitly taught the English label. With Tier 1 words, Calderón et al.(2005) suggest that instruction can be as easy and direct as pointing out a picture of the word or demonstrating the word with gestures. Visuals are effective in L2 acquisition, especially for abstract concepts (Gersten & Baker, 2000). Along with visuals, graphic organizers, semantic maps, word banks, and concept and story maps may also be used.

For ELLs, a Tier 1 word can easily turn into a Tier 2 word, in that it has multiple meanings. Think of all the meanings for the work *bank* (e.g., put your money in the *bank*, on the *bank* of the river, he can *bank* the rebound, there's a *bank* of supplies, donate at the *blood* bank, put that in your memory *bank*, the students have a word *bank*, you can *bank* on it). Now, take, for example, the word *leg.* A picture of a person's leg or the leg of a chair might suffice to get at one meaning of the word, but it might take further explanation to get across the meaning of the metaphor *"the last leg* of the race," or of the idiomatic expression *"He's pulling my leg."* Idioms, similes, and metaphors often include Tier 1 words, so it is important to address these words with ELLs.

In addition, cognates (true and false cognates) also are often Tier 1 words. A *cognate* is a word in two or more languages that is derived from the same ancestral language. True cognates are words that are spelled similarly and have the same or related meanings, for example, *repose* and *reposar (*in Spanish). False cognates are words that look or sound like they might have the same meaning, but they in fact do not, such as *casual* or *casualty* and *casualidad* (by chance or luck in Spanish). If students' L1 shares cognates with English, teaching students true and false cognates is an effective method, and having students draw on cognate knowledge is also an effective strategy for increasing vocabulary development. According to August et al. (2005), cognate awareness benefits students who have L1 oral proficiency, as well as students who have L1 literatcy. It should be noted that cognates are more easily recognized in print as opposed to orally, and that "the ability to recognize cognates develops with age" (August et al., 2005, p. 52).

Tier 2 words that cannot be taught using a picture or gestures or by providing the word in the student's L1 (e.g., an abstract concept, such as *love,* or a word that cannot be demonstrated, such as *cousin*) need to be taught explicitly before reading.

The three-tiered model assumes that readers use vocabulary and comprehension strategies, such as structural analysis and context clues, to decipher Tier 3 words they encounter while reading. However, ELLs may not have the English language proficiency to decipher Tier 3 words. These words need to be translated, defined, and explained to ELLs. Specialized content-area vocabulary that falls under Tier 3 needs to be pretaught to build ELLs' conceptual knowledge.

Narrow reading has been found to be useful for ELLs (Schmitt & Carter, 2000). With this method, students read in depth about a topic from a variety of texts at different reading levels. The repeated exposure to the words benefits ELLs' vocabulary acquisition.

Cooperative Learning Groups and Peer Tutoring

Cooperative groups and peer tutoring are methods that engage students as participants in their own and each other's reading process. The methods are beneficial because they aid in the learning of academic skills. In the case of peer tutoring, both tutor and tutee benefit. The tutor shares, successfully interacts, and works cooperatively with others, while becoming a more skilled reader and writer, with improved discussion skills. The tutee benefits from improved fluency, instant feedback, exposure to a range of reading strategies, oral reading practice, increased confidence in reading and writing, and advanced conversational and interactional skills. When working with peers, ELLs often resort to using their native language with other students who speak the same language to draw support and construct meaning socially in English (Cohen, 1994). In addition, students often feel that other students explain or "say it" better than the teacher (Vaughn, Schumm, Klingner, & Saumell, 1995).

According to Klingner and Vaughn (1996) cross-age peer tutoring and cooperative learning groups are beneficial for improving the comprehension of ELLs. These grouping styles can lead to increased use of language. For the different grouping strategies to be effective, teachers need to establish clear expectations and provide frequent monitoring and immediate feedback (Gersten & Baker, 2000). Some teachers might prefer using a highly structured grouping method. Classwide peer tutoring (CWPT), developed at the Juniper Gardens Children's Project in Kansas City, is one such strategy that offers structure during peer tutoring. It is beneficial for both the tutor and the tutee and may be utilized with diverse learners.

To implement CWPT, ensure that paired students are sufficiently similar in ability and that they can mutually benefit from instruction. All students in the classroom are paired and work simultaneously. The teacher's role is to facilitate and to monitor. The more proficient reader begins by reading orally for 5 minutes, at the end of which time the roles are switched. In both cases, while the tutee reads, the student serving as tutor indicates errors in omissions, addition, and long pauses in saying the word. If the tutee self-corrects, then the error is not counted. After reading, each student is given 2 minutes to retell what he or she read. CWPT sessions last for approximately 15–30 minutes. This program requires initial intensive teacher and student training.

A strategy designed for ELLs that incorporates cooperative groups is Collaborative Strategic Reading (CSR; Klingner & Vaughn, 1999), an instructional technique that employs a combination of reading comprehension and cooperative learning strategies. In CSR, students of mixed reading achievement levels work in small, cooperative groups and assist one another in applying four reading strategies to facilitate their comprehension of content-area text. The strategies are called Preview, Click and Clunk, Get the Gist, and Wrap-Up.

Before reading, students in the Preview stage preview the text,using clues from the text and from their prior knowledge to develop predictions and to determine their purpose for reading. Click and Clunk is the strategy that is implemented during reading. Students monitor their reading and identify "clunks" or encounters in which students realize that they do not comprehend because they either do not know or do not understand a word or a concept within the text. Reading is "clicking" if students are comprehending. After reading, students indicate that they Get the Gist by summarizing the text through the creation of a gist statement or paragraph. During the Wrap-Up strategy, students generate teacher-like questions about the material they read.

Activating Background Knowledge

Special attention should be paid to background knowledge in work with ELLs (August & Shanahan, 2006). Experience–text–relationship (ETR; Au, 1979) is a strategy that draws on ELLs' background knowledge and prior knowledge and experience. It also allows teachers to guide and monitor the reading process.

During the first stage, E (experience), have students discuss their personal experiences that relate to the theme, topic, or main idea of the text to be read. Then have students generate predictions about the story. Collectively, formulate a purpose for reading. During the second stage, T (text), either read the text aloud as the students follow along or allow students to read silently on their own. Read only one section of the story at a time. Discuss the section read and confirm or change predictions. Make sure that students tie their thoughts, comments, and predictions back to the text. Clarify any misconceptions or miscomprehension. Ask if there were any sections or words that were confusing and clarify these. Continue to alternate between reading and discussing small sections. During the final stage, R (relationship), help students integrate the information from the text with their experiences to develop an understanding of the text.

Culturally Responsive Instruction

Incorporating/bridging home, school, and community similarities and differences engages students and increases their level of participation and learning (Goldenberg, Rueda, & August, 2006). Culturally responsive instruction is an approach that takes into account students' cultural values and practices. Incorporating an approach to instruction that reflects students' cultural values and knowledge leads to improved literacy by "helping students build bridges from knowledge and Discourses often marginalized in school setting to the learning of conventional academic knowledges and Discourses" (Moje & Hinchman, 2004, p. 323). Based on research, Moje and Hinchman have created six clear-cut principles that provide a framework for engaging in culturally responsive youth literacy pedagogy:

1. Culturally responsive pedagogy should begin with the formation of relationships between teachers and students.
2. Culturally responsive pedagogy should recognize and be respectful of the many different cultural experiences that any one person can embody.
3. Culturally responsive pedagogy works with youth to develop applications and to construct understandings that are relevant to them.
4. Culturally relevant pedagogy depends on knowledge of discipline-related concepts.
5. Culturally relevant pedagogy invites youth to participate in multiple and varied discipline-specific, cross-discourse experience that include reading, writing, speaking, listening, and performing in the service of increasingly sophisticated knowledge construction.
6. Culturally relevant pedagogy invites youth to develop and express new understandings of the world that merge mainstream content concepts with everyday knowledge in alternative, creative forms.

Better understanding of ELLs can lead to the design of learning environments that result in successful educational outcomes (Goldenberg et al., 2006).

Frequently Asked Questions

This section addresses teachers' frequently asked questions about how to best instruct ELLs.

- *What are the different educational programs for ELLs?* There are several programs for ELLs, and they fall under two categories: ESL or ESOL (English for speakers of other languages) programs, in which instruction is offered in English but catered specifically to ELLs, and bilingual programs, in which instruction is offered in two languages (Ernst-Slavit et al., 2002). ESL or ESOL programs provide instruction in English and may be structured in a manner whereby instruction is taught by a bilingual teacher either in an all-day self-contained classroom setting or in a pull-out program. In many middle and secondary schools, an ESL or ESOL program is considered a course in itself, and students attend ESL or ESOL for one or multiple class periods a day. ESL or ESOL may also be taught to secondary school students through content areas.

Within bilingual instruction programs, there are ranges of immersion programs—from partial to total immersion. In these programs, instruction in English occurs from 50 to 90% of the student's academic day. In bilingual programs, both ELL and language-majority students are in the same classes and receive instruction in the minority and majority language.

Some ESL/ESOL and bilingual programs utilized *sheltered English instruction*, which comprises teaching with clear, direct, simple English that connects learning to students' prior knowledge, and adapts delivery of lessons and content material to students' level of English proficiency.

• *What should I do if my students respond to questions in their L1?* When having students respond, accept answers in their L1 but encourage them also to respond in their L2 (Gersten, 1996). When correcting attempts in English, be sensitive in providing feedback, so that errors lead to improved oral production of English language and structure. Recall that use of the L1 can act as a scaffold, allowing students to work at a higher cognitive level.

• *With adolescent ELLs, to what extent should the teacher focus on phonemic awareness, phonics, oral language, fluency, and comprehension strategies?* Phonics assists with decoding. It is beneficial to provide support in phonics in the context of authentic literacy experiences, while teaching other components of literacy. For example, when preteaching vocabulary, provide letter–sound relationships. A teacher might say, "The letters *th* in birthday make the /th/ sound. To make the /th/ sound, stick out your tongue between your teeth. Let's all try making the /th/ sound. Now, let's say the word *birthday*.

According to Lesaux and Geva (2006), phonemic awareness, rapid naming, and phonological memory predict ELLs' word identification and pseudo-word reading skills. Additionally, oral language proficiency is foundationally important in the acquisition of another language and is associated with well-developed English reading comprehension skills (Lesaux & Geva, 2006). ELLs reading in an L2 are more likely to have underdeveloped skills in oral language and thus have difficulty with reading comprehension (Lesaux & Geva, 2006). If the word the ELL student is trying to decode is not in his or her oral language vocabulary, he or she may decode the word correctly but be unable to recognize the word. Thus, even though there is limited evidence, it might be beneficial to read aloud to your ELL students (Shanahan & Beck, 2006). It might also be beneficial for ELLs to read aloud and develop reading fluency. Again, not many studies address fluency with ELLs, but findings of the few that do are consistent with findings related to fluency and native English speakers (Shanahan & Beck, 2006). *Paired reading,* whereby ELLs are paired with proficient readers, has been found to be beneficial (Li & Nes, 2001). According to Shanahan and Beck (2006), there is not enough research to determine the best way to teach reading comprehension to ELLs. However, according to the research of Klingner and Vaughn (1996), comprehension strategies should be offered to ELLs. Once students learn the strategies, they can work together, with the teacher serving as facilitator.

- *Why do ELLs who struggle with reading in my science class tell me they are no longer required to attend their ESOL classes?* Often the test used to exit students from L2 acquisition support programs is an oral language proficiency test. Research indicates that ELLs can become proficient in conversational English in approximately 2 years. Even though some ELLs appear to be proficient in English, they may continue to struggle with academic reading. The ability to speak does not equate with the ability to utilize language for academic success (Samway & McKeon, 1999). It takes from 5 to 11 years to acquire proficient academic language and literacy. The number of years depends on many factors, one of which is the number of years the student completed formal instruction in his or her L1. Once students exit ESL or ESOL programs, they may still need language support to read and to comprehend English, but they may no longer qualify for those services because they have demonstrated oral English language proficiency.

Interestingly, according to Gersten and Baker's (2000) research analysis, a common theme found in research and among professionals is that English language development should be merged with content-area learning. The underlying thought is that students can learn academic English language and content material at the same time. However, results indicate that English language learning and content-area learning should be "distinct educational goals" (p. 460). When developing instructional goals for ELLs, we should dedicate specific objectives to language learning and separate objectives for content learning. We cannot assume that ELLs will automatically pick up the English language and all of the rules that govern it, *while* learning about content. It is helpful to develop an understanding of the "double demands" made on ELLs to learn both the language and academic content (Gersten & Baker, 2000, p. 463).

It is beneficial to connect with the teachers in the ESL/ESOL department. They can help you to incorporate instructional practices, to understand L2 acquisition, and to differentiate instruction for ELLs in your content-area classroom. Consider participating in professional self-development activities related to ELL topics. Explore the websites of professional organizations (e.g., ESOL, reading, English, and your content area).

- *What strategies can I use to promote independent writing with ELLs?* Moving from a Language Experience Approach (LEA; Rigg, 1981), where the teacher writes the words the students say about an experience they have all shared together, to cooperative writing experience where students write in pairs or interactive writing (McCarrier, Pinnell, & Fountas, 2000) where the teacher and students share in the actual writing, to independent writing, where the student writes on his/her own is a way that you can guide ELLs toward independent writing. As with oral language and reading, provide specific feedback on English language usage. Be sensitive when correcting errors.

• *Are there other strategies teachers can use?* Yes. Below, in no particular order, are other beneficial strategies that teachers can incorporate into their instructional practices for ELLs, but note that these are supported by limited research.

When the teacher is speaking to the class, he or she should give concise directions. The teacher should use clear, simple vocabulary and a simplified grammatical structure when speaking. Remember that gestures, facial expressions, body language, and real-life objects (*realia*) can be used to elaborate and to clarify the objectives and purposes of the lesson.

Reading can be an avenue toward growth in vocabulary and use of prior knowledge, two key components of comprehension for ELLs. To facilitate this, the teacher should encourage wide reading and writing for both in-school and out-of-school literacy. In class, the teacher should provide books with culturally familiar text. Listening centers may be incorporated in the classroom for ELLs, so that students hear models of proficient reading.

• When teaching content, the use of hands-on activities and experiments is highly encouraged. Computer programs and the Internet can be a rich source of videos and demonstrations to further clarify concepts for ELLs. The teacher may also reflect on the objectives of the lesson and create a simplified worksheet that focuses on the modified goals for ELLs.

QUESTIONS FOR DISCUSSION

1. Think about your classroom. What factors may be influencing the academic progress of your ELL students? What can you do bridge these factors and help your students succeed?

2. Think of *literacy* as a more global term. What literacy skills do your students bring into your classroom? What can you do to capitalize on these skills?

3. Make a list of instructional strategies you would like to incorporate into your teaching to better instruct ELLs. Communicate with the ESL/ESOL teacher at your school. Collaborate with him or her to create a learning team to support your integration of new instructional practices. Try out the new instructional practices and reflect on the results. Share your reflections with your learning team.

4. Visit three of the suggested websites. Create a list of new information you gained and how you would consider this information in your instructional practices with ELLs.

Resources

Further Reading

August, D., & Hakuta, K. (Eds.) (1997). *Improving schooling for language-minority children: A research agenda.* Washington, DC: National Academy Press.

August, D., & Shanahan, T. (2006). *Developing literacy in second-language learners: Report of the national literacy panel on language-minority children and youth.* Mahwah, NJ: Erlbaum.

Ernst-Slavit, G., Moore, M., & Maloney, C. (2002). Changing lives: Teaching English and literature to ESL students. *Journal of Adolescent & Adult Literacy, 46*(2), 118–128.

Fitzgerald, J. (1995). English-as-a-second-language learners' cognitive reading processes: A review of research in the United States. *Review of Educational Research, 65*(2), 145–190.

Gersten, R., & Baker, S. (2000). What we know about effective instructional practices for English-language learners. *Exceptional Children, 66*(4), 454–470.

Harper, C., & de Jong, E. (2004). Misconceptions about teaching English-language learners. *Journal of Adolescent & Adult Literacy, 48*(2), 152–162.

Klingner, J. K., & Vaughn, S. (2004). Strategies for struggling second-language readers. In T. L. Jetton & J. A. Dole (Eds.), *Adolescent literacy research and practice* (pp. 183–209). New York: Guilford Press.

Samway, K. D., & McKeon, D. (1999). *Myths and realities: Best practices for language minority students.* Portsmouth, NH: Heinemann.

Websites

www.tesol.org/s_tesol/cat_tapestry.asp?CID=1585&DID=8732—Tapestry for Teachers of English Language Learners. This web portal is hosted on the Teachers of English to Speakers of Other Languages (TESOL) website (*www.tesol.org*). It has research-based information to guide teachers toward improving instruction for language-minority students.

www.all4ed.org—Alliance for Excellent Education. This is a national policy and advocacy organization whose goal is to make every child a high school graduate. The website is filled with information and publications that describe the current crisis in adolescent education, and that include things teachers can do at the classroom level and to effect more global change.

www.alliance.brown.edu/tdl/index.shtml—Teaching Diverse Learners. This site has information to assist teachers in providing equitable and effective instruction to ELLs.

www.everythingesl.net—EverythingESL. This site was created by an ESL teacher and author. It has resources, teaching tips, lesson plans, and a blog, so that teachers and parents can discuss issues specific to ELLs.

www.eslcafe.com—Dave's ESL café. This website has information for teachers interested in professional development that focuses on ELLs. It also has activities and lessons that teachers can use in their classes, and links for students as well.

www.readwritethink.org—ReadWriteThink.org. This website, hosted by the International Reading Association (*www.reading.org*), offers free lesson plans, created by teachers, that have been used successfully with language-minority students.

References

Alliance for Excellent Education. (2007, February). *Urgent but overlooked: The literacy crisis among adolescent English language learners.* Washington, DC: Author.

Au, K. (1979). Using the experience–text–relationship method with minority children. *Reading Teacher, 32*(6), 677–679.

August, D., Carlo, M., Dressler, C., & Snow, C. (2005). The critical role of vocabulary development for English language learners. *Learning Disabilities Research and Practice, 20*(1), 50–57.

August, D., & Hakuta, K. (Eds.). (1997). *Improving schooling for language-minority children: A research agenda.* Washington, DC: National Academy Press.

August, D., & Shanahan, T. (2006). *Developing literacy in second-language learners: Report of the National Literacy Panel on Language-Minority Children and Youth.* Mahwah, NJ: Erlbaum.

Avalos, M. A. (2003). Effective second-language reading transition: From learner-specific to generic instruction models. *Bilingual Research Journal, 27*(2), 171–199.

Avalos, M. A. (2006). No two learners are alike: Learners with linguistic and cultural differences. In J. S. Schumm (Ed.), *Reading assessment and instruction for all learners* (pp. 59–86). New York: Guilford Press.

Batalova, J., Fix, M., & Murray, J. (2005). *English language learner adolescents: Demographics and literacy achievements: Report to the Center for Applied Linguistics.* Washington, DC: Migration Policy Institute.

Beck, I. L., McKeown, M. G., & Kucan, L. (2002). *Bringing words to life: Robust vocabulary instruction.* New York: Guilford Press.

Bernhardt, E. (2005). Progress and procrastination in second language reading. *Annual Review of Applied Linguistics, 25*, 133–150.

Bigelow, M., & Tarone, E. (2004). The role of literacy level in second language acquisition: Doesn't who we study determine what we know? *TESOL Quarterly, 38*(4), 689–710.

Calderón, M., August, D., Slavin, R., Duran, D., Madden, N., & Cheung, A. (2005). Bringing words to life in classrooms with English language learners. In E. Hiebert & M. L. Kamil (Eds.), *Teaching and learning vocabulary: Bringing research to practice* (pp. 119–134). Hilsdale, NJ: Erlbaum.

Cohen, E. G. (1994). *Designing groupwork.* New York: Teachers College Press.

Cummins, J. (1981). *Bilingualism and minority language children.* Toronto: Institute for Studies in Education.

Cummins, J. (2003). Reading and the bilingual student: Fact and friction. In G. G. García (Ed.), *English learners: Reaching the highest level of English literacy* (pp. 2–33). Newark, DE: International Reading Association.

Ernst-Slavit, G., Moore, M., & Maloney, C. (2002). Changing lives: Teaching English and literature to ESL students. *Journal of Adolescent & Adult Literacy, 46*(2), 116–128.

Fitzgerald, J. (1995). English-as-a-second-language learners' cognitive reading processes: A review of research in the United States. *Review of Educational Research, 65*(2), 145–190.

García, G. E., & Godina, H. (2004). Addressing the literacy needs of adolescent English language learners. In T. L. Jetton & J. A. Dole (Eds.), *Adolescent literacy research and practice* (pp. 304–320). New York: Guilford Press.

Gersten, R. (1996). The double demands of teaching English language learners. *Educational Leadership, 53*, 18–22.

Gersten, R., & Baker, S. (2000). What we know about effective instructional practices for English-language learners. *Exceptional Children, 66*(4), 454–470.

Goldenberg, C., Rueda, R. S., & August, D. (2006). Synthesis: Sociocultural contexts and literacy development. In D. August & T. Shanahan (Eds.), *Developing literacy in second-language learners: Report of the national literacy panel on language-minority children and youth* (pp. 249–267). Mahwah, NJ: Erlbaum.

Graves, M. F. (2004). Theories and constructs that have made a significant difference in adolescent literacy—but have the potential to produce still more positive benefits. In. T. L. Jetton & J. A. Dole (Eds.), *Adolescent literacy research and practice* (pp. 433–452). New York: Guilford Press.

Hadaway, N. L., & Mundy, J. (1999). Children's informational picture books visit a secondary ESL classroom. *Journal of Adolescent & Adult Literacy, 42*(6), 464–475.

Harper, C., & de Jong, E. (2004). Misconceptions about teaching English-language learners. *Journal of Adolescent and Adult Literacy, 48*(2), 152–162.

Hinkel, E. (2006). Current perspectives on teaching the four skills. *TESOL Quarterly, 40*(1), 109–131.

Jimenez, R. T. (2001). "It's a difference that changes us": An alternative view of the language and literacy learning of Latino/a students. *Reading Teacher, 54*(8), 736–742.

Klingner, J. K., & Vaughn, S. (1996). Reciprocal teaching of reading comprehension strategies for students with learning disabilities who use English as a second language. *Elementary School Journal, 96*(3), 275–293.

Klingner, J. K., & Vaughn, S. (1999). Promoting reading comprehension, content learning, and English acquisition through Collaborative Strategic Reading (CSR). *Reading Teacher, 52*(7), 738–747.

Klingner, J. K., & Vaughn, S. (2004). Strategies for struggling second-language readers. In T. L. Jetton & J. A. Dole (Eds.), *Adolescent literacy research and practice* (pp. 183–209). New York: Guilford Press.

Lesaux, N., & Geva, E. (2006). Synthesis: Development of literacy in language-minority students. In D. August & T. Shanahan (Eds.), *Developing literacy in second-langauge learners: Report of the National Literacy Panel on Language-Minority Children and Youth*. Mahwah, NJ: Erlbaum.

Li, D., & Nes, S. (2001). Using paired reading to help ESL students become fluent and accurate readers. *Reading Improvement, 38*(2), 50–61.

McCarrier, A., Pinnell, G. S., & Fountas, I. C. (2000). *Interactive writing: How language and literacy come together, K–2*. Portsmouth, NH: Heinemann.

Moje, E. B., & Hinchman, K. (2004). Culturally responsive practices for youth literacy learning. In T. L. Jetton & J. A. Dole (Eds.), *Adolescent literacy research and practice* (pp. 321–350). New York: Guilford Press.

Moll, L. C., & Greenberg, J. (1990). Creating zones of possibilities: Combining social contexts for instruction. In L. C. Moll (Ed.), *Vygotsky and education* (pp. 319–348). Cambridge, UK: Cambridge University Press.

Nagy, W. E. (1988). *Teaching vocabulary to improve reading comprehension*. Newark, DE: International Reading Association.

National Center for Education Statistics. (2007). *Status and trends in the education of racial and ethnic minorities*. Retrieved January 21, 2008, from *nces.ed.gov/pubs2007/minoritytrends*.

National Institute for Literacy. (2007). *English as a second language literacy facts.* Retrieved January 21, 2008, from *www.nifl.gov/nifl/facts/esl.html#char.*

National Institute of Child Health and Human Development. (2000). *Report of the National Reading Panel. Teaching children to read: An evidence-based assessment of the scientific research literature on reading and its implications for reading instruction.* Retrieved on July 29,2003, from *www.nichd.nih.gov/publications/nrp/smallbook. htm.*

Perie, M., Grigg, W. S., & Donahue, P. L. (2005). *The nation's report card: Reading 2005* (NCES 2006-451). Washington, DC: U.S. Government Printing Office.

Rigg, P. (1981). Beginning to read in English the LEA way. In C. W. Twyford, W. Diehl, & K. Feathers (Eds.), *Reading English as a second language: Moving from theory* (p. 81–90). Bloomington: Indiana University Press.

Rubinstein-Ávila, E. (2004). Conversing with Miguel: An adolescent English language learner struggling with later literacy development. *Journal of Adolescent & Adult Literacy, 47*(4), 290–301.

Samway, K. D., & McKeon, D. (1999). *Myths and realities: Best practices for language minority students.* Portsmouth, NH: Heinemann.

Schmitt, N., & Carter, R. (2000). The lexical advantages of narrow reading for second language learners. *TESOL Journal, 9*(1), 4–9.

Shanahan, T., & Beck, I. (2006). Effective literacy teaching for English-language learners. In D. August & T. Shanahan (Eds.), *Developing literacy in second-language learners: Report of the National Literacy Panel on Language-Minority Children and Youth* (pp. 415–488). Mahwah, NJ: Erlbaum.

Short, D. J., & Fitzsimmons, S. (2007). *Double the work: Challenges and solutions to acquiring language and academic literacy for adolescent English language learners* (A report to Carnegie Corporation of New York). New York: Alliance for Excellent Education.

Storch, N., & Wigglesworth, G. (2003). Is there a role for the use of the L1 in the L2 setting? *TESOL Quarterly, 37*(4), 760–770.

Temple, C., Ogle, D., Crawford, A., & Freppon, P. (2005). *All children read: Teaching for literacy in today's diverse classrooms.* Boston: Allyn & Bacon.

Thomas, W. P., & Collier, V. (1996). Language-minority student achievement and program effectiveness. *NABE News, 19*(6), 33–35.

Total Physical Response. Retrieved October 22,2008, from *www.tpr-world.com*

Vaughn, S., Schumm, J. S., Klingner, J. K., & Saumell, L. (1995). Students' views of instructional practices: Implications for inclusion. *Learning Disability Quarterly, 18*, 236–248.

Verhallen, M., & Schoonen, R. (1993). Lexical knowledge of monolingual and bilingual children. *Applied Linguistics, 14*(4), 344–363.

Chapter 8

Responsible Differentiated Instruction for the Adolescent Learner

Promises, Pitfalls, and Possibilities

Jeanne Shay Schumm
Mary A. Avalos

GUIDING QUESTIONS

---

1. What is differentiated instruction?
2. What is the rationale for differentiated instruction and the promises for enhancing learning for all students?
3. What are the potential pitfalls of differentiated instruction for adolescent learners and their teachers?
4. What are promising practices for planning and implementing differentiated reading instruction in secondary classrooms?
2. What is responsible differentiation?

Jeff Thompson teaches eighth-grade U.S. history in a middle school in a highly diverse urban community. His school is a microcosm of the school district, with a large Hispanic population (72%) comprising first- and second-generation immigrants from all over Central and South America, as well as the Caribbean. Other demographic groups include white non-Hispanic (10%), Black non-Hispanic (18%), and Asian/Indian multiracial (2%). In addition to the school's cultural and linguistic diversity, the student population is also diverse in terms of socioeconomic status (SES). Although the school is located in one of the most affluent areas of the city, 68% of the student body qualifies for free or reduced lunch.

The school has a placement system that groups students full-time in gifted, advanced, or regular tracks. Jeff teaches five classes of "regular" students. Despite the tracking, Jeff's students represent a full range of reading levels. His most diverse class in terms of academic levels is an inclusion class that he coteaches with special education teacher Thomas Ingram.

Jeff puts it this way: "I teach about 150 students each day. The range of student differences in my classes is amazing. Some students can read the textbook easily; others can't read it at all; and still others just won't read it. Some students are so new to the country that their background knowledge in U.S. geography and government is just not there. Finding the time and resources for meeting individual student needs is tough. I want to give the students the best, but the reality of meeting each student's individual needs is beyond what I can do."

Classrooms in the United States have become increasingly more diverse in recent years. Immigration of students from foreign countries, the movement toward inclusion of students with disabilities in the general education classroom, and insufficient funding for gifted education programs have all contributed to broadening the ranges of students that teachers like Jeff might expect to teach. Moreover, criticisms of tracking in secondary schools based on issues related to equity and access have also contributed to changing classroom composition. This growing diversity, coupled with the demands of standards-based instruction and high-stakes testing, has challenged secondary school classroom teachers in reading and in content-area classes.

Given this diversity, some have argued that "teaching to the middle" or "one-size-fits-all" instruction falls short of meeting the range of instructional needs in today's classrooms (Gregory & Chapman, 2007; Schumm, Vaughn, & Moody, 2000). Rather, differentiated instruction has been offered as way to accommodate the range of student needs that teachers encounter. However, the term *differentiated instruction* is often defined and operationalized in a variety of ways and from a wide range of disciplines, causing confusion among teachers, administrators, parents, and students. In this chapter we first provide an overview of and a rationale for definitional issues associated with differentiated instruction, and explore some of the potential pitfalls in planning and implementing differentiated instruction in secondary settings. We continue with an overview of promising practices of differentiated instruction for adolescent learners. Finally, we offer a modest proposal for responsible implementation of differentiated instruction in secondary school settings.

What Is Differentiated Instruction?

The call for differentiated instruction has come from a variety of perspectives, including reading (Walpole & McKenna, 2007), general education (Chapman & King, 2003; Nunley, 2006), special education (Bender, 2002; Dion,

Morgan, Fuchs, & Fuchs, 2004; Haager & Klingner, 2004), gifted education (Tomlinson et al., 2003; Weinbrenner, 2001), teaching English as a second language (ESL) (Avalos, Plasencia, Chavez, & Rascón, 2007; Hoover & Patton, 2005), and multiple intelligences (Gardner, 1993; Gibson & Govendo, 1999; Hickey, 2004). As Figure 8.1 indicates, a number of definitions for *differentiated instruction* have been offered in the literature. What most definitions have in common is the basic notion that different students have different instructional needs.

Definitions vary in terms of how individual differences are categorized and what is necessary for differentiation to occur (e.g., assessment, planning, instructional methods). What seem more problematic is that in some definitions, *differentiated instruction* is a philosophy (Chapman & King, 2003); in others, it is a process (Hall, 2002); in still others a method (Werderich, 2002), an instructional concept (Staff Development for Educators, 2006), or an approach (Starr, 2004; Tomlinson, 2000). Definitional disparity is not new to education, and it can potentially lead to lack of clarity in both research and practice (Afflerbach, Pearson, & Paris, 2008). In 1990, Bergeron examined definitions of *whole language,* found a range of definitional variations, and eventually developed a definition that merged key concepts from the field: "Whole language is a concept that embodies both a philosophy of language development as well as the instructional approaches embedded within, and supportive of that philosophy" (p. 319). We propose that the same may be said of *differentiated instruction.* To paraphrase: *Differentiated instruction* is a concept that embodies both a philosophy of addressing individual needs of students in heterogeneous classrooms and the instructional approaches embedded within and supportive of that philosophy.

We feel that this definition is appropriate for three reasons:

1. Differentiated instruction is not defined exclusively as a philosophy or an instructional approach; rather, it is a concept that incorporates both.

2. Many definitions focus on differentiated instruction in the general education classroom. However, at the secondary level, differentiated instruction can occur in many settings: the reading classroom, content-area classrooms, resource or pullout settings, and even in advanced placement classrooms (Dixon, 2006). Therefore, the term *heterogeneous* is used to broaden the scope of the definition.

3. The definition does not mislead teachers into thinking that differentiated instruction is a single approach. There are multiple ways to plan and to implement differentiated instruction.

This final point is particularly important and warrants further clarification. Teachers and administrators often refer to *differentiated instruction* as a research-based practice. Although leaders in the field claim that students

- We define the term *differentiation* as a philosophy that enables teachers to plan strategically in order to reach the needs of diverse learners in the classroom today (Chapman & King, 2003, p. 6).
- Differentiated instruction is changing the pace, level, or kind of instruction in response to learners' needs, styles, and/or interests (Heacox, 2007, p. 1).
- Differentiated instruction is a teaching approach in which educational content, process, and product are adapted according to student readiness, interest, and learning profile. Unlike individualized instruction, in which teaching must be directed to the specific needs and skills of each *individual* student, differentiated instruction addresses the needs of student *clusters* (Starr, 2004, p. 1).
- Teaching students based on their individual abilities and through various methods designed to fit their particular learning skills rather than through a one-size-fits-all model (Franklin, 2002, p. 1).
- To differentiate instruction is to recognize students' varying background knowledge, readiness, language, preferences in learning, interests, and to react responsively. Differentiated instruction is a process to approach teaching and learning for students of differing abilities in the same class. The intent of differentiating instruction is to maximize each student's growth and individual success by meeting each student where he or she is, and assisting in the learning process (Hall, 2002, p. 1).
- In a differentiated classroom, the teacher proactively plans and carries out varied approaches to content, process, and product in anticipation of and response to student differences in readiness, interest, and learning needs (Tomlinson, 2001, p. 7).
- Differentiated instruction is an instructional concept that maximizes learning for ALL students—regardless of skill level or background. It's based on the fact that in a typical classroom students vary in their academic abilities, learning styles, personalities, interests, background knowledge and experiences, and levels of motivation for learning. When a teacher differentiates instruction, he or she uses the best teaching practices and strategies to create different pathways that respond to the needs of diverse learners (Staff Development for Educators, 2006, p. 1).
- [Differentiated Instruction] refers to a variety of classroom practices that allow for differences in students' learning styles, interests, prior knowledge, socialization needs, and comfort zones (Benjamin, 2005, p. 1).
- The concept of *differentiated instruction* is based on the need for general education teachers to differentiate instruction to meet the needs of diverse learners in the general education class; this includes students with learning disabilities as well as a number of other disabilities (Bender, p. 1).
- First of all, we believe that all children (even children whose achievement is way ahead of grade level) deserve classroom-based literacy instruction that helps them accomplish challenging tasks that are just out of their reach. Second, we mean instruction that targets a particular group of children's needs directly and temporarily—differentiated instruction is both driven and monitored by assessment. Third, we mean instruction that applies a developmental model and assumes that children might have needs in word recognition, in fluency, in oral vocabulary, and in comprehension, but that in order to reach higher-level reading comprehension goals, we first must help children achieve automatic access to words. And, finally, we mean instruction that supplements high-quality, grade-level, whole-group instruction (Walpole & McKenna, p. 2).

FIGURE 8.1. Definitions of differentiated instruction.

of all ability levels benefit from differentiated instruction (e.g., students who are advanced exceed learning objectives to continue their explorations, and those who struggle are able to grasp key concepts and move closer to grade level benchmarks; Tomlinson, 1995a), such statements need to be made with caution. Differentiated instruction is not an individual practice. Proponents of differentiated instruction draw on a wide array of theories and research to provide validation (for a review, see Tomlinson et al., 2003). Although Tomlinson et al. advocate the use of individual, research-based practices with multilevel components, they conclude that the empirical basis for models of differentiated instruction and their impact on student outcomes is yet to be determined. Tracy Hall, of the National Center on Accessing the General Curriculum, wrote, "While no empirical validation of differentiated instruction as a package was found for this review, there are a generous number of testimonials and classroom examples authors of several publications, and Web sites provide while describing differentiated instruction" (2002, p. 5). Clearly, research in this area is in its adolescence, if not its infancy.

What Is the Promise of Differentiated Instruction?

As the gap between proficient and struggling readers increases over time, elementary school students who struggle with reading continue to fall further behind and are failing on measures of reading at widespread rates in secondary schools (Deshler, Palinscar, Biancarosa, & Nair, 2007). Indeed, in secondary classes the range of student reading levels is enormous. Singer and Donlan (1985) estimated that student reading levels in a general education classroom are roughly two-thirds the average chronological age of the students. Thus, in a class with 12-year-olds, a 9-year span of reading differences can be expected.

The National Assessment of Educational Progress (NAEP), known as the nation's "report card," highlights reading (and other content) achievement in grades 4, 8, and 12. Fourth-grade NAEP results indicated that more Asian/Pacific Islanders (42%) and Whites (41%) scored at or above "Proficient" on the reading assessment in 2005 when compared with Native Americans/Alaska Natives (18%), Hispanics (16%), and Blacks (13%) (National Center for Education Statistics, 2007d). Similar results were scored on the 8th- and 12th-grade NAEP exams, with more Asian/Pacific Islanders (40 and 36%, respectively) and Whites (39 and 43%, respectively) scoring at or above "Proficient" than other ethnic groups (Native Americans/Alaska Natives, 17% 8th graders, 26% 12th graders; Hispanics, 15 and 20%, respectively; and Blacks, 12 and 16%, respectively). Although recent NAEP data suggest that achievement scores among all 4th graders have made considerable gains, the percentage of 8th and 12th graders scoring at the proficient level has not changed. Adolescents from diverse backgrounds are particularly at risk for dropping out of high school when they experience limited academic success (Deshler et al., 2007). Factors that contribute to diversity of academic needs include the increased cultural and linguistic diversity in U.S. schools, as well as the growing practice of including students with disabilities and those identified as gifted and talented in the general education classroom. Advocates of differentiated instruction see it as a promising way to address the widening array of individual student needs that teachers like Jeff Thompson encounter.

Cultural and Linguistic Diversity

Changing school demographics/student populations is another important reason to differentiate instruction at the secondary level. In fall 1972, whereas 77.8% of the total K–12 school population was White, 14.8% Black, 6% Hispanic, and 1.4% was other races, in 2005, 57.6% was White, 15.6% was Black, 19.7% was Hispanic, 3.7% was Asian, and 3.4% was other races (National Center for Education Statistics, 2007a). Nearly one-half (42%) of the K–12 student population in 2005 was from a racially diverse background, an increase of 22% since 1979. In fall 2005, 20% of 5- to 17-year-olds came from homes in which a language other than English was spoken, compared with 9% in 1979 (National Center for Education Statistics, 2007b). The majority of students who spoke a language other than English at home spoke Spanish, followed by Indo-European (e.g., German, French, Portuguese) and Asian/Pacific Islander languages (National Center for Education Statistics, 2007c).

According to recent projections,[1] an 82% population increase in the United States is predicted from 2005 to 2050, largely due to newly arrived immigrants and their U.S.-born children (Pew Research Center, 2008). In addition, it is predicted that the Hispanic population will triple in size and account for the majority of population growth through 2050. Hispanics will make up 29% of the population in 2050, compared with 14% in 2005, and White, non-Hispanic populations will become a minority (47%) by 2050.

Adolescent English language learners (ELLs) who are struggling share the following characteristics: (1) They are older than their same-grade peers due to grade-placement based on weak academic skills or limited formal schooling; (2) they typically have academic needs that traditional English as a second language (ESL) teachers cannot meet; (3) they have little, or limited, literacy skills and content knowledge in their first language; (4) they need approaches and materials to help them catch up with and compete with mainstream students; and (5) they are at risk of dropping out of traditional academic programs (Freeman & Freeman, 2002). Historically, immigrant populations have been young; therefore, based on current trends, adolescent ELLs and the school-age population speaking a language other than English in the home will continue to grow.

---

[1]Numbers reported here are from a "high" immigration prediction. The report includes both the "high" immigration projection and a "lower" immigration projection.

Generally the federal free or reduced-price lunch program demonstrates a proxy measure of poverty among and between public school populations. In 2005, larger proportions of minority students (Blacks, 70%; Hispanics, 73%, and Native Americans, 65%) were eligible for the federal lunch program than Whites (24%) or Asian/Pacific Islanders (33%) National Center for Education Statistics,, 2006). Proportionately, Blacks and Hispanics attended the most highly impoverished schools compared with other racial/ethnic groups (Pew Research Center, 2008).

In summary, these facts and numbers make clear the growth of cultural and linguistic diversity among school-age children in the United States, as well as future challenges for teachers, with more diversity predicted for the future.

Inclusion

In 1975, the Congress of the United States passed Public Law 94-142, the Education for the Handicapped Act (EHA). This landmark act provided funding for free and appropriate education of students with special needs. This included students with high-incidence disabilities (i.e., communication disorders, learning disabilities, and behavioral disabilities) and low-incidence disabilities (i.e., multiple disabilities, sensory impairments, physical or health disabilities, traumatic brain injury, or autism). One of the key components of this law required an Individualized Education Program (IEP) for any student receiving federal funds for special education. The reauthorization of this legislation in 1997, entitled the Individuals with Disabilities Education Act (IDEA), included emphasis for education of students with disabilities in the least restrictive environment, thus increasing the numbers of students with disabilities included in general education classrooms for all or part of the school day.

Although, students with disabilities may receive services in part-time resource settings, self-contained classrooms, or special schools, increasing numbers are being served in the general education classroom. The U.S. government estimates that 90% of general education teachers are assigned at least three students with IEPs (U.S. Department of Education, 2005). This estimate does not take into account students who have undiagnosed disabilities or students in the referral pipeline. In addition, the 1997 reauthorization called for increased participation of general educators in the IEP planning and implementation to ensure increased access to the general education curriculum.

More recently, concerns about the procedures and criteria used to identify students with learning disabilities and the disproportionate number of minority students in special education have led to recommendations for altering traditional referral and assessment procedures and criteria (for discussion, see Haager, Klingner, & Vaughn, 2007). The recommended alternative, response to intervention (RTI), requires that before being placed in special education, students have the opportunity to receive intensive, research-based instruction. Successful interventions would ensure ongoing education in the general education setting and avoid the necessity for special education services. RTI involves tiers of instruction that become increasingly more intensive. Tier 1 involves high-quality instruction in the general education classroom. Tier 2 involves small-group instruction for students who were unsuccessful in Tier 1. Tier 3 involves more sustained intervention for students who need additional support in their learning (Vaughn & Klingner, 2007). Recently, RTI models have been offered as a way to provide intensive instruction for students in middle school settings (Johnson & Smith, 2008). Although researched on an elementary school level, RTI has little empirical evidence in secondary settings and is very much in the formative stages.

Gifted and Talented

Students who are identified gifted and talented have particular needs (Van Tassel-Baska, 2003), whether they are placed in general education settings or in gifted education settings for all or part of the school day. Identification procedures for students who are gifted and talented vary considerably from state to state (Davis & Rimm, 2004). Similarly, service provision varies as well. Nonetheless, the trend toward inclusion of more students with exceptional gifts and talents in the general education classroom is clear, and teachers need professional development to address the needs of students in their charge (Van Tassel-Baska, Quek, & Feng, 2007). The trend toward high-stakes testing and lack of funding for gifted education (Baker & McIntire, 2003) has subjected many highly able students in general education settings to skill and drill manuals on minimal standards, ignoring critical and creative thinking activities (Glass, 2000; Viadero, 2007).

Tomlinson (2001) maintains that modifications to the content, process, and products of learning can meet the needs of low, average, and highly able students. For highly able students, curricula can be compacted to meet their learning needs (Reis & Renzulli, 1992). Pretesting helps the teacher determine what students know and need to learn on a topic. Depending on pretesting outcomes, highly able student then participate in classroom instruction, independent learning, or extension activities, as appropriate.

Teachers who used differentiated instruction offer their students different ways and objectives to learn, based on varying readiness levels, interests, and learning profiles (Tomlinson, 1995a). Tomlinson (2003) further describes differentiated instruction as "responsive instruction" and states that "the goal of a differentiated classroom is to plan actively and consistently to help each learner move as far and as fast as possible along a learning continuum" (p. 2). Wormeli (2006) justifies the need for differentiated instruction, describing it as "doing what is fair and developmentally appropriate for students when the 'regular' instruction doesn't meet their needs" (p. 14). The promise of differentiated instruction is that students' individual needs can and should be met to help them succeed in academic life and in life beyond the classroom. However, like many secondary school teachers, Jeff Thompson might ask, "How can this realistically be accomplished?"

What Are Potential Pitfalls of Differentiated Instruction?

Earlier we defined *differentiated instruction* as a concept that embodies both a philosophy of addressing individual needs of students in heterogeneous classrooms and an instructional approaches embedded within, and supportive of, that philosophy. It is difficult to imagine that teachers would not have the desire to meet individual needs of their students (Boardman, Arguelles, Vaughn, Hughes, & Klingner, 2005). However, the pragmatics of how to meet those individual needs within the parameters of widening diversity in the classroom, standards-based instruction, and high-stakes testing are daunting.

Research in teachers' perceptions of implementing adaptations for mainstreamed students with disabilities (Schumm & Vaughn, 1991), flexible grouping strategies (Elbaum, Schumm, & Vaughn, 1997; Moody, Vaughn, & Schumm, 1997; Schumm, Vaughn, & Elbaum, 1996), textbook adaptations (Schumm, Vaughn, & Saumell, 1994), research-based instructional practices (Boardman et al., 2005), and modifications for students identified as gifted and talented (Brighton, 2003) indicate that teachers hit roadblocks in differentiated instruction. Concurrently, students of all achievement levels feel that their individual needs are not being addressed (Schumm, Vaughn, & Saumell, 1992; Vaughn, Schumm, Klingner, & Saumell, 1995). In her book on differentiating instruction at the high school level, Nunley (2006) identifies 18 obstacles that teachers face (see Resources), and practical solutions for overcoming these obstacles. These obstacles include content coverage demands, lack of planning time and funding, grading policies, and resistance to changing current practices. Indeed, previous research has indicated that some secondary school teachers do not use differentiated instruction, because they believe it would not prepare students for the "real world" (Schumm & Vaughn, 1991).

For differentiated instruction to occur, teachers may need to change both "beliefs about the nature of schooling and their resulting classroom practice" (Brighton, 2003, p. 177). Moreover, instructional strategies must be feasible for the classroom teacher to implement. Gersten and his colleagues refer to this as the *reality principle* (Gersten & Brengelman, 1996; Gersten, Woodward, & Morvant, 1992). As Gersten and Brengelman (1996) explain, "Research must be able to be translated into manageable and comprehensible teaching strategies and procedures, Further, these strategies must reflect and fit within the details of day-to-day classroom instruction" (p. 69). In the following section "feasible" practices for planning and implementing differentiated instruction are presented.

What Are Promising Practices in Differentiated Instruction?

This section begins with an overview of differentiated instructional practices for secondary students. It continues with three promising practices to serve as examples: the Planning Pyramid, Collaborative Strategic Reading, and Modified Guided Reading.

An Overview of Differentiated Instructional Practices

Tompkins (2006) lists students' interests, motivation, background knowledge, prior experiences, culture and language proficiency, and instructional reading and writing levels as possible variables by which instruction can be differentiated. Tomlinson (1995b) identified four characteristics that shape teaching and learning in differentiated instructional classrooms: (1) Instruction is concept-focused and principle-driven, and stresses understanding over memorization; (2) ongoing assessment of student readiness and growth is built into the curriculum, enabling support where needed, or extension when data demonstrate that the student is ready to move on; (3) flexible grouping consistently allows for multiple grouping options and formats; and (4) students are active explorers, with the teacher acting as facilitator of the learning. She also posited that differentiated instruction is appropriate for secondary school students, who typically differ in readiness, interests, and learning profiles, making a one-size-fits-all model inadequate to meet students' varying needs.

Wormeli (2006) takes this one step further for middle school students and advocates including five additional strategies when differentiating instruction for preteens. First, teachers should address students' developmental needs (e.g., promoting competence and achievement; opportunities for self-definition; creative expression; physical activity; positive social interactions with adults and peers; meaningful participation in the family, school, and community), so that basic needs are met and students are better able to focus on learning goals. Second, middle school teachers should treat academic struggle as a strength to foster risk taking and understanding about different learning styles that work for some, but not all, students (e.g., drawing, writing, speaking about the content). Provision of various paths to the learning objective is the third strategy. This allows students at different readiness levels to demonstrate their understanding of concepts, with the added support of the teacher or peers, if needed. The fourth strategy is provide prompt, formative feedback. Middle school students learn best when they are able to compare what they have done with what they were supposed to have done, then have time to revise or to redo the task. Finally, the fifth strategy is to approach instruction unconventionally. Wormeli advocates this to pique students' curiosity and to challenge their knowledge, motivating them to learn.

While reviewing studies of exemplary literacy teaching, Ankrum, Avalos, Morewood, and Conrad (2008) found certain characteristics pertaining to small-group instruction among identified exemplary teachers. For example, to differentiate instruction, exemplary teachers use classroom-based assessments to inform their instruction (Brimijoin, Marquisse, & Tomlinson, 2003). Grouping of students is based on individual strengths and needs determined by teacher-administered assessments. Groups also remain fluid and flexible, changing as needed. Furthermore, multiple assessments are the basis for teacher decisions regarding lesson content and focus. Exemplary teachers spend additional time on concepts and/or reteach as needed, assessing often to monitor progress.

Planning Pyramid

Planning is an important key to the success of differentiated instruction. Although it is frequently necessary for teachers to adjust their teaching to respond to students' needs, preplanning in differentiated instruction involves anticipating those needs in advance. A number of preplanning systems have emerged, largely because of the widespread inclusion of students with disabilities in today's classroom. Universal Design for Learning (Hall, Strangman, & Meyer, 2003; Rose & Meyer, 2002; Van Garderen & Whittaker, 2006), the Unit Planner (Lenz & Deshler, 2004), and the REACH framework (Reflect on will and skill, Evaluate the curriculum, Analyze the learners, Craft research-based lessons, and Hone in on the data; Rock, Gregg, Ellis, & Gable, 2008) are examples. What most systems have in common are emphases on assessment, content modifications, and preplanning for adaptation to individual student needs.

In preparing our preservice teachers to plan for a wide range of student needs, we have used the Planning Pyramid to plan units and lessons (Schumm, Vaughn, & Harris, 1997; Schumm, Vaughn, & Leavell, 1994). The Planning Pyramid Lesson Plan has changed considerably since its origins, based on feedback from classroom and preservice teachers. The present version (see Figure 8.2) includes checklists of frequently used strategies for ELLs, students with disabilities, and students who are academically advanced or gifted.

The "heart" of the Planning Pyramid is the belief that all students can learn, but that students can and will learn in different ways, at different rates, and in different amounts. There are several steps in using the Planning Pyramid. First, teachers take a careful look at the content to be taught and state curricular objectives to be met (Tomlinson, 2000). Then teachers determine what all students must learn, what most students will learn, and what perhaps only a few students will learn based on prior knowledge of students and or specific pretesting of the content to be learned (Brimijoin et al., 2003).

Second, teachers need to determine the level of intensity will be necessary for students to master content. Schumm and Arguelles (2006) have pro-

LESSON PLAN

Subject Area: _____ Grade: _____

Date(s) _____

*Curriculum Standard	Theme/Topic:
*Lesson Objective	

Agenda and Procedures (what the teacher will do) **Time Frame**	***In Class Activity/Assignment** (what the students will do) **Time Frame**

| Instructional Strategies
☐ Discussion
☐ Lecture
☐ Demonstration
☐ Learning or interest centers
☐ Simulation or role play
☐ Learning games
☐ Guided Independent Study
☐ K-W-L
☐ Graphic organizers
☐ Teacher read-aloud
☐ Student read-aloud
Other: | FCAT Connection*
☐ Vocabulary
☐ Context clues
☐ Main idea
☐ Details/facts
☐ Author purpose
☐ Persuasion
☐ Conflict resolution
☐ Compare/contrast
☐ Reference/research | Grouping Patterns
☐ Whole class
☐ Small, mixed ability groups
☐ Small, same ability groups
☐ Mixed ability pairs
☐ Same ability pairs
☐ One-on-one, individualized
☐ Independent work
Other: |
| *Evaluation/Assessment
☐ Observation of final product
☐ Interview with student
☐ Group assessment (critique)
☐ Observation of process (student working)
☐ Self-assessment by student
☐ Teacher generated assignment
☐ Written product
☐ Test/Quiz
Other: | Adaptations
☐ Audiovisual aids
☐ Hands-on activities
☐ Computer programs/Internet
☐ Peer teacher to student tutors
☐ After school homework buddy
☐ Simplified worksheets
☐ Simplified grammatical structures
☐ Incorporate prompts, cues, facial expressions, body language, concrete objects
☐ Curriculum compacting | Adaptations
☐ Short, concise directions
☐ Reinforce language
☐ Check for meaning
☐ Clarify multiple meanings
☐ Go over vocabulary before lesson
☐ Use extended time, if necessary
☐ Reduce text amount
☐ Charts/graphs
Other: |

(continued)

FIGURE 8.2. Planning Pyramid Lesson Plan form. *Note.* K-W-L (what you know already, what you want to know, and what you learned from your reading). Adapted from the work of Jeanne Bergeron, by permission.

Instructional Aids (Teacher) ☐ Board ☐ Overhead ☐ Computer ☐ Audiovisual ☐ Props ☐ Visuals Other: Related Literature: **Supporting Technology:**	Materials (Students) ☐ Textbook ☐ Workbook ☐ Notebook ☐ Handout ☐ Maps/graphs ☐ Computers Other: Related Literature: **Supporting Technology:**	Learning Pyramid SOME WILL LEARN MOST WILL LEARN ALL WILL LEARN
*Home Learning		
Reflection Use an additional page to complete your reflection.		

FIGURE 8.2. *(continued)*

posed an Intensity Index (see Table 8.1), with five dimensions of intensity that impact differentiated instruction: grouping, strategies and materials, instructor, time, and practice. Third, the actual planning begins with attention to agenda and procedures, selection of instructional strategies, evaluation and assessment, and home learning activities.

Finally, we encourage inservice and preservice teachers to reflect about differentiated lessons and think about (1) what follow-up needs to be done with students who still need assistance, and (2) how they would teach the lesson differently. Because differentiated instruction is new to many teachers, this type of reflection is vital to the ongoing quest to help all students be successful in school.

Collaborative Strategic Reading

Over the course of elementary and secondary schooling, students are presented with a variety of strategies to improve their reading comprehension. Often the strategies are mentioned but not always taught with sufficient modeling and practice to ensure that they are fully mastered, then applied during independent reading. Collaborative Strategic Reading (CSR), a peer-mediated learning experience, encompasses four reading comprehension

TABLE 8.1. Intensity Index

	Low	Medium	High

Grouping
    Size
    Composition
	Whole class
	Mixed ability
		Small group, pairs
		Mixed or same ability
			Individual
			Same ability

Strategies and materials	No evidence	Moderate scientific evidence or proven track record with classroom implementation	Strong scientific evidence with a similar population of students
Instructor	Untrained volunteer	Classroom teacher	Reading specialist
Time	Low length, frequency, duration	Moderate length, frequency, duration	High length, frequency, duration

Practice
    Support
    Feedback
	None
	None
		Peer supported
		Delayed and/or nonspecific
			Teacher guided
			Immediate and specific

Note. From Schumm and Arguelles (2006). Copyright 2006 by The Guilford Press. Reprinted by permission.

strategies that hold great promise for secondary school reading and content-area reading classes. Both the National Reading Panel (2000) and the RAND Report on Reading Comprehension (Snow, 2002) emphasize the potential impact of multiple strategies on reading comprehension. CSR is designed to bring multiple strategies together in a coherent way, helping students to develop solid habits in reading and learning from expository test.

CSR has been researched at elementary (e.g., Arguelles, Klingner, & Vaughn, 2004; Klingner, Vaughn, & Schumm, 1998; Klingner & Vaughn, 2000) and secondary school levels (e.g., Bryant et al., 2000; Klingner & Vaughn, 1996). Findings indicate positive CSR outcomes on both teacher-made and distal standardized test scores. More recently a computer application of CSR has been used successfully with middle school students (Kim et al., 2006). CSR requires little other than reading materials and is intended to balance with other instruction methods, such as lecture and hands-on learning projects.

CSR is an adaptation of Palinscar and Brown's (1984) reciprocal teaching. Although reciprocal teaching is designed as a teacher-led activity, CSR is "collaborative," in that students work in multilevel, cooperative groups to learn the strategies, then implement them as they read and study expository text. Students are assigned roles (e.g., group leader, timekeeper, encourager) and work in groups of five or six students for the duration of an instructional unit.

The four strategies are (1) Preview, (2) Click and Clunk, (3) Get the Gist, and (4) Wrap-Up. Students begin by previewing a reading assignment. The purpose of this strategy is to activate students' prior knowledge to help them predict what they are going to learn from the passage. Students then read the passage, stopping at logical points. When they stop, they first "click and clunk," or engage in metacognition, to identify and to clarify words, phrases, sentences, or paragraphs that seem confusing. Group members then "get the gist" when they agree on key points of the section they just read. This series of "clicking and clunking" and "getting the gist" continues as they work section by section through the passage. At the end, group members engage in a wrap-up, or a discussion of what they learned and what is most likely to be on a test. Each student in the group keeps a learning log that he or she uses to study for weekly or unit tests.

The promise of CSR is that it promotes active reading and active engagement of all learners. Secondary teachers frequently complain that their students simply do not complete reading assignments. CSR not only gets students reading but it also provides a format for ELL students, or for struggling readers whose voices may not be heard in whole-class settings (Vaughn, Klingner, & Bryant, 2001).

Modified Guided Reading

At the secondary school level, students are frequently called upon to read independently and are infrequently provided an opportunity for the guided reading they experienced in elementary school. For students who struggle with reading at the secondary level, guided reading provides the support and modeling they need to become more proficient readers. Recent interventions integrating language and literacy instruction have proven to be successful in differentiating instruction for culturally and linguistically diverse (CLD) students at the secondary school level (Avalos et al., 2007; Jacobson, Lapp, & Flood, 2007; Kiefer & Lesaux, 2008; Lester, 2008; Zipoli, Coyne, & McCoach, 2008). Avalos et al. (2007) and Lester (2008) have experienced success working with struggling adolescent ELL readers who are Spanish speakers and African American vernacular English speakers, using a modified guided reading approach. Modified guided reading builds on the work of guided reading experts (Cunningham, Hall, & Sigmon, 2000; Fountas & Pinnell, 1996; Knox & Amador-Watson, 2002) and on linguistics (Birch, 2007), providing multiple ways to differentiate reading instruction for CLD adolescents.

The modifications made to a typical guided reading lesson for CLD students include (1) assessing students in both the first (L1) and the second (L2) language for grouping and instructional purposes; (2) analyzing the text for possible linguistic obstacles; (3) reading the guided reading text aloud in a shared reading format and selecting culturally relevant texts; (4) using carefully chosen prompts to assist language learners with metacognitive strategies or word identification while they are reading the text; (5) applying word work that focuses on morphological awareness, phonemic awareness, or phonics connected to the language of the text; and (6) linking writing assignments with the content or story from the text.

Assessing students' reading proficiencies in both their L1 and L2 enables the teacher to identify instructional needs better in the L2 or target language. Assessments that provide data for both L1 and L2 are beneficial when planning differentiated instruction for CLD adolescents, because this knowledge allows teachers to focus on what the student does or does not know about reading and language structure in their L1 and L2.

After reading the text through, the teacher begins an analysis to search for possible linguistic barriers, anticipating sections in which CLD students may need additional L2 reading or language support. Features that should be noted during the text analysis are figurative language, unfamiliar content or concepts to be addressed, complex syntax or pronunciation, punctuation, and text structure (narrative or expository). Figurative language can be confusing, because similes and/or metaphors usually involve dense and complex syntax (word order). Words that have different pronunciation should also be a focus; CLD adolescents want to "say it right" when reading aloud or speaking. Since phoneme–grapheme correspondence in English varies, CLD students need explicit instruction with regard to spelling patterns.

Intonation and fluency can be taught when punctuation marks are highlighted during instruction. For example, in English, our voices go up at the end of a question (try asking "Do you want to go to the beach?" without raising your pitch or changing your tone). Intonation patterns differ across languages (Komar, 2005). CLD adolescents need to be taught explicitly how to "read" punctuation in English to be fluent readers. Text structure is another important variable to consider when planning instruction. As Derewianka (1998) points out, language features from expository texts (i.e., present or "timeless" tense, descriptive in nature, formal and infused with academic language) are different than those found in narrative texts (i.e., mainly action verbs, past tense, dialogic in nature, and often written in the first person). It is essential to provide a variety of texts, so that CLD students benefit from the differing language features and learn organizational structures of text. Also, when selecting vocabulary, it is important to emphasize words that have common English morphemes (e.g., affixes) or orthographic patterns during the lesson. Two to three of the words should be receptive (low frequency, not used in everyday speech) and five to seven words should be productive (commonly used, but may be new or easily confused).

Shared reading has been demonstrated to connect diverse learners to texts (Allen, 2002; Koskinen et al., 1999; Meier, 2003) and to provide them with needed support beyond an introduction to the text. Reading the guided reading text aloud in a shared reading format affords CLD adolescents a model of fluent reading, story and vocabulary discussion, connected demonstrations, and scaffolding of strategy use. Misinterpretations of texts based on an L1 framework or cultural knowledge (Bernhardt, 1991) may be discussed and compared with the author's intended meaning, while validating students' perceptions and the knowledge they bring with them to school. It is important to note that open-ended question formats (i.e., retelling) that do not lead students to certain interpretations should be used, so that CLD students openly share their comprehension of texts. We also suggest that curriculum materials reflect the populations served in teachers' classrooms, especially when working with emergent L2 readers. If, however, the texts have content or concepts unfamiliar to your CLD students, the introduction of the text is a great opportunity to frontload vocabulary and content information, using visuals and other resources (i.e., Internet) to build students' prior knowledge before they read the text. During shared reading is the time to connect information from the text and students' personal experiences, using open-ended questioning and discussion.

Prompts from teachers during a traditional guided reading lesson scaffold reading processes, providing explicit instruction that makes learning the responsibility of the student. Students make reading miscues when they misuse or are not aware of a cueing system (graphophonics, semantics, or syntax). CLD struggling readers often make syntactical (word order) and graphophonic (phoneme–grapheme) miscues because of their developing language proficiency. Knox and Amador-Watson (2002) state that prompts, such as "Does it make sense?" and "Does it sound right?" with CLD emergent readers call on an "intuitive grasp" of the language that English learners do not have (p. 95). Prompts for CLD readers should focus on word recognition and provide concrete support for the text to be comprehensible. For example, "What sound does *ch* make?" or, for those who have had instruction in morphological analysis, "Can you chunk the word into parts to figure it out?"

Word work focusing on morphological awareness, phonemic awareness, and phonics should be embedded within the text for CLD students (Cummins, 2003) and be taught after they have read the text. Explicit instruction about words assists in language development of morphemes, orthographical patterns, and phonological awareness. For example, if students read the word *each* in the guided reading text, word work may focus on word families that contain *each* (i.e., "reach," "peach," "breach," "teach," "beach"), building language and vocabulary knowledge.

Finally, writing assignments connected to the text give CLD students opportunities to write, using the vocabulary and concepts from the readings in meaningful contexts. Au (1993) recommends the integration of reading, writing, listening, and speaking across the curriculum for CLD students. Writing assignments can personalize the content, while providing practice and teacher feedback. For example, after reading a guided reading text about homes, students can brainstorm features about their homes with the teacher and record their ideas, then write about their homes to expand the idea of the text and provide contextualized use of vocabulary.

What Is Responsible Differentiation?

In examining the literature on differentiated instruction for adolescents, what became evident from the outset is that research on schoolwide efforts for differentiation, as well as specific instructional practices, is thin. Clearly, much needs to be done to create a substantive research base in this domain. This is particularly true in the case of teachers' use of technology to assess students, monitor student progress, plan differentiated instruction, and integrate systematic and purposeful use of technology to meet the needs of individual students (Ferguson, 2007; Kingsley, 2007; Ysseldyke & Bolt, 2007).

As schools and teachers try to meet the challenge of meeting a full range of student needs in general education settings, the tenets for responsible inclusion proposed in the early days of the inclusion movement seem relevant here (Vaughn & Schumm, 1995) and can provide guidance in thinking about responsible differentiation as it relates to program planning, implementation, and evaluation (see Table 8.2).

QUESTIONS FOR DISCUSSION

1. Read the definitions of *differentiated instruction* included in this chapter. What definition most reflects your own thinking about meeting the needs of diverse learners?

2. What do you believe are the pros and cons of differentiated instruction? What do you see as barriers and as facilitators to the successful implementation of differentiated instruction?

3. Use the Planning Pyramid form to develop a differentiated lesson. How would you modify the form to meet your own planning style?

4. This chapter provides examples of promising practices for differentiated instruction. What other methods might you use to meet individual needs of students?

TABLE 8.2. Parallels between Responsible Inclusion and Responsible Differentiation

Responsible inclusion	Responsible differentiation
Student first. The first thing is the extent to which the student with disabilities is making academic and/or social progress in the general education classroom. Ongoing assessment, monitoring, and placement considerations are critical to success.	*Student first.* The first thing is the extent to which students are making academic and/or social progress in the general education classroom. Ongoing assessment, monitoring, and placement considerations are critical to success.
Adequate resources are considered and provide for inclusive classrooms. Personnel understand that for inclusion to be successful, considerable resources related to both personnel and materials are required to develop and maintain effective inclusive classrooms.	*Adequate resources are considered and provide for inclusive classrooms.* Personnel understand that for differentiated instruction to be successful, considerable resources, related to both personnel and materials, are required to develop and maintain effective classrooms.
Models are developed and implemented at the school-based level. School-site personnel develop inclusive models that are implemented and evaluated to meet the needs of students and families in their community.	*Models are developed and implemented at the school-based level.* School-site personnel develop differentiated instruction models that are implemented and evaluated to meet the needs of students and families in their community.
A continuum of services is maintained. A range of educational programs is available to meet the needs of students with learning disabilities. It is not expected that the needs of all students will be met with full-time placement in the general education classroom.	*A continuum of services is maintained.* A range of educational programs is available to meet the needs of students. It is not expected that the needs of all students will be met with full-time placement in the general education classroom.
Service delivery model is evaluated on an ongoing basis. The success of the service delivery model is considered and fine-tuned in light of the nature of the students with learning disabilities and with consideration of the extent to which it meets their academic and social needs.	*Service delivery model is evaluated on an ongoing basis.* The success of the service delivery model is considered and fine-tuned in light of the nature of the students and with consideration of the extent to which it meets their academic and social needs.
Ongoing professional development. Personnel realize that for teachers and others to be effective at inclusion, ongoing professional development at the school level is required.	*Ongoing professional development.* Personnel realize that for teachers and others to be effective at differentiated instruction, ongoing professional development at the school level is required.
Teachers and other key personnel discuss and develop their own philosophy on inclusion. This philosophy on inclusion guides practice at the school and sets a tone of acceptance for all students.	*Teachers and other key personnel discuss and develop their own philosophy on differentiated instruction.* This philosophy on differentiated instruction guides practice at the school and sets a tone of acceptance for all students.
Curricula and instruction that meet the needs of all students are developed and refined. Successful inclusion provides for curricula and instructional practices that meet the needs of all students.	*Curricula and instruction that meet the needs of all students are developed and refined.* Successful differentiated instruction provides for curricula and instructional practices that meet the needs of all students.

Note. From Vaughn and Schumm (1995). Copyright 1995 by Sage Publications. Adapted by permission.

Resources

Further Reading

Benjamin, A. (2003). *Differentiated instruction: A guide for middle and high school teachers.* Larchmont, NY: Eye on Education.

Benjamin, A. (2005). *Differentiated instruction using technology: A guide for middle and high school teachers.* Larchmont, NY: Eye on Education.

Drapeau, P. (2004). *Differentiated instruction: Making it work.* New York: Scholastic.

Klingner, J. K., Vaughn, S., Dimino, J., Schumm, J. S., & Bryant, D. (2001). *From clunk to click: Collaborative Strategic Reading.* Longmont, CO: Sopris West.

Northey, S. S. (2005). *Handbook on differentiated instruction for middle and high school teachers.* Larchmont, NY: Eye on Education.

Nunley, K. F. (2006). *Differentiating the high school curriculum.* Thousand Oaks, CA: Corwin.

Tomlinson, C. A. (1999). *The differentiated classroom: Responding to the needs of all learners.* Alexandria, VA: Association for Supervision and Curriculum Development.

Tomlinson, C. A., & McTighe, J. (2006). *Integrating differentiated instruction and understanding by design: Connecting content and kids.* Alexandria, VA: Association for Supervision and Curriculum Development.

Turville, J. (2007). *Differentiating by student interest: Strategies and lesson plans.* Larchmont, NY: Eye on Education.

Tyner, B. (2004). *Small-group reading instruction: A differentiated teaching model for beginning and struggling readers.* Newark, DE: International Reading Association.

General Websites

www.ascd.org/ed_topics/cu2000win_willis.html—The Association for Supervision and Curriculum Development's Winter 2000 Curriculum Update on Differentiating Instruction: Finding Manageable Ways to Meet Individual Needs.

www.cast.org/publications/ncac/ncac_diffinstruc.html—The Center for Applied Special Technology (CAST) provides a definition and description of the essential features and attributes of differentiated instruction with additional links to websites.

www.internet4classrooms.com/di.htm#it—The Internet4Classrooms (i4c) provides updated links regarding the instructional theory, practical tips, multilinks, sample units, and other documents of differentiated instruction.

Research Websites

www.k8accesscenter.org/training_resources/readingdifferentiation.asp—Differentiated Instruction for Reading.

www.readingrockets.org/webcasts/ondemand/1001—Reading Rocket's 60-minute Webcast (free of charge) outlines effective strategies teachers can use to differentiate reading instruction. Presenters: Carol Ann Tomlinson, G. Michael Pressley, and Louise Spear-Swerling.

References

Afflerbach, P., Pearson, P. D., & Paris, S. G. (2008). Clarifying differences between reading skills and strategies. *Reading Teacher, 61,* 364–373.

Allen, J. (2002). *On the same page: Shared reading beyond the primary grades.* Portland, ME: Stenhouse.

Ankrum, J. W., Avalos, M. A., Morewood, A. L., & Conrad, N. K. (2008, December). Framework for "better practices" for comprehensive literacy teaching. Paper presented at the 58th Annual Meeting of the National Reading Conference, Orlando, FL.

Arguelles, M. E., Klingner, J. K., & Vaughn, S. (2004). Collaborative strategic reading: "Real-world" lessons from classroom teachers. *Remedial and Special Education, 25,* 295–301.

Au, K. H. (1993). *Literacy instruction in multicultural settings.* Orlando, FL: Harcourt Brace.

Avalos, M. A., Plasencia, A., Chavez, C., & Rascón, J. (2007). Modified guided reading: Gateway to English as a second language and literacy learning. *Reading Teacher, 61*(4), 318–329.

Baker, B. D., & McIntire, J. (2003). Evaluating state funding for gifted education programs. *Roeper Review, 25,* 173–179.

Bender, W. N. (2002). *Differentiated instruction for students with learning disabilities.* Thousand Oaks, CA: Corwin.

Benjamin, A. (2005). *Differentiated instruction using technology: A guide for middle and high school teachers.* Larchmont, NY: Eye on Education.

Bergeron, B. S. (1990). What does the term whole language mean?: Constructing a definition from the literature. *Journal of Reading Behavior, 22,* 301–329.

Bernhardt, E. B. (1991). *Reading development in a second language: Theoretical, empirical, and classroom perspectives.* Norwood, NJ: Ablex.

Birch, E. M. (2007). *English L2 reading: Getting to the bottom* (2nd ed.). Mahwah, NJ: Erlbaum.

Boardman, A. G., Arguelles, M. E., Vaughn, S., Hughes, M. T., & Klingner, J. K. (2005). Special education teachers' views of research-based practices. *Journal of Special Education, 39,* 168–180.

Brighton, C. M. (2003). The effects of middle school teachers' beliefs on classroom practices. *Journal for the Education of the Gifted, 27,* 177–206.

Brimijoin, K., Marquisse, E., & Tomlinson, C. A. (2003). Using data to differentiate instruction. *Educational Leadership, 60,* 70–73.

Bryant, D. P., Vaughn, S., Linan-Thompson, S., Ugel, N., Hamff, A., & Hougen, M. (2000). Reading outcomes for students with and without learning disabilities in general education middle school classes. *Learning Disability Quarterly, 24,* 251–264.

Chapman, C., & King, R. (2003). *Differentiated instructional strategies for reading in the content areas.* Thousand Oaks, CA: Corwin.

Cummins, J. (2003). Reading and the bilingual student: Fact and friction. In G. G. García (Ed.), *English learners: Reaching the highest level of English literacy* (pp. 2–33). Newark, DE: International Reading Association.

Cunningham, P. M., Hall, D. P., & Sigmon, C. M. (2000). *The teacher's guide to the Four Blocks: A multimethod, multilevel framework for grades 1–3.* Greensboro, NC: Carson-Dellosa.

Davis, G. A., & Rimm, S. B. (2004). *Education of the gifted and talented* (5th ed.). Boston: Pearson Education.

Derewianka, B. (1998). *Exploring how texts work*. Newtown, Australia: Primary English Teaching Association.

Deshler, D. D., Palinscar, A. S., Biancarosa, G., & Nair, M. (2007). *Informed choices for struggling adolescent readers: A research-based guide to instructional programs and practices*. Newark, DE: International Reading Association and Carnegie Corporation of New York.

Dion, E., Morgan, P. L., Fuchs, D., & Fuchs, L. S. (2004). The promise and limitations of reading instruction in the mainstream: The need for a multilevel approach. *Exceptionality, 12,* 163–173.

Dixon, F. (2006). Diffentiating instruction in AP: An important question?: Or, out of the question. *Gifted Child Today, 29,* 50–54.

Elbaum, B. E., Schumm, J. S., & Vaughn, S. (1997). Urban middle-elementary students' perceptions of grouping formats for reading instruction. *Elementary School Journal, 97,* 475–500.

Ferguson, R. F. (2007). Become sophisticated about diversity. *Journal of Staff Development, 28,* 33–34.

Fountas, I. C., & Pinnell, G. S. (1996). *Guided reading: Good first reading for all children*. Portsmouth, NH: Heinemann.

Franklin, J. (2002). The art of differentiation: Moving from theory to practice. *Education Update, 44,* 1–2.

Freeman, D. E., & Freeman, Y. S. (2004). *Essential linguistics: What you need to know to teach reading, ESL, spelling, phonics, grammar*. Portsmouth, NH: Heinemann.

Gardner, H. (1993). *Frames of mind: The theory of multiple intelligences*. New York: Basic Books.

Gersten, R., & Brengelman, S. U. (1996). The quest to translate research into classroom practice: An emerging knowledge base. *Remedial and Special Education, 17,* 67–74.

Gersten, R., Woodward, K., & Morvant, M. (1992). Refining the working knowledge of experienced teachers. *Educational Leadership, 49,* 34–39.

Gibson, B. P., & Govendo, B. L. (1999). Encouraging constructive behavior in middle school classrooms: A multiple-intelligences approach. *Intervention in School and Clinic, 35,* 16–21.

Glass, T. F. (2000). What gift?: The reality of the student who is gifted and talented in public school classrooms. *Gifted Child Today, 27,* 25–29.

Gregory, G. H., & Chapman, C. (2007). *Differentiated instructional strategies: One size doesn't fit all* (2nd ed.). Thousand Oaks, CA: Corwin.

Haager, D., & Klingner, J. K. (2004). *Differentiated instruction in inclusive classrooms*. Boston: Allyn & Bacon.

Haager, D., Klingner, J. K., & Vaughn, S. (Eds.). (2007). *Evidence-based reading practices for response to intervention*. Baltimore: Brookes.

Hall, T. (2002). *Differentiated instruction*. Wakefield, MA: National Center on Accessing the General Curriculum. Retrieved May 1, 2007, from *www.cast.org/publications/ncac/ncac_diffinstruc.html*.

Hall, T., Strangman, N., & Meyer, A. (2003). *Differentiated instruction and implications for UDL implementation*. Retrieved October 20, 2008, from *www.cast.org/publications/ncac*.

Heacox, D. (2007). *Differentiated instruction in the regular classroom.* Minneapolis, MN: Free Spirit.

Hickey, M. G. (2004). "Can I pick more than one project?": Case studies of five teachers who used MI-based instructional planning. *Teachers College Record, 106,* 77–86.

Hoover, J. J., & Patton, J. R. (2005). Differentiating curriculum and instruction for English-language learners with special needs. *Intervention in School and Clinic, 40,* 231–235.

Jacobson, J., Lapp, D., & Flood, J. (2007). A seven-step instructional plan for teaching English-language learners to comprehend and use homonyms, homophones, and homographs. *Journal of Adolescent & Adult Literacy, 51*(2), 98–111.

Johnson, E. S., & Smith, L. (2008). Implementation of response to intervention at middle school: Challenges and potential benefits. *Teaching Exceptional Children, 40,* 46–52.

Kiefer, M. J., & Lesaux, N. K. (2008, March). *English-language learners' growth in morphological awareness and vocabulary: A longitudinal analysis.* Paper presented at the annual meeting of the American Educational Research Association, New York, NY.

Kim, A., Vaughn, S., Klingner, J. K., Woodruff, A. L., Reutebuch, C. K., & Kouzekanani, K. (2006). Improving the reading comprehension of middle school students with disabilities through computer-assisted Collaborative Strategic Reading. *Remedial and Special Education, 27,* 235–248.

Kingsley, K. V. (2007). Twenty ways to empower diverse learners with educational technology and digital media. *Intervention in School and Clinic, 43,* 52–56.

Klingner, J. K., & Vaughn, S. (1996). Reciprocal teaching of reading comprehension strategies for students with learning disabilities who use English as a second language. *Elementary School Journal, 96,* 275–293.

Klingner, J. K., & Vaughn, S. (2000). The helping behaviors of bilingual fifth graders during collaborative strategic reading. *TESOL Quarterly, 34,* 61–98.

Klingner, J. K., Vaughn, S., & Schumm, J. S. (1998). Collaborative Strategic Reading in heterogeneous classrooms. *Elementary School Journal, 99,* 3–21.

Knox, C., & Amador-Watson, C. (2002). *Responsive Instruction for Success in English (RISE): Building literacy and content knowledge with English language learners: Participant's resource notebook.* Barrington, IL: Rigby Professional Development.

Komar, S. (2005). *The impact of tones and pitch range on the expression of attitudes in Slovene speakers of English.* Retrieved March 20, 2008, from *www.phon.ucl.ac.uk/home/johnm/ptlc2005/pdf/ptlcp31.pdf.*

Koskinen, P. S., Blum, I. H., Bisson, S. A., Phillips, S. M., Creamer, T. S., & Baker, T. K. (1999). Shared reading, books, and audiotapes: Supporting diverse students in school and at home. *Reading Teacher, 52*(5), 430–444.

Lenz, B. K., & Deshler, D. D. (2004). *Teaching content to all: Evidence-based inclusive practices in middle and secondary schools.* Boston: Allyn & Bacon.

Lester, B. T. (2008). *Standard English language acquisition among African American vernacular English speaking adolescents: A modified guided reading study.* Unpublished doctoral dissertation, University of Miami, Coral Gables, FL.

Meier, T. (2003). "Why can't she remember that?": The importance of storybook reading in multilingual, multicultural classrooms. *Reading Teacher, 57*(3), 242–252.

Moody, S. W., Vaughn, S., & Schumm, J. S. (1997). Instructional grouping for reading: Teacher's views. *Remedial and Special Education, 18,* 347–356.

National Center for Education Statistics. (2006). *Participation in education: Elementary/secondary education: Indicator 6. Concentration of enrollment by race/ethnicity and poverty.* Retrieved March 8, 2008, from *nces.ed.gov/programs/coe/2006/section1/indicator06.asp.*

National Center for Education Statistics. (2007a). *U.S. Department of Commerce, Census Bureau, Current Population Survey, October Supplement, 1972–2005.* Retrieved March 8, 2008, from *nces.ed.gov/programs/coe/2007/section1/table.asp?tableid=667.*

National Center for Education Statistics. (2007b). *U.S. Department of Commerce, Census Bureau, Current Population Survey, 1979 and 1989 November Supplement and 1992, 1995, and 1999 October Supplement, and American Community Survey, 2000–05.* Retrieved March 8, 2008, from *nces.ed.gov/programs/coe/2007/section1/table.asp?tableid=668.*

National Center for Education Statistics. (2007c). *Participation in education: Elementary/secondary education, Indicator 6, Language minority school-age children.* Retrieved March 8, 2008, from *nces.ed.gov/programs/coe/2007/section1/indicator06.asp.*

National Center for Education Statistics. (2007d). *Status and trends in the education of racial and ethnic minorities: Indicator 10. Reading and mathematics achievement.* Retrieved March 8, 2008, from *nces.ed.gov/pubs2007/minoritytrends/ind_3_10.asp.*

National Reading Panel. (2000). *Report of the National Reading Panel: Teaching children to read: An evidence-based assessment of the scientific research literature on reading and its implications for reading instruction.* Washington, DC: National Institute on Child Health and Human Development.

Nunley, K. F. (2006). *Differentiating the high school curriculum.* Thousand Oaks, CA: Corwin.

Palincsar, A. S., & Brown, A. L. (1984). Reciprocal teaching of comprehension-fostering and comprehension-monitoring activities. *Cognition and Instruction, 1,* 117–175.

Pew Research Center. (2008). *U.S. population projections: 2005–2050.* Retrieved March 8, 2008, from *pewhispanic.org/files/reports/85.pdf.*

Reis, S., & Renzulli, J. (1992). Using curriculum compacting to challenge the above average. *Educational Leadership, 50,* 51–57.

Rock, M. L., Gregg, M., Ellis, E., & Gable, R. A. (2008). REACH: A framework for differentiated classroom instruction. *Preventing School Failure, 52,* 31–47.

Rose, D. H., & Meyer, A. (2002). *Teaching every student in the digital age: Universal Design for Learning.* Alexandria, VA: Association for Supervision and Curriculum Development.

Schumm, J. S., & Arguelles, M. E. (2006). No two learners learn alike: The importance of assessment and differentiated instruction. In. J. S. Schumm (Ed.), *Reading assessment and instruction for all learners* (pp. 27–58). New York: Guilford Press.

Schumm, J. S., & Vaughn, S. (1991). Making adaptations for mainstreamed students: General classroom teachers' perceptions. *Remedial and Special Education, 12,* 18–27.

Schumm, J. S., Vaughn, S., & Elbaum, B. E. (1996). Teachers' perceptions of grouping practices for reading instruction. In D. J. Leu, C. K. Kinzer, & K. A. Hinchman (Eds.), *Literacies for the 21st century: Research and practice* (pp. 543–551). Chicago: National Reading Conference.

Schumm, J. S., Vaughn, S., & Harris, J. (1997). Pyramid power for collaborative planning. *Teaching Exceptional Children, 29*(6), 62–66.

Schumm, J. S., Vaughn, S., & Leavell, A. G. (1994). Planning Pyramid: A framework for planning for diverse student needs during content area instruction. *The Reading Teacher, 47,* 2–10.

Schumm, J. S., Vaughn, S., & Moody, S. W. (2000). Grouping for reading instruction: Does one size fit all? *Journal of Learning Disabilities, 33,* 477–488.

Schumm, J. S., Vaughn, S., & Saumell, L. (1992). What teachers do when the textbook is tough: Students speak out. *Journal of Reading Behavior, 24,* 481–503.

Schumm, J. S., Vaughn, S., & Saumell, L. (1994). Assisting students with difficult textbooks: Teacher perceptions and practice. *Reading Research and Instruction, 34,* 39–56.

Singer, H., & Donlan, D. (1985). *Reading and learning from text.* Hillsdale, NJ: Erlbaum.

Snow, C. E. (2002). *Reading for understanding: Toward an R&D program in reading comprehension.* Santa Monica, CA: RAND Corporation.

Staff Development for Educators. (2006). *Differentiated instruction.* Retrieved May 1, 2007, from *differentiatedinstruction.com.*

Starr, L. (2004). *Differentiated instruction.* Education World. Retrieved May 1, 2007, from *www.education-world.com/a_curr/strategy/strategy042.shtml.*

Tomlinson, C. A. (1995a). *Differentiating instruction for advanced learners in the mixed-ability middle school classroom.* Retrieved March 8, 2008, from *www.lausd.k12.ca.us/lausd/offices/di/burleson/workshops/differntiate/ecdigest_e536.htm* (ERIC EC Digest #E536).

Tomlinson, C. A. (1995b). *How to differentiate instruction in mixed-ability classrooms.* Alexandria, VA: Association for Supervision and Curriculum Development.

Tomlinson, C. A. (2000). Reconcilable differences?: Standards-based teaching and differentiation. *Educational Leadership, 58,* 6–11.

Tomlinson, C. A. (2001). *How to differentiated instruction in mixed-ability classrooms* (2nd ed). Alexandria, VA: Association for Supervision and Curriculum Development.

Tomlinson, C. A. (2003). *Fulfilling the promise of the differentiated classroom: Strategies and tools for responsive teaching.* Alexandria, VA: Association for Supervision and Curriculum Development.

Tomlinson, C. A., Brighton, C., Hertberg, H., Callahan, C. M., Moon, T. R., Brimijoin, K., et al. (2003). Differentiating instruction in response to student readiness, interest, and learning profile in academically diverse classrooms: A review of the literature. *Journal for the Education of the Gifted, 27,* 145–199.

Tompkins, G. E. (2006). *Literacy for the 21st century: A balanced approach* (4th ed.). Upper Saddle River, NJ: Pearson, Merrill/Prentice-Hall.

U.S. Department of Education. (2005). *Twenty-sixth annual report to Congress on IDEA.* Washington, DC: Author.

Van Garderen, D., & Whittaker, C. (2006). Planning differentiated, multicultural instruction for secondary inclusive classrooms. *Teaching Exceptional Children, 38,* 12–20.

Van Tassel-Baska, J. (2003). *Curriculum planning and instructional design for gifted learners.* Denver, CO: Love.

Van Tassel-Baska, J., Quek, C., & Feng, A. X. (2007). The development and use of a structured teacher observation scale to assess differentiated best practice. *Roeper Review, 29,* 84–92.

Vaughn, S., & Klingner, J. K. (2007). Overview of the three-tier model of reading intervention. In D. Haager, J. K. Klingner, & S. Vaughn (Eds.), *Evidence-based reading practices for response to intervention* (pp. 3–11). Baltimore: Brookes.

Vaughn, S., Klingner, J. K., & Bryant, D. (2001). Collaborative strategic reading as a means to enhance peer-mediated instruction in reading comprehension and content area reading. *Remedial and Special Education, 22,* 66–74.

Vaughn, S., & Schumm, J. S. (1995). Responsible inclusion for students with learning disabilities. *Journal of Learning Disabilities, 28*(5), 264–270, 290.

Vaughn, S., Schumm, J. S., Klingner, J. K., & Saumell, L. (1995). Students' views of instructional practices: Implications for inclusion. *Learning Disability Quarterly, 18*(3), 236–248.

Viadero, D. (2007). Study: Low, high fliers gain less under NCLB. *Education Week, 44,* 7.

Walpole, S., & McKenna, M. C. (2007). *Differentiated reading instruction: Strategies for the primary grades.* New York: Guilford Press.

Weinbrenner, S. (2001). *Teaching gifted kids in the regular classroom.* Minneapolis: Free Spirit.

Werderich, D. E. (2002). Individualized responses: Using journal letters as a vehicle for differentiated reading instruction. *Journal of Adolescent & Adult Literacy, 45*(8), 746–754.

Wormeli, R. (2006). Differentiating for tweens. *Educational Leadership, 63*(7), 14–19.

Ysseldyke, J., & Bolt, D. M. (2007). Effect of technology-enhanced progress monitoring on math achievement. *School Psychology Review, 36,* 453–467.

Zipoli, R. P., Coyne, M. D., & McCoach, D. B. (2008, March). *Enhancing vocabulary intervention for kindergarten students with semantically related and embedded word review.* Paper presented at the annual meeting of the American Educational Research Association, New York, NY.

Chapter 9

Engaging Texts and Literacy Practices for Adolescent Boys

William G. Brozo
Courtney Gaskins

GUIDING QUESTIONS

1. Why should teachers of youth pay special attention to boys' literacy development?
2. What is the relationship between reading engagement, academic achievement, and life and career opportunities for adolescent boys?
3. How are principles of reading engagement turned into effective practices for reluctant and low-ability male readers?

In Sam Cooke's 1960 hit "Wonderful World," a boy sings a refrain with a message that seems almost quaint nearly 50 years on. The young man in the song is working hard to become an academic standout to make himself worthy of a girl's affection. The singer actually believes he will become more attractive through reading, writing, and study. Love may be a powerful motivator, but it is doubtful the messages in popular songs and media today are telling male youth that if they want a girl's attention, they need to get better grades.

So what motivates boys to become better readers and better students? We take up this question in this chapter by exploring principles of reading and learning engagement for adolescent males. Buttressing the principles are practical envisionments of a teacher in an alternative high school, working with male youth to increase motivation and achievement.

Reading Engagement:
Research-Based Principles and Practices

What is reading engagement? In general it is the extent to which one has a positive regard toward reading, seeks out texts, and makes time to read. It comprises many variables, including interest, choice, and self-efficacy. Engagement has been found to be a critical variable in reading achievement (Brozo, Shiel, & Topping, 2007; Guthrie & Humenick, 2004).

Evidence for the benefits of engaged reading is quite compelling (Moje, 2006). Correlational data derived from the National Assessment of Educational Progress (NAEP) in the United States show that adolescents who identified themselves as being interested in reading not only achieved better scores on the NAEP but also had better high school grade point averages than their less interested peers (Donahue, Daane, & Grigg, 2003). Engaged reading leads to frequent print encounters, which improve reading skill and increase educational, professional, and civic opportunities for male youth (National Endowment for the Arts, 2007). For boys of color in particular, it has been shown that the longer they remain engaged academically, the higher the status they achieve in labor markets (Sum, 2007).

Reading engagement is also important to the maintenance and further development of reading skills beyond adolescence. The International Adult Literacy Survey found that reading skills can deteriorate after the completion of initial education if they are not used (Organisation for Economic Cooperation and Development & Statistics Canada, 1995). In other words, engagement in reading is a predictor of learning success throughout life. Guthrie and Wigfield (2000) assert that "as students become engaged readers, they provide themselves with self-generated learning opportunities that are equivalent to several years of education" (p. 204).

Engagement may be a particularly potent variable in the reading and academic lives of boys. Lack of engagement with literacy appears to be one of the most significant factors in accounting for boys' lower attainment in relation to girls (Frater, 1998). We know that boys of all ages fail in reading more often than do girls, and dominate the rolls in corrective and remedial reading programs (Gambell & Hunter, 1999). This same pattern holds true in programs for the learning disabled, the emotionally impaired, and the speech and language impaired (Harmon, 1992). Furthermore, boys are far more likely to be retained at grade level (Byrd & Weitzman, 1994).

In spite of what we know about the importance of gaining and sustaining students' attention to reading and learning, teachers of youth need ways to retard or even reverse the well-documented slump in achievement and motivation during the upper elementary and middle school years (Anderman, Maehr, & Midgley, 1999; Brozo, 2005a). The fallout from this slump appears to affect boys disproportionately (Alliance for Excellent Education, 2007; Brozo, 2002) and has the most negative consequences for boys of color (Fashola,

2005). In the following pages, we present five principles of engagement, with support from the professional literature. We assert that when used as guideposts for practice, these principles offer great promise for capturing boys' literate imaginations, and gaining and holding their attention. Along with a general discussion of these principles are scenes of teaching from a classroom in an alternative high school. The teacher Courtney Gaskins describes from a first-person perspective strategies that have proven effective in bringing behaviorally and learning challenged boys into the flow of instruction, and heightening their enthusiasm for reading and learning.

Principle 1: Elevate Self-Efficacy

School-related self-efficacy is the belief and confidence that one has the knowledge and skills to accomplish meaningful tasks and produce a desired result in academic settings. The research literature makes evident that students with a belief in their own capacity to achieve are more engaged and motivated than are students with low self-efficacy (Pajares, 1996). Teachers can create the conditions in classrooms that increase their male students' perceptions of competence, leading to sustained effort and a greater likelihood of academic success (Schunk & Zimmerman, 1997). Practices such as introducing new content in novel ways (Brozo & Simpson, 2007), creating numerous collaborative learning opportunities (Margolis & McCabe, 2004), allowing access to a range of interesting and readable texts (Brozo & Hargis, 2003; Ivey & Broaddus, 2001), connecting to everyday literacies of youth (Alvermann, 2003), and giving youth choices (Protheroe, 2004) may have an especially beneficial effect on adolescent boys' perceptions of themselves as readers and learners (Brozo, 2002; Tatum, 2005).

Building Self-Efficacy for Boys in a High School Classroom

Over the years, I have learned to use teaching styles that are more suited for boys and that keep them engaged in the learning process. Prior to my teaching at an alternative setting I was not well versed in the role boys' specific emotional and social needs play in academic settings, and often handled these needs inappropriately. Unfortunately, I tended to respond with punishment, often further exacerbating academic failure, low self-esteem, and other emotional and behavioral problems. I believe this lack of understanding of boys contributes to a cycle of failure and labeling, which stigmatizes boys as "troublemakers" or "hyperactive."

Fraser, a 16-year-old African American male, had been a student of mine several years earlier. He came to our school reading at a fourth-grade level. Fraser was raised by a single mother and ended up at our residential facility because of truancy and his mother's inability to deal effectively with his behavior. Fraser was extremely immature for his age and had attention problems, as well as a poor self-image regarding his academic failures. Fraser read with difficulty, often leaving words out or substituting words beginning with the same letter as the word he was having difficulty reading. When it came to reading or writing, especially copying notes from the board or writing down terms from the textbook, Fraser would refuse to participate and would often misbehave, until he was asked to leave the room. There were times when I would almost force Fraser to read or to copy notes from the board. I learned that reading and writing for Fraser were frustrating tasks that immediately led to disengagement. Not until I began to identify and to supply him reading materials at the fourth- or fifth-grade reading level did I begin to see a change in Fraser's attitude toward his own abilities as a learner and his classroom engagement. Fraser was extremely eager to engage in learning when I introduced books on tape, or used films or visual aids to introduce concepts, prior to reading short excerpts from his classroom text.

In addition, Fraser's participation increased considerably when I used a question–answer format in which he could showcase his new knowledge with his peers. Even when Fraser answered three or four questions incorrectly, he would remain engaged the entire period. Fraser's enthusiasm would often rub off on other students. At the end of the class, I would have Fraser write a brief summary of what he had answered incorrectly. It was then that Fraser wrote out the assignment with little or no defiance, because he believed that writing down things he did not know made more sense than writing down things he knew.

During Fraser's second year at my school, I introduced him to Inspiration software, which is a visual thinking and learning tool. Inspiration allowed Fraser to organize the information from class using outlines and to develop story maps. He was also allowed to search for information on the Internet related to topics discussed in class, and to use concept mapping or diagramming to organize the information. Because Fraser would speak out in class about the new information he was learning on the Internet, and because of his experience with the Inspiration software, I would have him present this information to the class on a regular basis using printable graphic organizers. I would also have him read his summaries aloud, along with excerpts from the text he had been reading.

After being at our school for 2 years, Fraser's reading fluency and comprehension improved by three grade levels. In the spring, prior to leaving our school, Fraser passed three of his standardized tests—one in reading, the others in earth science and history. Not until I began to allow Fraser to use his strengths, such as his strong auditory skills, did Fraser become a more engaged, willing participant in literacy development activities.

Principle 2: Engender Interest in New Reading

If there is one assertion the literature allows us to make about reading engagement, it's that students will expend the energy necessary to learn if they are interested in the material (Eccles, Wigfield, & Schiefele, 1998; Guthrie &

Humenick, 2004; Mosenthal, 1999). This may be especially true for adolescent boys who are disconnected from school, or who struggle to keep up with the demands of academic reading (Brozo, 2002). High-interest reading material captures boys' imaginations, sustains attention, and contributes to higher reading achievement (Sokal et al., 2005). Teachers who engage students take the time to make schoolwork interesting and fun, and this is recognized and appreciated by the boys (A. J. Martin, 2003).

Boys contribute significantly to a nationwide, and perhaps even a worldwide, decline in the interest of youth in print literacy, both for pleasure and for school purposes (Baker, 2002; Brozo, 2005a; Dreher, 2003). Compared with their female peers, adolescent males spend less time reading, read a narrower range of texts, and have less favorable attitudes toward reading in general (Brozo et al., 2007). Teachers who understand the importance of interest as a motivator for reading and learning prepare students for new texts with engaging strategies (Brozo & Simpson, 2007), demonstrate how the content of the reading material can relate to the lives and concerns of the youth (Bean, 2002), and provide multiple opportunities for youth to enjoy reading and learning (Ogle, 2003). These approaches to gaining interest in new reading have been found to be particularly effective with male youth of color (Tatum, 2005).

Engendering Interest in New Reading for Boys in a High School Classroom

Boys have a unique learning style that is different from that of girls. Research suggests that whereas many girls may prefer to learn by observing and listening, boys prefer to learn by doing, by engaging in some active task (Sax, 2007).

During my first year teaching at a residential facility, I had a student named Keith, who was so resistant to reading books in class that he would literally toss them across the room. Keith, a 15-year-old European American male, came to my school reading at a third-grade level. Even sitting at the computer was a frustrating task for Keith, because he could not read many of the words on the screen, and he had difficulty typing in words correctly to search for information. After several weeks, I learned that Keith's motivation to read increased when the pages had colored pictures. Keith would often spend an entire class period flipping through popular magazines I had brought from home. From a conversation I heard between Keith and another student in the hallway, I found out that he was interested in baseball. I sent out an all-recipients e-mail at my school, asking that individuals bring in sports magazines. With these new resources in hand, I soon learned that Keith's favorite team was the Baltimore Orioles. I spent the next week teaching him to spell *Orioles*, so that he could search for the team on the Internet, and to write out in a spiral notebook all of the baseball teams in the National Baseball League (NBL) and their home cities. I also showed Keith how to find baseball scores in the local newspaper. Every day during baseball season, Keith would copy the team names, the associated cities, and the scores in his spiral notebook. He then learned how to search the NBL website to find various teams' scores, using the information written in his notebook.

The following year, Keith started a new notebook on the National Football League (NFL) and the National Basketball Association (NBA). He began to copy information from the newspaper and the Internet about players and coaches. I then introduced Keith to series books on sports figures. Keith would bring stacks of these short, content-rich books to my classroom and copy information from them into his notebooks.

I remember pulling the cards from a sports Trivial Pursuit game and was amazed at the number of facts that Keith could recite. When Keith learned about my past interest in boxing, he and I would have lengthy conversations about boxers during the 1970s and 1980s. He then began a notebook on boxing. This exercise went on for almost 2 years and extended to Keith's academic course work. Keith began keeping spiral notebooks in all of his classes, even copying or gluing in handouts.

My effectiveness as a teacher increased when I found a way to spark Keith's interest in reading by making him aware of and giving him access to texts about sports. Students like Keith need to discover that reading can be an enjoyable and informative activity, one that engages their imaginations and leads to sustained effort and higher achievement.

Principle 3: Connect Outside-School with Inside-School Literacies

Many students are disinterested in school-based reading and writing but highly engaged and competent in literate activities outside of school (Alvermann, 2003). Unfortunately, students' everyday skills and abilities with literacy are not always sanctioned in academic settings (Moje, 2002). Disengagement may be due as much to unresponsive curricular and instructional practices as to students' inherent lack of motivation or laziness. Sturtevant and her colleagues (2006) argue that "by eliminating barriers between students' competencies with outside-of-school texts and classroom practices it is possible to increase engagement in learning and expand literacy abilities (p. 111).

Youth who are disconnected from academic life and are aliterate within the domain of school-related reading may in many ways engage in active literacy practices at home and in their communities. For example, outside of school, youth have been documented to find and read "cheat codes" for playing computer and video games, to read comic books and graphic novels, to read magazines related to their hobbies (skateboarding, collecting, sports), to listen to music and to read and write song lyrics, to write text- and instant-messages with cell phones and other handhelds, and to participate in chat rooms and blogs (Hinchman, Alvermann, Boyd, Brozo, & Vacca, 2003/2004; Williams, 2005).

Motivating disengaged and struggling boys to read and to learn in school settings may be possible by tapping into their everyday, multiliteracy practices (Brozo & Simpson, 2007; Smith & Wilhelm, 2002) and making connections between the texts and media they use in their worlds and academic texts (Brozo, 2006; Tatum, 2006). By exploring innovative ways to motivate male youth to become academically engaged, linking everyday literacies with traditional textbook reading and print media, teachers build boys' capacity and efficacy as learners (Alvermann, 2001; Brozo, 2002).

Connecting Outside- and Inside-School Literacies for Boys in a High School Classroom

Over the years, by partnering, I have learned to address who boys really are and what they really need. I take time to learn about their outside-school interests, such as the music they listen to, their career plans, the subjects they enjoy most, and their outside reading interests. Often, we spend the last 5–10 minutes of class time listening to their music, discussing musicians and television shows, and downloading movies or songs and computer game cheat sheets. Many of my students comment to me that this is the first time a teacher has shown an interest in what they enjoy outside of the classroom.

Several years ago, I devoted an entire summer reading and writing class to my students' favorite music artists. At the start of class, I had them list their top 10 singers, performers, and groups. We then spent 2 weeks just writing down all the information they knew about these individuals (e.g., where they grew up, the types of songs they sang, whether they wrote their own music), and stories (fact or fiction) about these individuals that the boys found in the news and entertainment magazines. Raging debates took place in the classroom regarding information that one student thought was a "lie" to what others knew as fact because "my cousin's friend was there" or a "guy in my neighborhood met" so and so. Many of my students were surprised by how much they could write, without even looking up these individuals on the Internet.

One of my students, Juan, was extremely interested in Latino music. He was the only Latino in my class at the time, and many of the artists he mentioned were unfamiliar to the other students. I was surprised to learn that my students, who usually were unwilling to listen or discuss anything other than rap music, wanted to learn about Juan's Latino music. All of the music that Juan introduced to the class was in Spanish, unintelligible to his classmates, but they listened as though they understood every word. With my help, Juan was able to translate into English on the whiteboard what the Latinos were singing. Then he would help his classmates pronounce the Spanish lyrics, enabling most of them to learn the chorus and sing along when we played the music in class.

We spent the next several weeks reading the truths and the lies associated with the musicians and writing about their lives. Students spent most of the summer learning processes for organizing the information. Students wrote expository, descriptive, and persuasive essays on 2 of the 10 artists they had selected as their favorites. Students used a one-page graphic organizer to develop and organize each paragraph containing nine empty blocks, in which they were to write six to nine sentences on one topic, such as the artist's hometown, childhood experiences, and so forth. Once students had written several sentences based on what they knew and what they had gathered from reading, each student easily filled all nine blocks with complete sentences. Often we would spend days developing students' sentences in each block, using the thesaurus and the dictionary to expand on their thoughts. Finally, we spent several days organizing these sentences into paragraphs. After students had filled 7 and sometimes up to 10 graphic organizers with information, they were surprised to realize they had written a 5- to 6-page essay on their chosen artists.

One of my more challenging students at that time was Carlos, who complained throughout the entire process. But after leaving my school, he returned a few years later and admitted that the work we had done—learning how to organize information and to draw on what he knew to research new topics—helped him get through writing his 12th-grade research paper. He realized how essential it was to choose a topic of interest and to begin by writing about something familiar.

This process not only helped the boys in my summer class expand their writing skills but it also helping me to acknowledge students' experiences outside of school. I witnessed these young men developing academically, feeling positive about their writing abilities, and developing a healthy sense of being learners.

Principle 4: Make an Abundance of Interesting Texts Available

On the National Assessment of Educational Progress (NAEP; Donahue et al., 2003) only 31% of U.S. eighth graders and 34% of 12th graders reported reading for enjoyment on a regular basis. A sizable percentage of students reported reading for fun only on a monthly or yearly basis, or not at all. Furthermore, adolescent males in the United States and across the globe are not reading as many different kinds of texts or as often as their female peers (Brozo et al., 2007).

What accounts for this phenomenon? Perhaps youth are turning to other media that they find more enjoyable than traditional print. These media may entail fairly sophisticated forms of literacy, but they are not easily accounted for on surveys such as those employed on the NAEP or the Programme for International Student Assessment (PISA).

An alternative explanation may be that the types of texts youth generally encounter in school have a negative influence on their attitudes toward reading. The books that youth prefer to read are rarely available in school libraries or included as instructional resources by teachers (Worthy, Moorman, & Turner, 1999; Ivey & Broaddus, 2001). This means most, if not all, of the print encounters youth have in classrooms and libraries may be with texts they are required to read, not texts of their own choosing. School-related texts can be difficult and uninspiring, reinforcing reluctant and struggling students' negative attitudes toward reading, and explaining in part why so many students indicated on the NAEP survey that they read for enjoyment so infrequently (Brozo & Simpson, 2007).

Since most of the required reading in middle and secondary schools is within the class textbook (Alexander & Jetton, 2000), teachers are urged to make textbook topics more interesting by using alternative texts, such as novels, graphic novels, topical magazines, and informational text (Brozo & Simpson, 2007; Franzak, 2006; Sullivan, 2001). Teachers are also urged to commit to ensuring that boys have access to high-interest reading material, because it leads to improvement in motivation and achievement (Lenters, 2007; Sokal et al., 2005). Stocking school and classroom libraries with a variety of interesting texts related to a host of topics at a wide range of difficulty levels, creating opportunities for self-selection of texts, and structuring time for sustained print encounters makes it possible for all youth to experience the pleasure of reading and learning (Brozo & Hargis, 2003; R. Martin, 2003; Sullivan, 2003).

Making an Abundance of Interesting Texts Available for Boys in a High School Classroom

Reading magazines or searching the Internet motivates most of the boys I teach. These resources allow students to be active, to flip through pages or to scroll through web content. I have also seen boys identified as "lazy" in the classroom become active and proficient readers when their teachers gave them reading material on subjects that interested them, such as sports, adventure stories, and murder mysteries. Most critically, I believe I am the best teacher I can be when I match instructional practices with the needs and interests of the boys in my classroom, making it possible for them to thrive academically and socially.

When I search for text that is relevant to class topics, I have to know a great deal about my students' personal interests, as well as their reading abilities or levels. I selected resources because of not only individual interests but also the various "communities" to which my students belong, inside and outside of the classroom. I typically look for these texts in our school library and on the Internet but have often had to visit local used bookstores and to schedule visits with local librarians. I also encourage my students to visit public libraries and bookstores to find material of interest to them.

Several years ago I had a student named Giles, an extremely troubled young man who typically kept to himself. If he interacted with anyone at school, then it was with an adult; very rarely did I ever find him in conversation with his peers. Giles had been in the foster care system for over 11 years, and our facility was his eighth placement in 5 years. Giles, was about to turn 18, ready to "sign" himself out of "the system" and school. Test results indicated a basic reading level of about 5th grade, but his overall achievement was as high as 10th grade.

Often, Giles and I would have deep, high-level conversations about life, and about topics in science and math. He had an extensive vocabulary, which he used more often in conversation than in his writing. When I talked with Giles about his vocabulary knowledge, he said that because he had a difficult time spelling many of the words he wanted to use, he typically chose words he knew how to spell in his compositions. I loaned him a pocket dictionary and Silverthorne and Perry's (1984) *Word Division Manual.* I also found a composition notebook that we tabbed alphabetically, so that Giles could record the words he had difficulty spelling and defining.

Giles's first semester at our school was rough; by its end he was failing all of his classes. This meant that he would not graduate in the spring, and greatly increased the likelihood of Giles signing himself out when he turned 18. Giles had a deep interest in Wicca (a pagan, nature-based religion) and had at his last placement developed several friendships with other students around his interest in the cult. He spent much of his class time reading books on the subject and writing letters to friends who shared his new belief. One of the reasons Giles had a difficult time developing friendships at our school was that none of the students were even remotely interested in Wicca, even after Giles for weeks attempted to bring others into his way of thinking.

During one of our discussions, I began to realize that Giles's interest was mainly in the philosophical and ethical teachings of Wicca. He liked the idea of debating issues and thinking deeply about subjects of great interest, especially those having to do with injustice. I started to turn many of our discussions to Western philosophy, such as the beliefs of John Locke, René Descartes, and Machiavelli. I made available to him several high-interest/low-level reading resources about these men and their philosophies. Giles and I looked at the indices of his classroom textbooks, and I showed him where these scholars and philosophers were most often found in history and literature books, and discussed their influence on American thought.

Eventually Giles wanted to read the original works, and he visited a local bookstore, where he found old, used copies. I introduced Giles to ideas of social justice and environmental and global issues that were prominent in newspapers and magazine. Finally, I made available readings and Internet sites that appealed to Giles's growing interest in various philosophies. He still had difficulty with the language and vocabulary, and often I would see him writing down these words in his vocabulary notebook. Giles also spent hours flipping through *Time, U.S.A. Today,* and other periodicals and journals, looking for influences of the thinking of these philosophers on current events. He started to see the value of history, language arts, science, and mathematics as means to promote a particular philosophy or idea.

Giles even began to share his views of social justice with other students, and he found many students who shared his beliefs and viewpoints. This enabled him to develop socially, as well as academically. Although Giles never became fully engaged in classroom learning, he passed all of his classes and graduated.

By being ensured access to interesting texts that had meaning for him, Giles was able to attain the learning tools he needed to remain in school and accomplish an important academic goal. Many of the texts Giles read in pursuit of his interest in philosophers and their influence on modern ideas were content-oriented, allowing him to engage in meaningful and critical reading of a wide range of texts. These interactions with text helped him to develop analytical skills, such as comparing and contrasting information, and interpreting and integrating differing viewpoints. Giles also learned to seek out on his own texts, similar to those I was sharing with him, in a process of discovery through self-selected reading.

Principle 5: Expand Student Choices and Options

As students enter preteen and teen years, their choices about many things outside of school increase significantly, yet options for them in school remain limited. Choice may be one of the most critical elements of reading motivation (Guthrie & Davis, 2003; Turner, 1995). A. J. Martin (2003) found that teachers who provide boys with choices are particularly valued, because it signifies to male students that the teacher respects them, and they develop a sense of ownership of what they are reading and studying.

Studies of gender-based reading choices (Doiron, 2003; Simpson, 1996) have revealed that girls read more than boys, mostly narrative fiction, whereas boys read less, but much more nonfiction, informational text. When asked to choose an informational book, boys appear to have a much easier time finding a book of interest (Simpson, 1996). Observing the same phenomenon, Coles and Hall (2002) suggest that "schools should recognize and value the type of information-rich reading that boys undertake away from school and should provide links between it and the socially oriented reading, preferred by girls, that makes up much of the English school curriculum" (p. 96).

Allowing adolescent males more input into curricular decision making and choice over what they read in academic settings can increase their sense of agency, heighten engagement (Brozo, 2005b), and build competence (Booth, 2002; Williams, 2005). Many researchers have documented the benefits of acquiring students' input into classroom practices and materials, then giving them choices based on this input. Youth feel empowered and motivated to participate constructively in their education when invited to help choose how and what they learn (Cook-Sather, 2002) and read (Hoffman, Boraks, & Bauer, 2000). Teachers who gather critical information that helps them better appreciate the lifeworlds of youth make their teaching more responsive to the experiences and perspectives of youth (Cook-Sather, 2003; Lee, 1999; Slade & Trent, 2000).

Expanding Student Choices and Options
for Boys in a High School Classroom

As a classroom teacher, I examine factors affecting my students' literacy practices and text choices on a daily basis. I become informed as I listen to the statements and conversations in my classroom, and as I notice the books, magazines, and Internet sites my students peruse throughout each day. I also have had opportunities to discuss with my students how their family and social support networks affect their choices in selecting various reading materials. The influence of social power and problem solving on their literacy choices in both peer and family contexts is evident. For example, I have witnessed students reading certain books or selecting certain magazines as a result of peer or family suggestions. I have found that most of my students need these support networks in their literacy choices.

Several of my students depend more on me to help them develop their literacy choices and options, such as Giles, discussed previously, who in some ways had lost the social network that supported his literacy choices and had to rely on his teacher to help him reengage or develop new interest. Another student of mine, Jon, a young man who I found learned best by reading alone in a quiet place, was 15 when he arrived in my class. Even though both his parents were high school dropouts and often referred to themselves as "illiterate" in meetings, Jon was a stronger reader than his background might predict. He read only slightly below grade level.

When we first met, Jon exhibited extremely hyperactive behaviors that most of the other students in my class could barely tolerate. He had a hard time sitting in his seat for long periods of time and would often find himself looking out the window during class, without even realizing it. On one of those rare occasions for teachers, I found myself in the classroom with Jon as my only student. His other classmates were off on a field trip with one of my colleagues, and Jon, because of his unwelcome behavior, was not permitted to go. He and I decided to go to the library and restack the piles of books that had accumulated on tables. Our library, although very extensive given the size of our school, lacked a librarian.

As Jon and I began to work, he wanted to talk about every book he picked up, saying things like "I know who Einstein was," "Ms. Gaskins, I didn't know we had a book on Michael Jordan," and "I remember learning about Rosa Parks on the bus." I asked Jon how often he visited the library, and he replied, "Oh, all the time, but I keep getting kicked out." I stopped what we were doing and asked Jon if he knew how many books we had on the National Association for Stock Car Auto Racing (NASCAR; knowing this to be his favorite topic). He said, "Probably none." I grinned as we began looking up NASCAR in the computerized catalog, where we found eight titles. I wrote down the call numbers and was surprised to see Jon go straight to the area containing the books on cars and drivers. He pulled all of them out and sat on the floor, looking like someone who had just hit the jackpot. He had six books on drivers, including one on Dale Earnhardt, one on NASCAR cars, and another about how to draw racing cars. As Jon began flipping through them, I left him alone and returned to stacking books.

After about 10–15 minutes of reading, Jon would take a break, walk around the room, then go back to his pile of books. Initially, I thought he was simply looking at the pictures, but I watched as his eyes moved down the page. I already knew that Jon worked best when he was given short breaks and allowed to get up from his seat, to get water from the fountain in the hall, to run an errand to the office or go to the restroom.

I also learned that Jon retained the information he learned from reading if given the opportunity to discuss the information afterward. As he read his NASCAR books, I asked him questions. Never turning to address me directly, but keeping his eyes locked to the page, Jon gave meaningful answers to all of them. By the time the period was over, Jon had spent at least 10 minutes on each book, even pulling a piece of paper from the printer in the library and attempting to draw his first NASCAR automobile. As I walked Jon to his next class, he began telling me about his family's history and interest in NASCAR. His dad was a mechanic, and Jon himself hoped to be a mechanic someday for NASCAR.

Once Jon discovered the library and what it had to offer, he would often ask my permission to go to the library to read for the last 10 minutes of class. If the library had other students present, Jon would bring a book back, and sit in the hallway and read. Other teachers began to use the library as a reward to get Jon to settle down, which in most cases worked.

Jon's story reminds us the importance of expanding choices and options for adolescent males to ensure they find texts that appeal to them. Jon's appetite for books about auto racing kept him reading and returning to these texts time after time. For students like Jon, who otherwise struggle with both reading and writing, tapping into their existing interest is essential to increase their motivation, as well as their literacy skills and abilities.

A Final Word about Engaging Male Youth in Reading and Learning

Because teen and preteen boys are at the greatest risk of turning off to reading, teachers need principled practices that keep boys engaged. It has been shown that engaged readers can achieve at high levels, in spite of risk factors such as low family income and lack of parental education (Brozo et al., 2007). Engaged and active readers are more likely to stay the course in school, and to be more successful in their personal and community lives (Hofstetter, Sticht, & Hofstetter, 1999; National Endowment for the Arts, 2007), as well as in the work world (Herbert, 2007). Practices guided by the five principles of engaged reading and learning outlined in this chapter made a positive change in the literacy development of Fraser, Keith, Juan, Giles, and Jon, adolescent males who attended an alternative high school, and can make a difference in the lives of boys in schools and classrooms across the country. As the teacher in the alternative school discovered, not all boys will become academic standouts, but if they feel that teachers care enough to make reading and learning interesting, are willing to try to understand them and help them connect with books and print, and hold high but attainable literacy expectations for them, they will become readers and remain engaged.

QUESTIONS FOR DISCUSSION

1. What indicators of reading disengagement have you seen in the boys with whom you interact?

2. What practices have you used to capture boys' reading imaginations and sustain their attention to text?

3. Based on this chapter, what new practices might you employ to motivate disengaged male readers?

4. How can you collaborate with colleagues and literacy coaches to increase your knowledge about practices that are more responsive to adolescent males' reading and learning needs?

Resources

Further Readings

Brozo, W. G. (2002). *To be a boy, to be a reader: Engaging teen and preteen boys in active literacy.* Newark, DE: International Reading Association.

Sax, L. (2007). *Boys adrift: The five factors driving the growing epidemic of unmotivated boys and underachieving young men.* New York: Basic Books.

Scieszka, J. (2005). *Guys write for guys read.* New York: Viking.

Tatum, A. W. (2005). *Teaching reading to black adolescent males: Closing the achievement gap.* Portland, ME: Stenhouse.

Websites

www.csse.ca/cje/articles/cje30-2.html—*Canadian Journal of Education* special issue on boys, schooling, and literacy.

mensbiblio.xyonline.net/growingup.html—Growing Up Male.

www.guysread.com—Guys Read created by children's book author, Jon Scieszka.

www.edu.gov.on.ca/eng/document/brochure/meread/meread.pdf—Me Read, No Way.

References

Alexander, P., & Jetton, T. (2000). Learning from text: A multidimensional and developmental perspective. In M. Kamil, P. Mosenthal, P. D. Pearson, & R. Barr (Eds.), *Handbook of reading research* (Vol. 3, pp. 285–310). Mahwah, NJ: Erlbaum.

Alliance for Excellent Education. (2007, January). *The high cost of high school dropouts: What the nation pays for inadequate high schools.* Washington, DC: Author.

Alvermann, D. (2001). *Effective literacy instruction for adolescents* (Executive summary and paper commissioned by the National Reading Conference). Retrieved August 4, 2005, from *nrconline.org/documents/2001/alverwhite2.pdf.*

Alvermann, D. (2003). *Seeing themselves as capable and engaged readers: Adolescents and re/mediated instruction.* Naperville, IL: Learning Point Associates.

Anderman, E. M., Maehr, M. L., & Midgley, C. (1999). Declining motivation after the transition to middle school: Schools can make a difference. *Journal of Research and Development in Education, 32,* 131–147.

Baker, M. I. (2002). Reading resistance in middle school: What can be done? *Journal of Adolescent and Adult Literacy, 45*, 364–366.

Bean, T. W. (2002). Making reading relevant for adolescents. *Educational Leadership, 60*, 34–37.

Booth, D. (2002). *Even hockey players read: Boys, literacy and learning.* Markham, Ontario, Canada: Pembroke.

Brozo, W. G. (2002). *To be a boy, to be a reader: Engaging teen and preteen boys in active literacy.* Newark, DE: International Reading Association.

Brozo, W. G. (2005a). Avoiding the "fourth-grade slump. " *Thinking Classroom/Peremena, 6*, 48–49.

Brozo, W. G. (2005b). It's okay to read, even if other kids don't: Learning about and from boys in a middle school book club. *California Reader, 38*, 5–13.

Brozo, W. G. (2006). Bridges to literacy for boys. *Educational Leadership, 64*, 71–74.

Brozo, W. G., & Hargis, C. (2003). Taking seriously the idea of reform: One high school's efforts to make reading more responsive to all students. *Journal of Adolescent and Adult Literacy, 43*, 14–23

Brozo, W. G., Shiel, G., & Topping, K. (2007). Engagement in reading: Lessons learned from three PISA countries. *Journal of Adolescent & Adult Literacy, 51*, 304–315.

Brozo, W. G., & Simpson, M. L. (2007). *Content literacy for today's adolescents: Honoring diversity and building competence.* Mahwah, NJ: Merrill/Prentice-Hall.

Byrd, R., & Weitzman, M. (1994). Predictors of early grade retention among children in the United States. *Pediatrics, 93*, 481–487.

Coles, M., & Hall, C. (2002, February). Gendered readings: Learning from children's reading choices. *Journal of Research in Reading, 25*(1), 96–108.

Cook-Sather, A. (2002). Authorizing students' perspectives: Toward trust, dialogue, and change in education. *Educational Researcher, 31*, 3–14.

Cook-Sather, A. (2003). Listening to students about learning differences. *Teaching Exceptional Children, 35*, 22–26.

Doiron, R. (2003). Boy books, girl books: Should we re-organize our school library collections? *Teacher Librarian, 30*, 14–16.

Donahue, P., Daane, M., & Grigg, W. (2003). *The nation's report card: Reading highlights 2003.* Washington, DC: National Center for Education Statistics.

Dreher, M. J. (2003). Motivating struggling readers by tapping the potential of information books. *Reading and Writing Quarterly, 19*, 25–38.

Eccles, J. S., Wigfield, A., & Schiefele, U. (1998). Motivation to succeed. In W. Damon (Series Ed.) & N. Eisenberg (Vol. Ed.), *Handbook of child psychology: Vol. 3. Social, emotional, and personality development* (5th ed., pp. 1017–1096). New York: Wiley.

Fashola, O. (2005). *Educating African American males.* Thousand Oaks, CA: Corwin Press.

Franzak, J. K. (2006). Zoom: A review of the literature on marginalized adolescent readers, literacy theory, and policy implications. *Review of Educational Research, 76*(2), 209–248.

Frater, G. (1998). Boys and literacy. In K. Bleach (Ed.), *Raising boys achievement in schools* (pp. 57–80). Herndon, VA: Stylus.

Gambell, T. J., & Hunter, D. M. (1999). Rethinking gender differences in literacy. *Canadian Journal of Education, 24*, 1–16.

Guthrie, J., & Davis, M. (2003). Motivating struggling readers in middle school through an engagement model of classroom practice. *Reading & Writing Quarterly, 19*, 59–85.

Guthrie, J. T., & Humenick, N. M. (2004). Motivating students to read: Evidence for classroom practices that increase reading motivation and achievement. In P. McCardle & V. Chhabra (Eds.), *The voice of evidence in reading research* (pp. 329–354). Baltimore: Brookes.

Guthrie, J. T., & Wigfield, A. (2000). Engagement and motivation in reading. In M. Kamil, P. Mosenthal, P. D. Pearson, & R. Barr (Eds.), *Handbook of reading research* (Vol. 3, pp. 403–424). Mahwah, NJ: Erlbaum.

Harmon, J. A. (1992). *Gender disparities in special education.* Madison: Wisconsin State Department of Public Instruction.

Herbert, B. (2007, March 5). Education, education, education. *New York Times.* Retrieved October 5, 2007, from *donkeyod.wordpress.com/2007/03/05/education-education-education.*

Hinchman, K. A., Alvermann, D. E., Boyd, F. B., Brozo, W. G., & Vacca, R. T. (2003/2004). Supporting older students' in- and out-of-school literacies. *Journal of Adolescent and Adult Literacy, 47,* 304–310.

Hoffman, A. R., Boraks, N. E., & Bauer, D. (2000). Hobbies and hobby-related reading: Exploring preferences, practices, and instructional possibilities. *Reading Research and Instruction, 40,* 51–66.

Hofstetter, C. R., Stitcht, T., & Hofstetter, C. H. (1999). Knowledge, literacy, and power. *Communications Research, 26,* 58–80.

Ivey, G., & Broaddus, K. (2001). "Just plain reading": A survey of what makes students want to read in middle school classrooms. *Reading Research Quarterly, 36,* 350–377.

Lee, P. W. (1999). In their own voices: An ethnographic study of low-achieving students within the context of school reform. *Urban Education, 34,* 214–244.

Lenters, K. (2007). From storybooks to games, comics, bands, and chapter books: A young boy's appropriation of literacy practices. *Canadian Journal of Education, 30,* 113–136.

Margolis, H., & McCabe, P. P. (2004). Self-efficacy: A key to improving the motivation of struggling learners. *The Clearing House, 77,* 241–249.

Martin, A. J. (2003). Boys and motivation. *Australian Educational Researcher, 30,* 43–65.

Martin, R. (2003). Connecting with boys at lunch: A success story. *Teacher Librarian, 30,* 27–28.

Moje, E. B. (2002). Re-framing adolescent literacy research for new times: Studying youth as a resource. *Reading Research and Instruction, 41,* 211–228.

Moje, E. B. (2006). Motivating texts, motivating contexts, motivating adolescents: An examination of the role of motivation in adolescent literacy practices and development. *Perspectives, 32,* 10–14.

Mosenthal, P. (1999). Understanding engagement: Historical and political contexts. In J. Guthrie & D. Alvermann (Eds.), *Engaged reading: Processes, practices and policy implications* (pp. 1–16). New York: Teachers College Press.

National Endowment for the Arts. (2007). *To read or not to read: A question of national consequence.* Washington, DC: Author.

Ogle, D. M. (2003). Reading and learning about our wonderful world: Information-rich resources and strategies to engage readers. *NERA Journal, 39,* 7–10.

Organisation for Economic Co-operation and Development & Statistics Canada. (1995). *Literacy, economy and society: Results of the first international adult literacy survey.* Paris and Ottawa: Author.

Pajares, F. (1996). Self-efficacy beliefs in academic settings. *Review of Educational Research, 66*, 543–578.

Protheroe, N. (2004). Motivating reluctant learners. *Principal, 84*, 46–49.

Sax, L. (2007). *Boys adrift: The five factors driving the growing epidemic of unmotivated boys and underachieving young men.* New York: Basic Books.

Schunk, D. H., & Zimmerman, B. J. (1997). Developing efficacious readers and writers: The role of social and self-regulatory processes. In J. T. Guthrie & A. Wigfield (Eds.), *Reading engagement: Motivating readers through integrated instruction* (pp. 125–136). Cresskill, NJ: Hampton Press.

Silverthorne, J. E., & Perry, J. P. (1984). *Word division manual.* Cincinnati, OH: South-Western.

Simpson, A. (1996). Fictions and facts: An investigation of the reading practices of girls and boys. *English Education, 28*(4), 268–279.

Slade, M., & Trent, F. (2000). What the boys are saying: Examining the views of boys about declining rates of achievement and retention. *International Education Journal, 1*, 201–229.

Smith, M., & Wilhelm, J. (2002). *Reading don't fix no Chevys.* Portsmouth, NH: Heinemann.

Sokal, L., Katz, H., Adkins, M., Grills, T., Stewart, C., & Priddle, G. (2005). Factors affecting inner-city boys' reading: Are male teachers the answer? *Canadian Journal of Urban Research, 14*, 107–130.

Sturtevant, E., Boyd, F., Brozo, W. G., Hinchman, K., Alvermann, D., & Moore, D. (2006). *Principled practices for adolescent literacy: A framework for instruction and policy.* Mahwah, NJ: Erlbaum.

Sullivan, E. (2001). Some teens prefer the real thing: The case for young adult nonfiction. *English Journal, 90*, 43–47.

Sullivan, M. (2003). *Connecting boys with books.* Chicago: ALA Editions.

Sum, A. (2007, March). *The educational attainment of the nation's young black men and their recent labor market experiences: What can be done to improve their future labor market and educational prospects.* Boston: Center for Labor Market Studies, Northeastern University.

Tatum, A. W. (2005). *Teaching reading to black adolescent males: Closing the achievement gap.* Portland, ME: Stenhouse.

Tatum, A. W. (2006). Engaging African American males in reading. *Educational Leadership, 63*, 44–49.

Turner, J. (1995). The influence of classroom contexts on young children's motivation for literacy. *Reading Research Quarterly, 30*, 410–441.

Williams, B. T. (2005). Leading double lives: Literacy and technology in and out of school. *Journal of Adolescent & Adult Literacy, 48*, 702–706.

Worthy, J., Moorman, M., & Turner, M. (1999). What Johnny likes to read is hard to find in school. *Reading Research Quarterly, 34*, 12–27.

Chapter 10

Paying Attention
to Girls' Literacy Needs

Marsha M. Sprague
Kara K. Keeling

GUIDING QUESTIONS

1. How well do girls in America read?
2. What are some of the issues that adolescent girls confront?
3. What literature has been written that speaks to these issues?
4. How can teachers and other school personnel integrate girls' literature into the school curriculum, or extend it beyond the classroom?

In this chapter we address the current status of literacy achievement of adolescent girls, arguing that most girls need to become better readers. We then illustrate the psychological issues that girls face during that time period, and how good adolescent literature tackles those issues. Finally, we suggest ways that teachers and other concerned adults can acquire and use that literature as a way both to help girls become better readers and help understand and navigate the difficult years of adolescence.

There has been a general belief among teachers that girls' reading achievement represents a real triumph of education. After all, girls have consistently outperformed boys on reading tests for at least 15 years. The National Assessment of Education Progress (NAEP, 2005) tests confirmed that eighth-grade girls in public schools scored an average of 10 points higher than males in reading scale scores (Average Scale Scores). This sense of self-satisfaction is so pervasive that in most of our workshops we have teachers expressing surprise that we are focussing on girls' literacy. After all, girls are "readers," ... aren't they?

A closer look at the 2005 NAEP data (NAEP Reading Achievement) undermines this sense of self-satisfaction. Although it is true that girls scored higher than boys in the reading assessment, the average score (267) actually has dropped from a high of 270 in 1998, and represents the same score that girls attained in 1992. When taking into consideration the fact that accommodations were not permitted prior to 1998, this is really saying that girls' reading achievement was worse in 2005 than in 1992. Even more disturbing is to review actual percentages of girls in the different categories of readers.

NAEP (2005) defines three potential categories of readers: Basic, Proficient, and Advanced (NAEP Reading Achievement Levels). *Basic* represents "partial mastery of prerequisite knowledge and skills that are fundamental for proficient work at each grade"; *Proficient* shows "solid academic performance for each grade assessment," including "competency over challenging subject matter"; *Advanced* means "superior performance" (paragraph 4). In 2005, 24% of eighth-grade girls scored below basic performance in reading— meaning that they did not even have partial mastery of skills needed to be able to read successfully at their grade level. Another 42% scored at the Basic level; they had only partial mastery of reading knowledge and skills critical for success at their grade level. This means that 66% of the girls tested did not have a solid base of reading knowledge and skills.

This is far from a rosy picture of successful reading achievement among our nations' girls. NAEP data offer little encouragement that somehow girls learn a great deal in high school and demonstrate mastery by the time they graduate; although girls did perform slightly better in grade 12, 59% of girls tested were at Basic level or below (Gender Gap Wider, paragraph 4.)

So there is a compelling reason to focus on girls' literacy: Over half of adolescent girls are not proficient readers. And in a society that requires more and more ability to read, understand, and analyze information quickly, this is a disaster. What is to be done? Myriad projects focus on the explicit teaching of reading skills to help adolescents become better readers, but the general agreement of literacy educators is that the best predictor of reading success is the amount of text that is read. Cunningham and Allington write: "In order to become literate, children must become readers. Readers are not just children who can read—they are children who do read. The amount of reading children do is highly correlated with how well they read" (2007, p. 12). Students who read avidly for pleasure almost always do exceptionally well on tests of reading achievement. The act of reading provides practice in the underlying skills of making meaning, predicting, clarifying, and so on, but more important, the more one reads, the more schemas are formed, creating prior knowledge that makes future reading easier. It is like economics; the rich get richer—the readers get more proficient.

Unfortunately, studies have shown that adolescents are reading less and less. In a 2004 survey of literary reading, fewer than one-fourth of 17-year-olds read every day for fun. Instead of using free time to read for pleasure, middle and high school students report that they "watch television, listen to music, or use other media" (Manzo, 2007, paragraph 7). This is no surprise to any parent or teacher of teenagers. Text, with its even rows of tiny black marks on white pages, falls far behind its competitors in ability to stimulate myriad senses and sustain attention. Yet we have seen student after student succumb to the wonderful world of story as she finds the right book.

One of our graduate students, a high school teacher, had been assigned a small, below-average class of ninth graders. She was extremely frustrated by the students' total lack of interest in reading any of the stories in the literature text. While taking a course at our university in Young Adult Literature, she encountered a number of books that she had never read, and she decided to try out these books in her class. Using her own money, she bought a variety of young adult books and brought them into the classroom. She asked her students just to pick up any book that looked appealing and read the book jacket. She asked them to read the first chapter, if the box looked interesting. She told us about watching one of her most apathetic female students read the first chapter and say aloud, "This is me! This is me! This is me!" Most of her students found books that they wanted to read, so she decided to let them read for a part of each class period. To her shock, she found that the students did not want to stop reading. Students whom she had considered nonreaders were in fact nonpracticing readers; when paired with the right books, they were motivated to read. And to no one's surprise, it has been shown that when students read books that they find interesting, the quality of experience and the amount they learn from the text is enhanced (Schiefele, 1996).

Books That Support Girls

Those of us who work with adolescents know that academic achievement is not the only major concern of this age. The emotional swings of adolescence often overshadow concerns about grades and tests. Girls, especially, seem vulnerable to depression, anger, and doubt. A report from the Office of National Drug Control Policy (2006) called *Girls and Drugs* asserts that over 1.5 million girls reported having at least one major depressive episode in 2004—more than twice as many episodes as boys had. The report indicated shows that teen girls' misuse of prescription drugs surpassed that of boys, and more girls than boys reported drinking alcohol over a 1-month period. The root of this problem seems to lie in the loss of self-esteem that occurs as girls progress through their teens. A hallmark American Association of University Women (AAUW) study, *How Schools Shortchange Girls*, found that 60% of girls in elementary school were "happy with the way I am"; by high school, that number had dropped to 29% (1995, p. 19).

There is more bad news. Teenage pregnancy, though somewhat reduced in the last decade, is still a real concern. Kirby (2001) put the statistics in perspective, noting that "despite the declining rates, more than four in ten teen girls still get pregnant at least once before age 20, which translates into nearly 900,000 pregnancies a year." The 2004 National Crime Victimization Survey indicated that one in six women in the United States had been a victim or rape or its attempt; of those, 44% were under age 18 and 15% were under age 12 (Rape, Abuse & Incest National Network, 2006). Eating disorders are rampant. Data gathered by ANRED, the Anorexia Nervosa and Related Eating Disorders Association (n.d.), reveal that 1 out of every 100 adolescent girls has clinical anorexia nervosa; up to 4% of college women exhibit bulimia, and many more experience disordered eating habits such as binge eating, extremely restrictive dieting, fasting, laxative abuse, or vomiting (ANRED, n.d.).

Why are girls exhibiting so many negative behaviors? Mary Pipher, author *of Reviving Ophelia* (1994), suggested that adolescent girls are under unprecedented attack from both advertising and entertainment media that suggests they should act, dress, and behave in ways that are blatantly sexual and mature. This is borne out by the use of very young models to advertise clothing that is extremely revealing, and by the fascination and media saturation with young actresses and singers (e.g., Lindsay Lohan, Britney Spears, and Paris Hilton) who engage in destructive behaviors. Girls are encouraged to follow these models; yet, if they do so, they are often castigated as "sluts" and "hos." Rap, the most popular music of the decade, delights in portraying women as wicked and manipulative. Pipher suggests that girls react to these negative forces either by withdrawing into themselves or by acting out, using alcohol and drugs and sexual experimentation as ways to deal with the pressures.

So girls are facing many problems. Fortunately, great writers are tackling these issues in young adult literature. Their books offer girls a chance to connect their experiences with good stories, offering them ways to deal with what they encounter, or at least reflect on what the issues are. Since the early 1990s, reading educators such as Adler and Clark have argued for the use of novels to encourage dialogue around the problems faced by adolescent girls. They reference Spache (1978, cited in Adler & Clark, 1991, p. 758): "It is through facilitated discussion that readers recognize that they are not the first to meet and solve problems, become aware of previously unrecognized problems, and find solutions without experiencing feelings of inferiority, guilt, fear or shame."

Where can these dialogues around great literature take place? A wonderful phenomenon occurred upon the publication of Shireen Dodson's *The Mother–Daughter Book Club: How Ten Busy Mothers and Daughters Came Together to Talk, Laugh and Learn through their Love of Reading* (1997). Dodson documented her experiences in creating a book club in which mothers and daughters read the same books, then came together to discuss them. She writes of the wonderful discussions that ensued, and the insights that the girls showed. She notes that "by talking about the impersonal—plots, characters and author's choices—we've heard the girls' candid thoughts on important issues like death and illness, friendship and marriage, family relationships and school and social issues" (p. 20). Dodson quotes a book club member: "Some of the issues in the books have been a little delicate, but we talk about them anyway.... If we don't talk about it, who will?" (p. 20). After Dodson's book was published, a number of these mother–daughter clubs have sprung up, one in our own neighborhood, and are still active.

But not all mothers can or will choose to institute book clubs. A much more logical place to bring books to girls, and to provide ways to help them discuss the issues, of course, is in our schools. Girls are in school many of their waking hours, so it is logical that schools should try to help girls address their issues. In *Girls in the Middle,* Cohen and Blanc (1996) studied a number of middle schools in the United States and looked at ways that schools could help girls deal with the challenges they face. The first three recommendations from their report include the following:

1. Expand the range of acceptable behaviors for girls, particularly "non-conforming" behaviors such as argumentation and assertion.

2. Create a mentor program for girls, and support adult mentors through funding and recognition.

3. *Build identity development into the school curriculum. Provide opportunities for girls and boys to explore and discuss gender issues* (emphasis added).

It is, of course, this last recommendation that interests us, because it provides the template for introducing literature into the classroom that addresses girls' challenges. Especially interesting is that the report suggests the inclusion of both boys and girls in the discussions.

Choosing Books That Address Girls' Issues

A number of writers have examined the many published books that contain compelling female characters. Kathleen Odean (1997) has created a wonderful resource in *Great Books for Girls.* In this text, she lists more than 600 books that feature strong girls—from picture books through works for older readers ages 12–14. Odean writes:

> In selecting these books, I looked for girls and women who faced the world without timidity, either from the first or after overcoming their fears. I found female characters who are creative, capable, articulate, and intelligent. They solve problems, face challenges, resolve conflicts, and go on journeys. These girls are not waiting to be rescued; they are doing the rescuing. Nor are they waiting for a male to provide a happy ending: They are fashioning their own stories. (p. 4)

Odean sorts the books into a number of different categories, such as sports stories, biographies, historical fiction, mysteries, science fiction, and fantasy.

Another excellent source for books that feature strong female characters is *100 Books for Girls to Grow On*, by Shireen Dodson (1998). The text provides a brief summary of a number of works, followed by suggested discussion questions that are thought provoking and lead to central issues that girls need to tackle. For example, in the discussion questions for Virginia Euwer Wolff's book *Make Lemonade* (1993), Dodson asks:

> Both LaVaughn and Jolly are teenagers born into very poor circumstances, yet they are very different. Compare the two girls. (p. 182)

> Describe LaVaughn's mother. Describe the mother–daughter relationship they have. Discuss some ways your own mother–daughter relationship is similar to or different from the one depicted in this book. (p. 183)

The 100 books, organized alphabetically, are designed for girls ages 9 through 13. Dodson wrote this book as a supplement to her successful publication *The Mother–Daughter Book Club* (1997), described earlier.

Another resource book, *Once upon a Heroine* (Cooper-Mullin & Coye, 1998), provides not only another list of books but also entries by noted American females who recount their favorite books growing up. In addition, the authors extend the range of books to include students in high school.

We have created a template to help teachers and other interested adults select books that may encourage helpful discussion:

- Does the book feature a young female as a protagonist?
- Does the book place the girl in a position where she is being asked to conform to certain expected behaviors because she is female?
- Does the book illustrate forces that limit her choices, such as parents, societal expectations, or peer pressure?
- Does the book show the girl struggling against those forces?
- Does the girl define herself by the end of the book in ways that reflect her choices?

We have found many books that answer "yes" to these questions. These books are of high interest to adolescent girls, and they form the perfect springboard to launch important discussions.

How to Structure Discussion

There are many books that may serve as discussion initiators of the key features vital in examining girls' development. The books listed earlier are great resources for teachers who choose to select books that can be focal points for discussion. But what is to be discussed? Although the lists of questions offered by some of the authors are helpful in establishing a general understanding of the characters and the books, we want girls to understand the forces at work in shaping their development of voice. We created a visual framework (Figure 10.1) to help us target these features, and to share with students reading the books. Each of the circles can provide a window into discussing the main character, or one of the other female characters in the book. For example, the character of Nancy Drew, heroine of many mysteries and subject of a recent feature film, is an interesting study. The framework discussion guide would look like Figure 10.2.

In all likelihood, these questions will elicit good discussion. Most students will argue that Nancy clearly is expressing her own voice, and is being helped to do so in many ways. Her boyfriend Ned is always understanding and supportive of her escapades, even when they take away her attention from him. Her best friends are admiring and try to be helpful, although Bess expresses her preference for more safe, traditionally feminine pursuits. Both of the adults in the stories (Nancy's dad and the housekeeper) are loving but try constantly to restrain Nancy's curiosity and daring. Will Nancy eventually stop her sleuthing and getting into trouble, or will she pursue a career in investigation? It is fascinating to read some of the earliest Nancy Drew stories from the 1950s and compare them to their modern counterparts: This is another wonderful source for discussion, especially around the topic of what society expects from its girls.

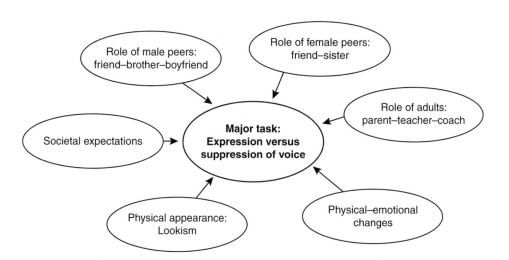

FIGURE 10.1. Elements influencing the development of voice.

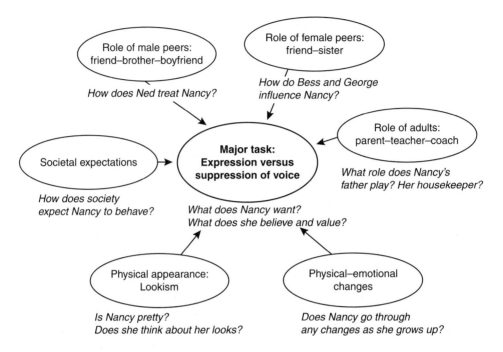

FIGURE 10.2. Using the framework discussion guide with Nancy Drew.

Genres That Offer Wonderful Reading Opportunities for Girls

Books that offer good opportunities for discussions about how girls can successfully negotiate the social pressures teens face on a daily basis fall into three major literary genres: contemporary realistic fiction, historical fiction, and fantasy. Although contemporary realism offers the most direct way to confront such topics, sometimes the more oblique approach of the other two genres creates a chance to see the issues in a clearer light. All three genres offer a wealth of books that are popular with young readers. Many of the books have female protagonists; it is, however, worth noting that books with male protagonists who have friendships or romantic relationships with strong girls also afford excellent chances for discussing how the girl characters deal with social pressures.

Contemporary Realism

Certainly contemporary realistic fiction provides characters with whom young audiences are likely to identify easily: The settings are familiar; the dilemmas the characters must resolve are often ones that readers have confronted personally (or they know someone who has dealt with them). The genre is popular for this reason: Many young readers feel reassured that they are not alone in their concerns, and they sometimes see realistic books as potential guides to answer questions about how to deal with issues that worry them or their friends (e.g., popularity, drugs, depression, suicide, self-mutilation, sex, rape and sexual abuse, teen pregnancy, eating disorders, dysfunctional families, physical abuse, the death of a parent or friend). These topics provide strong conflict to drive the plot of the novel; characters who face these serious issues inevitably change and grow substantially. Thus, the books provoke thoughtful discussion as readers weigh the protagonist's options, choices, limitations, and sources of support.

A brief discussion of three popular, contemporary novels suggests how to get young readers reading to learn how characters deal with family and social pressures to suppress their individuality, and to find ways to express their true voice instead. Jerry Spinelli's *Stargirl* (2004) features Leo, a high school junior, who becomes aware of how conformist his classmates—and he himself—are when a new girl, Susan Carroway, arrives at school. Stargirl, as she calls herself, dresses and acts utterly unconventionally; at the outset, no one knows what to make of her, because she does not fit in with any expected behaviors. She gains initial peer acceptance but soon becomes an outcast. Leo, in love with Stargirl, begs her to act like the other girls; she tries for a while but eventually refuses to deny her own personality. Unable to accept her deliberate decision to remain different from others, Leo breaks up with her, but later realizes that he has thrown away a relationship that enriched him, replacing it with the more sterile comfort of conformity. Although Stargirl is not the protagonist of the novel, readers appreciate her individuality through Leo's eyes, as well as see the cost of her attempts to conform to please him. They come to appreciate that she cannot shut down her own personality at the request of another person, no matter how much she cares for Leo. Stargirl makes a painful but conscious choice to remain true to her own eccentric personality, knowing that the cost of not doing so will be much higher, and Leo eventually learns to admire her strength of character and to regret pressuring her to be like everyone else.

Stargirl's expression of her voice is something that Melinda, in Laurie Halse Anderson's *Speak* (2001), must likewise learn to do. Raped by a popular athlete while drinking at a party before the beginning of her freshman year of high school, Melinda shuts down emotionally, becoming withdrawn and repressed. Her situation is exacerbated by both the isolation she experiences from her peers, who misunderstand her reason for calling the police to the party, and her parents' inability to communicate with her. Melinda does not, cannot "speak"—cannot tell anyone about the trauma she experienced. She silences herself in multiple ways: verbally, physically, emotionally. Over the course of the novel, she regains her voice, finding increasingly confident self-expression, first through gardening and art, then in her ability to confront her rapist in the novel's climactic scene.

Voice is likewise an important theme in Carolyn Mackler's *The Earth, My Butt, and Other Big Round Things* (2003). Virginia Shreves feels herself to be out of place as a large, somewhat chubby girl among her slim handsome family. Pressured by her family to diet, Virginia unsuccessfully tries to make herself over to fit their expectations for her. Upset by her brother's suspension from college for date rape and the continuing stresses from her mother to lose weight, Virginia rebels by finding ways to become a girl she likes being, with the support of her best friend, a teacher, and a boy who is interested in her: She pierces her eyebrow, dyes her hair purple, buys clothes that aren't frumpy, and founds a webzine, "Earthquack," where she and other frustrated teens can express their frustrations.

All of these books tell stories of teens facing multiple stresses: peer pressure, dysfunctional families, body image, depression, self-mutilation, sexual experimentation, rape, and eating disorders are just some of the difficulties with which Stargirl, Leo, Melinda, and Virginia must deal. Each novel shows realistic problems that the characters must confront; their struggles are quite painful at times, but ultimately, through the main characters' resolutions (and occasional minor characters' failures), they show that it is more liberating to find an honest way to express their own individuality than to adopt others' definitions of how they should act or who they should be.

Historical Fiction

Realistic stories set in the past offer readers a chance to think about how girls' opportunities have changed and to see how girls in far more restrictive societies were able to find fulfillment in their lives. Depending on the setting, a female protagonist in a historical novel may face limitations in her dress or behavior; her career and marriage options may be limited according to her race or class. Authors of good historical fiction try to find plausible ways for their protagonist to resist the pressures of past cultural conformity that will appeal to readers today. Some solutions are historically authentic; others are much less so. One can think of novels of historical fiction lying along a spectrum: At one end are stories of girls whose experiences are amusing but ultimately historically implausible; at the other are stories of girls whose experiences are historically accurate and representative. In the middle lie stories of characters who escape the societal limitations of their day in plausible ways; such novels are often set in times when traditional gender roles were in flux due to social upheavals.

Avi's *The True Confessions of Charlotte Doyle* (1992) is a delicious romp. Unexpectedly left without a chaperone, 13-year-old Charlotte crosses the Atlantic in 1832 as the only female on a ship whose crew mutinies. Charlotte joins the crew, dressing as a boy, learning to work as a sailor, even captaining the ship by the end of the voyage. Faced with returning to the repressive life of an ordinary middle-class girl at the end, Charlotte runs away from home to go back to sea. Charlotte finds a strong sense of self in rebelling against the culturally imposed role of a properly mannered young lady. But though impressively authentic in its portrayal of nautical techniques, this story is historically implausible on a number of levels. First, it is exceeding unlikely that a young girl would travel alone in the company of male sailors in the 1800s, and if she did, it is unlikely that she would escape being raped. Her choice to join a group of mutineers against the captain of a vessel, in violation of her natural class sympathies, is likewise improbable; nor is it credible that a girl of this time with no athletic experience could perform the incredibly demanding physical work required of a sailor. Charlotte carves out a place for herself in a man's world—by essentially becoming male in her dress and actions, and submerging her feminine identity. The book is popular because Charlotte is spunky and overcomes the restrictions placed on young girls in the 1800s, and society's conspiracy to silence the voices of girls: It fits 21st-century fantasies of empowerment rather than accurately portraying 19th-century female experience.

In contrast, in *Lyddie* (1991), Katherine Paterson situates its female character within an accurate historical context, and so demonstrates the constraints that earlier times imposed on girls, often impairing their chances to find their unique voices. Thirteen-year-old Lyddie goes to Lowell, Massachusetts, to work as a factory girl to try to earn enough money to pay off her family's debts. Paterson describes in minute, horrific detail the hard daily life of a factory girl in the 1840s. Lyddie learns to work the looms and teaches herself to read, yet she eventually loses her job when she tries to protect another girl from being raped by the factory manager. Luke, a Quaker neighbor, asks for Lyddie's hand in marriage, but instead of accepting his offer, she decides to travel to Oberlin College, which accepts women as students. She realizes that she cares for Luke and hopes that he will wait for her, but she is determined to free herself from ignorance and dependence before marrying anyone. *Lyddie* does not romanticize the past as does *The True Confessions of Charlotte Doyle* (1992); instead, it paints a clear and accurate picture of the lack of options that working-class young women faced in the 1800s. The inability of many girls to better themselves, despite their talents and ambitions, is evident in this novel. Paterson describes Lyddie's search for voice, which she equates with freedom and escape from slavery, as an almost insurmountable task. Because of Lyddie's spirit, however, she prevails. Although most girls of the time "escaped" only through marriage, Lyddie rejects that path as another type of slavery and seeks instead to continue her quest for self-development.

Some historical novels depict girls of the past who are temporarily freed from societal constraints because of unique historical events. In *Fever 1793* (2002), Laurie Halse Anderson tells the story of Mattie, a Philadelphia girl who lives through a particularly virulent outbreak of yellow fever. At the outset of the novel, 14-year-old Mattie lives a normal life for a girl of her age and class, feeling frustration with the limitations of her life: She tires of the chores she is expected to do, and she feels alarmed at her mother's attempts to marry her off to the son of a wealthy acquaintance when she has a crush on an artist's apprentice. When yellow fever strikes Philadelphia, hundreds of the city's inhabitants become infected and begin to die. Separated from her mother, Mattie survives her own bout with the fever, nurses other victims, then, as the epidemic abates, chooses to reopen the family coffeehouse with the help of friends. Throughout her ordeal, Mattie demonstrates strength, courage, and compassion.

Mattie's autonomy, though unusual for her time, is plausible because of the social breakdown caused by the epidemic; it contrasts with the much less likely scenario and ending of *The True Confessions of Charlotte Doyle*. Lyddie's experiences are far more typical for a girl of her time. Her final decision to earn her way through college rather than to marry is uncommon, though historically possible and convincing. Paterson comes up with an open-ended conclusion to the novel that reinforces her protagonist's commitment to self-improvement.

Fantasy

Fantasy stories have often been structured around the "heroic/romantic quest," in which a young person with hidden talents must go on a quest. After successfully completing a difficult task, the hero then returns home, often with a love interest in tow. Until very recently, heroes in the quest story have usually been male; young females were relegated to roles as beautiful, passive maidens waiting for rescue. But in the past several decades, a number of fantasy writers have created stories in which the hero is a girl. These new fantasy stories provide vehicles for exploring ways in which girls can find self-expression and develop agency, whether in revised versions of traditional female roles or in taking on roles once reserved for men.

Ella Enchanted, by Gail Carson Levine (1998), radically rewrites the traditional female-centered Cinderella story. Ella has been given a "gift" by her fairy godmother at birth: obedience. She cannot disobey a direct order from anyone. This makes her life miserable, especially after her father remarries a vindictive widow with two cruel daughters. When Ella falls in love with Prince Charming ("Char" for short), she realizes that her curse of obedience could cost him his kingdom. Although she loves him, she manages to resist his command to "Marry me," breaking the curse. This revision of the traditional submissive female, sex-object story offers a new look at obedience as a curse rather than a virtue, overtly challenging the idea that women should be passive and conforming. It makes Cinderella a resourceful, determined, innovative heroine. It also espouses the idea of doing rather than being—Ella would rather do work than be a princess.

In *The Blue Sword* (1982), Robin McKinley adapts the hero of the male quest into a "shero." In a world similar to colonial British India, the heroine Harry is kidnapped by Corlath, the king of the Hillfolk, because he has a vision that shows her fighting valiantly for the Hillfolk during battle with their Northern enemies. Trained in horseback riding and sword fighting by one of Corlath's riders, Harry becomes a skilled warrior, discovering that she has mystical powers of sight. Later, ignoring Corlath's command, she fulfills her destiny using magic as well as her skill in battle to defeat the invaders and save the Hillfolk. The novel raises fascinating questions about the nature of feminine power and agency. Harry takes on a male aspect matched by her name, but only after being kidnapped: Her makeover is not initially her own choice, yet she excels in it. The novel ultimately affirms the ability of a woman to function as both leader and warrior.

In *The Keeper of the Isis Light* by Monica Hughes (1980/2000), 16-year-old Olwen has been raised alone on the planet Isis by Guardian. When a colony ship arrives, Olwen makes friends with Mark, an attractive boy her age. However, when Mark accidentally discovers Guardian has genetically manipulated her, physically adapting her to life on Isis but turning her into a reptilian creature, he recoils in horror. Mortified by her physical differences from the colonists, Olwen isolates herself from them. After she heroically saves a child from danger, the colonists offer to restore her body to its original form, but Olwen refuses. She rejects her prior need to become like the colonists and chooses instead to return to her previous state of companionship and freedom. This story is remarkable in its stance that living alone may be a better choice for a girl than conforming to societal expectations. It especially challenges the idea of lookism, when Guardian tells Olwen, "You are not ugly at all. Form and function should be as one. You function perfectly. You are beautiful" (p. 111). Olwen comes to revel in her differences rather than seek to eradicate them.

Tamora Pierce, a noted fantasy writer for young adults, has written a powerful essay, "Fantasy: Why Kids Read It, Why Kids Need It" (1993), in which she argues that the genre fulfills several basic needs: Fantasy reinforces young people's idealistic belief that good should and does triumph; it offers them a chance to escape a restrictive society and create a new world for themselves; it is "a literature of empowerment" (p. 51), allowing ordinary protagonists to overcome huge obstacles and defeat in combat adversaries who are far more powerful. As shown by these three novels, fantasy can reveal to girls the possibilities of speaking out, of leading, and of overcoming obstacles—even those that seem insurmountable.

How to Integrate Girls' Literature into the Curriculum

Once a teacher identifies a number of books that will interest girls, and that will help both boys and girls make sense of the pressures that exist in navigating adolescence today, then it is important to find ways to use these books in school. With today's strong emphasis on reading achievement, this should not be difficult. These book selections can be used as part of the language arts curriculum, because many of them are award-winning texts, highly recommended by educators. The important addition is that they be used as vehicles to address some of the important issues we described earlier. We have found three distinct ways that teachers, reading and media specialists, and other personnel have been able to incorporate wonderful discussions into the life of the school. Two of these—the whole-class novel and literature circles—can be done within the classroom and involve both boys and girls; the other is an extracurricular book club.

The Whole-Class Novel

In the whole-class novel approach, the teacher assigns one novel that everyone reads. There are a number of advantages to this approach. The most important of these is that all students react to the same text, so the teacher can easily lead students to consider important points about how gender is handled in the book. This is appealing to teachers, especially when it is their first time grappling with this important theme. A second advantage to the whole-class novel approach is that most school libraries and English departments have "class sets" of books that have already been purchased, making it easy to provide the books to students. Teachers can use the template questions we listed earlier to determine which books might be appropriate to use.

Another advantage to using already-purchased class sets is that they have been preapproved by the district, so teachers don't have to worry about parental concerns or about not fulfilling district expectations for the curriculum. If class sets are not available, then the teacher can request that they be purchased. Choosing from already-identified book lists for a grade level, again, ensures that the books match the approved curriculum.

Most teachers begin the whole-class novel approach by doing an introductory activity before or during distribution of the novel. This serves both to pique student interest in the novel and to activate prior knowledge. Looking at the book jacket is an easy way to do this. For example, middle school students looking at the book *Lyddie* (Paterson, 1991) are able to discuss how the character is dressed and what she seems to be doing. They may wonder why a young girl is apparently working in a factory. This gives them an opportunity to share what they already know about child labor practices in the United States.

After the introductory activity, students are assigned readings based on the chapter divisions of the book. Typically, students read the chapters to be discussed in class for homework, spending several weeks on the class novel. When students simply do not do assigned homework reading, class time can be allocated for this. To hold students accountable for their reading, some teachers give a brief quiz on the assigned chapter (just a few questions with obvious answers, not obscure, miniscule details that frustrate struggling readers). Some teachers have students keep a response journal, writing their informal reactions after reading the material. Such activities that earn points toward a participation or homework grade are helpful in getting students to read the assigned text. During the class period, teachers frequently give minilessons on elements of the story they are teaching, such as plot, theme, characters, imagery, conflict, or historical factors.

What is most difficult about the whole-class novel approach is engaging all the students in discussion. In typical classes that we have observed, only a handful of students choose to answer discussion questions posed by the teacher. The remainder of the class sits apathetically and listens. To overcome this difficulty, we have seen teachers put students into small work groups (clusters of three to five students seem to work best) to discuss questions. The groups are given 10–20 minutes to answer these questions collaboratively. After the small groups have completed their discussions, the teacher then invites or requires responses from the class. This makes students much more willing to respond, because they are more confident of their ideas, having clarified them through sharing with other students. Teachers can also call on a variety of students, asking, "What did your group think about ... ?" and be likely to get thoughtful responses from all levels of students.

Questions for discussion are often found in the backs of novels. Educational publishers, such as Scholastic, are committed to providing quality discussion questions for teachers to use. Other provocative questions can be found on websites prepared by teachers that target the various texts. It is easy to add to this mix the questions we identified earlier:

- Who are the girls in this story? What are their voices (what do they say and do, and does this change during the book)?
- Is each girl able to express her own voice? Why or why not?
- Does the girl experience support or constraints from female peers? In what ways?
- Does the girl experience support or constraints from male peers? In what ways?
- Does the girl experience support or constraints from parents and other adults? In what ways?
- Does the girl experience support or constraints from societal expectations? In what ways?
- Does the girl experience lookism? In what way?

Because the majority of these books give girls a central role, it is reasonable to ask these questions during discussions of major characters.

One of the questions that teachers, especially male teachers, typically ask is how they can lead very sensitive class discussions of issues such as rape or pregnancy. A male high school teacher with whom we have worked says, "I try and create a safe environment.... I let the students do most of the talking. Of course, I monitor what they say, and don't let the discussion get off track or allow anything that is hurtful to be said. But overall, the kids are pretty respectful of one another. I think the key is getting a good book and letting students start to care about the characters. When my students read *Imani: All Mine* (Porter, 2006) and we get to what is a pretty graphic rape scene, the students really care about Tasha, and they want to talk about what happens to her. They are attached to her as a person. It's a powerful tool to open up student discussion" (P. Lawrence, personal communication, April 27, 2006).

Literature Circles

In the literature circle format, students are placed in small groups, then each group is assigned a book to read. Usually the books have some common thread. For example, a middle school teacher with whom we worked planned a unit on fantasy, using novels that featured strong female protagonists (Sprague & Risher, 2002). She selected the books *Dragonsong* (2003) and *Dragonsinger* (1997) by Anne McCaffrey; *Dealing with Dragons* (1990) by Patricia Wrede; and *Ella Enchanted* (1998) by Gail Carson Levine. Students are assigned randomly to one of the groups. Some teachers prefer to do short "book talks" and allow students to indicate their preferences for reading, which then guide the group assignments.

Authors generally agree that literature circles should have between four and eight members (Brabham & Villaume, 2000; Farinacci, 1998). A larger number of students makes it difficult for everyone to contribute. Also, groups should be as heterogeneous as possible. Once groups have been assigned, they are charged with setting up a reading schedule. The time allotted for discussion (usually 5–10 days) is divided into the total number of pages in the text, and each group sets up an agreed-upon reading schedule that is then turned into the teacher. Each night, students read the text, and during the following discussion period they respond to a series of questions prepared by the teacher. At that time, the teacher can introduce discussion of girls' issues, using the framework questions that we developed earlier in the chapter. The teacher is critical to the process; he or she can model how books may be discussed and provide input to groups that are struggling. As in the whole-class novel, teachers typically provide minilessons on "multiple literary elements such as plot, characterization, setting, point of view, tone and symbolism" (McMahon & Rafael, 1997, p. 61).

Once students complete their reading of the whole book, an important task is to provide a way that they may share with other members of the class who have not read the book. Some ideas for the sharing include posters advertising the book; dramatic performances based on scenes from the book; artwork—painting, sculpture, poem, mobile, collage, diorama—interpreting the book; or a diorama of the book (Daniels, 2002, pp. 48–49). Once these are shared, then the similarities and differences of the books can be discussed. In the case of the fantasy novels listed earlier, once the major theme of developing a voice was considered, ways in which the different female protagonists found their voices were contrasted.

Extracurricular Book Club

The out-of-school book club is another way that teachers or others can introduce girls to interesting literature. A recent text by Deborah Appleman, *Reading for Themselves: How to Transform Adolescents into Lifelong Readers through Out-of-Class Book Clubs* (2006), offers wonderful insight into how book clubs work and testifies to their power in engaging students in important discussions.

A number of excellent books describe how to start a book club, including *The New York Public Library Guide to Reading Groups* (Saal, 1995) and *The Reading Group Book* (Laskin & Hughes, 1995). Both books are written for adult clubs, so they may set different parameters than those appropriate for children's clubs, but the key tasks outlined are the same for book clubs targeting any age group. Some of the important questions that teachers and others may want to ask are outlined below.

Who Should Run the Club?

Unlike adult groups, in which hosts may rotate among members, school book clubs need adult sponsors. Even in high schools, where students often assume the role of discussion leader, an adult sponsor should be present for legal reasons, as is true for all extracurricular activities. School book clubs can be sponsored by a teacher (often an English teacher feels comfortable in leading discussions of literature); a reading specialist; a media specialist; a counselor; or another adult, such as a university researcher or a parent. Having two leaders may be optimal. According to Saal (1995), the Great Books program requires the presence of two coleaders, one whose task is to move the discussion along without giving his or her opinion, and the other whose job is to make sure that everyone in the group is participating.

Who Can Join?

Because school book clubs are voluntary, everyone who wants to join can probably do so. However, some conditions may limit membership. First of all, if the group is a "book club for girls," then it should be limited to girls only. This is a tough call to make, because both boys and girls benefit from discussing girls' issues. However, girls have expressed their appreciation for time and space to talk about their own special concerns. In research conducted in six middle schools, reported in the AAUW publication *Girls in the Middle*, Cohen and Blanc (1996) concluded,

> At least on a short-term basis, girls' groups appear to encourage girls to develop autonomy with the help of supportive adults and are places where girls can

address and even argue through their differences. As one girl explained, "We can say what we want. We don't have to worry about what the boys will say" (p. 82)

Regardless of whether the club is single- or mixed-gender, those writing about book clubs agree that the group should be limited to 20 members, and most prefer groups of 10 or 12.

When and Where?

Most school book clubs can easily meet in a classroom or at the school library. School book clubs can meet after school, at lunch, before school, on Saturdays, or even during the summers. Each has its own advantages and disadvantages. Appleman (2006) describes success with before-school clubs; many clubs meet after school, because most schools have extracurricular activity transportation for students who do not live near the school. It is fairly easy to find space and time to meet after school. However, many activities, especially athletics, meet at that time. We have lost some of our best book club members to sports practices.

Lunchtime offers another possible meeting slot, because it presents less potential conflict with other activities. One local school near us created a Brown Bag Book Club, in which students brought their lunch and a book, talking while they ate. However, many large schools have not one but multiple lunch periods, thus fracturing a single group and requiring more than one meeting time. Most student book clubs use less time than do adult book clubs, which often run for 2 hours; the most successful middle school student discussions often last an hour or less, whereas high school students are able to hold longer meetings.

Summer book clubs are obviously less constrained than those meeting during the school year; the students can meet every few weeks or more often. One writer noted that summer vacations and camps created attendance problems for some students. Another possible obstacle is the lack of a place to meet, because schools are sometimes closed in the summer.

Acquiring Books

Sponsors can provide books for members, if there are books available in the school library or if there are school funds to pay for them. With the very cheap books available through online booksellers, many members can purchase their own. Some of the active book club websites have suggested another way to accumulate reading materials: Clubs can raise money to buy books for their members. Car washes, bake sales, and used book sales are common ways to raise money for this purpose. Sponsors might be found to support the purchase of books. The Parent–Teacher Association and local chapters of state reading associations often are receptive to requests for the funding of small projects.

What to Do at Book Club Meetings

The main purpose of a book club is to *discuss the book*. *The New York Public Library Guide to Reading Groups* (Saal, 1995) suggests simple guidelines that, if followed, foster good discussion: "Speak up; listen thoughtfully to others; be brief; and come with questions in mind" (p. 32). These guidelines can be set at a club's first meeting or be used as a model for students who wish to create their own guidelines. The key to good discussion seems to lie in the quality of the questions asked by the facilitator and the willingness of members to openly share their ideas.

The New York Public Library Guide adopts the tenets of the Great Books program in advising its leaders to do the following:

> Ask questions that initiate, sustain, and try to conclude investigations into problems or issues found in the book.
> Ask questions that challenge all unclear, factually incorrect, or contradictory statements.
> Classify all responses according to your best judgment. Select those statements you want to question immediately; ignore those you find uninteresting, trivial, or irrelevant; and table those you may want to question later. (p. 35)

Devising questions that investigate the problems that girls face as they maneuver through adolescence is the most important duty of the leader of the girls' book club. The template questions we posed earlier provide an easy way to instigate discussion around girls' issues.

One of the most difficult challenges in leading girls through a series of thought-provoking questions is allowing them time to think. One New York Public Library book leader wrote:

> One of the most important things that I learned in working with reading groups is how to keep the discussion going along.... What is hard is to allow some silence. At first, I kept wanting to fill in with a question about the book. It took me a while to be able to allow a little silence, which gives people a chance to think an idea through and then express themselves. You get some of the most thoughtful observations that way. (Klucevsek, cited in Saal, 1995, p. 34)

Although discussion is the most important aspect of book clubs, other activities can be planned to keep students engaged. This is especially important for young students or for older students whose schedules force longer meeting times (it's hard to discuss a book with 12-year-olds for longer than 45 minutes). Some activities recommended in Chicago schools, which have a long history of book clubs, include drawing, writing, and finding other ways to respond to the book; watching videos or listening to audiotapes of books; inviting guest speakers to the meetings, such as authors and librarians; and conducting field trips to local bookstores or other venues (*Mayor Daley's Elementary Book Club*, 2003).

Maintaining Attendance at Club Meetings

A couple of generally agreed-upon tips for keeping attendance high at book clubs are to give students effective reminders and to provide food. If the book club meets only once a month, or even every 2 weeks, students are apt to forget about the meeting time. Using e-mail, intercom announcements, and phone trees are all helpful reminders for students. Most writers agree that food is a delectable and helpful addition to a book club. Laskin and Hughes (1995) favor some type of food; they note that "a reading group ... binds a group of readers together in personal as well as intellectual ways. So why not enjoy feeding the body as well as the soul?" (pp. 86–87). It is especially helpful if the food echoes the setting of the book; for example, a student might bring pita bread and hummus when members are reading *Habibi*, a novel about an American girl who moves to Palestine (Nye, 1999).

Preventing Problems

One of the most prevalent problems of book clubs, both for adults and for young people, is that members sometimes attend without having read the book, or after having read only part of it. This can lead to disinterest in the discussion and to members not wanting others to "give away the ending." *Teen-reads.com* recommends that group members decide for themselves what to do about this problem at the very beginning. A rule for the club might be that members should attend only if they have read the book; or that, if they have not finished the book, they must be prepared for discussions about the whole book.

   Although book clubs do require an extra time commitment on the part of students and their sponsors, they have proven to be an effective vehicle in providing a forum for girls to discuss interesting books.

Conclusions

We hope that this chapter has demonstrated that despite outperforming boys on tests of reading achievement, girls have many unmet needs. One of these needs is to become better readers; many girls exhibit very poor abilities in the area of reading. Another need is to understand the complexities and challenges that come with being a girl in America today. So much wonderful literature deals with many of the issues that girls confront—we need to connect girls to that literature. The chapter has considered the most useful genres for girls to read, identified examples within those genres, and has suggested specific ways for teachers and other concerned adults to initiate discussions around these important issues. Both in-school activities, such as literature circles, and out-of-school activities, such as book clubs, can introduce both girls and boys to compelling narratives that engage them in thinking through difficult problems.

QUESTIONS FOR DISCUSSION

1. How will I select and acquire good books that address girls' issues?
2. How will I incorporate and encourage the use of these books in my school/ classroom?
3. How can I get other teachers, reading specialists, administrators, and parents to support me in my efforts and add on others of their own?

Resources

Appleman, D. (2006) *Reading for themselves: How to transform adolescents into lifelong reader through out-of-class book clubs.* Portsmouth, NH: Heinemann.

Dodson, S. (1998). *100 books for girls to grow on.* New York: HarperCollins.

Johnson, N., Roberts, M. C., & Worell, J. (Eds.). (1999). *Beyond appearance: A new look at adolescent girls.* Washington, DC: American Psychological Association.

Pipher, M. (1994). *Reviving Ophelia: Saving the selves of adolescent girls.* New York: Ballantine.

Sprague, M. M., & Keeling, K. K. (2007). *Discovering their voices: Engaging adolescent girls with young adult literature.* Newark, DE: International Reading Association.

Websites

www.teenreads.com
www.ala.org/yalsa
www.edb.utexas.edu/resources/booksr4teens

References

Adler, E., & Clark, R. (1991). Adolescence: A literary passage. *Adolescence, 104* (26), 757-768.

American Association of University Women. (1995). *How schools shortchange girls*: *The AAUW report.* New York: Marlowe & Company.

Anderson, L. H. (2002). *Fever, 1793.* New York: Aladdin Paperbacks.

Anderson, L. H. (2003). *Speak.* New York: Puffin.

Anorexia Nervosa and Related Eading Disorders Association. (n.d.). Statistics: How many people have eating disorders? Retrieved February 23, 2008, from *www. anred.com/stats.html.*

Appleman, D. (2006). *Reading for themselves: How to transform adolescents into lifelong readers through out-of-class book clubs.* Portsmouth, NH: Heinemann.

Avi. (1992). *The true confessions of Charlotte Doyle.* New York: Avon Books.

Brabham, E. G., & Villaume, S. K. (2000). Questions and answers: Continuing conversations about literature circles. *Reading Teacher, 54*(3), 278–280.

Cohen, J., & Blanc, S. (1996). *Girls in the middle: Working to succeed in school.* Washington, DC: American Association of University Women Educational Foundation.

Cooper-Mullin, A., & Coye, J. M. (1998). *Once upon a heroine: 400 books for girls to love.* Chicago: Contemporary Books.

Cunningham, P. M., & Allington, R. L. (2007). *Classrooms that work: They can all read and write.* Boston: Pearson.

Daniels, H. (2002). Resource for middle school book clubs. *Voices from the Middle, 10*(1), 48–49.

Dodson, S. (1997). *The mother–daughter book club: How 10 busy mothers and daughters came together to talk, laugh and learn through their love of reading.* New York: HarperCollins.

Dodson, S. (1998). *100 books for girls to grow on.* New York: HarperCollins.

Farinacci, M. (1998). "We have so much to talk about": Implementing literature as an action-research project. *Ohio Reading Teacher, 32*(2), 4–11.

Hughes, M. (2000). *The keeper of the Isis light.* New York: Aladdin Paperbacks. (Original work published 1980)

Kirby, D. (2001). *Emergins answers: Research findings on programs to reduce teen pregnancy* (summary). Retrieved November 15, 2006, from *www.teenpregnancy.org/resourcs/ data/pdf/emeranswsum.*

Laskin, D., & Hughes, H. (1995). *The reading group book: The complete guide to starting and sustaining a reading group, with annotated lists of 250 titles for provocative discussion.* New York: Plume/Putnam.

Levine, G. C. (1998). *Ella enchanted.* New York: HarperTrophy.

Mackler, C. (2003). *The earth, my butt, and other big round things.* Cambridge, MA: Candlewick Press.

Manzo, K. K. (2007). Young people seen losing love of reading. *Education Week, 27.* [Electronic version]. Retrieved November 30, 2007, from *edweek.org/ew/articles/2007/11/19/13/reading.*

Mayor Daley's Elementary Book Club. (2003). Retrieved July 8, 2004, from *mdbc.cps.k12. il.us/about.html.*

McCaffrey, A. (1997). *Dragonsinger* (Harper Hall Trilogy, Vol. 2). New York: Spectra/ Bantam Dell. (Original work published 1977)

McCaffrey, A. (2003). *Dragonsong.* (Harper Hall Trilogy, Vol. 1). New York: Aladdin Paperbacks. (Original work published 1976)

McKinley, R. (1982). *The blue sword.* New York: Greenwillow.

McMahon, S. I., & Raphael, T. E. (Eds.). (1997). *The book club connection: Literacy learning and classroom talk.* New York: Teachers College Press.

National Assessment of Educational Progress. (2005). *Average scale scores and achievement-level results in reading by gender.* Retrieved January 11, 2008, from *nationsreportcard.gov/reading_math_2005.asp.*

Nye, N. S. (1999). *Habibi.* New York: Simon Pulse.

Odean, K. (1997). *Great books for girls.* New York: Ballantine.

Office of National Drug Control Policy. (2006). *Girls and drugs.* Retrieved January 13, 2008, from *www.mediacampaign.org/pdf/girls_and_drugs.pdf.*

Paterson, K. (1991). *Lyddie.* New York: Penguin Books.

Pierce, T. (1993). Fantasy: Why kids read it, why kids need it. *School Library Journal, 39,* 50–51.

Pipher, M. (1994). *Reviving Ophelia: Saving the selves of adolescent girls.* New York: Ballantine.

Porter, C. (2000). *Imani: All mine.* New York: Houghton Mifflin.

Rape, Abuse & Incest National Network. (2006). *Statistics.* Retrieved April 28, 2006, from *www.rainn.org/statistics.*

Saal, R. (1995). *The New York Public Library guide to reading groups.* New York: Crown.

Schiefele, U. (1996). Topic interest, text representation, and quality of experience. *Contemporary Educational Psychology, 21*, 3-18.

Spinelli, J. (2004). *Stargirl.* New York: Laurel Leaf.

Sprague, M., & Risher, L. (2002). Using fantasy literature to explore gender issues. *ALAN Review, 29*(2), 39–42.

Woolf, V. E. (1993). *Make lemonade.* New York: Scholastic.

Wrede, P. (1990). *Dealing with dragons* (Book 1 of *The Enchanted Forest Chronicles*). New York: Scholastic.

Chapter 11

Implications of Adolescents' Popular Culture Use for School Literacy

Alison Heron-Hruby
Donna E. Alvermann

GUIDING QUESTIONS

1. What perspectives have U.S. researchers taken on the implications of adolescents' popular culture use for school literacy?
2. What tensions exist among these perspectives?
3. How might these tensions inform the ways that U.S. middle and high school teachers incorporate popular culture into classroom literacy endeavors, especially when they face traditional, top-down notions of what reading and writing should look like in schools?

In recent years, there has been increased interest within the literacy field regarding the types of literacy practices in which adolescents engage when using popular culture (Alvermann, Moon, & Hagood, 1999; Morrell & Duncan-Andrade, 2002). For our purposes in this chapter, we define *popular culture* as a complex system involving interplay among people, texts, and technologies. This definition stems from cultural studies, a theoretical perspective that conceptualizes *culture* as a set of practices derived from "the production, circulation, and consumption of meanings" (Storey, 2003, p. 3). *Popular culture*, in particular, is defined in cultural studies as an arena for negotiation and struggle between dominant and subdominant groups along lines of gender, ethnicity, social class, sexuality, and generation (Storey, 2003). *Popular culture* texts themselves (e.g., television programs, video games, or songs) are secondary to what is done with them in the name of incorporation and resistance. Our focus, then, is on what adolescents do with texts in the interest of negotiating literacies of their own, within and outside the boundaries of school-sanctioned and other adult-dominated literacy practices, such as testing, mass marketing campaigns, and technology production.

Even more specifically, we focus this chapter on adolescent literacy research in the United States over the past 10 years. Although there is extensive international research available on adolescents' uses of popular culture (Alvermann, forthcoming; Beavis, Nixon, & Atkinson, 2005; Buckingham, 2003; Hagood, 2008; Sefton-Green, 2006), the opportunities, pressures, and constraints that U.S. secondary school teachers face in light of recent standards for literacy success, particularly those resulting from the No Child Left Behind Act of 2001 (NCLB), have presented unique research contexts for examining how—or if—adolescents' uses of popular culture might be incorporated into existing U.S. school curricula. As such, we believe it is useful to consider what the current U.S. research on that topic implies for educators working within those contexts, especially with the inherent emphasis on scientifically based literacy instruction and NCLB's rising expectations for schools to show adequate yearly progress (AYP).

Even if the NCLB sanctions were removed, other factors within U.S. schools influence possibilities for incorporating popular culture, such as U.S. teachers' tendency to be lukewarm about the idea of connecting students' popular literacies with school curricula (Hagood, 2002). This tendency may be due in part to the U.S. perspective that popular culture is often trite and coarse, or even potentially harmful (Trend, 2003; Quart, 2003), especially when compared to the attributes of elite culture, such as the literature, art, and music associated with high levels of taste and education (Bourdieu, 1979/1984). Consequently, teachers may not think of popular culture as a legitimate form of literate practice, especially if they discount the value of young people's knowledge about popular culture texts in a traditional, print-based environment.

The previously mentioned constraints, including the focus on AYP, present significant obstacles to the very idea of incorporating youth's popular culture in school curricula. Nonetheless, a small number of literacy researchers in the United States have in recent years given considerable attention to the role that popular culture plays in adolescents' literacy lives. Many of their findings challenge the utility of excluding students' own set of knowledge and experiences from school curricula, even in an era of high-stakes testing.

Indeed, the research itself reflects the late-20th-century shift in the U.S. literacy field away from a primary focus on how middle and high school students comprehend school-sanctioned materials, such as content-area text books and mandated literature anthologies, to an expanded focus that also includes how adolescents use reading and writing for myriad purposes across both in-school and out-of-school contexts (Moje, Overby, Tysvaer, & Morris, 2008). Indeed, authors of the International Reading Association (IRA) position statement on adolescent literacy (Moore, Bean, Birdyshaw, & Rycik, 1999) called for quality reading instruction for middle and high school students that attends to "the complexities of individual adolescent readers" (p. 8) and that provides access to "a wide variety of reading material that [adolescents] can and want to read" (p. 4). Accordingly, they suggested that teachers might incorporate adolescents' interests in popular culture into existing curricula to supplement school learning with what their students already care about and know.

Our review of the U.S. literacy research on adolescents' engagement with popular culture and the associated reading and writing practices reveals robust tensions regarding how teachers might go about purposefully incorporating aspects of adolescents' popular culture use into existing classroom endeavors. For example, some researchers have examined popular culture as a potential object of critical analysis that is meant to promote a heightened awareness among students about the effects of popular media on consumer culture (see Hobbs, 2007). In such a case, popular culture is positioned as a text to be examined using traditional modes of reading, writing, and discussion (Hobbs, 2007), and a venue for increasing students' skills in areas that reading and language arts teachers tend to value, such as the ability to analyze character or to understand and apply metacognitive strategies (Hobbs, 2001). Yet the work of literacy researchers who have considered the pleasure and play that adolescents derive from popular culture use (e.g., Hagood, 2002) suggests that classroom approaches focusing on rational–logical discourse, such as essay writing and cognitive strategy instruction, may limit or devalue the social and emotional significance that adolescents place on popular culture, undermining any attempt to connect school curricula to students' interests and experiences in the first place.

Other researchers have focused on the literacy practices inherent in popular culture use rather than on popular culture as an object of school study (e.g., Gee, 2003; Thomas, 2007). They argue that teachers might do well to design literacy activities that approximate some of adolescents' popular culture practices, an approach that adds challenge to the perhaps more superficial objective of adding popular culture texts (magazines, movies, song lyrics, etc.) to existing classroom reading lists. We don't view the tensions that arise when these perspectives are juxtaposed as necessarily problematic. In fact, in an era in which a single, uniform recommendation about how popular culture might be used in schools could easily falter in the face of teacher skepticism and top-down, AYP requirements, we believe it is important to consider the different ways popular culture might make its way into school curricula, especially if the goal is to connect students' own experiences and interests with what teachers present to them in classrooms. In this chapter, we assess such tensions and what they mean for classroom practice.

Framing the Intersection of Popular Culture and Literacy

Although there are differences in the theoretical frameworks that U.S. researchers use to study literacy practices, when they focus on young people's uses of popular culture in a digital environment, where multiple modes of communication (words, images, sounds, gestures) are available at the click of a mouse, researchers rely on a *social semiotic theory of multimodality* (Kress, 2003; Kress & Van Leeuwen, 1996). This theory, in a nutshell, accounts for how various resources (or available signs) are used to make meaning. Reading multimodal texts is a quite different process than reading in a single mode (most typically, the linguistic mode). As Lemke (2007) explains:

> Today more and more of what people value is codified multi-modally, as integrated combinations of images and text and sound, animations, videos, 3D virtual spaces, etc.... And you can't really get at the meaning of these forms piecemeal: you have to integrate the text with its fellow-travelers, cross-contextualizing them by one another, to get at the kinds of meanings being made and stored. (n.p.)

By drawing attention to the need to communicate using multiple modes of representation, not just language, in a world grown increasingly diverse and dependent on new information communication technologies, the New London Group (1996) envisioned a design of literate futures that calls for more than simply print-oriented instruction. From a multiliteracies perspective (New London Group, 1996), the term *text* itself has an expanded meaning, so that photographs, drawings, music, body language, and architecture, for example, become sources of meaning in the same manner as linguistic representations and, as a result, may be considered texts as well.

By defining *literacy* as a set of socially embedded practices with varying purposes and consequences, Street's (1984) ideological model of literacy provides researchers with a way to conceptualize reading as an act connected to the complex workings of social networks and varied outlets for communication, rather than as a set of autonomous skills reserved for written text. In contrast to the ideological model, the autonomous model of literacy, according to Street (1984), portrays reading as a cognitive act between an individual reader and a written text that holds to universal standards for logical thinking and transcends social customs. Popular culture, which so obviously is tied to social customs, would arguably be difficult to research as a set of autonomous reading and writing skills. Indeed, U.S. researchers who have studied popular culture tend to focus on social dynamics, such as power relations and cultural differences, rather than on decontextualized skills.

Also important to the study of the role of popular culture in adolescent literacy is the history of school-based literacy itself. A sweep of human history over the past 50,000 years reveals that only in the last 150 or so years did a call go out for universal education (Collins & Blot, 2003), one that conceivably would improve the lives of the so-called "illiterates" in the world. At the time the call was sounded, a high premium was placed on people's ability to comprehend the written word, inasmuch as writing was thought to be a marker of cognitive capacity and social functioning attributes that would lead to economic well-being and respect among peers. In the course of human history, this view of literacy is relatively new. As Collins and Blot pointed out prior to the privileging of written language over the spoken word, during a time that some scholars (e.g., Goody, 1986; Olson, 1994) refer to as the "Great Divide," oral communication was viewed as an equally valid indicator of human intellect and the competencies required for full membership in one's community. Once this order changed, however, the acts of reading and writing typically associated with schooled literacy became the norm. Because young people's literacy practices associated with popular culture texts are largely multimodal in form and function, they challenge the more traditional linguistic mode of school literacy. At the same time they present opportunities for teachers and students to reimagine what literacy in the 21st century involves.

Popular Culture as a Segue into School-Based Literacy Skills

A small number of studies have focused on possible relationships between popular culture and adolescents' literacy skills more generally. Included in these studies are several texts taken from the students' own popular culture, such as advertisements, popular film, and television programs. We would like to point out, however, that many of the texts were also selected by the teachers and/or researchers participating in the studies, and some of these do not fit easily into the category of participating students' popular culture, such the *Frontline* documentary on the Clinton sex scandal (see Hobbs, 2007). Nonetheless, the general focus of the studies was to have students "question information and authority" when it comes to mass and popular media (Tyner, 1998, cited in Hobbs & Frost, 2003, p. 331), therefore upholding Storey's (2003) definition of *popular culture* in the introduction of this chapter, which places consumers and producers in negotiation for positions of power and agency.

Alvermann et al. (1999), in their examination of teachers' instructional practices surrounding students' uses of popular culture at the middle school level, discussed four approaches. One approach views popular culture as detrimental to young people's development. Carmen Luke (1997), an Australian educator with many years of experience in researching and teaching critical media literacy, contends that when teachers think of popular culture in this way, their teaching becomes proselytizing about mass media's harmful effects. The second approach comprises teaching students how to analyze critically various forms of popular culture texts. For example, teachers may focus on teaching students how to become "the ideal" reader, viewer, listener—"the one who is never persuaded or fooled, who sees through the illusions the media provided—in effect, the [one] who is impervious to influence" (Buckingham, 1993, p. 146). In this approach, popular culture becomes an object that is useful primarily for the lessons it can teach. The third approach emphasizes the pleasures students take in various forms of media-produced texts (e.g., magazines, lyrics, videos, raps, TV, movies). Teachers who favor this approach typically shy away from asking students to critique what they find pleasurable in these texts. The underlying assumption is that everything is relative; thus, everyone is entitled to his or her own pleasures. Finally, the fourth approach (and the one that we favor) involves developing students' ability to be self-reflexive in their uses of popular culture. Teachers working from this perspective provide opportunities for students to explore issues such as "how media and the mass-produced icons of popular culture situate us into relations of power by shaping our emotional, political, social, and material lives" (Luke & Roe, 1993, p. 118).

A large-scale, mixed-methods study of 11th-graders media studies curriculum in a New Hampshire public high school demonstrated that when compared to students in traditional English/language arts programs at a high school with similar demographics and achievement levels, students in the media studies curriculum outperformed the control group on standardized measures of reading and writing achievement (Hobbs & Frost, 2003; Hobbs, 2007). The media studies students, who were heterogeneously grouped, read traditional literature texts, such as *Frankenstein* and *As I Lay Dying*, but studied these texts as part of theme-based units, with topics such as point of view and representation, which the teachers also had students apply to mass media texts, such as news reports, television sitcoms, and print ads. The emphasis was on critical media literacy, so that the students were continually engaged in analyzing media messages, addressing questions such as the following:

What techniques are used to attract and hold a viewer's (or reader's) attention?

What is the subtext of the author's message?

Students also produced their own multimedia artifacts—for example, documentaries that began with storyboards and scripts—to examine the unit's themes across the traditional literature and mass media. Qualitative data showed that the teachers had a high level of satisfaction in teaching the media studies units, and that students, who had not shown much enthusiasm for language arts in the past, appeared motivated and engaged (Hobbs, 2007).

The motivational aspect of using popular culture to promote literacy learning has also been addressed in research focused on the ways that teachers working with ethnically diverse groups of adolescents can make instruction more culturally relevant. Morrell (2002), for example, suggests ways that teachers can use hip-hop, popular culture films, and news media to engage urban youth in academic literacies, including debate, expository writing, and literary interpretation. Morrell and Duncan-Andrade (2002) describe how they used hip-hop music as a part of a unit they taught on poetry in an urban high school in northern California. In creating the unit, they emphasized the transfer of analytic skills from popular culture texts to canonical literature texts. By including literary and social analyses of popular culture music in the unit, they were able to have students use a genre with which they were already familiar to hone interpretive tools that they could then also apply to more typically valued genres in school. Morrell and Duncan-Andrade made it clear, however, that they did not use students' popular culture interests in ways that would signal they were appropriating them for their own ends as teachers.

Popular culture texts can also help students to portray themselves as competent readers and writers when they are portrayed as being otherwise in school. In one study, middle and high school students who were deemed to be underachievers at school, and who struggled to read school-assigned textbooks, indicated on reading logs that they actually read an average of 29–33 minutes daily outside of school (Alvermann et al., 2007). Thirty of the 60 students who participated in the study attended an out-of-school time media club at a local library. During the club meetings, participants had access to a wide array of media texts, including the Internet and the latest video games; popular music; and fashion, sports, and music magazines.

Similar texts were included as reading options on the daily reading logs they kept for the duration of the 14-week study. When compared to a 30-students control group that did not attend the media club meetings, an independent t-test revealed that club participants reported more often the statistically significant result that they read something on their own after school because they heard about it, and it had sounded interesting. The researchers concluded that providing adolescents with texts that they enjoy, and a social environment in which to share and use those texts, might help them not only to increase their perception of what literacy activities entail but also to take on a wider variety of literate behaviors, such as sharing texts and following up with peers' recommendations.

The analysis of literacy logs was only a small portion of the study; the researchers also looked at how the participating youth uses the popular media and technology texts provided them (Alvermann et al., 2002). Alvermann, Hagood, and Heron, who also served as the media club facilitators, found that choosing texts and accompanying activities for the students yielded quite different results than giving students control of what to use and how to use it. On their own, club participants became quite engaged in the texts, simultaneously critiquing and enjoying them. The activities the club facilitators designed, however, even when they involved popular culture texts that participants had chosen to be part of the media club materials, were met with little enthusiasm, especially when the focus was on critiquing representations of gender, race, and class in popular media.

A subsequent analysis that included data from the media club study (Alvermann et al., 2002) and two other studies of adolescents' uses of popular culture reinforced the significance of the media club participants' shift in enthusiasm when switching from adult-directed to youth-directed activities. The subsequent analysis (Heron-Hruby, Hagood, & Alvermann, 2008) demonstrated that expecting adolescents to analyze popular culture in ways that conform to adult expectations for mature thinking can lead to student resistance and resentment. Heron-Hruby et al. concluded that the tensions arising from differences in adult expectations and youth preferences make it difficult for teachers to include popular culture texts in the school curriculum, especially when teachers expect students to turn a critical eye on what they find enjoyable and useful (Luke, 1997). Thus, although there is some research to support teachers' use of popular culture texts in teaching students to become more skilled readers, there is also evidence to suggest that students' popular culture is not always a good medium for critical analysis, especially when the teachers decide how the critical analysis is supposed to look.

Popular Culture as a Complex Literacy Endeavor

Whereas in the previous section we focused on teacher and/or researcher-designed curricula, in this section we turn our attention to studies that offer insight into how adolescents use popular culture beyond, or in spite of, formal instruction initiated by adults. In these studies, researchers have been concerned with how adolescents use popular culture to form and to resist identities, or to "read" the world and themselves. The notion of "reading the world," as well as the word, which comes from political activist Paulo Freire (1993), situates reading as an ideological act that involves cultural understandings as much as it involves learning to decode words. In this sense, literacy practices associated with popular culture texts involve not only reading and writing (e.g., reading magazines and writing fan fiction) but also gaming and online social networking (e.g., MySpace, Facebook), along with the negotiation of identity and relations of power that accompany different standings within particular social, cultural, and/or political groups.

Studying Adolescent-Directed Uses of Popular Culture

Hagood (2002) focused on how adolescents' uses of popular culture texts, such as T-shirts emblazoned with the names and faces of famous rock musicians or Stephen King novels, played into their school identities (i.e., who they were as students, or, more specifically, who they were as readers during school hours). Hagood wrote, "Readers learn how to be a particular kind of person when using particular texts in particular ways," (p. 249) and, as such, focused on the different ways her research participant, Timony (a pseudonym), constructed himself, and was constructed, as a reader during school hours.

Timony, an eighth-grade student at the time of Hagood's study, was an avid reader who enjoyed a variety of texts, such as horror novels, biographies, and how-to books. His choices, however, which included the work of Stephen King and a biography of Kurt Cobain (the lead singer of Nirvana who committed suicide in the early 1990s) sometimes concerned his teachers who speculated that Timony "might be in some way disturbed" (Hagood, 2002, p. 249). Analyzing data from her observations of and interviews with Timony and his teachers, using poststructural definitions of identity and subjectivity (see, e.g., Butler, 1992), Hagood (2002) demonstrated how Timony's preferred texts and his actions surrounding those texts could be viewed as shifting, destabilized representations of a person in progress rather than as a set of predefined identities into which Timony could be sorted, either by himself or by others. In this way, his many possible identities (avid reader, horror fiction fan, dangerous teenager) appeared to be a superficial, easy way to categorize a complicated person who defied as much as he fit into these different roles.

Hagood (2002) concluded that taking a poststructual stance on subjectivity, which challenges the notion of stable identities, even the idea that people can have multiple identities at any given time, could restructure literacy instruction in schools to consider how adolescents use texts, including traditional literature texts, to push away staid meanings. The significance of students' engagement with literature texts in this way has been emphasized in other research as well, especially in the work of Cynthia Lewis (1999, 2000) and her coresearcher Jean Ketter (Lewis & Ketter, 2008), who examined ways that a small group of teachers in the rural Midwest upheld, then attempted to disrupt, White, middle-class ways of reading popular young adult fiction with young ethnic/minority protagonists.

In a subsequent study, Hagood (2004) analyzed the ways in which two female adolescents used popular culture texts both to affiliate with and to disrupt different identity groups—their Christian identity, in particular. Specifically, she presented visual analysis of these interactions, demonstrating how the girls "used popular culture to destabilize identities that limited their options and constricted them from being recognized as someone else, someone different, someone contradictory to another identity they held" (Hagood, 2004, p. 158); that is, the girls in Hagood's study used popular culture texts all at once to explore, to associate with, and to address limitations and contradictions within and across their chosen identities. Popular culture, in this sense, is much more than a mindless or dangerous dynamic for adolescents, as some adults have portrayed it in the past (e.g., Norton, 2001/2002; Quart, 2003).

Other researchers have also demonstrated ways that adolescents use popular culture in productive and complex ways. For example, Guzzetti (2006) worked within the perspective of literacy as a social practice to frame her case study of two young women who negotiated their social identities through website interactions (surfing, reading, posting their own content). Using data that she obtained from interviews, observations, and discourse analysis, Guzzetti showed how one girl (a self-identified activist) and the other (a punk rocker) used the interactive cybersites as entry points to gain acceptance and recognition in various affinity spaces (Gee, 2004), and to obtain information that portrayed them as "tech savvy" and "global citizens" prepared to fend for themselves.

Kamberelis (2004) provides insight into how adolescents' uses of popular culture (e.g., tagging and e-zine production) can be transformative, or politically effective. He depicts, in particular, how popular culture can function according to principles of rhizomes or pack multiplicities to effect ongoing social change (Deluze & Guattari, 1987). As such, adolescents' uses of popular culture, which, by definition, are exercises in subversion, "deterritorialize systems of authority by disrupting, circumventing, or subverting instruments of surveillance and regulation, and they reterritorialize the spaces in which these instruments operate" (Kamberelis, 2004, p. 192). Practices such as fashion choice and taste in music, for example, allow people to express nonmainstream ideas and to challenge authoritative ways of knowing. Adolescents' uses of popular culture texts, in this respect, can be conceptualized as political acts that transform spaces and instigate shifting perspectives.

Similarly, Knobel and Lankshear (2007) examined the ways in which Internet *memes*—cultural "matter" with staying power that is continually copied and passed among Internet users—involve social activist and other politically oriented behaviors. Examples of Internet memes such as Jibjab's "This Land!" (2004) and Black People Love Us (2002) are passed from person to person, interpreted and reinterpreted, and remain in circulation indefinitely. Knobel and Lankshear (2007) conclude that the memes' staying power, in part, has to do with their relationship to people's interests in political critique, advocacy, and citizenship. In exploring the significance that Internet memes have for school literacy, particularly activist literacy, Knobel and Lankshear emphasize the creativity of bottom-up contagious thought that seeks to usurp, or otherwise disrupt, top-down paradigms.

It is important to note, however, that celebrating young people's self-initiated uses of popular culture texts is only one aspect of studying the intersection of literacy and popular culture. Knobel and Lankshear (2007), for example, argue that educators should "equip students with important strategies for identifying the memes that infect their minds, and for evaluating the effects these memes have on their (ethical) decision-making, actions and relations with others" (p. 223). Simply using *popular culture texts*, according to Storey's (2003) definition of the term, is a critical activity in itself, because it involves a struggle between dominant and subordinate groups in a given society. However, inherent in the type of critical literacy pedagogy that Knobel and Lankshear (2007) describe is the stance that reading and writing should involve assessing texts for their role in illustrating various relations of power and domination (Hull, 1993). Integrating critical literacy pedagogy and popular culture, then, involves a sort of metacriticality, whereby young people's participation in popular culture is deemed an important struggle for power, but there is also a call for youth to step back and examine the implications of their participation in that struggle (see Buckingham, 2003).

Popular Culture as Literate Practice

As we mentioned earlier, U.S. literacy researchers who are interested in young people's uses of popular culture texts have focused to some extent on the potential fit of these texts in academic settings. In his research on the relationships between video games, literacy, and learning, Gee (2003, 2007) explored this potential in depth. It is important to note that Gee researched his own learning process while playing video games, then developed 36 principles based on that learning. In using those principles to write *What Video Games Have to Teach Us about Learning and Literacy*, he is careful to distinguish between the array of literacy practices reflected in gaming and the reading and writing activities often promoted in schools. For example, in discussing the video game *Full Spectrum Warrior*, he points out that the game "realizes that true knowledge in a domain (like warfare) is based on one's ability to build simulations ("models") in one's head, based on previous experiences and thoughtful conjecture, that prepare one for future action" (Gee, 2007, p. 109). Specifically, Gee emphasizes the importance of an embodied experience in learning, both with video games and more traditional modes, so that a player (or reader, or writer) enters the world of the text, experiences its contents (values, language, rules, etc.), and builds on those experience to acquire more sophisticated understandings of how the world (domain) functions. His argument is that video games provide just this type of experience, but that schools often fall short in providing the same type of embodied experience (Gee, 2003).

Stone (2007) and Thomas (2007) also examined the significance of the mismatches between students' in-school and out-of-school learning endeavors. Focusing on adolescents' popular culture practices, such as the creation of fan fiction and webpages, Stone and Thomas highlight how these practices involve several of the language arts endeavors valued in school, such as the reading and writing of narratives (Thomas, 2007), and the use of complex syntactical structures and sophisticated vocabulary, even when these skills don't show up in these students' work for school (Stone, 2007). Their findings are similar to those of Lewis and Fabos (2005), who observed seven youth, between ages of 14 and 17, use creative and strategic language practices to initiate and sustain instant messaging sessions with their friends. Thomas and Stone also demonstrated that adolescents' popular culture practices involve elements that educators do not typically emphasize, such as the use of reading and writing to forge friendships (Thomas, 2007), and intertextuality and multimodality (Stone, 2007), and suggested that teachers might include such elements in school curricula to enrich students' school literacy experiences.

Other work in the U.S. context that supports the potential benefit of popular culture in young people's learning has looked at Japanese animation (animé) (Chandler-Olcott & Mahar, 2003), comic book reading (Bitz, 2008; Botzakis, 2006); wrestling (Alvermann, Huddleston, & Hagood, 2004), spoken word poetry (Fisher, 2007), online journaling (Guzzetti & Gamboa, 2005), publishing ezines (Guzzetti & Gamboa, 2004), writing of fanfiction by English language learners (Black, 2006), constructing portfolios within instant messaging (Jacobs, 2006), and online gaming (Leander & Lovvorn, 2006). These studies, too numerous to do justice to in this short chapter, nonetheless reflect a larger trend in young people's interests in popular culture texts. This trend has been picked up in a series of PEW Internet studies, the latest of which (Lenhart, Madden, Macgill, & Smith, 2007) states the following:

> The use of social media—from blogging to online social networking to creation of all kinds of digital material—is central to many teenagers' lives. Some 93% of teens use the Internet, and more of them than ever are treating it as a venue for social interaction—a place where they can share creations, tell stories, and interact with others. (p. 1)

At the same time that young people are expressing their enthusiasm for creating online content, they are also reportedly aware of the different "standards" for writing online in contrast to writing to complete school assignments. In a combined focus group/survey study involving 700 youth, ages 12–17, and their parents, Lenhart, Arafeh, Smith, and Macgill (2008) found that the young people did not view e-mailing, text messaging, and posting to social network sites as "real writing." They viewed school writing as being important (as did their parents), and they had suggestions for ways that teachers could make formal writing instruction more engaging (e.g., by providing time to write in class, and by using computer-based writing tools).

There is still little known about how students' use of popular culture outside school curricula affects their in-school achievement. Recently, however, the potential impact of students' outside literacy interests on their formal school learning was tested in the Moje et al. (2008) large-scale, longitudinal study of predominantly Latino/a youth of middle and high school age. Based on the Moje et al. mixed-methods analysis of first- and second-wave datasets, the students surveyed and interviewed reportedly read a wide range of popular culture texts in their leisure time, but reading novels on a regular basis was the only literacy practice shown to have a statistically significant, positive relationship to their English grades. Although the Moje et al. reported only preliminary findings (there is one more wave of data to collect), the evidence is somewhat encouraging thus far, suggesting that reading popular novels is related to students' inschool achievement, at least in the area of English language arts. Less optimistically, it may be argued that this study demonstrates what many literacy scholars have suspected for years—that wide reading in materials closely resembling those used in school results in improved reading achievement. That this suspicion was not put to the test by the National Reading Panel (2000) is due to the fact that an insufficient number of studies on out-of-school reading practices existed at the time the Panel conducted its meta-analysis of effective reading instruction.

Implications for Practice in U.S. Schools

Different perspectives on how young people's uses of popular culture might fit within the regular school-day curriculum allow us to examine the tensions surrounding these perspectives and, in turn, the various possibilities for teacher intervention. They also provide insight into how a curriculum that invites students' popular culture texts can coexist in an era of high-stakes testing and AYP accountability.

Popular culture texts, just like any other kinds of text, are not neutral in the messages they send. As Luke and Freebody (1997) pointed out over a decade ago, "All language, all text, all discourse … 'refracts' the world; bending, shaping, constructing particular versions and visions of the social and natural world that act in the interests of particular class, gender, and cultural groups" (p. 193). A starting point in addressing the tension between a student's agency in reading a popular culture text and the structured message that *is* the text might involve creating "an awareness of how, why, and in whose interests particular texts might work [followed by strategies for developing] alternative reading positions and practices for questioning and critiquing texts and their affiliated social formations and cultural assumptions" (Luke & Freebody, 1997, p. 218). Teachers can then work to build on how students already use popular culture by fostering the higher-order thinking abilities valued in schools for use with both popular culture texts and more traditional texts. Two frameworks that encompass building awareness and taking alternative reading positions are the three-dimensional (operational, cultural, and critical) model of literacy (Damico, 2005; Green, 1988) and the four-resources model (code breaker, meaning maker, text user, and text analyst; Luke & Freebody, 1997; Luke, Freebody, & Land, 2000).

Perhaps the greatest tension in students' use of popular culture texts in school curricula is the conflict between potential criticism among teachers and students (through distancing oneself from violence, gender and racial stereotypes, sexually explicit song lyrics, etc.) and the pleasure that adolescents (and their teachers as well) derive from texts that contain arguably harmful ideas and images. The research we reviewed demonstrates that young people participate in creative and complex lines of thought when engaged in texts of which adults might be critical or skeptical. And we do believe that such findings are significant in understanding the importance of popular culture for literacy learning in general. However, more research is needed on how a critical approach to popular culture, one that is in line with the objectives for critical thinking in U.S. schools, might shape adolescents' already complex interaction with the popular culture texts they choose to read and write on their own.

In general, the research on how adolescents use poplar culture outside of school curricula demonstrates that what these young people are doing goes beyond mere entertainment, and it is certainly not simple. However, there is the challenge of deciding how adolescents' self-directed literacy endeavors, such as the ones associated with their uses of popular culture, relate to school success. The disassociation that adolescents perceive between online writing and writing in school, for example, and the suggestions they have for improving inschool formal writing instruction, suggests that, as educators, we need to tap into students' perceptions of what they know and need to know on a regular basis. Policies (whether local, state, or national) that treat youth as a monolithic group fail to take into consideration young people's commonsense knowledge about their own educational needs, especially in regard to reading and writing. Thus, whereas monitoring AYP may address federal policies that call for more strict accountability at the local level, such monitoring may provide little or no insight into what students themselves are thinking, such as the need for more inclass writing time and an integration of computer writing tools during formal writing instruction. The research on what adolescents know and do with popular culture may perhaps prove invaluable in creating ways to bridge educator and student knowledge.

QUESTIONS FOR DISCUSSION

1. What are some ways that middle and high school teachers can use popular culture as part of the school curricula, and still address local and national standards for school literacy success?

2. In what ways do adolescents "read" popular culture using the same literacy abilities that teachers want them to develop in school?

3. How might teachers go about learning from adolescents about youth literacy practices outside of school?

Resources

Further Reading

Black, R. W., & Steinkuehler, C. (2008). Literacy in virtual worlds. In L. Christenbury, R. Bomer, & P. Smagorinsky (Eds.), *Handbook of research on adolescent literacy* (pp. 271–286). New York: Guilford Press.

National School Boards Association. (2007, August). *Creating and connecting: Research and guidelines on online social and educational networking.* Retrieved November 13, 2007, from *files.nsba.org/creatingandconnecting.pdf.*

Skinner, E. (2007). "Teenage addiction": Adolescent girls drawing upon popular culture texts as mentors for writing in an after-school writing club. *National Reading Conference Yearbook, 56,* 345–361.

Websites

www.henryjenkins.org—This is Henry Jenkins's blog. A professor of humanities and founder of the Comparative Media Studies Program at Massachusetts Institute of Technology, Jenkins studies fan culture. Posts to this site range from practical observations to full-length research papers.

www.ernestmorrell.com—Ernest Morrell's website contains ideas on media, culture, and pedagogy. Morrell, a professor of urban education and cultural studies, and Associate Director of Youth Research at the Institute for Democracy, Education, and Access (IDEA) at UCLA, writes poems, plays, essays, novels, and academic books, book chapters, and articles. His website has links to critical pedagogy and media production.

References

Alvermann, D. E. (forthcoming). Popular culture in traditional and new literacies. In M. L. Kamil, P. Afflerbach, E. B. Moje, & P. D. Pearson (Eds.), *Handbook of reading research* (Vol. IV). New York: Erlbaum.

Alvermann, D. E., & Eakle, A. J. (2007). Dissolving learning boundaries: The doing, re- doing, and undoing of school. In D. Thiessen & A. Cook-Sather (Eds.), *International handbook of student experience in elementary and secondary school* (pp. 143–166). Dordrecht, Netherlands: Springer.

Alvermann, D. E., & Hagood, M. (2000). Fandom and critical media literacy. *Journal of Adolescent & Adult Literacy, 43,* 436–446.

Alvermann, D. E., Hagood, M. C., Heron, A., Hughes, P., Williams, K., & Yoon, J. (2002). *After-school media clubs for struggling adolescent readers: A study of youth's critical awareness* (Final Report submitted to the Spencer Foundation's Major Grants Program [Grant No. 199900278]).

Alvermann, D. E., Hagood, M. C., Heron, A., Hughes, P., Williams, K., & Yoon, J. (2007). Telling themselves who they are: What one out-of-school time study revealed about underachieving readers. *Reading Psychology, 28,* 31–50.

Alvermann, D. E., Hagood, M. C., & Williams, K. B. (2001). Image, language, and sound: Making meaning with popular culture texts. *Reading Online, 4*(11), n.p. Retrieved January 20, 2008, from *www.readingonline.org/newliteracies/lit_index.asp?href=/newliteracies/action/alvermann/index.html.*

Alvermann, D. E., Huddleston, A., & Hagood, M. C. (2004). What could professional wrestling and school literacy practices possibly have in common? *Journal of Adolescent & Adult Literacy, 47,* 532–540.

Alvermann, D. E., Moon, J. S., & Hagood, M. C. (1999). *Popular culture in the classroom: Thinking and researching critical media literacy.* Newark, DE: International Reading Association and the National Reading Conference.

Beavis, C., Nixon, H., & Atkinson, S. (2005). LAN cafes: Cafes, places of gathering, or sites of informal teaching and learning? *Education, Communication, and Information, 5*(1), 40–60.

Bitz, M. (2008). The comic book project: Literacy outside (and inside) the box. In J. Flood, S. B. Heath, & D. Lapp (Eds.), *Handbook of research on teaching literacy through the communicative and visual arts* (Vol. II, pp. 229–236). New York: Erlbaum/Taylor & Francis.

Black, R. W. (2006). Language, culture, and identity in online fanfiction. *eLearning Journal, 3*(2), 170–184.

Botzakis, S. (2006). *Reading when they don't have to: Insights from adult comic book readers.* Unpublished dissertation, University at Georgia, Athens, GA.

Bourdieu, P. (1984). *Distinction: A social critique of judgement of taste* (R. Nice, Trans.). Cambridge, MA: Harvard University Press. (Original work published 1979)

Buckingham, D. (1993). *Children talking television: The making of television literacy.* London: Falmer Press.

Buckingham, D. (2003). Media education and the end of the critical consumer. *Harvard Educational Review, 73,* 309–327.

Chandler-Olcott, K., & Mahar, D. (2003). "Tech-savviness" meets multiliteracies: Exploring adolescent girls' technology-mediated literacy practices. *Reading Research Quarterly, 38,* 356–385.

Collins, J., & Blot, R. K. (2003). *Literacy and literacies: Texts, power, and identity.* Cambridge, UK: Cambridge University Press.

Damico, J. S. (2005). Multiple dimensions of literacy and conceptions of readers: Toward a more expansive view of accountability. *Reading Teacher, 58,* 644–652.

Deluze, G., & Guattari, F. (1987). *A thousand plateaus: Capitalism and schizophrenia* (B. Massumi, Trans.). Minneapolis: University of Minnesota Press.

Fisher, M. T. (2007). *Writing in rhythm: Spoken word poetry in urban classrooms.* New York: Teachers College Press.

Freire, P. (1993). *Pedagogy of the oppressed* (Rev. 20th anniversary ed.). New York: Continuum.

Gee, J. P. (2003). *What video games have to teach us about learning and literacy.* New York: Palgrave/Macmillan.

Gee, J. P. (2004). *Situated language and learning: A critique of traditional schooling.* New York: Routledge.

Gee, J. P. (2007). Pleasure, learning, video games, and life: The projective stance. In M. Knobel & C. Lankshear (Eds.), *A new literacies sampler* (pp. 95–113). New York: Peter Lang.

Goody, J. (1986). *The logic of writing and the organization of society.* New York: Cambridge University Press.

Green, B. (1988). Subject-specific literacy and school learning: A focus on writing. *Australian Journal of Education, 32*(3), 156–179.

Guzzetti, B. J. (2006). Cybergirls: Negotiating social identities on cybersites. *eLearning Journal, 3*(2), 158–169.

Guzzetti, B. J., & Gamboa, M. (2004). Zines for social justice: Adolescent girls writing on their own. *Reading Research Quarterly, 39,* 408–436.

Guzzetti, B. J., & Gamboa, M. (2005). Online journaling: The informal writings of two adolescent girls. *Research in the Teaching of English, 40,* 168–206.

Hagood, M. C. (2002). Critical literacy for whom? *Reading Research and Instruction, 41*(3), 247–266.

Hagood, M. C. (2004). A Rhizomatic cartography of adolescents, popular culture, and construction of self. In K. M. Leander & M. Sheehy (Eds.), *Spatializing literacy research and practice* (pp. 143–160). New York: Peter Lang.

Hagood, M. C. (2008). Intersections of popular culture, identities, and new literacies research. In C. Coiro, M. Knobel, C. Lanankshear, & D. J. Leu (Eds.), *Handbook of research on new literacies* (pp. 531–551). New York: Erlbaum.

Heron-Hruby, A., Hagood, M. C., & Alvermann, D. E. (2008). Switching places and looking to adolescents for the formation of standardizing practices of school literacies. *Reading and Writing Quarterly, 24,* 311–334.

Hobbs, R. (2001). Improving reading comprehension by using media literacy activities. *Voices from the Middle, 8*(4), 44–50.

Hobbs, R. (2007). *Reading the media: Media literacy in high school English.* New York: Teachers College Press.

Hobbs, R., & Frost, R. (2003). Measuring the acquisition of media-literacy skills. *Reading Research Quarterly, 38,* 330–355.

Hull, G. (1993). Critical literacy and beyond: Lessons learned from students and workers in a vocational program and on the job. *Anthropology and Education Quarterly, 24,* 308–317.

Jacobs, G. E. (2006). Fast times and digital literacy: Participation roles and portfolio construction within instant messaging. *Journal of Literacy Research, 38,* 171–196.

Kamberelis, G. (2004). The rhizome and the pack: Liminal literacy formations with political teeth. In K. M. Leander & M. Sheehy (Eds.), *Spatializing literacy research and practice* (pp. 161–197). New York: Peter Lang.

Knobel, M., & Lankshear, C. (2007). Online memes, affinities, and cultural production. In M. Knobel & C. Lankshear (Eds.), *A new literacies sampler* (pp. 199–227). New York: Peter Lang.

Kress, G. (2003). *Literacy in the new media age.* London: Routledge.

Kress, G., & van Leeuwen, T. (1996). *Reading images: The grammar of visual design.* London: Routledge.

Leander, K. M., & Lovvorn, J. (2006). Literacy networks: Following the circulation of texts, bodies, and objects in the schooling and online gaming of one youth. *Cognition & Instruction, 24,* 291–340.

Lemke, J. (2007, February). *New media and new learning communities: Critical, creative, and independent.* Paper presented at the annual meeting of National Council of Teachers of English Assembly for Research (NCTEAR), Vanderbilt University, Nashville, TN. (Paper discussed online January 28, 2007; retrieved February 1, 2008, from *lchc.ucsd.edu/mca/mail/xmcamail.2007_01.dir/0354.html.*)

Lenhart, A., Arafeh, S., Smith, A., & Macgill, A. R. (2008, April). *Writing, technology and teens* (Pew Internet & American Life Project). Washington, DC: Pew Charitable Trusts. Retrieved April 24, 2008, from *www.pewinternet.org/ppf/r/247/report_display.asp.*

Lenhart, A., Madden, M., Macgill, A. R., & Smith, A. (2007, December). *Teens and social media* (PEW Internet & American Life Project). Washington, DC: Pew Charitable Trusts. Retrieved January 3, 2008, from *www.pewinternet.org/ppf/r/230/report_display.asp.*

Lewis, C. (1999). Teaching literature to adolescents. *Reading Research Quarterly, 34,* 114–127.

Lewis, C. (2000). Limits of identification: The personal, pleasurable, and critical in reader response. *Journal of Literacy Research, 32,* 253–266.

Lewis, C., & Fabos, B. (2005). Instant messaging, literacies, and social identities. *Reading Research Quarterly, 40,* 470–501.

Lewis, C., & Ketter, J. (2008). Encoding youth: Popular culture and multicultural literature in a rural context. *Reading and Writing Quarterly, 24,* 283–310.

Luke, A., & Freebody, P. (1997). Shaping the social practices of reading. In S. Muspratt, A. Luke, & P. Freebody (Eds.), *Constructing critical literacies: Teaching and learning textual practice* (pp. 185–225). Cresskill, NJ: Hampton.

Luke, A., Freebody, P., & Land, R. (2000). *Literate futures: Report of the literacy review for Queensland state schools.* Brisbane, Australia: Education Queensland. Retrieved March 28, 2008, from *education.qld.gov.au/curriculum/learning/literate-futures/pdfs/lf-review.pdf.*

Luke, C. (1997). Media literacy and cultural studies. In S. Muspratt, A. Luke, & P. Freebody (Eds.), *Constructing critical literacies: Teaching and learning textual practice* (pp. 19–49). Cresskill, NJ: Hampton.

Luke, C., & Roe, K. (1993). Introduction to special issues: Media and popular cultural studies in the classroom. *Australian Journal of Education, 37,* 115–118.

Moje, E. B., Overby, M., Tysvaer, N., & Morris, K. (2008). The complex world of adolescent literacy: Myths, motivations, and mysteries. *Harvard Educational Review, 78,* 107–154.

Moore, D., Bean, T. W., Birdyshaw, D., & Rycik, J. A. (1999). *Adolescent literacy: A position statement for the Commission on Adolescent Literacy of the International Reading Association.* Newark, DE: International Reading Association.

Morrell, E. (2002). Toward a critical pedagogy of popular culture: Literacy development among urban youth. *Journal of Adolescent & Adult Literacy, 46,* 72–77.

Morrell, E., & Duncan-Andrade, J. M. R. (2002). Promoting academic literacy with urban youth through engaging hip-hop culture. *English Journal, 91*(6), 88–92.

National Reading Panel. (2000). *Report of the National Reading Panel: Teaching children to read* (NIH Pub. No. 00-4769). Washington, DC: National Institute of Child Health and Human Development.

New London Group. (1996). A pedagogy of multiliteracies: Designing social futures. *Harvard Educational Review, 66,* 60–92.

Norton, B. (2001/2002). When is a magazine not a teen magazine? *Journal of Adolescent & Adult Literacy, 45,* 296–299.

Olson, D. R. (1994). *The world on paper: The conceptual and cognitive implications of writing and reading.* Cambridge, UK: Cambridge University Press.

Quart, A. (2003). *Branded: The buying and selling of teenagers.* New York: Basic Books.

Stone, J. C. (2007). Popular websites in adolescents' out-of-school literacies: Critical lessons on literacy. In M. Knobel & C. Lankshear (Eds.), *A new literacies sampler* (pp. 49–56). New York: Peter Lang.

Storey, J. (2003). *Cultural studies and the study of popular culture* (2nd ed.). Athens: University of Georgia Press.

Street, B. V. (1984). *Literacy in theory and practice.* New York: Cambridge University Press.

Thomas, A. (2007). Blurring and breaking through the boundaries of narrative, literacy, and identity in adolescent fan fiction. In M. Knobel & C. Lankshear (Eds.), *A new literacies sampler* (pp. 137–166). New York: Peter Lang.

Trend, D. (2003). Merchants of death: Media violence and American empire. *Harvard Educational Review, 73,* 285–308.

Part II

TEACHING THE ADOLESCENT LEARNER
RESEARCH-BASED INSTRUCTIONAL PRACTICES

Chapter 12

Research-Based
Instructional Literacy Practices
Challenges and Opportunities

Patricia L. Anders

GUIDING QUESTIONS

1. How do you define research-based practices?
2. What role does research play in your professional practice?
3. What are the processes you employ when selecting instructional practices?

This is a terrific time to be an educator in adolescent literacy: Adolescent literacy is considered to be among the "hottest" topics by members of the International Reading Association (IRA; Cassidy & Cassidy, 2007); foundations support the writing of literature reviews, research, and policy statements (e.g., Carnegie Foundation, Ford Foundation); the federal government is funding adolescent literacy–related research (e.g., the Institute of Educational Science's Striving Readers grants), and conference participants in unprecedented numbers are attending sessions that present information about adolescent literacy (Hinchman & Sheridan-Thomas, 2008). Topics related to adolescent literacy haven't always been of such high interest, although the topic has been around since the early 1900s. Edmund Huey (1908), for example, recommended that students read in the "central subjects," and E. L. Thorndike (1917) hypothesized that "perhaps it is in their outside reading of stories and in their study of geography, history, and the like, that many school children really learn to read" (p. 328). During the 20th century, scholarship and practice related to adolescent literacy have attended mainly to the teaching of reading across the curriculum or "in the content areas." But at the turn of the century, and currently, most scholars have broadened their interests to be more inclusive of the age group we are studying, youth and young adults, as they negotiate and engage in learning about their world and their place in it both in and out of school.

In this chapter I intend to provide a framework for Part II of this volume. Editors Karen D. Wood and William E. Blanton invited leading scholars to address topics such as assessment, motivation, differentiation of instruction, unique materials for instruction, vocabulary, comprehension, discussion, composition, grouping, use of the Internet and other technological innovations, and higher-order thinking. These topics are interesting to anyone involved in studying and teaching adolescent literacy. With standards of research and practice as a platform, innovative ideas suggested by these authors may be considered for implementation and critique. Even more fulfilling is that these ideas can be used to launch research to build on the lengthening chain of inquiry into adolescent literacy development and instructional practices.

This introductory chapter in Part II begins with the notion of "research-based instructional practices," addressing questions such as "Where did they come from?," "What are they?," and "Why are they important?" Next, I critiqued the concept of research-based instructional practices, reflecting on the nature of research and what it means when an instructional practice carries that stamp of approval. I do not mean to deride or diminish the importance of research-based instructional practices, but I do attempt to place in the foreground a perspective that often seems to be missing when policymakers, publishers, and others promote "research-based practices." Next, I summarize the literature related to research-based instructional practices in general and to adolescent literacy instruction in particular. I end with a strong recommendation: All adolescent literacy educators need to increase their research activity. All forms of research from multiple perspectives and situations are needed to enjoy the benefits of having research-based practices for adolescent literacy instruction.

Research-Based Instructional Practices

I first became conscious of the term *research-based practices* in the mid-1980s. Two events come to mind: first, a research project I codirected; and second, the publication of *Becoming a Nation of Readers: The Report of the Commission on Reading* (Anderson, Hiebert, Scott, & Wilkinson, 1985). The research project my colleagues and I conducted from 1986 to 1990 was the Reading Instruction Study (RIS; see Richardson, 1994, for a complete description of the study), sponsored by the Office of Educational Research and Improvement (OERI). Our purpose was to investigate why teachers reported that they did not use "research-based practices" when they taught reading. After all, the authors of the landmark volume *Becoming a Nation of Readers* had written that "the knowledge is now available to make worthwhile improvements in reading throughout the United States. If the practices seen in the classrooms of the best teachers in the best schools could be introduced everywhere, improvements in reading would be dramatic" (Anderson et al., 1985, p. 1). But, according to the OERI request for proposals, teachers who were asked whether they used research to make instructional decisions reported that they did not.

I think the term *research-based practices* began to gain currency in educational rhetoric at about this time, although Stewart (2002) reports finding the term referenced as early as the 1800s. Other common terms in the educational lexicon, such as *pedagogy, methods, skills instruction,* and *instructional strategies,* lost currency and did not connote the same evidentiary standard as the term *research-based.* No doubt, certain policymakers agreed with Anderson and colleagues (1985) that if teachers would simply use research-based practices, then all would be well. This shift in terminology challenges us to ponder questions such as the following:

What is a practice?

How does a practice differ from a method or an instructional strategy?

What is a sufficient research base to qualify a practice as "research-based"?

What are research-based practices?

These questions are considered in this chapter.

In 1998, about 10 years after the RIS study and the publication of *Becoming a Nation of Readers* (Anderson et al., 1985), policymakers and the U.S. Congress requested that a panel of reading researchers and interested others, including teachers, administrators, physicians, and parents, "convene … to assess the status of research-based knowledge" (National Reading Panel, 2000, p. 1-1) about teaching reading, and to address the questions "What is the knowledge base?" and "What research is available for teachers to make instructional decisions?" In 2000, the National Institute of Child Health and Human Development (NICHD) commissioned the National Reading Panel (NRP) to conduct a comprehensive review of reading instruction research. The panel chose a research paradigm that aimed, by purpose and design, to make causal claims:

> To sustain a claim of effectiveness, the Panel felt it necessary that there be experimental or quasiexperimental studies of sufficient size or number, and scope (in terms of population served), and that these studies be of moderate to high quality. When there were either too few studies of this type, or they were too narrowly cast, or they were of marginally acceptable quality, then it was essential that the Panel have substantial correlational or descriptive studies that concurred with

the findings if a claim was to be sustained. No claim could be determined on the basis of descriptive or correlational research alone. The use of these procedures increased the possibility of reporting findings with a high degree of internal validity. (National Reading Panel, 2000, p. 1-5)

Given the Congressional mandate, it is understandable why the panel made the decisions it did, although the minority report (National Reading Panel, 2000) raises provocative objections. Yatvin, the author of the minority report, points out that the panel did not review topics inherently integral to reading instruction, such as language development, accessibility to literature, and adolescent literacy.

Policymakers at the federal and state levels have interpreted the findings of the NRP and have recommended and, in the case of Reading First federal funding, required that instruction, materials, and assessments be used only if they are consistent with the findings and recommendations of the NRP report. In my own state of Arizona, the Department of Education promotes instruction, assessments, and instructional materials that, it believes, carry a stamp of approval based on the NRP report. In meetings with employees of the Arizona Department of Education, I have often been told that research proves that there are five components to the reading process, and that only instruction, programs, and assessments that aim to teach those components are "research-based" and endorsed by the state for teachers, teacher educators, and authors of instructional materials to use. According to the federal policymakers, then, the notion of research-based practices is grounded in the findings of the NRP, which used a particular theory of reading acquisition and the "gold standard" of clinical research to advocate for particular practices related to that theory, and includes the following components: phonemic awareness, phonics, vocabulary, fluency, and comprehension. This way of thinking and doing undermines the nature of research, teaching, and learning, and is a gross oversimplification of what constitutes a teacher's practice, particularly when considering research-based instructional practices for adolescents. In the next section I explain my distress over such a narrow conception of research-based practices, and end with an example from the RIS project.

Limitations of Policymakers' Definition of Research-Based Practices

The tightly woven, narrow construction of the term *research-based practices*, as conceived and implemented by Reading First and those associated with it, contradicts, first and foremost, the *nature* of research. Other concerns include the central role of curriculum in middle and secondary schools, the social nature of adolescents, and the heterogeneity of both teachers and students in middle and secondary schools.

The Purpose and Nature of Research

Policymakers and some uninformed educators assume that the purpose of research is to "prove" that something like a reading instructional practice "works." Commonly, they argue that if a teacher employs a particular practice, reading achievement will most likely increase. This is the claim that the authors of *Becoming a Nation of Readers* (Anderson et al., 1985) made, perhaps naively or innocently. Those who describe the nature of research, however, disagree (e.g., Fleck, 1979; Kuhn, 1962). Bateson (1979), for example, wrote that the purpose of research is to *dis*-prove; he explained that science does not prove—it probes. The point is that in the real world of research, there is no final, once-and-for-all answer to a research question. Researchers, and those who use research, know that research *suggests*, but that the finding remains open to question and to further research. The current status of research-based practices, as promulgated by many educational policymakers, ignores this basic presupposition about the nature of inquiry. Fortunately, those who are involved in research understand this abuse of the research enterprise; but literacy educators must remain steadfast, and not allow the abuse to continue. Policymakers, and those employed to implement policies, are misinforming the public and their constituents as to the purpose and value of research, and are doing a great disservice to public education by doing so.

The Central Role of Curriculum

The core purpose of the secondary school is to invite young people to become acquainted with the major ideas represented by the disciplines. Secondary education in the United States has a long tradition of introducing the sciences, social sciences, arts, languages, English language arts, and mathematics to its students. These disciplines are organized into Carnegie units, and each student is expected to engage and learn the central ideas of the curriculum. Standards are established by professional organizations representing these disciplines, resource materials (all forms of media, text, original sources, artifacts, experiments) are provided, and teachers are specialists in the subjects they teach.

Herber (1970, 1978) argued persuasively that separating reading instruction—especially content-area reading instruction—from the content to be engaged is impossible. He demonstrated that print content is organized rhetorically in ways that represent the conceptual hierarchy of the discipline—the organization of the text is the form of the ideas; hence, reading strategies/practices need to provide support, or scaffolding, for the engagement of those ideas.

Research-based literacy practices are typically researched and described in ways that isolate them from any sense of curriculum. This is one reason why content-area teachers are reluctant to be persuaded as to the value of the practices. Teachers do not see a link between research-based practice and conceptual content, and these teachers are committed to engaging their students in the ideas of the content.

The Secondary School Is Social

Research-based practices meet the criteria for being *research-based* because the conditions under which the practices are researched are rigidly controlled. Classic experimental studies focus on individual elements, such as the organization of information text instructional strategies, and create conditions that differ from the typical classrooms in which those elements will be placed. In addition, all students participating in a research study possess characteristics that set them apart from other students. Therefore, the elements studied must be considered in terms of their effects on individual students. In other words, classroom settings and students may look very much alike, but they are at the same time unique. Moreover, as Radenbush (2008) argues, "The social structure of instruction—the fact that it occurs within classrooms nested within schools—invalidates the canonical assumptions underlying the clinical trial" of the classical experiment (p. 207). Rarely will a research-based practice be transported into a classroom and "work" as it did in a research study. Teachers are called upon to modify research-based practices to fit their classroom conditions, the curriculum, and the needs of students.

If teachers use a research-based practice precisely as it was used in research studies, they are also limited in their capacity to take advantage of the social nature of young people and classroom interactions. As a high school teacher, I would not teach against the nature of my students, because doing so would invite student resistance and invite students to engage in power plays between them and me, resulting in dysfunctional classroom behavior. In addition, research suggests that students learn from each other, and that discussion strategies and critical thinking is often developed as students work together, either in small groups or as a whole class.

Moje (2007), who recognized and extended thinking about the social nature of the secondary school, curriculum, and instructional practices by identifying schools as a foundation of our democracy, asked what teachers do to teach for social justice and whether their teaching is socially just. Her question gets at the heart of what is wrong with a single-minded promotion of research-based practices. For example, some schools are assigning students to classes designed to teach them research-based practices in isolation from curricular content and their peers. Those of us who care about adolescents, and their literacy and learning, must weigh the value of any instructional practice we promote or use in terms of both our modeling of socially just behavior, and the opportunities that practices we use or programs we establish provide for youth.

Research-Based Practices Are a Small Part of What a Teacher Does

The typical high school teacher faces many challenges as she engages her students in the curriculum. Research-based strategies are but a small part of the

overall instruction. Shedd and Bacharach (1991) describe the "tangled hierarchies" in which teachers find themselves as they meet the demands of their
multifaceted roles, including being instructors, counselors, and supervisors.
As teachers fulfill these roles and orchestrate the many functions within each,
it is clear that teaching is not "merely technical and rule driven, and teachers are not simply passive recipients who carry research-based practice to the
classrooms. Rather, professional teachers are reflective; that is, they connect
knowledge to situations through processes of observation, understanding,
analysis, interpretation, and decision making" (Doyle, 1985, p. 32).

The Heterogeneity of the Students in the Secondary School

One thing that is known by anyone who has walked the halls of the modern
middle or high school is that differences and diversity abound. Many different languages are heard, ethnicities vary, and the socioeconomic differences
are great. It is necessary for teachers to make instructional and curricular
adaptations to meet the needs of these diverse students. For example, it is
common for teachers to have English language learners (ELLs) in their classroom. In such a classroom, the teacher needs to use and adapt practices to
support ELL students (Rubinstein-Ávila & Johnson, 2007). Some research,
such as that by Rubinstein-Ávila and Johnson, helps us to understand these
individual differences. Educators of adolescents (e.g., Wood & Muth, 1991)
suggest that unless we better understand what motivates and interests adolescents in developmentally appropriate ways, we can hardly begin to select
appropriate practices. Ivey (1999) provides insights into the complexities of
young adolescent readers.

Teachers are heterogeneous as well. Teachers' backgrounds, content
expertise, and theoretical orientations related to teaching and learning are
diverse. Research-based practices, as promulgated by many policymakers and
educators, tend to ignore this tremendous heterogeneity.

The RIS Example

Our experience in the RIS project (Lloyd & Anders, 1994) exemplifies each
of these limitations. As I noted earlier, the goal of the RIS study was to study
why teachers resist using research-based practices. First, we defined the term
practice, then searched the literature for research-based reading instructional
practices. We understood a *practice* to be an instructional strategy or method
employed by a teacher that could be named, observed, and described, and
whose research base suggested its value. Our search was governed by three
selection criteria: (1) We sought practices published in peer-reviewed publications; (2) the article needed to name and describe a reading instructional
practice, and provide evidence as to its efficacy in the classroom; and (3) the
purpose(s) of the stated practice must have been to affect reading comprehension. Practices meeting these criteria were located through the Education
Resources Information Center (ERIC) and the references cited in synthe-

ses and reviews of reading research published between 1970 and 1985. After locating the studies, we categorized 89 investigated practices in 15 categories. For example, in one category, "Background Knowledge," practices included providing advance organizers, confronting misconceptions, and predicting story events. Our analysis included an estimation of the efficacy of the practice for teaching reading comprehension in grades 4–8. As a result of this literature review and analysis, we were confident that we had found practices with a research base that adequately justified their use in the classroom. We prepared materials that we intended to use in professional development activities for upper elementary school teachers to use when teaching reading comprehension.

The program of professional development included both individual and group components. The group component involved meetings at each of six schools for teachers to discuss and explore the instruction of reading comprehension. One way we made the research-based practices available was to provide to teachers a list of the practices we had found. During an initial professional development meeting, we distributed the list of practices to each teacher, described the categories of practices informally, and discussed ways that the practices might help to solve some of the teachers' issues in teaching reading comprehension. They were asked to read over the list, to consider the description we had provided, and to come to the next session prepared to discuss the practices about which they wanted to know more. Then, as a group, we intended to set priorities based on their requests and develop an agenda for our subsequent sessions.

This never happened. Teachers did not refer to the list during any of the professional development sessions, although we tried several times to engage their interest in the list. We carefully prepared presentation after presentation of the research-based practices. We did the best presentation we could, using all the techniques and strategies promoted by the best professional developers. Participants would sit back, take notes, and pleasantly nod, as if they were compliant with the suggestions being made. When we finished, a participant would bring up another topic, make a joke, or occasionally say that what we had presented sounded fine, but it wouldn't work at *this* school or with *these* students. They perceived the research-based practices as being general and not applicable to their local situation.

In contrast, teachers responded very differently when they were offered a research-based practice in the context of a proffered issue or problem from their classrooms. They made eye contact with us and leaned forward, indicating that they were seriously considering both the theory and the details of the practice. We ended up bringing a box of handouts prepared for all the practices we had gathered, so that *in a meaningful context,* we could provide the details to get them started using the practice. Teachers did use the practices presented this way, and our discussions during the professional development meetings were enriched by the teachers discussing analytically and critically the strengths and weaknesses they found in the practices they attempted.

Analyses of the professional development meetings and other study-related data revealed three barriers to the use of the list of research-based practices: (1) The practices, as initially presented, were decontextualized; (2) teachers' theoretical stances differed from the theoretical stance of the literature; and (3) teachers' real concerns were different than those addressed by the professional development goals of the project. Our discovery of "context" is important. We gave the participants a list of practices and despite our attempts to present them in interesting and practical ways; the practices were meaningless until they were related directly to the instructional problems presented by students and content the teachers were teaching.

The second barrier, theoretical contradictions, is also important. According to our analysis of teachers' beliefs at the beginning of the professional development program, the teachers reported believing that to learn to read, a child needed to acquire a specific set of skills. More to the point, they believed that students needed to read at grade level and demonstrate good listening skills, word attack skills, grammar skills, dictionary skills, oral reading fluency skills, and comprehension skills, such as being able to recall the sequence of a story. They used a basal reading program, with children's and young adults' literature as supplemental materials. In contrast, the research-based practices we had found in the literature were not designed to teach isolated skills; rather, the research-based practices we provided were based on an interactive model of the reading process, which emphasized the importance of a reader using strategies, such as activating prior knowledge, making predictions, summarizing, questioning, and so forth. This contradiction made it difficult for the teachers to understand the practices and even more difficult to visualize doing them.

This theoretical disconnect can be extended to the content orientation of secondary teachers. Pam Grossman (1995) reported that, based on their disciplinary expertise, high school teachers bring distinctive beliefs, theories, and practices to the teaching of high school content. Hence, a "research-based practice" that was researched with little or no attention to the conceptual content or with a single discourse or structure, such as social studies, is likely to not be very meaningful to a teacher of another content area, such as mathematics. Jetton and Alexander (2007) extend Grossman's report and provide a convincing argument that little is understood about the complexities of disciplinary domains, literacy, and teaching, and that much research is needed.

This contradiction suggests another barrier to teachers' adoption of research-based practices: At the heart of the matter, they questioned whether the practices we were recommending would improve the scores their students received on high-stakes achievement test they were required to take (Anders & Richardson, 1992). In other words, if they shifted their instruction, would their students do better, the same, or worse on the state test? We were amazed at what we thought was a disproportional amount of time spent during our meetings on discussions about assessment, accountability, and high-stakes testing. In addition to teachers' concerns about student performance on the state test, they worried and disagreed about the importance of grades, how to give grades, and what grades meant to students and parents. Teachers wondered how to explain to parents the grades they had given to their children. They feared they would be "in trouble" with the principal or a school board member if they gave good grades to students who might not do well on the state test. Given the exponential increase in the amount of testing in schools today, almost 20 years after the RIS project, we can only imagine how much time and energy currently are driven by the emphasis on high-stakes testing and accountability.

What this all amounts to is that *research-based instructional practices* is a poorly constructed term that undermines the purpose of the research enterprise; oversimplifies teaching; and disregards the beliefs, theories, needs, and nature of teachers and students. Writing this chapter has forced me to struggle with what I believe the term means. Because of my experiences with the RIS project, I am reluctant to promote a practice, or a set of practices, without considering the teachers, students, subject area, and instructional norms of the school. Once these limitations are acknowledged and understood, reasonable educators can find value in the notion of research-based practices.

Toward a Definition of Research-Based Practices

A glance at the results of an Internet search on research-based practices on Google or another search engine provides some perspective as we struggle to arrive at a reasonable definition of *research-based practices*. Such a search reveals a preponderance of medical references among the tens of thousands of entries. It is common in everyday language to speak of a physician's or an attorney's practice. Physicians and attorneys have long established the standards of their practice (in this context, *practice* is conceptualized broadly and generally as the work of the professional), and they know that if they abide by those agreed-upon standards of practice, they remain in good standing with their peers. They are obligated by their standards of practice to use the findings from research to make informed decisions as they advise their patients or clients. This is a far cry from the way that "research-based practices" are currently being conceptualized and imposed on teachers and students.

For the purposes of this chapter, we might think of a teacher's practice as the work of the teacher, complex as it is, and research-based practices as tools the teacher has at his or her disposal to engage students in literacy efficaciously as they construct understandings in and across the secondary curriculum. In their struggle to define best practices, Hinchman and Sheridan-Thomas (2008) arrived at the following:

> We note, with some irony, that the phrase, best practices, can be contentious in the adolescent literacy literature because it hints of instructional practices suited to all youth, despite the fact that our youth themselves are about individuality,

with a wide array of differences in backgrounds, needs, and interests. Even so, research on literacy instruction does, indeed, either directly support or suggest a variety of tools that can be used selectively by responsive teachers to scaffold youth's development of self-regulated reading, writing, and alternative communication. We refer to best practices to signal the presence of such tools, not standardized practices to be used with every youth. (p. 1)

In other words, it seems that the intention of research-based practices might be more likely identified as *pedagogy*—the empirical reasoning and methods a teacher uses to engage students in learning though reading, writing, talking, and listening. Elizabeth Moje (2007) chose to use the word *pedagogy* rather than *practice* when comparing "socially just pedagogy" with "pedagogy for social justice" (p. 2). No doubt she chose the term *pedagogy* rather than *practice* to avoid the simplistic interpretations and implications of the term *practice*. What follows is a summary of the principles that seem to be fundamental to the selection of efficacious, research-based practices.

Principles Guiding Research-Based Practices

The literacy literature provides information to help understand the idea of research-based practices by providing guidelines and insights in sources such as policy statements, articles, books, and book chapters. For example, the IRA (2002) position statement, *What Is Evidence-Based Reading Instruction?*, emphasizes the importance of external validity when selecting research-based practices (Creswell, 2003); that is, in addition to the standard criteria for evaluating research (that the report of a research study demonstrate objectivity, internal validity, and reliability, and that the study be published in a peer-reviewed or refereed publication), teachers should ask questions:

Do the students in the study resemble the students I teach?

Is the teaching and learning context similar to mine?

Will this strategy provide scaffolding to help students negotiate the ideas about which they are reading?

This advice is well-taken, particularly if we accept that research-based practices are instructional tools from which a teacher selects to help deliver literacy instruction to meet the needs of students as they engage meaningful ideas. Teachers need to be critical readers of research. Staff developers, administrators, and policymakers should expect teachers to ask for the quality and quantity of evidence supporting their recommendations of research-based practices. Critical consumers ask the following:

Who says a practice is best? What is the philosophical orientation of the author?

What is the basis for the claim, and how is effectiveness determined?

Who does the practice benefit, and, just as importantly, who does not benefit?

When is the practice appropriate? What is the advantage of one practice over the another?

Do the authors address educators as professional decision makers or as assembly line workers? (Moje, Young, Readence, & Moore, 2000, pp. 403–404)

"Research says" is not an acceptable response to a teacher's inquiry. Research does not *speak*. However, researchers and practitioners can read, critique, and make informed decisions about the application of research-based practice.

In addition to using accepted standards to evaluate research, we in literacy have principles of practice that emanate from learning theory, linguistics, and psychology—the sciences of teaching and learning. Sturtevant et al. (2006) synthesized the literature related to adolescent literacy instruction and constructed eight principled practices representing that literature:

> *Principle 1:* Adolescents need opportunities to participate in active learning environments that offer clear and facilitative literacy instruction.
> *Principle 2:* Adolescents need opportunities to participate in respectful environments characterized by high expectations, trust and care.
> *Principle 3:* Adolescents need opportunities to engage with print and nonprint texts for a variety of purposes.
> *Principle 4:* Adolescents need opportunities to generate and express rich understandings of ideas and concepts.
> *Principle 5:* Adolescents need opportunities to demonstrate enthusiasm for reading and learning.
> *Principle 6:* Adolescents need opportunities to assess their own literacy and learning competencies, and direct their future growth.
> *Principle 7:* Adolescents need opportunities to connect reading with their life and their learning inside and outside of school.
> *Principle 8:* Adolescents need opportunities to develop critical perspectives toward what they read, view, and hear. (pp. viiviii)

These principles provide a gauge to choose and use practices, and to develop programs.

Moje and her colleagues (2000) had a similar idea when they commented that best practices in literacy needed to be selected with the mind-set of an ecologist. They suggested that an ecologist thinks in terms of relationships, and that this is what the educator concerned with adolescent literacy needs to think about. They write:

> To our way of thinking, any unqualified claim that an educational practice is effective is quite a bit like claiming that watering plants is effective: It depends. The value of watering plants depends on the circumstances. Similarly, the value of K-W-L [what you know, what you want to know, what you learned from read-

ing], Reciprocal Teaching, Questioning the Author, sustained silent reading, study guides, and reading and writing workshops depends on how these fit the teaching–learning situation. Thus, we assert that the notion of best practice should be considered ecologically, focusing on relationships in particular settings. (p. 403)

Key among these relationships are the face-to-face interactions among individuals and teachers around literacy events. Questions reflecting this perspective include the following:

Do classrooms display any passion for reading, writing, experiencing, and learning?

Are expectations rigorous yet reasonable?

Are individual learners' best interests foregrounded?

Are reasons for teachers and learners committing themselves to literacy growth clear and convincing?

Does a respectful and inviting community support self-expression?

This section has provided principles that may guide educators' consideration and selection of instructional practices promoted as being research based. These principles of professional practice go deeper than the overly simple and superficial notion of a research base. As I stated early on, however, I am not dismissing the notion that research-based practices do have utility.

Examples of Helpful Research-Based Practices

Dolores Perin (2007) provides an excellent model of the sort of research-based practice recommendations that are extremely helpful to teachers. She describes a meta-analysis by Graham and Perin (2007) that arrived at 11 recommendations for teaching adolescent writing. The principles are powerful and sensible, but the valuable contribution of Perin's chapter in *Best Practices in Writing Instruction* (2007) is that she contextualizes the findings of the meta-analysis, providing for possible considerations and limitations that the teacher should think about before, during, and after using the suggested practices and strategies. Each recommendation is explained, the effect size is reported, and one or two studies are provided as examples of the research included in the recommendation. The 11 recommended principles (with mean weighted effect sizes and grade levels for instruction) are the following:

- Teach adolescents strategies for planning, revising, and editing their compositions (mean weighted effect size = 0.82; grades 4–10).

- Teach adolescents strategies and procedures for summarizing reading material, because this improves their ability to present this information concisely and accurately in writing (mean weighted effect size = 0.82; grades 5–12).

- Develop instructional arrangements in which adolescents work together to plan, draft, revise, and edit their compositions (mean weighted effect size = 0.75; grades 4–12).

- Set clear and specific goals for what adolescents are to accomplish with their writing product (mean weighted effect size = 0.70; grades 4–8).

- Make it possible for adolescents to use word processing as a primary tool for writing (mean weighted effect size = 0.55; grades 4–12).

- Teach adolescents how to write increasingly complex sentences (mean weighted effect size = 0.50; grades 4–11).

- Provide teachers with training in how to implement the process writing approach when this instructional model is used with adolescents (mean weighted effect size = 0.46; grades 4–12).

- Involve adolescents in writing activities designed to sharpen their skills of inquiry (mean weighted effect size = 0.32; grades 7–12).

- Engage adolescents in activities that help them gather and organize ideas for their composition before they write a first draft (mean weighted effect size = 0.32; grades 7–12).

- Provide adolescents with good models for each type of writing that is the focus of instruction (mean weighted effect size = 0.30; grades 7–12).

- Use writing as a tool to facilitate adolescents' learning of content material (mean weighted effect size = 0.32; grades 7–12).

These recommendations are helpful to teachers, administrators, and policymakers. They are respectful of teachers' decision making when planning, implementing, and evaluating their instruction.

In terms of reading, no such meta-analysis of research-based practices was found; rather reading scholars have compiled books based on principles of practice, then suggest practices that are reasonable applications of those principles. Three examples focusing on adolescent literacy include Sturtevant et al. (2006), Hinchman and Sheridan-Thomas (2008), and Jetton and Dole (2007). Although not as concrete as the Graham and Perrin (2007) report, these books are respectful of decision-making capabilities and present theoretically based practices in context.

Summary and Conclusions

This chapter has posed questions and issues for adolescent literacy educators to ponder when considering research-based practices. My intention has been to open the discussion of what constitutes "research-based practices" by complicating and making the notion problematic. I do this in the spirit of inquiry and, by doing so, am consonant with the nature of the research enterprise and the realities of teachers' professional obligations, commitments, and responsibilities. Specifically:

- I have rejected the simplistic definition of research-based practices. This definition is promulgated by those who suggest that a practice affirmed by a clinical-type experimental study is superior to a practice that a teacher creates or adapts to fit particular curricula and specific students.

- I have promoted practices that are flexible and adaptable for teachers who use research-based principles of practice, grounded in theory, and sensitive to the curricular and social context of classrooms and schools.

- I have suggested that we recognize research-based practices as tools a teacher has at his or her disposal to engage students in literacy.

These arguments lead to the conclusion that teachers are in the best position to select and adapt practices that research *suggests* may be appropriate for their use. Wise teachers are adept at reading research, knowing their subject-area content and students, and choosing and adapting practices that are efficacious for their purposes to meet student needs. Furthermore, this position acknowledges teachers' professional obligations and responsibilities. Teachers who accept this responsibility will find themselves in the role of teacher-researcher as they create, adapt, and adopt practices. They will conduct their own inquiries to understand better instructional practices, their students, and their role as instructors. What a terrific time to be engaged in adolescent literacy!

QUESTIONS FOR DISCUSSION

1. Discuss possible teacher research projects to advance the field's understanding of adolescent literacy instruction.
2. Discuss your priorities when selecting practices to scaffold your students' reading and writing.
3. Discuss your commitment to implementing research-based practices in your instruction.

Resources

Alvermann, D. E. (Ed.). (2004). *Adolescents and literacies in a digital world*. New York: Peter Lang.

Alvermann, D. E., Hinchman, K., Moore, D., Phelps, S., & Waff, D. R. (Eds.). (2006). *Reconceptualizing the literacies in adolescents' lives* (2nd ed.). Mahwah, NJ: Erlbaum.

Mason, P. A., & Schumm, J. S. (Eds.). (2003). *Promising practices for urban reading instruction.* Newark, DE: International Reading Association.

Nichols, S. L., & Good, T. L. (2004). *America's teenagers—myths and realities. Mahwah, NJ: Erlbaum.*

Phelan, P., Davidson, A. L., & Cao Yu, H. (1998). *Adolescents' worlds: Negotiating family, peers, and school.* New York: Teachers College Press.

Pressley, M., Billman, A. K., Perry, K. H., Reffitt, K. E., & Reynolds, J. M. (Eds.). (2007). *Shaping literacy achievement: Research we have, research we need.* New York: Guilford Press.

Rush, L. S., Eakle, A. J., & Berger, A. (2007). *Secondary school literacy: What research reveals for classroom practice.* Chicago: National Council Teachers of English.

Smith, D., & Whitmore, K. F. (2006). *Literacy and advocacy in adolescent family, gang, school, and juvenile court communities.* Mahwah, NJ: Erlbaum.

References

Anders, P. L., & Richardson, V. (1992). Teacher as game show host, bookkeeper or judge?: Challenges, contradictions and consequences of accountability. *Teachers College Record, 94*(2), 382–396.

Anderson, R. C., Hiebert, E. H., Scott, J. A., & Wilkinson, A. G. (1985). *Becoming a nation of readers: The report of the Commission on Reading.* Washington, DC: National Institute of Education.

Bateson, G. (1979). *Mind and nature: A necessary unity.* New York: Dutton.

Cassidy, J., & Cassidy, D. (2007). What's hot, what's not for 2007. *Reading Today, 24*(4), 1, 10–12.

Creswell, J. W. (2003). *Research design: Qualitative, quantitative, and mixed methods approaches* (2nd ed.). Thousand Oaks, CA: Sage.

Doyle, W. (1985). Recent research on classroom management: Implications for teacher preparation. *Journal of Teacher Education, 36,* 31–35.

Fleck, L. (1979). *Genesis and development of a scientific fact.* Chicago: University of Chicago Press.

Graham, S., & Perin, D. (2007). *Writing next: Effective strategies to improve writing of adolescents in middle and high school.* Washington, DC: Alliance for Excellent Education.

Grossman, P. (1995). Content as context: The role of school subjects in secondary school teaching. *Educational Researcher, 24*(8), 5–23.

Herber, H. L. (1970). *Teaching reading in content areas.* Englewood Cliffs, NJ: Prentice-Hall.

Herber, H. L. (1978). *Teaching reading in content areas* (2nd ed.). Englewood Cliffs, NJ: Prentice-Hall.

Hinchman, K. A., & Sheridan-Thomas, H. K. (2008). Preface. *Best practices in adolescent literacy instruction* (pp. xiii–xvi). New York: Guilford Press.

Huey, E. B. (1908). *The psychology and pedagogy of reading.* Cambridge, MA: MIT Press.

International Reading Association. (2002). *What is evidenced based reading instruction: A position paper.* Newark, DE: Author.

Ivey, G. (1999). A multicase study in the middle school: Complexities among young adolescent readers. *Reading Research Quarterly, 34*(2), 172–192.

Jetton, T. A., & Alexander, P. A. (2007). Domains, teaching and literacy. In T. A. Jetton & J. A. Dole (Eds.), *Adolescent literacy research and practice* (pp. 15–39). New York: Guilford Press.

Jetton, T. L., & Dole, J. A. (Eds.). (2004). *Adolescent literacy research and practice.* New York: Guilford Press.

Kuhn, T. S. (1962). *The structure of scientific revolutions* (3rd ed.). Chicago: University of Chicago Press.

Lloyd, C. V., & Anders, P. L. (1994). Research-based practices as the content of staff development. In V. Richardson (Ed.), *Teacher change and the staff development process: A case in reading instruction* (p. 68–90). New York: Teachers College Press.

Moje, E. B. (2007). Developing socially just subject-matter instruction: A review of the literature on disciplinary literacy teaching. *Review of Research in Education, 31,* 1–44.

Moje, E. B., Young, J. P., Readence, J. E., & Moore, D. W. (2000). Reinventing adolescent literacy for new times: Perennial and millennial issues. *Journal of Adolescent & Adult Literacy, 43*(5), 400–410.

National Reading Panel (NRP). (2000). *Report of the National Reading Panel: Teaching children to read: An evidence-based assessment of the scientific research literature on reading and its implications for reading instruction* (NIH Pub. No. 00-4769). Washington, DC: U.S. Government Printing Office.

Perin, D. (2007). Best practices in teaching writing to adolescents. In S. Graham, C. A. MacArthur, & J. Fitzgerald (Eds.), *Best practices in writing instruction* (pp. 242–264). New York: Guilford Press.

Radenbush, S. W. (2008). Advancing educational policy by advancing research on instruction. *American Educational Research Journal, 45*(1), 206–230.

Richardson, V. (Ed.). (1994). *Teacher change and the staff development process: A case in reading instruction.* New York: Teachers College Press.

Rubinstein-Ávila, E., & Johnson, J. (2007). Meaningful content for middle school students for whom English is an *additional* language. In K. A. Hinchman & H. K. Sheridan-Thomas (Eds.), *Best practices in adolescent literacy instruction* (pp. 20–38). New York: Guilford Press.

Shedd, J. B., & Bacharach, S. B. (1991). *Tangled hierarchies: Teachers as professionals and the management of schools.* San Francisco: Jossey-Bass.

Stewart, M. T. (2002). *"Best practice?": Insights on literacy instruction from an elementary classroom.* Newark, DE: International Reading Association and the National Reading Conference.

Sturtevant, E., Boyd, F., Brozo, W. G., Hinchman, K. A., Moore, D. W., & Alvermann, D. E. (2006). *Principled practices for adolescent literacy.* Mahwah, NJ: Erlbaum.

Thorndike, E. L. (1917). Reading as reasoning: A study of mistakes in paragraph reading. *Journal of Educational Psychology, 8,* 323–332.

Wood, K. E., & Muth, K. D. (1991). The case for improved instruction in the middle grades. *Journal of Reading, 35,* 84–90.

Chapter 13

Assessing Adolescent Literacy

William Dee Nichols
Barbara J. Walker
Beverly K. McIntyre

GUIDING QUESTIONS

1. In the classroom, what types of assessment do you or the classroom teacher use, and who benefits most from these assessments?

2. Think about the assessments that you or the classroom teacher use. What are their characteristics?

3. What decisions are made from each of the assessments that you or the classroom teacher use?

David Pearson developed a framework (Figure 13.1) you can use to guide your reading (Pearson, 1998). As you read each section throughout this chapter, keep in mind the primary client or stakeholder; what decisions need to be made, based on the assessment; what questions can be answered; and which assessment tool is most beneficial to the client.

Teachers perform assessments frequently, but using them to change instruction or to provide feedback to students is more difficult. In a recent conversation, classroom teacher, Monica Hickman, who had just completed an assessment course, explained her current thoughts about assessment:

"Before taking this course on assessment, I would collect student assignments, data, if you will, and place it in their individual folders and then never look at it or examine it again. What good does that do? This procedure not only wasted my time, but the students' as well.... It was mere

Client	Decisions to be made Questions to be answered	Assessment tools
Students	• How am I doing? • What shall I do next?	• Portfolio entries (self-evaluated) and/or feedback from benchmark tasks
Teachers	• Have the kids met my learning goals? • How did my teaching go? • How can I help Amy? • Should Amy be in level ____?	• Portfolio entries and benchmark tasks • Curriculum-embedded tests • Informal diagnostic tools • Array of converging evidence
Parents	• How is my child doing? • Compared to the average student?	• Portfolios/work samples • Norm-reference test of some sort
Administrators	• How effective is our program? • How are our teachers doing?	• Aggregated data of some sort (portfolios, norm-referenced tests)
Policymakers	• How well are schools meeting public expectations?	• Trends, over time, on some aggregated data • Norm-referenced tests would do just fine
Taxpayers	• How well is our money being spent?	• Trends, over time, on some aggregated data • Norm-referenced tests would do just fine

FIGURE 13.1. The assessment needs of different clients of the assessment system. *Note.* From Pearson (1998). Copyright 1998 by The Guilford Press. Reprinted by permission.

documentation. However, I have learned that assessments really have the power to do so much more. They can be the foundation for knowledge, just as a concrete slab is the foundation of a house. Before a house can be built, it must have a steady foundation or it will simply crumble over a short amount of time. I have learned to use the students' assessments in order to identify their strengths and weaknesses, and then plan lessons built around those strengths, while attempting to alleviate the students' weaknesses in order to create a firm foundation for them and increase their academic ability" (personal communication, December 12, 2007).

Examining literacy needs, including reading, writing, and attitudes of adolescents, using assessments has received renewed attention during the past decade. Periodic national assessments obtained by the National Assessment of Educational Progress (NAEP), dating back to its induction in 1969, have attempted to provide reliable and valuable information about what American students know and can do. Starting in 1992, data on reading performance of students in grades 4, 8, and 12 have been collected periodically to provide information on students' reading comprehension performance, while additional data have examined writing ability and attitudes toward reading, especially self-selected reading reports.

In 1998, the NAEP reported that fewer than 7% of students in grades 4, 8, and 12 were able to comprehend, critically analyze, and apply information obtained by reading text beyond a proficient level (Donahue, Voelkl, Campbell, & Mazzeo, 1999). Other assessments have exposed deficiencies in the instruction of students on reading and thinking strategies (Campbell, Hombo, & Mazzeo, 2000) and reveal that only 29% of eighth graders were able to meet the standard for proficiency in reading (Donahue, Daane, & Jin, 2005). Although the report indicated slight improvements, most at a non-statistically-significant level, these results are disheartening to all stakeholders—educators, students, parents, taxpayers, and policymakers alike. The main concern as a result of these disheartening data is that students who fall behind in reading often do not catch up with their more successful peers, they have lower self-esteem, and they display less motivation to participate in reading and subject matter instruction.

Used appropriately and thoughtfully, classroom assessments can enhance student learning. Hart (1994) defines *assessment* as "the process of gathering information about students—what they know and can do" (p. 1), and differentiates it from *evaluation*, the process of interpreting the information gathered and using it to make judgments. Kingen (2000) states that assessment is diagnostic and formative, whereas evaluation is summative. According to Knowles and Brown (2000, p. 127), "Assessment is a comprehensive act that includes consideration of a student's goals for learning, processes of learning, progression toward established goals, and revision of goals when needed."

Regardless of the difference, one cannot examine classroom instructional practices without considering both instruction and assessment, because collectively they inform decision making and judgments about student performance. One of the key components of effective instruction is using a variety of assessments and evaluative instruments, and keeping in mind who is the primary beneficiary of each assessment or evaluation. From multiple assessments and evaluation instruments, middle and secondary school teachers can describe students' learning, examine and reflect upon their own teaching, and inform parents and policymakers about the progress of students. Assessments, when used by teachers in a thoughtful manner, can provide insight into students' performance in literacy. In this chapter, we discuss adolescent learners, summative evaluation, formative assessment, and assessments that affect engagement.

Adolescent Learners

Teaching the adolescent learner is not an easy task. Not only are these learners going through great physical change, but they are also progressing through continued cognitive, emotional, and social development. In addition, they are also developing attitudes and beliefs about books, and about how to approach reading tasks. Students who decide that the texts and reading tasks they encounter in school offer little value disdain reading and switch to other outlets and become more aliterate (unwilling to read) than illiterate (unable to read) (Moore & Hinchman, 2006). In other words, they disengage from literacy activities, because they lack realistic purposes to motivate them to learn.

Although the role of motivation in engaging readers is almost universally acknowledged as a crucial issue (Alvermann, 2002; Jetton & Dole, 2004; Strickland & Alvermann, 2004; Wigfield, 2004), it is largely neglected. Most instructional practices and interventions place a major emphasis on strategies and skills instruction that deal more with the notion of illiteracy than with aliteracy. Adolescents who struggle are defined almost exclusively in terms of their competence with a limited range of tasks related to reading print. This text-centered, skills-aligned position has shaped what is defined as competence, which in turn has negatively shaped struggling adolescents' perceptions of ability, while restricting their opportunities to engage in practices that might change their perceptions (Alvermann et al., 2007).

Outside the world of school, adolescents encounter a variety of reading opportunities, including billboards, advertisements, magazines, newspapers, comic books, interactive gaming, catalogues, and text messaging, just to name a few. Many of these adolescents who perform on a basic literacy level, according to assessment data gathered by the NAEP, use these alternative texts in sophisticated ways (Moje, 2000). Many students who are aliterate when it comes to school texts become quite literate as they adeptly navigate through technical manuals, gaming walk-throughs, websites, teen culture magazines, and other special interest publications (Moore & Hinchman, 2006).

From a sociocultural perspective, these new literacy practices are shaped by, and contribute to, the social contexts and discourses in which adolescents participate (Barton, Hamilton, & Ivanic, 2000; Gee, 1996). Adolescents have increasing opportunities to move beyond print to engage in media-rich activities within new literacy frameworks (Gee, 2003; Kist, 2005; Lankshear & Knobel, 2003; Strickland & Alvermann, 2004). Classifying struggling readers as illiterate often overgeneralizes their true reading identity and does not completely acknowledge their literacy capabilities. It is our goal to build on Pearson's framework and discuss ways to evaluate, assess, and determine affective factors that influence adolescent learners' success navigating literacy activities, keeping in mind that students are the primary stakeholders in assessment practices and need to be informed regarding how they are doing and what they need to do next.

Summative Evaluation

The terms *testing* and *evaluation*—more than any other facet of education—evoke strong emotional responses from educators, lawmakers, parents, concerned citizens, and students. To the uninformed teacher, the mere mention of words such as *assessment, evaluation,* or *testing* can bring about strong debate over when assessment and evaluation should occur, how often they should occur, and how much testing is enough. The debate over assessment and evaluation is often associated with feelings of dread from teachers and students alike. Thus, evaluation is foremost on the lips of educators, especially where summative evaluation is concerned.

Summative assessments or evaluations are the tests that judge learners' performance, and they are referred to as *student accountability testing* (Johnston & Costello, 2005). The primary stakeholders that benefit most from summative evaluation are school administrators, policymakers and, to some extent, taxpayers and parents. Although teachers and students benefit least from these forms of evaluation, teachers use summative evaluation to report on student learning, usually annually, at the end of a course, grade, or semester, and share the information with other primary stakeholders (FairTest, 2007). Formal or summative evaluations include traditional tests, quizzes, and criterion-referenced tests. For primary stakeholders, such as school administrators, these summative formats are used to evaluate the effectiveness of student work, programs, or services after their completion (Fisher & Frey, 2007). Most summative evaluations are standardized instruments used to measure performance of schools and students compared to that of others. Even though assessing and evaluating student performance is a highly critical component of effective instruction (Algozzine, Ysseldyke, & Elliott, 1997), this type of summative evaluation creates the most anxiety for the clients who benefit least from this form of evaluation (teachers and students alike).

Although middle and secondary school teachers are not the primary clients in summative evaluation, they nonetheless use summative evaluation, along with other assessments, to inform instruction and to evaluate students' growth. To meet the needs of stakeholders, such as parents, teachers record grades that students earn on classroom tests and quizzes for purposes of reporting and assigning report card grades.

Some summative evaluations are *criterion-referenced tests,* which measure student performance on a set of academic skills or objectives (Fisher & Frey, 2004; Hart, 1994). These standardized evaluations measure reading and writing achievement under very specific conditions. They report a student's performance in relation to the performance of a representative group. Thus, a score on a given standardized test indicates where a student stands in relation to a population of learners who have taken the test. This type of summative evaluation represents a snapshot of a student's reading performance on a specific day.

Although summative evaluation has its place in education, formative assessment, the driving force of daily instruction, is the most beneficial type of assessment to stakeholders, such as students and teachers. Formative assessment occurs periodically at various points during instruction and provides feedback for both students and teachers (FairTest, 2007; Johnston & Costello, 2005). According to Black and Wiliam (1998), *formative assessment* is diagnostic; it is used to redirect the path that instruction takes. It includes a variety of formats such as teacher observation, classroom discussion, and students' inclass work, as well as other teacher- or student-generated tests. Formative assessment is the focus of the rest of this chapter.

Formative Assessments

Teachers use formative assessment "to form an understanding of students' reading development and learning across lessons, units, marking periods or academic years" (Afflerbach, 2007, p. 49). *Formative* means that rather than following standardized procedures, assessment uses less formal procedures to provide rich information about learners' strengths and weaknesses. "The essence of formative assessment is noticing details of literate behavior, imagining what they mean from the child's perspective, and knowing what the child knows and can do" (Johnston & Costello, 2005, p. 262). Rather than a snapshot, which is what summative evaluations provide, formative assessments provide an ongoing video of students' progress. This approach is an "attempt to change the form and purpose of classroom assessment to make it more fundamentally a part of the learning process" (Shepard, 2000, p. 6). Thus, formative assessments include any type of assessment tool other than the traditional formal evaluation methods described previously.

The primary goal of formative assessment is to improve students' learning and achievement (Knowles & Brown, 2000; Neill, 1997). While the improvement of student learning is a goal of all educators, there is evidence of a deficiency in the use of formative assessments in many middle school classrooms (Black & Wiliam, 1998; Neill, 1997). Reasons for this remain unclear, but some researchers suggest that teachers misunderstand the value and purpose of formative assessment, and confuse it with summative evaluations, which are intended to inform other stakeholders (Black & Wiliam, 1998; Fisher & Frey, 2007; Natriello, 1987). This confusion and devaluation of formative assessment is unfortunate, because research clearly points to a link between the use of formative assessments and improved student learning that would warrant spending ample time on assessment and using the feedback it yields (Ames, 1992; Black & Wiliam, 1998; Black, Harrison, Lee, Marshall, & Wiliam, 2004; Fisher & Frey, 2007; Fuchs et al., 1997; Natriello, 1987).

An area of concern for any type of assessment is objectivity. Adolescents are especially sensitive when issues of fairness are concerned (Kingen, 2000; Knowles & Brown, 2000). Formative assessment techniques are especially well suited for adolescents, because students are likely to view them as being fair (Hart, 1994). In addition, the variety and flexibility of formative assessment allow for consideration of individual differences and cultural factors, such as language, interests, and learning styles.

For middle and secondary school teachers, assessment should be an essential daily activity. This ongoing, daily assessment continually informs teachers and allows them systematically to understand learners' strengths and knowledge. When teachers begin to design instruction around what students can do; both independently and with teacher support, learning progresses. If assessment is simply gathered and filed away, and does not result in improved teaching, then its value to the learner and the teacher alike diminishes greatly.

So, with this in mind, it becomes apparent that assessment and instruction occur simultaneously (Walker, 2008). For example, as a teacher conducts a lesson, he or she observes adolescent learners' strategy use and background knowledge. Observations are made as the learners are reading and interacting with teachers and peers. Afterward, the middle or secondary school teacher analyzes how he or she adapted instruction and the reader's behaviors. From this analysis, he or she makes decisions about the readers' strategies, as well as the suitability of the instructional techniques.

The Principles of Formative Assessment

The assessment process is complex and comprises more than just gathering data to provide feedback. Formative assessments are cyclical (Algozzine et al., 1997), occurring continuously throughout instruction (Walker, 2008). Because teachers need constant knowledge about what their students know and understand, the assessment process must be ongoing, conducted at various points during instruction (Black & Wiliam, 1998; Boston, 2002; Crooks, 1988; Fisher & Frey, 2007; Kingen, 2000; Lapp et al., 2004; Natriello, 1987; Walker, 2008). In a review of the literature, both Crooks (1988) and Natriello (1987) found evidence for the benefits of frequent assessment. By *monitoring student understanding* through continuous assessment, teachers are able to modify instruction on the spot, change the direction of instruction, or sometimes abandon an instructional technique and change it to another. Algozzine and his colleagues (1997) identify four principles of effective assessment that benefit teachers:

1. Monitoring student understanding.
2. Being attentive to time on task.
3. Recording student progress.
4. Using assessment feedback to make instructional decisions.

Teachers must keep abreast of students' understanding of expectations, directions, and both factual and strategic knowledge. Although the value *of monitoring student understanding* of content has already been established, the role of the other three principles cannot be underestimated.

Attentiveness to Time on Task

Because there is a positive link between the level of active student engagement with learning tasks and student achievement (Algozzine et al., 1997), it is important to monitor students' time on task. Noticing reduced task involvement can alert teachers to factors that may exert a negative influence over student engagement. Middle and secondary school students can also learn to monitor their own level of engagement in learning tasks through direct instruction and reinforcement of the desired behavior (Algozzine et al., 1997). Self-monitoring helps students to become aware of their level of participation and to increase it accordingly.

Recording Student Progress

Keeping records of student progress enables teachers to provide prompt and explicit feedback that keeps students up to date on their progress. During instruction, teachers judge whether their instructional methods are working, so that they know whether to make adjustments. Afterward, they record the adjustments and the resulting achievement. Thus, records of student performance make it possible for teachers to chart overall progress toward learning goals and to make informed decisions about future instruction. Middle and secondary school students can learn to chart their own progress for immediate feedback, aiding in the development of their metacognitive awareness. Doing so also fosters a sense of independence and self-efficacy (Algozzine et al., 1997).

Using Assessment Feedback

The use of formative assessments to provide constant and ongoing information about student progress keeps valuable information at a teacher's fingertips. Without receiving feedback and using it to plan the direction of future instruction or to redirect the current path of instruction, teachers are not able to provide activities at which their students can be successful (Lapp et al., 2004). In their review of the research literature surrounding feedback, Kluger and DiNisi (1996) found that 60% of the reviewed studies reported a positive link between supportive feedback and improved achievement. Hence, both teachers and students benefit when they use feedback to inform instruction.

Nicol and Macfarlane-Dick's (2006) review of the research literature on formative assessment led them to identify five principles of good feedback (p. 205):

1. Helps clarify what good performance is (goals, criteria, expected standards).
2. Facilitates the development of self-assessment (reflection) in learning.
3. Delivers high-quality information to students about their learning.
4. Encourages teacher and peer dialogue around learning.
5. Provides information that teachers can use to help shape teaching.

Once again, it becomes clear that the primary stakeholders (teachers and students) benefit from clear feedback practices. Feedback from formative assessments is valuable not only to teachers but also to students, especially when given immediately (Black & Wiliam, 1998; Boston, 2002; Natriello, 1987). The type of feedback given to students after an assessment is important. Black and Wiliam (1998, p. 141) state that "feedback to any pupil should be about the particular qualities of his or her work, with advice on what he or she can do to improve, and should avoid comparisons with other pupils." In their 1991 meta-analysis, Bangert-Drowns, Kulick, and Morgan found that when students receive feedback on their responses during instruction, they are more likely to respond appropriately on a later assessment. Most importantly, however, they found that when feedback provides information on the process behind an appropriate response, as opposed to just providing the answer, students have higher rates of success in future instructional tasks. Thus, feedback that focuses on the process rather than on just getting the right answers is especially beneficial to struggling students (Ames, 1992; Sawyer, Graham, & Harris, 1992). Giving students positive feedback that focuses on processes helps students to succeed.

Methods of Formative Assessment

Because a goal of formative assessment is to gather feedback continuously during instruction for the purposes of gaining information on student understanding, teachers need a variety of assessment tools. However, it is important to bear in mind that, to be formative, the assessment must help the teacher to determine where students are in the learning process, to give appropriate feedback, and to make decisions about what needs to happen next in the instructional process. Thus, assessments should be closely aligned with the curriculum and instruction. Knowles and Brown (2000) believe that assessment is more meaningful to the primary stakeholders when it possesses the following characteristics (p. 130):

- It begins with student goal setting.
- It provides choices for students in demonstrating what they know.
- It allows flexibility in its design.
- It is appropriate for each young adolescent.
- It provides opportunities for self-evaluation.
- It encourages development of students' thinking processes.
- It creates authentic connections.
- It permits demonstrations of learning that build on strengths.

With an appropriate mentor or teacher/guide, adolescent learners are increasingly able to recognize their own strengths and challenges, and to set personal goals for their learning. Receiving regular, informative scaffolding from teachers enables students to gain awareness of their own understanding and become self-regulated learners (Fisher & Frey, 2007; Nicol & Macfarlane-Dick, 2006; Walker, 2008). Over time, and with scaffolding, middle and secondary school learners become self-regulated learners.

Types of Formative Assessment

Many types of assessments fall within the formative assessment category. They are sometimes called *alternative assessments*, because they are an alternative to traditional standardized tests (Knowles & Brown, 2000). Formative assessments may also be termed *performance assessments, holistic assessments, outcome-based assessments*, or *authentic assessments* (Hart, 1994). We now review the most appropriate assessments for adolescent learners.

Teacher Questioning and Teacher-Made Tests

Questions have dominated summative evaluations, but teachers can use them in a formative system of assessment as well. In the classroom, teachers use questions to help them evaluate what students have learned from reading a passage. To reveal useful and accurate information about student understanding, teachers must exercise care by using effective questioning techniques that are free of biases based on culture, ethnicity, gender, or ability (Fisher & Frey, 2007). Effective questions require varying cognitive levels. Teachers allow several seconds of wait time for students to prepare a response. Prompts usually follow inaccurate answers to lead students to acceptable responses. Additionally, teachers are using higher level questions to describe students' reading development rather than to assess the response. Asking for predictions (What will happen?, Why do you think so?, What do you think the author is trying to help us discover?) provides information about the process of reading and learning. Teachers also use questions that focus on the important aspects of a passage rather than on minute details. Teachers create challenging questions that are thorough, that involve a multifaceted analysis of the important information in the passages.

Like teacher questioning, teacher-made tests are likely to align more closely with classroom instruction. The following guidelines have been adapted from Knowles and Brown (2000) to assist teachers in designing teacher tests:

- Students perform better on shorter than on longer tests.
- Give several tests over the course of a unit of study rather than one or two.
- Make certain that students understand your expectations before assessment.
- Use a variety of formats during a unit.

Observation

Observation is a time-tested, inexpensive, and sometimes undervalued assessment technique (depending on the stakeholder), yet it can yield a wealth of rich and varied detail about student performance. To provide useful information, observation must be systematic, focused in appropriate directions, and documented (Hart, 1994). To use this form of authentic assessment effectively, the middle and secondary school teacher should look for the strategies that adolescent learners use to make meaning. Many teachers can "read" their students; observing when they are frustrated or motivated. As a teacher observes these cues, he or she can adjust the instruction accordingly. Teachers who make the most out of observations make adjustments to instruction accordingly and record their observations afterwards. As the student is reading, the teacher can make quick notes about the sources of information the student is using as he or she answers questions or participates in discussion. When teachers write down their observations, they create anecdotal records that help them collate continuous information on both individual and group performance. Therefore, some teachers record their observations, using sticky notes that can be collated with other notes about individual learners.

For observational assessment to be effective, all students must be observed frequently and regularly. Multiple observations are needed to establish reliability and to recognize patterns. Observations of usual behaviors or occurrences must be noted, along with the unusual ones. Only then do observations provide the feedback necessary for recognizing patterns that impact instruction and learning. Teachers must know what to observe. The more knowledge a teacher has about students, and about what is developmentally appropriate for them, the easier it is to find meaning in observations. Observation notes must be recorded in some systematic way to be remembered and to be credible. A number of tools exist to minimize the amount of writing and time that record keeping consumes. In addition to sticky notes, some teachers use index cards, journals, or logs to record anecdotes. Checklists, which may be less time consuming and serve as a reminder of what behaviors to look for when observing, are especially beneficial to beginning teachers.

Oral Language

Oral language in the classroom is another valuable source of information on student understanding (Fisher & Frey, 2007). Classroom discussions, debates, and literature circles offer opportunities for students to express orally what they know and can provide teachers the opportunity to catch misconceptions. These oral language experiences afford students the chance to hear others' viewpoints, to expand their own, and to make connections with content. Nonverbal cues from body language and facial expressions often accompany oral language and can give teachers valuable insights into students' understanding. Discussions may involve the whole group, a small group, or pairs. Small-group discussions allow teachers the chance to move around the room, listening to conversations and making notes for anecdotal records.

Assessment Talks

One of the most authentic formative assessments is to ask the student about how learning is proceeding. This conversation can reveal much about the student's inner dialogue while reading and learning. Student conferences about books and writing projects serve as assessment talks. It is during these interactions that teachers can probe student thinking about both content and process. As middle and secondary school students and teachers discuss their literacy behaviors, students think about how they read and write. In this way, students think and talk about how they constructed meaning with text. In real life, people often explain their thinking and how they came up with an idea. Similarly, assessment talks encourage middle and secondary school students to talk about their thought process.

Performance-Based Assessment

Performance-based assessments allow students to engage in types of activity designed to demonstrate what they know. Performance assessments require students to integrate knowledge of specific process skills and content knowledge (Knowles & Brown, 2000). Such activities generally require creative and critical thinking, using higher-order skills. Performance assessments may be individual or collaborative within a group (Kingen, 2000; Knowles & Brown, 2000). Adolescents' penchant for social networking and peer relationships make group collaboration successful. Examples of performance-based assessment include drama projects, writing projects, debates, design of experiments, multimedia presentations, and readers' theater. For example, some teachers' performance assessments involve reading a long passage from a piece of authentic literature. After reading, students discuss the passage in a group setting and, finally, write a response and/or summary. Teachers then use rubrics to assess student performance (Pearson & Hamm, 2005; Pearson, Spalding, & Myers, 1998). Thus, these assessments focus on students' responses to authentic stories rather than on recognition of correct answers from a contrived text. Instead of scoring the "right answers," these assessments rely on informed judgments by teachers and other professionals. Many of the performance assessments involve use of rubrics, another form of assessment.

Rubrics

Rubrics have become popular ways to evaluate reading and writing. A *rubric* is a printed set of scoring standards for evaluating a performance or a product. The rubric rates specific aspects of a literacy task, such as orally retelling a story or writing a summary of expository text. The standards are described qualitatively, making differences apparent between excellent performances and weaker ones.

Sometimes, a group of teachers may want to evaluate a specific strategy, such as summarization. In this case, the teachers collaborate to develop a format based on a series of questions to evaluate the strategy. Often, teachers decide to collaborate in the development of a rubric, so that each grade-level teacher can evaluate the student's literacy behaviors in a consistent manner. For example, a middle school teacher developed a series of questions based on research (Irwin & Mitchell, 1983) similar to the one in Figure 13.2 to evaluate written summaries of expository text. Using these questions, a group of middle school teachers created a rubric. Using the rubric, the teachers evaluated middle school students' work and were then able to describe students' written summaries. For example, one middle school teacher reflected on Ron's summary:

> "Ron included important information, as well as relevant concepts about earthquakes, in his summary. Much of what Ron included in his written summary demonstrates excellent use of the text but little information that was not directly stated in the text. However, Ron's organization was exceptional, since main ideas were supported by key facts."

These statements describing Ron's summaries were based on the rubric. Rubrics help teachers and their students reflect on developing strategy use in relation to instructional goals.

Several things happened in the collaborative design of this rubric. First, the teachers developed their understanding of what is important in a summary. Second, they developed a standard for what a middle school summary should include. Third, the teachers learned how to evaluate differences within a rubric. They realized that all summarizes do not have to be alike, that a coherent and elaborate representation of the information is required to help students develop their ability to summarize material.

Did the summary have . . .
- Relevant content and concepts?
- A connection to prior knowledge?
- A focus on important information?
- Information directly stated in the text?
- Information inferred from the text?
- Appropriate language?
- An organizational structure?

FIGURE 13.2. Questions to evaluate summaries.

Think-Aloud Analysis

Analyzing how readers' construct meaning is critical to understanding their unique reading processes. Think-aloud analysis has been used extensively by teachers to help describe adolescent learners' thinking. In this process, middle and secondary school teachers observe students as they construct meaning. To analyze comprehension, the teacher evaluates how the reader thinks through the comprehension of a passage. Using a *think-aloud* format of interrupted reading, the teacher observes how students use the text and what they know to interpret the passage. Analysis of a think-aloud, therefore, is a tool for evaluating the reader's comprehension strategies in the context of the entire passage.

Student Self-Assessments

Opportunities for self-assessment enhance the appeal of assessment, creating a win–win scenario for teachers and students alike. These assessments engage students in the assessment process, asking them to evaluate and reflect on their progress toward literacy learning. In other words, students engage in self-assessment (Tierney, Crumpler, Bertlesen, & Bond, 2003), comparing their performance to their goals for reading development. In fact, adolescent learners need ample opportunities for self-assessment (Black et al., 2004; Black & Wiliam, 1998; Hart, 1994; Knowles & Brown, 2000). Adolescents seek increased opportunities for independent decision making and control over their life (Kingen, 2000; Knowles & Brown, 2000). Yet even as they strive for independence, adolescent learners need guidance in learning to set goals. One difficulty that teachers report with self-assessment is students' inability to view their performance in terms of a set of goals (Black et al., 2004). Assessing their own work helps students to internalize learning objectives, and the increased independence enables them to take ownership of their own learning (Hart, 1994).

Portfolios

Portfolios are another method to help students take ownership of their learning (Tierney et al., 2003; Walker, 2008). Because the primary purpose of formative assessment is to gather information about students' progress, portfolios provide an excellent tool for doing so. The assessment portfolio has a close relationship with instruction and learning. Afflerbach (2007) suggests that it is characterized by "its ability to provide detailed accounts of students' achievement in complex school tasks" (p. 72). Portfolios organize artifacts and information in a convenient format to demonstrate literacy.

   Portfolios document literacy using multiple sources of information (oral reading recorded on tapes, written think-alouds, writing, retelling, reflections, artwork, diagrams, etc.); multiple contexts (alone, with a partner, with a teacher or parent, with a group, etc.); and multiple types of assessments (self and peer evaluations, anecdotal records, and conference notes). In fact, artifacts can be drawn from many different aspects of the student's day. For instance, an adolescent learner might include a vocabulary map about China or excerpts from a response journal. This collection of student work samples highlights the student's strengths, weaknesses, interests, accomplishments, and growth (Fisher & Frey, 2004; Hart, 1994).

As schools have used portfolios, it has become increasingly clear that student-centered portfolios are important aspects of assessment. They shift the control of learning from test makers and teachers' manuals to students and teachers collaborating on reading growth. Portfolios assess literacy using artifacts from authentic activities. Each artifact includes a reflection about what it shows or what was learned; by this means, both adolescent learners and teachers begin to describe the process of learning. The contents of the portfolio are not items completed on a single day; rather, items are collected over a period of time, demonstrating student understanding during literacy activities.

Portfolios have many advantages as assessment tools and are especially well suited for adolescents (Hart, 1994). They facilitate communication between parents and teachers. They allow students to exercise control over the assessment process and to become a part of the parent–teacher conference. Portfolios provide a broad and detailed picture of students' strengths and weaknesses across a long period of time. Consequently, they are viewed as both fair and objective. They are particularly well suited for culturally and linguistically diverse students, who may struggle with more traditional evaluation techniques.

Assessing Affective Factors in Reading

As stated at the beginning of this chapter, the affective factors in reading are critical influences on reading achievement in adolescent learners. These factors affect the engagement and motivation of all students. When adolescent learners are motivated, they engage in extensive reading and usually improve as readers. Likewise, when students disengage from reading, they read and think less. Adolescents who become disengaged and aliterate not only miss worthwhile recreational and aesthetic reading experiences but also place their academic futures in jeopardy (Cunningham & Stanovich, 1998; Moore & Hinchman, 2006). Adolescents who avoid reading limit their vocabulary development, their knowledge of the world, and other literacy competencies.

Thus, interests, self-perception, and valuing literacy are critical to being engaged in reading. Several different types of assessments are designed to evaluate the affective aspects in literacy. Certainly, students' attitudes toward reading affect not only their motivation but also how they value literacy activities and perceive themselves as readers and writers. Furthermore, students who are interested in a topic are more motivated to read about it. The following frequently used indicators influence motivation.

Interviews and Interest Inventories

Many middle and secondary school teachers find that the most beneficial way to learn about their students' interests and attitudes is simply to make the time to talk and listen to them. Teachers who simply take the time to conduct informal, conversational interviews are provided with useful insight about family dynamics, interests, and demands placed on the student. One seventh-grade teacher reported that she did not find out until the middle of April that her student Justin's dad had left in October. She had no idea that lack of parental involvement and home life instability were the culprits in Justin's incomplete assignments, disruptive behaviors, and lack of engagement, until one day after school when she engaged in a meaningful conversation with Justin. The best way to get to know your learners is to talk with them.

Interest inventories also may be insightful and often serve as a springboard for informal interviews. These inventories can be especially helpful to the beginning teacher, who may not know what to look for or to ask. Interest inventories usually contain a list of statements or questions developed to indicate adolescent learners' interests. Adolescent students' interests differ widely. Some of these differences are based on adsolescents' level of knowledge related to the topic. In other words, they engage more intensively in topics in which they have more background knowledge and, in turn, more interest. Interest also influences the frequency and forms of strategic processing that students select.

Concept of Self as Reader

When students think of themselves as readers, they view themselves positively when reading. A positive view of self as a reader or writer increases students' engagement in literacy tasks. For instance, Addie had a positive reader self-perception but a negative writer self-perception. She pursued opportunities to read at home and in school. She expended more effort during reading assignments and demonstrated greater persistence in seeking reading proficiency. However, she had extremely immature handwriting; therefore, she avoided activities that required writing. She demonstrated very little effort when writing and gave up easily.

Although there are many self-perception scales, that ones designed to evaluate self-perception as a reader and writer are more informative to middle and secondary school teachers. Two that are exceptionally useful are the Reader Self-Perception Scale (Henk & Melink, 1995) and the Writer Self-Perception Scale (Bottomley, Henk, & Melink, 1997–1998). These self-perception scales are based on the theory that students' judgment of their ability to read or write affects their engagement and depth of interpretation of what they read. In other words, how students perceive themselves as readers and writers influences whether they engage in or avoid literacy activities. A positive self-perception indicates that students will engage in literacy activities, thus improving their literacy.

Motivation to Read

In addition to views of self-perception, adolescents' motivation to read also influences reading achievement. Two aspects that directly impact motivation are how adolescents view their competence, and how they value literacy activities. Self-competence is somewhat similar to reader self-perception, but it focuses adolescents' perceptions of their competence and performance relative to peers. Students are asked about the value they place on various reading activities. The Motivation to Read Profile (Gambrell, Palmer, Codling, & Mazzoni, 1996) is an assessment process that uses these concepts.

Based on the Motivation to Read Profile (Gambrell et al., 1996) for elementary school students, a group of researchers designed the Adolescent Motivation to Read Profile (Pitcher et al., 2007). They found that the value that adolescents assign to reading tasks is related to how they engage in literacy activities. In other words, how students value academic literacy activities influences whether they participate in these activities.

Summary

The middle and secondary school teacher and his or her students evaluate how literacy is progressing in the classroom. They use multiple types of assessments to provide a view of adolescent learners' literacy. The various assessments allow both the teacher and the students to describe and measure reading achievement. When measuring progress, the middle and secondary school teacher can use both summative evaluations and formative assessments to communicate to a wide range of stakeholders. Using a variety of assessments provides all stakeholders with a more comprehensive view of the adolescent learners in a class.

QUESTIONS FOR DISCUSSION

1. Is high-stakes evaluation really necessary?
2. How can teachers improve formative assessment?
3. Describe how teachers can get adolescent learners more engaged in learning activities?

Resources

Further Reading

Irvin, J. (1998). *Reading and the middle school student: Strategies to enhance literacy.* Boston: Allyn & Bacon.

Jetton, T. L., & Dole, J. A. (Eds.). (2004). *Adolescent literacy research and practice.* New York: Guilford Press.

Keene, E. (2006). *Assessing comprehension thinking strategies.* Carthage, IL: Shell. Education.

Lenski, S., Wham, M., & Johns, J. (2003). Reading and learning strategies: Middle school through high school. Dubuque, IA: Kendall/Hunt.

Rycik, J. A., & Irvin, J. L. (2005). *Teaching reading in the middle grades: Understanding and supporting literacy development.* Boston: Allyn & Bacon.

Websites

www.nifl.gov.
www.reading.org/resources/issues/focus_assessment.html.
www.ops.org/reading/secondarystrat1.htm.
www.literacy.uconn.edu/compre.htm.
www.literacymatters.org/adlit/intro.htm.
www.readingonline.org.
www.ncte.org.
suu.edu/faculty/lundd/readingsite/readingresources.
www.balancedreading.com.
readwritethink.org.
www.sitesforteachers.com.
www.reading.org.

References

Afflerbach, P. (2007). *Understanding and using reading assessment, K–12.* Newark, DE: International Reading Association.

Algozzine, B., Ysseldyke, J., & Elliott, J. (1997). *Strategies and tactics for effective instruction.* Longmont, CO: Sopris West.

Alvermann, D. E. (2002). Effective literacy instruction for adolescents. *Journal of Literacy Research, 34,* 189–208.

Alvermann, D. E., Hagood, M. C., Heron-Hruby, A., Hughes, P., Williams, K. B., & Yoon, J. C. (2007). Telling themselves who they are: What one out-of-school time study revealed about underachieving readers. *Reading Psychology 2,* 31–50.

Ames, C. (1992). Classrooms: Goals, structures, and student motivation. *Journal of Educational Psychology, 84*(3), 261–271.

Bangert-Drowns, R. L., Kulick, J. A., & Morgan, M. T. (1991). The instructional effect of feedback in test-like events. *Review of Educational Research, 61*(2), 213–238.

Barton, D., Hamilton, M., & Ivanic, R. (Eds.). (2000). *Situated literacies: Reading and writing in context.* London: Routledge.

Black, P., Harrison, C., Lee, C., Marshall, B., & Wiliam, D. (2004). Working inside the black box: Assessment for learning in the classroom. *Phi Delta Kappan, 86*(1), 9–21.

Black, P., & Wiliam, D. (1998). Inside the black box: Raising standards through classroom assessment. *Phi Delta Kappan, 80*(2), 139–148.

Boston, C. (2002). The concept of formative assessment. *Practical Assessment, Research and Evaluation, 8*(9). Retrieved January 11, 2008, from *pareonline.net/getvn.asp?v=8&n=9.*

Bottomley, D., Henk, W., & Melink, S. (1997–1998). Assessing children's views of themselves as writer using the Writer Self-Perception Scale. *Reading Teacher, 5,* 286–296.

Campbell, J. R., Hombo, C. M., & Mazzeo, M. (2000, August). *NAEP 1999 trends in academic progress: Three decades of student performance. Retrieved October 9, 2008, from nces.ed.gov/naep/pdf/main1999/200069.pdf.*

Crooks, T. J. (1988). The impact of classroom evaluation practices on students. *Review of Educational Research, 58*(4), 438–481. Retrieved November 30, 2007, from *www.jstor.org/stable/1170281.*

Cunningham, A. E., & Stanovich, K. (1998). What reading does to the mind. *American Educator, 22*(1), 8–15.

Donahue, P. L., Daane, M. C., & Jin, Y. (2005). *The nation's report card: Reading 2003* (NCES 2005-453). U.S. Department of Education, Institute of Education Sciences, National Center for Education Statistics. Washington, DC: U.S. Government Printing Office.

Donahue, P. L., Voelkl, K. E., Campbell, J. R., & Mazzeo, J. (1999). *NAEP 1998 Reading report card for the nation and the states* (NCES 1999-500). U.S. Department of Education, Office of Educational Research and Improvement, National Center for Educational Statistics. Washington, DC: U.S. Government Printing Office.

FairTest. (2007). *The value of formative assessment.* Retrieved November 3, 2007, from *www.fairtest.org/examarts/winter99/k-forma3.html.*

Fisher, D., & Frey, N. (2004). *Improving adolescent literacy: Strategies at work.* Upper Saddle River, NJ: Pearson/Prentice-Hall.

Fisher, D., & Frey, N. (2007). *Checking for understanding: Formative assessment techniques for your classroom.* Alexandria, VA: Association for Supervision and Curriculum Development.

Fuchs, L. S., Fuchs, D., Karns, K., Hamlett, C. L., Katzaroff, M., & Dutka, S. (1997). Effects of task-focused goals on low-achieving students with and without learning disabilities. *American Educational Research Journal, 34*(3), 513–543.

Gambrell, L. B., Palmer, B. M., Codling, R. M., & Mazzoni, S. A., (1996). Assessing motivation to read. *Reading Teacher, 49*(7), 518–533.

Gee, J. P. (1996). *Social linguistics and literacies: Ideology in discourses* (2nd ed.). Bristol, PA: Taylor & Francis.

Gee, J. P. (2003). *What video games have to teach us about learning and literacy.* New York: Palgrave/Macmillan.

Hart, D. (1994). *Authentic assessment: A handbook for educators.* Menlo Park, CA: Addison-Wesley.

Henk, W., & Melink, S. (1995). The Reader Self-Perception Scale (RSPS): A new tool for measuring how children feel about themselves as readers. *Reading Teacher, 48,* 470–482.

Irwin, P. A., & Mitchell, J. N. (1983). A procedure for assessing the richness of retell-ings. *Journal of Reading, 2,* 391–396.

Jetton, T. L., & Dole, J. A. (Eds.). (2004). *Adolescent literacy research and practice.* New York: Guilford Press.

Johnston, P., & Costello, P. (2005). Theory and research into practice: Principles for literacy assessment. *Reading Research Quarterly,* 40(2), 256–267.

Kingen, S. (2000). *Teaching language arts in middle schools: Connecting and communicat-ing.* Mahwah, NJ: Erlbaum.

Kist, W. (2005). *New literacies in action: Teaching and learning in multiple media.* New York: Teachers College Press.

Kluger, A. N., & DiNisi, A. (1996). The effects of feedback interventions on perfor-mance: A historical review, a meta-analysis, and a preliminary feedback interven-tion theory. *Psychological Bulletin, 119,* 254–284.

Knowles, T., & Brown, D. F. (2000). *What every middle school teachers should know.* Ports-mouth, NH: Heinemann.

Lankshear, C., & Knobel, M. (2003). *New literacies: Changing knowledge and classroom learning.* Buckingham, UK: Open University Press.

Lapp, D., Block, C. C., Cooper, E. J., Flood, J., Roser, N. L., & Tinajero, J. V. (2004). *Teaching all the children: Strategies for developing literacy in an urban setting.* New York: Guilford Press.

Moje, E. (2000). "To be a part of the story": The literacy practices of gangsta adoles-cents. *Teachers College Record, 102,* 651–690.

Moore, D. W., Hinchman, K. A. (2006). *Teaching adolescents who struggle with reading: Practical strategies.* Boston: Pearson Education.

Natriello, G. (1987. The impact of evaluation processes on students. *Educational Psy-chologist, 22*(2), 155–175.

Neill, M. (1997). Transforming student assessment. *Phi Delta Kappan, 79*(1), 34–41.

Nicol, D. J., & Macfarlane-Dick, D. (2006). Formative assessment and self-regulated learning: A model and seven principles of good feedback practice. *Studies in Higher Education, 31*(2), 199–218.

Pearson, P. D.(1998). Standards and assessment: Tools for crafting effective instruc-tion. In F. Lehr & J. Osborn (Eds.), *Literacy for all: Issues in teaching and learning* (pp. 264–288). New York: Guilford Press.

Pearson, P. D., & Hamm, D. (2005). History of reading comprehension assessment. In S. G. Paris & S. A. Stahl (Eds.), *Children's reading comprehension and assessment* (pp. 13–70). Mahwah, NJ: Erlbaum.

Pearson, P. D., Spalding, E., & Myers, M. (1998). Literacy assessment in the New Stan-dards Project. In M. Coles & R. Jenkins (Eds.), *Assessing reading to changing prac-tice in classrooms* (pp. 54–97). London: Routledge.

Pitcher, S. M., Albright, L. K., DeLaney, C. J., Walker, N. T., Seunarinesingh, K. Mogge, S., et al. (2007). Assessing adolescents' motivation to read. *Journal of Adolescent & Adult Literacy. 50*(5), 378–396.

Sawyer, R. J., Graham, S., & Harris, K. R. (1992). Direct teaching, strategy instruction, and strategy instruction with explicit self-regulation: Effects on the composition skills and self-efficacy of students with learning disabilities. *Journal of Educational Psychology, 84*(3), 340–352.

Shepard, L. A. (2000). The role of assessment in a learning culture. *Educational Researcher, 29,* 4–14.

Strickland, D. S., & Alvermann, D. E. (2004). Learning and teaching literacy in grades 4–12: Issues and challenges. In D. S. Strickland & D. E. Alvermann (Eds.), *Learning and teaching literacy in grades 4–12* (pp. 1–13). New York: Teachers College Press.

Tierney, R. J., Crumpler, T. P., Bertelsen, C. D., & Bond, E. L. (2003). *Interactive assessment: Teachers, parents and students as partners.* Norwood, MA: Cristopher-Gordon.

Walker, B. J. (2008). *Diagnostic teaching of reading: Techniques for instruction and assessment* (6th ed.) Upper Saddle River, NJ: Pearson Education.

Wigfield, A. (2004). Motivation for reading during the early adolescent years. In D. S. Strickland & D. E. Alvermann (Eds.), *Bridging the literacy achievement gap in grades 4–12* (pp. 56–69). New York: Teachers College Press.

Chapter 14

Motivating Adolescent Learners to Read

Pamela J. Dunston
Linda B. Gambrell

GUIDING QUESTIONS

1. How do middle and high school students' purposes for reading differ from children's purposes for reading?
2. How are motivation and reading related?
3. What constitutes *literacy*, and how is it defined?
4. How can classroom teachers motivate adolescent learners to read?

Adolescence and the Relationship between Motivation and Reading

Adolescence is a unique period in an individual's life. Those of us who teach and interact and/or live with adolescents know the daily challenges they provide in terms of attitude, behavior, and verbal communications (or lack thereof). Adolescence is a developmental period during which parents and teachers exist in an uncomfortable state of uncertainty about how to interact with, teach, and guide the young people in their lives. One hallmark of adolescence is an increased interest in peers and social activities and decreased interest in school. Adolescents' disinterest in school is particularly troubling, because this is the time when individuals begin to acquire specific foundational knowledge, skills, and experiences that have the potential to lead to full and equitable participation in a global society. In terms of literacy, adolescence is when individuals learn practices associated with literacy (Gee &

Green, 1998; Moje, Young, Readence, & Moore, 2000; Mosenthal, 1998), and specialized practices associated with diverse forms and purposes of text and media within different disciplines, communities, and social situations (Luke & Elkins, 1998). Unfortunately, this is also the time when students tend to lose interest in reading, particularly school-related reading (Guthrie & Davis, 2003; Ivey & Broaddus, 2001; Luttrell & Parker, 2001; McKenna, Kear, & Ellsworth, 1995; Worthy & McKool, 1996). Disinterest in school, learning, and reading is frequently associated with motivation.

Teachers rank motivating students as one of their primary and overriding concerns (O'Flahaven, Gambrell, Guthrie, Stahl, & Alvermann, 1992; Veenman, 1984), and recognize that it is at the heart of many pervasive problems they face in educating today's youth. Motivation plays an important role in learning (Baker, 2003; Deci & Ryan, 1985; Dolezal, Welsh, Pressley, & Vincent, 2003; Wigfield, Guthrie, Tonks, & Perencevich, 2004), and makes the difference between learning that is superficial and shallow, and learning that is deep and internalized (Gambrell & Codling, 1997; Guthrie et al., 2004; Ryan & Deci, 2000).

Students' motivation to read is of particular concern for several reasons. First, we know that students who spend more time reading are better readers (Anderson, Wilson, & Fielding, 1988; Gottfried, Fleming, & Gottfried, 2001; Taylor, Frye, & Maruyama, 1990; Strommen & Mates, 2004). Second, we know that students' intrinsic motivation to read is related to their overall reading achievement (Guthrie et al., 2004; Guthrie, Wigfield, Metsala, & Cox, 1999; Sweet, Guthrie, & Ng, 1998). Third, students who have more experiences with books and book language, more developed reading comprehension skills, and have strong home support for literacy development are better prepared than others for reading success (Allington, 1991) and have more opportunities for academic progress (Alvermann & Earle, 2003). Finally, we know that students who struggled to learn to read have better educational prospects when teachers support and nurture their motivation to read and reading achievement (Allington, 1986; Donahue, Voelkl, Campbell, & Mazzeo, 1999; Smith-Burke, 1989).

There is particular concern about reading motivation during the middle and high school years. Research reveals that students' intrinsic motivation for particular subject areas diminishes as they move through the grades. In a longitudinal study, Gottfried et al. (2001) assessed changes in the academic intrinsic motivation of 96 students who had participated in the study since they were 1 year of age. Results indicate that at ages 9, 10, 13, 16, and 17, academic intrinsic motivation declined in science, math, and reading. The researchers suggest that declines in adolescents' academic intrinsic motivation may be related to school curriculum, and may not be changed easily.

In addition to changes in reading motivation, in the move into the middle and high school grades, some students begin to lose self-confidence, become anxious about school, and engage in activities that inhibit rather than facilitate literacy learning. Many students who were successful readers in the elementary grades may begin to experience reading difficulties in middle and high school and come to view themselves as poor readers or nonreaders (Hughes-Hassell & Rodge, 2007). One possible reason for changes in adolescents' reading success may be due to changes in the structure of middle and high school classrooms and the nature of reading tasks. Middle and high school classrooms tend to be less personal and more formal than elementary school classrooms, and teachers tend to be subject matter specialists, with little background in reading instruction. Middle and high school classroom tasks place greater demands on students' linguistic, cognitive, and conceptual abilities, and teachers expect students to engage in independent reading, writing, and learning activities. Reading tasks in middle and high school classrooms are less familiar and include specialized vocabulary that represents abstract ideas and concepts (Allington & Johnston, 2002). Students who learned basic literacy skills in elementary school (i.e., how to read, recall, write, and spell) are now required to learn how to "read, write, and think in the complex and critical ways needed in a postindustrial democratic society" (Allington & Johnston, 2002, p. 14).

In the 1990s, motivation gained prominence in numerous models of learning. Because depth and breadth of literacy learning are influenced by motivational factors (Wigfield & Guthrie, 1997; Ford, 1992; McCombs, 1991; Oldfather, 1993), researchers have attempted to explain why different students expend different amounts of time and effort on literacy tasks (Gambrell, 1996; Wigfield & Guthrie, 1997). Wigfield and Guthrie extended the work of researchers in the achievement motivation field to develop a framework for reading motivation that comprises three broad categories and 11 dimensions. Although Watkins and Coffey (2004) question the soundness of the 11 dimensions as measures of discrete aspects of reading motivation, the framework provides a springboard for discussion (see Figure 14.1).

According to Wigfield and Guthrie (1997), the first broad category of reading motivation, Competency and Efficacy Beliefs, takes into account students' personal beliefs about their reading ability (self-efficacy), their willingness to take on difficult reading material or tasks (challenge), or their desire to avoid difficult reading activities (work avoidance). Adolescents who have confidence in their reading ability are more likely not only to read but also to read challenging texts. Adolescents' perceptions of their reading ability tend to affect their level of motivation in all subject areas. Those who lack confidence are more likely to avoid reading tasks; especially reading tasks perceived to be difficult. Literacy tasks and events that focus on what students can do well and that are challenging help them develop feelings of literacy competence.

The second category, Purposes for Reading, addresses students' reasons for reading and includes the constructs of intrinsic and extrinsic motivation. Motivation theorists make a distinction between extrinsic and intrinsic motivation. *Extrinsic motivation* refers to forces external to individuals that influence their inclination to engage in a particular behavior, such as reading or

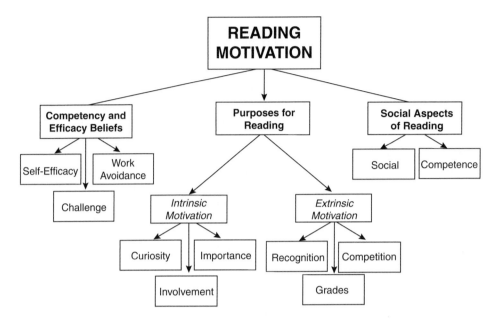

FIGURE 14.1. Components of reading motivation.

writing. Behavior that is motivated by internal needs, desires, or feelings is considered *intrinsic motivation*. The concepts of intrinsic and extrinsic motivation are very broad and can be applied to many aspects of literacy behavior. Specifically, research indicates that a student's perception of intrinsic or extrinsic value associated with literacy tasks is an important aspect of literacy motivation (Cameron & Pierce, 1994; Gambrell, 1996; Gambrell & Marinak, 1997).

Wigfield and Guthrie (1997) found that students are intrinsically motivated to read when the reading material (1) is presented or written in such a way that students become engaged in it and have satisfactory encounters with texts (involvement), (2) addresses a topic that interests them (curiosity), or (3) is relevant/important to their lives and central to success (importance). On the other hand, students are extrinsically motivated when they engage in reading for the sake of what it brings to them in the form of rewards or praise (recognition and grades) or achievement of a goal (competition). Deci, Vallerand, Pelletier, and Ryan (1991) demonstrated the effects of extrinsic motivation on learning in a study in which some students were told that learning text material would help them on an upcoming test (i.e., bribe), whereas other students were simply told that the text material was relevant and important. Findings suggest that emphasizing the relevance and value of learning to students is a more powerful motivational force than external forces, such as getting a better grade on a test. Marinak and Gambrell (2008) investigated the use of extrinsic rewards to motivate elementary school students to read. They found that giving students reward choices that are proximal to reading (a reward closely tied to the desired behavior, such as a book, in the case of reading motivation) increased intrinsic reading motivation.

In the Social Aspects of Reading category, students engage in reading to meet others' expectation (compliance) and/or to share literacy activities with friends and family (social). Adolescents report that family and friends influence what they read and write, and indicate that they talk about what they read with others through a variety of social interactions, such as informal conversations, e-mails, and instant messages (Pitcher et al., 2007). "Sharing books with friends or family is an important motivator for reading… and it is an activity in which even struggling readers can take the role of 'expert' reader" (Baker, 2003, p. 96).

The Changing Nature of Literacy Practices

To understand the average citizen's current thinking about reading, ask anyone outside the field to explain what reading means and/or what it involves. The typical response will probably focus on pronouncing words and understanding printed text. However, over the last 15 years, reading researchers have reconceptualized our understandings of reading, writing, and literacy, and the social practices involved (see the New London Group [1996] for "a programmatic manifesto" [p. 63] forming the basis for the International Multiliteracies Project). The term *literacy*, prior to the 1970s, was applied to adult education programs that were designed to teach reading and writing to illiterate or marginally literate adults. Reading was viewed as a means for communicating through and attaining meaning from print, as well as a means for learning. During the 1970s, literacy (rather than reading) became the central focus of formal education in America due to the public's growing awareness of low literacy levels in our society. Literacy programs gained attention as vehicles for teaching adults to read and write words, so that they could function within society and increase their economic opportunities. In some societies, literacy programs emphasized teaching individuals how the world works, and how to understand and question social and cultural practices that affect economic and political power structures (Lankshear & Knobel, 2003). During the 1980s and 1990s, socioculturally oriented theorists, researchers, and educators adopted the term *literacy* in an effort to move beyond the narrow educational activities associated with reading to encompass the social practices involved in reading and writing activities. At the same time, a variety of practices came to be associated with literacy. Because many of these practices are rooted in electronic information and communication technologies, and include posttypographic ways of generating, manipulating, distributing, receiving and sharing text, they are considered new literacies and tend to be associated with popular culture.

Current literacy definitions include the ability to read and understand signs, symbols, images (Stevens, 2001), written messages, visual images, sound bites (Alvermann & Hagood, 2000), telephones, textbooks, pagers, cell phones, computers, electronic mail, the Internet, art, music, drama, film, video games, and digital aids as avenues of adolescent literacy (Bean, Bean, & Bean, 1999). These *texts* play prominent roles in adolescents' lives and appeal to their interests. Even students who view themselves as nonreaders in school actively engage in out-of-school reading when the text is popular culture (Alvermann, Young, Green, & Wisenbaker, 1999). Researchers interested in adolescent literacy have pointed to a disparity between out-of-school literacy practices and in-school literacy (Bintz, 1993; Ivey & Broaddus, 2001; Knobel, 2001; Lewis & Fabos, 2005). Unlike in-school reading that focuses on literal-level tasks with academic texts, out-of-school reading is critical in nature (Ivey & Broaddus, 2001), more complex, and involves authentic purposes (Knobel, 2001). Students' out-of-school reading may differ from in-school reading due to increased motivation, engagement, and improved attitude when reading nonstandard texts in nonacademic settings.

The relationship among adolescents' motivation to read, new forms of literacy (particularly digital technologies), and out-of-school literacies is not readily apparent and may seem far-fetched. However, many researchers contend that a relationship exists, and that it has a direct bearing on what adolescents read and write, and the frequency with which they engage in literacy practices (e.g., Alvermann, 2001; Hinchman, Alvermann, Boyd, Brozo, & Vacca, 2004; Knobel, 2001). Many adolescents regularly engage in literacy practices that are not part of the academic curriculum and not sanctioned as appropriate, educational, or worthwhile activities during school time. For instance, many middle and high school students text-message their friends numerous times throughout the day when not in school but are not allowed to use cell phones in school. Parents and teens often do not see eye to eye on the value of digital literacies, and teachers worry that digital forms of communication ruin students' spelling and sense of grammatical correctness. However, some researchers (Dunston & Alvermann, 2006; Lewis & Fabos, 2005) have found that adolescents use and extend their schooled literacy practices in positive ways when engaging in digital communications. Lewis and Fabos (2005) and Dunston and Alvermann (2006) investigated the nature of adolescents' digital communications within the phenomenon of instant messaging (IM) in an effort to determine the function of online reading and writing practices in adolescents' lives, and to document the different ways in which IM mirrors or makes use of school literacy. Findings from both studies suggest that adolescents use school-acquired knowledge of language (including knowledge of appropriate, inappropriate, public, and private vocabulary, grammar, and spelling), social interactions, and gender relationships (social practices) when engaging in IM. Participants' understandings of how IM mirrors spoken dialogue, the roles of "speaker" and "listener," and male–male/female–female/male–female social interactions influence the nature of the

adolescents' IM. Participants in the studies "used linguistic features to manipulate the written tone, voice, word choice, subject matter, and structure of
messages in order to sustain interesting conversations and cut off those that
were not of interest" (Lewis & Fabos, 2005, p. 482). The IM of adolescents in
these studies provides evidence that schooled literacy practices are extended
in out-of-school literacy activities and include the ability to search, locate,
read, comprehend, apply, share, and extend new knowledge from a variety of
print sources, including books, newspapers, music, and websites.

Awareness of the role of reading, writing, and meaning construction
in the multitude of activities in which adolescents actively engage on a daily
basis has broadened our view of literacy. Given adolescents' level of interest
and the frequency with which they actively engage in these activities, clearly,
we must consider the relationship between adolescents' out-of-school literacies and reading motivation. If we ignore adolescents' motivation to engage
in out-of-school literacy practices, we run the risk of placing a greater divide
between traditional, school-related literacy and its relevance to adolescents.

Increasing Adolescents' Motivation to Read

Efforts to increase middle and high school students' intrinsic motivation to
read in academic settings may be difficult in a time when high-stakes testing takes center stage in the lives of classroom teachers. High-stakes testing
emphasizes student performance in the form of scores that administrators and
policymakers use for accountability and comparative purposes (i.e., comparisons between students, teachers, and school districts), and decision-making
regarding individuals' qualifications, potential, and suitability for education
and training programs, advanced degrees, and jobs. The design and purpose
of high-stakes testing does little to enhance adolescents' natural curiosity or
desire to learn. On the other hand, classroom teachers who address goals
beyond assessment, by creating environments and planning activities that
allow adolescents to take risks, ask questions, and engage in learning tasks
for the sake of developing personal expertise, tap adolescents' natural curiosity and desire to learn (Guthrie & Davis, 2003), thus increasing intrinsic
motivation. Several researchers in the field of literacy (e.g., Guthrie & Davis,
2003; Hinchman et al., 2003/2004; Hughes-Hassell & Rodge, 2007; Ivey &
Broaddus, 2001; Worthy, Moorman, & Turner, 1999) have identified specific
instructional practices that have the potential to increase adolescents' motivation to read.

Build Perceptions of Competence

Although conventional wisdom suggests easy tasks that result in success will
lead to increased motivation to learn, Colvin and Schlosser's (1997/1998)
research suggests that the opposite may be closer to the mark. Their work

revealed that students' perceptions of themselves as less capable learners are often reinforced when they are given literacy tasks that are "easy" and less challenging than those assigned to their peers. Colvin and Schlosser found that students respond positively to learning tasks that challenge them and required them to make an investment of time and effort. They suggested that teachers think in terms of Vygotsky's (1986) zone of proximal development and provide students with reading material that is slightly beyond their level to complete when working alone, but that they can successfully read when they receive assistance. In general, research suggests that feelings of competence and increased motivation result from completing tasks that require effort and investment of time and energy, rather than tasks that are easy and quickly completed.

Teachers can build adolescents' sense of competence by taking stock of what their students already know and can do in other aspects of life. Teachers may find that students previously viewed as "struggling" with literacy in a classroom setting may be competent in literacy activities that are not related to school. They may be surprised to learn that their students eagerly and easily engage in reading and writing many forms of text (e.g., text messages, blogs, music, poetry, MySpace webpages) on a regular basis. An important aspect of learning about adolescents' out-of-school literacies is the need to understand why these literacies are appealing to adolescents and how they differ from school literacies. Aiding adolescents in transferring out-of-school competencies to academic contexts is an important task for teachers (Hinchman et al., 2004).

One way to learn about adolescents' abilities and expertise is to listen to, watch, and engage them in conversations about their interests, hobbies, and extracurricular and free-time activities (Hughes-Hassell & Rodge, 2007; Hinchman et al., 2004; Moje et al., 2000; Weinstein, 2006/2007). Many teachers find interest inventories and surveys useful for gaining information about students' interests and activities in order to choose reading materials and plan activities for the classroom. Face-to-face conversations in hallways and cafeterias or at school dances, concerts, and sporting events offer greater opportunities for teachers to learn about and get to know students. In addition, face-to-face conversations tend to generate a sense of caring on the part of the teacher and student, and provide teachers with opportunities to discuss different ways of being a reader. Personal conversations can influence the way adolescents see themselves as readers and may change their perceptions of others' competencies.

Build "Real" Purposes for Reading

Because middle and high school students frequently view school literacy as unrelated to their personal lives or as having no relevance to their future lives, literacy is neither important nor worth the effort. They do what they "have to" to meet teachers' and parents' expectations, and to earn grades. When adolescents are not interested in classroom reading activities, and assignments and do not make direct connections between school-related reading and their "real" lives, they are less likely to be motivated to engage in reading (Guthrie & Davis, 2003; Hinchman et al., 2004; Ivey, 1999). "Adolescent students who participate in programs that connect literacy with real-life out-of-school issues and personal interests indicate more positive feeling about reading and writing in school" (Ivey & Broaddus, 2001, p. 354). Experiential and participatory forms of learning, such as inquiry-oriented or interdisciplinary thematic projects in middle and high school classrooms, may be key to increasing adolescents' motivation to read. Instruction that provides real purposes for learning and accomplishing tasks requires students to engage actively in the learning process. Participatory and experiential instructional approaches allow students to learn content, while connecting what they learn to their own lives (Hinchman et al., 2003/2004; Ivey, 1999; Moje et al., 2000; Thakkar, Bruce, Hogan, & Williamson, 2001).

Guthrie and Davis (2003) note the importance of real-world interactions in building adolescents' intrinsic reading motivation. They refer to real-world interactions as "providing opportunities for students to have sensory interactions (e.g., seeing, hearing, feeling, or smelling) with tangible objects or events as they appear or could appear in a natural environment" (p. 73). For teachers to build intrinsic reading motivation through real-world interactions, Guthrie and Davis stress the importance of linking texts to the real-world interactions. Because of students' including the use of supporting texts (newspapers, Internet websites, textbooks, maps, letters, etc.) and real-world interactions, reading and writing activities become contextualized, and students are intrinsically motivated to engage in literacy events.

Eagleton, Guinee, and Langlais (2003) offer a detailed description of a 6-week Hero Inquiry Project that engages adolescents in using the Internet in conjunction with traditional print. The focus of the project is on teaching students to choose a topic of personal interest (in this case, a personal hero), setting goals, developing research questions, applying Internet search strategies, identifying relevant information, note taking, and synthesizing and integrating information. Projects of this nature increase adolescents' intrinsic motivation to read, because they are relevant and important to students (self-selection of personal heroes) and involve real purposes (sharing personal heroes with peers).

Build Choice with Interesting Texts

Research has firmly established the importance of interest as a factor related to intrinsic motivation and reading. Adolescents who are interested in a topic and have access to an array of reading materials they find personally interesting are motivated to read and to put forth more effort to read (Worthy et al., 1999). Even though the general perception of parents and the public is that adolescents do not enjoy reading and do not engage in leisure-time reading,

Hughes-Hassell and Rodge (2007) found that 72% of the urban adolescents responding to their questionnaire indicated that they do engage in reading as a leisure-time activity. Respondents indicated that their leisure time reading is for fun, for educational purposes, and/or to relieve boredom. Adolescents who do not engage in leisure-time reading prefer to watch television, spend time with friends, or engage in other activities, such as playing video games and surfing the Web.

Considering the number of adolescents who do enjoy leisure-time reading, the next logical question is: Where do they find reading materials that appeal to their interests? Most adolescents report using school and public libraries to find reading material that interests them (Hughes-Hassell & Rodge, 2007; Ivey & Broaddus, 2001; Worthy et al., 1999). Fifty-three percent of the urban adolescent respondents in the Hughes-Hassell and Rodge (2007) study reported using the classroom library as a source for reading materials, whereas adolescents in other studies (Ivey & Broaddus, 2001; Worthy et al., 1999) ranked classroom libraries as poor sources for reading materials. Nearly 50% of the adolescents who responded to the Hughes-Hassell and Rodge (2007), Ivey and Broaddus (2001) and Worthy et al. (1999) surveys indicated that they purchased books through bookstores.

In the Ivey and Broaddus (2001) survey of sixth-graders, 42% of the responding students indicated that having good reading material was an important factor in motivating them to read. However, the reading materials that adolescents prefer are frequently different from the reading materials available at school (Worthy et al., 1999). Adolescents enjoy reading scary series books, comics, magazines (Worthy et al., 1999), graphic novels, manga (Japanese-style comics), and the Internet (Hughes-Hassell & Rodge, 2007). Schools do not provide funding to purchase the reading materials that rank high on adolescents' list of preferences, because these materials do not support the academic curriculum. Yet providing an ample supply of interesting and diverse texts that includes both traditional and nontraditional text forms within the school and classroom is an important way to facilitate motivation (Guthrie & Davis, 2003). Classrooms should have an abundance of print and digital materials, representing a broad range of genres, including literary, informational, and documentary texts. Literary texts include reading materials such as novels, poetry, short stories, letters, diaries, folktales, fables, speeches, plays, autobiographies, legends, personal essays, and biographies. Informational texts in the form of printed textbooks and digital texts include reading materials such as trade books, textbooks, reference materials, government documents, historical documents, manuals, pamphlets, editorials, Internet websites, and personal webpages. Documentary texts include reading materials such as illustrations, photographs, diagrams, tables, cartoons, graphs, time lines, schedules, and reference access systems (e.g., indices).

Two factors that affect students' use of materials are access and level of difficulty. Gambrell and Codling (1997) found that students are motivated to select books when they can view the cover. Face-front displays of books draw readers' attention to titles, favorite authors, and interesting topics. The importance of visual appeal may carry over to digital literacies and influence the choices adolescents make when surfing the Web; that is, visual appeal may influence adolescents' tendencies to navigate particular websites. Visual appeal aside, most adolescents have access to Internet-connected computers through local libraries or home computers; therefore, they have ready access to a range of digital texts that includes both easy and challenging reading materials. Whether the texts are digital or traditional forms of print, adolescents want and need access to texts that interest them.

In addition to access to interesting reading materials, adolescents need opportunities to make choices about what they read. Research indicates that students exhibit positive motivational patterns when their teachers provide them with opportunities to make choices about their learning. Teel, Debruin-Parecki, and Covington (as cited in Guthrie & Davis, 2003) found that when African American adolescents were given responsibility and opportunities to make choices about learning, they displayed significant increases in learning engagement. Research by Gambrell, Dromsky, and Mazzoni (1998), Midgley (1993), and Mizelle (1997) suggests that choice is positively related to motivation to read. Across all these studies, students were more motivated to read when they chose their own reading materials.

In studies by Gambrell and colleagues (Gambrell, 1996; Gambrell et al., 1998), fifth- and eighth-grade students were asked to tell about the "most interesting" narrative and informational text that they had read recently. The overwhelming majority of both fifth- and eighth-grade readers reported that they had self-selected these materials. Students frequently commented that they had selected a book because a teacher or friend had recommended or told them about it. The responses of these students suggest an important relationship between choice and social interactions with others about text. Choice allows students to voice preferences for engagement in reading and writing activities, and to experience some control over their learning environment. Students need to play an important role in suggesting and selecting reading materials.

Evidence from a number of studies suggests a strong correlation between choice and the development of intrinsic motivation (Paris & Oka, 1986; Rodin, Rennert, & Solomon, 1980; Spaulding, 1992). In addition, research related to self-selection of reading materials supports the notion that the books and stories that students find "most interesting" are those they have selected for their own reasons and purposes (Worthy, 1998; Worthy & McKool, 1996; Worthy et al., 1999). In a study by Schiefele (1991), students who were allowed and encouraged to choose their own reading material expended more effort in learning and understanding the material. It seems clear that providing adolescents with opportunities to select their own reading materials increases task engagement and intrinsic literacy motivation.

Build Time for Reading and Opportunities for Social Interactions

Studies by Heathington (1979), Hughes-Hassell and Rodge (2007), Ivey and Broaddus (2001), Midgley (1993), and Mizelle (1997) found that time is a primary factor in motivational literacy environments. Across surveys, observations, and student interviews, the amount of time actually devoted to reading and writing is related to students' level of motivation. The time allotted to reading and writing influences students' perceptions of the value of literacy. A primary goal for creating a classroom culture that fosters literacy motivation should be to ensure that all students have opportunities to engage in sustained reading events. To send the message that reading is valued, appropriate periods of time must be provided for students to engage in sustained reading activities. In-school sustained silent reading programs are important in a number of ways. First, students who spend more time reading become better readers (Allington, 2006), so in-school reading programs provide opportunities for students to enhance their reading competence. Second, reading programs are important to students who have little or no time for reading outside school. Third, in-school reading programs allow students the time to make sense of what they read, and to concentrate and reflect on their reading (Ivey & Broaddus, 2001).

Opportunities to talk about what they are reading are as important to middle and high school students as inclass time for engaging in independent reading. Adolescence is a developmental stage characterized by an increasing need to feel related, especially with respect to peers. This strong desire for relatedness refers to the development of relationships with others in the social context in which the activity occurs. One of the most robust findings in the research literature is the positive effect of social interaction on learning (Almasi, 1995; Gambrell, 1996; Johnson & Johnson, 1985; Slavin, 1984). Opportunities for social interactions with peers foster feelings of relatedness. When creating literacy events for adolescents, we need to keep in mind the importance of having them engage in informal, student-centered discussions that allow them to express opinions and entertain the opinions of others. Some researchers (e.g., Alvermann et al., 1999; Worthy, 1998; Worthy & McKool, 1996) have found that adolescents' out-of-school discussions about books are very different from inclass discussions. Informal classroom discussions about reading offer middle and high school students opportunities to learn about the texts their peers are reading and find compelling, and have the potential to motivate adolescents to engage in independent reading more frequently.

Build Connections between In- and Out-of-School Literacies

The everyday literacy practices of middle and high school students are changing rapidly due to interactive communication technologies and multimedia. Currently, there is little research to support the integration of new technologies in literacy instruction. However, some researchers have found that "adolescents who appear most 'at risk' of failure in the academic literacy arena are sometimes the most adept at (and interested in) understanding how media texts work, and in particular; how meaning gets produced and consumed" (Alvermann, 2002, p. 200). Incorporating new forms of technology into the academic curricula and expanding our views about what it means to be "literate" may have important consequences for adolescents' futures. Ryan (2005) posits that male adolescents' affinity for technology and "doing," as opposed to reading novels, may better prepare them for adult careers. Certainly, digital technologies should not be the primary focus of literacy instruction in middle and high school classrooms, but teaching strategies for locating information on the Internet, for thinking critically about the accuracy and reliability of information, and for considering the producer's purposes is a worthwhile endeavor (Hinchman et al., 2004).

Linking adolescents' out-of-school literacies to the classroom makes sense from a motivational perspective. Because students are interested in and motivated to engage in literacy practices that center on digital technology and multimedia, perhaps teachers can harness that motivation and channel it in a direction that includes traditional printed texts. Some adolescent literacy practices may not be appropriate for inclusion in the curriculum (e.g., IM, chat rooms, and text messaging), but others can be included and will help to bridge the gap between out-of-school and in-school reading. Alvermann, Huddleston, and Hagood (2004) argue that "to bind literacies by category, as personal or school based, is to divide up engagement with text" (p. 539).

QUESTIONS FOR DISCUSSION

1. Discuss obstacles that stand in the way of teachers incorporating suggestions for increasing motivation presented in this chapter into their classrooms. How can teachers diminish or eliminate these obstacles?

2. After considering why adolescents are motivated to engage in literacy activities with technology, discuss whether that motivation can be channeled to include traditional print. If so, how?

3. Discuss the different kinds of literacy in which middle and high school students engage, distinguishing between those that are and are not part of the classroom literacy program. What are the strategies for incorporating into the curriculum appropriate out-of-school literacy practices with the potential to motivate adolescents' in-school reading?

Resources

Further Reading

Guthrie, J. T. (2001, March). Contexts for engagement and motivation in reading. Retrieved June 4, 2008, from *www.readingonline.org/articles/handbook/guthrie/index.html*.

Watkins, M. W., & Coffey, D. Y. (2004). Reading motivation: Multidimensional and indeterminate. *Journal of Educational Psychology, 96*, 110–118.

Wigfield, A., & Guthrie, J. T. (1997). Relations of children's motivation for reading to the amount and breadth of their reading. *Journal of Educational Psychology, 89*, 420–432.

Wigfield, A., Guthrie, J. T., Tonks, S., & Perencevich, K. C. (2004). Children's motivation for reading: Domain specificity and instructional influences. *Journal of Educational Research, 97*, 299–309.

Website

www.pewinternet.org

References

Allington, R. L. (1986). Policy constraints and effective compensatory reading instruction: A review. In J. Hoffman (Ed.), *Effective teaching of reading: Research and practice* (pp. 261–289). Newark, DE: International Reading Association.

Allington, R. L. (1991). The legacy of "slow it down and make it more concrete." In J. Zutell & S. McCormick (Eds.), *Learner factors/teacher factors: Issues in literacy research and instruction* (pp. 19–30). Chicago: National Reading Conference.

Allington, R. L. (2006). *What really matters for struggling readers: Designing research-based programs* (2nd ed.). Boston: Allyn & Bacon.

Allington, R. L., & Johnston, P. H. (2002). *Reading to learn: Lessons from exemplary fourth-grade classrooms.* New York: Guilford Press.

Almasi, J. (1995). The nature of fourth-graders' sociocognitive conflicts in peer-led and teacher-led discussions of literature. *Reading Research Quarterly, 30*, 314–351.

Alvermann, D. E. (2001). Reading adolescents' reading identities: Looking back to see ahead. *Journal of Adolescent and Adult Literacy, 44*, 676–690.

Alvermann, D. E. (2002). Effective literacy instruction for adolescents. *Journal of Literacy Research, 34*, 189–208.

Alvermann, D. E., & Earle, J. (2003). Comprehension instruction: Adolescents and their multiple literacies. In A. P. Sweet & C. Snow (Eds.), *Rethinking reading comprehension* (pp. 12–30). New York: Guilford Press.

Alvermann, D. E., & Hagood, M. C. (2000). Critical media literacy: Research, theory, and practices in "new times." *Journal of Educational Research, 93*, 193–205.

Alvermann, D. E., Huddleston, A., & Hagood, M. C. (2004). What could professional wrestling an school literacy practices possibly have in common? *Journal of Adolescent & Adult Literacy, 47*, 532–540.

Alvermann, D. E., Young, J. P., Green, C., & Wisenbaker, J. M. (1999). Adolescents' perceptions and negotiations of literacy practices in after-school read and talk clubs. *American Educational Research Journal, 36*, 221–264.

Anderson, R. C., Wilson, P. T., & Fielding, L. G. (1988). Growth in reading and how children spend their time outside of school. *Reading Research Quarterly, 23*, 285–303.

Baker, L. (2003). The role of parents in motivating struggling readers. *Reading & Writing Quarterly, 19*, 87–106.

Bean, T. W., Bean, S. K., Bean, K. F. (1999). Intergenerational conversations and two adolescents' multiple literacies: Implications for redefining content area literacy. *Journal of Adolescent & Adult Literacy, 42*, 438–448.

Bintz, W. P. (1993). Resistant readers in secondary education: Some insights and implications. *Journal of Reading, 36*, 604–615.

Cameron, J., & Pierce, W. D. (1994). Reinforcements, reward, and intrinsic motivation: A meta-analysis. *Review of Educational Research, 64*, 363–423.

Colvin, C., & Schlosser, L. K. (1997/1998). Developing academic confidence to build literacy: What teachers can do. *Journal of Adolescent & Adult Literacy, 41*, 272–281.

Deci, E. L., & Ryan, R. M. (1985). *Intrinsic motivation and self-determination in human behavior.* San Diego: Academic Press.

Deci, E. L., Vallerand, R. J., Pelletier, L. G., & Ryan, R. M. (1991). Motivation and education: The self-determination perspective. *Educational Psychologist, 26*, 325–346.

Dolezal, S. E., Welsh, L. M., Pressley, M., & Vincent, M. M. (2003). How nine third-grade teachers motivate student academic engagement. *Elementary School Journal, 103*, 239–267.

Donahue, P. L., Voelkl, K. E., Campbell, J. R., & Mazzeo, J. (1999). *The NAEP 1998 reading report card for the nation and the states.* Washington, DC: National Center for Education Statistics.

Dunston, P. J., & Alvermann, D. E. (2006, November). *OMG!! I'm LOL :-D j/k Got 2 go ttyl: Literacy messages within teenagers' instant messages.* Paper presented at the National Reading Conference, Los Angeles, CA.

Eagleton, M., Guinee, K., & Langlais, K. (2003). Teaching Internet literacy strategies: The Hero Inquiry Project. *Voices from the Middle, 10*, 28–35.

Ford, M. E. (1992). *Motivating humans.* Newbury Park, CA: Sage.

Gambrell, L. B. (1996). Creating classroom cultures that foster reading motivation [Distinguished Educator Series]. *Reading Teacher, 50*, 14–25.

Gambrell, L. B., & Codling, R. M. (1997). Fostering reading motivation: Insights from theory and research. In K. Camperell, B. L. Hayes, & R. Telfer (Eds.), *Yearbook of the American Reading Forum* (pp. 17–28). Logan, UT: American Reading Forum.

Gambrell, L. B., Dromsky, A. J., & Mazzoni, S. A. (1998). *Middle school students' motivation to read narrative and expository texts.* Unpublished raw data.

Gambrell, L. B., & Marinak, B. (1997). Incentives and intrinsic motivation to read. In J. Guthrie & A. Wigfield (Eds.), *Reading engagement: Motivating readers through integrated instruction* (pp. 205–217). Newark, DE: International Reading Association.

Gee, J. P., & Green, J. L. (1998). Discourse analysis, learning, and social practice: A methodological study. In P. D. Pearson & A. Iran-Nejad (Eds.), *Review of research in education* (Vol. 23, pp. 119–170). Washington, DC: American Educational Research Association.

Gottfried, A. E., Fleming, J. S., & Gottfried, A. W. (2001). Continuity of academic intrinsic motivation from childhood through late adolescence: A longitudinal study. *Journal of Educational Psychology, 93*, 3–13.

Guthrie, J. T., & Davis, M. H. (2003). Motivating struggling readers in middle school through an engagement model of classroom practice. *Reading & Writing Quarterly, 19*, 50–85.

Guthrie, J. T., Wigfield, A., Barbosa, P., Perencevich, K. C., Taboada, A., Davis, M. H., et al. (2004). Increasing reading comprehension and engagement through concept-oriented reading instruction. *Journal of Educational Psychology, 96*, 403–423.

Guthrie, J. T., Wigfield, A., Metsala, J. L., & Cox, K. E. (1999). Motivational and cognitive predictors of text comprehension and reading amount. *Scientific Studies of Reading, 3*, 231–256.

Heathington, B. (1979). What to do about reading motivation in the middle school. *Journal of Reading, 22*, 709–713.

Hinchman, K. A., Alvermann, D. E., Boyd, F. B., Brozo, W. G., & Vacca, R. T. (2003/2004). Supporting older students' in- and out-of-school literacies. *Journal of Adolescent & Adult Literacy, 47*, 304–310.

Hughes-Hassell, S., & Rodge, P. (2007). The leisure reading habits of urban adolescents. *Journal of Adolescent and Adult Literacy, 51*, 22–33.

Ivey, G. (1999). Reflections on teaching struggling middle school readers. *Journal of Adolescent & Adult Literacy, 42*, 372–381.

Ivey, G., & Broaddus, K. (2001). "Just plain reading": A survey of what makes students want to read in middle school classrooms. *Reading Research Quarterly, 36*, 350–377.

Johnson, D., & Johnson, R. (1985). The internal dynamics of cooperative learning groups. In R. Slavin, S. Sharan, S. Kagan, R. Hertz-Lazarowitz, C. Webb, & R. Schmuck (Eds.), *Learning to cooperate, cooperating to learn* (pp. 103–124). New York; Plenum Press.

Knobel, M. (2001). "I'm not a pencil man": How one student challenges our notions of literacy "failure" in school. *Journal of Adolescent and Adult Literacy, 44*, 404–414.

Lankshear, C., & Knobel, M. (2003). *New literacies: Changing knowledge and classroom learning.* Philadelphia: Open University Press.

Lewis, C., & Fabos, B. (2005). Instant messaging, literacies, and social identities. *Reading Research Quarterly, 40*, 470–501.

Luke, A., & Elkins, J. (1998). Reinventing literacy in "new times." *Journal of Adolescent & Adult Literacy, 42*, 4–7.

Luttrell, W., & Parker, C. (2001). High school students' literacy practices and identities, and the figured world of school. *Journal of Research in Reading, 24*, 235–247.

Marinak, B. A., & Gambrell, L. B. (2008). Intrinsic motivation and rewards: What sustains young children's engagement with text? *Literacy Research and Instruction, 47*, 9–26.

McCombs, B. L. (1989). Self-regulated learning and academic achievement: A phenomenological view. In B. J. Zimmerman & D. H. Schunk (Eds.), *Self-regulated learning and achievement: Theory, research, and practice* (pp. 51–82). New York: Springer-Verlag.

McKenna, M. C., Kear, D. J., & Ellsworth, R. A. (1995). Children's attitudes toward reading: A national survey. *Reading Research Quarterly, 30*, 934–956.

Midgley, C. (1993). Motivation and middle level schools. In M. L. Maehr & P. R. Pintrich (Eds.), *Advances in motivation and achievement* (Vol. 8, pp. 217–271). Greenwich, CT: JAI Press.

Mizelle, N. B. (1997). Enhancing young adolescents' motivation for literacy learning. *Middle School Journal, 24*(2), 5–14.

Moje, E. B., Young, J. P., Readence, J. E., & Moore, D. W. (2000). Reinventing adolescent literacy for new times: Perennial and millennial issues. *Journal of Adolescent & Adult Literacy, 43*, 400–410.

Mosenthal, P. P. (1998). Reframing the problems of adolescence and adolescent literacy: A dilemma-management perspective. In D. E. Alvermann, K. A. Hinchman, D. W. Moore, S. F. Phelps, & D. R. Waff (Eds.), *Reconceptualizing the literacies in adolescent's lives* (pp. 325–352). Hillsdale, NJ: Erlbaum.

New London Group. (1996). A pedagogy of multiliteracies: Designing social future. *Harvard Educational Review, 66*, 60–92.

O'Flahavan, J., Gambrell, L. B., Guthrie, J., Stahl, S., & Alvermann, D. (1992, August). Poll results guide activities of research center. *Reading Today*, 12.

Oldfather, P. (1993). What students say about motivating experiences in a whole language classroom. *Reading Teacher, 46*, 672–681.

Paris, S. G., & Oka, E. R. (1986). Self-regulated learning among exceptional children. *Exceptional Children, 53*, 103–108.

Pitcher, S. M., Albright, L. K., DeLaney, C. J., Walker, N. T. Seunarinesingh, K., Mogge, S., et al. (2007). Assessing adolescents' motivation to read. *Journal of Adolescent &Adult Literacy, 50*, 378–396.

Rodin, J., Rennert, K., & Solomon, S. (1980). Intrinsic motivation for control: Fact or fiction. In A. Baum, J. E. Singer, & S. Valios (Eds.), *Advances in environmental psychology II* (pp. 177–186). Hillsdale, NJ: Erlbaum.

Ryan, J. (2005). Young people choose: Adolescents' text pleasures. *Australian Journal of Language and Literacy, 28*, 38–47.

Ryan, R. M., & Deci, E. L. (2000). Intrinsic and extrinsic motivations: Classic definitions and new directions. *Contemporary Educational Psychology, 25*, 54–67.

Schiefele, U. (1991). Interest, learning, and motivation. *Educational Psychologist, 26*, 299–323.

Slavin, R. (1984). Students motivating students to excel: Cooperative incentives, cooperative tasks, and student achievement. *Elementary School Journal, 84*, 23–63.

Smith-Burke, T. M. (1989). Political and economic dimensions of literacy: Challenges for the 1990s. In S. McCormick & J. Zutell (Eds.), *Cognitive and social perspectives for literacy research and instruction* (pp. 1–18). Chicago: National Reading Conference.

Spaulding, C. L. (1992). The motivation to read and write. In J. W. Irwin & M. A. Doyle (Eds.), *Reading/writing connections: Learning from research* (pp. 177–201). Newark, DE: International Reading Association.

Stevens, L. P. (2001). *South Park* and society: Instructional and curricular implications of popular culture in the classroom. *Journal of Adolescent & Adult Literacy, 44*, 548–555.

Strommen, L. T., & Mates, B. F. (2004). Learning to love reading: Interviews with older children and teens. *Journal of Adolescent & Adult Literacy, 48*, 188–200.

Sweet, A. P., Guthrie, J. T., & Ng, M. M. (1998). Teacher perceptions an student reading motivation. *Journal of Educational Psychology, 90*, 210–223.

Taylor, B. M., Frye, B. J., & Maruyama, G. M. (1990). Time spent reading and reading growth. *American Educational Research Journal, 27*, 351–362.

Thakkar, U., Bruce, B. C., Hogan, M. P., & Williamson, J. (2001). Extending literacy through participation in new technologies. *Journal of Adolescent & Adult Literacy, 45*, 212–219.

Veenman, S. (1984). Perceived problems of beginning teachers. *Review of Educational Research, 54*(2), 143–178.

Vygotsky, L. S. (1986). *Thought and language.* Cambridge, MA: MIT Press.

Watkins, M. W., & Coffey, D. Y. (2004). Reading motivation: Multidimensional and indeterminate. *Journal of Educational Psychology, 96,* 110–118.

Weinstein, S. (2006/2007). A love for the thing: The pleasures of rap as a literate practice. *Journal of Adolescent & Adult Literacy, 50,* 270–281.

Wigfield, A., & Guthrie, J. T. (1997). Relations of children's motivation for reading to the amount and breadth of their reading. *Journal of Educational Psychology, 89,* 420–432.

Wigfield, A., Guthrie, J. T., Tonks, S., & Perencevich, K. C. (2004). Children's motivation for reading: Domain specificity and instructional influences. *Journal of Educational Research, 97,* 299–309.

Worthy, J. (1998). "On every page someone gets killed!": Book conversations you don't hear in school. *Journal of Adolescent & Adult Literacy, 41,* 508–517.

Worthy, J., & McKool, S. S. (1996). Students who say they hate to read: The importance of opportunity, choice, and access. In D. J. Leu, C. K. Kinzer, & K. A. Hinchman (Eds.), *Literacies for the 21st century: Research and practice. Forty-fifth yearbook of the National Reading Conference* (pp. 245–256). Chicago: National Reading Conference.

Worthy, J., Moorman, M., & Turner, M. (1999). What Johnny likes to read is hard to find in school. *Reading Research Quarterly, 34,* 12–27.

Chapter 15

Using Picture Books
with Older Learners

Miriam Martinez
Nancy Roser
Janis M. Harmon

GUIDING QUESTIONS

1. Do picture books belong in middle and secondary school classrooms?
2. What roles can picture books play in middle and secondary school classrooms?
3. What textual and pictorial features might make picture books appropriate for older learners?
4. What needs of older learners might be met through the use of picture books?

Teachers of adolescents all too often overlook picture books as they seek out materials to support their curricula, assuming that picture books are intended only for young children (Kiefer, 1995). In earlier decades, children's literature experts would likely have agreed with these teachers. The topics and themes explored in the picture books of years past made them most appropriate for younger children. These topics included family stories; familiar everyday experiences; stories of the country and city, weather and the seasons; realistic and fanciful animal stories; humorous and fanciful stories; and stories of other lands (Huck & Kuhn, 1968; Sutherland & Arburthnot, 1977). Likewise, the illustrative and textual features of picture books written in earlier eras made them most appropriate for a younger audience (Goldstone, 2001/2002). These features included clearly focused illustrations, uncluttered page design, and linear texts with a clearly articulated beginning, middle, and end.

Many of today's picture books continue to exhibit these same features, but increasingly publishers are producing complex and sophisticated picture books. This new breed of picture book often explores mature themes and challenging subject matter, exhibits complex picture–text relationships, and contains demanding text with subtle meanings (Osborn, 2001). Peter Sis's picture book *The Wall* (2007) is one such book. This award-winning book depicts the author's life behind the Iron Curtain in Prague, Czechoslovakia. His intricate illustrations include photographs, posters, child artwork, and adult drawings that subtly use color to convey symbolic meanings. This complex artwork is integrated with diverse text formats that include journal entries, accompanied by shifts in text font that signal shifts in text function. Picture books like *The Wall* confirm that "dramatic changes in children's and YA [young adult] publishing over the last decade have blurred the lines between children's and adult books" (Zvirin, 1998, p. 1716). In effect, picture books have become books for all ages (Huck, Hepler, Hickman, & Kiefer, 1997), with increasing numbers being written for an older audience.

The more complex picture book that has evolved in recent decades would appear to be well suited for supporting older learners' literacy development and content learning. Yet researchers in large part have not focused on the role that picture books may play in the education of adolescents. There is extensive anecdotal evidence and testimonials of middle- and secondary-level teachers who sing the praises of picture books for literacy development and content learning (Billman, 2002; Costello & Kolodziej, 2006; Crum, 2007; Hadaway & Mundy, 1999; Heitman, 2005; Osborn, 2001; Steiner, 1998). However, no systematic research has directly explored the impact of using picture books to support the learning and literacy development of older readers. Nonetheless, related bodies of research suggest picture books have the potential to play an important role in promoting literacy and learning. These include studies about the nature and complexity of this text type and about the reader—particularly studies on older students' motivation and preferences in reading. We also include research on the impact of illustrations on readers' comprehension and related literature about publishing trends.

Related Research

In this section we review the research on picture books, examine what we know about the motivations, interests, and reading preferences of older learners, the impact of illustrations on their comprehension, and trends in picture book publishing.

Research on Picture Books

Scholars of children's literature define the *picture book format* as one in which there is an interdependence of illustrations and text. Illustrations and text each reflect and expand on the meaning of one another, together creating greater meaning than either can convey independently (Bader, 1976; Galda & Cullinan, 2001). Expanding on this conceptualization of the picture book, Wolfenbarger and Sipe (2007) observe that although picture and text work together, they also "create tension as each creates constraints on the other" (p. 273) in turn, requiring greater attention by the reader to picture–text relationships and the intended meanings of the picture book creator.

Close analyses of the relationships between text and illustrations in picture books reveal the potential complexity of this text format. Nikolajeva and Scott (2001) identified five relationships between illustrations and text: (1) *symmetry*, in which words and illustrations convey similar meaning; (2) *complementary*, in which words and illustrations provide different but complementary information; (3) *enhancement*, in which words and illustrations extend each other's meaning; (4) *counterpoint*, in which words and illustrations tell different stories; and (5) *contradiction*, in which the words and illustrations appear to contradict one another. The latter two types of word–illustration relationships in particular point to a potential complexity of picture books that can challenge adolescent and even adult readers.

The analysis of illustrations further reveals the potential complexity of picture books (Sipe, 2008). Using a semiotic perspective, Moebius (1986) analyzed the signs or tools used by illustrators to convey meaning through visual text. He calls these signs *codes*, which he grouped into five clusters:

1. *Codes of position.* Information about characters (e.g., status and emotional state) is conveyed through their positioning in an illustration, as well as their relative size. For example, a character who is feeling dejected, may be depicted as small in size and be placed at the bottom of the frame.

2. *Codes of perspective.* Illustrators can employ perspective for different purposes. For example, shifts in perspective can communicate a sense of action, heighten excitement or emotion, or reveal shifts between reality and fantasy.

3. *Codes of the frame.* Framed illustrations provide readers of picture books a sense of looking into the story world, whereas unframed illustrations express a sense that the reader is within the story world.

4. *Codes of line.* Illustrators convey particular meanings through their use of lines. For example, movement may be depicted when illustrators use diagonal lines, in contrast to vertical and horizontal lines that convey stillness. The type of line an illustrator uses can also serve as a sign: Thick, heavy lines call to mind boldness, whereas thin, curving lines depict a sense of delicacy.

5. *Codes of color.* Color is an especially powerful sign because of strong cultural associations with this visual element. In particular, color is frequently used in picture book illustrations to depict mood, emotions, and even status. For example, red is often associated with anger, whereas green and blue call to mind tranquility and peace.

In light of Moebius's analysis of illustrations, it is evident that picture books are open for interpretation and engagement at many different levels; therefore, they may be especially well suited for older readers.

Postmodern picture books also hold promise for use with older learners. The term *postmodern picture book* refers to picture books that "deliberately work against a linear storytelling pattern" (Wolfenbarger & Sipe, 2007, p. 273), hence requiring readers to engage with the text in new ways (Anstey, 2002; Trites, 1994). Although postmodern picture books do not adhere to a single variant structure, they frequently "develop more than one narrative line by including two or more sets of separate pictures on the page" (Trites, 1994, p. 225; e.g., *Black and White* by Macaulay, 1990) and may be additionally complicated by the inclusion of more than a single strand of text (e.g., *The Wall: Growing Up Behind the Iron Curtain* by Sis, 2007). In the last two decades, there have been increasing numbers of picture books with such variant structures (Trites, 1994), and the complexity of this text format may make the postmodern picture book suitable for older readers (Anstey, 2002).

Close analyses of postmodern books (Dresang, 1999; Goldstone, 1999; Lewis, 2001) have identified a number of distinctive features. Goldstone (2001/2002) has identified four features that distinguish the format:

1. *Nonlinear structure.* Postmodern narrative texts may contain jumbled or missing story elements, as well as multiple storylines. In parallel fashion, informational postmodern texts may also contain multiple pictorial and textual strands. The nonlinear structure typically requires readers/viewers to move back and forth through the text rather than reading in a sequential or linear fashion.

2. *Self-referential text.* Whereas the author of a traditional story deliberately attempts to pull the reader into the story world, the creator of the postmodern picture book deliberately breaks the story spell by calling attention to the text as a constructed object. For example, in Jon Scieszka's *The Stinky Cheese Man and Other Fairly Stupid Tales* (1992), the author begins with a story excerpt and does not include the table of contents until several pages into this story, at which point the table of contents actually falls on a character in the story.

3. *Cynical or sarcastic tone.* Postmodern picture books are typically characterized by a playfulness that "mocks in sarcastic or ironic tones" (Goldstone, 2001/2002, p. 365). This feature is evident in books such as *The True Story of the Three Little Pigs* (Scieszka, 1989), which mocks *The Three Little Pigs* by telling the story from the wolf's perspective.

4. *Antiauthoritarian text.* Postmodern picture books "make it clear that the author is not solely in charge" (Goldstone, 2001/2003, p. 365). Postmodern picture books actively invite the reader/viewer to co-construct or coauthor the text. For example, such an invitation is explicitly extended by Macaulay through the warning he places on the title page of *Black and White* (1990):

WARNING
>   This book appears to contain a number of stories that do not necessarily occur at the same time. Then again, it may contain only one story. In any event, careful inspection of both words and pictures is recommended.

Anstey (2002) argues that the distinctive features of postmodern picture books require a similar reading stance to that of reading hypertext on the Internet. By their very nature, these books position the reader/viewer to cocreate the story with the author and illustrator. Hence, these picture books appear to require complex reading operations (Trites, 1994; Wolfenbarger & Sipe, 2007).

Research on Readers

Several important studies lend indirect support for the use of picture books in middle- and secondary-level classrooms, especially studies that examine student motivation for reading. Motivation to read involves several constructs, including interest, choice, and variety of texts. First, interest in a topic is a motivating factor in getting students to read. Guthrie and Wigfield (2000) define *interesting books* as texts that match "the topic interest and cognitive competency of the reader" (p. 412), and argue that students are more apt to spend time reading when the topic is personally relevant and the text is easy to understand. Furthermore, some studies that address older readers' motivation and interest in reading consistently report the need for student choice, and the need for teachers to have a variety of reading materials available in the classroom—selections of reading texts that are varied in terms of format, topic, and level of difficulty (Ivey & Broaddus, 2001; Pitcher et al., 2007; Oldfather, 1993). In her qualitative study of three young adolescent readers of varying ability levels, Ivey (1999) found that these students displayed unique, complex, and varied behaviors as readers. She also found that the students' propensity for and level of engagement in reading were influenced by the classroom instructional environment. In particular, students' personal choices of books to read during independent reading indicated preferences for a variety of reading texts, especially texts that were accessible to the readers, such as picture books, as mentioned by one participant. Students, regardless of ability level, gravitate toward books that are easy to read, a finding supported by Guthrie and Wigfield (2000).

In another study, Ivey and Broaddus (2001) surveyed over 1,700 middle-level students to investigate aspects of classroom instruction and environment that influence students' motivation to read. Their analysis of student responses to the survey and individual interviews revealed several positive findings, one of which emphasized the importance of having high-quality, diverse reading materials available in the classroom. In response to the question "What types of books do you like to read?", students mentioned a variety of favorite genres and particular text types, such as comic books and informational books. Of particular interest to us, 27% of the respondents indicated a preference for picture books.

Illustrations have been found to play a role in the reading process. We know that illustrations in texts can serve a motivating function, resulting in promotion of "positive attitudes toward reading in general and toward illustrated text in particular" (Hibbing & Rankin-Erickson, 2003, p. 762). Illustrations have also been found to influence positively the time that readers invest in a text. Furthermore, illustrations in picture books may directly support readers' comprehension by providing background information that readers may lack (Schallert, 1980). Illustrations may play an especially supportive role for struggling readers. Rusted and Coltheart (1979) found that struggling readers move between text and illustrations when reading, whereas good readers pay little attention to illustrations.

Related Literature

Experts in the field of children's literature have observed publishing trends that indicate changes in the subject matter and genres of picture books. One consequence of these changes is that increasing numbers of picture books are appropriate for use with older learners.

Picture books of earlier decades tended to highlight the everyday experiences and concerns of young children, but in the 1990s, what Elleman (2004) has termed *blunt realism* (p. 33) began to make its way into picture books. Blunt realism is evident in Huck et al.'s (1997) list of topics explored in recent picture books—topics that include appreciation of cultural diversity, social and environmental concerns, and war and its aftermath. Some of the particular topics that authors choose to explore in picture book format include the Holocaust, the bombing of Hiroshima, life in war-torn Beirut, apartheid, homelessness, alcoholism, AIDS, and even suicide. Pictures books addressing such topics have stirred considerable controversy in both professional circles and the popular press (Krauthammer, 1995; Sutton, 1996). Yet the controversy appears to arise in part from the entrenched belief that picture books are intended for young children. When picture books are viewed as being for all ages, however, addressing serious issues in picture book format seems not only appropriate but also even desirable.

Yet another change in picture book publishing trends is the proliferation of genres in picture book format that, until recent years, appeared primarily as lengthier texts. This trend is especially evident in biographies and historical fiction (Bishop & Hickman, 1992; Temple et al., 2006). Diane Stanley, Kathryn Lasky, Peter Sis, Pam Muñoz Ryan, and Kathleen Krull are among the outstanding writers producing biographies in picture book format. Fine writers such as Patricia Polacco, Ann Turner, Emily Arnold McCully, Deborah Wiles, and Karen Ackerman have produced historical fiction in picture book format. Although some of the picture books in these genres are appropriate for young children, many are better suited for older students given their length, complexity, and subject matter. Biography and historical fiction may be especially well suited to a picture book format, because an enormous amount of historical information can be conveyed through a book's illustrations.

Using Picture Books with Older Learners

The research and related literature we have reviewed suggest that many picture books may be valuable resources for middle and high school teachers. Older students may initially view picture books as "baby books," but if teachers "consider picture books as literature—not children's literature—but as *literature*" (Newkirk, 1992, p. 13), and if they share their own genuine enthusiasm for the genre, students will also come to value picture books. Then, perhaps, picture books may help to fill a variety of niches (and gulfs) across the curricula in classrooms that serve older students. In the next section, we explore some of those niches and provide examples of literature that can fill them.

Picture Books in Language Arts/English/Reading Classrooms

Picture books can play a host of roles in language arts, English, and reading classrooms. Carefully selected picture books can provide rich material for literature discussion. Teachers can use high-quality picture books as models for students' writing and to teach various language arts and reading skills and strategies. Picture books can be an important resource for independent reading, especially for struggling readers and for English language learners. Finally, postmodern picture books hold promise as vehicles for fostering students' visual literacy.

Literature Discussion

Learning to read and respond insightfully to literary texts are critical objectives in the English/language arts curriculum. Rich and perceptive thinking about literature is most likely to occur when students are invited to talk about carefully crafted texts that explore significant themes (Daniels, 2001; Eeds & Wells, 1989). In middle and high school classrooms, literature discussion typically centers around novels. However, many picture books also have the potential to evoke equally rich literature discussion. Carlisle (1992), who has used picture books to engage older students in philosophical thinking, argues that picture books are "an easy place to think" (p. 58). Picture books may be an especially ideal "place to think" for reluctant readers, who, although quite capable of insightful thinking in response to text, nonetheless actively avoid the challenges presented by lengthier works of literature. In fact, our own experiences with older struggling readers support Carlisle's assertion that picture books can serve as a way to engage these students in meaningful discussions. For example, one resistant reader who had read *December* (1997), Eve Bunting's book about homelessness, had this to say: "I didn't like how the other kids were making fun of her." While her comment may seem somewhat unremarkable, it is indeed noteworthy coming from a student who rarely, if ever, contributed to class discussions. In one more instance, another disengaged older reader posed several questions while reading *The Dinosaurs of Waterhouse Hawkins* (Kerley, 2001): "What's a pigeon pie?", "How does he make the models?", "So he decided to just do art?", "So is the park still here?" These questions are indicative of an engaged reader who willingly and naturally participated in a discussion about the picture book.

A wide variety of picture books explore the kinds of significant themes that are likely to lead to rich discussions. In one example, *The Girl Who Loved Caterpillars*, author Jean Merrill (1992) retells the 12th-century Japanese story of Suzumi, a girl whose passion for learning about caterpillars flies in the face of her society's values. Her parents long for her to develop more conventional interests, but Suzumi steadfastly clings to her passion. Because *The Girl Who Loved Caterpillars* explores issues that still confront many young women, today's students are likely to have a great deal to say in response to this very sophisticated picture book.

Other examples of picture books with the potential to evoke rich conversation include Demi's *The Greatest Power* (2004), which invites readers to consider the greatest power in the world—possibilities such as beauty, technology, and money. Readers of Anthony Browne's *Voices in the Park* (1998) are likely to engage in discussions about the divisions between social classes. In *An Angel for Solomon Singer* (1992), Cynthia Rylant explores the power of a helping hand in overcoming the loneliness and isolation that too often occur in large cities.

From a time perspective, relying on picture books for literature discussion offers middle and high school teachers a genuine advantage. Because students are reading longer works on their own, the teacher who uses picture books in class does not have to wait for students to finish a work before inviting them to talk about literature. A picture book can be read aloud and discussed in a single class session. Thus, students may well participate in more literature discussion than they do in classes where only longer works are discussed.

Carlisle (1992) identified yet another advantage of picture books for literature discussions. By using picture books, a teacher can bring more diverse perspectives to bear on a topic than is possible when using a single extended work of literature to explore the topic. This in turn offers students the opportunity to make intertextual connections. If a teacher wants students to explore, for instance, the impact of war on the lives of people, then numerous picture books about World War II might be used to achieve this goal. For example, various picture books about World War II explore life in concentration camps (e.g., Wild's [1991] *Let the Celebration Begin!*), the impact of the war on German civilians (e.g., *Rose Blanche*; Innocenti, 1985), the resistance movement in the Netherlands (e.g., *The Greatest Skating Race*; Borden, 2004), the persecution of the Japanese Americans (e.g., *Baseball Saved Us*; Mochizuki, 1993), and the devastation suffered by the people of Hiroshima (e.g., *Hiroshima No Pika*, Maruki, 1980).

English and language arts teachers may also use picture books to contextualize the study of classic literature, which students often find inaccessible. Before students read the works of William Shakespeare, for example, teachers can use picture books to introduce the playwright and the time in which he wrote. Examples include *William Shakespeare and the Globe* (Aliki, 1999), *Shakespeare and Macbeth: The Story behind the Play* (Ross, 1994), and *Bard of Avon: The Story of William Shakespeare* (Stanley & Vennema, 1992). Picture book retellings of Shakespeare's classics, such as *William Shakespeare's Twelfth Night* (Coville, 2003) and *William Shakespeare's Macbeth* (Coville, 1997), may be appropriate for use with struggling readers.

Student Writing

Picture books can make an especially important contribution to English/language arts programs when they are used as writing models. Even when students are successfully reading longer works of literature, the complexity of novels can make it difficult to stand back and see how authors have crafted their work. Furthermore, more extended works may not serve as appropriate models, because most students are not likely to write extended works of their own. The relative brevity of picture books makes it easier for students to read as writers, inspecting the picture books for structure, form, and the author's use of various literary devices. For example, to explore how sentence length contributes to mood, students might compare the texts of *When I Was Young in the Mountains* (Rylant, 1982) and *Flight* (Burleigh, 1991). In writing about an idyllic childhood spent in the mountains, Rylant uses lengthy sentences and repetition that contributes to a calm and peaceful mood. By contrast, through his use of short, staccato sentences, Burleigh captures the drama and tension that surrounds Charles Lindbergh's solo flight across the Atlantic. After studying the way these authors structure sentences for particular effects, students might want to experiment with the same techniques. Immersing students in literature *units* structured around sets of picture books can be an especially effective way to help them make discoveries about literary craft. For example, reading the picture books of Van Allsburg is likely to heighten students' awareness of the effectiveness of the unexpected twist at the end of a story.

Picture books can support the writing program in yet another way. Quality writing relies on rich experience, and although rich experiences can take many forms, good literature can certainly constitute such experiences. Teachers can take advantage of the meaningful experiences offered by well-crafted picture books to foster their students' writing. Of particular note are picture books that feature "universal" experiences. *The Relatives Came* (Rylant, 1985), which describes the delights of a family reunion, is one such book. Though relatively simple, this picture book has the potential to evoke memories that many students hold dear—memories that can be shared through writing. The special family experiences celebrated in *Family Pictures/Cuadros de Familia* (Garza, 1990) may inspire middle and secondary school students to write about their own special childhood memories.

Picture books with novel structures (or story content) can also serve as engaging springboards for students' writing. *The Mysteries of Harris Burdick* (Van Allsburg, 1984) is such a book. It comprises a series of intriguing illustrations, with captions created to accompany stories. The stories, the author explains, have been lost. Each illustration and accompanying caption serves as an enticing invitation to write. Another example, *The Jolly Postman or Other People's Letters* (Ahlberg & Ahlberg, 1986), an equally novel picture book, comprises a series of humorous spin-off letters and postcards written to or by characters from European folklore. This picture book begs for older students to write their own spin-offs. For instance, an attorney writes to the Big Bad Wolf, informing him of a lawsuit the Three Little Pigs plan to bring against him. Jack sends the Giant a postcard, and Goldilocks mails Baby Bear an invitation to her birthday party. In Diane Stanley's *Rumpelstiltskin's Daughter* (1997), the protagonist is so clever that she has no need to call for help when the king asks her to spin straw into gold.

Still other stories leave readers with so much to think about that they are eager to write in response to the story. Who can finish *The Stranger* (Van Allsburg, 1986) without speculating about who this peculiar man is? Readers of Barbara Cooney's *Miss Rumphius* (1982) may want to write about how they envision themselves making the world a better place. After listening to poems in Eve Merriam's (1996) provocative *The Inner City Mother Goose*, students might write about the social problems they see in their own society; some may even want to attempt to write using Merriam's nursery rhyme format.

Teaching Literary Concepts

Because of their brevity, picture books are wonderful vehicles for teaching literary concepts. As one example, perspective can be taught through Jeanne Willis's (1988) *Earthlets* or Chris Van Allsburg's (1988) *Two Bad Ants*. It is hard to imagine a better example of irony than Alan Benjamin's adaptation of Somerset Maugham's (1993) *Appointment*. *Tough Cookie* (Wieniewski, 1999), which lampoons the detective genre, is a wonderful tool for introducing "spoofs."

Skill and Strategy Instruction

Picture books can be excellent vehicles for English/language arts reading skills and strategy instruction, especially if the books are experienced first for their artistry. Using literature ensures that instruction is done in a meaningful context, and picture books are typically brief enough to be used in mini-lessons. Also, it is relatively easy to find picture books that serve as clear-cut examples of the target skill or strategy. For example, the teacher who is targeting cause-and-effect relationships will find that David Macaulay's (1995) *Shortcut* provides a humorous context for a lesson.

The English/language arts teacher who wants to help students understand the way language works can turn to Ruth Heller's poetic picture book series on parts of speech, including titles such as *Up, Up and Away* (1991) and *Many Luscious Lollipops* (1989). There is simply no more entertaining way to teach punctuation than through Lynne Truss's books *Eats, Shoots and Leaves* (2006) and *The Girl's Like Spaghetti* (2007).

Independent Reading

Picture books may be just what the struggling reader in upper elementary or middle school needs for independent reading. Because picture books come in all levels of difficulty and contain texts of varying lengths, there is bound to be a "right fit" for each struggling reader. In fact, struggling readers who have not finished a book in years (or perhaps have never finished one) may be able to do just that when reading picture books. A caution: If picture books are brought into the classroom only for struggling readers to read during independent reading, then students may believe there is a stigma attached to reading picture books. When the genre is used to support other facets of the curriculum, however, students view picture books with new respect and value the opportunity to read them.

Visual Literacy

Literacy is increasingly being defined to include new literacies, such as hypertext, and Anstey (2002) argues that the rapidly changing nature of texts in the modern world requires students to understand that "all texts are consciously constructed and have particular ... purposes" (p. 446). Postmodern pictures books are "more closely aligned to hypertext than they are to traditional pictures books" (Goldstone, 2001/2002, p. 367), as evidenced by their nonlinear structure and the way that text forms change the roles of both writer and reader (Landow, 1992). Given this, experiences with postmodern picture books may help to prepare students for critical explorations of other texts they encounter, especially those on the Internet. Student awareness of the nature of postmodern picture books (and their similarity to hypertext) is likely to be heightened when teachers talk with students about the reading demands of nonlinear texts, and guide them to discover postmodern elements in books, such as *Black and White* (Macaulay, 1990), *Saint George and the Dragon* (Hodges, 1984), or *Moses: When Harriet Tubman Led Her People to Freedom* (Weatherford, 2006).

Picture Books in Social Studies and History Classrooms

Many educators have made a persuasive case for incorporating literature into the social studies curriculum (Steffey & Hood, 1994). Textbooks continue to play an important role in social studies instruction by offering a broad overview of many topics, and thereby providing general, but essential, background knowledge. Textbooks, however, tend to be stylistically dry and poorly written (Beck & McKeown, 1991; Freeman & Person, 1998; Tomlinson, Tunnell, & Richgels, 1993). Well-written works of children's literature, both fiction and nonfiction, stand in direct contrast to textbooks. Rather than taking a broad view of a subject, authors of children's literature are more likely to focus on a single subject and examine it in depth. Stylistically, quality works of children's literature are written to engage readers. Writing about history instruction in particular, Tomlinson et al. (1993) argue that readers need historical empathy to develop historical understanding. They hold that readers "must be able to perceive past events and issues as they were experienced by the people at the time" (p. 54). Temple and his colleagues (2006) believe that "helping readers develop historical empathy is what historical fiction does best, by emphasizing human motives and ordinary people" (p. 310).

Children's literature in general is an important tool in the social studies curriculum, and picture books in particular are valuable resources. Earlier in this chapter we discussed recent shifts in topics and techniques that make certain picture books especially (or only) appropriate for use with older students. Some of these same changes underscore their usefulness as resources in the social studies program. Two of these changes are of particular note: the increasing numbers of picture books dealing with cultural diversity and social concerns, and historical fiction and biographical subjects. The last two decades in U.S. publishing have witnessed an unprecedented number of books that highlight diverse cultures in both the United States and other countries. For example, the Caldecott Honor Book *Henry's Freedom Box* (Levine, 2007) depicts the true story of Henry Brown's escape from slavery via mail. In *Days of the Dead* (1994), Kathryn Lasky writes about the celebration of this important cultural event in Mexico. Florence Parry Heide and Judith Heide Gilliland bring the city of Cairo to life in *The Day of Ahmed's Secret* (1990).

Picture book authors also address current social issues (Steiner & Cobiskey, 1998). In *Amazing Grace* (1991), Mary Hoffman has created a moving account of the way in which racial prejudice affects a child. Eve Bunting uses the picture book format to look at the human side of still other contemporary social issues; she explores homelessness in *Fly Away Home* (1991), aging in *Sunshine Home* (1994), and immigration in *How Many Days to America* (1988). The Los Angeles riots are the topic of *Smoky Night* (Bunting, 1994).

The human side of history is increasingly being addressed in historical fiction and biographies in picture book format, many of which are best suited for older students. One of the reasons that picture books in these genres can be so valuable to content teaching is that they frequently address facets of history not often included in textbooks. For example, *Coolies* (Yin, 2001) and its sequel *Brothers* (Yin, 2006) are works of historical fiction that depict the experiences of early Chinese immigrants in the United States. Walt Whitman's role in the American Civil War is the focus of Kerley's (2004) beautifully crafted biography *Walt Whitman: Words for America*, which won the 2005 Sibert Informational Book Award from the American Library Association. In *The Queen's Progress*, Mannis (2003) brings Elizabethan times to life using an alphabet format to organize information. The human side of history is also depicted from a humorous perspective, as in Lane Smith's fictionalized antics of great American icons in *John, Paul, George, and Ben* (2006).

Because of its brevity, historical fiction in picture book format allows the teacher to bring more diverse perspectives into the curriculum. In *Katie's Trunk* (Turner, 1992), the reader meets a Tory family and comes to think about Revolutionary War issues from the perspective of the family. In *Encounter* (1992), Jane Yolen views the arrival of Columbus's ships in America from the perspective of the Taino boy who greeted the explorer. In addition, when historical fiction in picture book format is used in the social studies program, hard-to-imagine historical scenes are brought to life through illustrations. For example, the illustrations in Candace Christiansen's *The Ice Horse* (1993) help readers understand how ice was "harvested" from rivers in the early 20th century. Illustrations may help readers get a feel for an era in ways that words do not. The illustrations in *Dandelions* (Bunting, 1995) play a critical role in helping readers grasp the loneliness of life on the prairie for early settlers. Keifer (1995) has found that illustrations contribute in important ways when picture books dealing with sensitive issues, such as war, death, and the Holocaust, are used as part of classroom studies of these topics. According to Kiefer:

> In *Hiroshima No Pika, Sadako, Sami and the Time of the Troubles*, and *Rose Blanche* the pictures provide more than information, they provide the context for telling of human brutality in ways that do not repel or frighten but that evoke the deepest intellectual and emotional response. (p. 59)

Picture Books in Science Classrooms

Quality informational books in picture book format have proliferated in recent years (Elleman, 1992). The wide range of readily available topics in science—from plant to animal life, to geology, to ecology, to space, and more— make engaging additions to science programs. Still others address the history of science. In the Caldecott Honor Book *Starry Messenger* (Sis, 1996), students discover how Galileo's scientific explorations changed the way people looked at the galaxy.

As is true of social studies textbooks, science textbooks typically offer broad rather than in-depth coverage. Picture books can be used to amplify, illustrate, and intrigue. For example, although a science text might briefly discuss ecosystems and provide a few short examples, students could turn to Barbara Bash's *Desert Giant* (1989) for a rich description of the way in which the saguaro cactus functions as an ecosystem. Still another difficulty is that science textbooks have traditionally been stylistically dry and uninteresting, but this is not true of the best contemporary science picture books. For example, in describing the ways a variety of creatures construct their homes, the author of *And So They Build* (Kitchen, 1993) achieves lyricism through the repetition of the phrase "and so they build." Aliki captures the interest of readers from the very beginning of *Wild and Woolly Mammoths* (1977/1996), with an early scene describing the discovery of a mammoth so well preserved in a glacier for 39,000 years that dogs were able to eat the flesh of the uncovered creature. Picture books like these entice older students in the study of science.

Picture books can fill a variety of needs in the science program. They can serve as important resources for students' research. Equally important, teachers can use picture books to help students discover novel formats for organizing and relaying information in reports. Freeman (1991) notes that well-designed picture books containing features, such as headings, indices, and glossaries, serve as excellent models of well-organized reports. She also notes that some picture book authors use creative formats, such as the alphabet, for reporting information. One particular science alphabet book, *Q Is for Quark* (David Schwartz, 2001) contains fact-filled descriptions from "A for atom" to "Z for zzzzz (sleep)," accompanied by lighthearted and amusing illustrations. In books like *Hummingbird Nest* (George, 2004) and *Song of the Water Boatman and Other Pond Poems* (Sisman, 2005), students can see how observations of nature may be recorded through poetry. Such novel formats can spark far more interest in report writing than do traditional reports. Finally, on the lighter side, readers will find themselves chuckling many times as they read Jon Scieszka and Lane Smith's *Science Verse* (2004), a collection of humorous poems about various science topics.

Picture Books in Mathematics Classrooms

Although fewer in number, there are mathematics picture books that may be incorporated into the curriculum. Some of these picture books address the discipline from a historical perspective. One such picture book is Kathryn Lasky's *The Librarian Who Measured the Earth* (1994), which features the life and work of the Greek Eratosthenes. Other books explore particular concepts. For example, *Anno's Mysterious Multiplying Jar* (Anno & Anno, 1983) explores factorials. Demi uses a simple folktale about a village girl and a *raja* in India to illustrate the mathematical principle of exponential notation. In addition, David Schwartz explains various mathematical terms in his math alphabet book *G Is for Googol* (1998), such as "A for abacus," "B for binary," and "C for cubit." Still other picture books extend opportunities for students to solve problems. Readers of Jon Scieszka's *Math Curse* (1995) are challenged to solve a host of different problems involving fractions, estimation, binary numbers, and algebraic formulations. Teachers can also use *Math Curse* to challenge their students to generate their own math problems based on their daily lives. Greg Tang's *The Grapes of Math* (2001) and his more recent *Math Potatoes* (2005) contain riddles that keep readers engaged as they try to solve clever math puzzles.

Conclusions

The research reviewed in this chapter supports the placement of carefully selected picture books in middle and secondary school instruction, and picture books appropriate for use with older learners abound. In the latter portion of this chapter, we have offered only a small sampling of currently available picture books. We believe that time spent seeking out other appropriate picture books for older learners will be time well spent in light of the numerous ways these books can be incorporated into the curriculum. Certainly, instructional programs for older students should not be built exclusively around picture books, but we believe that because picture books have the potential to engage older readers, they are an especially valuable resource for teachers.

QUESTIONS FOR DISCUSSION

1. Various relationships can exist between texts and illustrations in pictures, some of which can be very complex. What types of relationship might you consider in selecting picture books that challenge and engage older readers?

2. To ensure thoughtful reading of a picture book, what do older readers need to understand about the tools or "codes" used by illustrators?

3. Select a picture book that you think is appropriate for older learners.

    a. Persuade your colleagues that this book should be one used in the classroom.

    b. Persuade your students that this picture book is not for young children.

Resources

Further Reading

Benedict, S., & Carlisle, L (Eds.). (1992). *Beyond words: Picture books for older readers and writers.* Portsmouth, NH: Heinemann.

Costello, B., & Kolodziej, N. J. (2006). A middle school teacher's guide for selecting picture books. *Middle School Journal, 38,* 27–33.

Goldstone, B. P. (2001/2002). Whaz up with our books?: Changing picture book codes and teaching implications. *Reading Teacher, 55,* 362–370.

Hibbing, A. N., & Rankin-Erickson, J. L. (2003). A picture is worth a thousand words: Using visual images to improve comprehension for middle school struggling readers. *Reading Teacher, 56,* 758–770.

Osborn, S. (2001). Picture books for young adult readers. *ALAN Review, 28*(3), 24–26.

Wolfenbarger, C. D., & Sipe, L. R. (2007). A unique visual and literary art form: Recent research on picturebooks. *Language Arts, 84,* 272–280.

Websites

www.childrenslit.com/childrenslit/th_picbkolder.html
www.ci.cerritos.ca.us/library/booklists/picture_books.html
www.californiayoungreadermedal.org/booklist_picturebooks_older_readers.htm
www.education.wisc.edu/ccbc/books/detailListBooks.asp?idBookLists=259

References

Anstey, M. (2002). "It's not all black and white": Postmodern picture books and new literacies. *Journal of Adolescent & Adult Literacy, 45,* 444–457.

Bader, B. (1976). *American picturebooks from* Noah's Ark *to* The Beast Within. New York: Macmillan.

Beck, I. L., & McKeown, M. G. (1991). Research directions: Social studies texts are hard to understand: Mediating some of the difficulties. *Language Arts, 68,* 482–490.

Billman, L. W. (2002, November). Aren't these books for little kids? *Educational Leadership,* pp. 48–51.

Bishop, R. S., & Hickman, J. (1992). Four or fourteen or forty: Picture books are for everyone. In S. Benedict & L. Carlisle (Eds.), *Beyond words: Picture books for older readers and writers* (pp. 1–10). Portsmouth, NH: Heinemann.

Carlisle, L. R. (1992). Picture books: An easy place to think. In S. Benedict & L. Carlisle (Eds.), *Beyond words: Picture books for older readers and writers* (pp. 49–58). Portsmouth, NH: Heinemann.

Costello, B., & Kolodziej, N. J. (2006). A middle school teacher's guide for selecting picture books. *Middle School Journal, 38,* 27–33.

Crum, S. (2007, March). Using picture books to teach literary techniques. *Book Links,* pp. 57–60.

Daniels, H. (2001). *Literature circles: Voice and choice in book clubs and reading groups* (2nd ed.). Portland, ME: Stenhouse.

Dresang, E. T. (1999). *Radical change: Books for youth in a digital age.* New York: Wilson.

Eeds, M., & Wells, D. (1989). Grand conversations: An exploration of meaning construction in literature study groups. *Research in the Teaching of English, 23,* 4–29.

Elleman, B. (1992). The nonfiction scene: What's happening? In E. B. Freeman & D. G. Person (Eds.), *Using nonfiction trade books in the elementary classroom* (pp. 26–33). Urbana, IL: National Council of Teachers of English.

Elleman, B. (2004). The picture-book story in twentieth-century America. In L. Pavonetti (Ed.), *Children's literature remembered: Issues, trends, and favorite books* (pp. 27–38). Westport, CT: Libraries Unlimited.

Freeman, E. B. (1991). Informational books: Models for student report writing. *Language Arts, 68,* 770–473.

Freeman, E. B., & Person, D. G. (1998). *Connecting informational children's books with content area learning.* Boston: Allyn & Bacon.

Galda, L., & Cullinan, B. (2001). *Literature and the child* (6th ed.). Boston: Wadsworth.

Goldstone, B. P. (1999). Brave new worlds: The changing image of the picture book. *New Advocate, 12,* 331–344.

Goldstone, B. P. (2001/2002). Whaz up with our books?: Changing picture book codes and teaching implications. *Reading Teacher, 55,* 362–370.

Guthrie, J. T., & Wigfield, A. (2000). Engagement and motivation in reading. In M. L. Kamil, P. B. Mosenthal, P. D. Pearson, & R. Barr (Ed.), *Handbook of reading research* (Vol. III, pp. 403–422). Mahwah, NJ: Erlbaum.

Hadaway, N. L., & Mundy, J. (1999). Children's informational picture books visit a secondary ESL classroom. *Journal of Adolescent & Adult Literacy, 42,* 464–475.

Heitman, J. (2005, April/May). Picture this: Using picture books to teach writing skills. *Library Media Connection,* pp. 36–38.

Hibbing, A. N., & Rankin-Erickson, J. L. (2003). A picture is worth a thousand words: Using visual images to improve comprehension for middle school struggling readers. *Reading Teacher, 56,* 758–770.

Huck, C. S., Hepler, S., Hickman, J., & Kiefer, B. (1997). *Children's literature in the elementary school* (6th ed.). Madison, WI: Brown & Benchmark.

Huck, C. S., & Kuhn, D. Y. (1968). *Children's literature in the elementary school* (2nd ed.). New York: Holt, Rinehart & Winston.

Ivey, G. (1999). A multicase study in the middle school: Complexities among young adolescent readers. *Reading Research Quarterly, 34,* 172–193.

Ivey, G., & Broaddus, K. (2001). "Just plain reading": A survey of what makes students want to read in middle school classrooms. *Reading Research Quarterly, 36,* 350–377.

Kiefer, B. (1995). The disturbing image in children's picture books: Fearful or fulfilling? In S. Lehr (Ed.), *Battling dragons: Issues and controversy in children's literature* (pp. 51–62). Portsmouth, NH: Heinemann.

Krauthammer, C. (1995, March 27). Hiroshima, mon petit. *Time,* p. 80.

Landow, G. (1992). *Hypertext: The convergence of contemporary critical theory and technology.* Baltimore: Johns Hopkins University Press.

Lewis, D. (2001). *Picture text: The contemporary children's picturebook.* London: Routledge/Falmer.

Moebius, W. (1986). Introduction to picturebook codes. *Word and Image, 2,* 141–158.

Newkirk, T. (1992). Reasoning around picture books. In S. Benedict & L. Carlisle (Eds.), *Beyond words: Picture books for older readers and writers* (pp. 11–20). Portsmouth, NH: Heinemann.

Nikolajeva, M., & Scott, C. (2001). *How picturebooks work.* New York: Garland.

Oldfather, P. (1993). What students say about motivating experiences in a whole language classroom. *Reading Teacher, 46,* 672–681.

Osborn, S. (2001). Picture books for young adult readers. *ALAN Review, 28*(3), 24–26.

Pitcher, S. M., Albright, L. K., DeLaney, C. J., Walker, N. T., Seunarinesingh, K., Mogge, S., et al. (2007). Assessing adolescents' motivation to read. *Journal of Adolescent & Adult Literacy, 50,* 378–396.

Rusted, J., & Coltheart, V. (1979). The effect of pictures on the retention of novel words and prose passages. *Journal of Experimental Child Psychology, 28,* 516–524.

Schallert, D. (1980). The role of illustrations in reading comprehension. In R. J. Spiro, B. C. Bruce, & W. F. Brewer (Eds.), *Theoretical issues in reading comprehension* (pp. 503–524). Hillsdale, NJ: Erlbaum.

Sipe, L. R. (2008). *Storytime: Young children's literary understanding in the classroom.* New York: Teachers College Press.

Steffey, S., & Hood, W. J. (Eds.). (1994). *If this is social studies, why isn't it boring?* York, ME: Stenhouse.

Steiner, S. F. (1998, June). Who belongs here?: Portraying American identity in children's picture books. *Multicultural Review*, pp. 20–27.

Steiner, S. F., & Cobiskey, L. (1998). Refugees and homelessness: Nomads of the world. *Book Links, 7,* 55–62.

Sutherland, Z., & Arburthnot, M. H. (1977). *Children and books* (5th ed.). Glenview, IL: Scott, Foresman.

Sutton, R. (1996). Why is this a picture book? *Horn Book, 72,* 390–391.

Temple, C., Martinez, M., & Yokota, J. (2006). *Children's books in children's hands: An introduction to their literature* (3rd ed.). Boston: Allyn & Bacon.

Tomlinson, C. M., Tunnell, M. O., & Richgels, D. J. (1993). The content and writing of history in textbooks and trade books. In M. O. Tunnell & R. Ammon (Eds.), *The story of ourselves: Teaching history through children's literature* (pp. 51–62). Portsmouth, NH: Heinemann.

Trites, R. S. (1994). Manifold narratives: Metafiction and ideology in picture books. *Children's Literature in Education, 25,* 225–242.

Wolfenbarger, C. D., & Sipe, L. R. (2007). A unique visual and literary art form: Recent research on picturebooks. *Language Arts, 84,* 272–280.

Zvirin, S. (1998, June 1). Crossovers: Juvenile books for adult reading. *Booklist,* pp. 1716–1718.

Picture Books

Ahlberg, J., & Ahlberg, A. (1986). *The jolly postman or other people's letters.* Boston: Little, Brown.

Aliki. (1996). *Wild and wooly mammoths.* New York: HarperCollins. (Original work published 1977)

Aliki. (1999). *William Shakespeare and the globe.* New York: HarperCollins.

Anno, M., & Anno, M. (1983). *Anno's mysterious multiplying jar.* New York: Philomel.

Bash, B. (1989). *Desert giant.* San Francisco: Sierra Club Books.

Borden, L. (2004). *The greatest skating race* (Illus. by N. Daly). New York: Margaret K. McElderry Books.

Browne, A. (1998). *Voices in the park.* New York: DK Publishing.

Bunting, E. (1988). *How many days to America* (Illus. by B. Peck). New York: Clarion.

Bunting, E. (1991). *Fly away home* (Illus. by R. Himler). New York: Clarion.

Bunting, E. (1994). *Smoky night* (Illus. by D. Diaz). San Diego: Harcourt Brace.

Bunting, E. (1994). *Sunshine home* (Illus. by D. De Groat). New York: Clarion.

Bunting, E. (1995). *Dandelions* (Illus. by G. Shed). San Diego: Harcourt Brace.

Bunting, E. (1997). *December* (Illus. by D. Diaz). San Diego: Harcourt Brace.

Burleigh, R. (1991). *Flight* (Illus. by M. Wimmer). New York: Philomel.

Christiansen, C. (1993). *The Ice Horse* (Illus. by T. Locker). New York: Dial.

Cooney, B. (1982). *Miss Rumphius*. New York: Puffin.

Coville, B. (1997). *William Shakespeare's Macbeth* (Illus. by G. Kelley). New York: Dial.

Coville, B. (2003). *William Shakespeare's twelfth night* (Illus. by T. Raglin). New York: Dial.

Demi. (2004). *The greatest power*. New York: Margaret K. McElderry Books/Simon & Schuster.

Garza, C. L. (1990). *Family pictures/Cuadros de familia* (As told to H. Rohmer; version in Spanish by R. Zubizarreta). Emeryville, CA: Children's Book Press.

George, K. O. (2004). *Hummingbird nest* (Illus. by B. Moser). San Diego: Harcourt.

Heide, F. P., & Gilliland, J. H. (1990). *The day of Ahmed's secret* (Illus. by T. Lewin). New York: Lothrop, Lee & Shepard.

Heller, R. (1989). *Many luscious lollipops*. New York: Grossett & Dunlap.

Heller, R. (1991). *Up, up and away*. New York: Grossett & Dunlap.

Hodges, M. (1984). *Saint George and the dragon* (Illus. by T. S. Hyman). Boston: Little, Brown.

Hoffman, M. (1991). *Amazing Grace* (Illus. by C. Binch). New York: Dial.

Innocenti, R. (1985). *Rose Blanche*. Mankato, MN: Creative Education.

Kerley, B. (2001). *The dinosaurs of Waterhouse Hawkins: An illuminating history of Mr. Waterhouse Hawkins, artist and lecturer* (Illus. by B. Selznick). New York: Scholastic.

Kerley, B. (2004). *Walt Whitman: Words for America* (Illus. by B. Selznick). New York: Scholastic.

Kitchen, B. (1993). *And so they build*. Cambridge, MA: Candlewick.

Lasky, K. (1994). *Days of the dead* (Photographs by C. G. Knight). New York: Hyperion.

Lasky, K. (1994). *The librarian who measured the earth* (Illus. by K. Hawkes). Little, Brown.

Levine, E. (2007). *Henry's freedom box* (Illus. by K. Nelson). New York: Scholastic.

Macaulay, D. (1990). *Black and white*. Boston: Houghton Mifflin.

Macaulay, D. (1995). *Shortcut*. Boston: Houghton Mifflin.

Mannis, C. D. (2003). *The queen's progress: An Elizabethan alphabet* (Illus. by B. Ibatoulline). New York: Viking.

Maruki, T. (1980). *Hiroshima no pika*. New York: Lothrop.

Maugham, W. S. (1993). *Appointment* (Adapted by A. Benjamin; Illus. by R. Essley). New York: Green Tiger Press.

Merriam, E. (1996). *The inner city Mother Goose* (Illus. by D. Diaz). New York: Simon & Schuster.

Merrill, J. (1992). *The girl who loved caterpillars* (Illus. by F. Cooper). New York: Philomel.

Mochizuki, K. (1993). *Baseball saved us* (Illus. by D. Lee). New York: Lee & Low Books.

Ross, S. (1994). *Shakespeare and Macbeth: The story behind the play* (Illus. by T. Karpinski). New York: Viking.

Rylant, C. (1982). *When I was young in the mountains* (Illus. by D. Goode). New York: Dutton.

Rylant, C. (1985). *The relatives came* (Illus. by S. Gammell). New York: Bradbury.

Rylant, C. (1992). *An angel for Solomon Singer* (Illus. by P. Catalanotto). New York: Orchard Books.

Schwartz, D. M. (1998). *G is for googol: A math alphabet book* (Illus. by M. Moss). Berkeley, CA: Tricycle Press.

Schwartz, D. M. (2001). *Q is for quark: A science alphabet book* (Illus. by K. Doner). Berkeley, CA: Tricycle Press.

Scieszka, J. (1989). *The true story of the three little pigs*. New York: Viking Kestral.

Scieszka, J. (1992). *The stinky cheese man and other fairly stupid tales* (Illus. by L. Smith). New York: Viking.

Scieszka, J. (1995). *Math curse* (Illus. by L. Smith). New York: Viking.

Scieszka, J., & Smith, L. (2004). *Science verse*. New York: Viking.

Sis, P. (1996). *Starry messenger*. New York: Farrar, Straus, & Giroux.

Sis, P. (2007). *The wall: Growing up behind the Iron Curtain*. New York: Farrar, Straus & Giroux.

Sisman, J. (2005). *Song of the water boatman and other pond poems* (Illus. by B. Prange). Boston: Houghton Mifflin.

Smith, L. (2006). *John, Paul, George, and Ben*. New York: Hyperion Books.

Stanley, D. (1997). *Rumpelstiltskin's daughter*. New York: Morrow.

Stanley, D., & Vennema, P. (1992). *Bard of Avon: The story of William Shakespeare* (Illus. by D. Stanley). New York: Morrow Junior Books.

Tang, G. (2001). *The grapes of math* (Illus. by H. Briggs). New York: Scholastic.

Tang, G. (2005). *Math potatoes* (Illus. by H. Briggs). New York: Scholastic.

Truss, L. (2006). *Eats, shoots and leaves* (Illus. by B. Timmons). New York: Putnam.

Truss, L. (2007). *The girl's like spaghetti* (Illus. by B. Timmons). New York: Putnam.

Turner, A. (1992). *Katie's trunk* (Illus. by R. Himler). New York: Macmillan.

Van Allsburg, C. (1984). *The mysteries of Harris Burdick*. Boston: Houghton Mifflin.

Van Allsburg, C. (1986). *The stranger*. Boston: Houghton Mifflin.

Van Allsburg, C. (1988). *Two bad ants*. Boston: Houghton Mifflin.

Weatherford, C. B. (2006). *Moses: When Harriet Tubman led her people to freedom* (Illus. by K. Nelson). New York: Hyperion.

Wieniewski, D. (1999). *Tough cookie*. New York: HarperCollins.

Wild, M. (1991). *Let the celebrations begin!* (Illus. by J. Vivas). New York: Orchard Books.

Willis, J. (1988). *Earthlets* (Illus. by T. Ross). New York: Dutton.

Yin. (2001). *Coolies* (Illus. by C. Soentpiet). New York: Philomel.

Yin. (2006). *Brothers* (Illus. by C. Soentpiet). New York: Philomel.

Yolen, J. (1992). *Encounter* (Illus. by D. Shannon). San Diego: Harcourt Brace Jovanovich.

Chapter 16

Polysyllabic Words and Struggling Adolescent Readers

The Morphemic Link to Meaning, Reading, and Spelling "Big" Words

Patricia M. Cunningham

GUIDING QUESTIONS

---

1. How are morphemes the keys to unlocking the pronunciation, spelling, and meaning for big words?
2. What are the most common prefixes, suffixes, and roots, and how can these be taught to struggling adolescent readers?

The dictionary defines a *wimp* as a timid or ineffectual person. When you wimp out, you withdraw from or avoid an undertaking. Many adolescents become wimps when faced with alien big words. Just the sight of one of these big words can cause struggling older readers to put down the book and "give up without a fight." Not normally timid or ineffectual, these readers "wimp out" when faced with a strange and unfamiliar big word. They skip right over the word or flee the scene! These word wimps suffer from *morphophobia*—the irrational fear and dread of big words.

Morphemes are prefixes, suffixes, and roots—the meaningful chunks—that make up most big words. Pick up any newspaper or magazine, read the first few sentences of any article, and notice the big words—words with eight or more letters:

SAT—**Scholastic Aptitude** Test—**denounced** as biased and **ineffective** by consumers is still the **gatekeeper** in most **American** schools. College **admissions officers** often **downplay** the **significance** of the exam in the **application** process but then brag about their school's scores in **recruitment brochures**.

The first thing that strikes you in looking at these big words is that these big words are the "meaning-carrying" words. The second thing you should notice is that these are low-frequency words. You could read many articles and pages in books before once again encountering the words **recruitment**, **gatekeeper**, and **denounced**. Almost all the texts that adolescents read have a high percentage of polysyllabic, low-frequency words. Because these big words contain most of the meaning, students cannot comprehend what they read unless they can pronounce and access meaning for these words.

Morphemes are the keys to unlocking the pronunciation, spelling, and meaning for big words. *Morphemes* are roots, prefixes, and suffixes that combine in a variety of ways to make up big words. The word **admission** is the word **admit**—with the spelling changes that always occur when **sion** is added to words ending in **t**. The first time you saw **admissions**, your brain probably accessed similar words, such as **permission**, **omission**, and **emission**. Using these other similar words, you quickly pronounced **admission**. Because you were probably aware that when you **permit** something you give your **permission**, when you **omit** something you have an **omission**, and the fumes that your car **emits** are called **emissions**, you probably also recognized the relationship between the word you had read many times—**admit**—and this new word **admissions**. Similarly, pronouncing and making meaning for **recruitment** was not difficult if your brain recognized the root **recruit**. **Gatekeeper** is a compound word: Its pronunciation and meaning are obvious when you think of the pronunciation and meaning of the two root words, **gate** and **keeper**.

Morphemes—roots, prefixes, and suffixes—are the keys to unlocking the pronunciation, spelling, and meaning for big words. When you see a big new word you have never before encountered in your reading, you think of similar big words, and use these big words and your understanding about how these big words work to pronounce quickly and access meaning for the new big word. But what if you don't have very many big words stored in your brain? What if you have some big words, but you have never realized how they are related to your smaller words? The lack of big words that they can access quickly and associate meaning for renders many adolescents helpless when encountering big words.

A *wizard* is a person noted for his or her remarkable powers or exceptional ability within a certain sphere. *Word wizards* have remarkable powers and exceptional abilities to analyze words. When encountering a new big word, word wizards do not "wimp out" and skip over the word. Word wizards can pronounce, spell, and figure out a probable meaning for new big words—all through the magic of morphemes: prefixes, suffixes, and roots! This chapter provides you with activities filled with morpheme magic to turn your word wimps into word wizards.

What Research Tells Us about Morphemes and Big Words

In 1984, William Nagy and Richard Anderson published a landmark study in which they analyzed a sample from the Carroll, Davies, and Richman (1971) *Word Frequency Book* to determine the number and relationships of words found in "printed school English." They estimated that there are over 400,000 distinct words in printed school English. Many of these words are related semantically through their morphology. A person who knows the words *hunt, red, fog,* and *string* will have little difficulty with the meanings of *hunter, redness, foglights,* and *stringy.* Word relationships such as these are defined as *semantically transparent.* When you group the semantically transparent words together, instead of 400,000+ words, you have 88,500 word families. Other word relationships are not so transparent. Meaning relationships exist between *planet* and *planetarium, vicious* and *vice, apart* and *apartment,* but these are not as apparent to most readers. Nagy and Anderson (1984) defined these types of meaning relationships as *semantically opaque.* If readers understand these more complex morphological relationships, then, instead of 88,500 word families, there would be 54,000 word families. Nagy and Anderson estimate that of the 10,000 new words the average middle school student encounters each year, only 1,000 are probably truly new words, not related to other more familiar words.

White, Power, and White (1989) confirmed the importance of morphology by examining all words in the Carroll, Richman, and Davies (1971) list that began with the four most common prefixes: *un, re, dis,* and *in.* They concluded that if students knew the common meaning for the base word, then they would correctly infer the meaning of the prefixed word 81% of the time. They estimated that the average seventh grader would encounter 1,324 analyzable words containing just these four prefixes. The number of analyzable words would double if all common prefixes were included.

Other research that supports the importance of morphology was begun by Ed Henderson (1985) who wrote:

> Those who set out to remember every letter of every word will never make it. Those who try to spell by sound alone will be defeated. Those who learn how to "walk through" words with sensible expectations, noting sound, pattern and meaning relationships will know what to remember, and they will learn to spell English. (p. 67)

The work of Henderson and his followers, most clearly laid out in *Words Their Way* (Bear, Invernizzi, Templeton, & Johnston, 2007), shows children progressing through a number of stages as they become fluent spellers. The final stage is called *derivational constancy*. This is the stage in which morphology plays a dominant role.

Templeton (1991) reviewed the research into students' spelling development in the derivational constancy stage. In one set of studies, students were asked to decide whether pairs of words, such as *please/pleasant*; *limb/limber*, and *logic/logician*, were related. Some of these pairs were shown to the interviewees. Other students did not see the pairs, but they heard the interviewer pronounce the words. Students gave a variety of responses:

> "*Clinic* and *clinician* are related because of the spelling."
>   "I doubt that *sign/signal* come from one another. I don't think the origin sounds the same." (p. 259)

Based on these studies, Templeton concluded that most students are uncertain about the nature and application of this of derivational morphology knowledge.

Another set of studies (Templeton, 1992) investigated the ability of 6th through 10th graders to spell and read derived forms of nonsense words. Subjects were given a made-up word such as TEFAME and a suffix, such as *ation*. Some of the words and suffixes were shown to some students; for others, they were only pronounced. Subjects were then asked both to pronounce and to spell the pseudoword that would combine TEFAME with *ation* and fit in a sentence such as the following:

> "He was convinced by Jan's _____ of the book." (p. 256)

Students at all grade levels were more successful at spelling the word (*tefamation*) than at pronouncing it. The explanation for this is probably that spelling the word only requires you to know how to spell *ation*, and that you must drop the *e* at the end of TEFAME. To read the word *tefamation*, however, requires changes in the pronunciation of the first *a*, along with a change in accent (similar to the changes that occur as *profane* becomes *profanity*).

A number of studies have demonstrated that poor decoders have a difficult time reading polysyllabic words even when they can read single-syllable words (Just & Carpenter, 1987; Samuels, LaBerge, & Bremer, 1978). Anderson and Davison (1988) concluded that because longer words are morphologically complex, deficiencies in morphological knowledge may be a cause of poor readers' difficulties with long words. Freyd and Baron (1982) investigated the extent to which readers' use of structural analysis is related to their reading ability. They found a strong relationship and concluded that skilled readers use structural analysis in three ways: to recognize known words more efficiently, to remember the meanings and spellings of partially learned words, and to figure out the meanings and pronunciations of new words.

Shefelbine and Calhoun (1991) investigated how students decode polysyllabic words. They classified 36 sixth graders as high, moderate, or low on the basis of their ability to decode polysyllabic nonsense words. These sixth graders were then given a test of their ability to analyze real words. The 12 high decoders showed equal facility with beginning and ending syllables, and correctly pronounced 75% of the prefixes and suffixes. Moderate decoders were equally successful with the beginning syllables of words and with prefixes, but were only able to correctly pronounce ending syllables and suffixes correctly about half the time. Low decoders pronounced only one-third of beginning or ending syllables. The researchers concluded that "developing proficiency in identifying polysyllabic words entails a vicious circle in which students need to read many polysyllabic words successfully to learn letter patterns but knowing these same patterns is necessary for reading the words in the first place" (p. 176).

In an intervention study (Shefelbine, 1990), 14 fourth graders and 15 sixth graders identified as having difficulty decoding polysyllabic words received 5 hours of instruction in how to use vowels and affixes to pronounce polysyllabic words and practiced decoding words after identifying these parts. When compared with a similar group of control students, the group that had received this short intervention demonstrated significantly greater ability to pronounce polysyllabic words that had never been included in the lessons.

In another instructional study, Lenz and Hughes (1990) taught 12 seventh, eighth, and ninth graders with learning disabilities a seven-step strategy for decoding polysyllabic words. The seven steps of DISSECT were as follows: Discover the context; Isolate the prefix; Separate the suffix; Say the stem; Examine the stem; Check with someone; Try the dictionary. They reported that the DISSECT training was effective in reducing oral reading errors and, for most students, resulted in increased comprehension of passages on their reading level.

Based on the meaning vocabulary, spelling development, and word recognition research, it seems obvious that work with big words should focus simultaneously on meaning, spelling, and reading. Morphemes—prefixes, suffixes, and roots—are the link to meaning, spelling, and decoding big words. The remainder of this chapter describes activities designed to teach students the magic of morphemes.

Teaching Prefixes

White, Sowell, and Yanagihara (1989) found that 20 prefixes account for 97% of all prefixed words. Four prefixes—*un, re, in* (and *im, ir, il* meaning "not"), and *dis*—account for 58% of all prefixed words. Graves (2006) suggests teaching these four prefixes to all students. The prefixes accounting for the other 39% of the words were *en/em, non, in/im* (meaning "in"), *over, mis, sub, pre, inter, fore, de, trans, super, semi, anti, mid*, and *under.*

In many prefixed words, the meaning of the word is not easily figured out by simply combining the meaning of the prefix and the root. Often words begin with syllables that have the same spelling as prefixes but are not prefixes. Knowing the opposite meaning of **im** helps you build meaning for **impatient** and **improbable**, but not for **imagine** or **immense**. As students learn prefixes, they must also learn that not all words that begin like common prefixes will help them with the meaning of words.

In this section I suggest hunting and sorting activities that alert students to the common prefixes, teach the meanings of those prefixes, and make sure that students know that not all letter combinations that look like prefixes are prefixes.

Teaching the Prefix Un

Because words that begin with the prefix **un** are the most common, and students know a lot of words with the prefix **un**, prefix instruction should probably begin with words that begin with the prefix **un**. You might introduce your prefix instruction by reading to your students a short selection that contains several **un** words. Use a high-interest newspaper or magazine article, if you can find one that contains several **un** words, or write a paragraph describing something your students have experienced, perhaps a recent loss by your students' favorite team.

```
On Friday night, East High's unbeaten football team
was unable to score against Jonesboro High's unmer-
ciful defense. East High's head coach was unrestrained in
his praise for Jonesboro's team. "Their defense was our
undoing! All we needed was one touchdown, but we were
unsuccessful every time we got the ball. I'm also unhappy
that we kept getting untimely penalties that gave them
good field position. We didn't lose because we were unlucky,
but because we were unworthy!"
```

After reading the article the first time for the meaning, have students listen again to identify the words that begin with the prefix **un**. Help students notice that **un** often changes a word to its opposite meaning. Write these **un** words on large index cards and use them to begin an **un** bulletin board.

Next, put students in groups and give them 10 minutes to brainstorm as many words as they can that begin with **un**, and in which **un** turns the word into its opposite. Have students write the word with markers on one side of the card, and write on the other side with pencil a sentence illustrating that word's meaning. When the time is up, let the groups share their words and add these cards to your **un** bulletin board (see Figure 16.1).

The next step is to have students hunt for words beginning with the prefix **un**. Model for students that **un** sometimes is not a prefix. Using index cards of a different color, write several words in which **un** is not a prefix meaning "opposite."

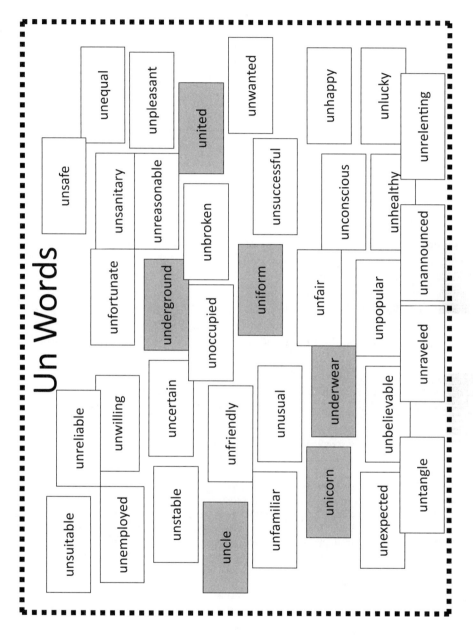

Un Words

unsuitable
unemployed
unreliable
unwilling
unstable
uncertain
uncle
unfriendly
unfamiliar
unicorn
unusual
underwear
unbelievable
unexpected
untangle
unfair
unpopular
unoccupied
underground
uniform
unraveled
unannounced
unhealthy
unconscious
unhappy
unlucky
unrelenting
unfortunate
unsanitary
unreasonable
unbroken
united
unsuccessful
unwanted
unequal
unpleasant
unsafe

FIGURE 16.1. *Un* bulletin board.

uncle   understand   uniform

Attach these index cards to your **un** board and explain to students that they should use the white cards for words in which **un** turns a word into its opposite meaning and the shaded (or whatever color you have chosen) index cards for any words they find that begin with **un** but in which **un** is not a prefix meaning "opposite" or "not." Have students write the **un** words they find on one side of an index card and the sentence in which they found the word on the back. Let the **un** collecting continue for a week or two, and take a few minutes at the end of each day to talk about the new **un** words added and read the sentences in which they were found. Model and remind students of this ongoing hunt by adding some **un** words you find, including some in which **un** is just a syllable and not a prefix meaning "opposite."

Teaching the Prefixes In and Dis

Two other common prefixes, **in** and **dis**, also mean "opposite" or "not." The complicating factor in teaching these prefixes is that there are many words in which **in** and **dis** do not mean "opposite" or in which the opposite meaning would not be clear to most students. To further complicate matters, the prefix **in** is spelled **il** before words beginning with *l*—**illegal, illogical, ir** before words beginning with *r*—**irrational, irreversible**, and **im** before words beginning with *p*—**impossible, impatient**. To teach these prefixes, students prob-

dis prefix meaning not or opposite	*dis* not a prefix	*in/im/il/ir* prefix meaning *not* or *opposite*	*in/im/il/ir* not a prefix
distance	impress	impossible	disapproval
illegal	discrimination	instrument	disappearance
innocent	impostor	incorrect	disagreement
discuss	impulsive	dishonest	disloyal
dislike	disaster	illustration	immeasurable
dispute	include	improve	insane
irritation	impure	disorder	irresponsible
inspire	imitate	immigrants	independent
immobile	distrust	inexpensive	irresistible
increase	displeased	immortal	improper
informal	inadequate	disprove	irrational
disconnect	illogical	irregular	impartial
incomplete	discourage	distasteful	important
illiterate	disobey	dissatisfied	impeachment
impatient	distributor	discussion	invitation

FIGURE 16.2. Lists of words with the prefixes *dis* and *in/im/il/ir* for students to sort into the proper categories.

re prefix meaning *back*		re prefix meaning *again*	re not a prefix
readjust	reappear	rearrange	rebound
rebuild	recall	receive	recess
recharge	reconsider	reconstruct	recycle
reduce	reelect	refill	refrigerator
refund	refuse	rehearse	relax
relay	relief	relocate	remainder
remember	remodel	remote	rename
reopen	reorder	reorganize	repaint
repair	repeat	replace	replacement
replant	reply	reporter	rewrite
reproduce	reread	rerun	responsibility
result	retire	return	reunite

FIGURE 16.3. Lists of words with the prefix *re* for students to sort into the proper categories.

ably need to be given a list of words to sort, rather than to come up with words on their own. Figure 16.2 presents a list of commonly known words and the four categories into which students working in groups might sort them.

Teaching the Prefix Re

Re, meaning "back or again," is another prefix that generates lots of words. Like **in** and **dis**, however, there are many words in which **re** is simply the first syllable, and not a prefix. Put students in groups and have them sort **re** words into three categories (see Figure 16.3).

Less Common Prefixes

Un, **in**, **dis**, and **re** are clearly prefixes that generate enough useful words to merit teaching them. Figure 16.4 lists some other prefixes that occur much less often. These prefixes are probably not worth a whole lesson, but it is help-ful to point them out to students when they occur and alert students to their meaning. As with **un**, **dis**, **in**, and **re**, be sure students understand that not all words beginning with these letters function as prefixes and help them with the meaning. As you teach prefixes, your message to students should be clear. Prefixes are chunks at the front of words that have predictable pronuncia-tions and spellings. Look for them and depend on them to help you spell and pronounce new words. Sometimes, they also give you meaning clues. If you are unsure about the meaning of a word, see whether a common meaning for the prefix can help. Check the meaning you figure out to make sure it makes sense in the context in which you are reading.

- *in* meaning "in": *inside income indent indoors infield insight intake inland*
- *mis* meaning "wrong" (wrongly): *mistake misbehave misdeal misjudge mistrust mistreat misspell misprint misplace mislead misunderstood misfortune*
- *non* meaning "not" or "opposite": *nonsense nonliving nonrenewable nonexistent nonessential nonstop*
- *de* meaning "not" or "opposite": *defuse detoxify deactivate dehumidify deflate deport decline*
- *pre* meaning "before": *preview pregame prepay pretest precook preexisting preschool preteen preheat premature*
- *en* meaning "make" or "put": *enjoy enforce enclose ensure enlarge enrich enlist enable encourage enroll enact endanger enrage endear*
- *over* meaning "over" or "too much": *overpower overdo overcome overweight overjoyed overhand oversleep overtime overpass overnight overreact*
- *under* meaning "under" or "below": *underdog undergo underground underage underhand underline underwear underestimate underpass underweight underwater undercover*
- *sub* meaning "under" or "below": *subway submarine subzero submerge subhuman*
- *super* meaning "above" or "beyond": *superman, superpower, supernatural*
- *semi* meaning "half" or "partly": *semiannual semicircle semifinal semisweet semitropical semiautomatic*
- *mid* meaning "middle" or "halfway": *midpoint midterm midair Midwest midnight midsemester*
- *fore* meaning "front" or "before": *forehead forecast foresee foretell forehand forewarn forerunner*
- *inter* meaning "between": *international interrupt intervene interface intersection*
- *trans* meaning "across": *transport transatlantic transmit transplant transform transaction*
- *anti* meaning "against": *antifreeze antibiotic antihistamine antitrust antitoxic antiaircraft*

FIGURE 16.4. Less common prefixes.

Teaching Suffixes

Once students are in the habit of using common prefixes to access word meanings, they can profit from instruction with the common suffixes. Most students easily learn the inflectional suffixes *s, es, ed,* and *ing,* because they are so common in speech and writing. These endings do not change meaning or part of speech. Derivational suffixes, however, add meaning or change the grammatical function of the word. One complication with suffix instruction is that, unlike parts of a compound word or prefixes, suffixes often require spelling and pronunciation changes. **Funny** becomes **funniest, beauty** becomes **beautiful,** and **sign** becomes **signature.** These changes not only make words with suffixes difficult to spell but also often result in readers not recognizing the common root words.

The most common and easy to understand suffixes that change meaning are **er** and **est**, meaning "more" and "most," respectively; **er**, meaning "person or thing that does something"; **ful** and **less**; and **able/ible**. Because **er** and **est** are so common and predictable, they probably don't need to be taught explicitly, even to struggling older readers. **Er**, meaning "person or thing" is also known to most adolescents and can be taught as part of a lesson on less common suffixes indicating "person or thing"—**or**, **ian**, and **ist**. Figure 16.5 lists some common **er**, **ian**, **or**, and **ist** words for students to categorize.

Teaching the Suffixes Ful and Less

Two other common suffixes that add meaning to words are **ful** and **less**. Some root words make new words with both **ful** and **less**, and each new word takes on its opposite meaning. *Hopeful* and *hopeless* are perhaps the best example of this. Other words combine with one but not the other, as in **beautiful** and **homeless**. Most students know a lot of words that end in **ful** and **less**, and understand the meanings of these suffixes, so they are relatively easy to teach. To teach these suffixes quickly and effectively, have students work in groups to

er person or thing	*er* (not suffix)	*or* person	*or* (not suffix)	*ist* person	*ist* (not suffix)	*ian* person	*ian* (not suffix)

actor		comedian		electrician		insist	
alligator		conductor		enlist		inventor	
beautician		conqueror		exist		Italian	
biologist		counselor		favor		fiber	
Californian		cyclist		flavor		librarian	
Canadian		custodian		florist		magician	
collector		teacher		governor		Martian	
colonist		director		guardian		meteor	
color		editor		historian		musician	
rescuer		speaker		Indian		consumer	
odor		professor		lumber		dentist	
optimist		psychiatrist		sculptor		freezer	
organist		psychologist		senator		journalist	
toaster		razor		specialist		manager	
persist		resist		survivor		disaster	
pessimist		Russian		tourist		filter	
pianist		sailor		typist		skater	
politician		scientist		visitor		warrior	

FIGURE 16.5. Lists of words with the suffixes *er, ian,* and *ist* for students to sort into the proper categories.

words with suffix *less* meaning *without*		words with suffix *ful* meaning *full* or *having*	
arm	bottom	care	cloud
beauty	breath	cheer	color
doubt	home	penny	speech
dread	hope	pity	spoon
end	limit	play	thank
fear	meaning	plenty	thought
forget	mercy	power	truth
fruit	mouth	price	use
harm	pain	rest	waste
help	peace	score	wonder

FIGURE 16.6. Lists of words for students to combine with the suffixes *less* and *ful* and sort into the appropriate columns.

decide which roots make a word with *ful* and which with *less*, and write them in the appropriate columns (see Figure 16.6). Be sure students know that some words can be combined with both, and remind them that if the root word ends in **y**, the **y** changes to **i** before the suffix is added. When the chart is complete, have students write sentences contrasting the words that have the same root and the opposite meaning in the same sentence. Give them an example or two to get them started:

```
We were powerless when we got hit by the powerful storm.
I was hopeful our team would win but the other team was
so hot it was hopeless.
```

Teaching the Suffixes **Able** and **Ible**

Able and **ible** add meaning to words and are relatively easy for students to understand. Have students work in groups to sort words into four categories (see Figure 16.7).

Teaching the Suffixes **Ous, Al,** and **Y**

Ous, **al**, and **y** are common suffixes that don't change the meaning of a word, but they do change the word's grammatical function or part of speech. Something that is **poison** is called **poisonous**. A problem for a **nation** is a **national** problem. A day with lots of **sun** is a **sunny** day. Have students work in groups to categorize the root words by what suffix can be added to them. Have them write the whole word—root and suffix—in the appropriate column (see Figure 16.8). Remind them of spelling changes that some of these words will need.

able suffix meaning able	able not suffix	ible suffix meaning able	ible not suffix
acceptable	agreeable	capable	corruptible
adjustable	available	comfortable	dependable
adorable	believable	compatible	desirable
affordable	breakable	convertible	digestible
distractible	inseparable	reasonable	uncomfortable
dishonorable	laughable	recyclable	undesirable
eligible	likable	reliable	unfavorable
enjoyable	lovable	resistible	unforgettable
excitable	miserable	respectable	unstable
fashionable	movable	responsible	unsuitable
favorable	permissible	sensible	unavoidable
flexible	possible	suitable	usable
gullible	predictable	syllable	valuable
horrible	preferable	reusable	vegetable
impossible	profitable	terrible	washable
indescribable	questionable	unavoidable	workable

FIGURE 16.7. Lists of words with the suffixes *able* and *ible* for students to sort into the proper categories.

ous words	al words	y words
adventure	ambition	bump	bury
caution	fun	luxury	politics
chill	fury	magic	rain
cloud	globe	mountain	region
coast	glory	music	risk
comic	grass	mystery	rust
continue	grouch	nation	spine
curl	hair	nature	stick
danger	hazard	navy	sun
dirt	humor	nerve	thirst
dust	industry	nutrition	tribe
electric	joy	option	tropics
fame	juice	person	water
fog	logic	poison	wind

FIGURE 16.8. Lists of words for students to combine with the suffixes *ous, al,* and *y* and to sort into the appropriate columns.

Teaching the Suffixes Ment, Ance, Ness, and Tion

Ment, **ance**, **ness**, and **tion** are common suffixes that don't change the meaning of a word, but they do change the word's grammatical function or part of speech. We try to **equip** our army with the very best **equipment**. The money we are **allowed** to spend each week is our **allowance**. When you feel **happy**, you are experiencing **happiness**. We hold **celebrations** to **celebrate** weddings and birthdays. Have students work in groups to categorize the root words according to what suffix can be added to them. They should write the whole word—with root and suffix—in the appropriate column (see Figure 16.9). Remind them of spelling changes that some of these words will need.

ment words	*ance* words	*ness* words	*tion* words
accept	complete	encourage	insure
act	connect	endure	interact
adjust	construct	engage	interrupt
adopt	contradict	enjoy	intervene
advertise	contribute	equip	introduce
agree	convict	excite	invent
allow	correct	execute	invest
amaze	corrupt	fair	isolate
annoy	dark	fit	kind
appear	develop	forgive	lazy
argue	devote	good	locate
arrange	direct	govern	manage
assign	disagree	great	measure
attach	disappear	guide	migrate
attend	disappoint	happy	move
attract	distort	ill	mutate
aware	distract	illustrate	open
bitter	disturb	impeach	pave
bright	donate	improve	subtract
clear	educate	indicate	persecute
collect	elect	inflate	place
command	employ	inject	predict
prevent	ready	require	select
produce	reduce	resist	settle
promote	reject	restrict	ship
punish	rely	rotate	sick
quest	replace	sad	state

FIGURE 16.9. Lists of words for students to combine with the suffixes *ment, ance, ness,* and *tion* and write in the appropriate columns.

Teaching the Suffix ly

Ly is the other suffix that occurs often enough to merit teaching it. Words that end in **ly** are often adverbs that modify verbs, adjectives, or sometimes other adverbs. Because students know a lot of **ly** words, and because almost all words that end in **ly** are adverbs, you can use the procedure described earlier for **un**. Read an article to your students and have them stop you when you read a word that ends in **ly**.

Write these **ly** words on index cards and talk about how **ly** changes how a word can be used in a sentence. Put students in groups and have them brainstorm some **ly** words to begin the **ly** bulletin board. They should write the word with a marker on one side of an index card and write a sentence with that word in pencil on the other side. Attach to the bulletin board the cards with **ly** words from the article you read to students and those brainstormed by each group. Let students hunt for **ly** words in everything they read for a week or two. Because some words that end in **ly** are not adverbs—**silly**, **hilly**, **family**—provide some index cards of a different color on which students can write these words. Be sure that students write the sentence in which they found the word on the back of the card. This encourages them to look for **ly** words when reading, and discourages them from just writing any **ly** words that come to mind.

Teaching Greek and Latin Roots

There is disagreement among vocabulary experts in terms of teaching Latin and Greek roots to students. Although it is true that these roots do contain clues to meaning, the meaning relationships are often hard to figure out, and students may become discouraged if they cannot "ferret out" the meaning of a word based on the meaning of the root. Perhaps the most sensible way to approach Greek and Latin roots is to be aware of them, and to point out relationships that you think will be understandable to most of your students. When encountering the word *spectacle*, for example, a teacher might point out that a spectacle is something you see that is quite striking or unusual. Furthermore, the teacher might point out that the root *spect* means to "watch," and invite students to think about how words they know, such as *inspection* and *spectators*, are related to this meaning. The word *constructive* might be explained as "helpful" or "building up" as opposed to *destructive*, which means "unhelpful" or "tearing down." Students might be told that the root *struct* means to "build" and be asked to think about how other words they know, such as *structure* and *reconstruction*, are related to this meaning. Figure 16.10 lists roots that have high utility. When a word containing one of these roots occurs, it may be worth exploring the root meaning with your students.

Root	Meaning	Common examples
dict	say	dictator, contradict, dictionary, unpredictable, verdict
duct	lead	duct, conductor, reduce, deduction, abduct, educate
fac/fec	do, make	factory, manufacture, benefactor, effect, defect
ject	throw	inject, reject, interject, object, subject, eject
loc	place	locate, location, relocate, dislocate, local
port	carry, take	report, heliport, transportation, export, import, portable
press	press	impress, depression, pressure, express, oppression, compress
scrib	write	scribble, describe, prescription, subscribe, transcript
sens	feel	sense, sensitive, insensitive, sensation, consent, nonsense
spec	look	inspector, spectacle, respect, spectator, suspect, prospect
struct	build	structure, construct, reconstruction, instructor, destruction
tract	drag, pull	tractor, extract, contract, contraction, attract, subtraction
vis/vid	see	vision, revise, invisible, video, evidence
voc	voice, call	vocal, vocalize, advocate, vocation, convocation, provoke
meter	measure	metric, kilometer, barometer, thermometer, diameter
micro	small	microphone, microscope, micromanage, microcosm
phon	sound	telephone, phonics, symphony, microphone, phonograph
photo	light	photograph, photography, telephoto, photosynthesis
tele	far	television, telegraph, telepathy, telephoto, telecommunication

FIGURE 16.10. Greek and Latin roots with highest utility.

Word Detectives

Teaching the most common prefixes, suffixes, and roots will go a long way toward helping older readers overcome morphophobia. Once students start to realize how word parts can help them with meaning, spelling, and decoding, they need to get into the habit of looking for patterns in words. Becoming *word detectives* teaches students to ask themselves two questions when they encounter a new word:

> "Do I know any other words that look and sound like this word?"
>
> "Are any of these look-alike/sound-alike words related to each other?"

The answer to the first question should help students with pronouncing and spelling the word. The answer to the second question should help students discover what, if any, meaning relationships exist between this new word and others in their meaning vocabulary stores. These two simple questions can be used by any teacher in any subject area. Imagine that students in a mathematics class encounter the new word/phrase:

```
improper fraction
```

The teacher demonstrates and gives examples of these kinds of fractions and helps to build meaning for the concept. Finally, the teacher asks the students to pronounce and to look at both words and see whether they know any other words that look and sound like these words: For *improper*, students think of the following words:

```
impossible, important, impatient, imported
property, properly, proper
super, paper, kidnapper
```

For *fraction*, they think of the following:

```
fracture, motion, vacation, multiplication, addition,
subtraction
```

The teacher lists the words, underlining the parts that are the same, and has students pronounce the words, emphasizing the parts that are pronounced the same. The teacher then points out to the students that thinking of a word that looks and sounds the same as a new word will help them quickly remember how to pronounce the new word and also help them to spell it.

Next the teacher explains that words, like people, sometimes look and sound alike but are not related.

> "Not all people who look alike are related but some are. This is how words work, too. Words are related if there is something about their meaning that is the same. After we find look-alike/sound-alike words that will help us spell and pronounce new words, we try to think of any ways these words might be in the same meaning family. "

With help from the teacher, students discover that *impossible* is the opposite of *possible*, *impatient* is the opposite of *patient*, and *improper* is the opposite of *proper*. *Proper* and *improper* are clearly relatives! *Impossible*, *impatient*, and *improper* are probably "distant cousins," because they all have *im*, which makes the word mean the opposite. Depending on their word sophistication, some students might be able to point out that a *fracture* is a break into two or more parts, and that *fraction* also involves parts.

Imagine that the same students who were introduced to improper fractions by their math teacher and asked to think of look-alike/sound-alike words, and to consider whether any of these words might be "kinfolks," had a science teacher who was beginning a unit on weather, and did some experiments with the students using *thermometers* and *barometers*. At the close of the lesson, the teacher pointed to these words and helped students notice that the *meters* chunk was pronounced and spelled the same, and asked them whether they thought these words were just look-alikes or related to one another. The students conclude that both were used to measure things, and the *meters* chunk must be related to measuring, like in *kilometers*. When asked to think of look-alike/sound-alike words for the first chunk, students thought of *baron* for *barometers*, but decided these two words were not related. For *thermometer*, they thought of *thermal* and *thermostat*, and decided that all these words had to do with heat or temperature.

Now imagine that this lucky class of students had a social studies teacher who pointed out the new word *international* and asked the two critical questions, an art teacher who was having them do some *sculpture*, and an English teacher with whom they encountered the new word *foreshadowing*.

Throughout their school day, middle and high school students encounter many new words. Because English is such a morphologically related language, most new words can be connected to other words by their spelling and pronunciation, and many new words have meaning-related parts already known to the student. By modeling the use of these two simple questions for key vocabulary in any subject area, teachers demonstrate how students can become word detectives and "solve" the mystery of unknown words.

The Nifty Thrifty Fifty List

The final teaching suggestion I have for turning word wimps into word wizards is to post in your classroom "key words" for all the common prefixes and suffixes. The Nifty Thrifty Fifty List (Cunningham, 2009) includes all the prefixes and suffixes determined to be most common in the White, Sowell, and Yanagihara study (see Figure 16.11). It also includes key words containing some other common word parts, such as *con/com, per, ex, ture*. These prefixes and suffixes often do not help students access meanings, but they are useful spelling/pronunciation chunks. Finally, a key word is included for the common spelling changes that occur when suffixes are added to words.

You might use any words your students know as your key words. The key words I included for each part are the words that students are most apt to know according to *The Living Word Vocabulary* (Dale & O'Rourke, 1981). All 50 of these words were known by at least two-thirds of eighth graders. Once the list of key words is posted, draw students' attention to these key words whenever you encounter another word with that prefix, suffix, or spelling change. Many big words occur infrequently, but when they do occur, they carry most of the meaning and content of what is being read. In English, many words are related through their morphology. Students who learn to look for patterns in big new words will be better spellers and decoders. If they learn to look fur-

antifreeze	anti	
beautiful		ful (y-i)
classify		ify
communities	com	es (y-i)
community	com	
composer	com	er
continuous	con	ous
conversation	con	tion
deodorize	de	ize
different		ent
discovery	dis	y
dishonest	dis	
electricity		ity
employee	em	ee
encouragement	en	ment
expensive	ex	ive
forecast	fore	
forgotten		en (double t)
governor		or
happiness		ness (y-i)
hopeless		less
illegal	il	
impossible	im	
impression	im	sion
independence	in	ence
international	inter	al
invasion	in	sion
irresponsible	ir	ible
midnight	mid	
misunderstand	mis	
musician		ian
nonliving	non	ing (drop e)
overpower	over	
performance	per	ance
prehistoric	pre	ic
prettier		er (y-i)
rearrange	re	
replacement	re	ment
richest		est
semifinal	semi	
signature		ture
submarine	sub	
supermarkets	super	s
swimming		ing (double m)
transportation	trans	tion
underweight	under	

FIGURE 16.11. The Nifty Thrifty Fifty List.

ther and consider possible meaning relationships, they will increase the size of their meaning vocabulary stores. Word wimps can become word wizards through the magic of morphology!

QUESTIONS FOR DISCUSSION

1. How fluent are your students with decoding and spelling polysyllabic words?
2. What do you notice in your students' reading and writing that suggests polysyllabic words may be a stumbling block for many of them?
3. Which of the activities in this chapter seem best to meet the needs of your struggling adolescent readers? How can you fit these activities into your curriculum?

Resources

Further Reading

Lists of words with common prefixes and suffixes can be found in the following:

Ganske, K. (2000). *Word journeys.* New York: Guilford Press.
Johnston, F., Bear, D. R., & Invernizzi, M. (2006). *Words their way: Word sorts for derivational spellers.* Upper Saddle River, NJ: Pearson.

Activities to teach the Nifty Fifty Thrifty List can be found in:

Cunningham, P. M., & Hall, D. P. (1998). *Phonics for upper grades.* Greensboro, NC: Carson Dellosa.

References

Anderson, R. C., & Davison, A. (1988). Conceptual and empirical bases of readability formulas. In G. Green & A. Davison (Eds.), *Linguistic complexity and text comprehension* (pp. 23–54). Hillsdale, NJ: Erlbaum.
Bear, D., Invernizzi, M., Templeton, S., & Johnston, F. (2007). *Words their way: Word study for phonics, vocabulary, and spelling instruction* (4th ed.). New York: Pearson.
Carroll, J. B., Davies, P., & Richman, B. (1971). *Word frequency book.* New York: American Heritage.
Cunningham, P. M. (2009). *Phonics they use: Words for reading and writing* (5th ed.). Boston: Allyn & Bacon.
Dale, E., & O'Rourke, J. (1981). *The living word vocabulary.* Chicago: Worldbook.
Freyd, P., & Baron, J. (1982). Individual differences in acquisition of derivational morphology. *Journal of Verbal Learning and Verbal Behavior, 21,* 282–295.
Graves, M. F. (2004). *The vocabulary book.* Newark, DE: International Reading Association.
Henderson, E. H. (1985). *Teaching spelling.* Boston: Houghton Mifflin.

Just, M. A., & Carpenter, P. A. (1987). *The psychology of reading and language comprehension*. Boston: Allyn & Bacon.

Lenz, B. K., & Hughes, C. A. (1990). A word identification strategy for adolescents with learning disabilities. *Journal of Learning Disabilities, 23*, 149–163.

Nagy, W., & Anderson, R. C. (1984). How many words are there in printed school English? *Reading Research Quarterly, 19*, 304–330.

Samuels, S. J., LaBerge, D., & Bremer, C. D. (1978). Units of word recognition: Evidence for developmental change. *Journal of Verbal Learning and Verbal Behavior, 17*, 715–720.

Shefelbine, J. (1990). A syllable-unit approach to teaching decoding of polysyllabic words to fourth- and sixth-grade disabled readers. In J. Zutell & S. McCormick (Eds.), *Literacy theory and research: Analysis from multiple paradigms* (pp. 223–230). Chicago: National Reading Conference.

Shefelbine, J., & Calhoun, J. (1991). Variability in approaches to identifying polysyllabic words: A descriptive study of sixth graders with highly, moderately, and poorly developed syllabication strategies. In J. Zutell & S. McCormick (Eds.), *Learner factors/teacher factors: Issues in literacy research and instruction* (pp. 169–177). Chicago: National Reading Conference.

Templeton, S. (1991). Teaching and learning the English spelling system: Reconceptualizing method and purpose. *Elementary School Journal, 92*, 185–201.

Templeton, S. (1992). Theory, nature and pedagogy of higher-order orthographic development in older children. In S. Templeton & D. Bear (Eds.), *Development of orthographic knowledge and the foundations of literacy: A memorial Festschrift for Edmund H. Henderson* (pp. 253–278). Hillsdale, NJ: Erlbaum.

White, T., Power, M., & White, S. (1989). Morphological analysis: Implications for teaching and understanding vocabulary growth. *Reading Research Quarterly, 24*, 283–304.

White, T., Sowell, J., & Yanagihara, A. (1989). Teaching elementary students to use word-part clues. *Reading Teacher, 42*, 302–308.

Chapter 17

Comprehension Is More Than a Strategy

Douglas Fisher
Nancy Frey
Donna Ross

GUIDING QUESTIONS

1. What factors contribute to reading comprehension?
2. Do readers comprehend differently in different reading situations?
3. What instructional routines are useful in developing students comprehension?

Kaila sits in front of a computer, researching primary source documents to answer an essay question she selected for U.S. History Class: What role did Thomas Jefferson play in the development of national identity in the United States? No one else in the class has this particular question, because there are enough questions for each student to have one of his or her own. One of the documents she finds on her Internet search is Jefferson's first inaugural speech (*www.bartleby.com/124/pres16.html*). It is a fairly complex document, with language and syntactic structure unfamiliar to an 11th grader today. The first sentence, for example, is 86 words long, and reads:

> CALLED upon to undertake the duties of the first executive office of our country, I avail myself of the presence of that portion of my fellow-citizens which is here assembled to express my grateful thanks for the favor with which they have been pleased to look toward me, to declare a sincere consciousness that the task is above my talents, and that I approach it with those anxious and awful presentiments which the greatness of the charge and the weakness of my powers so justly inspire.

When asked about what she has read, Kaila explains:

"Thomas Jefferson's first inaugural speech basically says that everything he plans to do will be for the benefit of the country. He describes the principles of the government and states that there should be justice to all men. He sets the basis for things, like freedom of religion and freedom of the press, that ended up making the new country strong and created a national identity. And, by the way, these are still the main points of what our government is about today. Jefferson is realistic in saying that it will be hard to maintain these things at all times but that as long as people continue to follow the beliefs he talks about, the country will prosper."

How is it that an 11th grader today understands a message from 1801? What factors exist to ensure that Kaila understands the text she has found, and what might teachers do to ensure that all students develop this level of understanding related to reading? These are the questions we hope to answer in this chapter.

Of course, reading for understanding—comprehension—isn't this easy for all students; some students struggle significantly with making meaning from texts. Whereas other chapters in this book address important components of reading, such as decoding, fluency, motivation, and such, this chapter focuses on comprehension. Unlike the many "how-to" chapters on reading comprehension found in the popular press, we don't think that it's simple to *teach* comprehension. In fact, we're pretty sure that Kaila didn't learn to comprehend Jefferson's speech because a few teachers along the way visualized, predicted, summarized, or inferred. Although most readers probably use these cognitive processes, our money is on the fact that it takes a lot more than a few strategies to ensure that students read and understand what they read.

Reflecting on the ease with which Kaila understood the text, we notice that at least three factors influenced her comprehension. Let's consider each of these factors, and what teachers might do about these factors, before we delve further into classroom instructional routines that are useful in secondary schools.

Factors Influencing Comprehension

In general, the research base on comprehension suggests that specific variables related to comprehension include the following:

(a) reader variables (age, ability, affect, motivation)
(b) text variables (genres, types, features, considerateness)
(c) educational-context variables (environment, task, social grouping, purpose) and
(d) teacher variables (knowledge, experience, attitude, pedagogical approach). (Flood, Lapp, & Fisher, 2003, p. 931)

It is the interaction of these variables that influences comprehension. Of course, some of these variables are beyond the control of the individual teacher. You cannot change the fact, for example, that Kaila is 16. But as Kaila sits in front of the computer as she is, some very specific factors influence her reading comprehension. And more important, there are things that her teachers can do related to these factors to ensure that Kaila continues to understand the texts she's reading.

Background Knowledge

Most noteworthy is the background knowledge Kaila needed to understand the text she read. She had to understand the newness of the country at that time, the election process, the reason Presidents give these types of speeches, the context for the speech, and how the U.S. Constitution and the Bill of Rights work. In addition, she had to be able to place Jefferson in context, to understand the issues facing the country at the time and how those issues were or were not resolved over the 200+ years since he spoke.

The relationship between background knowledge and reading comprehension has been studied extensively. A significant body of knowledge supports the claim that what a reader already knows about a topic predicts comprehension (e.g., Droop & Verhoeven, 1998; Weber, 1991). For example, Stahl, Chou Hare, Sinatra, and Gregory (1991) examined background knowledge in relation to vocabulary knowledge among 10th graders. Their analysis suggested that background (or domain) knowledge and vocabulary knowledge have independent effects on comprehension, in terms of both what and how much is comprehended. Similarly, Reynolds, Taylor, Steffensen, Shirley, and Anderson (1982) showed that eighth-grade students from a White, agricultural area struggled with comprehension when reading an ambiguous text referring to a cultural aspect of students from a Black, working-class area. The reverse was not true; the Black students had no trouble comprehending the text.

If background knowledge plays such as significant role in reading comprehension, which we believe it does, what should teachers do? We can't ask middle and high school teachers to create for students experiences that they did not have. We also can't change the fact that our students have different experiences with the world when they arrive in our classrooms. What we can do is get them to read, and to read a lot.

Of course, there are a few caveats to this solution. First, students have to read things that they can read. Reading hard books doesn't build background knowledge, or as Allington (2002) suggests, "You can't learn much from books you can't read" (p. 16). Although this may seem to be counterintuitive, building background knowledge requires that students read a lot from books they can read that relate to the topic under investigation (Marzano, 2004).

This is exactly what worked with Andrew. When we first met him, Andrew was an average student who identified himself as "a solid C guy." Andrew went through the motions of school, doing some homework and earning average grades. Then he met a neuron. In biology, he basically fell in love with the central nervous system and wanted to know everything he could about it. He started reading books on the subject and was open to recommendations from his teachers. Despite the fact that Andrew said he hadn't read a book "since like elementary school," Andrew read the following three books in a month:

- *The Complete Idiot's Guide to Understanding the Brain* (Bard & Bard, 2002)
- *Another Day in the Frontal Lobe: A Brain Surgeon Exposes Life on the Inside* (Firlik, 2006)
- *My Lobotomy: A Memoir* (Dully & Fleming, 2007)

As might be expected, Andrew did very well on the unit exam related to the central nervous system. He had a lot of background knowledge about the brain, because he had read a number of books, starting with a book that provided a basic level of information that Andrew could understand. Before reading these books, Andrew's level of understanding was minimal. By the end of the unit, it was significant.

But perhaps even more important than the unit grade in biology, Andrew started doing well in his other classes. He had read two memoirs of his own choosing, and he could talk about them in his English class. In fact, he was able to describe the difference between a memoir and an autobiography. He was also able to produce a very interesting paper about his own life for an assignment that focused on an autobiographical event. His grades started to rise in math and history as well. As he said, "I realized that I had to get better grades if I was going to be a brain worker like the people I was reading about."

Purpose

Returning to Kaila and her reading of primary source documents related to Jefferson's presidency, the second factor in her favor was purpose. Kaila had a very specific purpose for reading the texts she selected. This purpose was authentic, in that she had a choice in both the question she selected and the primary source documents she read to answer the question. Kaila accomplished the task of reading and understanding the 10 required documents because she knew what she was looking for when she started reading.

Unfortunately, too many middle and high school students don't know why they are reading what they have been assigned to read. Without purpose, the reader isn't sure what to pay attention to; therefore, the brain has a hard time remembering the information (Banikowski & Mehring, 1999). As Byrnes (1998) points out, the purpose one has for reading determines in large part the appropriate approach to comprehension. A person who needs to know whether she can afford to eat at a particular restaurant needs to understand the pricing information provided on the menu, but she does not need to recognize the name of every food item listed.

When our students question the importance of an established purpose for reading, we ask them to read a short piece of text called "House" (see Figure 17.1). As they read, we ask them to identify important facts and main ideas. When they have finished reading, we provide them with a specific purpose for reading—either as a homebuyer or as a burglar. Suddenly, as Pichert and Anderson (1977) found when they used this piece of text for their research, our students understand that having a specific purpose guides their reading and aids their comprehension.

Like Kaila, Amanda had a very specific purpose in mind when she read *The 10 Most Revolting Parasites* (Clark, 2007). In her health careers elective, she heard about a worm that burrows into human skin. Amanda wanted to know more about this parasite called a guinea worm, or *Dracunculiasis medin-*

The two boys ran until they came to the driveway. "See, I told you today was good for skipping school," said Mark. "Mom is never home on Thursday," he added. Tall hedges hid the house from the road so the pair strolled across the finely landscaped yard. "I never knew your place was so big," said Pete. "Yeah, but it's nicer now than it used to be since Dad had the new stone siding put on and added the fireplace."

There were front and back doors and a side door which led to the garage which was empty except for three parked 10-speed bikes. They went in the side door, Mark explaining that it was always open in case his younger sisters got home earlier than their mother.

Pete wanted to see the house so Mark started with the living room. It, like the rest of the downstairs, was newly painted. Mark turned on the stereo, the noise of which worried Pete. "Don't worry, the nearest house is a quarter of a mile away," Mark shouted. Pete felt more comfortable observing that no houses could be seen in any direction beyond the huge yard.

The dining room, with all the china, silver and cut glass, was no place to play so the boys moved into the kitchen where they made sandwiches. Mark said they wouldn't go to the basement because it had been damp and musty ever since the new plumbing had been installed.

"This is where my dad keeps his famous paintings and his coin collection," Mark said as they peered into the den. Mark bragged that he could get spending money whenever he needed it since he'd discovered that his dad kept a lot in the desk drawer.

There were three upstairs bedrooms. Mark showed Pete his mother's closet which was filled with furs and the locked box which held her jewels. His sisters' room was uninteresting except for the color TV which Mark carried to his room. Mark bragged that the bathroom in the hall was his since one had been added to his sisters' room for their use. The big highlight in his room, though, was a leak in the ceiling where the old roof had finally rotted.

FIGURE 17.1. "House." From Pichert and Anderson (1977). Copyright 1977 by the American Psychological Association. Reprinted by permission.

ensis. Along the way, Amanda learned about a number of other quite disgusting parasites, such as the filarial worm, the North American leech, and the human botfly larva.

As teachers, we can help students identify the various purposes for their reading, then guide the ways in which they read to meet those purposes. The most common question we can teach students to ask relative to purpose is: *Am I reading for enjoyment, to retell, to answer questions, or to gain information?* Based on the answer to this question, students might:

- Skim: read to gain an overall understanding of the content of the text
- Scan: read to locate specific information
- Reread: read to confirm meanings and understandings, and to clarify details

Regardless, having a clear purpose increases the likelihood that students focus on their reading and learn from it.

Word Knowledge

Once again, returning to Kaila and her essay on Jefferson, it's easy to see that she knows a lot of words. Like background knowledge, vocabulary is a significant predictor of reading comprehension (Baumann, Kame'enui, & Ash, 2003; Nagy, 1988). Quite simply, increasing vocabulary improves comprehension. For example, in their study of 77 fifth graders, Lubliner and Smetana (2005) demonstrated the positive effect of vocabulary instruction on reading comprehension. As Bromley (2007) noted, middle and high school teachers need to know a lot about words and their usage if they are to improve student achievement. Without attention to vocabulary across content areas, students do not comprehend the texts they need to read.

There are a vast array of ways that teachers can improve students' vocabulary, as outlined by Harmon, Wood, and Medina in Chapter 18, this volume. One of the most common ways involves the use of semantic maps and graphic organizers (Johnson & Rasmussen, 1998; Rosenbaum, 2001). Briana's science class was focused on immunity, which involves a number of technical and specialized vocabulary terms. Understanding the demands of word knowledge, Briana's teacher asked students to create semantic maps of their understanding of the various types of cells involved in immunity. Briana's map may be found in Figure 17.2. Briana clearly understands macrophages and their role in immunity, especially in relationship to T cells. Importantly, Briana does not yet have a complete understanding of B cells. One of the benefits of vocabulary instruction is the ability to use student products as a formative assessment tool that can guide instruction. Briana's teacher noticed that several students struggled with their representations of B cells, and decided that the class needed additional instruction in antibodies.

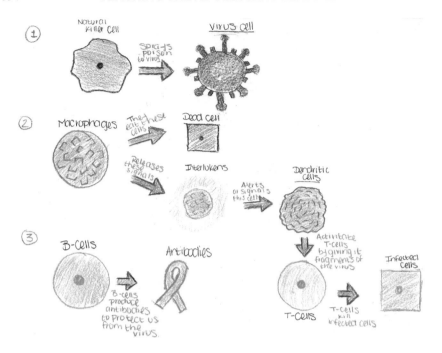

FIGURE 17.2. Student semantic map.

Useful Instructional Routines in Comprehension

In the first part of this chapter, we described three factors related to comprehension. Each of these factors has instructional implications, and attention to these factors will likely improve students' reading comprehension and, as a result, their achievement. Having said that, we'd like to turn our attention to some instructional routines that teachers can use with their classes to facilitate further students' comprehension. Each of these instructional routines is dependent on the factors we identified while observing Kaila negotiate meaning on a website. We call them *instructional routines*, rather than strategies, to distinguish between classroom procedures and behaviors that readers use to understand texts.

Modeling Thinking

Modeling is one of the most powerful ways that teachers facilitate students' use of cognitive strategies (Duffy, 2002). We cannot simply tell students to make connections with the text, for example. Nor can we continually question students about the texts they are reading. And, worst of all, we cannot ask students to stop while they are reading to fill out paperwork related to their predictions or visualizations. Students need to witness a skilled reader explaining the various ways that he or she makes meaning from the text. Students need a number of examples of visualizing, predicting, determining importance, solving unknown words, reading graphs and charts, and so on, if they are ever to incorporate these behaviors into their reading repertoires (e.g., Dole, Brown, & Trathen, 1996; Duffy, 2003).

In their study of 25 teachers recognized for their modeling, Fisher, Frey, and Lapp (2008) identified four components that readers use to make meaning from texts: comprehension strategies, vocabulary (specifically, word solving), text structure, and analysis of text features. A description and a number of examples of each may be found in Figure 17.3.

Before we explore modeling much further, let's listen in while life science teacher Kari Thompson models her thinking as she reads a text related to worms and mollusks. Excerpts from the text she used, what she said to the class, and which strategies she modeled can be found in Figure 17.4. From observing Kari and teachers like her, we know that comprehension modeling, and comprehension instruction in general, should do the following:

Component	Definition	Subtypes
Comprehension	Strategic and active moves to understand the text	Activating background, inferencing, summarizing, predicting, clarifying, questioning, visualizing, monitoring, synthesizing, evaluating, and connecting
Vocabulary	Focus on solving an unknown word, not providing the definition of the word	1. Inside the word strategies: Word parts such as prefix, suffix, root, base, cognates, and word families 2. Outside the word strategies: Context clues 3. Use of resources: peers, dictionaries, Internet
Text structures	Structures used in presenting information that readers can use to predict the flow of information	1. Compare–contrast 2. Problem–solution 3. Cause–effect 4. Chronological/sequence 5. Descriptive 6. Story grammar (plot, setting, character, conflict, etc.)
Text features	Components of the text added to increase understanding or interest	Headings, captions, illustrations, bold or italic words, charts, tables, diagrams, glossary, index, or graphs

FIGURE 17.3. Components of modeling. From Fisher, Frey, and Lapp (2008). Copyright 2008 by the International Reading Association. Reprinted by permission.

Text	Teacher commentary during the think-aloud	Strategies modeled/practiced
Segmented Worms [photo of bristleworm and fan worm]	As I look over this piece of text, I see photos of some rather interesting worms. The title of this reading is *Segmented Worms*. I wonder how these are different from the flatworms and roundworms we've already read about. I'll read the first paragraph.	Predicting, using titles and graphics, providing focus and motivation to read further.
Body Structure *Earthworms are annelids and belong to the phylum Annelida, which is characterized by animals with a body plan consisting of segments.*	So, these types of worms are part of a different phylum. Their bodies have parts, or segments. Since the author told me this first, I bet it is the distinguishing feature.	Synthesizing and predicting.
	The segments remind me of a train that has lots of cars connected together. Do you have any examples of things that are connected in segments? [Kari listens as the students share possibilities with their partners. Melody, a student in the class, says "I don't really see a train, I think it's more like those blocks that connect together." Mario added, "You mean Lego's?"]	Making connections to familiar items.
As you can see on the evolutionary tree in Figure 25.22, both mollusks and annelids undergo protostome development, and therefore are considered close relatives.	*Protostome*—Wow, that's a word! I'll break it apart. I remember that *proto* is the first of its kind, like prototype. I also know that *stome* means mouth. So the word really means "mouth first." This helps me remember these creatures—the first opening that occurs during their development is the mouth.	Segmenting words into word parts brings attention to root words and/or affixes that might offer clues to meaning.
	On the figure, it shows that there are three types of protostomes: mollusks, annelids, and arthropods. The one that has a segmented body is called the annelids. I remember that mollusks aren't segmented, but we haven't learned much about arthropods yet. I wonder if they segmented or not.	Using a text feature to add meaning. Making connections with previous texts. Asking questions.
	I'll continue to read. Maybe I'll gain a better understanding of the meaning of this word if I read on.	Additionally, understanding that clarification might come from context or from continued reading.

(continued)

FIGURE 17.4. Sample modeling event.

There are over 11,000 species of annelids, most of which live in the sea. Most of the remaining species are earthworms. Annelids live just about everywhere except in the frozen soil of the polar regions and in the sand of dry deserts.	Well, this didn't tell me more about protostome, but I found it interesting that most annelids live in the sea. It makes sense that they can't live in frozen soil or dry sand as they look awfully soft. And I know that soft things can't live in those harsh conditions.	Acknowledges what they text offers and does not offer. Connections to prior knowledge.
Figure 25.23. Sections of an earthworm	Oh, now that's a cool illustration. I see from this illustration that the earthworm has five hearts. That's a major difference from other creatures we've studied. I'll add that difference to our chart of similarities and differences here [writes on a large chart paper labeled as such]. Take a minute, with your partner, to notice additional similarities and differences between the earthworm, mollusk, and human.	Using a text feature to add meaning. Records information for later retrieval

FIGURE 17.4. *(continued)*

- *Not* focus on one strategy at a time. As Pressley (2002) explained, good readers use multiple strategies as they read. Readers must learn to coordinate the various cognitive processes that are necessary to make meaning from texts. It's not as simple as saying, "Now we'll focus on inferences for the next 4 weeks." This "curricularized comprehension" approach is akin to the saying that when one has only a hammer, every problem looks like a nail. Inferencing, like a hammer, works some of the time for some situations, but certainly not all of the time in all situations. That's not to say that students don't need an explanation of a specific strategy. Rather, students should be taught to use the clues in the text to determine which strategies would be useful.

- Provide opportunities for students to attempt the strategies that are modeled. As Fisher and Frey (2008) note, modeling is only part of a strong instructional model. Students need opportunities to practice the behaviors that are modeled. They also need opportunities to use these cognitive processes, both with their peers and individually, if they are ever really going to become independent comprehenders. Incorporating discussion, partner talk, and note taking during modeling ensures that students apply the strategies they see modeled and use academic language while doing so.

- Be interesting! No readers want to attempt strategies they see modeled if the text is boring. Students, especially struggling readers, have to be regularly and routinely invited into reading (Ivey, 1999). Modeling provides students with a sense of what is possible, in terms of both comprehension and what the world of reading has to offer.

• Think like a scientist, mathematician, historian, artist, fitness expert, mechanic, or literary critic. In addition to being interesting, texts that are chosen should have content value. Modeling doesn't mean that everyone suddenly has to be a reading or English teacher. Instead, students need to see how content experts process text. This elevates the modeling, because teachers show students how comprehension is influenced by what they know about the content.

Reciprocal Teaching

In addition to modeling, reciprocal teaching, a highly effective instructional routine for facilitating reading comprehension, enjoys a significant research base, dating back over 20 years (Palincsar, 1984; Palincsar & Brown, 1984). Interestingly, this approach continues to be the focus of research studies as it is applied to new student populations (Alfassi, 1998). For example, in Scandinavia, Takala (2006) demonstrated the effectiveness of reciprocal teaching for students with and without disabilities. In addition, reciprocal teaching has been used successfully to help students understand multiple-choice questions in biology (Jensen et al., 2006) and word problems in mathematics (Van Garderen, 2004), and to help struggling adolescents with reading and writing (Slater & Horstman, 2002).

Reciprocal teaching allows students to become the leaders and guide their reading with peers. In essence, they become instructors of the content they are studying. The four steps of reciprocal teaching are as follows (adapted from Palincsar, 1986):

1. *Summarizing,* which provides students an opportunity to identify and to integrate the most important information from the text. The text may be summarized across sentences, paragraphs, or the passage as a whole. When students first begin reciprocal teaching, their efforts are generally focused at the sentence and paragraph levels. As they become increasingly proficient, they are able to summarize at the paragraph and passage levels.

2. *Questioning,* which reinforces summarizing and carries the reader one step further in comprehension activity. When students generate questions, they first identify the kind of information that is significant enough to provide the substance for a question. They then pose this information in question form to determine that they can indeed answer questions related to the reading. Question generating is a flexible strategy to the extent that students can generate questions at many levels. For example, some school situations require that students master supporting detail information; others require that students be able to infer or to apply new information from text.

3. *Clarifying*, which is a particularly important activity when working with students who have a history of comprehension difficulty. These students may believe that the purpose of reading is saying the words correctly; they may not be particularly uncomfortable that the words and in fact, the passages are not making sense. When the students are asked to clarify, their attention is called to the fact that there may be many reasons why text is difficult to understand (e.g., new vocabulary, unclear reference words, and unfamiliar and perhaps difficult concepts). Students are taught to pay attention to the effects of comprehension barriers and to take the necessary steps to restore meaning (e.g., reread, ask for help).

4. *Predicting*, which occurs when students hypothesize what the author will discuss next in the text. To do this successfully, students must activate the relevant background knowledge. While predicting, students have a purpose for reading: to confirm or to disprove their hypotheses. Furthermore, the opportunity has been created for students to link the new knowledge they encounter in the text with the knowledge they already possess. The predicting strategy also facilitates use of text structure as students learn that headings, subheadings, and questions imbedded in the text are useful means of anticipating what might occur next.

It is important to note that all reciprocal teaching groups meeting in a given classroom do not have to read the same text. When reciprocal teaching is first introduced to a group of students, the teacher usually identifies discussion points in advance of the conversation. As students become skilled with reciprocal teaching, they identify where they want to stop and talk about the text. Over time, reciprocal teaching becomes a natural, four-part conversation that students have about a text.

Consider the conversation that four students had about *Reptiles and Amphibians* (Howell, 1993) as part of their self-selected reading during biology. Having just finished several pages about reptiles, they stop to talk with one another.

JAY: The main point here that the author is making is we don't have to be afraid of reptiles. Just because they have a bad reputation, from movies and stuff, doesn't mean that the world doesn't need them.

STEPHANIE: I agree, but I don't want one touching me. I'm not sure why I'm afraid of them alive. This was interesting, but I have to say that I still don't want to touch a snake or lizard. Do you? Okay, I have a better question. Of all of the reptiles we've studied, which would you have as a pet?

MIA: A box turtle—they're even kinda cute.

JAY: A tuatara, but that's really not a text-based question.

STEPHANIE: I know, but I'm interested. Okay, so an even better question would be about the best environments for reptiles. Where do you think that they'll survive best?

MIA: Because they're cold-blooded and have dry skin, I think that they'll live best in the desert.

JAY: Yeah, lots do. But remember that they like to lay their eggs on land, so some of them probably need to be near water.

BOBBY: But I need clarification. What does it mean that they look like their parents at birth? I looked like my mom as a baby, but I'm not a reptile.

MIA: I think that the author means that they don't have stages to develop, like the frogs that start as tadpoles and stuff.

The conversation continues, and the group reads further and further in the book. Along the way, they negotiate meaning with one another. And this is the power of reciprocal teaching—students' incorporation of specific cognitive processes as habits while they read. Parenthetically, there is a fair amount of evidence that talking about what you read also improves comprehension and remembering (e.g., Adler & Rougle, 2005).

Conclusions

There is no doubt that Kaila understood the passage she read. We have evidence, in her own words, of comprehension. Kaila likely used a number of invisible cognitive processes along the way, such as decoding, creating mental images, mapping words onto images, and synthesizing information. She was also fortunate to have teachers who understood the need to focus on background knowledge, purpose, and vocabulary. She also experienced countless examples of teacher modeling and the opportunity to work with her peers as they constructed meanings of texts.

Several decades ago, Rieck (1977) demonstrated that content teachers "telegraph messages against readers" (p. 646). In choosing the word telegraph, Rieck implied that the message wasn't explicit, or perhaps even intentional. Instead, by their behaviors, teachers sent a message to students that reading wasn't important. This message was sent when teachers did not have a purpose for the readings they assigned, did not discuss the readings with students, and did not require that students ever do anything with the materials they were assigned to read. In the years since Rieck exposed this unfortunate message, we believe that teachers have begun to telegraph a new message. In the classrooms we observe, where students are engaged with texts, the message is loud and clear: Reading is important. In these classrooms, students comprehend texts because they have been taught to do so, and they have been encouraged to read widely from books they both want and are able to read.

QUESTIONS FOR DISCUSSION

1. Given the importance of background knowledge, what can teachers to do develop and activate it?

2. How might school faculty work together to improve students' comprehension?

3. Select a piece of text related to the standards for a class and develop a modeling lesson in which comprehension, vocabulary, text structures, and text features are evidence.

Resources

Block, C. C., & Parris, S. R. (Eds.). (2008). *Comprehension instruction: Research-based best practices.* New York: Guilford Press.

Fisher, D., & Frey, N. (2008). *Word wise and content rich: Five essential steps to teaching academic vocabulary.* Portsmouth, NH: Heinemann.

Oczkus, L. D. (2003). *Reciprocal teaching at work: Strategies for improving reading comprehension.* Newark, DE: International Reading Association.

References

Adler, M., & Rougle, E. (2005). *Building literacy through classroom discussion: Research-based strategies for developing critical readers and thoughtful writers in middle school.* New York: Scholastic.

Alfassi, M. (1998). Reading for meaning: The efficacy of reciprocal teaching in fostering reading comprehension in high school students in remedial reading classes. *American Educational Research Journal, 35,* 309–332.

Allington, R. L. (2002). You can't learn much from books you can't read. *Educational Leadership, 60*(3) 16–19.

Banikowski, A. K., & Mehring, T. A. (1999). Strategies to enhance memory based on brain-research. *Focus on Exceptional Children, 32*(2), 1–16.

Bard, A. S., & Bard, M. G. (2002). *The complete idiot's guide to understanding the brain.* New York: Alpha Books.

Baumann, J. F., Kame'enui, E. J., & Ash, G. E. (2003). Research on vocabulary instruction: Voltaire redux. In J. Flood, D. Lapp, J. R. Squire, & J. M. Jensen (Eds.), *Handbook of research on teaching the English language arts* (2nd ed., pp. 752–785). Mahwah, NJ: Erlbaum.

Bromley, K. (2007). Nine things every teacher should know about words and vocabulary instruction. *Journal of Adolescent & Adult Literacy, 50,* 528–537.

Byrnes, H. (1998). *Reading in the beginning and intermediate college foreign language class.* Washington, DC: Center for Applied Linguistics.

Clark, L. (2007). *The 10 most revolting parasites.* Markham, ON: Scholastic Canada.

Dole, J. A., Brown, K. J., & Trathen, W. (1996). The effects of strategy instruction on the comprehension performance of at-risk students. *Reading Research Quarterly, 31,* 62–88.

Droop, M., & Verhoeven, L. (1998). Background knowledge, linguistic complexity and second language reading comprehension. *Journal of Literacy Research, 30,* 253–271.

Dully, H., & Fleming, C. (2007). *My lobotomy: A memoir.* New York: Crown.

Duffy, G. G. (2002). The case for direct explanation of strategies. In C. C. Block & M. Pressley (Eds.), *Comprehension instruction: Research-based best practices* (pp. 28–41). New York: Guilford Press.

Duffy, G. G. (2003). *Explaining reading: A resource for teaching concepts, skills, and strategies.* New York: Guilford Press.

Firlik, K. (2006). *Another day in the frontal lobe: A brain surgeon exposes life on the inside.* New York: Random House.

Fisher, D., & Frey, N. (2008). *Better learning through structured teaching: A framework for the gradual release of responsibility.* Alexandria, VA: Association for Supervision and Curriculum Development.

Fisher, D., Frey, N., & Lapp, D. (2008). Shared readings: Modeling comprehension, vocabulary, text structures, and text features for older readers. *Reading Teacher, 61,* 548–557.

Flood, J., Lapp, D., & Fisher, D. (2003). Reading comprehension instruction. In J. Flood, D. Lapp, J. R. Squire, & J. M. Jensen (Eds.), *Handbook of research on teaching the English language arts* (2nd ed., pp. 931–941). Mahwah, NJ: Erlbaum.

Howell, C. H. (1993). *Reptiles and amphibians.* Washington, DC: National Geographic Society.

Ivey, G. (1999). A multicase study in the middle school: Complexities among young adolescent readers. *Reading Research Quarterly, 34,* 172–192.

Jensen, M., Duranczyk, I., Staats, S., Moore, R., Hatch, J., & Somdahl, C. (2006). Using a reciprocal teaching strategy to create multiple-choice exam questions. *American Biology Teacher, 68,* 67–71.

Johnson, A. P., & Rasmussen, J. B. (1998). Classifying and super word web: Two strategies to improve productive vocabulary. *Journal of Adolescent & Adult Literacy, 42,* 204–207.

Lubliner, S., & Smetana, L. (2005). The effects of comprehensive vocabulary instruction on Title I students' metacognitive word-learning skills and reading comprehension. *Journal of Literacy Research, 37,* 163–200.

Marzano, R. (2004). *Building background knowledge for academic achievement: Research on what works in schools.* Alexandria, VA: Association for Supervision and Curriculum Development.

Nagy, W. E. (1988). *Teaching vocabulary to improve reading comprehension.* Newark, DE: International Reading Association.

Palincsar, A. S. (1986). Reciprocal teaching. In A. S. Palincsar, D. S. Ogle, B. F. Jones, & E. G. Carr (Eds.), *Teaching reading as thinking.* Alexandria, VA: Association for Supervision and Curriculum Development.

Palincsar, A. S., & Brown, A. (1984). Reciprocal teaching of comprehension fostering and comprehension monitoring activities. *Cognition and Instruction, 2,* 117–175.

Pichert, J. W., & Anderson, R. C. (1977). Taking different perspectives on a story. *Journal of Educational Psychology, 69,* 309–315.

Pressley, M. (2002). Comprehension strategies instruction: A turn-of-the-century status report. In C. C. Block & M. Pressley (Eds.), *Comprehension instruction: Research-based best practices* (pp. 11–27). New York: Guilford Press.

Reynolds, R. E., Taylor, M. A., Steffensen, M. S., Shirley, L. L., & Anderson, R. C.

(1982). Cultural schemata and reading comprehension. *Reading Research Quarterly, 17,* 353–366.

Rieck, B. J. (1977). How content teachers telegraph messages against reading. *Journal of Reading, 20,* 646–648.

Rosenbaum, C. (2001). A word map for middle school: A tool for effective vocabulary instruction. *Journal of Adolescent & Adult Literacy, 45,* 44–49.

Slater, W. H., & Horstman, F. R. (2002). Teaching reading and writing to struggling middle school and high school students: The case for reciprocal teaching. *Preventing School Failure, 46,* 163–166.

Stahl, S. E., Chou Hare, V., Sinatra, R., & Gregory, J. F. (1991). Defining the role of prior knowledge and vocabulary in reading comprehension: The retiring of number 41. *Journal of Reading Behavior, 23,* 478–508.

Takala, M. (2006). The effects of reciprocal teaching on reading comprehension in mainstream and special (SLI) education. *Scandinavian Journal of Educational Research, 50,* 559–576.

Van Garderen, D. (2004). Reciprocal teaching as a comprehension strategy for understanding mathematical word problems. *Reading & Writing Quarterly, 20,* 225–229.

Weber, R. (1991). Linguistic diversity and reading in American society. In R. Barr, M. L. Kamil, P. Mosenthal, & P. D. Pearson (Eds.), *Handbook of reading research* (pp. 97–119). New York: Longman.

Chapter 18

Vocabulary Learning in the Content Areas

Research-Based Practices for Middle and Secondary School Classrooms

Janis M. Harmon
Karen D. Wood
Adriana L. Medina

GUIDING QUESTIONS

1. Why is the teaching of content-area vocabulary so important?
2. What are the common vocabulary features shared across subject matter domains?
3. What are the key understandings of content vocabulary instruction?
4. What does effective vocabulary instruction look like?

Content-area classrooms are critical learning environments for middle and high school students. Jetton and Alexander (2004) assert that content areas are subject matter domains that heavily influence middle and secondary students' academic achievement. To achieve academic success, students must demonstrate proficiency in mathematics, science, and social studies through both receptive and expressive communicative skills. To read, write, and speak competently about specific content topics, students must have command of the language in each domain (Fang, 2006; Jetton & Alexander, 2004). In other words, students need the linguistic knowledge that is unique to various subject matter areas, in addition to the topic knowledge to be successful lifelong learners in these domains. To handle the demands of text-based learning, a student must develop the independent learning strategies tied to linguistic and topic knowledge, strategies that will enable him or her to read like a mathematician, a historian, and a scientist.

The linguistic knowledge needed for successful content learning includes not only a command of specialized language structures, such as complex sentences, dependent clauses, paragraph variations, and the unique structures of expository texts (Fang, 2006), but also the vocabulary needed to represent concepts. Unlike narrative texts, in which students can still comprehend the gist of a story even though some words might be unfamiliar, informational texts require students to have a functioning knowledge of many conceptually loaded terms, as well as familiarity with new and unique meanings for common terms (Blachowicz, Fisher, Ogle, & Watts-Taffe, 2006). Content-area classrooms, then, are also learning environments in which vocabulary knowledge and conceptual understandings are inextricably woven. Unfortunately, such contexts create daunting challenges for not only many students, especially English language learners (ELLs) and students with learning disabilities, but also for teachers who strive to provide effective instruction for content learning.

Although teachers across all disciplines and grade levels have their own personal beliefs concerning vocabulary acquisition and personal orientation toward what they consider to be effective vocabulary instruction (Hedrick, Harmon, & Linerode, 2004; Konopak & Williams, 1994), they share common concerns and challenges about vocabulary instruction. For example, in a recent survey, 390 middle school teachers representing major content areas were asked to provide the most critical questions they had about vocabulary instruction (Wood, Vintinner, Hill-Miller, Harmon, & Hedrick, 2006). The five most critical questions follow:

"How do I motivate students to learn new words?"

"How do I provide multiple exposures to help students internalize word meaning?"

"How do I help students understand how extensive reading impacts their vocabulary knowledge?"

"How do I teach context clues, so that students use this strategy independently?"

"How do I teach students to self-select words they need to learn?"

When other content-area teachers were asked informally to voice their questions about vocabulary instruction, the results were varied. Their questions included the following:

"What technique will help my students understand and recognize the word in any setting?"

"How do we find the time? Is there ever enough time to teach vocabulary?"

"Is using the vocabulary in everyday activities enough for the students to learn the vocabulary?"

"How can I make better use of word walls?"

The challenges of providing effective instruction are also varied, as illustrated by the following comments made by middle school teachers:

"My greatest challenge in teaching vocabulary is knowing for sure that my students really understand. I mean, they look lost sometimes." —*Special education teacher*

"My greatest challenge in teaching vocabulary is making sure that the students know not only content vocabulary but also words that tend to trip them up in the word problems that they read, [words] such as *descending* and *ascending.*"—*Mathematics teacher*

"My greatest challenge in teaching vocabulary is having the students actually take home the words to study and having them apply the content words accurately."—*Science teacher*

"Teachers have so much content to cover that I feel like many of my students hear the word or a brief definition and then we have to move on. So many students who learn a little slower are not hearing and seeing the words enough."—*Special education teacher*

These challenges and questions that practicing teachers have about content-area vocabulary instruction reflect the close and complex relationship between words and concepts and, on a broader level, the role of literacy in content learning. These concerns are also found in the literature on content literacy. For example, Gomez and Madda (2005) observed that the greatest difficulty facing a middle school science teacher in offering appropriate instruction for ELL Latino students was vocabulary. In the area of mathematics, Gullatt (1987) acknowledges that success in this domain requires specific reading strategies, as well as a working knowledge of mathematics vocabulary. In a more recent study, Borasi, Siegal, Fonzi, and Smith (1998) found that students' mathematical understandings were enhanced when they constructed their own interpretations through writing, drawing, dramatic presentations, and class discussions. In these activities, students had multiple opportunities to apply the language of mathematics, therefore internalizing mathematics vocabulary.

Given the importance of vocabulary in content-area classrooms and the need to examine effective vocabulary instructional practices that may offer viable solutions to the challenges and questions of practitioners, the remainder of this chapter is an extension of our previous work in this area (Harmon, Wood, & Hedrick, 2008) that examines the nature of vocabulary and the features of effective vocabulary instruction, and then concludes with concrete examples of effective instructional practices. We begin with the nature of content vocabulary, which includes a close look at the distinctive language of various content areas, as well as common features that are shared across various subject matter domains. We then present eight key understandings of effective vocabulary instruction and include specific examples of vocabulary instructional practices that target particular features of content vocabulary instruction.

What Is the Nature of Content Vocabulary?

Vocabulary and the Language of Content Areas

Similar to learning in general, learners acquire language and vocabulary development unique to a subject matter and new conceptual understandings simultaneously (Vygotsky, 1994). Although the language and vocabulary found in different content areas have some similar features, there are distinct differences that we now address. We then examine similar features across all subject matter domains.

Mathematics

Mathematics language is unique and tends to be used only in mathematical contexts, with very few, if any, occurrences outside of school (Thompson & Rubenstein, 2000). As a result, students have even fewer opportunities to use and reinforce newly learned concepts. Nonetheless, the language of mathematics, like that in all content areas, is inseparable from the learning of that discipline (Krussel, 1998; Steele, 1999; Tracy, 1994). Furthermore, students' *metalinguistic abilities*, the capacity to use knowledge about language, are also tied to this learning. For example, MacGregor and Price (1999) examined the relationship between language proficiency and algebra learning and found a positive correlation between students' metalinguistic awareness and achievement in learning algebraic notations. Their results indicated that students with low metalinguistic awareness scored low on assessments of algebraic knowledge.

Learning mathematics vocabulary is a challenge for many students because of the nature of the vocabulary itself—largely abstract, unequivocal, collective, and compact (Monroe, 1997). Many mathematics terms have precise meanings that are highly abstract. For example, one abstract term in geometry is *trapezoid*, a quadrilateral plane figure having two parallel and two nonparallel sides. A thorough understanding of the term *trapezoid* requires that students have a cumulative, experiential knowledge base that incorporates knowledge of lines; planes; the concepts of parallel, polygons, and quadrilaterals; as well as an understanding of how these concepts are interrelated. It is obvious from this example that effective vocabulary instruction in mathematics becomes more and more hierarchical, relying heavily on prior knowledge of concepts as mathematical concepts become more multifaceted in middle and secondary classrooms. As a result, mathematics teachers are obliged to infuse effective vocabulary instruction in their teaching to help students acquire the necessary language for communicating and learning mathematics.

Science

Science language is widely varied given the various disciplines that are subsumed under the heading of science. For example, science disciplines include physical science, physics, life science, medicine, earth science, chemistry, biochemistry and even astronomy—all of which have their own particular vocabulary and language patterns. Although science vocabulary is still considered to be low frequency vocabulary, limited to use in specific contexts, Miller (2005) asserts that today's students encounter many scientific terms outside of school from places such as advertisements and television commercials featuring pharmaceutical drugs and products, and other media outlets. Such exposures enable many students to become familiar with scientific terms, albeit at only a superficial and generalized level of understanding. However, such knowledge can serve as a familiar starting point for exploring deeper and more complex understanding about a concept. For example, Itza-Ortiz, Robello, and Zollman (2003) studied students' awareness of conceptual physics word meanings used in everyday life (e.g., the words *force* and *momentum*), and how these perceptions impact students' understanding of physics concepts. Their findings indicate that students with greater background knowledge about the physics concepts were able to articulate the differences between common, everyday meanings of physics terms and their more specific scientific meanings.

Social Studies

Social studies vocabulary, another unique and varied corpus of words that is language dependent, is particularly important in classrooms where instruction is largely in lecture format and requires individual textbook reading (Short, 1995). In addition, like the domain of science, social studies encompasses a variety of fields, including government, political science, geography, economics, and civics. These unique domains all contain rich and unique vocabulary terms representing both familiar and unfamiliar concepts (Graves, 2000). Social studies vocabulary in general also has distinctive features that set it apart from other disciplines. For example, students are inundated with many specific names and titles for people, places, and events—names and titles that are connected to specific time periods and geographic areas.

Features of Content Vocabulary

Although the vocabulary of each subject matter domain is distinct and unique, all share some common features that we describe in this section. Based on the work of others (Itza-Ortiz et al., 2003; Monroe & Panchyshyn, 1995), we present one way to examine domain-specific vocabulary in terms of the following categories: (1) technical terms; (2) nontechnical words; (3) function words, and word clusters and phrases; (4) unique representations; and (5) common roots.

Technical Terms

Technical terms are those words and phrases that represent particular concepts. Knowledge of these terms cannot be separated from knowledge of the concept itself. Examples of technical terms include words such as *coefficient, nuclear fusion, revolution,* and *socialism.* As labels for concepts, technical terms must be addressed in rich instructional activities that help students to develop a sound understanding of the concept itself.

Nontechnical Terms

Subject matter domains also contain many general words that represent multiple meanings. Although these nontechnical words are found in different content areas, their meanings may change, depending upon the subject. For example, words such as *organization, time line,* and *race* hold special meanings in social studies contexts, just as *crust, force,* and *table* have different meanings in science.

Function Words and Word Clusters and Phrases

The writing in every content area contains frequently occurring word clusters or phrases, and we sometimes assume that students already know what they mean. Nonetheless, these function words and phrases, which correlate conceptual ideas and signal specific relationships, can be roadblocks to student learning and should be addressed (Marco & Luzon, 1999). Examples include *are composed primarily of* and *that extends beyond* in science, *the result of* and *another example of* in social studies, and *more than twice a number* and *is divisible by* in mathematics.

Unique Representations

All content areas contain specific symbolic representations and abbreviations for precise meanings of a concept. For example, the language of mathematics includes numerical representations that are highly abstract (Monroe &

Panchyshyn, 1995). Many of these numerical representations are read differently, such "six squared" or "six to the second power" for 6^2.

Common Roots

Another feature of content-area vocabulary is the many common roots found in terms across the subject matter domains. Words with common roots abound in mathematics, science, and social studies texts. In particular, Milligan and Ruff (1990) analyzed the content of five glossaries in elementary and secondary school social studies textbooks and estimated that approximately 71% of the terms contained common roots. Examples include *demo-*, as in *democracy* and *demographer*, and *merc-*, as in *merchant* and *mercantile*.

What Key Understandings Are Essential in Content Vocabulary Instruction?

Over the past 25 years, extensive research efforts have resulted in a rich body of knowledge about what constitutes effective vocabulary teaching and learning—information that is applicable to teaching and learning vocabulary in the content areas. Various facets of the vocabulary research are pertinent, including the following: (1) what we now know about the intricacies of vocabulary acquisition in terms of what it means to know a word (Baumann, Kame'enui, & Ash, 2003) and how words are representations of concepts (Vacca & Vacca, 2008); (2) the complex relationship between vocabulary and reading comprehension that involves intricate connections to a reader's prior knowledge, commonsense notions that unknown words interfere with reading comprehension, and the impact of general ability on word learning (Stahl, 1999); and (3) specific dimensions of vocabulary learning and teaching that involve effective instructional features and the role of incidental word learning and wide reading for building vocabulary (Beck, McKeown, & Kucan, 2002; Nagy, 1988).

We highlight eight key understandings, grounded in the findings of this body of research, that guide effective vocabulary instruction in the content areas:

- Vocabulary learning is closely tied to conceptual understanding.
- Explicit instruction in content-area vocabulary builds and supports conceptual understandings.
- Explicit instruction involves multiple, varied, and meaningful experiences with words.
- Vocabulary learning occurs implicitly in content-area classrooms.
- The structure of expository texts can impact vocabulary learning.

- Classroom instructional time for learning vocabulary is necessary and must be sufficient.
- Metacognitive awareness of vocabulary learning fosters independent learning in the different content areas.
- Different content-area words require different types of instruction.

Vocabulary Learning Is Closely Tied to Conceptual Understanding

In particular, Vacca and Vacca (2008) clearly point out that "words are labels for concepts" (p. 147); therefore, they are critical for comprehending informational texts. In fact, because vocabulary learning in the content areas cannot be separated from conceptual understanding, it is an embedded component of concept teaching. Furthermore, because concepts are related to other concepts, the vocabulary representing these ideas must also be taught in relation to other vocabulary.

For example, to acquire a thorough understanding of the Underground Railroad in American history, students need to have a knowledge base of closely related concepts, such as the slave trade, the United States economy of the 1700s and the first half of the 1800s, the abolitionist movement, the Fugitive Slave Act of 1850, the Civil War, and people like Harriet Tubman. Students need to have a grasp of the accompanying vocabulary—*slavery, abolition, fugitives, Quakers, Civil War, safe houses, free states*—not only to describe this historical event but also to engage in critical, higher-level thinking activities (Jetton & Alexander, 2004). Through effective instruction, students internalize this specialized vocabulary that in turn enables them to process texts more efficiently as they read and to express their thoughts more clearly when they speak and write.

Explicit Instruction in Content-Area Vocabulary Builds and Supports Conceptual Understandings

Reading in the content areas can be a daunting task for many learners in middle and high school classrooms as they face more sophisticated texts; more complex, domain-specific topics; and more challenging vocabulary for representing these topics (Jetton & Alexander, 2004). Learners use their topic knowledge, vocabulary knowledge, and their repertoire of comprehension strategies and metacognitive strategies to make sense of these formidable, demanding texts. However, struggling learners—those less proficient in reading and ELLs—may lack the necessary requisites to read such texts successfully and would benefit from explicit instruction in comprehension (Duke & Pearson, 2002; National Reading Panel, 2000; RAND Reading Study Group, 2002). In what he calls the "visible aspects of learning," Vacca (2002) advocates explicit literacy instruction in all content-area classrooms, exhorting teachers to embed cognitive strategy instruction in their content-area instruction. The gradual release of responsibility model for explicit instruction, with explanation, modeling, guided practice, and independent application of strategies (Graves, Juel, & Graves, 2004), provides the instructional framework for teaching cognitive reading strategies, such as predicting, questioning, inferring, and clarifying word meanings. Although the primary goal of content-area instruction is to impart new knowledge and understanding about the concepts of a particular discipline, teachers can still achieve this goal, while simultaneously interjecting these cognitive strategies to guide struggling readers as they "read like a historian, or scientist, or mathematician."

Moreover, Vacca's visible aspects of learning also apply to vocabulary instruction. Explicit instruction of vocabulary results in comprehension gains (National Reading Panel, 2000) and is critical for conceptual learning to occur. Students, especially those who struggle with reading, need teachers who use effective instructional techniques for introducing, contextualizing, connecting, demonstrating, and applying word meanings. Furthermore, students deserve explicit instruction in independent word-learning strategies that are useful for unlocking word meanings across different subject matter areas.

The critical features of explicit vocabulary instruction, as outlined by Graves (2006), are relevant to content-area vocabulary instruction. These features include the careful selection of terms to teach, the ways to introduce terms, the impact of levels of word knowledge, and the selection of appropriate word learning tasks to match selected words. In light of instructional time constraints, Graves argues for the prudent selection of words—words that are both critical for conceptual understanding and transferable to other content areas. In regard to introducing words to students, Graves views initial instruction as teacher-directed tasks that involve the presentation of a definition that students can understand, accompanied by a meaningful context. The meaningful contexts illustrate how the terms may be used in written texts or may include a representation of concept, such as a visible item, photograph, or video.

Another feature of explicit instruction, levels of word knowledge, is based on the idea that words are known in different degrees. Some words demand a rich, decontextualized knowledge base (Beck et al., 2002), whereas other words can remain at a general level of understanding and still enable learners to comprehend a passage. Still another feature of explicit instruction is the kinds of tasks associated with learning word meanings—tasks that require different instructional approaches. Two particular word-learning tasks are important for content-area vocabulary: tasks for learning words that represent familiar concepts, and tasks for new words that represent complex and difficult concepts (Graves, 2006). For example, in mathematics, concepts such as *absolute value* and *order of operations* require different instructional approaches.

Many investigations have examined the efficacy of explicit instructional techniques for teaching content vocabulary; techniques range from frontloading activities to use before reading to a variety of graphic representations. For example, Carney, Anderson, and Blackburn (1984) found that fifth-grade students' comprehension skills improved when they were pretaught the social studies terms in selected passages. Key word mnemonic approaches were also effective in helping struggling readers learn and remember science vocabulary (King Sears, Mercer, & Sindelar, 1992).

Furthermore, the literature on vocabulary instruction also indicates the usefulness of visual representations, such as semantic maps, structured overviews, and semantic feature analysis grids for teaching content-area vocabulary. For example, Snouffer and Thistlethwaite (1979) documented the effectiveness of structured overviews as a preteaching tool with science and social studies texts. Similarly, the concept of *definition map*, a specific type of graphic organizer, proved useful in helping students with mathematics vocabulary, especially when used as part of classroom discussions (Monroe, 1997).

Explicit Vocabulary Instruction Involves Multiple, Varied, and Meaningful Experiences with Words

The extensive research of Beck, McKeown, and their colleagues has revealed that vocabulary learning and comprehension occurs when teachers invest in an extensive, long-term vocabulary program that includes multiple exposures to words in varied and meaningful contexts (Beck & McKeown, 1983; Beck, Perfetti, & McKeown, 1982; McKeown, Beck, Omanson, & Perfetti, 1983; McKeown, Beck, Omanson, & Pople, 1985). In regard to multiple exposures, McKeown et al. (1985) found that the more frequently students were exposed to words in meaningful contexts, the greater the impact on their word learning and comprehension. In fact, McKeown and her associates define these multiple opportunities to mean at least 12 or more meaningful encounters.

The meaningful contexts involved manipulation of word meanings that moved beyond the definitional level and included tasks such as presenting words in semantically related categories, using scenarios in which students use the meaning of a word to provide a reasonable completion to a partial sentence, and having students consider the connections between the targeted word and other, related words. The variability and frequency of the tasks were critical for enhancing not only word knowledge but also comprehension of passages containing the targeted words.

For example, in a World History unit on the Holocaust, students encounter terms such as *Holocaust, genocide,* and *propaganda.* The following tasks are representative of the meaningful contexts described in the research of Beck, McKeown, and their associates:

Meaningful prompt: Things you would not have expected to occur during the Holocaust.

Meaningful question: Did Hitler's use of propaganda lead to Jewish genocide?

Sentence completion: Propaganda led to the genocide of Jewish people because …

In each example, students must move beyond simply providing a definition for a term, and instead engage in higher cognitive processing that requires an understanding of a term to provide a correct response to the prompts and questions.

A few content-area studies illustrate the variety of ways that students can be actively engaged in vocabulary learning. For example, Lloyd and Contreras (1985) found that when fourth-grade students participated in hands-on experiences and class discussion, they expanded their vocabulary knowledge and reading comprehension of science texts. When compared to a dictionary group and a control group that received no instruction, the students in the hands-on/discussion instruction attained significantly higher gains in vocabulary and comprehension. Similarly, Stahl and Clark (1987) found encouraging results concerning the benefits of discussion for promoting vocabulary learning of science terms with fifth-grade students. Class discussion was also important in Grubaugh and Metzer's (1986) Spoken Word activity, in which students defined words and used personal examples. In still another science vocabulary study, conducted by Stahl and Kapinus (1991), Possible Sentences, an instructional strategy that directs students to use two or more vocabulary terms in a single sentence, was effective in vocabulary learning and in the recall of science facts. Active participation in mathematics vocabulary learning through student explanations, writing activities, and cooperative learning techniques to encourage classroom talk has also been documented (Miller, 1993).

Vocabulary Learning Occurs Implicitly in Content-Area Classrooms

Vocabulary learning is embedded in the rich and dynamic contexts of content-area classrooms in ways that mirror Vacca's (2002) description of the invisible aspects of content-area reading. Vacca notes that support for literacy before, during, and after reading activities is evident in instructional formats. Vocabulary support can also parallel this format by engaging students in activities in which they seek word meanings by activating background knowledge or drawing inferences from texts, associate word meanings by making connections and asking questions while reading, and ultimately apply word meanings by summarizing and synthesizing newly learned concepts after reading.

Vacca also describes the invisible aspects of content literacy in terms of rich classroom instructional techniques that support concept learning, techniques such as Questioning the Author (Beck et al., 1997), Socratic seminars (Copeland, 2005), and critical literacy perspectives (McLaughlin & DeVoogd, 2004). These instructional frameworks are fertile grounds for exposure to and reinforcement of content vocabulary. Active participation in classroom discussions requires that students use appropriate language and vocabulary to communicate their ideas to others.

The implicit nature of vocabulary learning in content-area classrooms also takes into account incidental word learning through context. Some research studies provide evidence that vocabulary is learned incidentally through reading and listening (Nagy & Herman, 1987; Sternberg, 1987). In particular, Swanborn and de Glopper (1999) estimate that readers acquire some understanding of approximately 15% of the unfamiliar words they encounter while reading. On the other hand, other studies indicate the unreliability of contexts for helping readers determine appropriate word meanings (McKeown, 1985; Schatz & Baldwin, 1986).

Nevertheless, reading widely and frequently impacts not only achievement but also students' vocabulary acquisition, as demonstrated by Anderson, Wilson, and Fielding (1988) in their study of the amount of time students spend reading. They found a correlation between the amount of time spent reading and reading achievement measured by a standardized reading test. Students scoring at the 98th percentile on the test read approximately 5 million words per year compared with about 600,000 words read by students scoring at the 50th percentile. These findings offer strong support for exposing students to a variety of books on different topics and encouraging them to read.

However, there is one qualification concerning the amount of background knowledge a student possesses about a content topic. Several studies have documented a positive correlation between students' prior knowledge of a given topic and their ability to learn word meanings incidentally while reading about the topic (Carlisle, Fleming, & Gudbrandsen, 2000; Swanborn & de Glopper, 1999). For example, Carlisle et al. (2000) found that fourth-grade and eighth-grade students with some topical knowledge learned word meanings incidentally in their science classes as they participated in hands-on activities and class discussions. At both grade levels, students with some background knowledge about the topic fared better in learning new words and concepts than those students who had limited topical knowledge.

The Structure of Expository Texts Can Impact Vocabulary Learning

Vocabulary learning in the content areas is also impacted by the type and amount of passage support for vocabulary in content textbooks (Cardinale, 1991; Gordon, Schumm, Coffland, & Doucette, 1992; Konopak, 1988). Both Konopak's investigation of text passages and Gordon et al.'s (1992) replication of Konopak's work revealed that students' comprehension increases when new terms in targeted passages are explicitly defined. The findings of these studies indicate the need for specific and obvious context clues for clarifying word meanings, especially in close proximity to the word. Such features, Konopak argued, would create texts that are more considerate to the readers. In another study on text-based features for supporting vocabulary, Cardinale (1991) not only confirmed Konopak's findings (1988) but also found that teachers need to attend to the students' cognitive demands in processing text information to construct meaning. In particular, Cardinale found the following descriptions to be useful: (1) clarification of cause-and-effect relationships; (2) use of analogies to connect familiar concepts with new and unfamiliar ideas; and (3) explanations of the morphemic structure of words containing Greek and Latin roots and other affixes. She argued that these embedded features of text are especially critical for helping students handle the cognitive demands of reading complex concepts.

Classroom Instructional Time for Learning Vocabulary Is Necessary and Must Be Sufficient

Although a limited number of studies document the amount of classroom time given to vocabulary, the few studies that have been conducted revealed disappointing results. Both Durkin (1978–1979) and Watts (1995) found that vocabulary received little instructional time in classrooms. In a more recent study, Scott, Jamieson-Noel, and Asselin (2003) observed that only a small percentage of instructional time specifically included a focus on vocabulary across both language arts and content-area classrooms. Moreover, only 1.4% of total instructional time in science, social studies, and mathematics classrooms accounted for specific attention to vocabulary. Scott and her associates also noted that the type of vocabulary instruction in these content classrooms was similar to what Vacca and Vacca (2008) describe as the "assigning and telling" mode, which provides little support for conceptual understanding and even less for word study.

Whereas these studies indicate that teachers in upper elementary school grades appear reluctant to use instructional time for vocabulary, we expect that this same situation exists at the middle and secondary school levels. Nevertheless, students across all grade levels need and deserve classroom time for increasing their vocabulary knowledge, especially in content-area classrooms, where domain-specific vocabulary is closely tied to conceptual understanding.

Metacognitive Awareness of Vocabulary Learning Fosters Independent Learning in the Different Content Areas

Helping students become independent word learners is a shared responsibility of all teachers across all subject matter disciplines. To enhance metacognitive awareness, teachers should consider two important facets of word learning: (1) direct instruction in independent word-learning strategies; and (2) attention to raising word consciousness. First, the strategies involved in word learning are useful for helping a student read like a mathematician, a historian, or a scientist. Specifically, these strategies—using context clues to unlock word meanings; studying the structure of words; considering word origins; and using references, such as dictionaries and glossaries—help students to become proficient word learners. Embedding independent word-learning strategies in the content-area instruction benefits all students, especially the striving readers who are challenged by the reading demands in particular content areas.

Although the research concerning the use of context clues as an independent word-learning strategy still remains somewhat limited and inconclusive (see Baumann et al., 2003, for a review of this research), there is enough evidence to support using context to infer possible word meanings. The investigations of Konopak (1988), Cardinale (1991), and others about considerate texts have led many publishers today to write textbook passages that offer readers more contextual aids for unfamiliar vocabulary. Nevertheless, struggling readers still require direct instruction that addresses text clues for unlocking word meanings.

Another independent word-learning strategy, morphemic and structural analysis, cannot be overlooked in regard to content-area vocabulary learning. A high percentage of subject-matter-specific words (roughly 60%) contain common affixes and roots (Milligan & Ruff, 1990), such as *micro, scribe,* and *scope.* Several studies have also documented the value of morphemic analysis instruction in content-area classrooms. In a comparison of morphemic and contextual analysis with typical textbook instruction, Baumann, Edwards, Boland, and Olejnik (2003) found that fifth graders in social studies classes had similar scores on a social studies content assessment. However, students in a typical vocabulary instruction group learned the meanings of targeted words, but students in a morphemic and contextual analysis group were more effective at inferring the meanings of new words.

ELLs in particular need to acquire not only semantic knowledge of content-area vocabulary but also morphological and syntactical knowledge about words (Robinson, 2005). Understanding these facets of word use requires explicit instruction, so that ELLs can actively engage in class discussions that promote deeper cognitive processing that result in conceptual understandings. These striving readers need and deserve such instruction from all teachers.

Attention to word origins is another independent word learning strategy that applies to content-area vocabulary. Rubenstein (2000) notes several advantages for teaching word origins in mathematics, including attention to cognates for ELLs and the connection between the precise meanings of mathematical words and their roots.

Metacognitive awareness is also enhanced when teachers focus on helping students develop word consciousness. Defined by Scott and Nagy (2004) as "an interest in and awareness of words" (p. 202), word consciousness comprises several types of knowledge and skills, including semantic and syntactic awareness of words. Exceeding a basic definitional understanding of a word, metalinguistic awareness involves knowing that word knowledge increases over time, and that different words require different strategies to decipher their meanings. Content-area classrooms are fertile grounds for fostering word consciousness that, in turn, may enhance content learning. There are several good reasons for raising the level of word awareness in content-area classrooms. First, students who develop an interest in words are more apt to use the language of the discipline in their speaking and writing. In addition, students become more aware of multiple-meaning words that are frequently found across subject matter areas. Finally, elevating students' awareness of words can be fun and motivating. Word play activities work well in review sessions and can even challenge students' thinking, as in the use of puns and riddles.

Different Content-Area Words Require Different Types of Instruction

In an examination of content-area vocabulary, Harmon, Wood, and Hedrick (2006) recognized distinctive features in the kind of word learning needed in the content areas. The nature of the words, as well as the knowledge level of the students, must be taken account when planning vocabulary instruction for building conceptual understandings in the content areas. With this in mind, Harmon, Wood, and Hedrick (2006) have described four major features of vocabulary instruction to help teachers determine the focus of instruction: integration, clarification, identification, and linguistic attention. We briefly describe each feature and provide an instructional example for each.

Integration

Integration lies at the heart of effective content-area instruction, with a focus on the semantic relationships that exist between words and ideas. When vocabulary instruction highlights these relationships, students are more apt to understand the interconnectedness among ideas as they use their own knowledge to construct meaning. When the goal is to help students grapple with new concepts, vocabulary instruction should focus on integration.

One effective instructional strategy for supporting integration is the use of concept circles. To get an idea of the conceptual relationships among vocabulary terms, concept circles provide a means to understand the terms. First, the teacher demonstrates four related words by putting a related text word in each quadrant of a circle, then directs the students to name the concept relationship among them. Another option is to put each of three related words in one quadrant of the circle and leave one quadrant empty. Students write in the empty quadrant a word that relates to the others, then identify the overall concept that the circle represents. Figure 18.1 provides an example of concept circles.

Answer: Toothed Whales

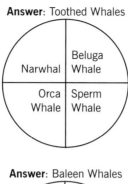

Answer: Baleen Whales

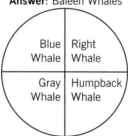

FIGURE 18.1. Example of concept circles. *Directions:* What concept is illustrated in each circle?

Clarification

The focus shifts when the goal of vocabulary instruction is to refine word meanings and to clear up possible confusions. In this case, the feature of clarification would be appropriate for guiding instruction. Clarification is especially needed when students encounter *polysemous*, or multiple-meaning words, in their reading. Mathematical terms, such as *table, graph*, or *complementary*, can be stumbling blocks for students, especially those whose first language is not English. Furthermore, words and phrases that signal relationships among concepts can also be problematic. For example, students may have difficulty understanding common phrases, such as *is increased by* or *in contrast to*. In these cases, vocabulary instruction would have a focus on clarification.

Contextual redefinition is a useful clarification strategy that works well with subject matter terminology. The students must carefully examine both word-level clues and contextual clues from a passage to make a reasonable prediction, as well as an ultimate verification of a word's meaning. The teacher can select important terms, then guide students as they complete the following chart:

Word	Word-level clues	Context clues	Predicted word meaning	Actual word meaning
Hydrosphere	*Clues:* hydro means water *Guess:* something about water	*Clues:* Water portion of the earth; seas and oceans	Study water on Earth	The portion of the Earth, or other planet, that is water

In this example, the students initially examine word-level clues and notice that *hydro* means water. Then they carefully read the text containing the term and use the context to find more clues to the meaning of the word. At this point, they make a reasonable prediction about the meaning, then verify their thoughts by consulting an outside source, such as the teacher or a glossary or dictionary.

Identification

Another goal of vocabulary instruction may be to help students identify and remember a myriad of important terms, such as people, events, and places in social studies, descriptions and labels in science, and mathematical procedures for solving problems. The feature of identification addresses this goal by emphasizing the need for students not only to make associations between their existing knowledge and the new concepts but also to have a personal way to hold on to the newly learned concepts. The feature of identification highlights visualization and mnemonic devices to help with recall and to reinforce learning.

A classic technique for helping students remember important terms is the well-researched instructional strategy, the key word method. This mnemonic technique has students creating images that they associate with the meaning of the word to remember the word. To teach the approach, the teacher first introduces the key word approach by providing examples of words whose meanings are difficult to remember. Next, the teacher asks students to think of familiar words or phrases that sound similar to the words or perhaps to make connections with word parts and word meanings. The teacher then directs students to use their newly created associations to remember the meanings of the words. Figure 18.2 contains several examples of the key word method.

Linguistic Attention

The last feature of content vocabulary instruction, linguistic attention, takes into account the wide-ranging effect that teaching common roots and affixes can have on vocabulary acquisition. Since approximately 60% of words have recognizable meaning units (Nagy & Anderson, 1984), it is important to include morphemic analysis instruction in all content-area classrooms. In

Word	Definition	Key word	Explanation	Image
fractals	shapes that are irregular or broken	fractured bone	Fractals are broken shapes—fractured bones are broken bones.	Broken bones of all different shapes
coplanar	points on the same plane	co-pilot	Coplanar refers to points on the same plane—co-pilots fly the same plane.	Two pilots flying a plane with a geometric plane below it
acute angle	angle whose degree measure is less than 90	a cute angel	Acute angles are small—and cute angels are small, too.	An little angel with a skirt drawn like an angle
hemisphere	each great circle separates a plane into two congruent parts called hemispheres	half-a-sphere	Hemi-sphere refers to half a sphere.	A circle cut into two pieces
obtuse angle	angle whose degree measure is greater than 90	moose angle	Obtuse angles are big—moose are big, too.	A moose with an angle drawn between his antlers

FIGURE 18.2. Keyword method: Geometry terms. From Harmon, Wood, and Hedrick (2006). Copyright 2006 by the National Middle School Association. Reprinted by permission.

addition, these units of meaning are not context specific; therefore, they can be applied to words across various disciplines. Furthermore, this feature works well with ELLs, because many cognates can be recognized through meaningful word parts.

An instructional tool for teaching word parts is the Word Family Tree (Buehl, 1999). This graphic organizer helps students connect key words to their origin and to other, related words. As can be seen in Figure 18.3, a Word Family Tree might look like a genealogical family tree. To create the Word Family Tree, students are provided with the target word and appropriate resources (dictionary, thesaurus, Internet, textbook, etc.). The form of the Word Family Tree may be provided, or students can make their own. The parts of the tree are the word, definition, pronunciation, memory clue, ancestor or root word, related words, words with a similar meaning, and three sentences using the word and the author of each sentence. Students can work in dyads to complete the tree. Then, students can share their tree with others, who may add to the information.

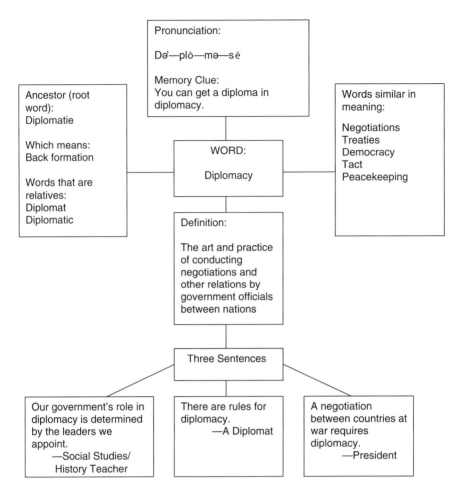

FIGURE 18.3. Word Family Tree.

Final Thoughts

Content-area teachers in middle and secondary school classrooms are professional educators, with expert knowledge about their particular field and knowledge of instructional practices for teaching the concepts in their domain. Vocabulary acquisition, as a critical aspect of all content-area learning, must also be a priority in content-area instruction. In this chapter we have emphasized the importance of content-area vocabulary, illustrated differences in the types of words found in various content areas, and highlighted several key understandings about effective vocabulary instructional practices. These key understandings, which can be easily embedded in the instructional practices of content-area teachers, call for explicit and implicit vocabulary instruction, multiple opportunities for meaningful engagement with words and concepts, close examination of how authors use words to explain concepts, time on task in classrooms, and development of metacognitive awareness in learning about concepts. Furthermore, the uniqueness of conceptually loaded terminology in the content areas also calls for different types of instruction to match the nature of the terms—as illustrated in the instructional features we described in this chapter. Such practices do not diminish content-area teaching; instead, they enrich student opportunities for developing the language of the discipline—a necessary attribute for understanding concepts.

QUESTIONS FOR DISCUSSION

1. Describe effective content vocabulary instruction.
2. How can teachers foster metacognitive awareness of vocabulary learning?
3. Design a lesson in which you implement instructional strategies that can help students build essential content vocabulary.
4. As a content-area teacher, describe how you would incorporate vocabulary instruction into classroom instructional time?

Resources

Further Reading

Beck, I. L., McKeown, M. G., & Kucan, L. (2002). *Bringing words to life: Robust vocabulary instruction.* New York: Guilford Press.

Graves, M. F. (2006). *The vocabulary book: Learning and instruction.* Newark, DE: International Reading Association.

Greenwood, S. (2002). Making words matter: Vocabulary study in the content areas. *Clearing House, 75*(5), 258–263.

Rupley, W. H., & Nichols, W. D. (2005). Vocabulary instruction for the struggling reader. *Reading and Writing Quarterly, 21,* 239–260.

Scott, J. A., Skobel, B. J., & Wells, J. (2008). *The word-conscious classroom: Building the vocabulary readers and writers need.* Mahwah, New York: Scholastic.

Stahl, S. A., & Nagy, W. E. (2006). *Teaching word meanings.* NJ: Erlbaum.

Wagner, R. K., Muse, A. E., & Tannenbaum K. R. (2006). *Vocabulary acquisition: Implications for reading comprehension.* New York: Guilford Press.

Websites

itcenter.clemson.edu/ceall/—Center of Excellence for Adolescent Literacy and Learning.

www.literacymatters.org/content/readandwrite/vocab.htm—Literacy Matters.

www.readwritethink.org—International Reading Association and the National Council of Teachers of English.

www.vocabulary.com; www.wordsmith.org/awad—Teaching resources.

www.flocabulary.com—Hip-Hop in the Classroom.

References

Anderson, R. C., Wilson, P. T., & Fielding, L. G. (1988). Growth in reading and how children spend their time outside of school. *Reading Research Quarterly, 23*, 285–303.

Baumann, J. F., Edwards, E. C., Boland, E. M., & Olejnik, S. (2003). Vocabulary tricks: Effects of instruction in morphology and context on fifth-grade students' ability to derive and infer word meanings. *American Educational Research Journal, 40*(2), 447–494.

Baumann, J. F., Kame'enui, E. J., & Ash, G. E. (2003). Research on vocabulary instruction: Voltaire redux. In D. J. Flood, D. Lapp, J. R. Squire, & J. M. Jensen (Eds.), *Handbook of research on teaching the English language arts* (2nd ed., pp. 752–785). Mahwah, NJ: Erlbaum.

Beck, I. L., & McKeown, M. G. (1983). Learning words well—a program to enhance vocabulary and comprehension. *Reading Teacher, 36*, 622–625.

Beck, I. L., McKeown, M. G., Hamilton, R. L., & Kucan, L. (1997). *Questioning the author: An approach for enhancing student engagement with text.* Newark, DE: International Reading Association.

Beck, I. L., McKeown, M. G., & Kucan, L. (2002). *Bringing words to life: Robust vocabulary instruction.* New York: Guilford Press.

Beck, I. L., Perfetti, C. A., & McKeown, M. G. (1982). Effects of long-term vocabulary instruction on lexical access and reading comprehension. *Journal of Educational Psychology, 74*, 506–521.

Blachowicz, C. L. Z., Fisher, P. J. L., Ogle, D., & Watts-Taffe, S. (2006). Vocabulary: Questions from the classroom. *Reading Research Quarterly, 41*(4), 524–539.

Borasi, R., Siegal, M., Fonzi, J., & Smith, C. F. (1998). Using transactional reading strategies to support sense-making and discussion in mathematics classrooms: An exploratory study. *Journal of Research in Mathematics Education, 29*(3), 275–305.

Buehl, D. (1999). *Word Family Tree.* Wisconsin Education Association Council News and Views. Retrieved April 2008, from *www.weac.org/news?1999-00/oct99/read.htm.*

Cardinale, L. A. (1991). *The facilitation of vocabulary acquisition by embedding explication in expository text.* Washington, DC: Educational Resources Information Center. (ERIC Document Reproduction Service No. ED 334978)

Carlisle, J. F., Fleming, J. E., & Gudbrandsen, B. (2000). Incidental word learning in science classes. *Contemporary Educational Psychology, 25*(2), 184–211.

Carney, J. J., Anderson, D., & Blackburn, C. (1984). Preteaching vocabulary and the comprehension of social studies materials by elementary school children. *Social Education, 48*, 195–196.

Copeland, M. (2005). *Socratic circles: Fostering critical and creative thinking in middle and high school.* Portland, ME: Stenhouse.

Duke, N. K., & Pearson, P. D. (2002). Effective practices for developing reading comprehension. In A. E. Farstrup & S. J. Samuels (Eds.), *What research has to say about reading instruction* (3rd ed., pp. 205–242). Newark, DE: International Reading Association.

Durkin, D. (1978–1979). What classroom observations reveal about reading comprehension instruction. *Reading Research Quarterly, 14*(4), 481–533.

Fang, Z. (2006). The language demands of science reading in middle school. *International Journal of Science Education, 28*(5), 491–520.

Gomez, K., & Madda, C. (2005). Vocabulary instruction for ELL Latino students in the middle school science classroom. *Voices from the Middle, 13*(1), 42–47.

Gordon, J., Schumm, J. S., Coffland, C., & Doucette, M. (1992). Effects of inconsiderate versus considerate text on elementary students' vocabulary learning. *Reading Psychology, 13*, 157–169.

Graves, M. F. (2000). A vocabulary program to complement and bolster a middle-grade comprehension program. In B. M. Taylor, M. F. Graves, & P. van den Broek (Eds.), *Reading for meaning: Fostering comprehension in the middle grades* (pp. 116–135). Newark, DE: International Reading Association.

Graves, M. F. (2006). *The vocabulary book: Learning and instruction.* Newark, DE: International Reading Association.

Graves, M. F., Juel, C., & Graves, B. B. (2004). *Teaching reading in the 21st century* (3rd ed.). Boston: Pearson Education.

Grubaugh, S. J., & Metzer, D. J. (1986). Increasing comprehension. *Social Education, 50*, 543–544.

Gullatt, D. E. (1987). How to help students in reading mathematics. *Education Digest, 52*(5), 40.

Harmon, J. M., Wood, K. D., & Hedrick, W. B. (2006). *Instructional strategies for teaching vocabulary in the content areas.* Columbus, OH: National Middle School Association.

Harmon, J. M., Wood, K. D., & Hedrick, W. B. (2008). Vocabulary instruction in middle and secondary content classrooms: Understandings and direction from research. In A. E. Farstrup & S. J. Samuels (Eds.), *What research has to say about vocabulary instruction.* Newark, DE: International Reading Association.

Hedrick, W. B., Harmon, J. M., & Linerode, P. M. (2004). Teachers' beliefs and practices of vocabulary instruction with social studies textbooks. *Reading Horizons, 45*(2), 103–125.

Itza-Ortiz, S. F., Robello, N. S., & Zollman, D. A. (2003, March). *The vocabulary of physics and its impact on student learning.* Paper presented at the National Association for Research in Science Teaching, Philadelphia, PA.

Jetton, T. L., & Alexander, P. A. (2004). Domains, teaching, and literacy. In T. L. Jetton & J. A. Dole (Eds.), *Adolescent literacy research and practice* (pp. 15–39). New York: Guilford Press.

King Sears, M. E., Mercer, C. D., & Sindelar, P. T. (1992). Toward independence with keyword mnemonics: A strategy for science vocabulary instruction. *Remedial and Special Education, 13*(5), 22–33.

Konopak, B. C. (1988). Eighth graders' vocabulary learning from inconsiderate to considerate text. *Reading Research and Instruction, 27*(4), 1–14.

Konopak, B. C., & Williams, N. L. (1994). Elementary teachers' beliefs and decisions about vocabulary learning and instruction. In C. K. Kinzer & D. J. Leu (Eds.), *43rd Yearbook of the National Reading Conference* (pp. 485–495). Chicago, IL: National Reading Conference.

Krussel, L. (1998). Teaching the language of mathematics. *Mathematics Teacher, 91*(5), 436–441.

Lloyd, C. V., & Contreras, N. J. (1985). *The role of experience in learning science vocabulary.* Paper presented at the 35th Annual Meeting of the National Reading Conference, San Diego, CA.

MacGregor, M., & Price, E. (1999). An exploration of aspects of language proficiency and algebra learning. *Journal of Research in Mathematics Education, 30*(4), 449–467.

Marco, M. J., & Luzon, M. J. (1999). Procedural vocabulary: Lexical signaling of conceptual relations in discourse. *Applied Linguistics, 20*(1), 1–21.

McKeown, M. G. (1985). The acquisition of word meaning from context by children of high and low ability. *Reading Research Quarterly, 20,* 482–496.

McKeown, M. G., Beck, I. L., Omanson, R. C., & Perfetti, C. A. (1983). The effects of long-term vocabulary instruction on reading comprehension: A replication. *Journal of Reading Behavior, 15,* 3–18.

McKeown, M. G., Beck, I. L., Omanson, R. C., & Pople, M. T. (1985). Some effects of the nature and frequency of vocabulary instruction on the knowledge and use of words. *Reading Research Quarterly, 20,* 522–535.

McLaughlin, M., & DeVoogd, G. L. (2004). *Critical literacy: Enhancing students' comprehension of text.* New York: Scholastic.

Miller, J. S. (2005). The language of science in daily conversation. *Science Activities, 42*(2), 3–4.

Miller, L. D. (1993). Making the connection with language. *Arithmetic Teacher, 40*(6), 311–316.

Milligan, J. L., & Ruff, T. P. (1990). A linguistic approach to social studies vocabulary development. *Social Studies, 81,* 218–220.

Monroe, E. E. (1997). Effects of mathematical vocabulary instruction on fourth grade students. *Reading Improvement, 34,* 120–132.

Monroe, E. E., & Panchyshyn, R. (1995). Vocabulary considerations for teaching mathematics. *Childhood Education, 72*(2), 80–83.

Nagy, W. E. (1988). *Teaching vocabulary to improve reading comprehension.* Newark, DE: International Reading Association.

Nagy, W. E., & Anderson, R. C. (1984). How many words are in printed school English? *Reading Research Quarterly, 19,* 304–330.

Nagy, W. E., & Herman, P. A. (1987). Breadth and depth of vocabulary knowledge: Implications for acquisition and instruction. In M. G. McKeown & M. E. Curtis (Eds.), *The nature of vocabulary acquisition* (pp. 19–35). Hillsdale, NJ: Erlbaum.

National Reading Panel. (2000). *Report of the National Reading Panel: Teaching children to read: An evidence-based assessment of the scientific research literature on reading and its implications for reading instruction.* Retrieved January 20, 2007, from *www.nichd.nih.gov/publications/nrp/smallbook.htm.*

RAND Reading Study Group. (2002). *Reading for understanding: Toward an R&D program in reading comprehension.* Retrieved March 31, 2008, from *rand.org/pubs/monograph_reports/mr1465/mr1465.pdf.*

Robinson, P. J. (2005). Teaching key vocabulary in geography and science classrooms: An analysis of teachers' practice with particular reference to EAL pupils' learning. *Language and Education, 19*(5), 428–445.

Rubenstein, R. N. (2000). Word origins: Building communication connections. *Mathematics Teaching in the Middle School, 5*(8), 493–498.

Schatz, E. K., & Baldwin, R. S. (1986). Context clues are unreliable predictors of word meanings. *Reading Research Quarterly, 21,* 439–453.

Scott, J. A., Jamieson-Noel, D., & Asselin, M. (2003). Vocabulary instruction throughout the day in twenty-three Canadian upper-elementary classrooms. *Elementary School Journal, 103*(3), 269–286.

Scott, J. A., & Nagy, W. E. (2004). Developing word consciousness. In J. F. Baumann

& E. J. Kame'enui (Eds.), *Vocabulary instruction: Research to practice* (pp. 201–217). New York: Guilford Press.

Short, D. (1995, February). *The academic language of social studies: A bridge to an all-English classroom.* Paper presented at the National Association for Bilingual Education, Phoenix, AZ.

Snouffer, N. K., & Thistlethwaite, L. L. (1979, November). *The effects of the structured overview and vocabulary pre-teaching upon comprehension levels of college freshmen reading physical science and history materials.* Paper presented at the National Reading Conference, San Antonio, TX.

Stahl, S. A. (1999). *Vocabulary development.* Cambridge, MA: Brookline Books.

Stahl, S. A., & Clark, C. H. (1987). The effects of participatory expectations in classroom discussion on the learning of science vocabulary. *American Educational Research Journal, 24*(4), 541–555.

Stahl, S. A., & Kapinus, B. A. (1991). Possible sentences: Predicting word meanings to teach content area vocabulary. *Reading Teacher, 45*(1), 36–43.

Sternberg, R. J. (1987). Most vocabulary is learned in context. In M. G. McKeown & M. E. Curtis (Eds.), *The nature of vocabulary acquisition* (pp. 89–105). Hillsdale, NJ: Erlbaum.

Steele, D. F. (1999). Learning mathematical language in the zone of proximal development. *Teaching Children Mathematics, 6*(1), 38–42.

Swanborn, M. S. L., & de Glopper, K. (1999). Incidental word learning while reading: A meta-analysis. *Review of Educational Research, 69*(3), 261–285.

Thompson, D. R., & Rubenstein, R. N. (2000). Learning mathematics vocabulary: Potential pitfalls and instructional strategies. *Mathematics Teacher, 93*(7), 568–574.

Tracy, D. M. (1994). Using mathematical language to enhance mathematical conceptualization. *Childhood Education, 70*(4), 221–224.

Vacca, R. L. (2002). Making a difference in adolescents' school lives: Visible and invisible aspects of content area reading. In A. E. Farstrup & S. J. Samuels (Eds.), *What research has to say about reading instruction* (3rd ed., pp. 184–204). Newark, DE: International Reading Association.

Vacca, R. T., & Vacca, J. L. (2008). *Content area reading: Literacy and learning across the curriculum* (9th ed.). Boston: Pearson Education.

Vygotsky, L. S. (1994). *Thought and language.* Cambridge, MA: MIT Press.

Watts, S. (1995). Vocabulary instruction during reading lessons in six classrooms. *Journal of Reading Behavior, 27*(3), 399–424.

Wood, K. D., Vintinner, J. P., Hill-Miller, P., Harmon, J. M., & Hedrick, W. B. (2006, November–December). *What middle school teachers want to know about vocabulary instruction and what the professional literature is telling them.* Paper presented at the National Reading Conference Annual Convention, Los Angeles, CA.

Chapter 19

Discussion-Based Instruction in the Middle and Secondary School Classroom

Thomas DeVere Wolsey
Diane Lapp

GUIDING QUESTIONS

1. Why is it important to design instructional experiences that support authentic oral language development for every student?
2. Why is time for oral language development/conversation needed in school?
3. What promising instructional practices support classroom discussion for high school and middle school students?

Have you ever been in a conversation where you were asked questions like, "What did you think about …?," "What caused you to think … ?," "Did you notice …?" When this happens, you know that you're engaged in a good conversation; one with an interchange that causes you to question, to evaluate, and to extend your thinking. Designing instruction that provides opportunity for conversations within classrooms is the goal of most secondary teachers, and providing examples of such instruction is the primary focus of this chapter. To accomplish this, we address the guiding questions listed earlier.

Why Is It Important to Design Instructional Experiences That Support Authentic Oral Language Development for Every Student?

Before introducing examples of best practices designed to support oral language development in the secondary school classroom, we should first establish the significance of oral language as the base for other learning within the classroom and also throughout one's life experiences. To do so, we begin with the following quote, which, we think, illustrates the importance of ensuring that all students are supported through instruction as they learn to present their oral ideas fluently.

> If there is a full rich literacy for everyone, we can discover what literacy is good for. It's what people do with their reading and writing that is important. Language makes so many things possible. (Margaret Meek, Emeritus Professor of Education at the Institute of Education, Literacy Changes Lives, 1996)

This quote becomes reality through nonthreatening listening and speaking classroom interchanges that offer the foundation for all other literacy development (Loban, 1963; Menyuk, 1984; Nichols, 2006). One becomes better able to convey ideas orally when involved in conversational exchanges that support practice, self-evaluation, and self-modification. Therefore, participation in conversational exchanges is very important for students throughout the grades (Pinnell & Jaggar, 2003). A significant feature is that these experiences should be designed to support and to build on the home languages that students bring to school (Au, 1993; Ball & Farr, 2003; Edwards, 2007).

Although classrooms comprise students who have had a wide array of language experiences (Ball, 2002; Taylor & Doresey-Gaines, 1988; Weber, 1991) including native English speakers whose home registers may differ from their peers' (Baugh, 2000; Taylor & Doresey-Gaines, 1988) and English language learners (ELLs) who speak languages other than English (Allen, 1991; Gonzales, Moll, & Amanti, 2005), all must be provided opportunities for language expansion through classroom experience that acknowledges they come to school with language that must be added to, not erased. This belief in diversity of experience as the foundation for language development becomes reality through classroom practice that helps students to understand that audience matters, and that the words, tone, and messages they wish to share must appropriately share the target message with the target audience. More specifically through classroom practice

> People who say *cuz, watchamacalit, jeet,* and *gonna* must learn to recognize their counterparts in written language as *because, what you may call it, did you eat, and going to.* The oral forms are not sloppy renditions of the written forms, they are different forms representing the same meanings. *Each reader must learn the set*

> *of relationships that exists between his or her oral language and its written counter-parts: the phonics of language.* The relationships are not the same for all speakers because of differences in dialects, as well as idiosyncratic differences. (Good-man, Watson, & Burke, 1996, p. 11; bold and italic emphasis in original)

As this quote suggests, one's oral language provides the foundation on which additional language and literacy skills can be built. A person's language illustrates the development and organization of his or her thinking (Berry, 1985; Lee, 2005; Lyle, 1993) and provides the means to acquire, as well as to share, ideas (Lee, 2006; Lemke, 1989).

Why Is Time for Oral Language Development/Conversation Needed in School?

Conversation and discussion promote independent and deep thinking, and are at the same time social activities. When students are engaged in discussion, the learning that occurs can increase in exponential ways because of the interchanges with peers and teachers. As a result, participants can carefully shape the discussion through responses and additional contributions that invite others to react and question. Paying attention in conversation to the contributions of others is very important and should begin at an early age. For example, Clark (2007) found that young children acquire new words in conversation with adults by first noticing, then repeating, the words, usually in the very next speech turn. The context of the conversation permits participants to build concepts by viewing specific objects or pictures, or by questioning one another about intended meanings and purposes. Through repetition and acknowledgment of a new word, the child maps the concept and begins to assign meaning to it. This language expansion through conversation is not limited to young children. Greenman (2004) proposed that even doctoral students improve their performance with academic English in environments that provide substantial context for production of the target language and information. This supports our belief that conversation is a very appropriate activity for the secondary classroom, in which one of the major goals is to support students as they develop their use of content and academic language registers.

In school, language production is critical to successful acquisition of the academic register; in other words, simply hearing or reading about science or social studies is not sufficient for students, who must be able to retrieve from long-term memory the concepts, and the relations among concepts, needed to make sense of the discipline. Opportunities for language production often occur through discussion. In the following sections, we examine an ineffective classroom discussion or discourse pattern, then turn our attention to a rationale and to best practices for increasing discussion as a means to support academic language development.

What Promising Instructional Practices Support Classroom Discussion for High School and Middle School Students?

Lessons prepared by teachers are frequently characterized by the instructional objectives and standards by which achievement is measured; at the same time, teachers design their lessons to promote good thinking about and through content. The result may be a dichotomy that leaves students and teachers struggling to establish the purposes and outcomes of authentic discussion. Consider the teacher who must help students understand the ethical dilemmas of genetics research and at the same time is charged with the task, via a set of educational standards, to teach students about genetic variation. Discussion, in general, flows when the participants take the lead and the teacher does not attempt to control the outcome. The life science teacher who attempts to impose direction on a discussion of genetic variation will be frustrated as students explore the topics of interest to them, or the students in that life science course may find that, if they are to succeed, they must replicate the discourse in lectures or in the textbook.

Good teachers since the time of Socrates have employed discussion as a means of helping students learn. We have found that when teachers clearly communicate expectations about identified outcomes, classroom discussions are more focused. And teachers and students from Socrates' time to the present have grappled with the best means to promote learning through discussion. As the populations of schools have become more diverse, so have the languages spoken at home by these students. This sociocultural dimension has highlighted the need to make classroom discourse an additive rather than a subtractive feature of these home languages. In the following sections, we examine an ineffective classroom discussion or discourse pattern, then turn our attention to a rationale for increasing discussion and designing suitable purposes for doing so.

Discussion in the Classroom: A Non-Example

Teachers often think of classroom discussion in terms of dialogue; that is, everyone in the class has an opportunity to say something. Although this generalization is useful to a point, researchers describe a discourse pattern called initiate (or input)–respond–evaluate, or IRE, in which a teacher initiates a verbal exchange by posing a question or making a statement that calls for a response (Cazden, 2001; Mehan, 1979). When a student responds, the teacher evaluates the response for correctness. The pattern is so prevalent that most teachers who think they are having a discussion are actually engaged in a recitation model (*recitation* refers to the notion that students are reciting what they have learned in response to the teacher's query). When a teacher has a set of correct answers in mind, the questions posed are often only a prompt for students to guess or to predict what the teacher is thinking. Questions to which the teacher knows the answer, and the students may not, have been characterized as *pseudoquestions* (cf. Green, 1983; Mehan, 1979), because the purpose is to quiz or to assess students rather to obtain new information or to initiate and engage them in conversation. Tharp and Gallimore (1989) found that this model existed in schools at the beginning of the 20th century and persisted to the time that they wrote. In many of the classrooms we observe, this type of interaction is still seen often. When this occurs, student responses are short, reinforcing the primacy of the teacher in the interaction and enforcing classroom management (Alvermann & Hayes, 1989). Discourse such as the IRE pattern legitimizes the power relationship, with teacher as authority figure, even though the teacher may be unaware that this is the effect of the recitation model (Fairclough, 2001). Notice that the teacher's right to preempt a student in the following example is unquestioned:

> TEACHER: What is the phase in mitosis after interphase?
>
> STUDENT: I think the phase is preprophase, but, um, I was thinking ...
>
> TEACHER: It is in some cases. Who can tell the class what Jamie is missing?

A discussion with the teacher at the head of a room full of students in neat rows facing the teacher's lectern reinforces the power relationship, too. Twenty-five years ago John Goodlad (1984) found the same arrangement of desks in rows in many of the classrooms he studied. In observational data of high school classrooms, 25.3% of the activities in the classrooms were lectures. Discussion was only observed 5.1% of the time, and was seventh on the list of classroom activities that Goodlad observed. It was also the first activity listed in which student talk was explicitly included in the observed activity (p. 107). Because teachers often replicate the pattern of instruction that is most familiar to them from their own days as students, it is difficult to change the habits that reinforce the recitation model. Whereas recitation serves as an assessment tool (whether the student read the text, etc.) of the individual student (Hollander, 2002), discussion serves as a tool to construct and negotiate understanding with peers and with the teacher, and offers teachers insights about the additional topical information that should be shared with students continually to scaffold their learning and language development.

Supporting Classroom Discussion: A Positive Example

Classroom discussion can be a form of inquiry. Teachers who want students to construct an understanding of a topic through discussion may face difficulty, because discussion takes time. When pacing and sequence guides insist that students proceed through a curriculum within short time frames, teachers may become frustrated, and pseudodiscussion techniques may replace authentic discussion. There are no simple answers, as readers of this chapter know, for how best to address time spent on any given activity. Decisions about how much time to spend are often dictated by how much autonomy teachers are given, local and state curricular decisions, and so on. However, when teachers make decisions about instructional activities, such as discussion, in relation to the purpose of the activities and the need for their students to understand topics and concepts, we can see that classroom discussion is an important part of learning about content.

Ferguson and Young (1996) found that dialogue improvisations, in which students extended the dialogue of a story at the conclusion of the written narrative, helped ELLs increase proficiency in English. Grainger (1999) discovered that students use prosodic features of oral language to capture emotionally significant events, to experiment with language, and to express aspects of the cultural world they inhabit through conversation. Discussion has been correlated with high performance on literacy assessments. Applebee, Langer, Nystrand, and Gamoran (2003) found that discussion-based approaches with high academic demands result in improved performance on literacy measures for both high-achieving and low-achieving students. Applebee et al. also provide a useful definition of *"open discussion"*: *"free exchange of information* [our emphasis] among students and/or between at least three participants that lasts longer than 30 seconds. The three participants may include the teacher, although the teacher may be deliberately silent during some discussions" (p. 700). For discussion to be effective, students must be free to explore aspects of the target concept while listening to peers and building mental models of the target concept.

Discussion as Inquiry

Discussion is inquiry, and inquiry takes time. A primary reason for this is that inquiry starts from a position of uncertainty. When the answers are known, there is little need for discussion. In discussion, students become intellectual explorers with questions whose answers they do not know, and that might take them to terrain they had not realized existed. Defining the terrain and the essential nature of the questions takes time, but if students are to think in ways that result in better understanding of the topic and the important attributes of the object of inquiry, the time spent is often worth the investment. To make discussion a part of your lesson plan, we suggest that you determine the purposes for the activity in advance:

1. What background knowledge do students have about the topic? How should the instruction be tiered to support differences?

2. To what knowledge might students need to be exposed before they can engage in meaningful discussion about the topic?

3. What discussion skills might students need to develop to participate in an effective discussion?

4. Will discussion help to promote learning and inquiry about this topic? Are multiple constructions of knowledge possible?

What Are the Processes and Elements
of Classroom Discussion?

Two questions that teachers consider when planning for discussion have to do with what students know and what they need to know for a discussion to proceed. The background knowledge that students bring to the discussion shapes the outcome and may help teachers plan instruction that supports the discussion. In many cases, teachers use texts to help support or inform the discussion. In other cases, discussion is a means of developing the questions that students may want to explore through follow-up reading and research. In most cases, discussion is also a means to shape thinking. This occurs as participants express their thoughts and listen attentively to other participants in the discussion. All these processes draw on the brain's capacity to store and retrieve concepts as well as to hold conceptualizations and change them as new information is encountered.

Useful approaches to reading texts include the directed reading activity (DRA; Betts, 1946) and the structured reading lesson (SRL; Ryder & Graves, 2003). These approaches suggest that reading be situated within a framework of activities that builds or activates background knowledge and sets purposes in advance of reading, activities that promote critical thinking while reading, and activities that follow up or extend concepts learned as a result of reading. We suggest that discussion is a useful tool during all phases of reading, because it provides for students an opportunity to hear what they think about a topic, or as Forster (1927) suggested long ago in his famous quote, "How can I tell what I think till I see what I say?" The clarity of one's ideas may occur while speaking. Therefore, good instruction should provide time for this conversational chatting, while being sensitive to what students already know, and what they need to know, if the discussion is to be engaging and supported by productive reading activities.

An example may be helpful here. Often students hold misconceptions about science topics; for example, students, and some adults, believe that the Earth's seasons are a result of the distance between the Earth and sun rather than the alignment of the Earth on its axis (e. g., Henriques, 2000). A teacher who wishes to teach students about the seasons may use discussion as a way to uncover students' misconceptions about the nature of Earth's movements in space to provide a purpose for reading a textbook on the topic or watching a video. During a discussion, students can be asked what they believe (prior knowledge) about the identified topic. During this conversational chat students can clarify, expand, practice, and refine their developing conceptions as they interact with their peers and the teacher, who may offer other information. In this way, discussion is a preparation for the reading activity. After reading a text that explores complex ideas, students might discuss the new information they acquire from viewing videos and reading. This supports students' attempts to refine their earlier thinking.

After students read, discussion can help them situate their understanding of the text with that of others, further deepening what they have learned. For example, when students in an English class read *The Old Man and the Sea* (Hemingway, 1952), discussion after reading helped them to identify and to share the connections they made to their own experiences, and to notice patterns shared with other texts they had read. Students also built their notions of the story's theme as each contributed and listened to the ideas that others contributed. Notice how their discussion was scaffolded by what they read and the responses of their peers:

TEACHER: So, you're thinking that …

STUDENT A: Well, that Santiago [the story's protagonist] is a bit like Superman, who goes to a lonely place to learn about himself in his fortress of solitude. See, yeah, just like Santiago, who has to go to sea by himself and learn what he can do by pushing himself. Hemingway has Santiago say, "I am sorry that I went too far out" (p. 115).

STUDENT B: Yeah, like Superman, but Hemingway has a lot of religious images, too. He has Santiago battle the bad things that happen in life, the sharks, you know? And when Santiago is so tired after reaching the land, he falls over with the mast on his shoulder. The picture reminds me of the Bible where Jesus is walking to Calvary … a thing he had to do alone.

What Qualifies as Participation in the Discussion?

If we agree that authentic discussion is pedagogically useful, some exploration of what qualifies as participation in a discussion is required as well. Moguel (2004) studied his college classrooms and found that students in his teacher education courses fell into two categories: passive participants and active participants. *Passive participants* felt that there should be no pressure to speak, and that facilitators for discussions should take a primary role in moving the discussion along. *Active participants* talked over their peers, or spoke so often that peers' opportunities for interaction were limited. Moguel suggested that teacher preparation should include good models of classroom discourse and that teacher-candidates should be told why the models are important. We add that active participation must not include behaviors that shut down the participation of others.

Several approaches have been advocated for encouraging productive participation. Some teachers award points for participation; usually, this is simply a tally sheet of the number of times a person speaks. Welty (1989) and Nichols (2006) caution that such grading schemes may seem necessary, but they come with a cost. Assigning a point value to participation is an ill-defined venture at best. How does one rate the short but well-thought out response of a student who contributed just one very insightful comment but listened carefully to everything? What value should be attached to the person who talks a lot but contributes little? Is there participatory value in listening? How would a teacher know whether good listening occurred or did not occur? According to Kohn (1993), rewards, such as points toward a grade, are unlikely to produce the desired effect of increased participation. Indeed, if Kohn is correct, and we believe he is, points only serve to reduce risk-taking behavior, and to increase attention to surface features of discussions and the likelihood that students compete with their peers to utter more words, even if what they contribute is of lesser value. Hollander (2002) points out that when students must compete to speak, the purpose of a collaborative and constructive classroom environment is made moot.

Another consideration revolves around who will have the floor and for how long. If the teacher acts as moderator, a potential danger is that an authentic discussion will quickly devolve to the default recitation mode (Cazden, 2001), with the teacher as the center of attention. Cold calling on students is characteristic of the recitation model. John Holt (1982) employs a metaphor for describing how students feel when called on to respond to a question. Asking such a question is like shining a flashlight on the student, he asserts. The teacher's attention is on that student, requiring that he or she perform. More important, the remainder of the students know that, at least for now, they are in the dark, where the teacher cannot see them—no thinking required. An alternative is cool calling, in which the teacher asks a question of a particular student but provides wait time to give the student an opportunity to think through a possible answer. We make use of cool calling in our own teaching by further extending the time from question to response. Because some students are very shy or unsure of their command of the curriculum, we often meet the student at the door and mention that we will be asking a particular question later in the class. The advance notice provides time for the student contributor to look up facts, think about possible responses, and even write notes. If it appears that this is causing too much pressure for students, we first have them share their ideas with a partner, before sharing it with the whole class. Welty (1989) suggests that another student can be primed to serve as a "backstop" to elaborate or to build on what the first student contributed. Because participants often look for others to note what they've said and elaborate further, the backstop technique can further bolster the participation of reluctant students. A graphic organizer, completed by the instructor to track the shape and scope of the discussion, is a useful means to help students think about the topic under consideration. Honoring students' contributions by writing their key points on the board is another way to encourage reluctant students to participate vocally more often (Welty, 1989).

Finally, if we think of discussion as a collective endeavor to understand a concept or to solve a problem, we can begin to move away from the notion that those who don't talk much are not participating or are unprepared. Perhaps we can rely on volunteers to build the conversations we want to encourage. Because some students don't talk enough, others talk too much, and still others don't pay attention at all, we may attribute this dynamic to students who have grown accustomed to the recitation model. Cohen (1986, 1994) suggested that group norms could promote effective interactions in collaborative group work. These norms might include making sure everyone in the group understands the task, keeping everyone on task, and having students assist each other with the task. Cohen's insights about group tasks inform classroom discussions in at least two ways.

Group Configuration

First, the problem of participation in whole-class discussion means that large numbers of students who may want to contribute are unable to do so because of limited amounts of time. Small-group discussion helps put the odds of participating with limited time in favor of the small-group participants. One stands a much better chance of participating if there are just four other people in the group, rather than 30 others in the whole class. This also alleviates the pressure of having to speak publicly for ELLs who do not feel quite ready to address the whole class. They can try on the language and build security through these smaller group interactions. As they gain confidence in their new language production, they become more ready and able to speak to a larger group. As teachers interact with these smaller groups, they can more fully differentiate the sharing of difficult concepts (Raphael, Brock, & Wallace, 1996). Second, norms for participation are more easily implemented in small groups. In small groups, the discussion management strategies needed for whole groups tend to fade into the background. For example, in small groups, there is less need for students to raise their hands and wait to be recognized. The students themselves monitor the discussion behaviors that permit the group to work together and accomplish the task. Figure 19.1 is an easy-to-use tool that enables group members to reflect on their discussion practices.

Participatory Practices

Whether discussion occurs in small groups or with a whole class, norms or participatory practices (which are not rules) help students understand how best to learn through discussion. Some norms, such as listening carefully and contributing one's ideas, are somewhat obvious. Others take some practice. In planning a discussion, teachers might also think about the norms to be taught or reinforced. For example, how does one respectfully challenge a classmate's ideas? What rhetorical devices might a student use to add to or elaborate on an idea introduced by someone else? How can students learn to keep discussions focused? What ways can peers encourage others to participate? Each of these ideas presented as questions can be phrased as a rule (Keep the

The discussion (yes = 3; almost = 2; no = 1)			The group (yes = 3; almost = 2; no = 1)
• Each person understood the concept.			• Everyone participated.
• We used our time productively.			• We are pleased with the discussion outcome.
• We built on each other's ideas.			• We are ready for the next discussion.
Task total			Group total
Job + Group =			

FIGURE 19.1. Goal 18 discussion evaluation. Adapted from Lapp, Fisher, and Wolsey (2009). Copyright 2009 by The Guilford Press. Adapted by permission.

discussion focused!), but norms are a bit more flexible and take the learning context into account in ways that rules cannot. Norms suggested by Cohen (1986) include ideas such as "everyone helps" and "everyone asks for help." We suggest that it is worthwhile to teach students how to be good discussion participants. Perhaps the best way to do that is to conduct a discussion about discussions. By modeling norms for group participation and providing tools for reflection on how well the group's discussion went (e.g., see Figure 19.1), students slowly begin to accept the norms, and discussions become increasingly productive. Discussion skills may be taught, learned, and inferred.

Think–Pair–Share

Sometimes whole-class discussion is warranted. In these situations, there are some techniques that teachers can use to increase participation and improve the effectiveness of the discussion. To help students be prepared with something to say, many teachers have students write a brief journal entry about the topic before discussion begins. Doing so gives students an opportunity to think through what they already know and to compose potential responses for starting a discussion. To increase participation and thinking about the topic, another tool, described by Kagan (1994), permits students to explore a concept in small groups or dyads before contributing to the whole-class discussion. In the think–pair–share structure, the teacher or discussion leader(s) poses a problem, provides some time for students to think individually, then asks students to share their thoughts with a neighbor and, finally, with the whole class. In this way, discussion participants are not put on the spot in front of the whole class, without an opportunity to think individually and compare their thinking with a partner. Whole-class discussions then build on the combined contributions of each pair.

Sensitivity to English Language Learners

English language learners (ELLs) may employ communication strategies that teachers may also want to notice in discussion. Arias (2008) reviews eight of these. In *approximation*, students may use a similar sounding word for the intended word (*illusion* for *allusion*). *Word coinage* occurs when the phrase or word commonly used is not in the student's lexicon (*lunch place* instead of *lunch room* or *cafeteria*). Another strategy, *circumlocution*, is to talk around the word when the concept is known but the word is not ("I'm taking, you know, a yellow car with a light on top, to go downtown, today" for *taxi*.). Literal translation of some words or idioms can confuse students who don't understand why something that "costs a pretty penny" is very expensive. When the word is known in the first language but not the second, students may *code-switch*; that is, use a word from the first language in place of English ("I've got to buy new *camisas* before school starts"). Three other strategies are to avoid or change the topic of discussion, to give up the topic completely, or to mime the intended meaning. Wise and sensitive teachers know how and when to assist the ELL to improve performance in English and honor the language the student brings to the classroom.

Classroom Arrangement

Furniture arrangement in the classroom needs to support conversation. In small groups, students often sit at tables or turn their desks to face one another to facilitate interaction. As we mentioned earlier in this chapter, row-by-row arrangement, with students facing the teacher, inhibits student-to-student interaction. At the same time, it makes the teacher the center of authority and knowledge—an undesirable effect, if students are to learn to think critically as members of a class and on their own. This effect may be minimized if students are seated in a horseshoe shape or in a circle. Another effective seating arrangement is the fishbowl, in which students sit in two concentric circles. The inner circle comprises the discussion participants, whereas members of the outer circle observe the process and comment on it after the discussion. Later, the students switch from inner circle to outer circle, and vice versa.

Student Status

One problem to which teachers must attend, whether the discussion involves the whole class or small groups, is students' status as members of the class. Cohen (1994) describes *status* as an agreed-on rank order within a class or group. The rank may be based on perceptions that students, and sometimes the teacher, hold about academic ability, socioeconomic status, gender, race, and language ability. Students who are perceived as low in status are less likely to participate in discussions, and students high in status are less likely to attend to the contributions of low-status peers. Students may perceive status based on gender, socioeconomic factors, race, culture, and so on. Note that low status has little, if anything, to do with actual ability or quality of low-status students' contributions. Students perceived to be of low status are often silenced or systematically excluded from discussions. One solution to this problem has traditionally been the assignment of roles, in which each student serves as a facilitator, for example. Another solution is the establishment of norms or participatory behaviors, discussed earlier, that promote the notion that everyone should participate (Cohen, 1986). Teachers might improve a student's status by recognizing his or her contribution to the discussion, or by making a low-status student a group expert on a specific topic.

Grading and Discussions

We have explored the problems with assigning points for actual discussion contributions, but the problem that often remains is to encourage students to participate and to transform discussion into learning that they retain. Norms and seating arrangements that encourage discussion also encourage participation, of course. If grades or scores must be assigned, students might be asked to complete a journal entry summarizing the discussion, or predicting the topics for the next day's discussion. We suggest providing a rubric or scoring criteria in advance. In addition to the content of the discussion, students can write about their own contributions to the discussion. They might write about the discussion tools they used to build on or to disagree with a peer, for instance. Following Fisher and Frey's (2004) ideas for journal entries, students can also write about discussions held in class that day as an admission slip for entry to class the next day, as an exit slip to leave the class on that day, or as part of an ongoing reflective journal. These ideas provide an opportunity for students to transform their thinking and promote the norm of participation, without actually intruding on the discussion itself.

Using Texts

Discussion and texts share a complicated relationship in the classroom. Often, a text of some type is introduced to students, and discussion of the concepts raised in that text follows. Before going further, a brief explanation of the term *text* is in order. A text can be a textbook, of course, but other texts are also useful, including an archived photograph from a newspaper (see, e.g., the Calisphere project at *www.calisphere.universityofcalifornia.edu*), a video clip from the news, an article downloaded from the Internet, or a poem from an anthology. Typically, a text is a result of media production and often is produced by someone outside the classroom. Discussion can result in close reading of texts and the contexts in which they were produced. More important, discussion of texts may result in good questions for further discussion. Discussion not only promotes thinking about texts but it also promotes thinking beyond the text in significant ways. Alvermann, Dillon, O'Brien, and Smith (1985) studied how teachers use textbooks in class discussions and developed a checklist to help teachers think about the purposes or motives for using textbooks in discussion. Indeed, Nuthall (2005) described how he came to understand that students need more than a single presentation of material (i.e., a teacher explains something and expects students to understand based on a single presentation). The conversational interaction helped students to revisit and clarify representations about which their understanding was imperfect. Alvermann and her colleagues (1985) suggest that no single purpose is best. If teachers ask students to rely solely on the textbook, for example, students come to believe that the book is the only source of information. Instead, teachers might demonstrate how the textbook fits a range of purposes, through use of the checklist. Some of these purposes also inform how other texts besides textbooks might be used.

In a study of fourth-grade students' use of collaborative reasoning, Anderson et al. (2001) found that students used 13 different argumentation stratagems, or the tactics of six different forms, which we've noted in Figure 19.2. When any of the stratagems appeared in discussion, the use of the technique snowballed. As these researchers noted, once an argument stratagem emerges in a discussion, it tends to spread to other children and to occur with increasing frequency (Anderson et al., 2001, p. 41). The stratagems identified in this study may usefully inform what teachers may model or expect for

Managing participation of classmates	• What do you think, John? • Now, let's hear what Samantha thinks.
Positioning in relation to a classmate's argument	• I agree/disagree with Sabrina because. . . . • I've got something [an idea] for you, Tamika. • Yes/no, but [counterargument]. . . .
Acknowledging uncertainty	• Probably/might/maybe [counterargument hedging the argument through conditional terms]. • I am confused because. . . .
Extending the story world	• What if . . . [a scenario] . . . ? • Placing the self in the story: "I would still. . . ." • Placing classmate in the story: "If you were. . . ."
Making arguments explicit	• I think [proposition] because [reason given]. • Valid inference: If [action], then [consequence], so [new action].
Using story evidence	• In the story, it said [cites evidence].

FIGURE 19.2. Stratagems.

discussions in their classrooms. The argument stratagems can be applied to both nonfiction texts and fiction narratives, but the researchers found that students may be more likely to use stratagems that occur in student-directed rather than teacher-directed discussions. Moreover, students were more disposed to employ a stratagem that had previously been directed to them personally.

Promising Discussion Practices

Some tools may help the teacher plan for and promote effective discussions in middle and secondary classrooms. Good questions are required tools. In addition, in this section we describe the instructional conversation, the Socratic seminar, and discussions in electronic environments. We introduce a tool, called the *interactive schema board*, that promotes discussion over a period of time.

Questions

If recitation models start with questions to which teachers already know the answers, what role should questions have in effective discussion? In a discussion model called *shared inquiry* (cf. Wheelock, 1999), teachers pose questions for which they don't have a preconceived answer, encouraging students to explore together the texts they read. Welty (1989) suggests that teachers prepare questions in advance that encourage students to avoid the recitation mind-set, with the correct answer known by the teacher. The teacher prepares questions for the beginning of the discussion, the transitions, and the closing of the discussion.

Four kinds of questions were found in a study describing the questions that teachers asked of students; Daines (1986) reported on the questions asked by 38 teachers in grades 2–12 in their classrooms. Interpretive questions included those that required students to make inferences, compare or contrast, determine cause-and-effect relationships, make predictions based on trends, and so on. Of the 5,289 questions teachers asked, 93% were at the literal level. Less than 7% were interpretive questions. Teachers asked about 78 questions per hour, with second-grade teachers asking the most questions and tenth-grade teachers asking the fewest. Teachers waited only 2 seconds, on average, from the time the question was asked until a student responded. Higher-order questions did not result in longer wait times. More important, the average student's response was only 3 seconds long, with the longest average range being 5 seconds for 10th graders. A more recent study found that students who were deaf did not need their teachers to ask literal-level questions to support their comprehension at more advanced levels (Schirmer & Woolsey, 1997). These findings have implications for teachers. First, teachers should plan questions that promote higher-order thinking; and second, teachers, when they ask questions, should give students more time to think. Through their questions, teachers model how students can come up with their own questions. When students learn to identify questions, to inquire, to problematize (Freire, 1993; Raphael, 1986), they learn to think about their world differently and in depth.

The Instructional Conversation

A goal of discussion in classrooms is promotion of the idea that students have something far different to contribute than simply replicating known answers in an oral format. Tharp and Gallimore (1989) shared ideas about the role of the teacher in assisting performance and engaging in joint activity with students. Their *instructional conversation* approach encourages students to converse in comfortable and culturally cognizant ways, while keeping instructional goals in mind. The right to determine who talks is not the decision of just the teacher, who may recognize that students often speak in overlapping turns rather than waiting to be recognized. Such conversations were found to support increased understanding among Hispanic students with learning disabilities, for example (Echevarria, 1996). In science, Beisenherz, Dantonio, and Richardson (2001) effectively used instructional conversations to assist students in developing a shared understanding of the critical characteristics of science concepts. Although discussion resists the application of rules, some promising practices may be helpful. In this section, we explore the Socratic seminar, electronic discussions, and the interactive schema board.

The Socratic Seminar

One reason for classroom discussion, as we suggested earlier, is to promote deep and critical thinking among students. The Socratic seminar, properly implemented, is one promising practice toward achieving this end. A defining feature of the Socratic seminar is collaboration as opposed to debate, in which competition is highlighted (e.g., Adams, n.d.). In the Socratic seminar, participants read a common text and are encouraged to develop questions to bring to the discussion session. The teacher or leader has three responsibilities: (1) Prepare the questions that define the discussion; (2) probe the responses of the participants to elicit reasons, support, or implications of their claims; and (3) engage the participants with one another, especially if ideas presented seem to be in conflict (Adler, 1984). Metzger (1998) set up inner and outer discussion circles for her seminars. Students in the inner circle conducted their discussion for a set period of time, and students in the outer circle provided feedback when the discussion ended. Then the groups changed positions. Students in the outer circle might ask questions about the oral discourse of students in the inner circle; for example, "What can be done to get everyone involved in this discussion?" (Cornett, 1997, p. 257). This procedure keeps the discussion focused and helps to ensure that all students have the opportunity to participate. The teacher who wants students to understand the concept of genetic variation can successfully employ the Socratic seminar to engage students as they discuss the ethical dilemmas such research might provoke.

Discussion in the Electronic Era

One of the great strengths of the digital age is that technology has the potential to span geography and the constraints of time. Students in 21st-century classrooms have the opportunity to participate in real-time discussions with students in other classrooms, other states, or even other countries via Web cameras, instant messaging and chat software, and voice-over Internet technology. In addition, students can expand their discussions beyond the bounds of school through asynchronous tools, such as blogs and discussion boards (Boling, Castek, Zawilinski, Barton, & Nierlich, 2008; English, 2007; Grisham & Wolsey, 2006; Wolsey, 2004). In threaded discussions, for example, students can explore in depth the topics they began discussing in class, start new discussions, and find additional resources to support and illustrate the positions they've taken. It's not uncommon for students to find links to important online objects and texts to support their assertions.

Students in Lynn Johnson's class at Maple Crest Middle School in Kokomo, Indiana, participated in threaded discussions with the author of a book for young adults, who provided chapters of a manuscript in process for students' reactions. The book's author posted chapters from her manuscript and asked students to respond. In Figure 19.3, students discuss the author's use of German and French words to make the dialogue seem authentic in the story. A student responds to the author in Figure 19.4 and encourages her to write another book. The student poses questions left in her mind as a reader. Figure 19.5 shows a student inferring the emotions of a character from the story.

Thread:Chapters 11 - 13	Date:Saturday, September 22, 2007
Post:RE RE RE SPECIAL QUESTION	Status:Published
Author:S	Overall rating: Not rated

Some of the German and French is hard to understand but I can still understand the story even if I don't understand a few of the words.

Thread:Chapters 11 - 13	Date:Sunday, September 23, 2007
Post:RE RE RE SPECIAL QUESTION	Status:Published
Author:El	Overall rating: Not rated

I agree with Shelby. Some of the words I can't understand, but the story still flows.

Thread:Chapters 11 - 13	Date:Thursday, September 27, 2007
Post:RE RE RE RE SPECIAL QUESTION	Status:Published
Author:E	Overall rating: Not rated

I really did like these chapters. Sara talking helps you feel her excitment. Also the girls trying to figure out baseball was kind of funny.

Thread:Chapters 11 - 13	Date:Friday, November 2, 2007
Post:RE RE RE RE RE SPECIAL QUESTION	Status:Published
Author:E	Overall rating: Not rated

The way that Evelyn is trying to protect her sister is very sweet. It is also very sad that she wants to do that just to make her sister happy.

FIGURE 19.3. Students use threaded discussion to explore a novel.

Thread:Chapters 21 - 23	Date:Friday, November 2, 2007
Post:RE:Chapters 21 - 23	Status:Published
Author:m␣	Overall rating: Not rated

Yea, I like this book a lot too! Like Josie said, I too was very sad when I finished the book. I just hope you are planning to write a sequel to " A ␣ ␣ ␣e ", because I would love to find out if their mother comes to America or not and if Sarah makes other friends besides, Nancy. But, I have one question, does John like Evelyn or does Evelyn like John? But, at the very end, it was a very happy time when they finally got a letter from their mother!

FIGURE 19.4. A student responds to the novel's author.

Thread:Mrs. Johnson's Discussion Starter	Date:Sunday, September 9, 2007
Post:RE:Mrs. Johnson's Discussion Starter	Status:Published
Author:CO	Overall rating: Not rated

I liked everything in these chapters. Sara was getting very annoying when she didn't even let Evelyn go to her classes. I guess she was just scared. Nothing in the chapters confused me. I really enjoyed it. I also noticed all the mean comments from the kids in Sara's class, It showed how the kids in America felt about kids from different countries, just like brittany said earlier.

FIGURE 19.5. A student infers the emotions of a character in the novel.

Interactive Schema Boards

Maggie Hunter, an art teacher at Powell County High School in Montana, uses discussion to help her students understand complex topics in her content area. The schema board she describes builds on existing knowledge and gives students a visual tool to help shape discussions. The schema board is patterned after the know–want to know–learned (K-W-L) chart that is familiar to many readers of this text (Ogle, 1986). In this adaptation, students use the schema board to frame their thinking and, subsequently, to support their discussion of the topic—Piet Mondrian, in this example. Mrs. Hunter shares this description of how she used the schema board to promote discussion over a period of several weeks:

> During class I began the introduction on Piet Mondrian. Working in their cooperative learning groups, students shared with their partners what they knew about Mondrian, then they wrote the information on yellow sticky notes, placing them on the schema board under activating schema on Mondrian. Some responses were "He is French," "he is a man," and "Mondrian is an abstract artist." Next we discussed what students might need to know about Mondrian that they didn't know. Those responses, written on the sticky notes, were placed under Building Schema on Mondrian on the schema board. Then I drew my students' attention to the new vocabulary words, which were displayed on a large piece of poster board at the front of the room; for example, *organic shape, geometric shape, simplified, stylized,* and

abstract. Students read the first article on Piet Mondrian and discussed with their partners what they learned, wrote the information on sticky notes, and placed them on the schema board under Revising Schema on Mondrian. When this was completed, each group shared with the class what it had learned about Mondrian, and whether group members' original assumptions about him were correct.

This process was repeated for the next 3 weeks as students read new texts and worked on their own art projects. The revised schema sticky notes were eventually moved to the "activating schema" section and the building of knowledge on Mondrian continued (see Figure 19.6). As the students continued to build their schemata board about Mondrian, they initiated a whole-class discussion about his work, using the vocabulary words and theories they had read earlier.

STUDENT 1: He [Mondrian] removed man and nature from his paintings.

STUDENT 2: And Mondrian removed all curved lines and organic shapes from his paintings, too.

STUDENT 1: Right, Piet Mondrian was searching for artistic truth, and his images became more and more abstract.

The interactive schema board reminded students of important vocabulary words they could use in discussion and writing. Because this unit took several

FIGURE 19.6. Photo of interactive schemata board.

weeks, students used the interactive schema board to keep track of their discussion topics, to revise their thinking, and to continue where they had left off on previous days.

At the beginning of this unit, one student asked me to explain abstract art, because he did not understand it. After the project was completed, he began to understand how Mondrian looked at the world, and he could appreciate another style and form of artistic impression. The schema board demonstrated to the students their understanding of the concepts presented in the articles, because they could see how their thinking changed as a result of the discussions and reading.

Summing It Up: Classroom Conversation Matters

Classroom discussion can promote learning by engaging the minds of all the participants. This aspect of instruction bears further research and time, for classroom discussion in a crowded curriculum may seem like a luxury. However, the depth of learning and the appeal of constructing understanding with others may be a critical key to vibrant communities of learners fostering the sense of inquiry we desire. Learning through speaking and listening doesn't easily lend itself to prepackaged programs, as Pinnell and Jaggar (2003) assert, and the classroom conversation requires thoughtful attention to the contexts of the discussion. Few instructional activities are as disappointing as the lesson plan that calls for "discussion," without attention to the contexts and purposes of the discussion, and how they may resonate with student participants. At the same time, few instructional activities are as rewarding as the discussion in which the teacher, having done the work of preparing students, ensuring adequate resources, and assisting students' acquisition of the skills of academic discourse, can finally step outside the discussion as students engage in intellectual exploration on their own.

QUESTIONS FOR DISCUSSION

1. Think of a unit you plan to teach soon. What concepts might students better understand as a result of classroom discussion? Why is discussion a good fit for this content?

2. What are your current practices in discussion? How might you change your teaching practices to include more student-centered discussion?

3. What benefits do students realize as a result of participatory practices, such as authentic discussions in the classroom?

4. Consider a recent discussion from your teaching experience. What might you change to improve active participation?

5. How might you use engage students in meaningful discussions as they work in small groups?

6. In what ways might you use technology to promote discussion as inquiry in your classroom?

Resources

McKenzie, J. (Publisher). (1997). A questioning toolkit. *From Now On, 7*(3). Available at *www.fno.org/nov97/toolkit.html.*

Nobis, K. S. (n.d.). Blogging with photovoice: Sharing pictures in an integrated classroom. Available at *www.readwritethink.org/lessons/lesson_view.asp?id=1064.*

Shea, R. H. (n.d.). Exploring language and identity: Amy Tan's "Mother Tongue" and beyond. Available at *www.readwritethink.org/lessons/lesson_view.asp?id=910.*

References

Adams, C. (n.d.). Socratic seminars. *Studyguide.org: A website for Mrs. Adams' English classes.* Retrieved May 29, 2008, from *www.studyguide.org/socratic_seminar.htm.*

Adler, M. (1984). *The Paideia Program: An educational syllabus.* New York: Macmillan.

Allen, V. G. (1991). Teaching bilingual and ESL children. In J. Flood, J. M. Jensen, D. Lapp, & J. R. Squire (Eds.), *Handbook of research on teaching the English language arts* (pp. 356–364). New York: Macmillan.

Alvermann, D. E., Dillon, D. R., O'Brien, D. G., & Smith, L. C. (1985). The role of the textbook in discussion. *Journal of Reading, 29*(1), 50–57.

Alvermann, D. E., & Hayes, D. A. (1989). Classroom discussion of content area reading assignments: An intervention study. *Reading Research Quarterly, 24*(3), 305–335.

Anderson, R. C., Nguyen-Hahiel, K., McNurlen, B., Archodidou, A., Kim, S., Reznitskaya, A., et al. (2001). The snowball phenomenon: Spread of ways of talking and ways of thinking across groups of children. *Cognition and Instruction, 19*(1), 1–46.

Applebee, A. N., Langer, J. A., Nystrand, M., & Gamoran, A. (2003). Discussion-based approaches to developing understanding: Classroom instruction and student performance in middle and high school English. *American Educational Research Journal, 40,* 685–730.

Arias, J. (2008). Multilingual students and language acquisition: Engaging activities for diversity training. *English Journal, 97*(3), 38–45.

Au, K. H. (1993). *Literacy instruction in multicultural settings.* Orlando, FL: Harcourt Brace Jovanovich.

Ball, A. (2002). Three decades of research on classroom life: Illuminating the classroom communicative lives of America's at-risk students. In W. Secada (Ed.), *Review of research in education* (Vol. 26, pp. 71–112). Washington, DC: American Educational Research Association.

Ball, A., & Farr, M. (2003). Language variations, culture and teaching the English language arts. In J. Flood, D. Lapp, J. Squire & J. Jensen (Eds.), *Handbook of research on teaching the English language arts* (2nd ed., pp. 435–445). Mahwah, NJ: Erlbaum.

Baugh, J. (2000). *Beyond ebonics: Linguistic pride and racial prejudice.* New York: Oxford University Press.

Beisenherz, P. C., Dantonio, M., & Richardson, L. (2001). The learning cycle and instructional conversations. *Science Scope, 24*(4), 34–38.

Berry, K. S. (1985). Talking to learn subject matter/learning subject matter talk. *Language Arts, 62*(1), 34–42.

Betts, E. A. (1946). *Foundations of reading instruction with emphasis on differentiated guidance.* New York: American Book Company.

Boling, E., Castek, J., Zawilinski, L., Barton, K., & Nierlich, T. (2008). Collaborative literacy: Blogs and Internet projects. *Reading Teacher, 61*(6), 504–506.

Cazden, C. B. (2001). *Classroom discourse: The language of teaching and learning* (2nd ed.). Portsmouth, NH: Heinemann.

Clark, E. (2007). Young children's uptake of new words in conversation. *Language in Society, 36,* 157–182.

Cohen, E. G. (1986). *Designing groupwork: Strategies for the heterogeneous classroom.* New York: Teachers College Press.

Cohen, E. G. (1994). *Designing groupwork: Strategies for the heterogeneous classroom* (2nd ed.). New York: Teachers College Press.

Cornett, C. E. (1997). Beyond retelling the plot: Student-led discussions. *Reading Teacher, 50*(6), 527–528.

Daines, D. (1986). Are teachers asking higher level questions? *Education, 106,* 368–374.

Echevarria, J. (1996). The effects of instructional conversations on the language and concept development of Latino students with learning disabilities. *Bilingual Research Journal, 20*(2), 339–363.

Edwards, P. A. (2007, November). *The education of African American students: Voicing the debates, controversies and solutions.* Presidential address to the National Reading Conference, Austin, TX.

English, C. (2007). Finding a voice in a threaded discussion group: Talking about literature online. *English Journal, 97*(1), 56–61.

Fairclough, N. (2001). *Language and power* (2nd ed.). London: Pearson Education.

Ferguson, P. M., & Young, T. A. (1996). Literature talk: Dialogue improvisation and patterned conversation with second language learners. *Language Arts, 73*(8), 597–600.

Fisher, D., & Frey, N. (2004). *Improving adolescent literacy: Strategies at work.* Upper Saddle River, NJ: Pearson/Prentice-Hall.

Forster, E. M. (1927). *Aspects of the novel.* Orlando, FL: Harcourt.

Freire, P. (1993). *Pedagogy of the oppressed, 30th anniversary edition.* New York: Continuum.

Gonzales, N., Moll, L. C., & Amanti, C. (Eds.). (2005). *Funds of knowledge: Theorizing practice in households, communities, and classrooms.* Mahwah, NJ: Erlbaum.

Goodlad, J. (1984). *A place called school: Prospects for the future.* New York: McGraw-Hill.

Goodman, Y., Watson, D., & Burke, C. (1996). *Reading strategies: Focus on comprehension* (2nd ed.). Katonah, NY: Richard C. Owen.

Grainger, T. (1999). Conversations in the classroom: Poetic voices at play. *Language Arts, 76*(4), 292–297.

Green, J. L. (1983). Research on teaching as a linguistic process: A state of the art. *Review of Research in Education, 10,* 151–252.

Greenman, C. (2004). Coaching academic English through voice and text production models. *ReCALL, 16* (1), 51–70.

Grisham, D. L., & Wolsey, T. D. (2006). Recentering the middle school classroom as a vibrant learning community: Students, literacy and technology intersect. *Journal of Adolescent & Adult Literacy, 49,* 648–660.

Hemingway, E. (1952). *The old man and the sea.* London: Jonathan Cape.

Henriques, L. (2000, April 29). *Children's misconceptions about weather: A review of the literature.* Paper presented at the annual meeting of the National Association of Research in Science Teaching, New Orleans, LA. Retrieved January 18, 2008, from *www.csulb.edu/~lhenriqu/narst2000.htm.*

Hollander, J. A. (2002). Learning to discuss: Strategies for improving the quality of class discussion. *Teaching Sociology, 30*(3), 317–327.

Holt, J. (1982). *How children fail* (rev. ed.). New York: Dell.

Kagan, S. (1994). *Cooperative learning.* San Juan Capistrano, CA: Kagan Cooperative Learning.

Kohn, A. (1993). *Punished by rewards: The trouble with gold stars, incentive plans, A's, praise and other bribes.* Boston: Houghton Mifflin.

Lapp, D., Fisher, D., & Wolsey, T. D. (2009). *Literacy growth for every child: Differentiated small-group instruction for K–6.* New York: Guilford Press.

Lee, C. D. (2005). Double-voiced discourse: African American vernacular English as resource in cultural modeling classrooms. In A. Ball & S. W. Freedman (Eds.), *New literacies for new times: Bakhtinian perspectives on language, literacy, and learning for the 21st century* (pp. 129–147). New York: Cambridge University Press.

Lee, C. D. (2006). Every good-bye ain't gone: Analyzing the cultural underpinnings of classroom talk. *International Journal of Qualitative Studies in Education, 19*(3), 305–327.

Lemke, J. L. (1989). Making text talk. *Theory Into Practice, 28*(2), 136–41.

Loban, W. D. (1963). *The language of elementary school children.* Champaign, IL: National Council of Teachers of English.

Lyle, S. (1993). An investigation into ways in which children talk themselves into meaning. *Language and Education, 7*(3), 181–87.

Meek, M. (1996). Literacy changes lives. National Literacy Trust. Retrieved October 20, 2008, from *www.literacytrust.org.uk/Database/quote.html.*

Mehan, H. (1979). *Learning lessons: Social organization in the classroom.* Cambridge, MA: Harvard University Press.

Menyuk, P. (1984). Language development and reading. In J. Flood (Ed.), *Understanding comprehension* (pp. 101–121). Newark, DE: International Reading Association.

Metzger, M. (1998). Teaching reading beyond the plot. *Phi Delta Kappan, 80*(3), 240–256.

Moguel, D. (2004). What does it mean to participate in class?: Integrity and inconsistency in classroom interaction. *Journal of Classroom Interaction, 39*(1), 19–29.

Nichols, M. (2006). *Comprehension through conversation: The power of purposeful talk in the classroom.* New York: Heinemann.

Nuthall, G. (2005). The cultural myths and realities of classroom teaching and learning: A personal journey. *Teachers College Record, 105*(5), 895–934.

Ogle, D. (1986). K-W-L: A teaching model that develops active reading of expository text. *Reading Teacher, 39,* 564–570.

Pinnell, G. S., & Jaggar, A. M. (2003). Oral language: Speaking and listening in the classroom. In J. Flood, D. Lapp, J. R. Squire, & J. M. Jensen (Eds.), *Handbook of research on teaching the English language arts* (2nd ed., pp. 881–913). Mahwah, NJ: Erlbaum.

Raphael, T. (1986). Teaching question answer relationships, revisited. *Reading Teacher, 39*, 186–190.

Raphael, T. E., Brock, C. H., & Wallace, S. M. (1996). Encouraging quality peer talk with diverse students in mainstream classrooms. Learning from and with teachers. In J. R. Paratore & R. L. McCormack (Eds.), *Peer talk in the classroom: Learning from research* (pp. 176–206). Newark, DE: International Reading Association.

Ryder, R. J., & Graves, M. F. (2003). *Reading and learning in content areas* (3rd ed.). New York: Wiley.

Schirmer, B. R., & Woolsey, M. L. (1997). Effect of teacher questions on the comprehension of deaf children. *Journal of Deaf Studies and Deaf Education, 2*(1), 47–56.

Taylor, D., & Doresey-Gaines, C. (1988). *Growing up literate*. Portsmouth, NH: Heinemann.

Tharp, R. G., & Gallimore, R. (1989). Rousing schools to life. *American Educator, 13*(2), 20–25, 46–52.

Weber, R. (1991). Language diversity and reading in American society. In R. Barr, M. L. Kamil, P. Mosenthal, & P. D. Pearson (Eds.), *Handbook of reading research* (97–119). New York: Longman.

Welty, W. M. (1989). Discussion method teaching: How to make it work. *Change, 21*(4), 40–49.

Wheelock, A. (1999). Junior Great Books: Reading for meaning in urban schools. *Educational Leadership, 57*(2), 47–50.

Wolsey, T. D. (2004, January/February). Literature discussion in cyberspace: Young adolescents using threaded discussion groups to talk about books. *Reading Online, 7*(4). Retrieved October 10, 2008, from *www.readingonline.org/articles/art_index.asp?href=wolsey/index.html*.

Chapter 20

Writing Instruction for Adolescent Learners

Jane Hansen
Brian Kissel

GUIDING QUESTIONS

1. What are some decisions that adolescents make as they engage in writing?
2. In what ways does writing for different audiences benefit adolescent writers?
3. Why is it important for adolescent writers to be able to evaluate their own drafts?

Writing instruction can take many forms. Teachers can say, "After we have finished our study of Jamestown you will take an essay test. We'll devote a day to the format I require for high-quality answers, and your test will have five questions. I will score your work when you are finished." Or they might say, "We have been studying Jamestown for 2 days now, and after our fourth day, you will each choose an aspect of life there that intrigues you. You'll write a five-page essay on it, following the guidelines I give you. I'll provide a small amount of inclass time to work on these, but mostly you will work on them as homework. You'll hand them in 2 weeks from now, and I'll correct them."

Or, "We have been studying Jamestown for 2 days now, and after our fourth day, we will each choose an aspect of life there that intrigues us. We will study it and work on it for 2 weeks within our writers' workshop. Each of us will choose the format we want to create for our final product, and after we have shared our final products, we will write a self-evaluation. You will hand in both the self-evaluation and a copy of your final product. I will write a letter of evaluation to you about your work."

Students as writers must engage in various processes to complete the different writing tasks. In the first, students engage in a task restrained by the teacher—to answer test questions by following a required format. The teacher wants to know what they learned, and wants this information delivered in a certain manner. The task is based primarily on a view of writers as persons who show authorities what they know. In the second situation, students engage in a task guided by the teacher—to write an essay for homework, following guidelines. The teacher wants to know what they can learn by their own study and wants their information delivered in a certain manner. This task is based primarily on a view of writers as persons who work on their own to produce writing that adheres to a particular set of guidelines, and it will be read by one authority.

In the third situation, students engage in a task guided by a teacher who engages in the task with them. This teacher has taught them to study mentor texts and to consider audiences. The writers make decisions about a format to use that conveys their information to their chosen audience. This teacher has taught the writers to interact with each other along the way, and to evaluate their own work. This task is based primarily on a view of writers as persons who seek the influence of various texts and persons, including their classmates, published authors, and audiences—including the teacher. Plus, these writers seek to influence their classmates and audiences—including the teacher.

In the section that follow we present three research-based guidelines for writing instruction for adolescents; relate the research that underpins each, and provide examples of instruction that illustrate each guideline; and show a classrooms in which the students and teacher bring together all three guidelines.

Research-Based Guidelines for Writing Instruction for Adolescents

Given the scenarios presented above, how do teachers decide on the kind of instruction to provide for their writers? What views of writers do they decide to honor? Writers and writing are complex, and research suggests many guidelines. Three rose to the surface when we researched writing instruction for adolescents:

- *Guideline 1*: Writers are decision makers. Thus, effective writing teachers of adolescents teach their students to generate options and to make choices about various aspects of what they do as writers.

- *Guideline 2*: Writers consider their audience. Thus, effective writing teachers of adolescents teach their students ways to adapt their writing so that it is reader-friendly for the particular audience they choose for each piece they write.

- *Guideline 3*: Writers evaluate their drafts. Thus, effective writing teachers of adolescents teach their students to read various kinds of writing by diverse authors, so that they can learn to read their own work with the ear of a writer.

Guideline 1: Writers Are Decision Makers

This guideline is supported by research in several areas: Writers make decisions about the topics/ideas on which they write, about the genre(s) that convey their ideas most effectively, about the process they use, and about how to adapt to restrictions. Writing instruction that stresses the importance of the adolescent writer as the person who determines what to write, in what form, and how to go about the task, is more authentic—more true to the behaviors of writers of the world—than writing instruction wherein the teacher determines these parameters.

Adolescent Writers Make Decisions about Their Topics

Of all the decisions that writers make, the choice of what to write about receives the most attention in the research and appears to be the most crucial. Writers do their most effective work when they are passionate about what they have chosen to compose. To learn how to choose, and to have the nerve to write about what is important, can be challenges for teachers and adolescents.

To illustrate this point, Linda Rief (2007), a middle school teacher-researcher, writes about a 2-week teaching endeavor in which she taught seventh graders in Estonia. To initiate writing, she wanted the students to talk. She found the desks, however, bolted to the floor. Undaunted she scoured the building for loose chairs and created a circle. The students felt uncomfortable facing each other and had nothing to say. They only knew how to give back information as the teacher presented it.

Eventually, students whispered, "Are you sure we may say what we think? You want us to write what we think? Will it not be trouble?" (Rief, 2007, p. 190). With Linda's assurance, they talked and wrote. She heard their joys, sorrows, aspirations, and concerns. Their previously unheard voices resounded as the students wrote about what they chose as central in their lives.

For choice to influence adolescent writers, their classrooms must be safe places in which they can truly write about what is important to them. Some researchers have started to question whether this is usually the case in schools. They fear that topic choice is actually perceived—by teachers and students—as topics within a certain range of acceptability. Ralph Fletcher (2006), a writer-researcher, focuses on this concern in relation to boys.

To show what he means Fletcher (2006) describes three pieces of student writing. The first, written by a boy, is a memoir about a time he threw snowballs at his cousin and broke a window. The second, also written by a boy, is about a time the cat peed in his mother's coffee—guaranteed to bring laughs to the class. The third, a story written by a girl, is about the time she cleaned out the freezer with her mother and discovered soup that her grandmother made before she died. They defrosted the soup and ate it, while talking about their memories of the grandmother.

Fletcher (2006), a consultant in the classroom, chose one student to share from the Author's Chair—the girl, because her story was poignant. Now, he argues, that was a mistake on his part; he devalued the work of the boys who wrote for other purposes that he (Fletcher), at that time, did not value as much as the work of the girl. Fletcher elaborates:

> This feature of the writing workshop (student-selected topics) would seem to be relatively simple and straightforward. But today for boys, it's not simple. Many boys find that the "choice coupon" in the writing workshop contains a great deal of small print listing many types of writing they are *not* allowed to do. Boys get an unfriendly response from their teachers when they try to write about high-interest boy topics such as hunting, favorite movies, comics, outer space adventures, video games, war. (p. 42)

In addition, Fletcher writes about cultural and test fears. Because of Columbine, for example, some schools have No Tolerance policies regarding speaking or writing about violence, when it could be that students might benefit from writing about these fears. Also, our nation's current test frenzy tends to restrict choice; teachers feel they need to assign topics—the types that will be on tests—to prepare their students. Either of these fears may lead to more restrictions on boys than on girls.

Overall, many boys go "underground" to write about topics that interest them. This restriction may be responsible for the disengagement we tend to see in adolescent males.

In addition to concerns about boy writers, some researchers fear that what is seen as choice of topics tends to restrain urban writers. Tammy Schwartz (2004) conducted a participatory action research project with sixth-grade adolescent girls in an urban Appalachian neighborhood. Initially, to try to understand the language and the voices of the girls, Schwartz asked them to write words or phrases they used in their homes, community, and school. When she compared the languages used in all three settings, she found that the girls' voices were restricted in their classrooms. Their teachers asked them to write about what they knew, but the students felt these to be false requests.

Choice, as practiced in those settings (Schwartz, 2004), did not lead to voices that were "hot, complicated, rude, or uncomfortable" (p. 16). The only voices heard in this urban Appalachian school were those typically represented in traditional, middle-class curricula. In other words, the choices did not reflect the voices of the students in the classroom. Schwartz wonders whether writing instruction, as often practiced, immerses students in settings where differences, difficulties, and childhood burdens are not accepted.

To change classrooms and schools so that they are more student-friendly is becoming a goal. Danling Fu (2003), a consultant-researcher in Chinatown, in New York, writes about one middle school where that occurred. The students, who come daily from a particular area of rural China, write every day, starting the day they arrive. They write in Chinese, then their texts become Chinese–English, then English–Chinese, and, finally, English.

Several of the teachers work together to support the students as they use their writing to enable their transitions from rural to city settings, and from homes where parents are ever-present to homes where parents are ever-away at multiple jobs. With consistent support the students put forth their concerns and use their writing to learn about the United States. Their voices direct the writing curriculum: They study what they write about—they write about what they study.

Maureen Barbieri (2002), a staff developer-researcher with the New York City public schools, also studied middle school students in Chinatown. She started by reading to students, and asking them to draw something they remembered. This touched their lives, and they began writing. Through a collection of case studies, we see the struggles and successes of the students— and of Barbieri—as they learn to write their own stories. Barbieri knew the importance to writers of writing about their "obsessions," but she sometimes found herself interfering. She wanted the students to write about New York City, to gain a deeper understanding of their new home, but they returned to China when they wrote, and Barbieri heard the urgency of their concerns in their words. She writes about what she learned as a teacher of English language learners. Over time, her "primary focus was always on the content of what they read, wrote, and discussed. In other words, my first goal was not the development of greater English proficiency. ... There are no bigger questions than What has my life meant so far? or What matters to me? ... These were the kinds of questions [the students] addressed in their writing" (pp. 59–60).

In a somewhat similar vein, teacher-researcher John Gaughan (2001) invites his high school students' voices, fears, and outrageous joys into their classroom. In his book, *Reinventing English: Teaching in the Contact Zone*, he begins with assumptions, such as "students need to examine where they are and where they're coming from" (p. 7), and Gaughan feels it is his responsibility to "help them empathize with people of different races, religions, and sexual orientation" (p. 9).

These beliefs, of course, led to some difficult days. Gaughan (2001) says his book is about the "clashing and grappling my students and I have done when we meet in the contact zone of the classroom. It is about opening minds to difference" (p. 9). His account is about his efforts to encourage his students to air their views honestly and forthrightly. Plus, they explore the assumptions that underlie their opinions, and consider how those assumptions relate to their peers, their community, and their country. "Essentially, this book is about social justice" (p. 11).

Fairness, issues of control, and concern with self-authority often appear in adolescents' writing when they determine what to write about. Then, to strengthen the import of their words, students consider the form, or genre, that best conveys their passions.

Adolescent Writers Make Decisions about Their Genre(s)

Adolescent writers make decisions about the genre(s) that convey their messages most effectively. If I'm afraid of being shot, do I convey that fear most effectively as a poem, a narrative, or a letter to the editor? This decision is crucial, and effective teachers of adolescents teach their students to consider alternatives. To tell students to write about a compelling topic within the restraints of a particular genre does not honor all passions.

The students of Nancie Atwell (1998), a middle-school teacher-researcher, write in depth about their own ideas and choose the kind of writing in which to frame them. To aid those decisions, they read different kinds of writing. Overall, as Nancie teaches her students about topic development and genre, she helps them realize the significance of events, people, themes, and goals in their lives.

Genre choice is, however, in danger. Lisa Scherff and Carolyn Piazza (2005) conducted a study in four high schools in Florida—a state with a 30-year history of high-stakes testing. To determine the secondary students' perceptions of their writing and writing instruction, the researchers asked them to complete surveys. Through analysis of the students' responses, they determined that the instructional focus on testing limited the number of genres that students explored. They mostly wrote responses to literature, summaries, and expository and persuasive essays—reflecting the genres most frequently tested. They "never" or "hardly ever" wrote business letters, responses to art/music, drama, poetry, or personal writing (p. 287). Students reacted negatively to this restriction in genre choice. One student noted, "We need to write more fiction. There were far too many five-paragraph essays with banal topics to actually feel any true connection with the work" (p. 286). Another student responded, "Unfortunately, IB (International Baccalaureate) has destroyed all creativity I once possessed. I never had the chance to write essays, poetry, or any other such creative work. Instead we got to write about symbols and structure. ... They have turned art into math and science" (p. 287).

They, thankfully, does not apply to all. Teacher-researcher Tracy Rosewarne writes about her decision, in the face of state tests in Michigan, to teach writing effectively to her high school students (Sipe & Rosewarne, 2006). She alternates units, with 2 weeks on a teacher-directed topic with student choice of genre, then 2 weeks in which students have complete choice of both topic and genre. Throughout the units on teacher-directed topics, the class devotes time to reading, writing, and talking about various genres in which professional writers have written within that topic.

In their first unit of this kind, they all read *Night,* by Elie Wiesel, and Rosewarne (Sipe & Rosewarne, 2006) directed them to write about an important event that had occurred since 1930—one they could learn about via interview and reading. As they focused in on their topics, students considered various genres, and chose one that would convey their message in the most compelling manner. Rosewarne worked with her students to "examine the ways authors choose genre and use genre to help shape a message" (p. 137). This represented a change for her as a teacher. Like most other teachers, she had taught genre and thematic studies as separate organizing structures, but now she melded them—as real writers do. Her instruction—and her students' experiences as writers—became more authentic.

Genre choice, however, does not have to mean that writers must choose one genre by which to convey a message. Tom Romano (2000), a passionate writer/teacher-researcher created multigenre papers as a way to address genre choice, and several other teachers (e.g., Allen & Swistak, 2004; Dickson, DeGraff, & Foard, 2002; Putz, 2006) now engage their students in this form of exploration. Students choose their own topics, and then the genres—as distinct from genre—in which to convey their passion. One paper may contain an essay, a poem, an epitaph, and a fictional narrative—all pieces of writing that stand on their own and, at the same time, when presented as one paper, tell a particularly compelling tale or present a persuasive, dramatic argument.

Choice of genre and topic is a must for writers who have strong beliefs, joys, and concerns to convey. To do so, however, they must make decisions about the journey they will take as they compose. Some meander, whereas others take a more direct route, from a fuzzy initial idea to a clear final draft. Many factors encourage adolescent writers as they engage in the process of writing.

Adolescent Writers Make Decisions about Their Process

Donald Murray (1999), who wrote extensively about writing, says:

> There is not one writing process but many. ... Sometimes I write away with a river flood of fluency, other days I build a draft slowly like a bricklayer. No matter. I am a writer. I write. ... Change your process as your thinking style evolves, as you face a new writing task, or as you become more experienced with a particular writing task. (p. 10)

He lists the features of the writing process he used for that book (focus, explore, plan, draft, clarify), but he insists that we understand: He adapts that writing process when he engages in other writing tasks, depending on his experience with that task, and the way his head works on that day.

There is no such thing as *the* writing process. This principle of writing instruction for adolescents sometimes gets lost in the shuffle. Sometimes we see posters in classrooms with five or seven steps the students are to follow when they write. No! Writing teachers who write don't post posters with steps for their students to follow. They know, as writers, that they don't always use the same process every time they write. Different topics and genres beget different processes. Sometimes the following acts become part of a writer's process, and sometimes not: brainstorming, mapping, free writing, interviewing, adjusting the distance, finding information, finding a title, creating a lead, finessing an ending, outlining, and revising.

To come to an understanding of the complexity of writing can take years. Erika Daniels (2007), a middle school teacher-researcher, considers her journey to be similar to that of many. She used to teach writing in a prescribed way: She gave writing assignments, then provided feedback on final drafts. Then she started to think aloud as she demonstrated her writing processes in front of her students, realized the importance of mentor texts, and learned about the power of peer response. Her students started to flourish. They not only learned about the various ways to approach and to engage in writing tasks, but they also became excited and created a Literacy Café as a venue in which to publish and celebrate their writing.

Critical literacy can bring the passions of some adolescents into writing, and it can bring additional elements of their writing processes to the forefront. Students are not simply writing about topics of their choice, in genres of their choice, via processes they adapt to their task. They are driven to critique situations in their lives. Rosary Lalik and Kimberly Oliver (2007) studied the complexities of a yearlong study of *Health* as conducted by Oliver and four eighth-grade girls. They engaged in journal writing, the creation of a survey, analysis of the results of it, and weekly conversations. The importance of the journal writing and conversations varied among the girls, showing the importance of setting up a unit of study with allowances for differences, so that various students can engage in a learning process that works for them.

Overall, the researchers learned that critical literacy is difficult to teach; the idea is to pursue topics that arise from the heartfelt concerns of the adolescents, which Oliver did, but, at the same time, she found herself walking across a tightrope. Always, she listened to and learned about the girls' viewpoints. Always, she carefully presented hers, and sometimes the girls rejected them. In such cases, she tended to drop her ideas; she learned the importance of not insisting on exercising influence. The power of being decision makers came to the forefront when these adolescents *and* their teacher engaged in critical literacy.

Adolescent Writers Make Decisions about How to Adapt to Restrictions

The current restrictive atmosphere in which we educators find ourselves immersed is contrary to the exploration that leads knowledge seekers forward. It is especially anathema to writers. Authors devote their lives to creating their own voices, their own stances, and their own ways with words. These traits of writers nestle at the heart of effective writing classrooms for adolescents.

AP (advanced placement) English teacher-researcher P. L. Thomas (2003) studied the effects of restrictions and choices on his writers. He divided his syllabus into three areas: a required novel that they all read; a poetry unit in which each student chose to focus on women poets, ethnic poets, or traditional poets; and an independent study of a literary work that students chose from a list of books on a theme selected by Thomas. He designed the three assignments to introduce the students gradually to the notion of choice and, at the same time, teach them what they needed to know to do well on the AP test.

Thomas (2003) was initially disappointed in the results. Compared to previous years, his students' scores on the AP test had dropped. In previous years, he restricted his students throughout the year to the type of writing required on the AP test, and their scores, though not as high as Thomas wanted, were higher than scores with his new approach. His effort to boost them failed. Upon further thinking, he realized that the success that he saw in his students' writing throughout the year was important to them as persons and writers, though not revealed in ways that the test measured. To learn to finesse choice and restrictions successfully became the goal that he now works on as a teacher—goals that may represent those of many teachers. Given the importance of high-stakes tests, and given the importance—to writers—of choice, what does a teacher do?

Testing has narrowed the curriculum in many classrooms, resulting in a loss of teacher autonomy (Campbell, 2002). This happens in spite of evidence that students who are engaged in effective writing instruction—instruction that includes choice in topics, exposure to multiple genres, and time to write and revise—score higher on state writing tests (Shelton & Fu, 2004). Nancy Shelton, a teacher-researcher in Florida, worried about her writers. They had performed poorly on their state tests, she wanted their scores to rise, and they did!

To make this happen, Shelton created one approach to the teaching of writing for the fall and another for the spring. During the fall, students engaged in a daily writers' workshop, during which they chose their topics, genres, and the processes they used as they worked on their drafts. They became engaged as writers and looked forward to this time each day. Then, in the spring, Shelton taught her writers to use the format required for the state test. They studied it as a genre, learned how to write in that format, and performed better than her students had in previous years.

Engagement as writers for several months, in which students made decisions about their topics, genres, and processes, prepared these students to write for the evaluators of their state test entries. To understand more fully the importance of audience, our next section focuses on it.

Guideline 2: Writers Consider Their Audience

This guideline is supported by research in several areas: Adolescent writers write for a variety of audiences; they write with passion for some audiences, adjust their language for all, and experience restrictions. In many circumstances, our guideline about audience is intertwined with the guideline in the previous section on the importance of choice. Often writers' choices are influenced by the reader(s) the writer has in mind for drafts and, especially, for a final product.

Adolescent Writers Write for a Variety of Audiences

As our profession learned about the importance of audience to writers, we saw great change begin within writing instruction. Instead of the teacher being the only reader/audience, students started to write for a wider range of persons. In particular, when writers intend to take a piece of writing to the public, they consider who will read their final drafts. To polish a piece of writing is not a ritual—the task is accomplished with specific readers in mind.

Often, the first audience that adolescents experience—beyond their teacher—is their classmates. William Bintz and Karen Shelton (2004) write about a teacher-researcher project in which seventh- and eighth-grade students engaged in written conversations. Based on the well-known fact that middle school students are social, this project placed them in a situation where they interacted. Plus, their writing was not assessed.

This particular conversation started with the book *Baseball Saved Us*, by Mochizuki, about a Japanese American boy sent to an internment camp during World War II. The teacher (Blintz & Shelton, 2004) read a portion, the students conversed in writing, she read again, and the cycle continued throughout the book. Overall, they made personal connections, presented their own views, and considered those of the other. Within the safety of these conversations the students' voices were more confident, their perspectives gained breadth and depth, and their sense of responsibility to their writing increased.

The students of middle school teacher-researcher Denise Maltese (2006) wrote for their classmates—and beyond. They each researched a "mover and shaker" in the world, chose an audience outside the classroom for whom to write, and also wrote for a classroom presentation. One girl researched Barbara Aiello, a pioneer in special education, and created a newsletter about Aiello for parents. She performed, for the class, a dramatic reenactment of Aiello as a teacher. The choice of person helped to create a situation in which students were engaged, and the choice of their outside audience further encouraged their commitment. Plus, their choice of how to present their movers and shakers to their classmates helped them to consider this audience in a way that felt comfortable to each of them.

Currently, it is possible to publish adolescent writers' creations by accessing publishers online. Teacher-researcher Dawn Putnam (2001) wanted to engage her 10th-grade students in a writing project that meant something to them. She chose a company that would publish their final drafts in a book. Each student chose a piece of his or her writing to revise, edit, and submit.

Putnam noticed that her students' engagement increased along the way, and they were excited when each person in the class received a copy of the anthology.

Putnam (2001) expanded on this idea the following year. Students' creation of an anthology that others (businesses in the community) could purchase influenced the topics they addressed. In addition, because of this larger audience, other writing choices became important: cover color, design, title, font, and acknowledgments for the book. The students wrote letters to the business owners explaining why they should consider purchasing these books and how their businesses could benefit from selling them—again, they considered authentic audiences.

Adolescents Write with Passion for Some Audiences

Teacher-researcher Donna Mahar (Chandler-Olcott & Mahar, 2001) and her suburban, seventh-grade English students established pen pal relationships with primary children from an urban area. The young adolescents became personally attached to their new, little friends, and planned two celebrations for them. For these events the seventh graders wrote memos and produced a book of poetry for the children, experiences that required the students to work for real purposes and with real audiences that were important to them. The young adolescents cared about the little children and about their writing.

Literacy in the lives of adolescents, however, is often complex. A 5-year ethnographic research study by Theresa McGinnis (2007) helps us see situations in which immigrant middle school writers consider their audiences—and when they don't. McGinnis observed two students in their public middle schools, their homes, and their communities. In their homes, McGinnis saw these students engaged; they wrote with an audience in mind; their writing counted. Most of it was social—notes, messages, letters, e-mails. They wrote to connect with others and to remain connected; their writing mattered.

In school, however, the students' writing did not engage them; they had few writing experiences, and when they did write, they responded to texts. Absent were literacy experiences in which they explored critical, important issues to them as poor, urban, immigrant adolescents. McGinnis (2007) speculated that these students, who had been engaged during their earlier school years, would have remained so had their teachers involved them in critical literacy projects. That happened when Hannah Mancina (2005), a high school, freshman English teacher-researcher took advantage of an unexpected opportunity to engage her students in a social action project. Prior to this, the adolescents in her alternative high school for students who had not been successful in regular settings saw little value in themselves and were unengaged in her classroom. Too often, she reflected, she had been not only their sole audience but she had also served as a "compliance officer," who judged the correctness of their writing.

That role changed the day Mancina (2005) walked into her classroom and found the students engaged in a newspaper article about a marijuana bust that involved some of their peers. The students continued to read the article despite her pleas to put it away. Rather than impose her curriculum, she engaged the students in their curriculum and used the newspaper article as an opportunity to immerse the students in a social action project.

Mancina (2005) brought in articles from the newspaper that addressed their high school. None of the articles were positive accounts. The students became angry when they learned that the press portrayed them negatively. In response, they wrote letters to the editor and to the community, informing them about the school as they viewed it. When no noticeable change occurred as a result of their letters, the students moved forward.

The students hypothesized that the community in general had negative feelings about their school. So Mancina (2005) challenged them to discover whether those perceptions were accurate. When the students interviewed community members, they received a pleasant surprise: They heard nothing but positive comments about their school. They then questioned the sincerity of those thoughts; they wondered whether the interviewees sugarcoated their responses. These concerns informed their research reports in class and led them to write to various members of the community.

Mancina (2005), excited about this social action project, asked her students to write about the benefits and drawbacks of writing from their hearts, for real audiences. Every one of them felt that these experiences had positively influenced them as writers. One student wrote, "It made me feel great because I knew that I might actually be able to make a difference"; another stated that writing to a real audience made him feel "important" (p. 35).

Similarly, high school English teacher-researcher Lori Kixmiller (2004) conducted a case study of Teresa, a writer in one of her classes, who became engaged when she "discovered an audience that cared about her topic" (p. 30). Teresa's story began when Kixmiller started to allow choices and one student, an African American boy, shared his story about being pulled over by the police when he drove his car through a wealthy suburban neighborhood. He felt that he was being profiled. Upset by this, Teresa asked, "Can I write about police brutality in Indianapolis?" She chose her peers as her audience, hoping to persuade them to be advocates against racial profiling. Teresa, who had always been disinterested in writing, became engaged. "She dove into her research for the first time all year because she found a topic that mattered to her and a sympathetic audience to appeal to" (p. 29).

Writing passionate letters can also bring adolescents into writing. Kate Kessler (2005) studied high school students who wrote to persons at establishments that had wronged or slighted them in some way. In each case, the students received reparations from the company! Few had ever written for an audience other than a teacher, and they now certainly realize "they have the power to effect change through their writing" (p. 91). Kessler expands "Teaching writing is not just about a teacher audience. One of our goals as writing teachers should be to prepare students to write beyond the academic class-room. They need to be prepared to enter the world of civic literacy" (p. 95).

Ernest Morrell (2006) devotes his research to the study of urban adolescents who engage in critical participatory action research in their communities. Because of their work for change, their passion about their causes, and development of a sense of empowerment, their literacy achievement benefits. Some of these young researchers work to make sense of violence in their communities; others strive for environmental justice; and still others try to resolve the lack of access for people with physical disabilities.

Typically, students work in groups, and each group chooses a project—a cause within their community to work on together. Students collect data and write it up for publication (letters, reports) and presentation to the authentic audiences. These causes are important to them, and their voices gain confidence. Their participatory action research (Morrell, 2006) inspires both individual transformation and social action as the students gain a sense of empowerment. The overall intent is to engage youth in projects in which they use their literacy and realize its value. Overall, participation in projects such as these may decrease the achievement gap between urban adolescents and their more affluent counterparts.

A slightly different approach to the study of community issues marks the initiative of high school teacher-researcher Heather Brown (2004), who taught her Native American students to create personal webpages that included pictures, original writings and artwork, and other items that expressed their likes and backgrounds. Then each student created a link to another webpage that presented his or her own research project, which was about some aspect of identity—a concern in the communities, a reality in their culture.

This writing project "transformed" the classroom (Brown, 2004, p. 48) in part because the students wrote about concrete information—themselves, real issues in their communities, and real aspects of their culture—that was unfamiliar to Brown. They were very interested in their own and each other's work, and the talk patterns in the classroom changed as students began to ask one another for help and even to offer it when they saw someone struggling. Ultimately, Brown attributed her students' level of engagement to the world-wide audience the Web provides.

Nowadays, however, students often find their audiences on their own and write on their own, with their friends serving as their only audiences. Gloria Jacobs (2006) studied high school students' uses of instant messaging. Lisa, a student whom Jacobs featured, used instant messaging to study for a midterm exam. As she studied for her test, she sent instant messages to her friends with questions. The audience was authentic, the task was authentic, and the commitment was real. The language that students use for instant messaging is direct and convincing.

Many adolescents engage in various technology-based literacies. Mahar's (Chandler-Olcott & Mahar, 2001) students—mentioned earlier in this chapter—all of whom kept writer's notebooks in which they wrote about whatever they chose, selected something from it each week to expand upon and send to authentic audiences, many of which fell within the new literacies of their age. They created digital videos, animation-inspired fanfictions, and blogs.

The era of new literacies expands the range and nature of the audience in writing. When students blog, send instant messages, and reveal details of their lives via social networking websites, the audience response is written, immediate, and anonymous. This technology expands the audience possibilities for adolescents who wish to connect to a larger, global online community.

These young people, as hypothesized by Gee (2000), are on their way to becoming workers who design, implement, and transform networks and systems. When Lisa (Jacobs, 2006) uses instant messaging, she is able to take up the roles of text producer, consumer, and distributor. The digital world takes our students beyond our print-based notions of audience.

Adolescent Writers Adjust Their Language for Their Audiences

Writing for real audiences gives students occasions to pause and consider the exact language they use. When Maltese's (2006) students—referred to earlier in this chapter—wrote about "movers and shakers," they wrote two renditions, one for each of two audiences. This experience not only engaged them in a situation where they needed to adjust their language, it gave them an opportunity to study language itself.

For another project, her students wrote letters to authentic audiences, and one boy wrote a complaint letter to the superintendent. While doing so, he asked, "Can I use slang?" Such considerations (e.g., when to say what in which language) are decisions that writers must make over the course of time, for a variety of audiences.

To become adept, students need to experience the universe of discourse (Moffett, 1968). The variety of languages available to writers is wide, and the breadth and depth to which adolescents engage can improve their ability to adapt to any single situation.

In addition to variance in discourse, editing language for preciseness becomes especially important when the audience matters. Mancina (2005) reported that her students—mentioned earlier in this chapter—improved their pieces of writing via editing when they wrote to audiences in their community. They wanted their work to make a good impression. The process of editing, often a dreaded task, becomes less so when the audience is valued.

Fortunately, the number of adolescents who find themselves in classrooms with such opportunities is increasing. Kessler (2005) writes about this change as an extension of the change from product to process writing, and argues that we are now in an age of postprocess writing, in which discovery and meaning making (process), and writing conventions (product) are both important. Then, she acknowledges the canons of rhetoric (invention, arrangement, style, memory, and delivery), and focuses on the fifth canon—delivery—as an important postprocess action. Thus, *audience*—the reader to whom the creation is delivered—becomes an important consideration within our new age of writing.

Adolescent Writers Experience Restrictions

National American College Testing (ACT) survey results (Patterson & Duer, 2006) reveal that many in our profession create an unhealthy situation for some students. ACT researchers collected data from secondary and postsecondary teachers of reading and writing, and the most significant finding they present to us pertains to the difference in types of instruction in high school classrooms of college-bound and non-college-bound students. In classes of college-bound, students, individuals are taught to "change the focus of their papers, depending on the audience they are addressing" (p. 84). This, unfortunately, is not taught in classes of non-college-bound students. The difference between the two tracks is amazing. To consider various audiences needs to be added to the repertoire of instructors who teach non-college-bound students.

Nowadays, however, such restrictions placed on some students by their teachers receive less attention than those placed on all students because of mandated tests. A new form of audience has become important. Students must write for the readers of state tests. Although this does not necessarily have to be a negative factor, it has become so. Typically, the writing these readers want to read does not place students in a position to choose topics or genres, or to engage in processes that appeal to them. The audience that students must write for in these situations places restrictions on students' passions; the students often write from duty rather than from their hearts.

Especially important is the danger that we educators will devote overly large chunks of instructional time to satisfying the readers of tests. Teresa's case (Kixmiller, 2004), presented earlier in this chapter, shows the importance of not limiting our teaching to practice for tests. "Effectively teaching audience appeal is vital, especially given our current educational climate of formulaic writing for standardized assessment (p. 30). ... If we simply design assignments as vacuous writing prompts such as *Design your favorite place; use specific examples*, we do not acknowledge the rhetorical power that invoking an audience can have for students" (p. 33). If Kixmiller had taught only vacuous prompts, Teresa might not have become a writer.

Such projects, however, provide a backdrop against which students can study the language they need when they write for state tests. Maltese (2006) worries that the mandates of No Child Left Behind (NCLB) limit authenticity and narrow the curriculum. The only response that students receive from standardized tests (if they receive any response) is their score; they don't know the impact of their language on their audience. A number is not an appropriate response from an audience to a writer; it disregards the essence of the art of writing. It disregards the crucial importance of the audience to adolescent writers.

"Kids write with purpose and passion when they know that people they care about reaching will read what they have to say. More importantly, through using writing to reach out to the world, students learn what writing is good for. ... They discover why writing matters in their lives and in others' and what it can do for them and the world" (Atwell, 1998, p. 489).

Guideline 3: Writers Evaluate Their Work

This guideline is supported by research in several areas: Writers benefit from supportive evaluation; their self-evaluations can enable them as writers; they may suffer when evaluation is claimed to be precise; and they prosper when they value a wide range of discourses. In many circumstances, our guideline about evaluation is intertwined with the guidelines of the previous sections on the importance of choice and audience. When adolescent writers evaluate their work, they often do so with their intended audiences in mind, as they consider the choices/decisions they made throughout the process of writing when they created the particular draft at hand.

Adolescent Writers Benefit from Supportive Evaluation

Evaluation of writers and their writing, above all else, is supportive of the writer's intent. Gone are the days of the Red Pen that highlights the negative; we found nothing in defense of that approach to evaluation. Evaluation that tells the writer what the reader learned and appreciated is evaluation that energizes the writer. To discourage is not the goal of a writing teacher. Typically, this supportive response, because of the variance our global community values among writers, occurs in classrooms where writers are known by their teachers and peers. They all engage in busy work sessions, and the teachers work and confer amid the adolescents.

For many who are new to the teaching of writing, this classroom is very different than those in which they found themselves as students. Colleen Ruggiere (2000), a high school teacher-researcher, writes about the dramatic changes in her classroom when she totally changed her way of teaching to move herself from the center. She was no longer the only evaluator. Throughout the periods of time when her students were engaged in the process of writing, they interacted in support and appreciation of each others' efforts. And, they read their final drafts aloud for additional confirmation.

Instead of focusing on the modes of communication, as she had in her previous form of teaching, she focused on encouraging her students to voice their thoughts. Ruggiere (2000) did not grade their weekly assignments, so her students worried less about their grades and concentrated more on voicing their ideas. The class grew as a community: Students came to value each other as writers/persons. They worked together to support each others' explorations into the world of writing.

Sometimes, when confirmation is not a feature of students' English classes, researchers create alternative experiences. Thus, Emily Skinner (2007) created an afterschool writing club for nine adolescent girls in the Bronx. As the White facilitator for a diverse group of nonwhite girls, Skinner provided support that showed she valued them. She listened and learned about them and their culture, much of which was new to her. Skinner permitted the girls to engage in conversations that might be considered off-task in classrooms. In doing so, she showed the value she placed on their conversations, interactions, and identities. This overall context provided a foundation for the success of the writing workshop Skinner created for the girls in their sessions. They knew that her evaluations supported them as writers.

Alfred Tatum (2005) realizes that middle school classrooms that include several Black males who live in turmoil need to be tightly structured settings in which students' self-identities become strong. This led him to create a different instructional environment than he would provide for students who do not live amid unrest. His passionate belief in the importance of support for adolescent boys began with his own beginnings. An African American middle school teacher who grew up in poverty, Tatum used literacy to become strong. Based on his own experiences, he set up his classrooms so that his students, similarly, used literacy to gain strength.

With supportive response Tatum's (2005) students find value in themselves; therefore, they see a reason to work hard—to close their own achievement gaps. Black adolescent males who don't have a strong self-image have to prove themselves to others; in so doing, they often, much too often, become involved in negative social engagements, and get shot. Because their sense of identity is formed both outside and inside school, literacy instruction that focuses on enabling them to believe in their own self-worth is a matter of life or death.

In Tatum's classroom, his African American males find materials in which they see themselves; the content supports their culture and provides a way to a different, better reality. Importantly, he sets high academic standards. The value he sees in his students—and their realization that he values them—leads to their literacy growth.

Adolescent Writers' Self-Evaluations Can Enable Them as Writers

Self-evaluation takes writers beyond being the recipients of supportive response; instead, they become the creators of the situation in which they work. Self-evaluators see their work as worthwhile, know what they can do well, and intentionally place themselves in positions where they will become increasingly proficient. Writers who can evaluate their own work can independently move ahead: They can figure out what they want and need to do next on their journey within the world of writing. In classrooms where students are taught to evaluate their own work, the writers learn to use their self-evaluations to determine their own goals.

Janet Emig (1983) may have originated the notion of writers/students as evaluators of their own work. In her groundbreaking dissertation/study *The Composing Processes of Twelfth Graders*, published in 1971, she brought adolescents into the field of research on writing instruction. After evaluating students' processes and finding that their composing processes were governed by what they thought their teacher wanted, and that it hadn't occurred to them that there may be something they would want, she wrote:

> Finally, a shift may consequently come in who evaluates whom, and to what end. ... American high schools and colleges must seriously and immediately consider that the teacher-centered presentation of composition, like the teacher-centered presentation of almost every other segment of a curriculum, is pedagogically, developmentally, and politically an anachronism. (pp. 88–95)

Emig's (1983) commitment to a shift may not yet be a reality. A recent group of researchers (Pajares, Johnson, & Usher, 2007) studied the sources of students' self-efficacy beliefs about themselves as writers. They administered a true–false, 28-item, Likert-formatted instrument to elementary- and secondary-level, White, middle-class students in various parts of the United States. Their multiple regression analyses showed that students, especially middle school students, believe they are good writers if their teachers think they "master" their assignments. Self-evaluation—the ability to find value in one's own work—still may not be an outcome of composition instruction, 30 years after Emig urged change.

This research was, unfortunately, confirmed by interviews of 49 high school boys, conducted by Michael Smith and Jeffrey Wilhelm (2004). The boys do embrace literacy—the kinds they engaged in outside of school. As they said, "I just like being good at it," but "good at it" they are not when the measure is mastery, as defined by their teachers, on what the boys considered to be inauthentic tasks. The authors end with these sentences: "Within this bleak picture there is a seed of hope. Our data suggest that at least some boys reject literacy ... because of the way they encounter literate activity in school—and that is in our power to change" (p. 461).

Jane Hansen (1998) writes about teachers who do change. In a junior high school English class of students who either did not do their assignments or completed them in a perfunctory fashion, the teacher decided to teach students how to set reasonable goals for themselves. They designed lesson plans for work they cared about, and they engaged in it. Then, when the teacher added assignments to those students created for themselves, they started to become involved in her tasks as well—more so than ever before. About their newfound enthusiasm, their teacher wrote, "I can't believe how directed my students continue to be about their goal-setting lesson plans. ... I have to tell you, I don't have any regrets with this new strategy" (p. 66).

Overall, as the students in that English class (Hansen, 1998) learned to evaluate their drafts, they learned to find value in them. Their teacher taught them to read drafts with the following intentions: (1) to find value in their own work, (2) to find value in the work of the other writers in their classroom, and (3) to find value in the work of published writers. The central form of evaluation that guided these writers forward was self-evaluation. They saw themselves as writers, and writers, by definition, work to become better. The information they needed to improve was determined to a large intent by the experiences their teacher provided.

Top-notch writing teachers engage their students in reading, and in the study of those texts. Writers learn to find value in the texts of others, and they find value in many genres. As instructors, we teach them to use the writing they read/hear as mentor texts to guide them as they intentionally become better writers. Research by Korat Ofra and Rachel Schiff (2005) shows the influence of reading on students' ability to articulate qualities of good writing. They studied readers to find out whether children who read more books (as indicated on a Title Recognition Test) are better able to recognize "good writing" (as determined by answers to open-ended questions). They collected data from sixth-grade students from low and high socioeconomic status (SES) populations.

Overall, the low-SES students read less than the high-SES students, and this did affect their ability to identify and to produce good writing. Importantly, the smaller amount of reading by the low-SES students negatively influenced them as writers more than the higher amount of reading positively influenced the high-SES children, supposedly because the latter were influenced by many factors in life. Their higher amount of reading, in other words, didn't influence them as writers as much as the lower amounts of reading affected the low-SES students. This research brings to our attention the importance of reading for low-SES students if they are to produce good writing. Writers read. And, writing teachers provide for this in their instruction.

Linda Rief and Sarah Jasinski (1996), a middle school teacher–student duo, write about Sarah, a 14-year-old girl who creates a portfolio to show who she is as a person, who she is as a writer, and who she is as a reader—although, as a writer, she is a reader. She chose the items for her portfolio and wrote a commentary about each choice. Overall, they show two reasons why students' self-evaluations are important. First, as Rief states, "We must guide and teach students how to evaluate their own processes and products if we want them to be thoughtful, articulate, literate, and independent" (p. 42). To move forward—to become independent writers—adolescents must be able to evaluate their own drafts and processes in order to improve their work. Second, for teachers to move forward—to become teachers who provide authentic, direct instruction tailored to what their adolescent writers see as their needs— teachers must know their writers' perceptions of themselves, their work, and the work of other writers.

Overall, these encounters allow writers to evaluate their own work effectively, but the dynamic changes these teachers and students experience involve courage, especially in our current era of high-stakes tests. Unfortunately, these powerful assessments often evoke change in the opposite direction of that envisioned by these teachers and their adolescent writers.

Adolescent Writers May Suffer When Evaluation Is Claimed to Be Precise

Jean Ketter and Jonelle Pool (2001) examined the impact of high-stakes tests on three teachers and their students in two classrooms in a rural Maryland high school. They collected data via interviews, observations, and writing documents, and used their information to determine how high-stakes testing influence instruction.

They found that teachers adapt their writing instruction to meet the demands of the test. Because of this high-stakes climate, their instruction changes from being more reflective to being less reflective, and from being more sensitive to individual students to being less so. The criteria for passing the tests consider neither the various cultures within the school nor the complexity of literacy learning; thus, instruction assumes a homogeneous, simplistic stance. The learning environment changes from a place where students have choices as writers, to a place where choice is restricted, making the classroom less engaging for students.

The pressure that these teachers felt with regard to testing misled them into thinking they needed to alter their instruction. The tests changed the definition of success—from success by writers who engage in writing that is increasingly effective in the eyes of various real audiences, including the author, to success by writers who engage in writing that is effective in the eyes of one audience that may be performing an inauthentic task. The readers of the state test essays do not necessarily read as readers. They read as representatives of a rubric created by a composite of readers who may or may not represent the values of the evaluator as a reader.

To substantiate the negative influences of national tests, such as those sponsored by NCLB, Dorothy Suskind (2007) researched that scenario. NCLB legislation, with its increased scrutiny of school accountability, promotes a state/federal curriculum supported by published curricular programs rather than student-centered curricula in which students' work guides teachers' instructional decisions. This has serious implications for writing instruction. In an effort to achieve high quantitative scores on writing assessments, teachers feel pressured to teach writing in a way that is not authentic. The assessment, in other words, influences writing instruction in a negative manner. It narrows the possibilities for adolescent writers to make decisions about their work, to consider a wide range of audiences, and to develop internal standards, so that they can become independent writers.

Overall, NCLB contradicts the principles that serve as the foundation for evaluation in literacy (Johnston & Costello, 2005). Current understandings indicate that the ability to guide and to monitor one's own learning is essential to learners. Plus, it is essential for teachers to teach evaluation practices in which adolescents become able to "self-regulate" their forward motion—and their literacy achievement. This our profession knows. This, however, is not necessarily what happens in our current era.

Johnston and Costello (2005) write, "The U.S. has currently reached the highest volume of testing and the highest stakes testing in its history. We are reminded of a definition of fanaticism as the act of redoubling one's efforts while having forgotten what one is fighting for" (p. 265).

Rubrics, the typical means of scoring high-stakes tests, claim precision—an impossible claim for an endeavor that strives for difference, and for which there are no precise expectations. It would be ludicrous to apply a rubric to all novels of a given year to determine the Pulitzer Prize. Gradually, teachers are acquiring the courage to reject rubrics—to not be a part of the fanaticism of testing. Yet for state tests—a huge number of which are essays—all entrants are judged by one standard.

Maja Wilson (2007, 2006), a high school teacher in Michigan, presents a passionate argument in "Why I Won't Be Using Rubrics to Respond to Students' Writing" (2007). Wilson writes, "While numbers work pretty well for communicating certain kinds of precise information, we have kept words around for their evocative, emotive, associative power. Increased pressure to standardize our reactions to words violates their nature" (p. 63).

With this in mind, Wilson (2006) provides the following example:

> The rubric's attempt to reduce our reaction to a text to a number goes counter to every instinct we have about reading and response. Imagine how quickly the conversation in a book club would be cut short if our meetings revolved around representing our responses to the latest best-seller in numbers: *Poisonwood Bible*—voice, 5; or organization, 3. We might introduce these rankings as an inside English teacher joke, but the numbers would never be the focus of our time together; peeling back the layers in the text and the pure pleasure of the words experienced together would keep us coming back for more. (p. 29)

Yes, to escape that scary reality is a must—for the sake of our students. Randy Bomer (2006) joins the chorus of professionals who lament the repressive nature of testing. It silences adolescent voices and scares teachers into prescribed, scripted curricula. When students write for inauthentic purposes, about topics that are disconnected from their lives, they receive not-so-subtle messages that their lives are meaningless. Their test scores become their identity in a "culture of accountability based upon lack of trust, suspicion that people are not trying hard enough or learning well enough, suspicion of every type of learning that cannot be easily measured and controlled" (p. 11).

Meanwhile, as high-stakes tests measure the very basis of students' literacy knowledge, adolescents busy themselves redefining and inventing new forms of literacy via blogs, webpages, social networking, and e-mail. This is the literacy that affects the lives of adolescents. When these discourses are not regarded as legitimate forms of expression, communication, and thinking, school becomes inconsequential.

Adolescent Writers Prosper When They Value a Wide Range of Discourses

Since they were children, adolescents have automatically adjusted their spoken language when they talk to different people. Their ability to adjust, however, depends on the range of people with whom they engage. This carries over into writing. If teachers create classrooms in which adolescents write for different audiences, their range of competence should broaden.

James Gee (2000), however, presents the difficulty of this in the concept of *social languages*. The discourses in which people engage on a daily basis can breed elitism, insecurity, or a welcoming approach to others, depending on the value a person places on the importance of diverse discourses. Gee exemplifies his claim in relation to today's workers. There are three types of workers in our current, capitalist economy: (1) symbol analysts (persons who design, implement, and transform networks and systems), (2) enchanted workers (product/service employees who must collaborate and redesign their work as a whole process), and (3) backwater workers (part-time or on-demand workers who perform the low-level service jobs, or jobs that require brute strength but little knowledge).

The increasingly common scripted curriculum in today's classrooms, Gee (2000) declares, prepares children (labeled "at-risk" by schools and the dominant culture) to be backwater workers. "The New Literacy Studies would argue that these children, in fact, never learned to read in the sense of being able to actively recruit distinctive oral and written social languages for learning within socioculturally recognizable and meaningful academic Discourses" (p. 413).

The situation worsens. All students suffer. In our tendency to view test scores and position in the work force through the eyes of "higher is better," we tend to overlook the elitism we breed. In his study, Gee (2000) looked at two sets of middle school teenagers, those from working-class families and those from upper-middle-class families. He interviewed them, analyzed their I-statements, and used them to illustrate how students fashion themselves according to the world in which they live.

The upper-middle-class students viewed their social situation as more acceptable—more value-able—than that of the working-class students. Gee (2000) includes transcripts from two upper-class White students, who say things like "[Even though low-income students don't have as good a school system] I believe every person has equal chances, um, to become what they want to be" (p. 418). Another White student says (about the lack of African American and Hispanic doctors),

> Well, they're probably discriminated against, but, but it's not really as bad as, as people think it is, or that it once was. Because, uh, I was watching this thing on TV about this guy that's trying to … How colleges and some schools have made a limit—and they've increased the limits on how many black and Hispanic students they have to have. So, a bunch of white people [rising intonation] are

getting—even if they have better grades than the black or Hispanic student, the black or Hispanic student gets in because they're black or Hispanic. So, I think that that kinda plays an effect into it. (p. 417)

It appears that adolescents of the dominant culture are oblivious to those who are not members, that somehow they think everyone has equal chances despite the inequality that still exists. This implies that writing teachers have a task to consider: In what ways can we fashion our classrooms and the writing tasks so that our students interact with, acknowledge, and value a variety of persons and discourses? In so doing, research shows, our students may become more effective writers.

Students who are not from the dominant White culture, however, continue to find themselves in troubled classrooms, where their teachers do not appreciate their culture, do not value their discourse patterns. Sarah Beck (2006), who collected the data for her dissertation in a high school, found urban students who were at odds with their "traditional" teacher. The culture of many of the students differed from that of the teacher, who had not reflected on who he was, who his students were, and what this meant for him as a teacher.

To incorporate the literacies of adolescents into our teaching shows them we care, and it helps us to value their world. J. Bucky Carter (2007) incorporates graphic novels as reading and writing material. In particular, he uses *Ultimate Spider-Man*, including the longtime Spider-Man mantra "with great power comes great responsibility." Adolescents want great power, and think about this when they use the long-standing notion of "show and tell" as they create their comics. They test their writerly voices, while they explore the possibilities of this new discourse.

Another new medium about which teens tend to know more than their teachers is blogging. Sylvia Read (2006) examined the literature on blogging and participated in the blogs of several young adolescents to understand their motivation to engage in this literacy act. She maintained digital correspondence with six adolescent bloggers (ages 13–18) throughout several weeks. Read charted the content, format, frequency of comments, and motivation for each blogger. Overall, she found that students were motivated by an innate, basic human need to relate and to connect with others about their lives. Blogs provided them with an outlet to do so.

The adolescents used blogs to communicate with friends, share feelings, get responses from peers, and seek validation for their lives (Read, 2006). For most of these adolescents, responses from the audience motivated them to continue writing. For Sean, however, who wrote about his feelings, his girlfriend, and his feelings about his girlfriend, blogging to an invisible audience did not fulfill his need for response. He explains, "Subtly, perhaps subconsciously, I asked for people to contact me, to talk to me, to validate my existence. … I stopped, uh, blogging because I was confessing my problems to an invisible audience without coming to terms with them first" (p. 42). Shortly after Read studied Sean's blog, he quit blogging indefinitely.

New literacies, however, redefine evaluation for many adolescent writers. In blogging, the audience remains at a "digital distance"—close enough for immediate and intimate responses but far enough to avoid face-to-face interaction. Many adolescents feel secure with the distance of the audience and are empowered to record their life histories onto a permanent space. They can write about what is important to them without fear of being put down. And the writer who no longer feels compelled to seek continued validation, as was the case with Sean, can leave that space behind without consequence.

Another of our adolescents' current literacies is zines. Tobi Jacobi (2007) studied adolescent girls that her college students worked with as they created their version of *zines* (publications that originated as underground venues for free expression, often conveyed in multiple genres on a singular topic chosen by the writer). After 6 weeks of writing, each person examined her body of work, chose pieces for her zine, and collaborated with others as they revised, edited, and prepared to read aloud for their invited audience of teachers and families. It was an amazing event. The value the adolescents saw in their work became contagious. One audience member was so touched that she stood and read a piece of her own writing to the audience.

The adolescents felt valued. That is the key to evaluation. Evaluation that energizes, that brings an adolescent to feel larger, that leads to confidence—this is the kind of evaluation that effective educators use in classrooms where adolescents write. Cindy Aguilar (Aguilar, Fu, & Jago, 2007) talks about the complicated nature of this. To find value in adolescent writers is to see their writing nested within their selves. We close this section of our chapter with her words:

> Teaching [adolescent] English language learners means understanding and valuing our students' cultural backgrounds and life experiences, as well as knowing their literacy in their home language and school experience. (p. 116)

Concluding Thoughts

What compels adolescents to write? Who do they write for? How do adolescents know they have connected with their audiences? These questions guide writing instruction in adolescents' classrooms. When students are empowered with choice, understand that they write for authentic audiences, and engage in evaluation (both self- and teacher-directed), they realize that writing serves a real purpose in their lives.

Writing is a social process—and this is especially important to most adolescents—that serves multiple purposes in the lives of those who engage in it. It allows adolescents to inform, communicate, entertain, think, connect, respond, critique, explain, persuade, and express. And this current adolescent generation finds brand new ways to engage in these writing acts via blogs, social networking websites, instant messaging, multigenre papers, graphic novels, anime, and electronic journal entries. Most adolescents engage in this type of writing from home, and teachers who define literacy in expansive terms find ways to bring these student interests into the classroom. Engagement in writing comes when students are empowered with choices, write for multiple audiences, and receive constructive and connective responses to their words. This is what compels writers to write.

QUESTIONS FOR DISCUSSION

1. Write a list of your students on the left side of the paper. On the right side of the paper, create a list of their interests. Was this easy or difficult for you to do? What are some ways you can find out more about your students' interests? How can knowing their interests guide you in helping them connect with topics for writing?

2. Besides choices in topics, what are some other choices that can empower adolescent writers?

3. Although choice is often indicated in the research literature as crucial for writers, why is choice often so limited in writing classrooms? What role has high-stakes testing played in limiting choices for writers? In what classroom circumstances might you feel justified to limit choice?

4. Ask students to determine the audience for several pieces of their writing. Who are they writing for? How often is the teacher the only audience for the writing? In what ways might teachers help students expand their audiences for writing?

5. What role do you think the teacher has when evaluating student writing? What role does the student have when engaging in self-evaluation?

Resources

Further Reading

Elbow, P. (1998). *Writing without teachers*. New York: Oxford University Press.
Ellis, L., & Marsh, J. (2007). *Getting started: The reading–writing workshop, grades 4–8*. Portsmouth, NH: Heinemann.
Kaufman, D. (2000). *Conferences and conversations*. Portsmouth, NH: Heinemann.
Moje, E. (2000). "To be part of the story": The literacy practices of gangsta adolescents. *Teachers College Record, 102*, 651–690.
Murray, D. (2004). *Write to learn* (8th ed.). Boston: Heinle.
Romano, T. (2008). *Zigzag: A life of reading and writing, teaching and learning*. Portsmouth, NH: Heinemann.
Rief, L. (2007). *Inside the writer's–reader's notebook*. Portsmouth, NH: Heinemann.

Website

www.nwp.org—The National Writing Project.
www.learner.org—Anneburg Media.
www.ncte.org—The National Council of Teachers of English.

www.noflyingnotights.com
ublib.buffalo.edu/lml/comics/pages/reading.html
www.informationgoddess.ca/comics@graphicnovels/index.htm

References

Aguilar, C. M., Fu, D., & Jago, C. (2007). English Language Learners in the classroom. In K. Beers, R. E. Probst, & L. Rief (Eds.), *Adolescent literacy: Turning promise into practice* (pp. 105–125). Portsmouth, NH: Heinemann.

Allen, C., & Swistak, L. (2004). Multigenre research: The power of choice and interpretation. *Language Arts, 81*(3), 223–232.

Atwell, N. (1998). *In the middle: New understandings about writing, reading and learning* (2nd ed.). Portsmouth, NH: Heinemann.

Barbieri, M. (2002). *"Change my life forever": Giving voice to English language learners.* Portsmouth, NH: Heinemann.

Beck, S. W. (2006). Subjectivity and intersubjectivity in the teaching and learning of writing. *Research in the Teaching of English, 40*(4), 413–460.

Bintz, W. P., & Shelton, K. S. (2004). Using written conversation in middle school: Lessons from a teacher researcher project. *Journal of Adolescent & Adult Literacy, 47*(6), 492–507.

Bomer, R. (2006). Stories in our classrooms: Diverse human lives, as narrated by standardizing policies. *Voices from the Middle, 13*(3), 8–14.

Brown, H. (2004). Walking into the unknown: Inquiry-based learning transforms the English classroom. *English Journal, 94*(2), 43–48.

Campbell, M. (2002). Constructing powerful voices: Starting points for policy driven literacy assessment reform. *Journal of Reading Education, 27,* 17–23.

Carter, J. B. (2007). *Ultimate Spider-Man* and student-generated classics: Using graphic novels and comics to produce authentic voice and detailed, authentic texts. In J. B. Carter (Ed.), *Building literacy connections with graphic novels: Page by page, panel by panel* (pp. 145–155). Urbana, IL: National Council of Teachers of English.

Chandler-Olcott, K., & Mahar, D. (2001). A framework for choosing topics for, with, and by adolescent writers. *Voices from the Middle, 9*(1), 40–47.

Daniels, E. (2007). Literacy Café: Making writing authentic. *Voices from the Middle, 14*(3), 12–19.

Dickson, R., DeGraff, J., & Foard, M. (2002). Learning about self and others through multigenre research projects. *English Journal, 92*(2), 82–90.

Emig, J. (1971). *The composing processes of twelfth graders.* Urbana, IL: National Council of Teachers of English.

Emig, J. (1983). *The web of meaning: Essays on writing, teaching, learning, and thinking.* Upper Montclair, NJ: Boynton/Cook.

Fletcher, R. (2006). *Boy writers.* Portland, ME: Stenhouse.

Fu, D. (2003). *An island of English: Teaching ESL in Chinatown.* Portsmouth, NH: Heinemann.

Gaughan, J. (2001). *Reinventing English: Teaching in the contact zone.* Portsmouth, NH: Boynton/Cook.

Gee, J. P. (2000). Teenagers in new times: A new literacy studies perspective. *Journal of Adolescent & Adult Literacy, 43*(5), 412–420.

Hansen, J. (1998). *When learners evaluate.* Portsmouth, NH: Heinemann.

Jacobi, T. (2007). The Zine Project: Innovation or oxymoron? *English Journal, 96*(4), 43–49.

Jacobs, G. (2006). Fast times and digital literacy: Participation roles and portfolio construction within instant messaging. *Journal of Literacy Research, 38*(2), 171–196.

Johnston, P., & Costello, P. (2005). Principles for literacy assessment. *Reading Research Quarterly, 40*(2), 256–267.

Kessler, K. (2005). Composing for delivery. *English Journal, 95*(2), 89–96.

Ketter, J., & Pool, J. (2001). Exploring the impact of a high-stakes direct writing assessment in two high school classrooms. *Research in the Teaching of English, 35*(3), 344–393.

Kixmiller, L. (2004). Standards without sacrifice: The case for authentic writing. *English Journal, 94*(1), 29–33.

Lalik, R., & Oliver, K. (2007). Differences and tensions in implementing a pedagogy of critical literacy with adolescent girls. *Reading Research Quarterly, 42*(1), 46–70.

Maltese, D. (2006). Out of the narrow tunnel and into the universe of discourse. *Voices from the Middle, 14*(2), 47–56.

Mancina, H. (2005). Empowering students through a social-action writing project. *English Journal, 94*(6), 31–35.

McGinnis, T. (2007). Are urban middle schools leaving bright immigrant youth behind? *Voices from the Middle, 14*(4), 32–38.

Moffett, J. (1968). *Teaching the universe of discourse.* Boston: Houghton-Mifflin.

Morrell, E. (2006). Critical participatory action research and the literacy achievement of ethnic minority groups. In J. Hoffman, D. Schallert, C. Fairbanks, J. Worthy, & B. Maloch (Eds.), *55th yearbook of the National Reading Conference* (pp. 60–77). Oak Creek, WI: National Reading Conference.

Murray, D. (1999). *Write to learn* (6th ed.). Fort Worth, TX: Harcourt Brace College.

Ofra, K., & Schiff, R. (2005). Do children who read more books know "what is good writing" better than children who read less: A comparison between grade levels and SES groups. *Journal of Literacy Research, 37*(3), 289–324.

Pajares, F., Johnson, M. J., & Usher, E. L. (2007). Sources of writing self-efficacy beliefs of elementary, middle, and high school students. *Research in the Teaching of English, 42*(1), 104–120.

Patterson, J. P., & Duer, D. (2006). High school teaching and college expectations in writing and reading. *English Journal, 95*(3), 81–87.

Putnam, D. (2001). Authentic writing using online resources: Selling our words in the community. *English Journal, 90*(5), 101–106.

Putz, M. (2006). *A teacher's guide to the multigenre research project: Everything you need to get started.* Portsmouth, NH: Heinemann.

Read, S. (2006). Tapping into students' motivation: Lessons from young adolescents' blogs. *Voices from the Middle, 14*(2), 38–46.

Rief, L. (2008). Writing: Commonsense matters. In K. Beers, R. E. Probst, & L. Rief (Eds.), *Adolescent literacy: Turning promise into practice* (pp. 189–208). Portsmouth, NH: Heinemann.

Rief, L., & Jasinski, S. (1996). Sarah: Speaking for herself. *Voices from the Middle, 3*(4), 32–46.

Romano, T. (2000). *Blending genre altering style: Writing multigenre papers.* Portsmouth, NH: Heinemann.

Ruggiere, C. A. (2000). The value of voice: Promoting peace through teaching and writing. *English Journal, 89*(5), 47–54.

Scherff, L., & Piazza, C. (2005). The more things change, the more they stay the same: A survey of high school students' writing experiences. *Research in the Teaching of English, 39*(3), 271–304.

Schwartz, T. (2004). Writing and neighborhood voices: It depends on where you grow up at. *Voices from the Middle, 12*(1), 16–22.

Shelton, N., & Fu, D. (2004). Creating space for teaching writing and for test preparation. *Language Arts, 82,* 120–128.

Sipe, R. B., & Rosewarne, T. (2006). *Purposeful writing: Genre study in the secondary writing workshop.* Portsmouth, NH: Heinemann.

Skinner, E. (2007). "Teenage addiction": Adolescent girls drawing upon popular culture texts as mentors for writing in an after-school writing club. In D. W. Rowe & R. T. Jiménez (Eds.), *56th yearbook of the National Reading Conference* (pp. 345–361). Oak Creek, WI: National Reading Conference.

Smith, M., & Wilhelm, J. D. (2004). "I just like being good at it": The importance of competence in the literate lives of young men. *Journal of Adolescent & Adult Literacy, 47*(6), 454–461.

Suskind, D. (2007). Going public: NCLB and literacy practices in teacher education. *Language Arts, 84*(5), 450–455.

Tatum, A. (2005). *Teaching reading to black adolescent males: Closing the achievement gap.* Portland, ME: Stenhouse.

Thomas, P. L. (2003). When choice failed—or did it? *English Journal, 92*(6), 17–19.

Wilson, M. (2006). *Rethinking rubrics in writing assessment.* Portsmouth, NH: Heinemann.

Wilson, M. (2007). Why I won't be using rubrics to respond to students' writing. *English Journal, 96*(4), 62–66.

Chapter 21

Grouping in the Middle and Secondary Grades

Advancing Content and Literacy Knowledge

Jeanne R. Paratore
Rachel L. McCormack

Jeanne R. Paratore
Rachel L. McCormack

GUIDING QUESTIONS

1. What do we know about effects of various grouping practices?
2. What organizing principles should guide us as we group students for literacy instruction?
3. How might the experiences of two teachers guide others in grouping students for literacy instruction?

During a recent classroom visit, Joel, an eighth-grade social studies teacher, offered the following explanation for his practice of reading the social studies text aloud to all of his students:

> "I know that what I am doing is wrong. I know it's not best practice. *I'm* doing all the reading, and they [students] aren't getting any practice reading the social studies text. I'm not even sure how much they are paying attention. I just know that I am covering the material."

We were struck by Joel's comment, not because it was unique or unusual, but because it was not. We have heard some variation of this explanation numerous times in our conversations with middle-grade teachers, likely because "covering the material" in today's high-stakes assessment climate is considered fundamental to preparing students for the test. In many middle-grade classrooms, the outcomes follow a familiar pattern: Students are provided a single exposure to important content, usually in some sort of whole-class context, and those who are capable learners acquire essential information (but not much more), whereas students who are less capable learn very little (Ornstein, 1995). So what's a teacher to do? In classrooms of 25–30 students representing a wide range of literacy abilities, topical interests, and motivation to learn, how might various grouping strategies and instructional practices help teachers not only respond to students' literacy strengths and needs but also develop deep understanding of requisite content knowledge?

   In this chapter, we begin by considering ways teachers might organize students for instruction and also examine briefly the types of tasks and activities that are likely to support engagement and learning. Then, we describe the ways that two teachers put the research to work in their classrooms.

Organizing Students for Instruction

There are essentially four ways to organize students for instruction: ability grouping, cooperative learning, peer tutoring, and whole-class learning. Each option has advantages and disadvantages.

Ability Grouping

Studies of traditional ability grouping (i.e., groups formed on the basis on students' abilities that are maintained over long periods of time) generally fail to indicate a pattern of achievement gains associated with the practice of ability grouping (Good & Marshall, 1984; Slavin, 1990). For low-performing learners, evidence indicates "a consistent pattern of deprivation" (Good & Marshall, p. 25). Although a meta-analysis by Lou, Spence, Poulsen, Chambers, and d'Apollonia (1996) showed a slightly different pattern of results, researchers noted a lack of uniformity across the 20 findings they examined. Twelve findings favored homogeneous groups, one found no effect, and six favored heterogeneous groups. Lou et al. found that results differed by ability level: Low-ability students learned more in heterogeneous groups; medium-ability students learned more in homogeneous groups; and there were no differences for high-ability learners.

   Some researchers have sought to understand the outcomes associated with ability grouping by examining the teaching actions and instructional tasks that students experience during the various levels of groups. Studies (Allington, 1983, 1994; Barr & Dreeben, 1991; Hiebert, 1983; Oakes, 1985) consistently find that students in high-performing groups benefit from higher quality teaching actions (e.g., fewer interruptions, brisk pacing), texts (i.e., more interesting topically and linguistically), and instructional tasks (e.g., more time spent reading connected and interesting texts; more time in discussion; more intellectually challenging questions). Given the lower quality of instructional experiences, it is not surprising that students in low-performing groups often experience low self-esteem and negative attitudes toward reading and learning (Braddock & Dawkins, 1993; Eder, 1983; Hiebert, 1983). The fact that a disproportionately high percentage of students from economically poor and linguistic and cultural minority groups is represented in low-ability classes (Braddock & Dawkins, 1993; Gamoran, 1992; Gamoran, Nystrand, Berends, & LePore, 1995; Oakes, 1985)—the same students who remain mired in generally low rates of literacy achievement—increases concerns about ability grouping as a routine practice.

Cooperative Learning

Cooperative learning, as defined by Johnson and Johnson (1987), has four basic elements. The first is *positive interdependence,* the understanding that the success of any individual member of the group is dependent on the success of all members of the group. The second is *face-to-face interaction.* The third is *individual accountability* for mastering assigned material. The fourth is the need for students to have and appropriately use *interpersonal and small-group skills.* Studies (Johnson, Maruyama, Johnson, & Nelson, 1981; Sharan, 1980; Slavin, 1980; Stevens & Slavin, 1995) that compare the effects of cooperative, competitive, and individualistic learning on achievement found that, in most cases, cooperative learning techniques yield significantly greater achievement than traditional grouping practices. Cooperative learning also had strong and consistent effects on self-esteem and ability to work cooperatively. Slavin (1990) noted that such positive findings are most likely to occur when two particular elements are in place: group goals and individual accountability. A close examination of the evidence indicates that effective implementation of cooperative learning requires not simply physical regrouping of students, but careful selection of the learning task, collaborative planning of the task, and a requirement that every individual display knowledge and understanding upon task completion.

Peer Tutoring

Another grouping practice commonly used is that of peer tutoring or peer dyads. Cohen, Kulik, and Kulik (1982) conducted a meta-analysis of 65 studies of peer tutoring. They included studies that took place in actual elementary or secondary schools, that reported on quantitatively measured outcomes in both tutored and untutored groups, and that were free of methodological flaws, such as differing aptitude levels and teaching of the test to one group. In 45 programs, they found that tutored students performed better than their peers in a conventional class. In 20 of these cases, the differences in achievement gains were statistically significant, but the effect sizes were modest. In most cases, both tutors and tutees experienced increased achievement gains. Notably, strong effects were consistently associated with certain features, including highly structured programs and programs of shorter duration that focused on lower-level skills, on mathematics rather than reading, and on programs evaluated on the basis of locally developed rather than standardized achievement tests.

Peer tutoring, then, can lead to higher levels of achievement for both members of tutoring dyads, but such effects are likely to be documented only when the learning task is highly structured and explicit in nature, and measured with an instrument that is highly congruent with the learning activity.

Whole-Class Learning

Most studies indicate that whole-class instruction for long periods of time does not serve students well (Lou et al., 1996). However, there are times when working with students in a whole-class context is beneficial. For example, when introducing a topic or strategy for the first time, or when the instructional purpose is to build a shared experience or common understanding, whole-class instruction might be most effective. For the most part, though, research indicates that motivation and achievement increase when teachers create conditions that prompt students to work in smaller groups (Ornstein, 1995). Ornstein's review of related studies indicated that working with students in small groups rather than as a whole class prompted changes in a number of factors associated with learning consequences. For example, most whole-class settings were marked by a high degree of teacher control, by a single task during which students worked alone, and by tasks that focus on lower-level skills "to keep things simple so that the majority of students can perform the task without frustration" (p. 107). When classes were divided into smaller groups (homogeneous or heterogeneous), tasks changed from single to multiple (more easily tailored to individual needs); from independent to collaborative and social; and from low-level, "right answer" assignments to more intellectually challenging tasks requiring integration of present information with previous topics of study.

Creating Contexts That Motivate and Engage

When asked to name the factor that is most influential in their students' success or failure, many middle-grade teachers first mention students' motivation, which often is perceived as low and as a characteristic that resides within students and their prior (and often individual) experiences, and as being largely outside the control of teachers. But studies of motivation and engagement largely dispute this perception. In their review of studies of motivation for reading, Guthrie and Humenick (2004) found that motivation is explained by four factors, all of which are fully within the control of most classroom teachers: knowledge goals, student choices, interesting texts, and collaboration. A full discussion of strategies and approaches that support motivation and engagement (and deepen content learning) is outside the scope of this chapter. However, central to most practices that successfully support both literacy and knowledge learning are those that emphasize concept-based learning (e.g., concept-oriented reading instruction [CORI]; Guthrie, McRae, & Klauda, 2007), strategy-based instruction (De Corte, Verschaffel, & Van de Ven, 2001; Duke & Pearson, 2002; Harvey & Goudvis, 2000; Kim, Vaughn, & Wanzek, 2004; Palincsar & Brown, 1984; Van Keer, 2004), and discourse strategies that engage students with each other and with the teacher (Blum, Lipsett, & Yocom, 2002; Brice, 2002; Goatley, Brock, & Raphael, 1995; Miller & Legge, 1999; Nystrand, 2006; Raphael, 1997; Raphael & McMahon, 1994).

Responding to Research: Applying the Evidence to the Classroom

To summarize, we interpret the evidence related to grouping to mean that different instructional goals and needs are likely to require different grouping options. The appropriateness of any particular grouping context depends on the fit between the specific learning task and the chosen grouping strategy; students' preparedness to work within the selected context; and the extent to which teachers monitor, support, and challenge students as they work within any of the grouping options. As described elsewhere (e.g., Paratore, 1994; Radencich, McKay, & Paratore, 1995), we perceive effective classrooms to be those in which learning is guided by some basic organizing principles: (1) groups are flexible and changing, with no student functioning as a permanent member of any group; (2) grouping options are selected in response to both individual and curricular needs; (3) the use of different grouping frameworks, which ensures that no student is consistently "left out" of any grouping plan because he or she lacks a specific literacy or social behavior; and (4) a "global" plan characterized by the balanced use of the full range of grouping options. In the next section, we visit classrooms in which teachers put this evidence to work.

We interpret the evidence about motivation and engagement to mean that, as teachers, we have control over factors that, at least over time, might override an individual or a group predisposition to disengage from reading or learning. In the next section, we visit two classrooms in which teachers choose different grouping and instructional strategies to reach the same goal: high levels of engagement and achievement of their middle-grade learners.

The Classroom Context: Research into Practice

Rebecca's Fifth-Grade Classroom

In Rebecca's fifth-grade classroom there are 21 children who represent a wide range of literacy abilities. As Rebecca watched them during the first weeks of school, she found that whereas some students could read and respond to the regular curricular materials with ease, others struggled mightily because of word-level difficulties, comprehension difficulties, or general learning difficulties.

As Rebecca began to consider the instructional contexts and strategies that would be most appropriate to this particular group of fifth graders, she examined many issues. First, as she watched the reluctance with which some students, particularly some of the boys, approached reading tasks in the early days of school, Rebecca was reminded of research indicating that students' motivation and interest in reading often are diminished during later elementary school years (Gambrell, Palmer, & Codling, 1996). She was determined to frame instruction in ways that would, in the best circumstance, spark (or respark) her students' interest in reading, both in and out of school, or, in the worst circumstance, at least engage them during the time they were in her classroom.

Second, Rebecca wanted instruction to reflect what we know as *best practice* in literacy instruction. She planned the classroom instructional routines on the basis of what she understood to be effective practices at all levels of instruction:

1. Students need to read or reread complete text (e.g., story, excerpt, chapter) every day.

2. Students need opportunities to talk to their peers about what they read every day.

3. Students need opportunities to write in response to what they have read and heard every day.

4. Students need opportunities to read something at their comfort level every day.

5. Students need direct instruction in becoming strategic readers and writers every day.

Third, Rebecca understood that if students were to develop the essential comprehension and language knowledge to advance their literacy abilities, it was fundamental for all students to have access to high-quality, grade-appropriate text, either through reading or listening, and for all students to be given equal opportunity to respond through writing and language experiences (Cazden, 1992; Fielding & Roller, 1992).

Fourth, Rebecca recalled what she knew about grouping practices and set out to devise grouping models that incorporated a variety of configurations: whole class, peer-led cooperative groups, needs-based groups, peer dyads, and independent. She knew that the students could move from one grouping situation to another, based on both her own and students' assessment of their needs and interests.

The following section describes three models that Rebecca implemented as a result of this planning. Although the models are alike in the basic literacy and grouping principles outlined earlier, each is unique in its focus and becomes increasingly more demanding in its expectations for student involvement and decision making. Therefore, the models are hierarchical and sequential. To participate effectively in the second model, students must first be accustomed to the literacy and learning strategies of the first; successful participation in the third model assumes familiarity and accomplishment with the second.

The Take-Five Model

The Take-Five model (Wood, McCormack, Lapp, & Flood, 1997) is presented in Figure 21.1. Designed after Paratore's (2000) flexible grouping prototype, it is largely teacher-directed and intended to provide all students opportunities

Literature	Content Areas
Get Ready (Whole Class)	
Review previous work	Review previous work
Activate/build background	Activate/build background
Develop vocabulary	Develop vocabulary
Make predictions	Make predictions
Question	Question
Minilesson	Minilesson
Introduce/implement graphic organizers	Introduce/implement graphic organizers
Comprehension monitoring	Survey text
Read (Various Groupings)	
Read with a focus	Read with a focus
Main idea	Main idea
Reread (Various Groupings)	
With a different focus	For detail
For detail	Skim
To identify areas of confusion	Complete graphic organizers
Verbalize/think aloud	K-W-L
Talk/discuss	Answer questions in text orally
Respond (Various Groupings)	
Response journals	Learning logs
Dialogue journals	Response journals
Arts	Convert graphic organizer to connected text
React (Whole-Class or Various Groupings)	
Share journal entries	Share responses or graphic organizers
Teacher-led or peer-led discussions	

FIGURE 21.1. The Take-Five model.

to learn and practice essential literacy strategies. In addition, it is designed to familiarize all students with various grouping contexts and the types of learning behaviors that are appropriate to each. The same format is carried out each day, allowing students to become knowledgeable about useful, basic instructional routines as they progress to other, more complex instructional models. The planning sheet displayed in Figure 21.2 is helpful in preparing each day's lesson.

The Take-Five model is so named because of its five daily components: get ready, read, reread, respond, and react. In this model, all students read the same high-quality, grade-appropriate text. When the text is a chapter book, students read one chapter, generally 15–20 pages, every day. When the text is a basal reading anthology, the focal selection may be divided into two

---

Title: _____

Chapter/Pages: _____ Date: _____

Get Ready

    ____ Review

    ____ Build and access background knowledge

    ____ Vocabulary:

        _____

        _____

        _____

    ____ Predict

    ____ Self-question

    ____ Minilesson

    ____ Quick write:

Read

    ____ Read aloud ____ Silent ____ Pairs ____ Other

    ____ Modifications: _____

Reread

    ____ Set new purpose: _____

    ____ Read aloud ____ Silent ____ Pairs ____ Other

Respond

    ____ Discussion prompt:

    ____ Whole class ____ Groups ____ Pairs

    ____ Writing prompt:

    ____ Whole class ____ Groups ____ Pairs ____ Individual

React—Share Written Responses

FIGURE 21.2. Teacher planning sheet.

or more sections, depending on length. The procedure for each component follows.

GET READY

This part of the lesson helps students get ready to read. Strategic reading is at the center of the design, and there is a great deal of teacher modeling and many opportunities for guided practice. Prereading activities include activating and building background knowledge, developing vocabulary, making predictions, and posing questions. Students, along with the teacher, often do a *quick write*—a short, one-draft, prereading writing piece—to motivate them to read the selection for the day. In addition, students are sometimes provided a "minilesson" (Calkins, 1994) on a reading or writing strategy. When reading informational text, students may also be guided to survey the text further by filling in a graphic organizer, such as K-W-L (what you know, what you want to know, and what you learned from your reading; Ogle, 1986).

READ

Although the ultimate goal is for all students to read the text independently, in this model, the first few pages are read aloud to provide the whole class a foundation for successful independent reading. During the read-aloud, comprehension monitoring strategies, such as reading ahead, visualizing, summarizing, confirming predictions, rereading, and adjusting reading rate are modeled by the teacher, and students are invited to think aloud and think through the strategies as well. Students are then given a focus to continue reading and are asked to read on independently. A small group of students may remain with the teacher to receive additional support. Depending on individual needs, such extra help may take the form of a read-aloud of the entire selection, partner reading with the teacher or a peer, or listening to the selection on tape.

REREAD

In this component, students reread the selection in whole or in part for different reasons. It may be necessary, for example, to reread the text, or a portion of it, to retrieve specific information, to answer a question from the study guide, to respond to a prompt, or to complete a graphic organizer. For those students who listened to the text on tape or while the teacher was reading aloud, repeated readings of a small section can help to build fluency.

RESPOND

After the readings, students respond to a writing prompt. The prompts are recorded in journals. They can be written in groups led by peers or by the teacher, or they can be composed individually.

REACT

Using their journals as prompts, the students meet in small, peer-led groups or larger, teacher-led groups to share what they wrote in their journals, to express reactions to each other's work, or to extend their thinking.

The Literature Circles Model

As children acquire autonomy in literacy and learning strategies, they progress to the literature circles model. Using strategies suggested by Short (1990) and McMahon and Raphael (1997), this model focuses on literacy learning through peer talk. In literature circles, students are provided ample opportunities to interact with both their peers and their teacher through planning, responding to, and discussing the books they read. Students also get many opportunities to practice the reading strategies they learned and used during the Take-Five model.

In this model, heterogeneous groups of four to six students join together to read a book they have chosen from a selection of several thematically related titles. Prior to reading, students determine how much they will read each day and who will be the student leader of the day. They use a student planning sheet (Figure 21.3), completed by the group leader prior to the first group meeting, to help structure their activities and interactions. Although some group leaders are able to complete the planning sheet on their own, others require teacher assistance to do so.

CLASS MEETING

Literature circles begin each day with a class meeting. Led by the teacher, students share their group plans, ask questions about procedures, and discuss common themes evident throughout the texts. For example, a class reading various texts about the Civil War might benefit from a review of the key incidents surrounding that war, especially if it is part of a thematic unit integrating social studies and literature. In addition, students might be offered a minilesson to introduce or review a skill or strategy of particular importance in understanding the focal texts.

PEER-LED GROUPS

Next, the students meet in their peer-led groups, and the student leader takes over, using the student planning sheet as a guide. Students follow procedures they learned in the Take-Five model: They get ready, read, reread, respond in their writing journals, and react through peer-led discussions.

During the peer-led groups, a phase-in, phase-out model is used by the teacher (Lapp, Flood, Ranck-Buhr, Van Dyke, & Spacek, 1997). As the students read and interact, the teacher observes and redirects students as

Title: _____

Chapter/Pages: _____

Date: _____

Student Leader: _____

Get Ready

Say: (1) Let's review.

        (2) Let's make predictions

        (3) Let's talk about these words: _____

        (4) What questions do we have before reading?

Read

        Let's read.

            ____ In pairs   ____ Alone   ____ In groups

Reread

        Let's think about this while we reread: _____

            ____ In pairs   ____ Alone   ____ In groups

Respond

        Let's respond in our response journals.

React

        What shall we talk about?

FIGURE 21.3. Student planning sheet.

needed. Students who have difficulty reading the text are paired with more able peers or with the teacher during the reading segment. If a student leader is unprepared or incapable of managing the group, the teacher temporarily joins that group. Such teacher interventions are brief and relatively rare, particularly as students gain experience and expertise in leading and participating in the groups.

DEBRIEFING

The whole class reconvenes in a debriefing session to discuss what happened in their groups. Students respond to the themes that tie their groups together, similarities and differences among the books they are reading, and connections to other books they have read individually or as a class. In addition, they sometimes use the debriefing to raise questions about procedures and tasks.

Students' reactions to this model are instructive. They liked working in groups, they liked the format, and they liked the way everyone in the group had a chance to be student leader. One student, Jennifer, expressed her approval in this way:

> "I really like how we get to work with other people. I really enjoy that. They help you fix mistakes in your reading and writing. They're there also to tell you that you did a good job."

The students also learned a great deal about themselves after working so closely with their peers. Alison felt that she learned much more than how to be a better reader; she learned to be part of a group:

> "I learned that sometimes I have to open up and do stuff like this because I am shy. I also learned that I am good in a group."

The students also learned that reading together enriches their understanding of the text. What is difficult to accomplish alone is often made easier through the interactions with peers. Consider Peter's remarks:

> "I have become a better reader. I like to read in groups because you can talk about the books in the groups and ask questions to other group members. It's harder to do that when reading alone."

The Genius Club Model

The Genius Club model derived its name by accident. The students initially misread the word *genus*—selected to indicate that the focus would be on reading books of the same genre—and instead identified the word as *genius*. Although Rebecca promptly corrected the misunderstanding, the students liked referring to themselves as *geniuses*, and the label stuck. The Genius Club model differs from the literature circles model in the following ways:

1. As the original name implies, focal texts are related by genre rather than by theme.
2. Focal texts are differentiated by readability level, enabling lower-performing readers to participate with no teacher or peer support during the reading segment of the lesson.
3. Students pace themselves by reading as quickly or as slowly as is individually comfortable.
4. Students engage in two separate response groups: first with peers who have read different books, then with peers who have read the same book.
5. The response groups are not led by a designated student leader, and each member of the group has equal responsibility in achieving a successful discussion.

The model has two phases. In the first phase, students meet in heterogeneous groups of five or six. Each group is given the same set of five or six books. Within each text set, the books are characterized by the same genre but represent a variety of reading levels. With the teacher's guidance, each student chooses the book he or she will read.

CLASS MEETING

Genius Club begins each day with a teacher-led class meeting. During this time, the teacher leads the students in a discussion of the genre being read. They discuss the characteristics of a particular genre and the ways those characteristics might differ among the books they are reading. For example, if the genre is biography, the teacher might help students understand the difference between factual and fictionalized biographies. In addition, students discuss the similarities and differences they encounter in the books they are reading.

PEER-LED GROUPS

The students then meet in their peer-led groups. For the first 15 or 20 minutes, they read silently. Sometimes they reread what they have read, revisiting parts that they found confusing or that they particularly liked and simply wish to read again. They might also reread and take notes in their journals for discussion later on, recording new or unfamiliar words, jotting down particular ideas, or recording questions they might have.

When students convene to discuss their books, they relate both their general responses and their thoughts about literary elements and the ways their particular books conformed (or did not) to what they have learned about genre. These discussion groups are more cognitively demanding than those that took place during the literature circles model in two ways: (1) The absence of a student leader requires each student to be skilled at entering the discussion in appropriate ways, and (2) the individuality of the text assignments requires students to construct and share their own meaning, with little peer support or assistance.

As with the literature circles, the teacher circulates around the classroom throughout this time and, when necessary, becomes a participant observer by redirecting students to stay on task, answering questions, or assisting lower performing readers in reading the text.

DEBRIEFING

The class ends with a debriefing session. At this time, groups share what they have learned about literary elements and the particular genre they are studying. They might also share snippets of information about their own books, and why they like or do not like them. Teachers comment on and contribute to the students' ideas, and also share their observations about the ways the students are interacting in groups. The first phase of the Genius Club model is planned to take approximately 2 weeks. Because students read at very different rates, some students finish reading only one book during this period, whereas others may choose to read several. At the end of 2 weeks, all students should be ready to enter the second phase.

REGROUPING

At the start of the second phase, students are regrouped so that they can join with other students who have read the same book. Now the groups resemble those in the literature circles model. For the next few days, students meet in their new groups to share their responses to the ideas, characters, events, writing styles, and literary elements of their particular books. Students conclude this phase with a cooperative learning assignment, in which they are required to devise a way to present the information from their books and their group's discussions to the rest of the class. Figure 21.4 presents a sample presentation task sheet for this cooperative activity.

There are many advantages to the Genius Club model. Students read books at their own pace and comfort level. They have an opportunity to discuss the same text from two different perspectives, and with two different groups of peers, and they experience multiple texts in a single genre through interaction with their peers.

Students have been predictably enthusiastic about this alternative format. The flexibility of the groups is appealing to them. They like choosing to be with their friends during the first phase of the model, yet they are happy

---

For your presentation, you will need to do the following:

1. Join other students who have read the same biography.
2. Discuss the person you read about. What did you like about the biography? How is this person like you? How did the person's accomplishments make you feel? What was the person's greatest contribution?
3. Share your vocabulary notebooks. Choose three new words that you all agree are important or interesting words to teach to the class.
4. Plan your 5- to 10-minute presentation. You need to do the following activities:
   - Using your individual summaries as a guide, write a group summary on a 5-by-7 inch index card. Choose someone in your group to read it.
   - Think of a way to present a main event in that person's life to the rest of the class.
   - Think of a way to teach three new words to the rest of the class.
5. Practice your presentation.

FIGURE 21.4. Presentation task sheet.

to share what they have read with students who have read the same book in the second phase of the model. They especially like being able to read at their own pace. As one student stated:

> "We got to read at our own level and speed. Sometimes when I read, I have to go back and reread something I've read. I could do that without worrying about slowing my group down."

Joel's Eighth-Grade Social Studies Classroom

Joel, the teacher whose comment we used to begin this chapter, is an eighth-grade teacher with 24 students who represent a wide range of reading abilities. Similar to many other middle school social studies teachers with whom we have worked, Joel often regrets the amount of content he needs to teach in his eighth-grade social studies classroom and that he has "so little time to do it." He acknowledges that he had "all but eliminated" the students' reading of the course text. Instead, he said, he read the text aloud to the whole class, stopping periodically to paraphrase the important information. Occasionally, he asked some students to read aloud. He explained that (1) the text is too hard for some of the students to read, and (2) the students preferred that he read the text aloud, then paraphrase the contents so they could understand it. As he indicated in the earlier quote, Joel was aware that many of his students were disengaged, but, as he explained, "I just know that I am covering the material."

We agreed with Joel's evaluation that the practice of reading aloud to all of his students was probably not helping most of them to learn the content, at least not in the way that he was implementing it. (For examples of effective strategies for reading aloud to adolescents, see Allen, 2002.) Moreover, we were concerned that Joel was not teaching his students to read (and understand) the text, which they would surely have to do on their own as they advanced to higher grades. We wanted to help Joel teach his students the social studies content without reading the text aloud to all of his students—or at least not *only* reading the text aloud. We also wanted to help Joel engage his students in text reading, talking about the text, and working collaboratively in flexible groups. During our work with Joel, the eighth graders were studying the American Revolution. They were about to learn about the early colonists, who were categorized as either Patriots or Loyalists. As we took a look at the text Joel used, we noticed that the chapter began by explaining what the terms *Loyalist* and *Patriot* meant, and continued with an explanation of which colonists would most likely be a Loyalist or a Patriot. Joel said,

> "I can explain the terms. But the next several pages in the text include biographical sketches of six important historical figures who represent Loyalists and Patriots. I just can't do them justice by having the students read the pages for homework. I'm better off reading the pages aloud."

We suggested using a cooperative grouping format and teaching technique called *jigsaw* (Aronson & Patnoe, 1997) to engage the students in reading and talking about the text (see Figure 21.5). In a jigsaw grouping format, students participate in two different grouping configurations. In the first, students read and discuss a section of a text and become experts on that portion. In the second grouping configuration, one member from each of the original groups joins with others to form a group that comprises members who each have read a different section of text. They take turns being instructors, teaching the other group members what they have read and learned about the text.

Joel's Students in Grouping 1

There were six historical figures presented in the text, so Joel formed six groups, with four students in each. He heterogeneously grouped five of the groups according to reading ability. For the sixth group, Joel selected the four

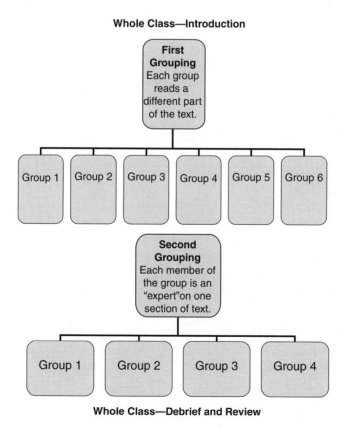

FIGURE 21.5. Joel's jigsaw grouping (based on Aronson & Patnoe, 1997).

students in the class who needed support reading the text. He did this so he could provide the support for reading to those students who needed it most. They would be reassigned to heterogeneous groups later.

Each group was assigned a different colonist. Some were Loyalists; the others were Patriots. In addition, the students were given a data sheet (see Figure 21.6) to fill out information about the colonist. Each student was also given a number from one to four to remember. The students were directed to (1) read (and reread) the text assigned to them silently, (2) work collaboratively to fill in their data sheet, and (3) practice using information on the data sheet as "talking points" to describe the colonist they read about. He also asked students to be prepared to answer questions beyond what they had recorded on the data sheet, and to feel free to make comparisons between the colonist they studied and the others presented in the group.

To help the students in the sixth group contend with the text, Joel sat in on the group and assisted them in reading the text. Then, he guided them in recording the responses on their data sheet.

Joel's Students in Grouping 2

The students were then directed to regroup according to the number each had been previously assigned. All the 1's formed a group, the 2's formed a group, and so on. This grouping configuration resulted in four groups of six students. Each student in the group had read about a different colonial figure and was considered the "expert" for that colonist in the group. Using their data sheets as notes, students took turns describing the colonists, relating the

---

Name of colonist:

Circle one: Loyalist   Patriot

Physical description:

Profession/Occupation:

Contributions or actions taken:

Argument *for* or *against* independence:

Other important information:

FIGURE 21.6. Joel's data sheet.

important actions they took, and presenting the arguments each colonist had for or against independence from England.

Joel circulated from one group to the next, redirecting the discussions when necessary. We watched Joel as he paid particular attention to the students with whom he had read the text and facilitated the discussion and completion of the data sheet. Dispersed among four groups, they had to make their presentations to their groups without Joel's help. Their participation in the groups was effectively scaffolded through the use of the data sheets, and they performed as well as their peers. In Joel's words, "They really held their own. I'm proud of them."

Reconvening the Whole Class: Reactions from the Students

Joel and his students reacted favorably to the jigsaw format. The discussion that ensued when they reconvened was lively and robust. They seemed to have a clear grasp of the content, and enthusiastically offered ideas and comments about the information they shared in the groups. One student stated, "That was so much fun! I learned a lot about all the colonists, but I only had to read about one." We reminded Joel that although they had only read a few pages of the text, it was more than many of the students had read on their own all year.

Conclusions

Studies indicate that classroom grouping practices matter in the ways that students learn to read, think, respond, and interact with teachers and with their peers. In the last three decades, we've seen grouping practices shift from an emphasis on homogenous grouping (i.e., ability grouping) to emphasis on whole-class instruction (to provide access and equity) and, in many classrooms, back to homogeneous grouping (in the form of guided reading groups). Although other forms of grouping (cooperative learning and peer tutoring) have solid evidence to support their effectiveness, in many classrooms, they continue to be used sparingly. In middle grades, especially in content-area classrooms, teachers remain largely dependent on whole-class instruction as a structure for "guaranteeing" the delivery of curriculum to every student.

The alternative models we have presented, both in published research and in the context of Rebecca's and Joel's classrooms, suggest that there are many ways to "cover the curriculum" and meet the needs of students, without resorting to either whole-class instruction or some form of rigid ability grouping. As we continue to work to learn more about effective classroom grouping practices, it is important to remember that there is no "right" way and that different grouping options support different learning goals. Thus, effective teachers have a repertoire of organizational strategies on which to

draw as they plan and implement instruction. Of fundamental importance—
and, we believe, the essential catalyst for committing to a dynamic approach
to grouping—is a deeply held belief that covering the curriculum does not
require leaving some of our students behind. Rather, if we, as teachers, make
good decisions about the contexts, tasks, and texts we assign, we will engage,
motivate, and advance knowledge of all of our students.

QUESTIONS FOR DISCUSSION

1. Consider the students in your classroom and the next curriculum topic you will
   teach. How might you use your understanding of research, the experiences of
   Rebecca and Joel, and your own prior knowledge and experiences to organize
   students, texts, and tasks in ways that advance both content and literacy
   knowledge?

2. Imagine a conversation with a teacher who says something like this: "Well,
   I tried having my students meet in small groups. But it just doesn't work.
   The good students participate and the poor students just sit there. Sometimes everyone is off-task, talking about everything but the text. I just think
   it's a waste of time." What do you suppose accounts for the behavior this
   teacher observed and the behaviors observed in the classrooms described in
   this chapter. If you were going to "coach" this teacher toward more effective
   implementation of peer-led groups, what recommendations would you make?

3. Suppose a parent calls you to say that her daughter has told her that, in your
   class, she is sometimes grouped with students—not all of whom are the
   "good" students—to discuss what they have read. The daughter is confused
   by this and so is the parent. How will you explain your grouping plan to this
   parent?

Resources

Further Reading

Allen, J. (2002). *On the same page: Shared reading beyond the primary grades.* Portland,
   ME: Stenhouse.
Knapp, M. (1995). *Teaching for meaning in high-poverty classrooms.* New York: Teachers
   College Press.
Swan, E. A. (2003). *Concept-oriented reading instruction: Engaging classrooms, lifelong
   learners.* New York: Guilford Press.

References

Allen, J. (2002). *On the same page: Shared reading beyond the primary grades.* Portland,
   ME: Stenhouse.
Allington, R. L. (1983). The reading instruction provided readers of differing read-
   ing ability. *Elementary School Journal, 83,* 548–559.

Allington, R. L. (1994). Content coverage and contextual reading in reading groups. *Journal of Reading Behavior, 16*, 85–96.

Aronson, E., & Patnoe, S. (1997). *The jigsaw classroom: Building cooperation in the classroom* (2nd ed.). New York: Addison-Wesley/Longman.

Barr, R., & Dreeben, R. (1991). Grouping students for reading instruction. In R. Barr, M. L. Kamil, P. B. Mosenthal, & P. D. Pearson (Eds.), *Handbook of reading research* (Vol. II, pp. 885–910). New York: Longman.

Blum, H. T., Lipsett, L. R., & Yocom, D. J. (2002). Literature circles: A tool for self-determination in one middle school inclusive classroom. *Remedial and Special Education, 23*(2), 99–108.

Braddock, J. H., & Dawkins, M. P. (1993). Ability grouping, aspirations, and attainments: Evidence from the National Educational Longitudinal Study of 1988. *Journal of Negro Education, 62*, 324–336.

Brice, L. (2002). Deliberative discourse enacted: Task, text, and talk. *Theory and Research in Social Education, 30*(1), 66–87.

Calkins, L. M. (1994). *The art of teaching writing.* Portsmouth, NH: Heinemann.

Cazden, C. B. (1992). Whole language plus: *Essays on literacy in the United States and New Zealand.* New York: Teachers College Press.

Cohen, P. A., Kulik, J. A., & Kulik, C. L. C. (1982). Educational outcomes of tutoring: A meta-analysis of findings. *American Educational Research Journal, 19*, 237–248.

De Corte, E., Verschaffel, L., & Van de Ven, A. (2001). Improving text comprehension strategies in upper primary school children: A design experiment. *British Journal of Educational Psychology, 71*(4), 531–559.

Duke, N. K., & Pearson, P. D. (2002). Effective practices in developing reading comprehension. In A. E. Farstrup & S. J. Samuels (Eds.), *What research as to say about reading instruction* (pp. 205–243). Newark, DE: International Reading Association.

Eder, D. (1983). Ability grouping and students' academic self-concepts: A case study. *Elementary School Journal, 84*, 149–161.

Fielding, L., & Roller, C. (1992). Making difficult books accessible and easy books acceptable. *Reading Teacher, 45*, 678–685.

Gambrell, L. B., Palmer, B., & Codling, R. M. (1996). *Elementary students' motivation to read* (Reading Research Report No. 52). Athens, GA: National Reading Research Center, Universities of Georgia and Maryland.

Gamoran, A. (1992). Is ability grouping equitable? *Educational Leadership, 50*, 11–17.

Gamoran, A., Nystrand, M., Berends, M., & LePore, P. C. (1995). An organizational analysis of the effects of ability grouping. *American Educational Research Journal, 32*, 687–715.

Goatley, V. J., Brock, C. H., & Raphael, T. E. (1995). Diverse learners participating in regular education Book Clubs. *Reading Research Quarterly, 30*, 352–380.

Good, T. L., & Marshall, S. (1984). Do students learn more in heterogeneous or homogeneous groups? In P. L. Peterson, L. C. Wilkinson, & M. Hallinan (Eds.), *The social context of instruction: Group organization and group processes* (pp. 15–38). New York: Academic Press.

Guthrie, J. T., & Humenick, N. M. (2004). Motivating students to read: Evidence for classroom practices that increase reading motivation. In P. McCardle & V. Chhabra (Eds.), *The voice of evidence in reading research* (pp. 329–354). Baltimore, MD: Paul H. Brookes.

Guthrie, J. T., McRae, A., & Klauda, S. L. (2007). Contributions of concept-oriented reading instruction to knowledge about interventions for motivations in reading. *Educational Psychologist, 42*(4), 237–250.

Harvey, S., & Goudvis, A. (2000). *Strategies that work: Teaching comprehension to enhance understanding.* York, ME: Stenhouse.

Hiebert, E. H. (1983). An examination of ability grouping for reading instruction. *Reading Research Quarterly, 18*, 231–255.

Johnson, D. W., & Johnson, R. T. (1987). *Learning together and alone: Cooperative, competitive, and individualistic learning.* Englewood Cliffs, NJ: Prentice-Hall.

Johnson, D. W., Maruyama, G., Johnson, R., & Nelson, D. (1981). Effects of cooperative, competitive, and individualistic goal structures: A meta-analysis. *Psychological Bulletin, 89*, 47–62.

Kim, A. H., Vaughn, S., & Wanzek, J. (2004). Graphic organizers and their effects on the reading comprehension of students with LD: A synthesis of research. *Journal of Learning Disabilities, 37*(2), 105–118.

Lapp, D., Flood, J., Ranck-Buhr, W., Van Dyke, J., & Spacek, S. (1997). Do you really want us to talk about this book?: A closer look at book clubs as an instructional tool. In J. R. Paratore & R. L. McCormack (Eds.), *Peer talk in the classroom: Learning from research* (pp. 6–25). Newark, DE: International Reading Association.

Lou, Y., Spence, P. C., Poulsen, C., Chambers, B., & d'Apollonia, S. (1996). Within-class grouping: A meta-analysis. *Review of Educational Research, 66*, 423–458.

McMahon, S. I., & Raphael, T. E. (Eds.). (1997). *The book club connection: Literacy learning and classroom talk.* Newark, DE: International Reading Association.

Miller, S. M., & Legge, S. (1999). Supporting possible worlds: Transforming literature teaching and learning through conversations in the narrative mode. *Research in the Teaching of English, 34*(1), 10–64.

Nystrand, M. (2006). Research on the role of classroom discourse as it affects reading comprehension. *Research in the Teaching of English, 40*(4), 392–412.

Oakes, J. (1985). *Keeping track: How schools structure inequality.* New Haven, CT: Yale University Press.

Ogle, D. M. (1986). K-W-L: A teaching model that develops active reading of expository text. *Reading Teacher, 39*, 564–570.

Ornstein, A. C. (1995). Synthesis of research: Teaching whole-group classrooms. *Peabody Journal of Education, 70*, 104–116.

Palincsar, A. S., & Brown, A. L. (1984). Reciprocal teaching of comprehension-fostering and comprehension-monitoring activities. *Cognition and Instruction, 1*, 117–175.

Paratore, J. R. (1994). Flexible grouping. In A. Purves (Ed.), *Encyclopedia of English studies/language arts.* Urbana, IL: National Council of Teachers of English and Scholastic.

Paratore, J. R. (2000). Grouping for instruction in literacy: What we've learned about what's working and what's not. *California Reader, 33*(4), 2–10.

Radencich, M. C., McKay, L. J., & Paratore, J. R. (1995). Keeping flexible groups flexible. In M. Radencich & L. McKay (Eds.), *Flexible grouping for literacy in the elementary grades* (pp. 25–41). Boston: Allyn & Bacon.

Raphael, T. (1997). Balanced instruction and the role of classroom discourse. In J. Osborn & F. Lehr (Eds.), *Literacy for all: Issues in teaching and learning* (pp. 134–169). New York: Guilford Press.

Raphael, T., & McMahon, S. (1994). Book Club: An alternative framework for reading instruction. *Reading Teacher, 48*(2), 102–116.

Sharan, S. (1980). Cooperative learning in small groups: Recent methods and effects on achievement, attitudes, and ethnic relations. *Review of Educational Research, 50*, 241–271.

Short, K. (1990). Creating a community of learners. In K. Short & K. Pierce (Eds.), *Talking about books: Creating literate communities* (pp. 33–52). Portsmouth, NH: Heinemann.

Slavin, R. E. (1980). Cooperative learning. *Review of Educational Research, 50*, 315–342.

Slavin, R. E. (1990). Ability grouping in the middle grades: Achievement effects and alternatives. *Review of Educational Research, 60*, 471–499.

Stevens, R. J., & Slavin, R. E. (1995). Effects of a cooperative learning approach to reading and writing on academically handicapped and nonhandicapped students. *Elementary School Journal, 95*, 241–262.

Van Keer, H. (2004). Fostering reading comprehension in fifth grade by explicit instruction in reading strategies and peer tutoring. *British Journal of Educational Psychology, 74*, 37–70.

Wood, K. D., McCormack, R. L., Lapp, D., & Flood, J. (1997). Improving young adolescent literacy through collaborative learning. *Middle School Journal, 28*, 26–34.

Chapter 22

Promising Practices
for Supporting Adolescents'
Online Literacy Development

Julie Coiro

GUIDING QUESTIONS

1. What are some ways that literacy instruction might differ as readers move from the printed page to learning on the Internet?
2. What are some of the biggest challenges that adolescents face as they turn to the Internet for academic information?
3. How might the use of online information and communication technologies in your classroom challenge your thinking about how adolescents learn to be proficient readers and writers?

Having the ability to comprehend and to create online information texts will play a central role in our students' success in a digital information age. Although some characterize the use of the Internet for learning as aspects of information literacy (American Library Association, 2003), technology use (International Society for Technology in Education, 2007) or life skills required for the 21st century (Partnership for 21st Century Skills, 2007), this chapter conceptualizes the use of the Internet as a reading issue. More specifically, *online reading comprehension*, or *online literacy*, in this chapter, is defined as a complex, problem-based inquiry process that involves a changing set of skills, strategies, and dispositions needed to ask important questions, then to locate, evaluate, synthesize, and communicate information to answer those questions using the Internet (Leu, Kinzer, Coiro, & Cammack, 2004).

Unfortunately, few studies have framed the use of the Internet as a reading issue, and even fewer have formally investigated how students acquire these online literacies or which classroom practices most effectively foster their development (see Castek, in process; Kuiper, 2007; Leu et al., 2007; New Literacies Research Team, 2005). To date, much of the literature has been either theoretical in nature, arguing that real differences exist between online and offline reading (e.g., Coiro, 2003, 2007a; Coiro & Dobler, 2007; Spires & Estes, 2002), or it has focused on how individuals interact with information on the Internet, illustrating that many students struggle with online informational reading tasks (see Bilal, 2001; Coiro, 2007b; Eagleton & Dobler, 2007).

Studies comparing online and offline reading comprehension indicate that the cognitive skills and strategies students use to read and learn effectively from online informational text are both similar to and more complex than what previous research suggests is required to comprehend offline informational text. On the one hand, observational and interview data (Coiro & Dobler, 2004, 2007; Schmar-Dobler, 2003) have revealed that skilled adolescents who read on the Internet often apply many of the same comprehension strategies used by strategic readers of printed offline texts (see Pearson, Roehler, Dole, & Duffy, 1992). These strategies include activating prior knowledge, making inferences, monitoring and repairing comprehension, asking questions, and determining important ideas.

However, findings from these same studies and a growing collection of other research suggest that offline reading strategies are no longer sufficient to read effectively and learn from Internet text (e.g., see Afflerbach & Cho, 2008; Burbules & Callister, 2000; Leu, 2007; RAND Reading Study Group, 2002; Wolfe, 2001). Coiro and Dobler (2007), for example, found that in addition to more conventional reading comprehension strategies, successful Internet reading experiences require new applications of prior knowledge, inferential reasoning, and comprehension monitoring. Similarly, Schmar-Dobler (2003) reported that skilled online readers are aware of different textual features that aid their navigation through digital environments. More recently, Coiro (2007a) found that among 118 economically and academically diverse seventh graders, offline and online reading comprehension skills made significant and *independent* contributions to performance on a series of three online reading tasks. These data suggest that new (or at least statistically unique) reading comprehension skills and strategies may be required to comprehend and use informational text on the Internet.

Studies that have examined how students interact with information on the Internet report that many adolescents are less than proficient in their ability to complete online informational reading tasks successfully (Eagleton & Dobler, 2007; Goldman & Lawless, 2007; Leu et al., 2007). Often, students mistake their ability to move around on the Internet as the ability to read and comprehend online information (Burke, 2002). Equally discouraging are emerging reports that even some traditionally higher-performing offline

readers have difficulty adapting their use of offline comprehension strategies to online reading tasks. Several studies (Bilal, 2000, 2001; Coiro, 2007a;
Kuiper, 2007; Leu, Zawilinski, Castek, et al., 2008; Wallace, Kupperman, Krajcik, & Soloway, 2000) have revealed cases of proficient offline readers who
were unable to navigate hypertext efficiently, critically evaluate the relevancy
and reliability of online information, and/or flexibly monitor and adapt their
strategy use to changing online reading environments. Thus, we can no longer assume that higher-performing offline readers will succeed in online
reading environments.

In addition to these two areas of work, some research has begun to
investigate how learning in middle and high school classrooms is facilitated
through the use of information and communication technologies, including
the Internet. This chapter seeks to translate the preliminary patterns emerging from the literature in a first attempt to inform instruction that prepares
students to succeed in a globally networked, online world of information.
In these early stages, research in this area often characterizes instructional
programs as "innovative" rather than "effective" (see, e.g., Kozma, 2003),
because the field has not readily developed ways to evaluate learning success
with new technologies (Sherry, Jesse, & Billig, 2002). Consequently, readers
should proceed with caution, understanding that recommended guidelines
and related promising practices in this chapter reflect the preliminary nature
of research findings in this area. With this limitation in mind, a review of the
literature suggests that at least five instructional guidelines show promise for
fostering adolescents' online literacy development:

- *Guideline 1*: The effective online literacy teacher understands and
  makes explicit for students relationships between offline and online
  reading comprehension strategy use.

- *Guideline 2*: The effective online literacy teacher honors the literacies
  that students bring to school from their daily lives.

- *Guideline 3*: The effective online literacy teacher explores and clarifies
  expectations about new classroom roles and relationships embedded
  in problem-based online collaborations.

- *Guideline 4*: The effective online literacy teacher provides time for students to develop positive dispositions toward learning and communicating on the Internet.

- *Guideline 5*: The effective online literacy teacher uses self-, peer-, and
  teacher assessments as inquiry to inform reading strategy use and
  classroom instruction.

In the sections that follow, I examine each guideline in turn, presenting
an evidence base and associated promising practices to guide instruction and
future research.

Guideline 1: Understand and Make Explicit for Students the Relationships between Offline and Online Reading Comprehension Strategy Use

To date, empirical intervention studies (Castek, in process; Kuiper, 2007; Leu et al., 2005, 2007) and several international reviews of innovative practices of information and communication technology (ICT) use (e.g., Becta, 2007; Harrison, 2005; International Association for the Evaluation of Educational Achievement, 2000; Organisation for Economic Co-operation and Development, 2001) have documented characteristics of instructional programs that appear to positively influence adolescents' development of online literacy skills and strategies. Across these studies, at least two conclusions are pertinent to this chapter. First, explicit strategy instruction that emphasizes reflective dialogue and the flexible use of offline and online comprehension skills often yields gains in online reading comprehension ability and content-area learning for a diverse range of students in grades 5–12. Second, although many other contextual variables influence student learning outcomes, more effective programs of strategy instruction provide modeling of *when* and *how* to use particular reading strategies during collaborative, inquiry-based online learning tasks embedded in content-area instruction. Importantly, however, one study (Kuiper, 2007) found that 10 weeks of instruction was not enough to help fifth graders consistently apply their new repertoire of comprehension strategies in a follow-up series of similar online reading tasks.

In many ways, these recent findings about how best to develop online reading comprehension reflect what we already know about effective strategy instruction that facilitates offline reading comprehension (e.g., Duke & Pearson, 2002; Paris, Cross, & Lipson, 1984; Pressley, 2000): (1) Explicit instruction in how, when, and why to coordinate multiple strategies in a particular context, and (2) multiple opportunities for guided and independent practice and feedback lead to the acquisition and use of self-regulated reading comprehension strategies. With these research-based findings in mind, three classroom practices show promise toward teaching students about the relationships between offline and online reading comprehension strategy use.

• *Encourage students to compare offline and online text features and the reading purposes they engender.* As noted by Patterson (2000), we need to help our students think reflectively about the different features and purposes of reading and writing hypertext. Online texts have several unique characteristics that set them apart from traditionally printed offline texts (Afflerbach & Cho, 2008; Alexander & Jetton, 2000; Wolfe, 2001). Online readers, for example, may encounter at least a dozen additional cueing systems (e.g., navigational buttons, digitized speech, interactive supports) and informational text structures beyond the three conventional cueing systems (syntactic, graphophonic, and semantic cues) that skilled readers apply to comprehend printed text

(Eagleton & Dobler, 2007). Compared to printed texts, some Internet texts also prompt new purposes for reading, more critical thought processes during reading, and new examples of authentic responses after reading (Coiro, 2003).

Several lessons designed by classroom teachers for the ReadWriteThink online lesson database (*www.readwritethink.org*) effectively illustrate reflective classroom assignments that prompt students to notice the similarities and differences between offline and online texts, and their associated range of reading purposes. Beyersdorfer (2007), Karchmer (2007), and Seitz (2006), for example, provide excellent models of how adolescents might compare and contrast offline and online text features (e.g., graphics, hyperlinked headings, digitized speech, and video) to gain a deeper understanding of how to navigate and to comprehend information on the Internet.

Other lessons help students address the challenge of where to focus their attention online (Lankshear & Knobel, 2002), with strategy discussions about how to skim and scan effectively while searching for specific online information (see Kolodziej, 2007a, 2007b). Some of these lessons include self-assessment forms that ask students to summarize how and when each skill might be most useful. Another online lesson (Mozambite, 2005) incorporates an interactive program that invites upper-level elementary school students to explore a range of informational texts (including websites) and identifies suitable reading purposes and audiences for each.

Teachers can adapt any of these lessons to develop similar activities using printed texts and websites that are more consistent with their grade level or unit of study. Over time, strategy lessons that compare and contrast offline and online texts can help students recognize, label, and define a range of more and less familiar online cueing systems and related reading purposes. In turn, students can begin to actively consider new strategies for effectively comprehending and using the range of informational texts they encounter on the Internet.

- *Provide explicit teacher and peer think-aloud models of effective online reading comprehension strategy use.* For some students, online metacognitive strategy use may not be improved without explicit training in how to search for and interact with information on the Internet (Castek, in process; Tsai & Tsai, 2003). One solution is for teachers to provide explicit think-aloud models of effective online reading strategy use. A *think-aloud* is a technique in which the teacher pauses while reading to verbally model the thought processes of a skilled reader as he or she interacts with a text (Davey, 1983). Teachers use think-aloud models to call attention to often overlooked or hidden comprehension strategies that are useful in particular reading situations. Highly focused and well-planned, strategy think-alouds can provide readers of all ages a common language for sharing important metacognitive strategies that facilitate comprehension (Kelly & Clausen-Grace, 2007; Wilhelm, 2001).

Guided by an emerging taxonomy of online reading comprehension strategies that adolescents use to solve online information tasks (see Leu et al., 2007), teachers can develop instructional think-alouds to model how to formulate online questions effectively; to generate effective search terms; to evaluate critically the relevancy, reliability, and stance of website information; to integrate information from multiple resources; and to use one or more online communication tools to share a response with others (see also Coiro, 2005a; Eagleton & Dobler, 2007). Figure 22.1, for example, provides a model of how a teacher might think out loud to explain how to preview a website for relevant information.

Several researchers also suggest inviting students to construct their own think-aloud models of comprehension strategy use as they read on the Internet

---

Teacher: (*Arrives at a website.*) First, I'm going to read the title of the page and the title of the website in the bar at the top of the window. This gives me an idea of what the whole website might be about. I might also look at the first part of the website address or the "About this site" button here in the corner to see what I can learn about who created the information at this website. Then, I'm going to scan over the menu choices that run down the left side of the screen. This helps me understand what topics might be covered at this website. I can also try to visualize how big this website is and how much information it covers.

Student: Okay, so let's just click on the third link to see what's there.

Teacher: Well, I'm not going to click yet. I'll just scroll my mouse over each choice while I think about the information I might find behind that link. This is kind of like making predictions as you read a story, but here it's with information rather than narrative text. See how I also try to hold my mouse over each choice without clicking? That's because sometimes another menu or graphic will pop up to give me even more choices for where to read next. See—oh, there's one of those pop-up menus right there that was hidden before! Now, I am going to think about my question and pick the link that will most likely lead me closer to information that I need.

Student: (*Scans the menu list.*) I don't see any words that match the words I am looking for in the left menu. I think we should just go back and try a different site.

Teacher: We could do that, but I see a word that means something similar to my question, even though it doesn't match the words exactly. I am going to click on this link first to see if it leads me a little closer to information about my topic. (*Clicks and scans the page.*) Yes, see here, the name of the hyperlink didn't match exactly, but because it was about a similar topic, I clicked on it and now I see my topic listed as one of the links to another page that will help me answer my question. So sometimes looking for synonyms or broader categories about your topic can help you find relevant information several levels from the homepage of the website.

FIGURE 22.1. Excerpt from a teacher think-aloud for previewing a website for relevant information.

(Damico & Baildon, 2007; Dwyer, 2007; Kymes, 2005). Thinking aloud about their own reading of offline texts serves to enhance students' comprehension-monitoring abilities (Baumann & Jones, 1993) and improve overall reading competence (Rosenshine & Meister, 1994). In addition, helping adolescents to see themselves as online experts with important skills can encourage even weaker offline readers to take leadership roles in classroom strategy discussions (Leu, Coiro, Castek, et al., 2008; New Literacies Research Team, 2005).

Exploratory work in this area indicates that teacher and peer think-aloud models can be shared by a whole class with a projector and one common text; by a small group of students as part of an Internet workshop session, where students share and compare information they discovered online (see Leu, Leu, & Coiro, 2004); or by a sequence of guided lessons, during which teachers gradually transfer to students most of the responsibility for modeling online reading comprehension strategies. (You can read more about this sequence of lessons, called *Internet reciprocal teaching*, in Leu, Coiro, Castek, et al., 2008). In each situation, insights gleaned from both effective and ineffective strategy use can inform future lessons and highlight online reading experts (teachers *and* students) to whom others can turn for additional support.

• *Embed explicit strategy lessons within curriculum-based, online information challenges.* As noted by Guthrie, Wigfield, and Perencevich (2004), students are motivated by authentic and intentional reading purposes that are situated in the context of interesting texts. In addition, students are more likely to transfer what they learn from strategy instruction to new informational texts when it is embedded within inquiry activities with content-specific goals (Guthrie & Cox, 2001). Strategy instruction that is embedded within themed units about science or health, for example, has been documented to build conceptual knowledge, while promoting strategic reading comprehension in both offline (Guthrie et al., 2004) and online information environments (Castek, in process; Kuiper, 2007; New Literacies Research Team, 2005).

These findings highlight the potential of using what might be called "curriculum-based online information challenges" to link strategy instruction with authentic, content-specific issues and interesting online texts. Rather than teaching online reading strategies as part of an isolated technology lesson with the computer teacher, a curriculum-based online information challenge invites students to use a range of Internet technologies to locate and interact with online informational texts linked directly to a particular content theme or learning objective (see Leu, Coiro, Castek, et al., 2008). Small groups of students are presented with content-related information problems designed both to develop conceptual knowledge and elicit important online reading comprehension skills (e.g., asking questions, locating, evaluating, synthesizing, and communicating). Introductory challenges may ask students in a middle school U.S. History course, for instance, to incorporate only two or three of these procedures (e.g., locate, evaluate relevance, communicate) to solve a problem: (1) Locate the name of one American who might be considered a hero of the Civil War and provide an explanation of what makes that person a hero; (2) send your partner an e-mail with the name you located, evidence from the text that supports your opinion, and the address of the website(s) where you found the information.

More complicated challenges may require students in a high school science class, for example, to incorporate several online reading strategies to solve a more controversial (or complex) problem:

1. What is the main cause of global warming?
2. Find another answer to this same question.
3. Which answer do you think is most accurate and how did you determine that it was?
4. Post your answers on our classroom blog.

Students in either challenge are guided to discuss their solutions in small groups, while they exchange reading comprehension strategies for locating, critically evaluating, and synthesizing online information. Lessons are designed to minimize teacher talk, maximize student engagement, and provide time at the end for students to debrief and to exchange strategies with the entire class, after having already done so in their small groups (for more information, see Leu, Coiro, Castek, et al., 2008).

Guideline 2: Honor the Literacies Students Bring to School from Their Daily Lives

Youth play a key role in establishing the emerging nature of Internet-related practices and texts (Livingstone, 2002). As of 2005, some 93% of teens in the United States used the Internet (Lenhart & Madden, 2005). Of those online teens, nearly 40% knew how to use the Internet to create and share digital stories and videos; 28% had created their own blog or online journal; 27% maintained their own personal webpage; and 27% knew how to remix content they found online into their own creations.

Unfortunately, many schools fail to acknowledge the online information and communication literacies that adolescents bring to classrooms from their daily lives (e.g., Alvermann, Jonas, Steele, & Washington, 2006; Levin & Arafeh, 2002). To many educators, the creative and social literacy practices that often take place outside school classrooms are unrelated to values associated with more privileged informational or print-based literacies inside school classrooms (Burnett & Wilkinson, 2005; Lankshear & Knobel, 2003). Furthermore, out-of-school online practices, and their associated texts, are often perceived as immoral or deviant (Moje & van Helden, 2004) and literacy progress is difficult to measure in ways to which teachers are accustomed in an era of accountability (Tierney, Bond, & Bresler, 2006).

Yet, as Selfe and Hawisher (2004) point out: "If literacy educators continue to define literacy in terms of alphabetic practices only, in ways that ignore, exclude, or devalue new-media texts, they … run the risk of their curriculum no longer holding relevance for students who are communicating in increasingly expansive networked environments" (p. 233). Consequently, we need new frameworks and associated instructional models that bridge in-school and out-of-school practices to exploit the multiple literacy competencies that adolescents bring to school (Hull & Schultz, 2002; O'Brien & Bauer, 2005). So what can teachers do to ensure that instruction in online reading comprehension is relevant and meaningful to adolescents who are technologically savvy in their daily literacy practices? Three classroom practices show particular promise in this area.

• *Foster a classroom culture that recognizes the multiple literacy contributions of every student.* Although many adolescents have difficulty navigating school-based online reading tasks, these same students bring with them different literacy experiences that have shaped their identities as social and literate individuals outside the classroom (Alvermann et al., 2006; Anstey & Bull, 2006). Perry (2006) refers to these different literacy experiences that students practice at home and/or during their own personal time as the *hidden literacies* that often go unnoticed by teachers, without a focused effort to learn about them (see also Voss, 1996). Perry (2006) explains that when hidden literacies are given a place in the school curriculum, they may actually enhance student learning and serve as springboards to authentic academic literacies required for inquiry and deep understanding.

Consequently, it is important that teachers foster a classroom culture that welcomes variation and capitalizes on the unique literacy talents that each student offers to the classroom learning community (Cope & Kalantzis, 2000). Teachers should make time to learn about what students are reading and writing outside of school, and make space for students to demonstrate their knowledge of digital literacies, linking to students' identities as competent learners. Time might be provided weekly during class for adolescents to share texts they have constructed, for example, while writing fan fiction (e.g., *www.fanfiction.net*), remixing photos (e.g., *worth1000.com*) or moving images (e.g., *www.animemusicvideos.org/home/home.php*); creating three-dimensional virtual worlds (e.g., *www.alice.org*); maintaining a personal website (e.g., *www.angelfire.com/egomrtastee18/index.html*) or online magazine (*www.agirlsworld.com*); or composing graphic novels that integrate manga (Japanese comics) and anime (Japanese animation) (e.g., *www.koyagi.com/Libguide.html*).

By learning more about adolescents' online literacy experiences outside the classroom, teachers are better equipped to connect to the ways students use literacies to construct meaning and pursue their own interests (Alvermann et al., 2006). In addition, opportunities to perceive themselves as literacy experts, with important skills to share, encourage students' greater investment in classroom activities, increase their engagement with texts, and, in some cases, improve their self-confidence and motivation in school (Brader, 2008; New Literacies Research Team, 2005; Schulz-Zander, Buchter, & Dalmer, 2002).

- *Help students connect and compare effective literacy strategies for engaging in personal and academic online reading tasks.* In her work with developing online readers, Kuiper (2007) found that adolescents tended to overestimate their abilities to construct academic knowledge based on their abilities to engage in out-of-school literacy practices. She also found the way the Internet is used at school often does not fit in with students' likes and dislikes about particular topics, websites, and tasks (see also Stone, 2006). Consequently, Kuiper explains, although it is important to recognize and encourage use of the texts and practices from students' daily lives, teachers should not overestimate adolescents' ability to engage in higher-level academic inquiry tasks without explicit support (see also Hinostroza, Guzman, & Isaacs, 2002; Tsai & Tsai, 2003). This support should clearly explain the differences between students' use of information and communication technologies for topics and purposes of their own choice, and their use of the Internet to achieve academic research goals.

Adolescents are often quite savvy, for example, in navigating chatrooms and online role-playing games (Chandler-Olcott & Mahar, 2003); varying their language and voice when composing instant messages for different audiences and purposes (Lewis & Fabos, 2005); producing creative e-zines to share with their peers (Guzzetti & Gamboa, 2004); and "multimediating" across a range of online texts and technologies (Beach & O'Brien, 2008). However, as stated earlier, adolescents often lack the skills necessary for school-related online information tasks. Thus, effective online literacy teachers can help by anticipating the connectedness between academic expectations and students' personal experiences with Internet technologies to predict aspects of online reading (e.g., discrepancies, new functions, or purposes) that may frustrate students or conflict with their use of the Internet (Kuiper, 2007). Then, students can sometimes be given opportunities to choose their own topics and/ or texts, while they receive explicit and reflective strategy instruction in how to comprehend, critically interpret, and respond to each type of text for different purposes and audiences.

Emerging research highlights the potential of connecting personal and academic online reading tasks to facilitate conventional learning outcomes, new literacies, and student engagement (e.g., O'Brien, Beach, & Scharber, 2007; Perry, 2006; Tierney et al., 2006). Over time, students begin to understand how to use literacy differently for different purposes, in and out of school, and realize the need to apply these skills and strategies flexibly for new purposes and new contexts using new technologies. In turn, instruction that explicitly links effective strategies for engaging in personal and academic online reading tasks may prompt a more connected and relevant classroom culture for today's youth—a culture in which "students explore, challenge, test, and critique knowledge in ways that make sense for themselves in their own lived experience" (Hunsberger, 2007, p. 422).

• *Provide space for students to explore, interpret, and create multiple forms and genres of texts.* Moje (2007) has proposed that adolescents prefer multimodal texts that blend print information with visual, audio, spoken, and other non-verbal forms of expression. Research (Beach & O'Brien, 2008) suggests that adolescents also tend to spend a large part of their personal lives multitasking or, more appropriately, *multimediating* between instant messaging conversations, social networking sites, online video games, and online popular culture texts (e.g., fanfiction, Japanese animae). Consequently, Tierney et al. (2006) propose that teachers who want to support adolescents' new literacy development in the classroom should provide opportunities for students to interact with "images, soundtracks, and text interconnected in very complex, multi-faceted ways using a plethora of image, sounds, and print" (p. 361). They argue that including reflective interactions with multimodal texts as part of collaborative school projects can prompt more sophisticated uses of these texts.

A number of researchers have documented the potential of encouraging students to explore, interpret, and create multiple forms and genres of texts as part of the classroom curriculum. Burn and Leach (2004), for example, summarized findings from 12 case studies and reported that the incorporation of moving image media in the curriculum led to gains in print literacy and also prompted students' developing identities as learners capable of determining their own meanings from text. Hobbs and Frost (2003) reported that 11th graders who received extensive instruction in how to analyze critically a combination of print, audio texts, and visual texts improved in their ability to identify the purpose, target audience, point of view, and construction techniques of media messages compared to a control group that received no media analysis instruction.

Elsewhere, Chandler-Olcott and Mahar (2003) found that opportunities to create multimodal texts had positive benefits for students, who came to see themselves as capable text producers, especially when such texts were constructed for an audience of peers, as well as for teachers. In addition, O'Brien et al. (2007) reported preliminary findings that some reluctant adolescent readers who participate in a combination of traditional reading assignments and novels and media-rich digital projects not only made gains in conventional reading and writing skills but also developed a stronger self-image as readers and writers. Overall, these findings reinforce Moje's (2007) conclusion that classroom settings that "provide the freedom to explore multiple forms and genres of text for expressing identity and representing understanding ... may engender the motivation necessary to push so-called struggling readers" (p. 210) toward the higher levels of thinking required to comprehend online texts across a range of personal and academic purposes.

Guideline 3: Explore and Clarify Expectations for New Classroom Roles and Relationships Embedded in Problem-Based Online Collaborations

This guideline is prompted by research suggesting that innovative uses of the Internet for collaborative inquiry prompt new classroom literacy learning opportunities and new relationships among teachers, students, and peers (Erstad, 2002; Schulz-Zander et al., 2002). Students and teachers who are more accustomed to didactic approaches may have difficulty negotiating the multiple roles and responsibilities that accompany collaborative problem-based uses of the Internet in school classrooms (Mioduser, Nachmias, Tubin, & Forkosh-Baruch, 2002). Because literacy contexts change so quickly on the Internet (Leu, Kinzer, et al., 2004), teachers should continue to be flexible in exploring and clarifying what they expect of themselves and of their students as they negotiate changing roles and relationships for student–student and teacher–student collaborations. Below, new characteristics of each type of relationship are paired with emergent findings about how best to create a classroom culture that exploits the full potential of online, problem-based collaborations to support adolescents' online literacy development.

• *Clarify new student roles and relationships for collaborating with peers.* For teachers who design online classroom literacy collaborations, it is important to clarify for students how to interact effectively with others in an online, collaborative learning community. When working in face-to-face partnerships with their peers, students should understand two issues in particular. First, students should come to appreciate that each of their peers brings to the group a different, but valuable, set of skills and experiences (Cope & Kalantzis, 2002). Thus, any preconceived notions about a classmate's ability (or inability) to contribute to online collaborations based on his or her offline reading performance may hinder the group's overall ability to solve complex problems with the Internet. Rather, teachers help students understand that the most effective online collaborative groups appreciate individual differences, determine each student's strengths for the particular task at hand, then distribute responsibilities to exploit these strengths (Schulz-Zander et al., 2002).

Second, students should understand the new affective literacy roles and responsibilities for which they will be held accountable in an online collaborative learning community. Drawing from recent frameworks (see American Association for School Librarians, 2007; International Society for Technology in Education, 2007; Partnership for 21st Century Skills, 2007), today's online literacy learners are expected to be self-determined, critical, and reflective. In addition to learning new information, they should know how to use the Internet to seek divergent perspectives, make ethical decisions, and to contribute actively to the exchange of ideas and new knowledge construction. Moreover, online learners are expected to display creativity, initiative, persistence, and confidence as they work collaboratively with new technologies to solve real problems. Law, Lee, and Chow (2002) suggest that affective and sociocognitive learner outcomes may be even more important than "knowledge-based competencies" in preparing students for lifelong learning in the 21st century. Consequently, teachers should clearly communicate these expectations to students as part of literacy instruction.

In addition to face-to-face peer relationships, online collaborations may also invite students to work with adolescents from different countries or different backgrounds (e.g., cultural, linguistic, geographic, or economic). In these situations, students are expected to be aware of and appreciate different perspectives as they initiate and/or respond to online exchanges. Here teachers play an important role in making sure students go beyond surface-level discussions about their similarities and differences to truly understand the complex contexts in which online collaborations take place (for further discussion, see Fabos & Young, 1999). The most meaningful cross-cultural conversations "extend cultural exploration beyond tourism or the fascination with the 'other' to help students understand economic, political, social, and imperialistic pressures on different world populations" (Fabos & Young, 1999, p. 238).

Preliminary studies of classrooms in which teachers clarified and supported new online collaborative roles and peer relationships during inquiry-based projects reported increases in students' interest and acquisition of academic content, as well as cultural competence, self-esteem, and motivation in school (Erstad, 2002; Harrison, 2005; Hinsotroza et al., 2002; Schulz-Zander et al., 2002). O'Brien et al. (2007) found that both high- and low-performing students seemed to do better in new literacy environments, where "collaborative social allegiances" (p. 68) attracted and engaged even those students who were disenchanted with traditional instructional literacy programs (see also Erstad, 2002; New Literacies Research Team, 2005).

• *Clarify new roles and relationships between students and teachers.* Consistent with a new literacies perspective of online reading comprehension (Leu, Kinzer, et al., 2004), teachers become more important, though their roles change, in new literacies classrooms. It is not just the online technologies themselves, but characteristics of the classroom learning culture, and the design of student-centered learning contexts within which they are situated, that appear to matter most (Castek, in process; Law et al., 2002; Mioduser et al., 2002). Consequently, teachers should be aware of their own roles and changing relationships with students as they introduce online literacy collaborations into the curriculum.

In these new contexts, successful teachers perceive their role as designer and orchestrator of authentic online projects to initially minimize the complexities of online problem-based inquiry (Kuiper, 2007; Schulz-Zander et al., 2002). In addition, effective online literacy teachers stimulate knowledge construction over an extended period of time (as opposed to just a few lessons), with tasks inspired by students' questions and personal interests about a topic or issue (Erstad, 2002; Law et al., 2002). A critical role for teachers is to outline and to make explicit for students several intermediate steps in the online research process (Law et al., 2002). These steps may include, for example, stopping to elicit feedback from peers that informs group members' efforts to refine their questions, revise preliminary survey questions, or edit their finished projects. Pausing like this at each phase of research ensures opportunities for students to work with others throughout the process rather than only at the end, and increases the interdependence of students' work (Law et al., 2002).

As teachers explore how to plan and orchestrate these complex online learning tasks, they must also consider how best to negotiate more equalized relationships with students. Schulz-Zander and colleagues (2002) noted that in several innovative learning environments a distinguishing feature was that "the students' self-activity increased while the teacher moved further to the background" (p. 441) to give structure to learning activities, scaffold the students' work processes, and reflect on student progress. Others recommend that teachers provide authentic opportunities for students to join them as literacy leaders and technology experts, while they explore the changes taking place in literacy and learning on the Internet (Erstad, 2002). For instance, teachers recognized for their successful integration of technology into their literacy curricula are not afraid to ask their students for help in using a particular tool, and they often make space for students to teach online literacy skills to each other (see Coiro, 2005a). Elsewhere, technology-savvy students can work as partners with teachers to support their use of technology in classrooms (see, e.g., the Generation YES [Youth and Educators Succeeding] program described by Harper, 2006). Ten years of data collected by the Northwest Regional Educational Laboratory (NWREL) show that Generation YES (*www.genyes.com*) is "an effective alternative for schools wishing to integrate technology into their regular curriculum and increase their use of project-based, student-centered learning practices" (Harper, 2006, p. 3). Overall, a careful combination of explicit instruction and efforts to make space for students to share and collaborate with peers and teachers appears to have contributed to or hindered the success of most online collaborative projects (Law et al., 2002; Mioduser et al., 2002; Schulz-Zander et al., 2002).

Guideline 4: Provide Time for Students to Develop Positive Dispositions toward Learning and Communicating with the Internet

Positive *dispositions*, or attitudes and beliefs, are key dimensions of effective learning (Guthrie et al., 2004), particularly for students growing up in a digital information age (Carr & Claxton, 2002; Johnston, 2005). In the context of challenging *offline* reading comprehension tasks, affective variables, such as attributions of success and failure, self-judgments, and self-efficacy beliefs, are positively related to strategy use and self-regulation (Schunk & Zimmerman, 2003). Skilled offline readers are often characterized as curious, engaged learners who are confident in their ability to tackle difficult texts (Guthrie et al., 2004). Learners with positive dispositions often seek out challenging reading tasks, and each successful experience reinforces their initiation and use of the comprehension skills and strategies applied.

Similarly, as learners transition into *online* reading environments, their attitudes and self-efficacy relative to the Internet appear to be important factors that affect their motivation, interests, and performance in Internet-based learning environments (Peng, Tsai, & Wu, 2006; Tsai, 2004; Tsai & Lin, 2004). Moreover, some of the motivational factors that influence students' success on the Internet appear to be significantly unique compared to reading dispositions that are useful in offline learning environments (Terry & Doolittle, 2006; Whipp & Chiarelli, 2004).

In open-ended Internet reading environments, successful online readers are those who manage rapidly changing text forms with persistence, flexibility, patience, critical stance, and self-reflection (see Bilal, 2000, 2001; Eagleton, 2003; Eagleton, Guinee, & Langlais, 2003; Kuiper, 2007). Others highlight the importance of affective dispositions, such as creativity (Loveless, 2002) and cognitive flexibility (Anderson, 2002; Coiro & Dobler, 2007), to construct meaning successfully from disparate online texts.

Notably, Tsai and Tsai (2003) reported that college students with high Internet self-efficacy had better information search strategies and learned better than those with low Internet self-efficacy in a web-based learning task. They observed behavioral, procedural, and metacognitive differences between two groups of college freshman with higher and lower levels of Internet self-efficacy. More specifically, they found that students with higher Internet self-efficacy tended to (1) use computers more correctly and efficiently; (2) be more willing than peers with lower self-efficacy to try new search approaches when a previous strategy had not worked; (3) solve problems independently rather than asking for help; (4) read more purposefully to select necessary information; and (5) be more apt to criticize and question information they encountered on the Internet.

Unfortunately, little research has closely examined how classroom teachers can help to develop positive student dispositions toward reading and learning with the Internet. However, related work in how to develop students' positive reading dispositions in print reading environments suggests that at least two practices may similarly facilitate important dispositions required for comprehending information on the Internet.

• *Attend to personal reading dispositions as part of a framework for online reading comprehension strategy instruction.* As noted by Schoenbach, Greenleaf, Cziko, and Hurwitz (2000), students' self-awareness and personal reading identity are critical dimensions of classroom life that support adolescent reading development. Recent findings highlight the potential of attending to personal reading dispositions as part of a framework for offline reading comprehension strategy instruction. Guided by the notion that efforts to promote self-efficacy beliefs should support self-regulated reading, Souvignier and Mokhlesgerami (2006) designed three different reading interventions that complemented strategy knowledge with varying levels of cognitive and motivational aspects of self-regulation. The researchers then examined the effects of each intervention on the comprehension levels of three groups of fifth graders across 20 classrooms. Overall, they found that classroom instruction emphasizing both "cognitive and motivational self-regulatory competence" (p. 58) produced significant and long-terms gains in fifth graders' reading comprehension, understanding of reading comprehension strategies, and competence for application of reading strategies compared to a control group. In addition, although there was no direct evidence of separate gains in self-efficacy, Souvignier and Mokhlesgerami believed that "promoting motivational aspects of self-regulation was realized by integrating motivational and cognitive principles" (p. 69).

Other programs that combined affective and cognitive aspects of strategy instruction to promote students' engagement and offline reading comprehension achievement across the curriculum reported significant changes in students' attitudes and behaviors related to reading (Greenleaf, Schoenbach, Cziko, & Mueller, 2001; Guthrie & Davis, 2003). In these programs, teachers supported personal reading dispositions by embedding regular routines and opportunities for conversations about reader habits, attitudes, and personal reading goals into their content-area curricula: "Classroom activities support individual students in developing increased awareness of themselves as readers, inviting them to discover and refine their own goals and motivations, likes and dislikes, and hopes and potential growth in relationship to reading" (Schoenbach et al., 2000, p. 27).

Moreover, the focus on student effort, rather than on ability, may prompt high self-efficacy beliefs that may support positive dispositions toward reading and learning (Souvignier & Mokhlesgerami, 2006). Thus, as individual students gain a sense of themselves and their efforts as readers, they should be encouraged to understand how their habits and attitudes influence their ability to comprehend challenging texts. Over time, teachers can facilitate strategy conversations that integrate the focus on personal dimensions with social, cognitive, and knowledge-building dimensions of classroom life to support students as they work to make sense of texts.

Given the success of these programs in promoting students' positive dispositions toward offline reading and learning, we now need research that examines how these interventions play out as adolescents face the challenges of reading and learning on the Internet. As we journey forward, students ought to benefit from classroom discussions that integrate cognitive reading strategy use with the beliefs, attitudes, motivations, and habits that appear to characterize confident and capable online learners.

• *Design online inquiry projects that prompt interdisciplinary connections to 21st-century life skills to improve learning and motivation.* Current work indicates the need for interdisciplinary curricular connections that prompt students to look across multiple issues to solve the broader complex problems of the 21st century (Barton & Smith, 2000; Jackson & Davis, 2000). In 2007, the Partnership for 21st Century Skills revised its learning framework to recommend that classroom teachers "move beyond a focus on basic competency in core subjects to promote understanding of academic content at much higher levels by weaving 21st century interdisciplinary themes into core subjects" (paragraph 2). More specifically, the organization suggests that teachers design learning tasks that empower students to solve important problems by integrating their knowledge of several subject areas with emerging opportunities to apply their developing financial, global, and civic literacies in real academic learning contexts. Consequently, effective online literacy teachers seek to promote adolescents' self-efficacy and online reading confidence, while providing authentic opportunities to practice entrepreneurial skills, to develop a mutual respect for diverse cultures and lifestyles, and to participate effectively in civic life experiences.

Models of how teachers are addressing the complexities of designing online interdisciplinary projects that integrate 21st century life skills have begun to emerge around the world. For example, distinguished educators associated with the Apple Learning Interchange (see Glaude et al., 2007) share details of their Inspire to Inquire project, which challenges adolescents to find interdisciplinary connections in their environments. Curtis (2004) describes school projects in Hawaii that integrate art, writing, and computer animation to work on real-world problems related to conservation and cultural heritage. And Pearlman (2007) outlines the fundamentals of technology-embedded interdisciplinary projects and reminds teachers to focus on developing online reading dispositions that include collaboration, critical thinking, problem solving, and citizenship. In addition, teachers may wish to explore online resources such as the Global Virtual Classroom (*www. virtualclassroom.org*), Global Education Collaborative (*globaleducation.ning. com*), and Global SchoolNet (*globalschoolnet.org/index.cfm*), which seek to foster international dialogue about new literacies and the sharing of resources among students and teachers around the world.

Guideline 5: Use Self-, Peer, and Teacher Assessments as Inquiry to Inform Online Reading Strategy Use and Classroom Instruction

This guideline is informed by work suggesting that assessment in a digital age should be framed as a process of inquiry, whereby students and teachers work together through observation, reflection, and feedback to understand their academic progress and document learning over time (Johnston,

1997; Serafini, 2000/2001). As we move into the next millennium, Tierney (2000) argues for a shift toward more learner-centered assessment practices that "afford students opportunities to engage with teachers, caregivers, and stakeholders in meaningful partnerships involving genuine decision making" (p. 244). Consequently, students learning how to read successfully on the Internet should have opportunities to engage in self-, peer-, and teacher assessments of their online comprehension strategy use as part of a reflective learning process. By more actively participating in the assessment process, students begin to accept more responsibility for their learning and to reflect more thoughtfully on their literacy efforts and performance (Afflerbach, 2007; Chappuis & Chappuis, 2007/2008). From this perspective, three classroom practices guide our thinking about assessment as inquiry to inform online reading strategy use and classroom instruction.

• *Encourage students to reflect actively on their online reading strategy use during each phase of the inquiry process.* Successful online readers monitor and reflect on their abilities to generate questions effectively, and to locate, evaluate, synthesize, and communicate information as they interact with multiple texts in online reading environments (Coiro & Dobler, 2007; Kuiper, 2007). Reflection that takes place while students are engaged in the activity, and after completing it, promotes continuous learning in authentic contexts and is integral to the online inquiry process (Hughes, Bruce, & Edwards, 2006).

Notably, online readers often vary in their strategy use across the phases of an online reading task (Coiro, 2007a); that is, sometimes readers who can efficiently search, locate, and communicate where they found a text may have difficulty critically evaluating the information within that text or synthesizing information across multiple texts. Likewise, a reader who struggles to locate and communicate online texts using search engines, blogs, or e-mail may sometimes be able to critically evaluate and synthesize information when taken directly to the website(s). Thus, teachers should provide opportunities for students to reflect on their ability to use reading strategies aligned with each phase of online reading comprehension, and to integrate and coordinate strategies across the phases while using different online technologies.

One idea for creating opportunities for student and peer reflection of online reading strategy use is to use a software program such as Camtasia (see *www.techsmith.com/camtasia.asp*) or iShowU (see *www.shinywhitebox.com/home/home.html*). These programs create a video recording of an individual's or a small group's actions and voices as participants complete an online reading task, just as if you were watching over their shoulder. At the end of the task, teachers, students, and/or peers can replay the video recording, stopping to reflect on effective and ineffective reading comprehension strategy use during each step in the reading process. Viewers are able to pause, for example, at the end of each phase of an online reading task (e.g., after an online text has been located, but before it has been read more closely) and before or after certain reading decisions (e.g., text entry, mouse clicks, scrolling, scan-

ning text, pressing the back button) to explain their reasons for using particular strategies or to ask others for suggestions about what they might have
done in a similar online reading situation. Through dialogue and discussion,
students come to understand and internalize their own strengths and areas
for online reading improvement.

• *Teach students how to set and monitor realistic online comprehension goals.*
As stated earlier, adolescents often overestimate their abilities to read on the
Internet and are easily frustrated when they realize their perceptions do not
match their abilities (Kuiper, 2007). Once students begin reflecting on their
use of effective online reading strategies to solve academic inquiry tasks, they
should have opportunities to set realistic online comprehension goals as part
of the learning process. Students who set and monitor their own reading goals
are able to internalize and organize their reading strengths and difficulties
(Johns & Lenski, 2001). In addition, the students are more determined to
learn, and they feel a sense of accomplishment when they reach their goals
(Afflerbach, 2007).

Checklist assessments are one effective way to help students determine
their strengths and areas of improvement for a particular reading task (Afflerbach, Reutschlin, & Russell, 2007). Thus, teachers might consider adapting
research-based checklists of effective online reading strategy use (see Eagleton & Dobler, 2007; Illinois Mathematics and Science Academy, 2007; Leu,
Coiro, Castek, et al., 2008) to develop criteria for successful performance
in a number of different online reading scenarios. Students can then refer
to these checklists, while they are completing the comprehension task, and
after they have finished, to monitor their current level of online reading
comprehension ability. During reflective strategy discussions, teachers and
peers can also provide feedback to students and help to set realistic goals for
particular strategies on which to focus next. Over time, students may create
learning portfolios (see Valencia, 2007) of recorded online reading sessions,
paired with audio descriptions of their progress on specific learning targets,
and develop insights into themselves as online readers and learners (Coiro,
2005b). These types of formative assessment practices enable students to
more actively adjust and improve their own learning (Chappuis & Chappuis,
2007/2008) and more deeply understand effective online information use for
learning (Hughes et al., 2006).

• *Employ multiple and alternative forms of assessment that evaluate online learning products and processes for both individuals and groups.* Another set of recommended practices for using assessment to inform instruction integrates three
purposeful decisions about how to measure online reading comprehension
ability. First, because the benefits of collaborative online inquiry tasks are
rarely captured with traditional assessments (Harrison, 2005; Johnston, 2001),
it is important to use *multiple* and *alternative* assessment instruments to measure comprehension strategy use and collaboration in online reading environments. Alternative assessments of online reading processes (e.g., Coiro,

2007a; Leu et al., 2005) can capture high levels of strategic processing not typically measured by multiple-choice measures of reading comprehension ability (see Johnston, 1983; Pearson & Hamm, 2005). Similarly, alternative measures of collaborative learning experiences can capture new 21st-century learning outcomes that may include "newfound respect for classmates and their opinions, understanding work team dynamics and using them for high-quality outcomes, taking turns, and recognizing the different learning that can occur in the collaborative and cooperative context" (Afflerbach, 2007, p. 170). Data from multiple assessment formats in technology-rich learning environments can then be triangulated to demonstrate learning outcomes that map onto state standards of academic achievement (Sherry et al., 2002).

Second, informative assessments of online reading comprehension ability should be designed to capture both the *processes* that occur during authentic online inquiry tasks and the resulting learning *products*. If effective reading assessments reflect our understanding of how students read in relation to a particular task, text, and setting (Afflerbach, 2007), effective online literacy teachers should create assessment situations that require students to use online reading comprehension strategies during real learning tasks, while providing new insights about how students effectively process online information and create final learning products. Likewise, effective online literacy teachers must be able to observe student behavior carefully and continually refine measures of performance-based processes and products to evaluate student work as it occurs in different online learning environments (Sherry et al., 2002).

Third, teachers should use informative assessments to capture both a student's *individual* online reading ability or contribution to an assigned online reading task and the quality of his or her working *group's* interactions and discussion. Johnston (2001) claims that the shift in our thinking about online literacy development as part of a social process prompts the need for assessments of group collaboration and productivity. Moreover, "the movement from individual assessment to group interaction and discussion provides for more active learning and allows [teachers to] assess students' growth [in strategy use] throughout the process" (Wood, Taylor, Drye, & Brigman, 2007, p. 196).

Concluding Comments

As we come to the end of this chapter, it is clear that teachers play a central, albeit somewhat different, role within new literacy classrooms. Learning how to foster adolescents' online literacy development most effectively is a complex and gradual process that requires innovation, reflection, and flexibility. Effective use of information and communication technologies in the classroom involves both knowing the technical aspects of how to operate continually emerging technologies and understanding how to use the technologies to bring about higher-order thinking and collaboration (Harlen & Deakin Crick, 2003). Instead of being the single source for all literacy knowledge, the teacher's role becomes that of mediator supporting self-reflection and self-regulation in ways that enable adolescents to gain greater control over their own literacy practices with networked information technologies.

Because of these changing teacher roles, greater attention needs to be placed on teacher education and professional development in a digital information age. As the Internet continues to challenge conventional definitions of reading comprehension, we need more research that systematically examines how to define and measure the skills, strategies, and dispositions required for comprehending a wider, and continuously evolving, range of offline and online informational texts. Likewise, future studies that build on what we have learned about how adolescents spend their time outside of school would help teachers realize new possibilities for teaching and learning in school. And finally, we need a series of rigorous research studies, with more statistical analyses to determine the extent to which the five promising practices outlined in this chapter positively impact adolescents' online literacy and learning across a number of classroom settings. As we venture forward in these areas, the journey will no doubt be challenging. Yet it is a challenge that can no longer be ignored, if we, as educators and researchers, seek to prepare today's adolescents for their literacy futures in a globally networked, digital information world.

QUESTIONS FOR DISCUSSION

1. Observe students working together while reading on the Internet to complete a problem-based online reading task that you designed. What dispositions do students demonstrate as they interact with each other and the information? At what are students most successful, and what appears to be most challenging? Document your findings with specific anecdotes that occur during the activity. Share your results with colleagues, and outline a series of steps to facilitate more successful collaborative online learning experiences.

2. Select a comprehensive website that you find useful for students in a particular content area. Skim the website to look for challenges adolescents may face as they navigate the information. Create a teacher think-aloud that provides an explicit model of the literacy strategies you believe are most helpful for learning from the information at that website. Conduct your think-aloud with students, and write down your reflections on what worked and what did not. How would you modify what you did?

3. Describe three specific actions that you will initiate to learn about and validate the literacies that students bring to your classroom from their daily lives. As you follow through with these actions, keep a journal to reflect on the unique skills sets you discover among your students. Recruit a colleague to do the same, and take time to exchange your reflections over time. Summarize how the information from this shared experience can inspire adolescents to contribute more actively to classroom reading and writing activities.

Resources

Further Reading

Coiro, J., Knobel, M., Lankshear, C., & Leu, D. J. (Eds.). (2008). *Handbook of research in new literacies*. Mahwah, NJ: Erlbaum.

Eagleton, M. B., & Dobler, E. (2007). *Reading the Web: Strategies for Internet inquiry*. New York: Guilford Press.

Kajder, S. (2006). *Bringing the outside in: Visual ways to engage struggling readers*. Portland, ME: Stenhouse.

Stevens, L. P., & Bean, T. W. (2007). *Critical literacy: Context, research, and practice in the K–12 classroom*. Thousand Oaks, CA: Sage.

Websites

www.readingonline.org—Reading Online, sponsored by the International Reading Association, offers hundreds of articles about reading education and classroom instruction. Many of the articles focus on instructional practices that facilitate adolescents' literacy and learning with the Internet.

www.newliteracies.uconn.edu—The New Literacies Research Team at the University of Connecticut conducts research on the new reading comprehension and learning skills required by the Internet and other emerging information and communication technologies. Several projects mentioned in this chapter are described in more detail at this website.

21cif.imsa.edu—The 21st Century Information Fluency Project, affiliated with the Illinois Mathematics and Science Academy, seeks to support educators committed to mastering and teaching digital information fluency skills, including the ability to find, evaluate, and use digital information effectively, efficiently, and ethically.

www.globalschoolnet.org/index.cfm—Global SchoolNet. This website for children and adolescents hosts collaborative projects and scholarship competitions about diplomacy and global issues. Projects are designed to develop literacy and communication skills, to foster teamwork, to create multicultural understanding, and to prepare youth for critical life skills required for success in an increasingly global economy.

www.edutopia.org/index.php—Sponsored by the George Lucas Foundation, Edutopia documents and shares information about exemplary programs in K–12 public schools. Many of the featured programs promote adolescent literacy and content-area learning through classrooms projects with the Internet.

References

Afflerbach, P. (2007). *Understanding and using reading assessment*. Newark, DE: International Reading Association.

Afflerbach, P., & Cho, B. Y. (2008). Identifying and describing constructively responsive comprehension strategies in new and traditional forms of reading. In S. Israel & G. Duffy (Eds.), *Handbook of research on reading comprehension*. Mahwah, NJ: Erlbaum.

Afflerbach, P., Reutschlin, H., & Russell, S. (2007). Assessing strategic reading. In J.

R. Paratore & R. L. McCormack. (Eds.), *Classroom literacy assessment: Making sense of what students know and do* (pp. 177–194). New York: Guilford Press.

Alexander, P. A., & Jetton, T. L. (2000). Learning from text: A multidimensional and developmental perspective. In M. L. Kamil, P. Mosenthal, P. D. Pearson, & R. Barr (Eds.), *Handbook of reading research* (Vol. III, pp. 285–310). Mahwah, NJ: Erlbaum.

Alvermann, D. E., Jonas, S., Steele, A., & Washington, E. (2006). Introduction. In D. E. Alvermann, K. A. Hinchman, D. W. Moore, S. F. Phelps, & D. R. Waff (Eds.), *Reconceptualizing the literacies in adolescents' lives* (2nd ed., pp. xxi–xv). Mahwah, NJ: Erlbaum.

American Association of School Librarians. (2007). Standards for the 21st century learner. Retrieved October 1, 2008, from *www.ala.org/ala/mgrps/divs/aasl/aaslproftools/learningstandards/standards.cfm*.

American Library Association. (2003). *Introduction to information literacy.* Retrieved February 26, 2008, from *www.ala.org/ala/acrl/acrlissues/acrlinfolit/infolitoverview/introtoinfolit/introinfolit.cfm*.

Anderson, R. E. (2001). Guest editorial: International studies of innovative uses of ICT in schools. *Journal of Computer Assisted Learning, 18,* 381–386.

Anstey, M., & Bull, G. (2006). *Teaching and learning multiliteracies: Changing times.* Newark, DE: International Reading Association.

Barton, K. C., & Smith, L. A. (2000). Themes or motifs?: Aiming for coherence through interdisciplinary outlines. *Reading Teacher, 54,* 54–63.

Baumann, J. F., & Jones, L. A. (1993). Using think-alouds to enhance children's comprehension monitoring abilities. *Reading Teacher, 47,* 184–193.

Becta. (2007). Harnessing Technology Review 2007: Progress and impact of technology in education. Coventry, UK: Becta. Retrieved January 10, 2008, from *publications.becta.org.uk/download.cfm?resid=33979*.

Beach, R., & O'Brien, D. (2008). Teaching popular culture texts in the classroom. In J. Coiro, M. Knobel, C. Lankshear, & D. J. Leu (Eds.), *Handbook of research on new literacies* (pp. 775–804). Mahwah, NJ: Erlbaum.

Beyersdorfer, J. (2007). *Comparing electronic and print text about the Civil War soldier.* ReadWriteThink Lesson Plan. Retrieved January 10, 2008, from *www.readwritethink.org/lessons/lesson_view.asp?id=68*.

Bilal, D. (2000). Children's use of the Yahooligans! Web search engine: I. Cognitive, physical, and affective behaviors on fact-based search tasks. *Journal of the American Society for Information Science, 51,* 646–665.

Bilal, D. (2001). Children's use of the Yahooligans! Web search engine: II. Cognitive and physical behaviors on research tasks. *Journal of the American Society for Information Science, 52,* 118–136.

Brader, A. (2008). *Youth identities and new literacy practices: A double edged sword.* Retrieved January 10, 2008, from *www.andybrader.com/downloads/double%20edged%20sword_a_brader.pdf*.

Burbules, N. C., & Callister, T. A., Jr. (2000). *Watch IT: The risks and promises of information technologies for education.* Boulder, CO: Westview Press.

Burke, J. (2002). The Internet reader. *Educational Leadership, 60,* 38–42.

Burn, A., & Leach, J. (2004) ICT and moving image literacy in English. In R. Andrews (Ed.), *The impact of ICT on literacy education* (pp. 153–79). London/New York: Routledge/Falmer.

Burnett, C., & Wilkinson, J. (2005). Holy lemons!: Learning from children's uses of the Internet in out-of-school contexts. *Literacy, 39,* 158–165.

Carr, M., & Claxton, G. (2002). Tracking the development of learning dispositions. *Assessment in Education, 9,* 1–28.

Castek, J. (in process). *An examination of classroom instruction that integrates the new literacies of online reading comprehension: Exploring the contexts that facilitate acquisition and the learning outcomes that result.* Dissertation being completed at the University of Connecticut.

Chandler-Olcott, K., & Mahar, D. (2003). "Tech-savviness" meets multiliteracies: Exploring adolescent girls' technology-mediated literacy practices. *Reading Research Quarterly, 38,* 356–385.

Chappuis, S., & Chappuis, J. (2007/2008). The best value in formative assessment. *Educational Leadership, 65,* 14–19.

Coiro, J. (2003). Reading comprehension on the Internet: Expanding our understanding of reading comprehension to encompass new literacies. *Reading Teacher, 56,* 458–464. [OnlineSerial]. Available at *www.readingonline.org/electronic/elec_index.asp?href=/electronic/rt/2-03_column/index.html.*

Coiro, J. (2005a). Making sense of online text. *Educational Leadership, 63,* 30–35.

Coiro, J. (2005b). Scaffolding readers on the Internet: Pairing assessment and instruction of online reading comprehension. In B. Dalton (Chair), *Scaffolding readers on the web: Customizing comprehension and assessment experiences for diverse learners.* Paper presented at the 55th annual meeting of the National Reading Conference, Miami, FL.

Coiro, J. (2007a). *Exploring changes to reading comprehension on the Internet: Paradoxes and possibilities for diverse adolescent readers.* Unpublished doctoral dissertation, University of Connecticut, Storrs. Available online at *www.newliteracies.uconn.edu/coirodissertation.*

Coiro, J. (2007b). *Critical evaluation on the Internet: What's missing in the text? What's missing in our instruction?* Paper presented at the 52nd Annual Conference of the International Reading Association, Toronto, CA.

Coiro, J., & Dobler, E. (2004, December). *Investigating how less-skilled readers use reading strategies while locating information on the Internet.* Paper presented at the 53rd Annual Meeting of the National Reading Conference, Scottsdale, AZ.

Coiro, J., & Dobler, E. (2007). Exploring the comprehension strategies used by sixth-grade skilled readers as they search for and locate information on the Internet. *Reading Research Quarterly, 42,* 214–257.

Cope, B., & Kalantzis, M. (2000). *Multiliteracies.* London, UK: Routledge.

Curtis, D. (2004). *High tech in Hawaii: The real-world relevance of technology.* Retrieved October 1, 2008, from *www.edutopia.org/nuuanu.*

Damico, J., & Baildon, M. (2007). Examining ways readers engage with websites during think-aloud sessions. *Journal of Adolescent and Adult Literacy, 51,* 254–263.

Davey, B. (1983). Think aloud—modeling the cognitive process of reading comprehension. *Journal of Reading, 27,* 44–47.

Duke, N. K., & Pearson, P. D. (2002). Effective practices for developing reading comprehension. In A. E. Farstrup & S. J. Samuels (Eds.), *What research has to say about reading instruction* (3rd ed., pp. 205–242). Newark, DE: International Reading Association.

Dwyer, B. (2007). *"I've a load of questions in my head": Scaffolding the development of effec-*

tive search strategies for struggling readers during Internet Inquiry. Paper presented at the annual meeting of the National Reading Conference, Austin, TX.

Eagleton, M., Guinee, K., & Langlais, K. (2003). Teaching Internet literacy strategies: The hero inquiry project. *Voices from the Middle, 10,* 28–35.

Eagleton, M. B., & Dobler, E. (2007). *Reading the Web: Strategies for Internet inquiry.* New York: Guilford Press.

Erstad, O. (2002). Norwegian students using digital artifacts in project-based learning. *Journal of Computer Assisted Learning, 18,* 427–437.

Fabos, B., & Young, M. D. (1999). Telecommunication in the classroom: Rhetoric versus reality. *Review of Educational Research, 69,* 217–259.

Glaude, C., Dumont, K., Fletcher, T. J., Davies, J., Bigue, D., & Tully, C. (2007). *Inquire to inspire: 21st century skills through experiential learning projects.* Featured 21st Century Learning Collection from Apple Learning Interchange. Retrieved March 3, 2008, from *edcommunity.apple.com/ali/story.php?itemid=12054.*

Goldman, S. R., & Lawless, K. A. (2007). Assessing multiple-source digital literacy skills. In K. A. Lawless (Chair), *21st century literacy: What is it, how do students get it, and how do we know if they have it?* Symposium presented at the Annual Meeting of the American Educational Research Association, Chicago, IL.

Greenleaf, C. L., Schoenbach, R., Cziko, C., & Mueller, F. L. (2001). Apprenticing adolescent readers to academic literacy. *Harvard Educational Review, 71,* 1–42.

Guthrie, J. T., & Cox, K. E. (2001). Classroom conditions for motivation and engagement in reading. *Educational Psychology Review, 13,* 283–302.

Guthrie, J. T., & Davis, M. H. (2003). Motivating the struggling readers in middle school through an engagement model of classroom practice. *Reading & Writing Quarterly, 19,* 59–85.

Guthrie, J. T., Wigfield, A., & Perencevich, K. C. (2004). *Motivating reading comprehension: Concept-oriented reading instruction.* Mahwah, NJ: Erlbaum.

Guzzetti, B. J., & Gamboa, M. (2004). Zines for social justice: Adolescent girls writing on their own. *Reading Research Quarterly, 39,* 408–436.

Harlen, W., & Deakin Crick, R. (2003). *A systematic review of the impact on students and teachers of the use of ICT for assessment of creative and critical thinking skills.* London: Evidence for Policy and Practice Coordinating Centre Department for Education and Skills.

Harper, D. (2006). *Generation YES [Youth and Educators Succeeding]—Vision to action: Adding student leadership to your technology plan.* Retrieved March 3, 2008, from *www.genyes.com/media/programs/how_to_include_students_in_tech_plan.pdf.*

Harrison, C. (2005). ICT and classroom pedagogies. In M. Leask & N. Pachler (Eds.), *Learning to teach using ICT in the secondary school* (2nd ed., pp. 154–169). London: Routledge.

Hinostroza, J. E., Guzmán, A., & Isaacs, J. (2002). Innovative uses of ICT in Chilean schools. *Journal of Computer Assisted Learning, 18,* 459–469.

Hobbs, R., & Frost, R. (2003). Measuring the acquisition of media-literacy skills. *Reading Research Quarterly, 38,* 330–355.

Hughes, H., Bruce, C., & Edwards, S. (2006). Fostering a reflective approach to online information use for learning. In D. Orr, F. Nouwens, C. Macpherson, R. E. Harreveld, & P. Danaher. (Eds.), *Proceedings 4th International Lifelong Learning Conference: Lifelong learning: Partners, pathways, and pedagogies* (pp. 143–150). Yeppoon, Australia. Retrieved January 15, 2008, from *eprints.qut.edu.au/archive/00004556/01/4556_1.pdf.*

Hull, G., & Schultz, K. (Eds.). (2002). *School's out!: Bridging out-of-school literacies with classroom practice.* New York: Teachers College Press.

Hunsberger, P. (2007). New directions in research: "Where am I?": A call in "connectedness" in literacy. *Reading Research Quarterly, 42*, 420–424.

Illinois Mathematics and Science Academy. (2007). *21st century information fluency: Evaluation Wizard.* Retrieved January 17, 2008, from *21cif.imsa.edu/tools/evaluate/evalWizard_beta_1.1.html.*

International Association for the Evaluation of Educational Achievement. (2000). *SITES Module 2: Case studies of innovative pedagogical practices using Second Information Technology in Education Study.* Retrieved March 1, 2008, from *sitesm2.org/sites_research_projects/sites_research_projects.html.*

International Society for Technology in Education. (2007). *National educational technology standards for students: The next generation.* Retrieved March 1, 2008, from *www.iste.org/inhouse/nets/cnets/students/pdf/nets_for_students_2007.pdf.*

Jackson, A. W., & Davis, G. A. (2000). *Turning Points 2000: Educating adolescents in the 21st century.* New York: Teachers College Press.

Johns, J. L., & Lenski, S. D. (2002). *Improving reading: Strategies and resources.* Dubuque, Iowa: Kendall/Hunt.

Johnston, P. (1983). *Reading comprehension assessment: A cognitive basis.* Newark, DE: International Reading Association.

Johnston, P. (2001). How will literacy be assessed in the next millennium? *Reading Research Quarterly, 35*, 249–250.

Johnston, P. (2005). Literacy assessment and the future. *Reading Teacher, 58*, 684–686.

Johnston, P. H. (1997). *Knowing literacy: Constructive literacy assessment.* York, ME: Stenhouse.

Karchmer, R. (2007). *Compare and contrast electronic text with traditionally printed text.* Read, Write, Think Lesson Plan. Retrieved February 15, 2008, from *www.readwritethink.org/lessons/lesson_view.asp?id=90.*

Kelly, M. J., & Clausen-Grace, N. (2007). *Comprehension shouldn't be silent: From strategy instruction to student independence.* Newark, DE: International Reading Association.

Kolodziej, N. (2007a). *Skimming and scanning: Using riddles to practice fact finding online.* ReadWriteThink Lesson Plan. Retrieved March 1, 2008, from *www.readwritethink.org/lessons/lesson_view.asp?id=1079.*

Kolodziej, N. (2007b). *Developing searching, skimming, and scanning skills with Internet bingo.* ReadWriteThink Lesson Plan. Retrieved March 1, 2008, from *www.readwritethink.org/lessons/lesson_view.asp?id=1052.*

Kozma, R. (2003). A review of the findings and their implications for practice and policy. In R. Kozma (Ed.), *Technology, innovation, and educational change: A global perspective.* Eugene, OR: International Society for Educational Technology.

Kuiper, E. (2007). *Teaching web literacy in primary education.* Imskamp, Enschede: Herman Kuiper, Amsterdam. Retrieved February 15, 2008, from *dare.ubvu.vu.nl/bitstream/1871/10836/1/7533.pdf.*

Kymes, A. (2005). Teaching online comprehension strategies using think-alouds. *Journal of Adolescent and Adult Literacy, 48*, 492–500.

Lankshear, C., & Knobel, M. (2003). *New literacies.* Maidenhead, UK: Open University Press.

Lankshear, C., & Knobel, M. (2002). Do we have your attention? New literacies, digital technologies and the education of adolescents. In D. Alvermann (Ed.), *Adolescents and literacies in a digital world*. New York: Peter Lang.

Law, N., Lee, Y., & Chow, A. (2002). Practice characteristics that lead to 21st century learning outcomes. *Journal of Computer Assisted Learning, 18*, 415–426.

Lenhart, A., & Madden, M. (2005). *Teen content creators and consumers*. Washington, DC: Pew Internet American Life Project. Retrieved March 10, 2007, from *www.pewinternet.org/pdfs/pip_teens_content_creation.pdf*.

Leu, D. J. (2007). *What happened when we weren't looking?: How reading comprehension has changed and what we need to do about it*. Keynote research address presented at the 52nd Annual Meeting of the International Reading Association, Reading Research Conference, Toronto, CA.

Leu, D. J., Castek, J., Hartman, D., Coiro, J., Henry, L., Kulikowich, J., et al. (2005). *Evaluating the development of scientific knowledge and new forms of reading comprehension during online learning*. Final report presented to the North Central Regional Educational Laboratory/Learning Point Associates. Retrieved May 15, 2006, from *www.newliteracies.uconn.edu/ncrel.html*.

Leu, D. J., Coiro, J., Castek, J., Henry, L. A., Reinking, D., & Hartman, D. K. (2008). Research on instruction and assessment in the new literacies of online reading comprehension. In C. C. Block & S. R. Parris (Eds.), *Comprehension instruction: Research-based best practices* (2nd ed., pp. 321–346). New York: Guilford Press.

Leu, D. J., Kinzer, C. K., Coiro, J., & Cammack, D. (2004). Towards a theory of new literacies emerging from the Internet and other ICT. In R. B. Ruddell & N. Unrau (Eds.), *Theoretical models and processes of reading* (5th ed., pp. 1570–1613). Newark, DE: International Reading Association.

Leu, D. J., Jr., Leu, D. D., & Coiro, J. (2004). *Teaching with the Internet K–12: New literacies for new times* (4th ed.). Norwood, MA: Christopher-Gordon. Companion website at *www.sp.uconn.edu/~djleu/fourth.html*.

Leu, D. J., Reinking, D., Carter, A., Castek, J., Coiro, J., Henry, L. A., et al. (2007, April). *Defining online reading comprehension: Using think aloud verbal protocols to refine a preliminary model of Internet reading comprehension processes*. In D. Alvermann (Chair), *21st century literacy: What is it, how do students get it, and how do we know if they have it?* A symposium presented at the annual meeting of the American Education Research Association, Chicago, IL. Retrieved March 1, 2008, from *www.newliteracies.uconn.edu/event_files/ies_nrc2006_symposium.pdf*.

Leu, D. J., Zawilinski, L., Castek, J., Banerjee, M., Housand, B., Liu, Y., et al. (2008). What is new about the new literacies of online reading comprehension? In A. Berger, L. Rush, & J. Eakle (Eds.), *Secondary school reading and writing: What research reveals for classroom practices*. Chicago: National Council of Teachers of English.

Levin, D., & Arafeh, S. (2002). *The digital disconnect: The widening gap between Internet-savvy students and their schools*. Pew Internet and American Life Project. Retrieved February 13, 2005, from *www.pewinternet.org/pdfs/pip_schools_internet_report.pdf*.

Lewis, C., & Fabos, B. (2005). Instant messaging, literacies, and social identities. *Reading Research Quarterly, 40*, 470–501.

Livingstone, S. (2002) *Young people and new media: Childhood and the changing media environment*. London: Sage.

Loveless, A. (2002). *Literature review in creativity, new technologies, and learning: Report 4. A report for NESTA Futurelab*. Retrieved February 15, 2008, from *www.nestafuturelab.org/research/reviews/cr01.htm*.

Mioduser, D., Nachmias, R., Tubin, D., & Forkosh-Baruch, A. (2002). Models of pedagogical implementation of ICT in Israeli schools. *Journal of Computer Assisted Learning, 18*, 405–414.

Moje, E. (2007). Youth literacy, culture, and identify. In J. Flood, D. Lapp, S. B. Heath, & V. Chou, (Eds.), *Handbook of research on teaching literacy through the communicative and visual arts* (Vol. II, pp. 207–219). Mahwah, NJ: Erlbaum.

Moje, E. B., & van Helden, C. (2004). Doing popular culture: Troubling discourses about adolescence. In J. Vadeboncoeur & L. Stevens (Eds.), *Re/Constructing "the adolescent": Sign, symbol, and body* (pp. 211–248). New York: Peter Lang.

Mozambite, A. (2005). Developing a living definition of reading in the elementary classroom. ReadWriteThink Lesson Plan. Retrieved March 1, 2008, from *www.readwritethink.org/lessons/lesson_view.asp?id=2*.

New Literacies Research Team. (2005). *New literacies for learning.* A symposium presented at the annual meeting of the National Reading Conference, Miami, FL.

O'Brien, D., Beach, R., & Scharber, C. (2007). "Struggling" middle schoolers: Engagement and literate competence in a reading writing intervention class. *Reading Psychology, 28*, 51–73.

O'Brien, D. G., & Bauer, E. B. (2005). New Literacies and the institution of old learning. *Reading Research Quarterly, 40*(1), 120–131.

Organisation for Economic Co-operation and Development. (2001). *Learning to change: ICT in schools.* Paris: OECD's Centre for Educational Research and Innovation.

Paris, S. G., Cross, D. R., & Lipson, M. Y. (1984). Informed strategies for learning: A program to improve children's reading awareness and comprehension. *Journal of Educational Psychology, 76*, 1239–1252.

Partnership for 21st Century Skills. (2007). *Learning for the 21st century.* Retrieved January 10, 2008, from *www.21stcenturyskills.org.*

Patterson, N. G. (2000). Hypertext and the changing role of readers. *English Journal, 90*, 74–80.

Pearlman, B. (2007). *New skills for a new century: Students thrive on cooperation and problem-solving.* Retrieved October 1, 2008, from *www.edutopia.org/new-skills-new-century.*

Pearson, P. D., & Hamm, D. N. (2005). The assessment of reading comprehension: A review of practices—past, present, and future. In S. G. Paris & S. A. Stahl (Eds.), *Children's reading comprehension and assessment* (pp. 13–69). Mahwah, NJ: Erlbaum.

Pearson, P. D., Roehler, L. R., Dole, J. A., & Duffy, G. G. (1992). Developing expertise in reading comprehension. In S. J. Samuels & A. E. Farstrup (Eds.), *What research has to say about reading instruction* (2nd ed., pp. 145–199). Newark, DE: International Reading Association.

Peng, H. Y., Tsai, C. C., & Wu, Y. T. (2006). University students' self-efficacy and their attitudes toward the Internet: The role of students' perceptions of the Internet. *Educational Studies, 32*, 73–86.

Perry, T. B. (2006). Multiple literacies and middle school students. *Theory Into Practice, 45*, 328–336.

Pressley, M. (2000). What should comprehension instruction be the instruction of? In R. Barr, M. L., Kamil, P. Mosenthal, & P. D. Pearson (Eds.), *Handbook of reading research* (Vol. 3, pp. 545–562). Mahwah, NJ: Erlbaum.

RAND Reading Study Group. (2002). *Reading for understanding: Toward an R&D program in reading comprehension.* Santa Monica, CA: RAND Corporation.

Rosenshine, B., & Meister, C. (1994). Reciprocal teaching: A review of the research. *Review of Educational Research, 64*, 479–530.

Schmar-Dobler, E. (2003). Reading on the Internet: The link between literacy and technology. *Journal of Adolescent and Adult Literacy* [Online Serial]. Retrieved October 11, 2006, from *www.readingonline.org/newliteracies/jaal/9-03_column.*

Schoenbach, R., Greenleaf, C. L., Cziko, C., & Hurwitz, L. (2000). *Reading for understanding: A guide to improving reading in middle and high school classrooms.* San Francisco, CA: Jossey-Bass.

Schulz-Zander, R., Buchter, A., & Dalmer, R. (2002). The role of ICT as a promoter of students' cooperation. *Journal of Computer Assisted Learning, 18*, 438–448.

Schunk, D. H., & Zimmerman, B. J. (2003). Self-regulation and learning. In W. M. Reynolds & G. E. Miller (Eds.), *Handbook of psychology: Educational psychology* (pp. 59–78). New York: Wiley.

Seitz, S. K. (2006). *Traveling terrain: Comprehending nonfiction text on the Web.* ReadWriteThink Lesson Plan. Retrieved March 1, 2008, from *www.readwritethink.org/lessons/lesson_view.asp?id=98.*

Selfe, C., & Hawisher, G. (2004). *Literate lives in the information age: Narratives on literacy from the United States.* Mahwah, NJ: Erlbaum.

Serafini, F. (2000/2001). Three paradigms of assessment: Measurement, procedure, and inquiry. *Reading Teacher, 54*, 384–393.

Sherry, L., Jesse, D. J., & Billig, S. H. (2002). Creating a WEB of evidence of student performance in a technology-rich learning environment. *International Journal on E-Learning, 1*, 31–40.

Souvignier, E., & Mokhlesgerami, J. (2006). Using self-regulation as a framework for implementing strategy instruction to foster reading comprehension. *Learning and Instruction, 16*, 57–71.

Spires, H. A., & Estes, T. H. (2002). Reading in Web-based learning environments. In C. C. Block & M. Pressley (Eds.), *Comprehension instruction: Research-based best practices* (pp. 115–125). New York: Guilford Press.

Stone, J. C. (2006). Popular websites in adolescent's out-of-school lives: Critical lessons on literacy. In M. Knobel & C. Lankshear (Eds.), *A new literacies sampler: New literacies and digital epistemologies* (pp. 49–66). London: Peter Lang.

Terry, K. P., & Doolittle, P. (2006). Fostering self-regulation in distributed learning. *College Quarterly, 9* [Online Serial]. Retrieved March 1, 2008, from *www.senecac.on.ca/quarterly/2006-vol09-num01-winter/terry_doolittle.html.*

Tierney, R. J. (2000). How will literacy be assessed in the next millenuem. *Reading Research Quarterly, 35*, 244–250.

Tierney, R. J., Bond, E., & Bresler, J. (2006). Examining literate lives as students engage with multiple literacies. *Theory Into Practice, 45*, 359–367.

Tsai, C. C. (2004) Adolescents' perceptions toward the Internet: A 4-T framework. *CyberPsychology and Behavior, 7*(4), 458–463.

Tsai, C. C., & Lin, C. C. (2004). Taiwanese adolescents' perceptions and attitudes regarding the Internet: Exploring gender differences. *Adolescence, 39*, 725–734.

Tsai, M. J., & Tsai, C. C. (2003). Information searching strategies in web-based science learning: The role of Internet self-efficacy. *Innovations in Education and Teaching International, 40*, 43–50.

Valencia, S. W. (2007). Inquiry-oriented assessment. In J. R. Paratore & R. L. McCormack (Eds.), *Classroom literacy assessment: Making sense of what students know and do* (pp. 3–20). New York: Guilford Press.

Voss, M. M. (1996). *Hidden literacies: Children learning at home and at school.* Portsmouth, NH: Heineman.

Wallace, R. M., Kupperman, J., Krajcik, J., & Soloway, E. (2000). Science on the Web: Students online in a sixth-grade classroom. *Journal of the Learning Sciences, 9,* 75–104.

Whipp, J. L., & Chiarelli, S. (2004). Self-regulation in a Web-based course: A case study. *Educational Technology Research and Development, 52*(4), 5–22.

Wilhelm, J. D. (2001). *Improving comprehension with think-aloud strategies.* New York: Scholastic.

Wolfe, C. R. (2001). *Learning and teaching on the World Wide Web.* San Diego: Academic Press.

Wood, K. D., Taylor, D. B., Drye, B., & Brigman, M. J. (2007). Assessing students' understanding of informational text in intermediate- and middle-level classrooms. In J. R. Paratore & R. L. McCormack (Eds.), *Classroom literacy assessment: Making sense of what students know and do* (pp. 195–209). New York: Guilford Press.

Chapter 23

Technology and Literacy

*Current and Emerging Practices
with Student 2.0 and Beyond*

David G. O'Brien
Brock Dubbels

GUIDING QUESTIONS

---

1. What technology tools and Web 2.0 applications are important for literacy learning?
2. What are the best practices involving technology and literacies?
3. How can instruction in the classroom and curriculum be enhanced by using new and evolving technologies that support digital literacy practices?

This chapter provides an overview of evolving research and theoretical frameworks on technologies and literacy, particularly digital technologies, with implications for adolescents' literacy engagement. We suggest future directions for engaging students with technology and provide resources that support sound practices.

Evolving Research on Digital Technologies: From Frameworks to Best Practice

When Kamil, Intrator, and Kim (2000) tackled a synthesis of research on technologies and literacy, they termed the task a *conundrum*. Given the rapidly evolving landscape of various technologies, that review, now dated (as this chapter soon will be), is still insightful both in reviewing a diversity of topics and the evolving importance of each. For example, at the turn of the decade, these researchers gave us historical footing in matters such as how computers and software may be used to improve reading and writing (Kamil, 1982), and to motivate learners (Hague & Mason, 1986). They noted the rising significance of hypertext and hypermedia, and foreshadowed the explosion of interest in the intersection of traditional literacies and digital media, which, at the turn of the decade, comprised a new program of inquiry (Reinking, McKenna, Labbo, & Kieffer, 1998). Finally, they also highlighted the social and collaborative importance of students working on stand-alone computers or in collaborative network environments, cited the paucity of research overall on technologies and literacy, and expressed optimism about the future of computers as instructional tools.

In the same volume that featured the synthesis by as Kamil, Intrator, and Kim, Leu (2000) used the phrase "literacy as technological deixis" (p. 745) to refer to the constantly changing nature of literacy due to rapidly morphing technologies. Leu's characterization is crucial, because he posits that these literacies are moving targets, evolving too rapidly to be adequately studied. If best practices rest on a solid research foundation, then, in the case of technologies and literacy we haven't even begun to know what best practices *are*. Nevertheless, even in the midst of a shallow bed of "empirical" studies—that is, studies of specific effects, over time, with statistical power, or studies of carefully described and documented, contextualized practices—compelling frameworks have emerged, with implications for how technologies enable new literacy practices. Best practices, if based on solid frameworks rather than a carefully focused research program, can be extrapolated from the frameworks and be the basis for sound instruction and curriculum planning. In this chapter we bridge some of these frameworks with instructional practice.

The relatively brief evolution of technologies and literacy has led us from computers and software as self-contained instructional platforms to a networked virtual world that computers enable. In the past 10 years or so, we have moved from viewing the Web as primarily a source of information and as a sort of dynamic hypertext with increasingly sophisticated search engines, to *Web 2.0*. Albeit a fuzzy term that has accrued definitions ranging from simply a new attitude about the old Web to a host of perspectives about a completely new Web, Web 2.0 presents exciting possibilities for enhancing instruction and learning. This new Web is an open environment with virtual applications; it is more dependent on people than on hardware; it more participatory than a one-sided flow of information (e.g., blogging, wikis, social networks); it is more responsive to our needs (e.g., mapping a route to a previously unknown destination). Perhaps most important, Web 2.0 is more open to sharing of ideas, media, and even computer code (Miller, 2005). The presence of Web 2.0 is about the World Wide Web (WWW) as a platform for production. Software that users would normally purchase and install from a disk or download is now hosted on the Internet. In a sense, Web 2.0 affords anyone access to the largest stage yet conceived. Educationally, it has the potential to diminish the broadcast mode of information transmission that has reduced individual interests and engagement. Instead, learners can now have at their disposal studio-quality tools that enhance production, appreciation, recognition, and performance, and above all, provide access to a worldwide audience.

Whereas research on computers and reading and writing has remained sparse, research on the myriad literacy practices involved in the Web 2.0 phenomenon is sparse but growing rapidly and is informed by many theoretical frames and fields, most of which overlap—for example, multiliteracies (Cope & Kalantzis, 2000; New London Group, 1996), new literacies and new literacy studies (Coiro, Knobel, Lankshear, & Leu, 2008; Kist, 2005; Knobel & Lankshear, 2007), media studies and new media studies (Hobbs, 2007; Kress, 2003), and critical media literacy and popular culture (Alvermann, Moon, & Hagood, 1999; Beach & O'Brien, 2008), to name a few.

Each of these frameworks has its own dynamics for describing and studying literacy practices, and each is inextricably intertwined with other frameworks. In the rapidly emerging research base, most of the designs are highly contextualized and theoretically tantalizing, but few studies are gauged to identify specific generalizable practices. For example, the studies designed around some of the aforementioned frameworks vary in terms of methodology (spanning the full range of human and cognitive sciences); they vary in terms of which data are collected, which settings (physical and virtual) are studied, and how learners are defined (e.g., as information processors, real selves, virtual selves, identity constructors). Hence, we can present here only a small sampling and complement the descriptions with some "best practice" exemplars, reminding readers of the caveat that "research-based" practices represent glimpses or snapshots taken along the rapidly moving field.

Reader and Writer 2.0: New Literates and New Literacies

What is important about technologies and literacies, especially when considering adolescents? What should we cull from the myriad evolving frameworks and perspectives to be able to present something useful for teachers and learners at this point in time given this rapidly changing texture. First, we want to present the adolescent learner, the person we call Student 2.0, starting with a vignette.

> High school students in Eden Prairie, Minnesota, a suburb of Minneapolis, posted photos on Facebook revealing themselves partying with alcohol, in violation of school rules. Following an investigation by school officials, disciplinary action was taken against 13 students. Students who believed that that the administration went too far walked out of school in protest; some of the parents threatened legal action (Xiong & Relerford, 2008). Scholars of digitally mediated popular culture challenged the

adults, parents and school officials alike, to evaluate more critically what had happened: High school students felt a compelling need to express themselves as digital authors and document a relatively common practice, partying with alcohol. And issuing sanctions assumes that the practice had not been widespread before it was expressed publicly on Facebook. Prosecution of the rule offenders would only serve to remind the documentors to be more careful. The new media scholars also reminded the youth as authors to consider more carefully their audience in the future. When you post on Facebook, you create for everyone, including school administrators and parents. Some students who were interviewed on television reacted to the disciplinary measures by saying that their rights to free speech were violated, that the school administrators had no jurisdiction, because the activities happened off of school grounds. Others went back to Facebook to start a new group page to defend their actions.

The Eden Prairie incident, albeit intriguing as a local interest piece about controversial legal and ethical issues regarding the Web 2.0, illustrates the trend of online content creation among youth. Rather than just use the Web to locate information, students are involved in content creation, that continues to grow, with 64% of online "teenagers" ages 12 to 17 engaging in at least one type of content creation, up from 57% of online teens in 2004 (Lenhart, Madden, Macgill, & Smith, 2007). In this national survey by the Pew Internet and American Life Project, 55% of online teens ages 12–17 say that they have created a profile on a social networking site, such as Facebook or MySpace, and 47% of online teens claim to have uploaded photos where others can see them. Even though those students posting online photos sometimes restrict access, they expect feedback. Nearly 9 out of 10 teens who post photos online (89%) say that people comment on their postings at least some of the time. The number of teen bloggers nearly doubled from 2004 to 2006, with girls leading boys in blogging, and the younger, upcoming girls more likely to out-blog boys.

The important issue for teachers is that these student authors are composing in a visual mode and reading comments printed in response; their peer readers (who are also most likely composers) are increasingly "reading" images and composing text responses or print messages in blogs and expecting critical responses. In short, students increasingly seem to engage in the types of reading and writing they either don't engage in, or don't prefer, at school.

Experienced teachers can remember when stand-alone computers were going to revolutionize education; they can recall when the Internet was a cumbersome, text-based environment rather than an engaging graphical environment called the WWW. Those of us who, as literacy educators, have spent our careers studying how young people interact with printed texts are now faced with a new landscape that renders many of our theoretical models, instructional frameworks, and "best" practices based on these print models inadequate or even obsolete. Print text remains important but, as noted, expression is increasingly multimodal (Kress & Van Leeuwen, 2001). Reading and writing youth are increasingly likely to express ideas using different semiotic modes, including print, visual, and audio modes, and to create hybrid texts that defy typical associations between modes and what they traditionally represent.

> When David worked with struggling readers in a high school Literacy Lab, the students, many of whom did not choose to read and write using print, wrote complex multimodal texts on a range of topics. They were very articulate about the affordances of various modes, and how those affordances influenced their choices in composition. For example, one group of students working a project exploring the impact of violence in the medion in adolescents, decided when to use images instead of print to communicate their ideas more effectively and passionately. They carefully planned how to juxtapose images and print to convey meaning. What would traditionally have been termed a "report" was instead a multimedia project, which they presented to parents and others at the school Open House evening.

> Brock has created a game studies unit, in which students study the qualities of their video games and create a technical document called a Walkthrough using blogs, a wiki, video, and an animated slide show embedded into the blog. Students could read, compare, and evaluate other students' work. Brock used an RSS feed (*really simple syndication*, a feed link to syndicated content) and had the blogs collected with bloglines, a way to both aggregate the student work and provide social networking through the WWW-based platforms and the comment sections for students.

From these two examples, you can see that the reading and composition enabled by these digital technologies is spatial rather than linear. Linearity has been replaced by reading and writing in virtual textual space—where a hot link lures the reader away from one page and on to the next, and from print to images and video, deeper and deeper into one's unique textual experience, and writers can post, broadcast, and receive responses. Scholars are already starting to look at the new spatial and temporal dimensions of digital literacies, as well as the compatibilities and incompatibilities of these dimensions with traditional spatial and temporal dimensions of schools (Leander, 2007). Researchers are also studying new literacy environments such as webpages using research paradigms derived from reading print on paper—for example, Coiro and Dobler's (2007) work extending traditional comprehension theories to study online reading comprehension. Coiro and Dobler argue that although we know a lot about the reading strategies that skilled readers use to understand print in linear formats, we know little about the proficiencies needed to comprehend text in "electronic" environments. McEneaney (2006) cogently argues that the traditional theoretical frameworks, including so-called "interactive theories" (from cognitive or transactional perspectives) are too strongly based in a traditional notion of print to be useful. With what are the new literates interacting? McEneaney contends that the text can "act on" the environment: The text can create the reader, just as the reader through the dynamics of online environments, can create or change the text.

But the new literates also encounter new challenges. The new textual spatiality lacks the kinesthetic texture of books; readers lose their "places" and even the ability to feel the touch of the page as they do when they flip paper pages back, then reorient themselves on the page (Evans & Po, 2007). The feel of the text is replaced by the feel of a finger on a mouse or a key. The imaging that helps a reader maintain and access the previous page might be replaced by multiple mental images of more rapidly changing texts, or mental images replaced by actual images. What Evans and Po call the *fluidity* of the digital or electronic texts invites readers to alter the text more readily, more easily. We come full circle with a tension faced by readers of the digital texts. On the one hand, this text fluidity begs readers to alter texts, to pick alternative texts, and to mix and match texts; on the other hand, this new textuality, with texts unfolding at every mouse click, places the text itself more in the control of the reader. The text the reader creates, often unwittingly via a series of clicks or cuts and pastes, may address the reader/writer in unexpected ways. One of the most exciting prospects for educators is the unlimited range of texts, from traditional print modes to various hybrids, including print texts, visual texts, audio texts, and even various types of performance texts that students can now create, as they themselves are "created" or changed by those texts. The new literates can navigate through a collage of print, images, videos, and sounds, choosing and juxtaposing modalities, and bending old spatial and temporal constraints to communicate to peers and to others throughout the world.

Beach and O'Brien (2008), in drawing from both the philosophy of mind and neuroscience (e.g., Clark, 2003; Restak, 2003) propose that the students of the "digital generation" have more digitally adept brains; they read and write differently than youth from even 10 years ago, because their existence in the mediasphere, the barrage of multimodal information they encounter daily, the constant availability of multiple tech tools at their fingertips, and the convergence enabling immediate use and production of media have changed the way they process multimedially. Prensky (2001) has posited a similar scenario. The Beach and O'Brien proposal (2008), in response to a Kaiser Family Foundation study (Foehr, 2006) of young people ages 8–18 and widely disseminated in the popular press, shows that even though the total amount of time devoted to media use remains about the same as 5 years ago (6.5 hours a day), the amount of time devoted to *multitasking*, using multiple forms of media concurrently (e.g., surfing the Web while listening to an MPEG-1 Audio Layer 3 (MP3) and checking text messages), is on the rise. Beach and O'Brien (2008) contend that *multitasking* is not accurate, because it implies the ability to engage in several activities at the same time or, more accurately, to switch attention rapidly among activities to gain efficiency in completing work. They instead characterized this often seamless juggling as *multimediating* (Lankshear & Knobel, 2003), because it more accurately involves not only multimodal attention shifts but also seems to include a new facility and flexibility in processing and producing multimodal texts. The missing piece in characterizing the new literates is that we continue to appraise them using outdated models of reading, text processing, and learning. Instead, we need to think of them as more adept at using technologies to read, compose, and "socialize."

Texts 2.0: From the Page to the Screen

Let us revisit the question posed in the last section—What is important about technologies and literacies?—and this time consider the evolving kinds of texts that youth are reading and writing. Again, we have to choose among compelling frameworks and perspectives. One salient issue surrounding the evolving technologies is how the notion of "text" is changing. We are "moving from the page to the screen" (Kress, 2003). Kress notes that the screen privileges images. He also makes a case for the ambiguity of images and the necessity of print text for helping the viewer understand context and make a directed interpretation of images. As educators, we have to concede that texts are increasingly *multimodal* (Jewitt & Kress, 2003). In multimodal reading and composing, ideas and concepts are represented with print texts, visual texts (photographs, video, animations), audio texts (music, audio narration, sound effects), and even dramatic or other artistic performances (drama, dance, spoken-word) (O'Brien & Scharber, 2008).

A second change is the increasing popularity of hybrid texts that are unlike most of the longer, connected discourse with which many of us grew up. For example, *textoids* are on the rise. These texts were originally defined as specially created research texts that lacked the coherence and structure of naturally occurring texts from typical genres (Graesser, Millis, & Zwaan, 1997) or contrived instructional texts (Pearson, 2004). Ironically, these once-contrived texts are ubiquitous in online environments. The term *textoids* now refers to fleeting texts that are transported from one place to another and are constantly changing (e.g., Wikipedia entries, pasted into a student's report and edited to fit into the new textual context); they are also textual bursts of information sent to cell phones as text messages. Short textoids or text bursts are displacing longer discourse as readers expect more choices in accessing information and entertainment faster in quick clicks. At the same time, the sheer number and range of genres of these textoids, the juxtaposition of textoids with other media, and the retention of the more traditional, longer discourse, makes reading in online text environments more challenging than reading in traditional print environments.

The typical ways of describing and distinguishing texts from one another, such as using text structure, no longer apply (McEneaney, 2006). Electronic texts defy such classification, because they may be short and contrived to produce a targeted burst to get attention (the textoids); they are not linear but spatial (hypertexts, hypermedia). Single textoids or pages or articles are linear, but they exist in virtual space, with a multitude of other possible texts. In short, the texts have virtual structure that is much more dynamic than static structures assigned to single print texts.

Present Technology Tools and Web 2.0 Applications

As we noted, Web 2.0 tools are about production, and they are hosted on the Web to enable a range of activities. As the access to bandwidth increases, and computers are equipped with greater image/video processing capacity, these tools will become invaluable in engaging youth. Young people will use these tools not only to develop literacy and numeracy skills but also to continue to hone their technological skills in the production, communication networking, data mining, and problem solving that are increasingly valued in the global economy. In the past, many of the tools now available as Web-based tools were expensive, limited to single machines, and difficult to use. These same tools, such as word processing, multimedia production, and network communications tools are now free, shareable, collaborative, and perceived as both meaningful and enjoyable by young people. Moreover, the tools are part of young people's daily lives. In addition, the personal electronics that many young people carry in their pockets, backpacks, and purses are more powerful than the computers that inhabited labs not even 5 years ago. With the advent of new applications and relatively cheap storage on the Web, these portable devices neither perform the bulk of processing nor store the outputs of processing; they are access devices—Web portals, with small screens and keyboards or other ways to input data. For example if you want to work with pictures, you can access a portal such as Flickr to view and manage pictures; if you want to create a document of just about any stripe, you can go to Google Docs and make slide shows; engage in word processing; construct spreadsheets; and store, share, and collaborate with writing partners.

Teachers can use many of these tools to extend and to enhance the learning experience of their students. The tools present challenges in developing best practices because they are neither repositories of content nor self-contained curricula. Rather, they can be used by creative teachers who are able to draw from existing content domains, themes, and conceptual frameworks as they work within the applications; the tools can provide supportive environments for producing content, sharing and collaborating around content, and hosting public displays of users' productions. Hence, the tools are not useful without the context of a larger unit or lesson plan, and instructional and learning frameworks that support activities and literate practices enabled by the tools. Teachers must understand clearly their instructional and learning objectives and goals, and students must know how the tools can help them meet those goals. Otherwise, the tools, which students sometimes know well and can use for entertainment, revert to users' tools for pleasure and interests, easily circumventing instructional or learning practices desired by teachers. Next, we review some Web 2.0 tools that enable these practices, and describe the features of each, presenting examples of how we have used them with students.

MySpace

We start with the nemesis of most computer classrooms and labs. For example, Brock was observing another teacher's students during a drafting class. The students were working in a lab with high-end three-dimensional drafting software. During downtime between instructions that were broadcast over the public address system, students often checked their MySpace pages. Although the site was blocked in the district, many students easily overcame the obstacle by searching for a proxy server that granted them access. A *proxy server* is a website that has a name accepted by the firewall, so it is allowed—it is kind of like using a fake ID. Although students may not know how it works, they have learned how to do it. And no matter how savvy the information technology (IT) department, the almost infinite supply of new proxy servers and webpages, with directions targeting youth who want to jump the school restrictions, makes sites deemed objectionable by school districts difficult to block.

On the one hand, to the digital immigrants and the inhabitants of the Institution of Old Learning (O'Brien & Bauer, 2005), MySpace represents an uncontrolled virtual space that distracts students from work and enables socializing and forms of expression incompatible with the organization and temporal control of school. On the other hand, for digital natives, "assimilated" digital immigrants, and new literacies advocates, MySpace is a dynamic forum of multimodal expression. It is also a place where young people socialize with peers around the world, put pictures up, write in slang, stream music and video, and engage in instant messaging. They are able to blog, to embed flash animations—in short, to engage in almost limitless expression using a range of multimodal literacies. It is really an example of students expressing themselves in the same way they dress, decorate their rooms, or draw in their notebooks.

This does not mean that the space is benign. Although you can connect with friends and family, you can also get solicitations from unwanted characters. Most young people are aware of whom to talk to, and how they expect others to speak to them. Users know that others mask their true identities through the computer, which has led young people to be more savvy as well. The Kaiser Family Foundation *Generation M* report (Roberts, Rideout, & Foehr, 2005) notes that when kids come across inappropriate sites and solicitations, they move past them. For digital natives, experienced in social networking, these are just another distraction in the way of what they went to the site to do. MySpace sites can also be locked to persons other than those invited by the owner.

We don't expect sites like MySpace to be imported into the school curriculum. However, in the spirit of being more assimilated into Generation M's world, it makes sense for teachers to join MySpace, set up a page, and even let students know that you have done so. As teachers, we interact regularly with our students via MySpace. Through it, we are more in tune with their social worlds, their interests, and their creativity. You might also want to bridge media production in school with the sharing features of such social networking sites, so that students may use tools like MySpace as a way to share and to get feedback on their productions.

Facebook

You already know a bit about Facebook from the Eden Prairie vignette. It is a place where you can post your profile and surround yourself with friends, their activities (including photos of parties!) and favorite sites, and connect the dots to all of your websites. Brock has links to SlideShare, mogulus television station, Facebook social networking groups, and various blogs. Facebook also includes tons of little games, multiple ways you can communicate with others, and things you can share. Brock is a member of many groups, and when the mood catches him, he starts another group: How about people who have read this chapter and want to continue the discussion about literacies involved in applications for Student 2.0? It really is that easy, and he really did start that group.

In Facebook you can choose to keep up with friends you don't see often, as well as friends and acquaintances with similar interests and affinities. You can take surveys of movies and compare them to your friends; you can see what kind of German or French philosopher you are. You can share music, keep up to date with friends through instant messaging, and be alerted to activities of groups to which you belong. Facebook, like MySpace, is blocked in many school districts, although most of adolescents we know seem to prefer MySpace. As with MySpace, we encourage teachers to set up a Facebook account to see what it provides. Although it might be tricky if the site is officially blocked in school, we also encourage teachers to use it to network with both colleagues and students. One of the great revelations, if you are included as a "friend" to students classified as "struggling" in reading and writing, is the quality, the range of genres, and the passion with which these students compose and engage in reading others' compositions on social networking sites. It is possible that these same students, who have negative perceptions about their abilities and avoid reading and writing in school, might invite teachers to read what they have written online.

YouTube

Unfortunately, YouTube is much maligned in schools, not just because of the content, but also because streaming media consume bandwidth. This is the most complete compendium of online searchable video ever. Like any compendium, including the billions of webpages outer there, there are some videos that teachers may find either objectionable or a waste of time, just as there are thousands of interesting and informative videos. There are really many opportunities for using Web-based video in the classroom. Here are several ways that we have used it:

1. To show a video.
2. To host a video we have produced.
3. To engage in social networking.
4. To enhance engagement among students.
5. To provide content for a Web-based, TV-like network with Mogulus.

The real value of video is its impact due to availability of narrative, and the power of performing and presenting to the world—something that local and even national networks cannot do. YouTube not only hosts videos created by your students but also provides access to videos created by novices and professionals from all over the world. YouTube should be a part of classroom instruction designed to teach appropriate use of media and media savvy to young people. With YouTube you can embed video in your blog and your website, as well as upload your own creations—even from your cellular phone. We have observed that when students create for performance and presentation to an audience other than their teachers and immediate peers, they put forth much more effort and are much more creative and engaged, and the learning experience lasts long after the week-and-a-half extinction point of most test-driven curricula. Students can create, post, and share. In addition, teachers can create groups and utilize social networking to perform and to respond. The most powerful benefit is that this social networking and broadcasting function extends and deepens the possibility of participating in high-traffic media networks, where millions of people may view your work and send out links to invite their friends to see what you have done. With the right topic and a bit of luck, a cell phone with video capture and a good idea can start a person's career in video media. This prospect can be motivating, and the idea that students have done something that everyone can see leads them to some real street "media cred."

Flickr

This photo sharing website, web services suite, and online community platform was one of the earliest Web 2.0 applications. In addition to being a popular website for sharing personal photographs, the service is widely used by bloggers as a photo repository. Flickr's popularity has been fueled by its innovative online community tools that allow photos to be tagged and browsed by folksonomic means, a social/collaborative way to create and manage tags for content, in contrast to traditional subject indexing, in which content is fit to subjects predetermined by experts (Vander Wal, 2007). In Flickr, metadata are generated by not only experts but also creators and consumers of the content. Folksonomies became popular on the Web around 2004, with social software applications such as social bookmarking or annotating photographs. Typically, folksonomies are Internet-based, although they are also used in other contexts. Folksonomic tagging is intended to make a body of information increasingly easy to search, discover, and navigate over time.

As folksonomies develop in Internet-mediated social environments, users can discover who created a given folksonomy tag, and see the other tags that this person created. In this way, a folksonomy user may discover the tag sets of another user who similarly interprets and tags content. The result is often an immediate and rewarding gain in the user's capacity to find related content (a practice known as *pivot browsing*). Part of the appeal of folksonomy is its inherent subversiveness: Compared to the choice of the search tools that websites provide, folksonomies can be seen as a rejection of the search engine status quo in favor of tools that are created by the community. Obviously, in addition to being a place to share photos, Flickr is a great source of media for students' multimedia productions.

Blogger

Brock has used this one, putting his class blog (*www.5th-teacher.blogspot.com*) up on the screen, with images, examples, links to other resources, related news events, goings on in the class, his teaching manifesto, and global descriptions of assignments, as well as breakdowns of daily work. He also embeds his slide shows in the blog, along with video. This provides a resource for students to use both in class and outside of class. Because students have learned the format, and how to use pictures and other media from the Web, they have become proficient at creating reflective work and high-quality multimedia productions. Blogger gets a bad rap by some, but you can limit the audience of student blogs by closing them off from the world feature and selecting viewers by inviting specific people. This also allows the teacher to access the blog if there is questionable content for classroom blogs "gone rogue."

SlideShare

This Web application is great for getting students to see the opportunities of creating active multimedia products. Brock's students created slide shows in PowerPoint, using images, text, and animation and transition effects, then uploaded them to SlideShare. This allowed the class to create their own group (Washburn Introduction to Engineering Design [IED]) where they could see and comment on each others' slides, as well as use the chat function. Students also use SlideCast, in which they enter and synchronize an MP3 with their presentation, so that both teachers and students can create music videos or even do voice-over narration for telling stories and performance (dramatic) readings. SlideShare also lets you one-click to Blogger, so that students may embed their slide show in their blog. A cool feature is the ability to link this into Facebook.

Google Suite

Google provides a nice suite of tools for educators and students. Often your students have computers with Internet access at home but lack productivity software, such as Microsoft Office, or free tools such as OpenOffice. Students can use the Google Suite to create word processing, slide shows, and spreadsheets. The impressive feature is that this suite is available online, so students with an Internet connection can work at home on the document they created at school. And as with other Web 2.0 applications, students may invite others to cowrite and produce documents here. This allows groups to work on the same paper, and it also tracks each person's contributions as the document is created. We used Google Documents to collaborate on this chapter. In addition, Google Maps, Google Earth, and Google SketchUp, a three-dimensional modeling program, are other tools in the Google suite that deserve extra emphasis. Reading and writing practices are more engaging to students when tied to the creation of the places, people, and activities. Brock had students create scenes from the play *A Raisin in the Sun* using this tool. The class explored the role of place and lived space, and the way space influences how people feel, speak, and act. This high-tech diorama was reminiscent of the shoebox versions we sometimes made for fun or for school projects.

Zotero

Zotero, an easy-to-use yet powerful research tool, helps researchers gather, organize, and analyze sources (citations, full texts, webpages, images, and other objects), and share research results in a variety of ways. An extension of the popular open-source Web browser Firefox, Zotero includes the best parts of older reference manager software (like EndNote)—the ability to store author, title, and publication fields, and to export that information as formatted references—and the best parts of modern software and Web applications (like iTunes and del.icio.us), such as the ability to interact, tag, and search in advanced ways. Zotero integrates tightly with online resources; it can sense when users are viewing a book, article, or other object on the Web, and—on many major research and library sites—find and automatically save the full reference information for the item in the correct fields. Since it lives in the Web browser, it can effortlessly transmit information to, and receive information from, other Web services and applications; because it runs on one's personal computer, it can also communicate with software running there (e.g., Microsoft Word). It can also be used offline (e.g., on a plane, in an archive without Wi-Fi).

Scribd

This document-sharing community and self-publishing platform enables anyone to publish easily, distribute, share, and discover documents of all kinds. You can submit, search for, and comment on e-books, presentations, essays, academic papers, newsletters, photo albums, school work, and sheet music. A powerful feature of this tool is that you can upload documents in many different formats, including Microsoft Word, Adobe Portable Document Format (PDF), plain text, hypertext markup language (HTML), PowerPoint, Excel, OpenOffice, Joint Photographic Experts Group (JPEG), and many other formats. Once your documents are uploaded, you can embed them in a blog, Facebook profile, or other external websites, with your fonts, images, and formatting fully intact. Each document hosted at Scribd has its own unique uniform resource locator (URL), and you have unlimited storage, so you can upload as many documents as you like. Once these are up, they are also available for fast indexing by Google and other major search engines, so that your content can be found in simple searches. You can keep certain documents private or share with a limited number of friends, and you can automatically convert published content into PDF, Word, and plain text. What is engaging for young writers is that not only can they publish widely but they also can see how many people have viewed their documents by location. Through Google you find documents similar to your own, as well as connect with a community of writers working in the same content area, enabling feedback and dialogue about your documents yet allowing you to retain full copyright under Creative Commons licenses.

Other Web 2.0 Resources

Space limits preclude a more elaborate listing of the multitude of other Web 2.0 sites. We recommend that readers of this chapter peruse the following briefly annotated list of other sites promoting multimodal literacies:

- *Digg.* A community-based, popular news article website, where news stories and websites are submitted by users, then promoted to the front page through a user-based ranking system.
- *bubbl.us.* An online brainstorming tool that students and teachers can use to create colorful mind maps online, share maps and collaborate with friends, embed mind maps in blogs or websites, e-mail and print maps, and save maps as images.
- *BigHugeLabs.com.* A tool that makes using Flickr a lot more interesting by capitalizing on the site's existing functionality. Dozens of toys, games, and utilities allow you, for example, to create a magazine cover from a selected Flickr photo, create a motivational poster, and access huge amounts of user data (FlickrDNA).

- *Photoshop Express.* An application providing two gigabytes of storage to which you can link in your blogs or websites. You can edit images on the fly without having to up/download them each time or move from computer to computer, and you are just a login away from your library of photos.

- *SoundJunction.* A site where users can take music apart and find out how it works, create music, find out how other people make and perform music, learn about musical instruments, and look at the backgrounds of different musical styles.

- *del.icio.us.* (pronounced like the word *delicious*). A social bookmarking Web service for storing and sharing data with more than 3 million users and 100 million bookmarked URLs.

- *Ning.* A site that enables the creation of one's own social network, designed to compete with sites like MySpace and Facebook, by appealing to users who want to create networks around specific interests, or who have limited technical skills.

- *VoiceThread.* A versatile online media album that can hold essentially any type of media (images, documents, and videos) and allow people to make comments in five different ways—using voice (with a microphone or telephone), text, audio file, or video (with a webcam)—and share them with anyone they wish.

- *Many Eyes.* A tool for the visual representation of data that makes sharing data creative and fun, while tuning students into the relation between information presentation and interpretation.

- *Scratch.* A designing tool with a language that makes it easy to create interactive stories, animations, games, music, and art.

Classroom Vignettes of Practices with Technologies and Literacy

Junior High "Intervention" Class

We have studied our reading/writing intervention class in a suburban community of the Twin Cities for 3 years (O'Brien, Beach, & Scharber, 2007). The class uses a Literacy Lab setting with a reduced enrollment target of 15 students, previously assessed as struggling in reading, and mentored by two teachers, both of whom hold K–12 reading licenses. The class meets once a day in a block scheduling format, with 93-minute class periods. The curriculum juxtaposes traditional engagement activities with "new literacies" activities. For example, on the side of more traditional interventions, students use the Scholastic READ 180 program, read and discuss young adult novels as a group, and dramatize the texts and a range of activities to integrate reading and writing. They also engage in strategies instruction, such as the use of mind mapping and various activities designed specifically to help students achieve competence on state language arts standards and high-stakes assessments. On the new literacies side, using various technology tools, the students engage in writing activities, such as producing stories, comic books (using Comic Life), wikis (in Moodle) and poetry writing. They write journal responses to their reading and construct PowerPoint presentations about topics, such as their favorite video games or young adult novels, and share their poetry or story writing. They plan, design, and perform radio plays (using GarageBand for background tracks and sound effects). Recently, students completed place-based projects in which they used VoiceThread to publish photos of important places in their school, complete with audio or print commentaries. They publish their writing in the school district Moodle site. Some of the students also participate in afterschool computer gaming sessions. In the new literacies realm, the teachers include practices in which students engage to explore ideas, construct a classroom community, and develop agency in meeting personally relevant goals.

Media Class Rhythm and Flow Unit

This was the first unit that Brock created after transitioning from a language arts teacher to a media specialist. He found that the units he taught as a language arts teacher were still very applicable to the standards and benchmarks in media technologies when it came to teaching media or print texts, or the many opportunities that arise as a result of having access to computers. As a media specialist, Brock tried to link the media and technology activities to improvement in reading and writing. For example, he included Reading Friday, in which students had to create a music business persona/image, describe their style of music, and choose lyrics that they would perform and record into Garage Band. GarageBand is one option. Students could also use one of the Web-based products we have discussed. So the students took print texts—poems, paragraphs, dialogue, and lyrics they liked—and recorded themselves reading as a track on the music software. They also recorded *outtakes*, or descriptions of the experiences, and rated their oral interpretation performances. After students had shared their tracks with Brock, they began to practice putting a beat and music behind the tracks. This enabled a thorough interpretation and exploration of voice and oral expression. Students who had never really thought about the qualities of the voices in the narratives (e.g., the tone, theme, pitch, volume, emphasis in elongation and breaks) could better hear and understand dramatic pauses, tone and volume changes, diction and word choices, as well as format, organization, and punctuation. This activity began to make a difference in students' understanding of these concepts. As students began exploring pauses work, changing and emphasizing words, assonance, and resonance in rhyme structures, they were really looking at oral reading and fluency, and reading in general, in a much deeper and more playful way. Students then took photos and made their CD covers, using image manipulation software; they made their own liner notes and wrote their own copy for advertising; they conceptualized a MySpace design (because they were not permitted access to MySpace) and created tours, clothing, and so on. It turned into a game about being in the music business. This unit, which had originally been intended as a weeklong reward for the kids, so engaged students as they performed their lyrics and created their music careers that Brock extended it for 2 weeks.

What are "best practices" in these scenarios? First, students engage in activities, using technologies that support both the local curriculum and state standards. Rather than considering technologies and innovation as replacements for more traditional instructional and learning, the technologies provide more effective ways to engage students. Second, best practices dictate that the technologies *enhance* teaching and learning by providing access to media and enabling students to use various modalities to explore and publish ideas. Third, although we can already see a future in which digital literacies replace traditional print literacies, for now, given the realities of standards, print-centric assessments, and, particularly the predominately print-based curricula, best practices explore ways to bridge print and digital literacies effectively. Fourth, the notion of best practices, which we typically associate with teaching or facilitating learning, should be extended to include practices related to supporting infrastructures and increasing funding for technologies that do enhance teaching and learning.

Future Directions and Best Practices for Engaging Students in Literacy with Technology

Clearly, the future will bring a wider range of more accessible digital tools. What started as the Web 2.0 phenomenon will continue at a rapid rate as the analog television bandwidth is purchased by Web Portals, such as Google, to provide faster access to more and more data from small personal communication devices—things that we used to call "phones." As shown by current studies from the Pew Internet and American Life project, youth will continue to use more media and engage in more media multitasking or multimediating. As more young people have access to these tools, the digital divide will persist but not be as defined. As educators, we will slowly but surely start to redefine *learners* based on the experiences these young people have daily in the mediasphere, and the way their brains are changing as result. Similarly, we will start to redefine literacy more in line with the new literacies practices in which youth engage outside of school, and to think of better ways to connect out-of-school and in-school experiences with technologies and literacy.

Given the frameworks briefly described in this chapter for understanding technology-enabled or enhanced texts and new literacies practices, what are some possible practices that will not only produce more engaged and better readers and writers, as traditionally defined, but also facilitate practices that improve intertextual, intermedial, and multimodal understanding? We briefly outline some of these realizing that practices, they are morphing as we write, and that new ones will have emerged even before this chapter is published. We offer these not so much as static examples but as ways of thinking about best practices in the milieu of new and emerging technologies, and new literacies and literates. We want fellow educators to think in novel ways about how these new technologies may improve literacy practices, not because of their technical features, but because they are engaging. Although it is oversimplistic to state that technologies are worthwhile simply because they are motivating, we might cautiously state that technologies are *engaging* because they often incorporate aspects of play, are pleasurable, and are associated with leisure time outside of school. We also argue that good technology can guide and extend students' knowledge of the world and their relationship to it, and that the software and appliances it inhabits are means for guidance, creativity, and production. Here are some recommended practices as we to end this decade and head into the next.

Engaging Readers and Writers

Young people should have access to curricula and learning opportunities in which reading and writing strategies instruction is not always the focus; rather the focus is to provide high-interest engaging activities that allow young people to accomplish goals using a range literacy tools and practices, many of them enabled by technology. Young people can become very strategic about what tools they use and how they use them to engage in practices that produce personally relevant outcomes. Learners need to be strategic, but they do not always benefit most from being taught strategies. And, as we noted, it is quite possible that the learners we are trying to engage are harder to engage because of their experiences in the mediashpere. In Brock's teaching, texts aren't necessarily print texts; rather, they are multimodal messages (Dubbels, 2008). For example, Brock has even used allegorical paintings and text as movement activities and multimodal analogues to decoding and propositional levels of comprehension.

Connecting with Out-of-School Literacies

As educators, we should make a more concerted effort to connect school instructional practices and curricula to out-of-school practices. Literate practices involved in activities such as instant messaging, creating and reading images, authoring webpages, and participating in social networks are ignored, devalued, or even feared in schools. In contrast, students engagement in strategies instruction, skills instruction, and reading textbooks and answering questions is common. Although these traditional activities and assessments are important, and more directly tied to valued outcomes, such as performance on high-stakes tests, they are increasingly disconnected from the new literacies skills, knowledge, and abilities that youth use the most, and they are simply not as engaging as many of the digital literacies practiced outside of school. The digital tools, and the practices they support, some of which we present shortly, are not intended to turn youth completely away from traditional academic reading and learning; rather, they are intended to engage them in novel ways with important content and learning tasks. The goal, as we noted, is to engage students in these practices, to improve their learning, and to connect the learning to personally relevant goals.

Taking Advantage of Multimodality

Traditional print materials, such as textbooks, have changed little over the last 150 years, and they have performed admirably as the staple of the curriculum. But given the range of teaching and learning tools enabled by new and emerging technologies, print materials alone are increasingly inadequate, not to mention uninteresting, to young people. Students are increasingly able to use a range of tools to compose and to understand complex ideas, to convey beliefs and emotions, and to share their creations in print, visual, aural, and even tactile and kinesthetic forms. The most straightforward practice to capitalize on the multimodality of digital texts is simply to make the tools available (e.g., computers, digital cams and audio recorders, multimedia authoring tools, Web authoring tools, Web 2.0 tools) and provide practice in using them. A more involved approach is to think systematically of multimodal options for existing tasks and assignments (e.g., a media inquiry project in place of a report; a blog in place of a term paper), and to provide for students a choice in the modalities and tools they use. David and his colleagues did just this in the Literacy Lab at Jeff High School (O'Brien, 2006; O'Brien, Springs, & Stith, 2001) when they reconstructed an entire literacy curriculum to take advantage of a multimedia lab they set up.

Examining Stances toward Technology

Ideally, to construct digitally enabled curricula, youth need educators who are either capable of using the technologies or open to learning them (often with support of students!) and connecting the technology tools to literacy practices. Taking new stances requires new attitudes and familiarity with the frameworks we have briefly overviewed (e.g., frameworks in which texts are multimodal representations rather than just print, and reading and writing are socially and culturally embedded practices that can be enabled with digital tools). Prensky's (2001) characterization of *digital natives* (the students) and *digital immigrants* (teachers who did not grow up with the technologies that students use adeptly) is a useful, albeit forced, binary that speaks to stance. Digital immigrants need to be willing to jump into the fray and start to use the technologies that their students know. The practical side of this immersion is that teachers who use the technologies can understand how these tools enable teaching and learning; the more affective dimension is that the actualizing digital immigrants see the value of the tools and feel good about their own competence in using them.

QUESTIONS FOR DISCUSSION

1. What present technology tools and Web 2.0 applications may be used to extend and enhance the learning experience of students?
2. As a classroom teacher, what multimodal options can you incorporate into your existing tasks and assignments?
3. How would you design an entire literacy unit, incorporating multimodal options?

Resources

Further Reading

Beach, R. (2006). *Teachingmedialiteracy.com: A resource guide to links and activities.* New York: Teachers College Press. Available online at *teachingmedialiteracy.com.*

Burn, A., & Durran, J. (2007). *Media literacy in schools: Practice, production and progression.* London: Paul Chapman.

Coiro, J., Knobel, M., Lankshear, C., & Leu, D. J. (Eds.). (2008). *The handbook of research in new literacies.* New York: Erlbaum.

Kist, W. (2005). *New literacies in action: Teaching and learning in multiple media.* New York: Teachers College Press.

Websites

www.editlib.org/index.cfm?fuseaction=reader.frontpage—Editlib. The EdITLib Digital Library is a repository of peer-reviewed and published articles and papers on the latest research, developments, and applications related to all aspects of educational technology and e-learning.

www.aceworkshop.org—The Assembly on Computers in English is a long-standing assembly of the National Council of Teachers of English and is a nonprofit organization of English language arts teachers and teacher-educators dedicated to intelligent technology integration into the English language arts.

www.reading.org/resources/issues/focus_technology.html—IRA Focus on Technology: IRA Programs and Resources is a link to resources of the International Reading Association site, designed to help educators support students in the new literacies of information and communication technologies, as well as to help teachers who want to become more proficient in using the technologies. The resources include publications, online resources, and meetings and events that support the use of technologies and literacy.

References

Alvermann, D. E., Moon, J. S., & Hagood, M. C. (1999). *Popular culture in the classroom: Teaching and researching critical media literacy.* Newark, DE: International Reading Association.

Beach, R., & O'Brien, D. G. (2008). Teaching popular culture texts in the classroom. In J. Coiro, M. Knobel, C. Lankshear, & D. Leu (Eds.), *Handbook of research on new literacies* (pp. 775–804). New York: Erlbaum.

Clark, A. (2003). Natural born cyborgs? In J. Brockman (Ed.), *The new humanists* (pp. 70–77). New York: Barnes & Noble.

Coiro, J., & Dobler, E. (2007). Exploring the online reading comprehension strategies used by sixth-grade skilled readers to search for and locate information on the Internet. *Reading Research Quarterly, 42*(2), 214–257.

Coiro, J., Knobel, M., Lankshear, C., & Leu, D. J. (Eds.). (2008). *The handbook of research on new literacies.* New York: Lawrence Erlbaum.

Cope, B., & Kalantzis, M. (Eds.). (2000). *Multiliteracies: Literacy learning and the design of social futures.* London: Routledge.

Dubbels, B. R. (2008). Video games, reading and transmedial comprehension. In R. E. Ferdig (Ed.), *Handbook of research on effective electronic gaming in education* (pp. 251–276). Hershey, PA: IGI Global.

Evans, E., & Po, J. (2007). A break in the transaction: Examining students' responses to digital texts. *Computers and Composition, 24,* 56–73.

Foehr, U. G. (2006). *Media multitasking among American youth: Prevalence, predictors, and pairings.* Menlo Park, CA: Henry J. Kaiser Family Foundation.

Graesser, A. C., Millis, K. K., & Zwaam, R. A. (1997). Discourse comprehension. *Annual Review of Psychology, 48,* 163–189.

Hague, S. A., & Mason, G. E. (1986). Using the computer's readability measure to teach students to revise their writing. *Journal of Reading, 30*(1), 14–17.

Hobbs, R. (2007). *Reading the media: Media literacy and high school English.* New York: Teachers College Press.

Jewitt, C., & Kress, G. (Eds.). (2003). *Multimodal literacy.* New York: Peter Lang.

Kamil, M. L. (1982). Technology and reading: A review of research and instruction. In J. A. Niles & L. Harris (Eds.), *New inquiries in reading research and instruction. Thirty-first yearbook of the National Reading Conference* (pp. 251–260). Rochester, NY: National Reading Conference.

Kamil, M. L., Intrator, S., & Kim, H. S. (2000). Effects of other technologies on literacy and literacy learning. In P. M. M. Kamil, P. D. Pearson, & R. Barr (Eds.), *Handbook of reading research* (Vol. 3, pp. 773–788). Mahwah, NJ: Erlbaum.

Kist, W. (2005). *New literacies in action: Teaching and learning in multiple media.* New York: Teachers College Press.

Knobel, M., & Lankshear, C. (Eds.). (2007). *A new literacies sampler.* New York: Peter Lang.

Kress, G. (2003). *Literacy in the new media age.* London, UK: Routledge.

Kress, G., & Van Leeuwen, T. (2001). *Multimodal discourse: The modes and media of contemporary communication.* London: Edward Arnold.

Lankshear, C., & Knobel, M. (2003). *New literacies: Changing knowledge and classroom learning.* Buckingham, UK: Open University Press.

Leander, K. M. (2007). "You won't be needing your laptops today": Wired bodies in the wireless classroom. In M. Knobel & C. Lankshear (Eds.), *A new literacies sampler* (pp. 25–48). New York: Peter Lang.

Lenhart, A., Madden, M., Macgill, A. R., & Smith, A. (2007). *The use of social media—from blogging to online social networking to creation of all kinds of digital material—is central to many teenagers' lives.* Washington, DC: Pew Internet and American Life Project.

Leu, D. J. (2000). Literacy and technology: Deictic consequences for literacy education in an information age. In M. L. Kamil, P. Mosenthal, P. D. Pearson, & R. Barr (Eds.), *Handbook of reading research* (Vol. III, pp. 743–788). Mahwah, NJ: Erlbaum.

McEneaney, J. E. (2006). Agent-based literacy theory. *Reading Research Quarterly, 41*(3), 352–371.

Miller, P. (2005). Web 2.0: Building the new library. *Ariadne, 45.*

New London Group. (1996). A pedagogy of multiliteracies: Designing social futures. *Harvard Educational Review, 66*(1), 60–92.

O'Brien, D., Beach, R., & Scharber, C. (2007). "Struggling" middle schoolers: Engagement and literate competence in a reading writing intervention class. *Reading Psychology, 28*(1), 51–73.

O'Brien, D., & Scharber, C. (2008). Digital literacies go to school: Potholes and possibilities. *Journal of Adolescent & Adult Literacy, 52*(1), 66–68.

O'Brien, D. G. (2006). "Struggling" adolescents' engagement in multimediating: Countering the institutional construction of incompetence. In D. E. Alvermann, K. A. Hinchman, D. W. Moore, S. F. Phelps, & D. R. Waff (Eds.), *Reconceptualizing the literacies in adolescents' lives* (pp. 29–46). Mahwah, NJ: Erlbaum.

O'Brien, D. G., & Bauer, E. (2005). New literacies and the institution of old learning. *Reading Research Quarterly, 40,* 120–131.

O'Brien, D. G., Springs, R., & Stith, D. (2001). Engaging at-risk students: Literacy learning in a high school literacy lab. In E. B. Moje & D. G. O'Brien (Eds.), *Constructions of literacy: Studies of teaching and learning in and out of secondary schools* (pp. 105–123). Mahwah, NJ: Erlbaum.

Pearson, P. D. (2004). The reading wars. *Educational Policy, 18*(1), 216–252.

Prensky, M. (2001). Digital natives, digital immigrants. *On the Horizon, 9*(5). Accessed April 1, 2008, from *www.marcprensky.com/writing/Prensky%20-%20digital%20 natives,%20digital%20immigrants%20-%20part1.pdf.*

Reinking, D., McKenna, M., Labbo, L., & Kieffer, R. (Eds.). (1998). *Handbook of literacy and technology: Transformations in a post-typographic world.* Mahwah, NJ: Erlbaum.

Restak, R. (2003). *The new brain: How the modern age is rewiring your mind.* New York: Rodale.

Roberts, D. F., Foehr, U. G., & Rideout, V. J. (2005). *Generation M: Media in the lives of 8–18 year-olds.* Menlo Park, CA: Kaiser Family Foundation.

Vander Wal, T. (2007). Folksonomy Coinage and Definition. Retrieved October 26, 2007, from *www.vanderwal.net/folksonomy.html.*

Xiong, C., & Relerford, P. (2008, January 13). A minor walkout in Facebook flap. *Minneapolis Star Tribune.* Accessed October 24, 2008, at *www.startribune.com/local/ west/13677002.html.*

Chapter 24

Engaging Adolescents in Thoughtful Literacy Practices

Danielle V. Dennis
Evan Lefsky
Richard L. Allington

GUIDING QUESTIONS

1. Before you read, discuss with a colleague what a *thoughtfully literate* class-room might look like, then jot down some of your ideas. What were the similarities and differences between your thoughts and the ideas this chapter? What are you already doing in your classroom, and what would you like to add?

2. Think about your favorite high school content-area teacher for a couple of minutes. Jot down three things that he or she did when teaching that makes him or her stand out in your mind. Determine whether any of these things are discussed as you read this chapter.

3. Think about the challenges presented by the use of a single textbook in the classroom. What methods could be used to address this for the range of learners you might find in your classroom?

What Do We Mean by "Thoughtful Literacy"?

Discussions around the type of talk that pervades secondary school class-rooms often paint a picture of teachers as beholders of knowledge, asking directed questions with specific answers (Cazden, 2001; O'Brien, Stewart, &

Moje, 1995). These teachers are generally in control of the delivery and out-come of the instructional content, as well as the conversation that ensues from the topic (Applebee, 1996; Johnston, Woodside-Jiron, & Day, 2001; O'Brien, Stewart, & Moje, 1995). According to O'Brien et al., "The control provides an efficient way to respond to organizational and time constraints [teachers] face within the institutionalized curriculum" (p. 451). Not only does this level of control lead to student disengagement from the curriculum (Guthrie & Davis, 2003; O'Brien et al., 1995), but this focus on efficiency over engage-ment also does little to promote increased achievement on the new literacy standards.

Conversely, Langer (2004), in "Beating the Odds," describes dialogue between students and teachers in secondary schools as thoughtful, and pres-ents an image of classrooms in which students are generating and solving problems through conversation. These data support Allington and John-ston's (2002) notion of *thoughtful literacy*, in which teachers promote the use of language and student talk to aid in the understanding of text. *Thought-ful literacy*, then, is defined as, "engaging the ideas in the text, challenging those ideas, reflecting on them, and so on" (Allington, 2006, p. 135). This differs from comprehension tasks focused mainly on remembering material, instead focusing on the skills of analyzing, synthesizing, and summarizing text through literate conversation.

Teachers who engage students in thoughtful literacy practices explic-itly teach comprehension strategies in context rather than as discrete and discernable skills (Allington & Johnston, 2002; Allington & McGill-Franzen, 2009; Duffy, 1993; Pressley, 2000). Specifically, the teaching of higher-order thinking skills, and how to actively monitor the use of those skills, requires students to utilize questioning strategies as they negotiate text and converse with peers about the content within the text. It is these higher-order skills that are being tested on measures of accountability, so utilizing thoughtful literacy practices in secondary school classrooms may also lead to higher achievement scores for all adolescents.

Thoughtful Literacy in an Age of Accountability

Promoting the practice of thoughtful literacy in a climate of accountability and high-stakes testing requires teachers to be risk-takers, to deviate from the neo-norm of scripted reading programs, and to share with students the locus of control within the classroom. Since the inception of No Child Left Behind (NCLB), there has been much evidence of a narrowing of the curriculum, in which teachers are forced to utilize packaged reading programs to teach the material on which students will be tested by the state (Allington, 2002a; Linn, 2000; Shanahan, 2005). Researchers argue that this has led to an increased emphasis on the transmission model of teaching within our middle and high schools, in which teachers are in control of a directed curriculum, and students rely on teachers' answers for learning facts associated with the content (Alvermann, 2001; O'Brien et al., 1995).

Both Allington (2006) and Alvermann (2001) argue that thoughtful literacy practices are actually more effective approaches to increasing achievement on high-stakes assessments, because students are expected to utilize text as a tool rather than rely on the teacher to provide specific answers to explicit questions. In terms of accountability assessments, for example, on the Florida Comprehensive Assessment Test (FCAT), over 65% of questions asked of students on the reading test involve higher-order thinking skills, such as, application, analysis, synthesis, and evaluation (Florida Department of Education, n.d.). To respond accurately to these questions, students must be proficient at self-monitoring their questioning processes while reading unfamiliar text. Certainly, this does not exclude the teacher from the learning process of students. Rather, it relies on teacher expertise in terms of content and personal knowledge of students to provide texts that match student ability, interest, and topic. Furthermore, it relies on the teacher to engage students in conversations that reflect a more literate discourse—conversations that require them to think critically about the text being read.

Promoting Thoughtful Literacy with the Six T's

Richard, a researcher, often heralds the many exemplary teachers he has had the opportunity to learn from and observe through his research. He characterizes these teachers as possessing the ability to engage their students in thoughtful literacy practices that promote understanding of the required curriculum and demonstrate higher levels of proficiency on standardized assessments of reading and writing (Allington, 2002b, 2006; Allington & Johnston, 2002). Although his research has focused primarily on elementary school classrooms, his description of the six T's of effective elementary literacy instruction were well supported by research that emerged from and expanded the field of adolescent literacy. Thus, the following discussion focuses on the six T's of effective literacy instruction, concentrating specifically on what we know about the teaching and learning of middle and high school students.

Time

There is a long line of research demonstrating the positive relationship between time spent reading and reading improvement (Carroll, 1963; Davidson & Koppenhaver, 1993; Denham & Lieberman, 1980; C. W. Fisher & Berliner, 1985; D. Fisher, 2004; Knapp, 1995). Basically, the rule of thumb is that greater amounts of reading produce higher reading achievement. But, of course, it is not that simple, because students also need instruction to improve their reading. Observations of the classroom literacy instruction of exemplary teachers revealed that their students spent far greater amounts of time actually reading compared to students in less effective classrooms. If we consider that many less effective teachers allocate no class time for students to engage in reading, it does not take much additional reading in the exemplary classrooms to produce the differences. However, the differences in many cases were staggering (e.g., 0 minutes vs. 33 minutes of reading during a class period).

To foster such reading, the exemplary teachers worked to ensure that students had books they could actually read. They also worked to develop reasons for reading those books. Others have offered similar evidence for the benefits of extensive reading of appropriately matched books (Ehri, Dreyer, Flugman, & Gross, 2007; Fisher & Frey, 2007; Ivey, 2002; Moore, Bean, Birdyshaw, & Rycik, 1999; O'Connor et al., 2002). As Guthrie and Humenick (2004) noted, "Enabling students to become deeply immersed in and intrigued by the content of a passage or book is a central practice among teachers who are effective in motivating students" (p. 333). In other words, by linking appropriately difficult texts to course content, and by fostering situational interest, the most effective teachers created classrooms where students read (and read some more).

Extended engagement in reading activity during class time means that these students actually read much more about course content and read material at their reading levels. Thus, not only reading ability but also knowledge of key course content or principles improved. This is a win–win situation for content-area teachers. As Vellutino (2003, pp. 74–75) argues, the inclusion of extensive and diverse reading in the classroom establishes students who do the following:

1. Develop linguistic competencies.
2. Acquire discourse knowledge, or knowledge about the structural characteristics of text.
3. Acquire world and domain-specific knowledge.
4. Increase reading fluency and proficiency.

But it wasn't just general linguistic competence or reading ability that improved in the extensive reading classrooms. These classrooms expanded content knowledge as well. Think of it this way: Who is more likely to know American History or Earth Science content? Students who have read a single textbook, or students who have read the same textbooks and 10–20 other books on the topics studied? Imagine how reading *My Brother Sam is Dead* (Collier, 2005) or *Guns for General Washington* (Reit, 2001), two less difficult books about the American Revolution, might add to struggling high school readers' knowledge of that era. Imagine, for a moment, how much these books might benefit a grade-level reader in the same class.

Text

The issue of access is of great importance at middle and high schools in which overreliance on textbooks seems to be the standard. Successful practice is the key to developing understanding of content for adolescent readers. Unfortunately, textbooks that are written as much as two grades levels above the grade in which they are used do little to promote understanding or engagement for nearly two-thirds of the student population. Accurate, fluent reading with easy comprehension allows students to coordinate their knowledge of how reading works, and their reading skills and strategies, to engage in independent reading (Allington, 2002b).

Frequently, middle and high school teachers ask why adolescents didn't learn to read in elementary school, and whether it is indeed too late to help them become more proficient readers. In most cases, the answer to the first question is that they did receive instruction in elementary school. The answer to the second is that it's not too late to help them achieve literacy success. Many students who gain proficiency on reading tasks in the elementary grades do not continue that success in middle and high school, due in part to the changing demands of the texts and the tasks. In elementary schools, students who are exposed to a plethora of narrative texts with familiar structures become very successful at comprehending these genres of text (Duke, 2000). When the text load shifts primarily to informational and technical texts in content courses, many students are not prepared because of their lack of experience with those types of text. The cognitive demands of difficult concepts and vocabulary in content-area texts also present a unique and sometimes insurmountable challenge for many students, especially those who struggle with decoding and fluency. Their lack of practice with text in general equates to difficulties with not only the content words but also common words that are important to the meaning. One only has to look at the reading scores reported by the National Assessment of Educational Progress to understand that reading instruction and intervention must continue for all students as they move into middle and high school (National Center for Educational Statistics, 2006).

One of the key success factors in studies of exemplary teachers (Allington & Johnston, 2002) is the opportunities they provide for students to engage in reading, writing, and conversation through the use multiple level texts. When all students have texts they can read accurately with comprehension, they remain actively engaged in the subject's content. Additionally, when students are given the opportunity to choose and read texts on topics that interest them, they remain engaged throughout the course of study. It is important to note that exemplary teachers do not provide free choice; instead, they provide students with guidance in selecting texts that they can read successfully and that are of interest to them. In their meta-analysis, Guthrie and Humenick (2004) verified results regarding the impact of students' access to engaging text on outcomes, as well as the provision of a degree of choice in what they read. Although the use of multiple texts is not realistic for every topic covered in every subject area, exemplary teachers are skilled at scaffolding reading assignments when the text provides challenges for some students.

Additionally, content teachers who use multiple texts recognize the value of the multiple perspectives and issues that cannot be represented in a single textbook. They establish classrooms with a culture of safety (safe classroom) by reinforcing the importance of multiple perspectives and opposing ideas in building shared knowledge. The conversations that take place in these classrooms closely replicate those seen in the adult world and are important in the development of higher-order literacies. This framework for content learning lends itself to the type of intertextual and even interdomain connections that make learning relevant and engaging for students.

In many secondary school content-area classrooms, single text use is the predominant method of instruction (Alvermann & Moore, 1991), promoting the idea that the teacher or the textbook is the center of instruction. Not surprisingly, McKenna, Kear, and Ellsworth (1995) discovered a steady decline in students' attitudes toward academic and even pleasure reading as they moved up in grade level. The negative attitudes developed by students have led to decreased levels of reading frequency and avoidance of difficult reading tasks (Bean, 2000). For many students who read below grade level, content-area texts are extraordinarily difficult. These texts are often written four to five grade levels above students' independent reading levels. Because of this lack of experience and practice with text, many students do not read strategically and have not developed the endurance that high school literacy tasks require. To meet these challenges, increased use of thematic units incorporates a variety of topical literature and texts in secondary content classrooms. These classrooms can serve as a model that is likely to increase students' engagement in reading (Bean, 2000).

Bean (2000) has urged the research community to investigate further the impact of multiple texts on students' learning, interest, critical thinking, writing, and attitudes toward reading. As more and more states institute high-stakes testing for secondary school students, more and more teachers are requiring less and less reading in their content-area classrooms. The excuse is that because students are not capable of reading the textbook, teachers find ways to help students work around the reading. What these teachers do not realize is that in their effort to deliver the content, they are enabling students to avoid reading altogether. Thus, when students are asked to perform on standardized tests, their lack of frequent engagement in reading leads to poor comprehension (McKenna et al., 1995). Additionally, because these students have not built up a sufficient amount of reading endurance, they flounder when asked to read for prolonged periods of time in extended expository texts. It is easy to see that secondary school content-area literacy needs further exploration if we are determined not to exclude an entire generation of adolescents from a productive future.

Teach

The International Reading Association's Commission on Adolescent Literacy developed "Adolescent literacy: A position statement" to bring much needed recognition to adolescent literacy as a field, and to the types of instructional practices that adolescents deserve (Moore et al., 1999). One of the components noted within the position statement is that "adolescents deserve expert teachers who model and provide explicit instruction in reading comprehension ... across the curriculum" (p. 104). We believe that although most teachers of adolescents agree with this statement, many may find it difficult to uphold in the current context of middle and secondary school education. As previously noted, transmission models of education permeate middle and high school classrooms, and secondary students often rely heavily on teacher talk rather than text as their primary source of information (O'Brien et al., 1995). Moreover, the focus of instruction in these settings is more often the literal meaning of the text being read rather than employment of the strategies necessary for meaning making to occur.

The goal for teachers who engage students in thoughtful literacy practices is that students ultimately comprehend the text, but these teachers recognize the importance of teaching students the process for doing so on their own, rather than teaching the meaning of the text directly. To meet this goal, teachers must provide students with explicit strategy instruction and model methods for self-regulation of these strategies when reading (Pressley, 2002). Dole, Brown, and Trathen (1996) provide three instructional actions that increase the effectiveness of strategy instruction (p. 66):

1. Students benefit when teachers model, or "think aloud," about their reasoning as they read.

2. Students benefit when teachers gradually reduce their role until students are ready to assume independent control of the strategies they have been learning. Gradual release of responsibility is facilitated by the support teachers provide to help students accomplish an academic task.

3. Students are more likely to self-regulate strategy use when teachers inform them of its benefits and show them evidence of its contribution to improved performance.

Cris Tovani (2004), a Denver educator, writes about the "So what?" of reading comprehension. She argues that many secondary school students are uncertain of what they should be thinking as they read, and she encourages teachers to model the types of thinking they employ as expert readers of text.

Tovani asserts that, as educators, we must demonstrate the connections we make to text (text-to-text, text-to-self, and/or text-to-world) and the thinking strategies (questioning strategies, visualization, analyzing, recognizing confusion as we read) we use to integrate those connections into the text, then ask ourselves "So what?" to extend our thinking about the text. We discuss explicitly with students the ways our thinking helps us better to understand the text. Gradually, students will be able to follow these steps with the automaticity of an expert reader, but only after the steps have been modeled explicitly, and students have been given significant opportunity to practice those steps and engage in discussion with peers about the process of gaining meaning from text. Of course, the material being read must be texts that students can actually read accurately and fluently. Following this method of explicit instruction requires that teachers demonstrate the "strategies necessary for effective reading such as self-questioning, using background knowledge, comprehension monitoring, searching for information, and synthesizing multiple texts, [which] are learned as tools for content knowledge acquisition" (Guthrie & Davis, 2003, p. 73).

Fisher and Frey (2007) shadowed students throughout their school days at two middle schools. Both schools had high populations of at-risk students, and both initially demonstrated proficiency scores that were considerably lower than their respective district averages. One of these schools, however, mirrored what Langer (2004) labeled a "beating the odds" school, and gradually raised achievement scores of even its most at-risk students. According to Fisher and Frey (2007), literacy-based instructional strategies, and the consistency with which they were used, allowed this school to raise both engagement and achievement successfully across the board. Students in this successful school learned to use specific reading strategies across the curriculum, and all teachers integrated these strategies into their course work. Thus, students began to self-regulate use of these strategies, and were able to choose which strategy would be most appropriate with a particular text. More importantly, these students were engaging in conversation about the text they read, as well as externalizing the thinking processes they used as they negotiated an understanding of the text.

These observations support assertions presented by Guthrie and Davis (2003). They suggest that the disconnect between reading instruction and content knowledge in middle and secondary schools is a "clear contributor to the disengagement of students from books and necessary literacy practices" (p. 66). However, when content-area teachers successfully integrate interesting texts, which represent a variety of genres and build upon students' curiosities and interests, with stimulating tasks, both comprehension achievement and intrinsic motivation are shown to improve substantially (Guthrie & Davis, 2003; Guthrie & Humenick, 2004). Much of this improvement is directly tied to students' purpose for reading. Students who are reading with the purpose of understanding the content are more likely to comprehend the material than those who are reading with the sole purpose of raising test scores.

Talk

Recently, Danielle, a researcher, met with a group of friends for a Book Club discussion. All of the members had recently read *Beautiful Boy* by David Sheff (2008). Following a deep but lively discussion of this memoir, Danielle thought about club member Richard's sentiment that we don't engage in personal conversations of books the way we learned to respond to books in school. So she asked the other club members what they remembered about reading and responding to text in school. All of the women around the table were well-educated and represented myriad professions, yet unanimously they recalled rows of desks that faced a teacher who lectured about the topic of the day. Students would write verbatim notes, read a text selection related to the topic, then answer explicit questions about the reading. All of these professional women recounted memories of growing up in families where the expectation was to become a reader able to discuss the text thoughtfully, and all asserted a preference that their own children engage in discussion about books in school that supported the learning they experienced in the home.

The model of instruction described by the Book Club women that morning supported Cazden's (2001) description of classrooms dominated by an initiation–response–evaluation practice, in which teachers ask questions that require students to respond with an expected answer, then evaluate the responses for correctness. Although this practice has dominated secondary school classrooms (Alvermann, 2001; Guthrie & Davis, 2003; O'Brien et al., 1995), Johnston et al. (2001) emphasize that "discourse environments such as I-R-E are problematic because within them children are acquiring not simply facts and strategies, but also routines of behavior and patterns of values, beliefs, roles, identities, and ways of knowing" (p. 231). As noted by the discrepancy between the Book Club and the classroom, these learned patterns are not the ways of knowing represented outside the classroom.

Research emerging from the field of adolescent literacy, however, describes classrooms in which students are engaged in meaningful conversations about text, and teachers who are taking professional risks and generating higher standardized test scores in the process (Applebee, Langer, Nystrand, & Gamoran, 2003; Fisher & Frey, 2007; Johnston et al., 2001). Fisher and Frey (2007) describe a classroom in which students are participating in literate conversation that is teacher-directed but student-led, and involves the use of familiar instructional strategies that students have practiced and for which they assume responsibility in daily classroom interactions with peers. These students, who attend a "beating the odds" school, have also shown significant growth in their standardized test scores compared to students in other schools with similar demographics. Similarly, Applebee et al. (2003) reported on several approaches that contributed most to student achievement, including high academic demands and "those that used discussion to develop comprehensive understanding, encouraging exploration and multiple perspectives rather than focusing on correct interpretations and predetermined conclusions" (p. 722).

Affording students opportunities to create identities as readers and writers is an essential component of a thoughtfully literate, participatory classroom (Allington & McGill-Franzen, 2009; Applebee et al., 2003; Johnston et al., 2001). In thoughtfully literate classrooms, teachers facilitate learning by making their own thinking visible, generating questions based on students' interests, guiding students to texts of appropriate levels of difficulty, offering problem-solving strategies, scaffolding students' knowledge through instruction that cannot be scripted, and providing ample opportunities for students to discuss and to question what they are their learning with peers. Access to these experiences allows students to become members of a literate society, much like the women in the Book Club.

Tasks

Every teacher, regardless of time spent in the classroom or expertise with subject matter, has made errors in judgment relating to students' knowledge. We have assumed too much about the level of skills or background knowledge with which our students enter the classroom. As a high school literacy coach, Evan remembers many conversations with teachers that began as follows: "They're 16 years old. They must know that," or "How can he be in high school and not know that word?" Often the concepts that students were missing had been taught, or at least "covered." What was missing was the learning. Often this is the case when the concept is not presented in a way that is relevant for the students. Even given the best reading strategy or piece of content knowledge, students must see a deeper purpose to apply and integrate it in their knowledge base.

To promote thoughtful literacy experiences in the classrooms, it is necessary for teachers to allow students the opportunities to build deep knowledge on topics of interest within a specific domain. Fink (2006) suggests that it is this deep knowledge and engagement with text that provides the scaffolding for students to comprehend increasingly difficult texts and to apply strategies independently . Many of the instructional strategies taught to students are employed only when there is a strong motivation to understand the text. Allington and Johnson (2002) refer to this practice as *managed choice*, because the teacher remains involved in the selection of content being studied, which is based on both student interest and the required curriculum. Through the use of a variety of materials chosen (by the teacher) to support the topic, students are encouraged to make choices about their learning process. Teachers who are vested in the approaches and content they have developed are more willing to accept professional responsibility for developing reading proficiency when they have a high degree of autonomy (McGill-Franzen, 2000).

Texts on topics of interest that students can read provide the motivation and engagement for kids to read content by choice. This drastically increases the amount of reading in which students engage daily and allows students to build the necessary background, domain, and vocabulary knowledge required to continue on a successful trajectory of learning throughout adolescence. *Text sets*, or a collection of texts at varying levels of difficulty on a specific concept or theme, provide the opportunity for all students to participate completely in secondary classes, not just those who are able to read the textbook. Thus, students begin to view themselves as literate learners who have expertise in a particular area of study within the classroom.

Beyond the texts provided in the classroom, however, is a need to reconceptualize the way we think about the curricular mandates presented to classroom teachers. Applebee (1996) discusses curriculum as fragmented and decontextualized from the real world, as well as from itself, and suggests that "the structure of such a curriculum offers nothing to help the teacher and students sustain their conversations because each new element requires starting over—there are by definition no relationships among the parts" (p. 70). Teachers who accept professional risk taking as part of their growth within the profession, however, have the "with-it-ness" to scaffold the curriculum spontaneously with a continuous discourse. This requires a shift from the concept of curricular coverage to what Applebee refers to as a "significant set of conversations" (p. 47). In other words, inviting students to participate in the discourse of school asks teachers to begin looking at the curriculum as opportunities for student exploration to invoke interest in learning rather than as a set of facts and skills that must be covered to move on to the next set. Guthrie and his colleagues (2006) found that stimulating tasks, matched with books that were explored because of increased student interest in the topic, led to increased reading comprehension and increased intrinsic motivation, both of which often decline in the middle and high school years.

Test

As a former middle school reading teacher, Danielle was responsible for providing remedial instruction to students who did not pass the state test. After 1 month of teaching the packaged program that was the required curriculum, Danielle realized that although her students all scored below the proficient level on the test, they had very different abilities and needs. Furthermore, it became clear that rather than actually learning to *read*, her students were instead learning the discrete and decontextualized skills of phonics instruction and decoding. Fortunately, a supportive administration allowed Danielle to shelve the curricular script for an instructional plan that matched the needs of her students. However, only after Danielle administered several instructionally informative assessments did her administration embrace these changes.

Although no "scientific evidence" reveals a connection between testing and increased achievement, many school districts use the data from these assessments to make indiscriminate decisions about individual students

(Afflerbach, 2005; Allington, 2002a; Buly & Valencia, 2002; Dennis, 2008; Linn, 2000). According to Afflerbach (2005), use of results from standardized reading assessments as estimates of individual growth is "at best an approximation of the students' actual achievement level" (p. 158). However, students scoring below the proficient level on state assessments are often identified and placed in supplemental or remedial reading classes (Allington, 2001, 2006; Buly & Valencia, 2002; Klenk & Kibby, 2002), which often focus exclusively on phonemic awareness and decoding skills, regardless of the grade or reading level of the students being taught (Buly & Valencia, 2002; Pressley & Allington, 1999; Shanahan, 2005).

This practice does little to inform teachers of the individual abilities that students bring with them to the classroom, and it does much to take away the teacher's autonomy in instruction. What we know is that adolescents demonstrate a variety of abilities and needs with regard to literacy (Dennis, 2008). Many students who enter the classroom have the reading knowledge and skills necessary to earn proficient scores on statewide reading tests but are either disengaged from the curriculum (Guthrie & Davis, 2003; O'Brien et al., 1995) or experience difficulty in coordinating their reading knowledge and skills with reading informational text, which is the mainstay in most secondary school classrooms. Teachers have the ability to utilize assessment in a way that builds on what students already know. Evaluations of student work that measure effort, growth, and progress are often missing in secondary school classrooms (Afflerbach, 2004), but they are necessary if we are to provide the necessary instruction to engage students in thoughtful literacy practices.

In other words, if we want adolescent readers to activate their prior knowledge, apply reading strategies, and interact with and construct meaning from text, then we must administer classroom assessments that accurately reflect students' abilities in each of these areas. Additionally, these formative assessments must inform teaching and not be utilized solely as summative measures of student learning (Afflerbach, 2004; Allington & Dennis, 2007). Much of this assessment can be conducted informally through observation and anecdotal notes, and does not need to add to an already packed curriculum. As students engage in literate conversation, teachers are able to utilize checklists and anecdotal records to note the knowledge and skills that students are demonstrating, and those areas in which they require additional instruction.

A Thoughtfully Literate Classroom

We do not claim that transitioning from a traditional secondary school classroom to a participatory classroom is a simple process. Nor do we suggest that an entire secondary curriculum can be easily changed all at once. We do, however, believe taking small steps to engage adolescents in thoughtfully literate discussions is essential, and we offer five questions that teachers should consider when shifting classroom expectations:

1. Are students given plenty of time to explore topics and themes through reading, writing, and discussion?

2. Are all students provided with many books they can and want to read?

3. Are students offered opportunities to read and write about topics of interest?

4. When asked to perform literate tasks, are students provided with scaffolded instruction in how to perform the task and opportunities for practice, then afforded the opportunity to monitor their own use of strategies and skills?

5. Do classroom assessments demonstrate students' abilities, and are students given opportunities to demonstrate and use their strengths in reading and writing?

QUESTIONS FOR DISCUSSION

1. Tape-record a discussion of a book or magazine article with a friend (who has also read the book or article) as your conversation partner. Then tape a classroom of students discussing, or answering questions about, a class text. Listen to both audiotapes. What is different about the two events?

2. Utilizing multiple-level texts allows teachers to differentiate instruction in new ways. Think about one unit of instruction. How might you incorporate multiple-unit texts into that unit, so that all students have opportunities for engagement with the curriculum?

3. Students require explicit instruction and modeling before engaging in a thoughtful literacy in the classroom. Make a list of the six T's of thoughtful literacy, then plan how you will facilitate student engagement and learning in thoughtful literacy practices.

Resource

www.albany.edu/cela—The National Research Center on English Learning and Achievement offers educators access to its research, services, and classroom activities that support thoughtful literacy.

References

Afflerbach, P. (2004). Assessing adolescent reading. In T. L. Jetton & J. A. Dole (Eds.), *Adolescent literacy research and practice* (pp. 369–391). New York: Guilford Press.

Afflerbach, P. (2005). National reading conference policy brief: High stakes testing and reading assessment. *Journal of Literacy Research, 37*(2), 151–162.

Allington, R. L. (2001). Research on reading/learning disability interventions. In A. E. Farstrup & S. J. Samuels (Eds.), *What research has to say about reading instruction* (pp. 261–290). Newark, DE: International Reading Association.

Allington, R. L. (Ed.). (2002a). *Big brother and the national reading curriculum: How ideology trumped evidence.* Portsmouth, NH: Heinemann.

Allington, R. L. (2002b). You can't learn much from books you can't read. *Educational Leadership, 60*(3), 16–19.

Allington, R. L. (2006). *What really matters for struggling readers: Designing research-based programs* (2nd ed.). Boston: Pearson Education.

Allington, R. L., & Dennis, D. V. (2007). Assessment of adolescent reading proficiencies. In L. Rush, A. J. Eakle, & A. Berger (Eds.), *Secondary school reading and writing.* Urbana, IL: National Council of Teachers of English Press.

Allington, R. L., & Johnston, P. H. (2002). *Reading to learn: Lessons from exemplary fourth-grade classrooms.* New York: Guilford Press.

Allington, R. L., & McGill-Franzen, A. (2009). Comprehension difficulties of struggling readers. In G. G. Duffy & S. Israel (Eds.), *Handbook of comprehension research.* New York: Guilford Press.

Alvermann, D. E. (2001, December). *Effective literacy instruction for adolescents.* Paper presented at the meeting of the National Reading Conference. Chicago, IL.

Alvermann, D. E., & Moore, D. W. (1991). Secondary school reading. In R. Barr, M. L. Kamil, P. B. Mosenthal, & P. D. Pearson (Eds.), *Handbook of reading research* (Vol. II, pp. 951–983) New York: Longman.

Applebee, A. N. (1996). *Curriculum as conversation.* Chicago: University of Chicago Press.

Applebee, A. N., Langer, J. A., Nystrand, M., & Gamoran, A. (2003). Discussion-based approaches to developing understanding: Classroom instruction and student performance in middle and high school English. *American Educational Research Journal, 40*(3), 685–730.

Bean, T. W. (2000). Reading in the content areas: Social constructivist dimensions. In R. Barr, M. L. Kamil, P. B. Mosenthal, & P. D. Pearson (Eds.), *Handbook of reading research* (Vol. III, pp. 629–644). Mahwah, NJ: Erlbaum.

Buly, M. R., & Valencia, S. W. (2002). Below the bar: Profiles of students who fail state reading assessments. *Educational Evaluation and Policy Analysis, 24*(3), 219–239.

Carroll, J. B. (1963). A model for school learning. *Teachers College Record, 64,* 723–733.

Cazden, C. B. (2001). *Classroom discourse: The language of teaching and learning.* Portsmouth, NH: Heinemann.

Collier, J. L. (2005). *My brother Sam is dead.* New York: Scholastic Paperbacks.

Davidson, J., & Koppenhaver, D. (1993). *Adolescent literacy: What works and why* (2nd ed.). Hamden, CT: Garland Publishing.

Denham, C., & Lieberman, A. (1980). *Time to learn.* Washington, DC: U.S. Government Printing Office.

Dennis, D. V. (2008). Is assessment data really driving middle school reading instruction?: What we can learn from one student's experience. *Journal of Adolescent & Adult Literacy, 51*(7), 578–587.

Dole, J. A., Brown, K. J., & Trathen, W. (1996). The effects of strategy instruction on the comprehension performance of at-risk students. *Reading Research Quarterly, 31*(1), 62–88.

Duffy, G. G. (1993). Teachers' progress toward becoming expert strategy teachers. *Elementary School Journal, 94*(2), 109–120.

Duke, N. K. (2000). 3.6 minutes per day: The scarcity of informational texts in first grade. *Reading Research Quarterly, 35*(2), 202–224.

Ehri, L. C., Dreyer, L. G., Flugman, B., & Gross, A. (2007). Reading Rescue: An effective tutoring intervention model for language minority students who are struggling readers in first grade. *American Educational Research Journal, 44*(2), 414–448.

Fink, R. (2006). *Why Jane and Johnny couldn't read—and how they learned.* Newark, DE: International Reading Association.

Fisher, C. W., & Berliner, D. C. (1985). *Perspectives on instructional time.* New York: Longman.

Fisher, D. (2004). Setting the "opportunity to read" standard: Resuscitating the SSR program in one urban high school. *Journal of Adolescent & Adult Literacy, 48*(2), 138–151.

Fisher, D., & Frey, N. (2007). A tale of two middle schools: The differences in structure and instruction. *Journal of Adolescent and Adult Literacy, 51*(3), 204–211.

Florida Department of Education. (n.d.). *FCAT handbook.* Retrieved February 2, 2008, from *fcat.fldoe.org/handbk/fcathandbook.asp.*

Guthrie, J. T., & Davis, M. H. (2003). Motivating struggling readers in middle school through an engagement model of classroom practice. *Reading & Writing Quarterly, 19,* 59–85.

Guthrie, J. T., & Humenick, N. M. (2004). Motivating students to read: Evidence for classroom practices that increase reading motivation and achievement. In P. McCardle & V. Chhabra (Eds.), *The voice of evidence in reading research* (pp. 329–354). Baltimore: Brookes.

Guthrie, J. T., Wigfield, A., Humenick, N. M., Perencevich, K. C., Taboada, A., & Barbosa, P. (2006). Influences of stimulating tasks on reading motivation and comprehension. *Journal of Educational Research, 99*(4), 232–245.

Ivey, G. (2002). Meeting, not ignoring, teen literacy needs. *Education Digest, 68*(2), 23–25.

Johnston, P., Woodside-Jiron, H., & Day, J. (2001). Teaching and learning literate epistemologies. *Journal of Educational Psychology, 93*(1), 223–233.

Klenk, L., & Kibby, M. (2002). Re-mediating reading difficulties: Appraising the past, reconciling the present, constructing the future. In M. Kamil, P. Mosenthal, P. D. Pearson, & R. Barr (Eds.), *Handbook of reading research* (Vol. 3, pp. 667–690). Mahwah, NJ: Erlbaum.

Knapp, M. S. (1995). *Teaching for meaning in high-poverty classrooms.* New York: Teachers College Press.

Langer, J. A. (2004). Beating the odds: Teaching middle and high school students to read and write well. In R. B. Ruddell & N. J. Unrau (Eds.), *Theoretical models and processes of reading* (5th ed., pp. 1040–1082). Newark: DE: International Reading Association.

Linn, R. L. (2000). Assessments and accountability. *Educational Researcher, 29*(2), 4–16.

McGill-Franzen, A. (2000). Policy and instruction: What is the relationship? In M. Kamil, P. Mosenthal, P. D. Pearson, & R. Barr (Eds.), *Handbook of reading research* (Vol. III, pp. 891–908). Mahwah, NJ: Erlbaum.

McKenna, M. C., Kear, D. J., & Ellsworth, R. A. (1995). Children's attitudes towards reading: A national survey. *Reading Research Quarterly, 30,* 934–956.

Moore, D. W., Bean, T. W., Birdyshaw, D., & Rycik, J. A. (1999). Adolescent literacy: A position statement. *Journal of Adolescent & Adult Literacy, 43*(1), 97–112.

National Center for Educational Statistics. (2006). *The nation's report card.* Retrieved August 9, 2006, from *nces.ed.gov/nationsreportcard.*

O'Brien, D. G., Stewart, R. A., & Moje, E. B. (1995). Why content literacy is difficult to infuse into the secondary school: Complexities of curriculum, pedagogy, and school culture. *Reading Research Quarterly, 30*(3), 442–463.

O' Connor, R. E., Bell, K. M., Harty, K. R., Larkin, L. K., Sackor, S. M., & Zigmond, N. (2002). Teaching reading to poor readers in the intermediate grades: A comparison of text difficulty. *Journal of Educational Psychology, 94*(3), 474–485.

Pressley, M. (2000). What should comprehension instruction be the instruction of? In P. B. Rosenthal, M. L. Kamil, P. D. Pearson, & R. Barr (Eds.), *Handbook of reading research* (Vol. III, pp. 545–561). Mahwah, NJ: Erlbaum.

Pressley, M. (2002). *Reading instruction that works: The case for balanced teaching* (2nd ed.). New York: Guilford Press.

Pressley, M., & Allington, R. L. (1999). What should educational research be the research of? *Issues in Education: Contributions from Educational Psychology, 5*(1), 1–35.

Reit, S. (2001). *Guns for General Washington: A story of the American Revolution.* New York: Gulliver Books.

Shanahan, C. (2005). *Adolescent literacy intervention programs: Chart and program review guide.* Naperville, IL: Learning Point Associates.

Sheff, D. (2008). *Beautiful boy.* Boston: Houghton Mifflin.

Tovani, C. (2004). *Do I really have to teach reading?: Content comprehension grades 6–12.* Portland, ME: Stenhouse.

Vellutino, F. R. (2003). Individual differences as sources of variability in reading comprehension in elementary school children. In A. P. Sweet & C. E. Snow (Eds.), *Rethinking reading comprehension* (pp. 51–81). New York: Guilford Press.

Index

Page numbers followed by an *f* or *t* indicate figures or tables.

510